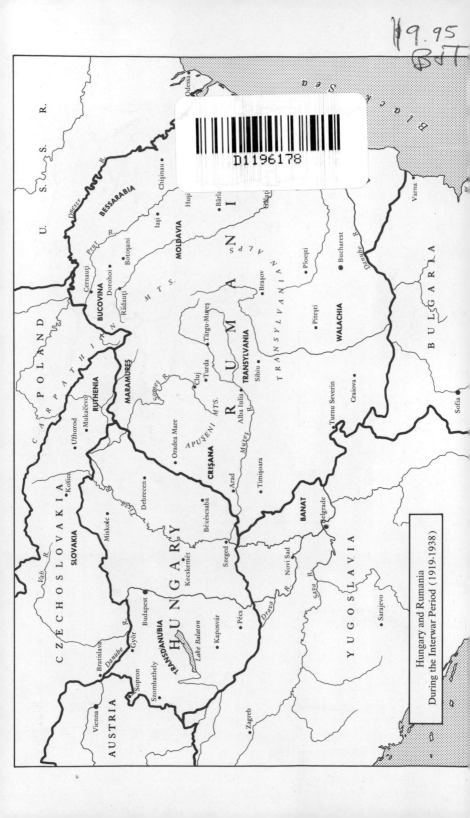

D1196178

Hungary and Rumania
During the Interwar Period (1919-1938)

Hoover Institution Publications

The Green Shirts and the Others

The Green Shirts and the Others

A History of Fascism in Hungary and Rumania

By

Nicholas M. Nagy-Talavera

Hoover Institution Press

Stanford University · Stanford, California

The Hoover Institution on War, Revolution and Peace, founded at Stanford University in 1919 by the late President Herbert Hoover, is a center for advanced study and research on public and international affairs in the twentieth century. The views expressed in its publications are entirely those of the authors and do not necessarily reflect the views of the Hoover Institution.

Hoover Institution Publications 85
Standard Book Number 8179-1851-5
Library of Congress Card Number 74-98136
Printed in the United States of America

To the memory of KOSSUTH,
The greatest of all . . .
And to that of Avram Iancu, the last *Tribunul,* whom the great Kossuth did not understand until it was too late.
To the memory of Ady, the poet, prophet and visionary who tried to bring the message of Paris and the West to Transylvania . . .
And to that of the lonely democrat, the pathetic martyr of Transylvania, Iuliu Maniu.

To my crushed Transylvania, which is slowly awakening from the long night . . .
And to her freedom, which is on the march . . .
And to the young Transylvanians; to the Rumanians, who are the majority; to the Hungarians and Saxons — all these to whom I hope the future belongs.

Contents

(Ethnic distribution map on page 117)

Preface

This purports to be the first more or less comprehensive and comparative work in the English language concerning the history of the Fascist movement in Hungary and Rumania — the only East European countries where fascism assumed the character of a mass movement. But it can serve also as more than a study of Fascist movements in two relatively unimportant East European countries: it hopefully can shed some light on contemporary political developments in several parts of the world as well.

Some of the readers of the manuscript would have preferred that this work consider the subject from an ideological point of view, i.e., from the point of view of an established theory. But one of the writer's primary aims was to gather as many facts as possible about these times in Hungary and Rumania and to present them as objectively as possible. Therefore, this work is anti-ideological because the writer considers ideologies in general, and in East Central Europe in particular, to be at best little more than distorted reflections of the real thing: the national sentiment. In other words, ideologies everywhere disguise only ambitions, and perhaps nowhere is this so patently true as in that part of the world where Hungary and Rumania are located.

But although this work is anti-ideological, it nevertheless tries to convey the importance of an idea — a quest, a yearning for a constructive nationalism, a nationalism compatible with humanity and with a recognized need for development. This quest seems to be the task of the second half of the twentieth century elsewhere, too. The problem which Hungary and Rumania faced between 1918 and 1945 were very similar to the problems in many countries in the underdeveloped world today. Hungary with its westernized structure presented problems similar to those of Spain and Portugal, and above all, Latin America. Rumania, on the other hand, thanks to Byzantine and Turkish Phanariote influences and traditions, was closer to the problems of the fifty-odd African and Asian countries.

In the second half of the twentieth century, everything seems to be uncertain except the existence of an all-pervading nationalism. Nationalism is stronger than Christianity or any established religion. It is stronger than the new secular religion, Marxism. What man should strive for is a nationalism that is compatible with humanity, that alleviates the problems of the industrial age, and that promotes what some historians call "inclusive diversity."

The author does not pretend to supply a blueprint for constructive nationalism — nor even to have said the last word about fascism in Hungary and Rumania. But hopefully, by examining the experience of the past in these two countries, this work may in some measure contribute to an understanding of relevant problems in the present.

Nicholas M. Nagy-Talavera

Chico, California
February, 1969

Acknowledgments

Twelve years ago I arrived in this country a penniless refugee just out of Siberian slave labor camps and the heat and tragedy of the Hungarian Revolution, my only armament for a new life a high school degree. Today I have a Ph.D. degree from the University of California at Berkeley and the Hoover Institution is publishing my first work. Obviously some acknowledgments must be made — fewer by far than should be made or than I would like to make. But limitations of space are more responsible for this than my forgetfulness or lack of appreciation.

The bulk of my gratitude goes to the great American people who created the conditions in which I could restore content and purpose to a shattered life. It would be extremely difficult to recall all the hundreds who proffered aid and encouragement, but I would like to mention some of those who helped me most along the long road that led to the writing of this book.

I will always remember gratefully Mr. István Barankovics of the Hungarian National Council, who convinced me early in 1957 to become a student; Mrs. Livia Barankovics and Mr. Charles Sternberg of the International Rescue Committee, who arranged the generous scholarships which enabled me to go to Berkeley; Kappa Nu Fraternity which, by "adopting" me for the first hard years of my academic career, removed the burden of room and board expenses and made it possible for me to study at an accelerated rate; and the dear families of my fraternity brothers who stood by me in every imaginable way.

Many thanks to Professors Charles and Cornelius Tobiás at Berkeley, who organized the academic career for me and 40 or 50 other Hungarian refugee students. I wish to thank the Department of Slavic Languages and Literature at the University of California in general and Professors F. J. Whitfield, G. P. Struve and O. A. Maslenikov in particular for what they did for me. I also wish to remember the two secretaries, Mrs. N. A. Shebeko and Miss Z. G. Pourtova. In the Department of History, my first token of gratitude goes to Prof. Charles Jelavich (who since 1962 has been at Indiana University) for his understanding and help. I will also always remember gratefully Professors N. V. Riasanovsky, J. F. King, G. D. Feldman and C. E. Schorske for what I received from them in understanding and knowledge during those years. Deep thanks also to Mrs. J. S. Purcell, the department secretary.

As far as the present book is concerned, many thanks to Prof. C. A. János in the Department of Political Science, Berkeley; Prof. Wayne S. Vucinich in the Department of History, Stanford University, and Prof. R. E. Zelnik in the Department of History, Berkeley, for their advice, encouragement and cooperation. Above all, my appreciation goes to Prof. W. B. Slottman in the Department of History, Berkeley, for his good will, advice and patience. He served as chairman of my Ph.D. committee, and my dissertation served as a basis for this work.

I wish to express my deep appreciation to the staff of the Hoover Institution on War, Revolution and Peace for their generosity, advice and confidence in me during the years — for giving me a chance. I have Prof. W. S. Sworakowski first in mind, but I also remember with gratitude the Hoover Library staff who did far more in assuring the success of my project than librarians are required to do. It was Mrs. Mary E. King who, as the English language editor of my work, bridged the gap which exists between the literary activity and the publishing house for almost anyone whose native language is not English. I am much obliged also to Prof. E. J. Weber of U.C.L.A.; although working on the same subject during the same time I was, he placed all of his research material, his warm hospitality, and his invaluable advice at my disposal. Finally, I wish to express my gratitude to Mrs. Eilen S. Grampp, secretary of the Center of Slavic and East European Studies at Berkeley, who through her deeply human understanding and encouragement and her advice in time of weakness and faltering fulfilled a humane duty in addition to a secretarial one.

CHAPTER I

Two Lands Within
The "No-Man's-Land" of Europe:
Hungary and Rumania

Asia begins with the Landstrasse *

Metternich

1

Does Europe end with Vienna? Probably there are few parts of Europe where people cling so desperately to their European identity and emphasize their belonging to the Christian West as do the peoples of the region between the German and Russian ethnic blocs — although the average Westerner knows little and cares less about them. Budapest is freely confused with Bucharest, and even for the educated Westerner the problems of the region represent little more than a nuisance. Bismarck, for example, in a statement which he probably did not mean to be taken literally, considered the bones of one Pomeranian infantryman more valuable than all of the Balkans. One could quote many others in the same vein. And it was partly because of this Western indifference and contempt that both world wars began in this region.

Because Europe does not end with Vienna. Vienna is a bastion, a bulwark beyond which the Tartars, the Turks and the Soviets failed to advance. But the confused region beyond it, the crossroads of Rome and Byzantium, of East and West, and of German and Russian expansion is an organic part of Europe. And woe to those Europeans who forget it.

Here in this middle zone, between Germans and Eastern Slavs on one hand and Scandinavia and Greece on the other, a tortuous history created a world vastly different from Vienna and the West both in its form and in its content. If we walk in a westerly direction from the Landstrasse, we see in most cases clearly defined nation-states, well established a long time ago, each with an identity of its own and with few insoluble problems, whether economic or political. If we walk in an easterly direction, however, we encounter a No-Man's-Land with multiple problems.

This No-Man's-Land contains roughly 570,000 square miles of territory. It is about the size of Alaska, or twice that of Texas, or little more than double the size of France, with her unitary political, ethnic and religious structure. In it dwells a conglomeration of twenty-four distinct national identities,

*The Landstrasse is the street that leads from Vienna eastward toward Hungary, to the Balkans and to Eastern Europe.

1

numbering 110 million people: Germans, Poles, Estonians, Latvians, Lithuanians, White Russians, Ukrainians, Czechs, Slovaks, Hungarians, Rumanians, Slovenes, Serbs, Croats, Bulgarians, Greeks, Macedonians, Albanians, Armenians, Jews, Turks, Russians, and Italians. And, of course, those idols of the romantics, the Gypsies. As for religion, we find every possible subdivision of Christianity, Judaism and Islam. To make things more complicated, thanks to the fact that the region was always a road of invasion and migration, the nationalities are not grouped in homogeneous, compact areas, but overlap and crisscross geographical and political boundaries. If for the West one Alsace-Lorraine problem seemed a burden, No-Man's-Land has at almost any time been confronted with at least twenty of like magnitude.

The peoples of the region, threatened by invasions originating more often than not on neighboring soil, have often looked for salvation to Vienna, St. Petersburg or Paris, but rarely to each other. Such a situation in a region not protected by a Monroe Doctrine of its own had to produce a violent nationalism. This nationalism in fact became the keynote of life, especially in the last eighty to a hundred years, in an area crippled by economic backwardness and the social dislocation that goes hand in hand with it, and torn by powerful internal and external pressures.

In that area are located the two countries, Hungary and Rumania, which provide the backdrop for this discussion of fascism, or to be more exact of the Fascist responses which their peculiar conditions created during the interwar period.

2

Hungary was structured on a Western pattern. She was a great power during the Middle Ages, and the Renaissance and Reformation left their mark on the Lands of the Holy Crown of St. Stephen.* Nevertheless, thanks to the long Turkish wars, Hungary lagged centuries behind the West at the dawn of the nineteenth century.

The ruling class of Hungary, the "Hungarian Nation," was born out of the terrible Jacquerie of 1514, after the suppression of which the oligarchy found it expedient to codify its rights and privileges.

The father of this nation within the nation was István Werböczy, a corrupt jurist, the man who supplied the codification. By his prescription there was to be no difference between nobles, whether of the lower or higher echelons.** Only nobles counted as "nations," and the rest of the people, those who paid the taxes and toiled and slaved on the land, were aptly called *misera contribuens plebs.**** The legal code****which Werböczy devised to regulate

*Szentkorona országai, historic Hungary (minus Croatia and Slavonia) as it existed before 1918.
**As Werböczy put it, *"Una eademque nobilitas."*
***Wretched taxpaying commoners.
****Called *Tripartitum*, the Bible of the "Hungarian Nation."

the relationship between these two classes of Hungarians (the proportion of which was roughly 5 percent to 95 percent) was to prevail until 1848 on paper and a hundred years longer in spirit.

From the time of the code's adoption, the Hungarian Nation monopolized political power in Hungary. Even the Habsburgs, who from 1527 wore the Holy Crown of St. Stephen as Apostolic Kings of Hungary, did not disregard this proud Hungarian elite. They were never deprived of their privileges within Hungary. They were hereditary leaders within their counties, and it became an integral part of their nature to expect obeisance from below and respect from above. They succeeded to an admirable degree — until the year 1945 demonstrated the hopelessly outdated nature of their social and political structure. On the positive side, it was the Hungarian Nation which set the example and the standards for the rest of the country as to what it meant to be Hungarian, and which prevented Hungarians from relapsing into the degradation of the Rumanian principalities. On the negative side, it was the same Hungarian Nation which, because it petrified the social and economic, and consequently the political, structure for all too long, prevented the rise of a truly Hungarian middle class — with dire consequences for the country during the twentieth century.

3

The Latins of the Balkans traveled a different road from Hungary with her medieval glories and her society structured on the European feudal model. Ever since Dacia had been cut off from Rome, this land had been a lost land, a sort of Atlantis, where people continued to speak the old Roman tongue and still called themselves Romans and their country Romania. But if they were cut off from Rome, they were not cut off from Byzantium. They weathered the nomadic floods with the same mysterious flexibility and indestructibility that were to become the cardinal traits of Rumanian national character. These qualities are reflected in Rumanian proverbs, which are more eloquent than any history book: "The flood runs down the riverbed — the rock remains in it"; or: "The tempest bends the grass roots, but does not tear them out"; and most telling of all: "O Lord do not make the Rumanian suffer as much as he can bear."

At the beginning of the eighteenth century, after centuries of indirect Turkish rule, the Phanariote period began in the principalities, a period which the Rumanian historian A. Xenopol could not remember without blushing.

Almost until the mid-nineteenth century, the Phanariote Greeks ruled the Rumanians. There was no counterpart of the Hungarian Nation among the higher boyars and the lower nobility in their relation to their princes. If Byzantine tradition coupled with their own historical experience taught the Rumanian people to be flexible, the Phanariote period, with its oppressive misrule and poverty through exploitation, profoundly undermined their belief in law, order and decency. It turned the peasantry into miserable slaves. No Rumanian could hope to survive unless he was willing to creep before his boyar master, who in turn groveled before the Hospodar, who in his turn

3

crawled literally on his hands and knees before the Turkish officials, who did the same before their superiors in Constantinople, who in their turn could be sent to the scaffold at the whim of a capricious Padishah. This period deprived the mass of people of all feeling of honor and independence. It made hunger, misery, injustice and personal abuse the normal state of human existence, until at last the average Rumanian, were he peasant or boyar, went about his business like a dog that has been beaten so often his spirit is broken and he dare not wag his tail without permission.

There was no escape: the Arnauts* were fast and merciless. The Rumanians had to bear in silence whatever their masters inflicted upon them, or run the risk of death. Only the Haiduci, the outlaw nationalist bandits whose exploits are perpetuated in folk songs that sigh of oppression, held out in a Robin Hood fashion here and there in the depths of thick forests.

Even the Rumanian language retreated into the huts of the peasants. Greek was spoken in the towns well up until the nineteenth century, and Greek was the language of the Orthodox Church. Foreigners, mostly Greeks and Armenians, took over every lucrative profession, giving the Rumanians a long-lasting national inferiority complex, a resentment against what their greatest national poet, Mihai Eminescu, called "Xenocracy." The aristocracy developed in this period and bequeathed to the independent Rumanian state was of Greek origin, as their names, Cantacuzino, Sturdza, Marghiloman, Duca, Mavromihali, Mavrocordato, etc., clearly show.

The Rumanians of Transylvania fared somewhat, but not much, better. The Hungarian landlords oppressed and exploited them, and the Habsburgs or the Uniate Church could do little to better their lot.

4

In Hungary, the legacies of Joseph II** and the quarter of a century of turmoil created by the French Revolution and the Napoleonic Wars left their traces deep in the souls of articulate Hungarians. The whole of Europe was in a state of ferment, and Hungary, which had undergone little change since the Turks left, showed all signs of awakening in the 1830s.

Since the suppression of the bloody uprising of 1514, there were, properly speaking, two nations in Hungary, the Hungarian Lords, as they were called in this period, and the millions of slaves, the working classes. The two nations glared with wolfish hatred at each other; the master did not regard his serf as a human being, whereas the latter waited like a shackled beast for the occasion of attacking his tyrant.[1]

*Albanian Moslem troops of the Turkish army, who often garrisoned the principalities.

**Strangely enough, when Joseph II, on the basis of purely practical considerations, substituted the widely spoken German for Latin in his domains, it gave rise to the vernacular among many of the fourteen-odd nationalities of the Habsburgs, independent of the French Revolution, a result very different from the goal of the Emperor. The vernacular is the most pregnant symbol and expression of nationhood.

In addition to the absence of absolute royal prerogative in Hungary since 1222 and the many rights and privileges resulting from it, the Hungarian Nation enjoyed exemption from taxation.* It should not be difficult to imagine what sort of economy complemented such a social structure. Industry, transportation and a money economy were practically nonexistent. Only about 5 percent of the population were town dwellers, the majority of them not Hungarians at all.[2] A primitive agriculture predominated, with the land owned almost exclusively by noblemen. And with the economic and political power in its hand, the Hungarian Nation was not eager for change, for it clearly understood that any change in the status quo would only decrease and not increase the privileges of nobility. No one, looking at the petrified state of Hungarian society in 1815, would have predicted the swift changes that were to occur in one or twoscore years under the impact of liberal and national ideas.

Then, in the 1830s, the Hungarian national genius made itself felt in an unprecedented manner, producing poets, musicians, writers, artists and leaders in a number and stature previously unknown to channel the energies of the Hungarian awakening. Because of the pathos which lingers over great moments in the history of small nations, some words should be said about the two Hungarians who tower over this great Hungarian decade, symbols of the two roads which were to be traveled in bringing Hungary from the sixteenth into the nineteenth century and in winning more independence from Austria. Count István Széchenyi stood on the conservative road, and Louis Kossuth on the liberal one.

Széchenyi was a conservative magnate, but not a reactionary. He loved his country with all her faults, which he criticized vehemently and which nobody saw more clearly than he. He was widely enough traveled to be able to discern important parallels. He was a man of absolutely sincere Catholic faith and of great spiritual purity. His remedy for Hungary's woes was: moderation; economic development first and national independence afterward, based on a strong domestic economy. He hoped to accomplish this through the leadership of the elite, the Hungarian Nation. It is this elite which he addressed and which he tried to reform.**

Louis Kossuth, like many great Hungarian patriots of the national awakening, was not of Hungarian but of Slovakian origin. A liberal nationalist in the nineteenth-century sense, he wished to transplant the ideals of the French Revolution to Hungarian soil. That meant the severance of ties with

*Out of nine million inhabitants, there were 136,000 who counted as Hungarian Nation in 1836. C.A. Macartney, *October Fifteenth* (Edinburgh, 1961), I, 7.

**In the twentieth century, when Széchenyi rather than Kossuth became the idol of the Hungarian Nation, they conveniently overlooked Széchenyi's acid criticism of the political nation, confusing the form with the content in Széchenyi's teachings, remembering only that he wanted "slow" progress under the leadership of the elite and that he was Catholic.

the Habsburg Dynasty and giving leadership to the Hungarian Nation, but only if it accepted liberal principles unreservedly.

Although a nationalist, Kossuth saw the pressing nationality problem which would arise in an independent Hungary after the supernational Dynasty was removed from the scene, for 50 percent of her people were not of Hungarian stock. French nationalism, a cultural nationalism rather than one of "blood and soil," seemed the appropriate solution for the problem. Kossuth hoped that the nationalities in the Lands of St. Stephen would find a liberal, independent Hungary attractive enough to become Hungarians. He was an eloquent orator, a brilliant publicist, and the strange inner flame which burned in him mesmerized the Hungarian Nation, who had been awakened by Széchenyi a decade before.

We see a unique phenomenon in Hungary between 1830 and 1848. The greater part of the gentry but also many of the magnates, especially the younger ones, now embraced liberal nationalism. This radical revolutionary elite won the sympathy of even Marx and Engels, who were in most cases less than enthusiastic about that class. But what these remarkable people did not realize was that nationalism was also on the rise among the nationalities of Hungary. Moreover, the French pattern did not apply in the Carpathian Basin for a number of reasons. The assimilation process of compact nationalities became almost impossible after the French Revolution in Europe. Also, France had never had 50 percent of Bretons, Alsatians or Savoyards to assimilate, and French culture, society and state were infinitely more attractive for assimilation than the Hungarian.[3] The supernational Dynasty understood this and skillfully used the discontent of the peasantry and the nationalities against Hungarian nationalism and the liberalism fostered by the radicals of the Hungarian Nation. The brilliant Hungarian elite realized the threat of the Habsburg schemes: in 1848, it voluntarily abolished serfdom. But it could or would not yield on the issue of intransigent nationalism — its very *raison d'être* — and this was to become the undoing of the hope for a democratic Hungary.

When the storm broke in 1848, Hungary had to stand up to defend herself against the Dynasty, using the only weapon left to her in her prostrate state: to inflame the wounds of every nationality in Hungary. Széchenyi, whom Kossuth himself called "the greatest Magyar," was hopelessly outdistanced by events, swept aside, and broken in soul and body. There was nobody to organize the life-and-death struggle of the nation but Kossuth.

A sublime euphoria swept through Hungary in those months which posterity can sense but cannot comprehend. The handful of Hungarians, a minority in their own country, challenged in victorious campaigns the strong military monarchies of Russia and Austria while simultaneously fighting off the onslaught of their own nationalities. That such an immortal feat was possible in the struggle for a free, democratic Hungary revealed the merit of Kossuth. It was he who united the Hungarian people with the Hungarian Nation, at least for a while, and it was he who exchanged privileges for freedoms. It was he who broke the tie with the Habsburgs and made Hungary a democratic republic. At the end, he tried to undo the errors of his nationality policy, but it was too late. "France was too far away," as he used to say, and Russian intervention crushed the noble attempt of the Hungarians, led by a revolutionary elite of aristocrats and intellectuals, to establish democracy in the Carpathian Basin. The Habsburgs thereupon instigated extraordinary court martials and hanged those Hungarian patriots whom they had not been able to defeat in open battle. Hungary was once more made safe for autocracy.

But the myth of Kossuth lived on in the hearts of his people, and it took a long time for the Hungarian ruling class, which in the next decade recovered from revolutionary euphoria and returned to its old ways, to undo the tremendous sympathy which Kossuth's struggle gained for Hungary in France, England, the U.S.A.* and the whole civilized West. On the walls of peasant huts his picture was still omnipresent, and every politician knew that the best way to get elected was to invoke the memory of Kossuth. Even in the 1956 uprising, the youth of a new Hungary went to the barricades singing the old songs glorifying the name of Louis Kossuth.

With the crushing of Hungarian democracy, Austria, which had seemed on the verge of collapse a year before, achieved a remarkable comeback, although this end could not have been achieved without Russian help. The feebleminded Emperor Ferdinand was replaced by young Francis Joseph, who with the help of a "government of prime ministers," as the Viscount of Ponsonby liked to call it, tried to modernize the Empire, relying only on the army and the police to transform it into a unified, centralized state. The personality of Prince Felix Schwarzenberg was a forceful one, and the other cabinet members, Alexander Bach, Count Franz Stadion, Anton Schmerling, Count Friedrich Thun and Karl Ludwig Bruck were brilliant statesmen. But their policy had a basic weakness: after the ordeal of 1848-49, they tried to assert Habsburg supremacy in Germany and Italy simultaneously and at the same time to hold Hungary. Such a task demanded resources the Dynasty did not have, and under the impact of Solferino and Königgrätz, Francis Joseph and his advisers were able to see, with the remarkable adaptability so characteristic of the Habsburgs, that in order to survive they would have to overhaul the Empire thoroughly and come to terms with their strongest and best-organized nationality, the Hungarians.

The year 1867 was a fateful year in the history of Hungary. The Compromise, which was concluded between the Dynasty and the Hungarian Nation, was a compromise in the true sense of the word. It gave the political nation a free hand within the Lands of St. Stephen over its own people and the nationalities. The Croats were forced against their will back into the Hungarian fold in a Hungaro-Croatian Compromise a year later. The architect of both compromises was Francis Deák, the last of the great representatives of the generation of 1848, who blended in his person the ideas of Széchenyi and Kossuth. He was a liberal conservative, a true Magyar patriot, who understood the necessity of finding a just and satisfactory solution for the

*The U. S. was the only country to send a minister to Kossuth, but he did not arrive until after the defeat of Hungarian democracy.

nationality problem. He was also a tactful and honest politician, a realist, and a man of irreproachable integrity. He did not survive his accomplishment for long, and even before his death in 1876, much of his work had been undone by the Hungarian Nation.

During the years of Absolutism (1849-67), the political nation managed to recover from its infatuation with liberal nationalism. It also recovered its traditional political instinct, which expressed itself in identifying its own economic and political predominance with the Hungarian national interest and doing so with a commendable inflexibility. Its economic and social predominance seemed secure in an alliance with the Dynasty, the Austrian industrialists, and the newly emerging class of assimilated Jewish industrialists in Hungary. This cooperation would make Hungary safe for the nobles against the possible aspirations of the lower classes or the evident aspirations of the nationalities, which were receiving increasing stimulus from the independent states of their kinsmen across the Carpathians and the Danube. For the short run, the policy of the nobles seemed to succeed. It is questionable whether in the changing, insecure atmosphere of the Danube Basin any policy based on the simultaneous repression of one's own people and one's nationalities could have prevailed for long. But this policy had to function within the framework of a capitalist system based on a semifeudal agriculture of great estates, a system that forced economic liberalism on an unwilling people while denying them political liberty.*

The result was a disconcerting and hopeless mixture of sixteenth- and nineteenth-century conditions. The very heart and soul was missing from the Western ideas which supposedly were applied in Hungary in those decades. This state of affairs continued in Hungary until 1918 and then with minor modifications until 1945. The aristocracy and gentry managed to keep its estates, its *de facto* serfs, and the privilege of political power despite the pseudo-parliamentary system. That on the national level.

On the local level, that peculiar administrative unit the *vármegye*, which corresponded roughly to the English county, was ruled entirely in the interest and absolute control of the Hungarian Nation. There was no secret balloting,** the elections were rigged and corrupt on both the local and national levels; consequently, the results did not even represent the will of the enfranchised 6 to 7 percent of the population.

The nationality laws of 1868 enacted by the farsighted Deák and Baron József Eötvös were never put into effect. Croatia, in complete disregard for

*In 1908, out of about 25 million inhabitants of Hungary, 971,202 were enfranchised. There were about 660,000 landowners, 136,000 other capitalists, 127,102 smallholders and artisans, and only 48,100 workers and intellectuals among them. The proportion of the propertied franchised was 796,000 against 175,000 who had no property. And that with 6 to 7 percent of the population having the vote. Oszkár Jászi, Gulya Rácz, and Zoltán Zigány, *A választójog reformja és Magyarország jövője* (Budapest, 1908), p. 63.

**The standard justification used was that Hungarians were upright enough to stand up for their political beliefs openly.

8

the letter and spirit of the Hungaro-Croatian Compromise, was ruled as a pashalik by Count Károly Khuen-Héderváry for two decades, and his removal in 1903 did not change things for the better. Although in the wild Magyarization campaign of the era degrees of intensity could be discerned, the trend of national oppression was a general one. Only among the Jews and the city-dwelling Germans was the drive to assimilate successful.

And here we arrive at a crucial point in our story. A modern Hungary was emerging in place of the old, and the Hungarian Nation could not cope numerically or intellectually with the problem of running this new twentieth-century state alone. Because of the speed of development, the elite needed help. But it did not recruit the Hungarian people, the peasantry, to fill the new openings in the army, industry, commerce, the professions and administration. It rightly feared that once the Hungarian peasantry developed its own middle class and intelligentsia, this new native middle class would sooner or later take over the country and usurp the power of the ruling class. Even a middle class consisting of neophytes was more desirable than such a challenge to the elite! The political nation turned to the newly assimilated Jews and Germans. The assimilation of Jews and Germans was an assimilation to the Hungarian Nation rather than to the Hungarian people, with the Jews forming an industrial, commercial and professional middle class in the Western sense of the word, and the Germans replenishing the ranks of the Hungarian Nation in the extended administration, army and bureaucracy. Both groups had the zeal of converts as far as their Hungarian nationalism was concerned, and together they became the motor force of Magyarization, their tactless zeal often exasperating the nationalities.

But here the parallel between the two groups ends. The Jewish middle classes became the propagators of reform; the German recruits came closer to approximating the traditional patterns of the Hungarian Nation and, perhaps because of their status as neophytes, emphasized their arrival into the ruling class with archconservatism, ultranationalism and eventually, fascism. Thus can be seen the grim consequences of the Hungarian Nation's failure to assume the responsibility of developing a native Hungarian middle class during the Compromise Era, and its equally important failure to extend the franchise and thus widen the basis of democracy. All this was considered inexpedient, contrary both to the iron determination of the political nation to preserve its commanding position and to the nationality policy. Even in 1867, if the Hungarian Nation had allowed political development to keep pace with economic progress, it could have laid a strong foundation for democratization.

Instead, in addition to all its other problems, Hungary entered the new era without a native middle class. Its middle class was divided between the Jewish segment, which truly can be considered a middle class in the Western sense, and a "middle class of Hungarian gentlemen" (úri magyar középosztály) as they used to call themselves, consisting of the gentry and the neophytes of German origin, occupying such middle class jobs as they considered appropriate to their status. Nevertheless, the economic, and to a lesser extent the social, progress of the Compromise Era was an impressive one.*

As we have mentioned, all this capitalistic progress, a nineteenth-century phenomenon, rested on the archaic basis of great landed estates of the type that existed in the sixteenth century. Prof. Oszkár Jászi calls them aptly *"Morbus Latifundi."***

Some 1,820,000 families did not have enough land for subsistence. If we count five people per family, this comes to 9,100,000 people — half the population. Conditions in Croatia were similar, if not worse. Agrarian disturbances and mass emigration to the United States***and other parts of the

*From 1867 to 1910 about 6 million *holds* were cleared for agriculture. Agriculture was modernized and fertilizers appeared. The yields increased in a spectacular fashion. The national production of agricultural products, especially cereals, doubled between 1870 and 1890. There was a sharp fall in the population employed in agriculture. By 1910 only 64.5 percent were employed in agriculture, compared to about 90 percent some decades before. Well over 20 percent of the population lived in towns, which were largely rebuilt. Budapest became a metropolis with more than a million inhabitants and another fifty towns were of a considerable size. After the financial crash of 1873, industry developed swiftly. By 1910, 3,361,000 people, including dependents, out of 18 millions derived their livelihood from industry. Of this number, 1,297,000 were genuinely employed in industrial enterprises and 44,770 in home industries. There were about 5,000 factories and 720,000 people worked in commerce and the by then fully developed banking system. A network of railroads and roads radiated from Budapest, reaching all parts of the country. Communications employed 630,000 persons. There were 680,000 employed in administration and the professions, connoting a not unimportant middle class. It was in the Era of Compromise that the great influx of Jews from the Polish provinces of Austria came to Hungary to find economic opportunity and freedom from the anti-Semitism prevalent in Poland. There was also an important leisure class in Hungary, but at least formally, all differences between noble and nonnoble were swept away and there was full religious freedom and equality. Macartney, *op. cit.*, I, 7-8.

**Forty percent of all Lands of the Crown of St. Stephen comprised large and extremely large estates, and if we add the medium-sized properties from 142 to 1,420 acres, the figure rises to 54.4 percent of the total area. Only 34.5 percent of the total belonged to those who personally cultivated their land. Many of these people leased their land, and it is no exaggeration that not even one-third of the land was in the hands of those who cultivated it. In Hungary proper (without Croatia), there were 2,280,000 farmer families. At best, only 460,000 had land over 20 acres, which would guarantee an independent livelihood. There were 1,820,000 families, that is four-fifths, who had less than 20 acres, and most of them had the so-called dwarfholdings or no land at all. Oszkár Jászi, *Dissolution of the Habsburg Empire*, pp. 222-23.

***During the interwar period, Fascist demagoguery would compare this figure of emigration with the figure of Jewish influx from Galicia during the same decades. As if the Jews, not the impossible structure of great

10

world were safety valves for the spreading discontent. Meanwhile the ruling classes never ceased to assert their love for the people in general, and for the peasant, "the backbone of the Hungarian state," in particular. Indeed this was the time when voices were heard about the need to create a Hungarian Nation comprising "thirty million Magyars."

The industrial proletariat lived through the privations of the Manchestrian period of Hungarian capitalism. There had been a Social Democratic Party in Hungary since the 1880s, but it adopted the rigid dogmatism of German and Austrain Socialists rather than the doctrine of the more flexible and adaptable Socialist movements in England and France. The party was never allowed to gain parliamentary representation, notwithstanding the fact that it had more than once proved its strength in strikes and through trade unions.*

The nationalities of Hungary were even more defenseless than the Hungarian people. Of the 413 deputies elected in 1910 by the enfranchised 8 percent of the Hungarian people, only eight represented the roughly half the population consisting of minorities.[4] The administration, the police and the gendarmeries of the nationality-inhabited areas consisted of 80 to 90 percent Magyars. Shortly before the war, the employees and the official language of the railroads in semiautonomous Croatia were Magyarized by decree, a foreshadowing of trends in the making. And while the adaptable Dynasty democratized and federalized the Austrian half of the empire, the Hungarian Nation centralized and Magyarized the Lands of St. Stephen, resisting democratization fiercely.

This Hungarian attitude was to count against the Dual Monarchy in its coming struggle for survival. It was not the social disolocation but the oppression of the nationalities that first drew Western attention to the fateful changes within the Hungarian ruling class that took place as a consequence of its interpretation of its national and social interests after 1867.

R. W. Seton-Watson (incidentally an admirer of Kossuth) went to Hungary to gain information to refute Western charges that Hungary was mistreating her nationalities. What he saw there changed his mind. He engaged in a thorough study of the nationality problem in Hungary, for which he became the target of vulgar abuse by the Hungarian Press.[5]

Other Western voices were also raised: Garibaldi's son, his father being a great friend of the Hungarians, reproached the Hungarians for their treatment of the Rumanians of Transylvania. Clemenceau considered the mass trial of Rumanian nationalists the "shame of the free Hungarian Nation."[6] (It is interesting to note that in referring to the "free Hungarian Nation" Clemenceau showed himself to be still under the impact of Kossuth and 1848.)

---

landed estates, had edged out the hundreds of thousands of Hungarian immigrants from their native land. In reality, it was almost exclusively the Jews who provided relief from agrarian overpopulation: a twentieth-century, industrialized economy.

*Meanwhile, because of electoral reforms, there were 87 Socialist deputies in the Austrian Parliament by 1910.

But by then the nationalities were almost as intransigent as their Hungarian overlords. In keeping with the spirit of the age there was no question about minority rights; what each nationality wanted was to redraw the map. And there were many voices in the Europe of 1910 expressing an opinion that in 1920 only facilitated the Trianon Treaty, which in its turn aggravated many of the injustices it was intended to remedy.

Such were the conditions, problems and social ills in Hungary as she approached World War I, fatefully tied to Austria and Germany. The leader of Hungary was Count István Tisza, a forceful personality and a strong leader, the quintessence of the Hungarian nobleman, but the kind the Compromise Era produced, for whom 1848 was nothing but a memory. Profoundly undemocratic, believing in the almost divine right of his class to rule unchallenged as it had for ages, utterly incapable of understanding the dynamics of economic change and the social upheaval which inevitably goes with it, he was nevertheless a person of great integrity, of genuine principle, and of stubborn bravery. It was said of him that he was the incarnation of his class and his race, with all its virtues and faults. To this evaluation the writer may only add that he was the embodiment of that which his class became after it turned its back on its own past, on Kossuth, and on the ideals of 1848.

5

Meanwhile, the Rumanians continued in a way of life which Prof. Nicolae Iorga calls *"Byzance après Byzance."* The line which separated the feudal but thoroughly Western class relationships in Hungary from the Oriental structure of the principalities was an almost brutally clear one. There was no talk in Rumania about any restriction of royal prerogative or about rights or privileges of the nobility. The principalities had only one thing in common with Hungary: they lacked a native midle class at the beginning of the modern era. Consequently, the ideas of the Enlightenment had to come to the Rumanians through the Greeks, the people of the Ottoman Empire who had the most contact with the West. The uncouth boyars listened to the ideas of the Jacobins with bewilderment but not without sympathy.

In the 1820s, more than two decades after the French Revolution, the Greek rebellion against Turkish rule had started from Russia under the leadership of Alexander Ypsilanti, who hoped to enlist Rumanian support for his "Sacred Battalion" on his way to Greece. Ypsilanti and his Greek idealists overlooked the fact that after hundreds of years of Phanariote rule the Rumanians would hardly welcome the Greeks as liberators. Yet their thrust had its repercussions in the principalities. An uprising took place under Tudor Vlădimirescu, who had pledged help to the Greek cause years before. His rebellion, which had perhaps stronger social than national motivations, came into conflict with the Greeks, and after they defeated him they killed him. Russian help, thanks to Metternich's swift intervention, did not materialize, and the Arnauts crushed the Greeks with ease. But when the Greeks of Greece proper rose, all Europe became involved. The flames of the Greek rebellion did not burn out before they reached the pale of civilization, as Metternich characterized the affair, and the Russian armies marched across the principalities on their way toward Tsargorod, which was the coveted prize Constantinople, the first teacher of the Eastern Slavs.

Once more they were to be denied the privilege of celebrating the "Te Deum" in the Hagia Sophia. But in the Adrianople Treaty of 1829, the Russians wrung many concessions from the Porte. The Sultan pledged not to appoint any more Phanariote princes, to appoint only native princes; and he agreed to appoint no one without Russian consent. With this, the Phanariote period of Rumania came officially to an end. But the most important concession from the enfeebled Turks was the right of the Russians to intervene on behalf of the Balkan Christians, a reaffirmation of the right granted to them in 1774. Another vital concession was the liberation of trade in the principalities, especially the grain trade, which had been a Turkish monopoly. The principalities were responsible for the food and grain supply of Constantinople and other Ottoman metropolises. Now they could freely export their grain, greatly increasing the income of the boyars. The treaty established Russian predominance in the principalities, and the Russian consuls in Bucharest and Iaşi ruled supreme from then on.

Tsar Nicholas I based his rule on the most reactionary *protîpendătă* boyar higher aristocracy. In 1831, he gave to this unhappy land a statute, the *Reglămăntul Orgănic,* which codified the existing privileges of the boyars, legalized the restrictions they practiced on the peasantry, and added new burdens to the ones already there. The peasants were bound to the soil, and their obligation to work greatly increased. Since the boyars could now export their produce at discretion, and at soaring prices, they naturally were interested in cheap and abundant labor, and the *Reglămăntul Orgănic* secured this for them. While the boyars spent their new-found wealth in the most irresponsible fashion, the peasants, 95 percent of them Rumanians, reached the rockbottom of their misery.

From the time the forces of Peter the Great reached the Pruth River in 1711, the danger of Russian expansion loomed ever larger on the Rumanian horizon. Thanks to their incessant expansionist drive, by the end of the eighteenth century the Russians had established themselves firmly on the shores of the Black Sea. In 1812, they wrenched from the weak Porte the eastern half of historic Moldavia, called Bessarabia, with an overwhelmingly Rumanian population for whom the Russians invented a new nationality: "Moldavian." But this was not all. The Rumanian people and rising Rumanian nationalism inconveniently blocked the general Russian expansion toward one of its key objectives: Constantinople, with its access to warm seas and direct contact with the Southern Slavs in particular. In those years, for the Rumanians Russia became the national enemy, an obsession, just as the Germans were for the Czechs. And no wonder. During the 240 years since 1711, Russian armies have passed through the principalities as friends or foes more than a dozen times, their friendship or "liberation" meaning the loss of one or two provinces for Rumania and their enmity something infinitely worse. During the nineteenth century, every time they passed through, the

Russian armies left in their wake a trail of suffering, plunder, disease, death and destruction in this dejected, suffering land. Except for a few Russians like the Resident Pavel Kisselev, who tried to do his best to mitigate these sufferings, Russo-Rumanian contacts of the past 150 years have been almost uniformly unpleasant for the Rumanians.

It was in the early decades of the nineteenth century that the young boyars (suddenly rich through the grain trade) began to travel abroad, which in most cases meant France, and many of them were shocked when they saw the differences between the West and their native land. It was during this time that the firm cultural bond between the Rumanian upper class and France was established. When these "bonjourists" came home, some were filled with revolutionary zeal. We shall see later what became of their peculiar brand of liberalism under the impact of the realities of their country. But in the years before 1848, those who lived in Paris listened avidly to the lectures of Michelet, kept in contact with Miczkiewicz, and when the February Revolution of 1848 came, they were on the barricades of Paris under the blue, yellow and red tricolor.

After a short propaganda effort for Rumania in revolutionary Paris, they hurried home to revolutionize their homeland. Taking advantage of the wavering attitude of the Wallachian Prince Bibescu, they seized control of Bucharest (for reasons to be discussed later, they failed to take Iaşi). The names of these young men — C. A. Rosetti, the republican; Ion Brătianu, who was a fiery revolutionary at that time; the great democrat Nicolae Bălcescu; Ion Ghica; Ion Heliade-Rădulescu; Ion Câmpineanu; Mihai Kogălniceanu; and Văsilie Alecsăndri in Moldavia — were prominent among the Rumanian reform generation which would bring about independence and unification later. Inside Rumania, the boyars were dead set against the revolution. Characteristically, they considered these young boyars insane, "otherwise how on earth could they rebel against their own privileges and interests?"[7] The peasants for their part were suspicious of these young ciocoi (a derogatory term for the ruling nobility and their helpers, partisans, etc.), who came to their villages and spoke to them about libertăteă, a word unknown and meaningless to them.

Finally, the boyars applied a well-known remedy against liberal change: they pointed out to Tsar Nicholas that every liberal move in the principalities was a pro-Turkish move, every conservative move a pro-Russian one. In 1849, a Russo-Turkish army entered the principalities and crushed the rebellion of doctrinaire idealists in Wallachia. Many of the leaders, among them Brătianu, fled to Paris, where they assured Louis Napoleon that there could be no better barrier against Russian expansion than an independent Rumanian state.* Developments soon confirmed their expectations. The general

*Despite the sympathy French liberals felt toward Brătianu, they were rather hazy about these remote regions. The French foreign minister, receiving young Brătianu, cut into his exposé by asking: "Pardon, Monsieur, what is the capital of your country?" "Bucharest, Excellency." "Ah, Bukhara? Bukhara, you say? Please, Monsieur, go on!"

fluidity that characterized the age and the area, Ottoman decay, Russian expansionist pressure, and the rising tide of nationalism gave them the chance they needed.

Russian defeat in the Crimean War removed the main obstacle to Rumanian nationhood. Part of Bessarabia was reannexed, and in the principalities the tremendous burst of nationalism of the late 1850s bore ample fruit. Brătianu returned to Bucharest in 1856. Supported by the French consul at Iaşi against complicated Russian and Austrian intrigues, and despite Stratford Canning's vice-regal diplomacy at the Porte, he unified the principalities in 1859 by electing Alexander Cuza as the ruling prince of both Wallachia and Moldavia. Although still nominally under the rule of the Sultan, the Rumanian state embarked on her existence as a European nation, armed with the Napoleonic Code, a French Group Theatre, and the novels of Dumas Père.

The father of modern Rumania was without a question Louis Napoleon, the self-appointed champion of nationalism all over Europe from the Balkans through Poland to Italy. He was impressed by the idea of a "Latin Sentinel on the Danube," a slogan skillfully planted by Brătianu and Nicolae Golescu in Paris.

It was one thing to gain national independence and foreign support and to adopt Western (French) trappings. To overcome a long continuity of tradition and the consequences of a very different heritage is another. Prince Cuza was the first, but by no means the last, Rumanian leader who was to learn this. He may have had some unendearing individual qualities, but he sincerely wished to curb the power of the boyars, to help the wretched peasants, and to restrict the merciless exploitation of national resources through the system of "dedicated monasteries," which drained away huge sums of the national income to Mount Athos. Cuza was farsighted enough to negotiate with Kossuth (who in exile had moderated his Hungarian nationalism), to arrive at a nationalism compatible with humanity and reason: the establishment of a Danube Confederation of Rumania, Serbia and Hungary as a balance to the huge German and Russian ethnic blocks weighing so heavily on No-Man's-Land.

In challenging the Church and the boyars in 1864 by liberating the serfs, Cuza counted on the support of the peasantry. But in the Rumania of his day, a prince could work for the peasants but not with them. After generations of long suffering, the spirit and backbone were missing from the peasant masses. One could expect a terrible *Jacquerie* from them when the burden became unbearable, but no constructive support. Cuza's dissolute private life was used skillfully against him, and his autocratic temper turned his faithful helper Kogălniceănu against him. In February 1866 a group of officers, representing the dissatisfied ruling class, forced him to abdicate.

It was Brătianu who took over the unchallenged leadership for the coming decades. But this Brătianu was no longer the handsome, somber émigré, the revolutionary idealist of 1848. He had "grown up" and seen the realities of Rumanian society; he also understood the interests of his class. He selected Prince Charles, of the Catholic branch of the House of Hohenzollern-

Sigmaringen, to ascend the throne of Rumania after Cuza — with the approval of Bismarck. Charles arrived in Rumania during the Austro-Prussian War and gave the country a liberal constitution modeled on the Belgian Charter of 1831, a constitution fated amid Rumanian realities to remain a piece of meaningless paper. The long reign of this Teutonic Spartan brought Rumania final independence from Turkey in 1881, after she had participated on Russia's side in the war against Turkey in 1878 — and been rewarded by losing to Russia the part of Bessarabia recovered in 1856. Rumania received the barren, windswept province of Dobrogea, with its Bulgarian and Turkish inhabitants, as a meager compensation. That experience, coupled with past ones, made Rumanian suspicions and fear of Russia almost insurmountable in the future. Therefore, Rumania adhered secretly to the Austro-Hungarian-German Treaty in 1883, a step not unwelcomed in Hungary, which hoped to keep the Rumanian irredenta under control.

After the difficulties of adjustment during the first years of his reign, Charles, from 1881 the king of an independent Rumania, proved to be a conscientious ruler, trying to do his best for his adopted country. But his task was not an easy one. Under the existing parliamentary system, a kind of political life developed in Rumania. There were "liberals" and "conservatives," the first representing the bourgeoisie and the second the landed estate owners, but these labels were meaningless. There was nothing like a genuine popular representation, for the inarticulate, illiterate masses were effectively denied participation in politics by bureaucratic methods. The criticism against Brătianu, *"la patrie veut être servie et non pas dominé,"* was a deserved one.[8] His methods and measures set a very bad precedent for future Rumanian politics. But to do him justice, the opposition was no better, and it is a question whether other methods would have worked under the circumstances.

In the economy, based as it was on agriculture, the peasant question was paramount, and it dominated the Rumanian scene from the time of independence up to World War I. Agrarian reforms did not improve the lot of the peasantry. The local bureaucracy knew how to get around them, and as a result the peasants were worse off fifty years after the Cuza reforms than before them. The land was owned almost exclusively by the boyars and their usurer tenants. The newly won personal freedom of the peasants was illusory because of their indebtedness to their former lords. A sharp population increase (54 percent between 1859 and 1899) weighed heavily on areas which had an agrarian overpopulation already.* The landowner could even enforce the agricultural "labor contracts" with the help of the military. In 1912, for example, 26,538 soldiers were "loaned" to landowners for this unsavory purpose.[9]

*The peasant masses did not take advantage of the safety valve of emigration possibilities overseas (to the U. S.) as hundreds of thousands in Hungary did. As in Russia, in Rumania, too, only the oppressed Jews migrated to the U. S. and to other countries, but not the peasants, despite their misery.

The misery of the peasants notwithstanding, the boom in grain export continued in these decades led to a superficial prosperity. The external attributes of European civilization were acquired with great rapidity. By 1914, 2,500 miles of railroad were built in a land where there were none in 1866. The Danube was bridged at Cernavoda with a ten-mile-long bridge in order to bring the seaport of Constanţa and the Dobrogea into the framework of the Rumanian economy. The crude oil production of Ploeşti gave some industrial character to a country which until then relied on agriculture alone.

But by 1914 only 1.5 percent of the national wealth was invested in industry. Foreign investment in industry was encouraged by tax exemptions and many other benefits. The oil industry was 99 percent in the hands of foreign investors (German, British, Dutch, French and American). The exploitation of the Carpathian forests went on in a wasteful manner, quite unchecked. A great deal of foreign debt was contracted to finance railroad construction and other public projects.[10] Bucharest began to acquire that *douce décadence,* that pseudo-Western aspect of sophistication, which earned her the questionable fame of being the Paris of the Balkans. But these twentieth-century trappings were ill equipped to cover up the sixteenth century and the Byzantine and Phanariote heritage. In 1906. when Rumania celebrated the fortieth anniversary of King Carol's rule with a magnificent exposition in Bucharest, *douce décadence* was in full bloom and Bucharest glittered before the many foreign guests. Karl Lueger, Mayor of Vienna and enemy of the "Judeo-Magyars," was among the most welcome.

What lay behind this imposing facade was exposed in the bloody peasant revolt of March 1907. Touched off by abuses by a Jewish tenant in Moldavia, disorders spread with lightning speed all over the country and widened into a great *Jacquerie.* The government panicked. There was talk of foreign intervention, but the minister of war, General A. Averescu, did not lose his head. He called on the military to quell the rebellion and did not hesitate to use artillery, to burn and destroy villages, and to kill an estimated 10,000 peasants. This spontaneous, unorganized, desperate outburst of the peasant masses showed better than anything else the reality behind the trappings of the artificially westernized salons of Bucharest.

After the highly instructive peasant revolt, a Liberal government was formed, and Brătianu's son declared himself in favor of a radical agrarian reform. The worst abuses of the peasantry by the landlords ceased. But the outbreak of the world war prevented the carrying out of more fundamental reforms. Rumania participated in 1913 in the Second Balkan War, gaining from hard-pressed Bulgaria a strip of land, Southern Dobrogea, which was mainly inhabited by Bulgarians and included Silistra, the important Danube fortress denied to Rumania by the Russians in 1878.

In Transylvania, the enlightened measures of the revolutionary Emperor Joseph II led to a fearful *Jacquerie* of the oppressed Rumanian serfs against their Hungarian masters. Perhaps their motives were more social than national; the leaders were Ion Horia from Albac, Ion Closca from Cărpinis and Gheorge Crişan. The army put down the rising — by no means less horrible than the much later one of 1907 in Rumania proper[11] — and Horia mounted the scaffold with simple words, "I am dying for my people."

After that, only the Uniate Church with its see in Blaj kept the national spirit alive. Rumanian intellectuals gathered under its protection and brought about a nationalist awakening. By the first decades of the nineteenth century, Gheorge Şincai had reformed the Rumanian language, adopting the Latin alphabet in place of the prevalent Greek one.*

During the revolution of 1848, the Rumanians, urged on by the Dynasty, rose against the intransigent Magyar nationalism of Kossuth. The Rumanians' spiritual leader was the Orthodox Metropolitan Andreas Şaguna, their political leader was Semeon Bărnuţiu, and their military leader the legendary Moţ Avram Iăncu. If in Wallachia the arrival of Russian interventionists meant the end of the liberal revolution, in Transylvania the Russians were greeted as liberators come to rescue the people from the intolerant Hungarian nationalist-revolutionaries. Many a Russian general stated later that their victory would scarcely have been possible without Iăncu's help.[12] But gratitude had as little place in Prince Schwarzenberg's designs as Rumanian nationalism did; the new Habsburg monarchy had to be a centralized state. When Iăncu protested, he was thrown into jail and manhandled. It was too much for the proud Moţ hero. His mind became clouded. He was finally released in this state to wander through his beloved mountains, playing his legendary flute, deeply revered by his unhappy people. But reverence for heroes does not last forever. Some years later, Iăncu was found by a roadside, dead of starvation. His fate is an instructive example of how much small nations count in the power politics of great nations.

Nor was that to be all. The *raison d'état* of the Habsburgs demanded further sacrifices from the nationalities of the Lands of the Holy Crown of St. Stephen, among them the Transylvanian Rumanians. In the Compromise of 1867 they were handed over to the Hungarian Nation. Bishop Şaguna advised passive resistance. But there was now a new generation of militant Rumanian nationalists who did not wish to live as their fathers lived. Their paper, the *Tribuna*, demanded rights for the Rumanian majority of Transylvania. The Hungarians usually dealt with demands for minority rights in an adminstrative manner, as they would deal with common crimes — the perpetrators were fined or imprisoned.

In 1890, the Rumanians decided to turn to the Emperor, who was in no position to challenge the Hungarian Nation on Transylvanian or any other minority rights. The members of the delegation who presented the memorandum in Vienna were tried for treason by the Hungarian authorities. The trial gained much sympathy for the Rumanian cause all over the West, and sympathy demonstrations followed it in Bucharest.

In the prewar decade it was already clear that Rumanian irredentism was irreconcilable and irrepressible. The leaders of the Transylvanian Rumanians,

*It was from Transylvania that the Latin alphabet conquered the Principalities, and where the Russians, understandably, did not welcome this proof of the unquenchable desire of the Rumanian people to belong to the West.

the poet Octavian Goga and the politicians Iuliu Maniu and Alexandre Vaida-Voevod, became the leaders of the future united Rumania.*

It was precisely the Transylvanian irredenta which spoiled the relations of the Dual Monarchy with her secret Rumanian ally. The Rumanian government could not ignore this question. It seems that by 1913 Brătianu had made his decision: the Bessarabian irredenta seemed to be impracticable. But he tried to enlist Russian support in case of the expected disintegration of Austria-Hungary. S. Sazonov's visit to Rumania and the meeting between Tsar Nicholas and King Charles in Constanţa in 1914 were milestones on this road. But not even the most sanguine optimist among Rumanian nationalists on either side of the Carpathians foresaw how soon their wildest dreams would be realized.

6

For all of Europe the First World War was a terrible calamity. It disrupted brutally a pattern of development, and it was the end of an era. Its material damage could be repaired. Even the colossal loss in life could be tolerated. But the damage it caused in intellectual values, the discredit it brought to reason, and hence to the intellectual, was irreparable in its consequences.

It would seem that the splendid, hopeful structure of Europe (that is, of the world as of 1914) had a weak spot — and the shot fired by Gavrilo Princip in Sarajevo struck into it. Mankind was not ready for the first full-fledged mechanized war. And from then on, "events passed very largely outside the scope of conscious choice. Governments and individuals conformed to the rhythm of the tragedy and swayed and staggered forward in helpless violence, slaughtering and squandering on ever increasing scales till injuries were wrought to the structure of human society which a century will not efface, and which may conceivably prove fatal to the present civilization."[13]

In a sense, the War of 1914-18 was worse than the Second World War. During its excruciating trench warfare, huge armies faced each other and month after month and year after year destroyed each other hopelessly and systematically with artillery, poison gas, barbed wire and machine guns. Ultimately, victory or defeat was more product of the mathematics of cannon fodder and slaughter than of leadership, skill or individual courage. The Second World War, on the other hand, contained much more movement, hope and adventure, and in 1939 came to a generation very different from the hopeful, idealistic generation that went to war in 1914.

In the hearts of those who fought or lived through the First World War, something froze irrevocably, resulting in a nihilism, a disillusionment, which produced on the winning side the Lost Generation in the United States, and the Maginot Line psychology and the Pétains in France. On the losing side,

*Vaida and Goga belonged to those Transylvanian Rumanian intellectuals who, after the Dynasty failed them, turned confidently to the demagoguery of Lueger and Georg von Schönerer in Vienna for ideas, ideas which never influenced Maniu.

the consequences were of a more radical character. Remarque foresaw this in his *All Quiet on the Western Front*, expressed in the words of a German soldier before the Armistice in the fall of 1918:

> All that meets me, all that floods over me are but feelings — greed of life, love of home, yearnings of the blood, anticipation of deliverance — but no aims.
>
> Had we returned home in 1916, out of the suffering and strength of our experiences we might have unleashed a storm. Now if we go back we will be weary, broken, burnt out, rootless, and without hope. We will not be able to find our way anymore.
>
> And man will not understand us — for the generation which grew up before us, though it has passed these years with us here, already had a home and a calling; now it will return to its old occupations, and the war will be forgotten — and the generation that has grown up after us will be strange to us and push us aside . . . .
>
> I stand up. I am very quiet. Let the months and years come, they bring me nothing, they can bring me nothing. I am so alone and so without hope that I can confront them without fear. The life that has borne me through these years is still in my hands and eyes. Whether I have subdued it, I know not. But so long it is there it will seek its own way out, heedless the will that is in me.[14]

These words were a grim forecast of things to come: the maladjustment of the veterans; the Horthys and the Hindenburgs who did not understand the postwar world, but who were nevertheless to wield power for too long; and the younger men, growing up in frustration, insecurity, and with a deeply wounded national pride after the defeat. The young would grow restless, and their pessimistic impatience would be strange to Horthy and his generation; consequently, they would try to "push him aside," as Remarque predicted. Because despite the shock to reason and intellect, World War I did not mean the end of things. On the contrary, a new day was dawning. With it came the rise of totalitarian ideas, especially in those areas of Europe where the defeat, the economic situation, and the lack of democratic tradition favored such a trend to an extraordinary degree.

Austria-Hungary, which seemed from the outside to be such a magnificent edifice, proved very weak in action — not so much on the Russian front (that could have been understood), but in the campaign against Serbia, in which the Serbians wrote one of the most glorious chapters of their history. Austria-Hungary was always saved only by German intervention. Italy and Rumania made much of their traditional policy of *sacro egoismo*, which continued with increasing vigor. By 1916-17, the initial general enthusiasm for the war had entirely disappeared. Nobody had counted on a long modern war with its requirements on the home front, and because of the relentless English blockade, there was widespread famine in both Germany and Austria. Hungary was spared the worst aspects of famine because of its agricultural character.

Surprisingly, the United States' entry into the war had its strongest effects in Austria-Hungary. After the Sixtus letter, the Dynasty's attempt to save the

Empire through a separate peace, the German General Staff took direct control. Austria's sovereignty had ended in everything but name.

But this did not concern Hungary. There was always a stronger martial spirit and enthusiasm for the war in centralized, unitary Hungary than in heterogeneous Austria, but as the years passed, it lost much appeal even there. Tisza, the dynamic leader of the Hungarian Nation, fell from power in 1917 over the issue of granting a wider franchise than he thought necessary or desirable, but not before he was able to block effectively any concession to the Rumanians.

The general war-weariness accentuated both the social ills and the nationality problem in Hungary. The voices of the small, democratic groups grew louder and louder. The disfranchised Social Democrats and the radical intellegentsia, under a predominantly Jewish leadership, became more and more vociferous, especially after the proclamation of Wilson's Fourteen Points.*

Ever since the mechanization of war, which coincided with broad popular participation in it, wars have not been conducted with small, professional armies. And when a debacle comes, the losing ruler can no longer return to his palace and continue his business pretty much as before. Not only he but the whole ruling class is made responsible for the defeat by the broad, popular masses, who have attained a degree of consciousness and power. That is what happened in France in 1870, and in Russia the misconduct of war coupled with long-standing social ills led to an outburst unprecedented in human history, not even waiting for the result of the contest on the field.

Both in Germany and in the Habsburg Empire, defeat had far-reaching and immediate effects on the position of the ruling elite and the dynasties. Germany, a fairly homogeneous state, could be saved as a national entity. But the Austro-Hungarian state, only four years older than the German one, could not overcome the temptation to pursue the glittering prospects of independent nationhood. This was a temptation harbored by most of her nationalities and carefully fostered in the highest quarters in the West in line with what the Western powers considered a liberal policy.

7

In mid-October, 1918, Tisza, the strongest statesman of the Dual Monarchy, declared in the Hungarian Parliament with his usual courage and staightforwardness, "We lost the war!" He put into words something

---

*There was a fatal flaw in this line of thought. Some days after the proclamation of the Fourteen Points, Secretary of State Robert Lansing (in conformity with the agreement concluded with T. G. Masaryk and other exiles), virtually proclaimed the dismemberment of the Austro-Hungarian Empire. And for good measure there were secret treaties between the Entente and Rumania and Italy dated 1915 and 1916 respectively. We shall see in the Trianon Treaty how much of Wilson's noble intentions were realized.

everybody had felt for a long time but had not dared to express. "Tisza said it" was the general reaction. In two weeks revolution engulfed Budapest, and in another two weeks the Dual Monarchy disintegrated. When the revolution came, Tisza was the man most hated by the masses, because they unjustly regarded him as the cause of the war. In the first days of the revolutionary turmoil, he was assassinated. It is interesting to think how Hungarian history might have developed if he had lived. He had tremendous integrity and character, which many of those lacked who in the next twenty-five years never tired of invoking his memory. Thus, the Hungarian Nation was left without a leader. It was also thoroughly discredited amid the bitterness of a lost war, amid suffering coupled with the ever present social dislocations which were accentuated by events. Under such circumstances there could be no question of leadership by anyone who even faintly resembled the old order.

So a progressive magnate, Count Michael Károlyi, formed a National Council of democratic, progressive elements, many of them members of the Jewish bourgeoisie, and some of them Social Democrats. Archduke Joseph, the last *homo regius* of the Habsburgs in Budapest, swore allegiance to the National Council. The Council severed Hungary's ties with Austria, proclaimed a republic, began an enlightened, democratic policy toward nationalities, and appealed to the Entente, which after all had fought the war under the slogan, "Let's make the world safe for democracy," to help to create a free, democratic Hungary on the basis of Wilson's Fourteen Points.

The new minister for the nationalities in Count Károlyi's deomocratic government, Professor O. Jászi, who for many years had advocated an enlightened policy toward Hungary's nationalities, thought the day had come to put his ideas into practice. During the months of November and December 1918, he tried his best to transform Hungary into his dream: an Eastern Switzerland. But the nationalities were beyond the point of being satisfied by concessions: the ideas of Czechoslovakia, Greater Rumania, and the "Yugoslav Idea" were too overwhelming for that. As far as the Entente was concerned, it became clear at an early stage of the peace settlement that the world first had to be made safe for France, and only then, if at all, for democracy. And it would not be fair to condemn the French after the heroic struggle and the sacrifices they had made during the war. After four years of an ordeal in which their soldiers bore the brunt of the burden, the French people had one thought, will and slogan: "Never again!" But French policy toward Czechoslovakia, Rumania and the Kingdom of the Serbs, Croats and Slovenes excluded any possibility of cooperation between the newest and oldest democracies of the continent. This fact did not add to the popularity of a government in Hungary which openly proclaimed its devotion to France, and under which the "Marseillaise" was played along with the Hungarian national anthem on festive occasions. All this had grave consequences later on.

But perhaps the greatest misfortune was the fact that the democratic and socialist intellectuals, although they meant well, did not have deep enough roots in Hungarian society. Most of them were not Hungarians by origin. In addition, Hungary was not ready for a liberal revolution. When it came, only the workers were an organized group, led by the Social Democrats. The bulk of the population, the peasants, were not organized because in the past the landlords on the local level could prevent their organizing themselves, and the government took care that they not be organized by the workers.

As F. Borkenau was quick to see, Károlyi had four tasks before him: (1) to make peace, (2) to carry through democratic elections, (3) to democratize the administration, and (4) to carry through an agrarian reform.[15] The agrarian reform was by far the most important measure to be carried out. In all countries where the feudal manorial system existed with its *de facto* if not *de jure* serfs, there was no room for democracy. Whether in Russia, Spain, Latin America, Hungary, Poland or Rumania, the first (but not the only) condition for a working democracy is a strong, land-owning, self-confident peasantry. Otherwise, the choice lies between an ultraleftist or a reactionary dictatorship. And even in Russia, Bolshevism could only live by giving land to the peasant.

Károlyi failed to fulfill any of his four tasks, partly because of the intransigency of the French, who cared nothing for the fate of Hungarian democracy. There was no moderation in the attitude of the Social Democratic party either. Because of the lack of mass support, the Károlyi regime was nothing but the dictatorship of the Social Democratic party, which had the only organized force, the workers, at its disposal with their framework of the trade unions. It was a sad spectacle that the Social Democrats, who had spent the last thirty years or so in criticizing electoral abuses, now made free elections impossible. They had the temerity to proclaim that "regardless of how the elections go, we intend to have a Red Parliament."[16] Also, they were narrow-minded enough to deny the peasants the right to organize their own party. Little did those Jewish intellectuals, who felt only an abstract kind of love for the Hungarian people, understand the bulk of it — the peasantry. There was no Lenin among them, not even a Trotsky. They prevented land reform on the basis of their dogmas, hoping to outdo Lenin by not allowing any capitalism in the villages as he did. They hoped to accomplish a direct transition to socialism.[17]

It is reasonable to assume that if the leadership of the Social Democratic party had come from the Hungarian people and had loved them with something more than abstract love, they would have had something more than a doctrinaire lack of understanding for the peasantry and would not by their errors have decided the fate of the democratic revolution from the outset. The consequences of this haughty contempt for the peasantry were to be far-reaching. If land reform had been carried out, there is little likelihood that the counterrevolution, even if victorious, would have been able to undo it subsequently. And the peasants would have remembered later those who gave them the land as they remembered Kossuth, who liberated their fathers and grandfathers from *de jure* serfdom.

But as is often the fate of small nations, the *coup de grace* for the new Hungarian democracy came from the outside. On March 20, 1919, the Entente demanded from Károlyi the surrender of new territories to the Succession States (this time purely Magyar-inhabited areas), declaring also that the lines of demarcation would have to be considered provisional frontiers. Károlyi was by that time thoroughly discredited. He could not get a decent peace from his Entente friends, he could not solve the social problems, and he could not even guarantee self-determination for his people. At that dark hour, there seemed only one solution — to ally Hungary with Soviet Russia and to drive out the intruders with the help of the Red Army and the solidarity of the international working class.

The national emergency gave the Bolshevik agent Béla Kun his chance. As a prisoner of war in Russia, he familiarized himself with Lenin's ideas, became an enthusiastic Bolshevik, and was sent by Lenin back to Hungary to start a Communist revolution. Lenin was an expert as far as the psychology of the Russian people was concerned, but for Hungary he could not have made a worse choice. It is hard to conceive of somebody farther away in thought, spirit and character from the Hungarian people than this little Jewish ex-journalist, who in addition did not have a winning personality.

He came to power on the national issue, but he quickly forgot the basis of his power. He started a bizarre experiment of doctrinaire war communism; for example, he threatened to punish the smallest commercial transaction with the death penalty.* In Russia, Kun must have observed Lenin's policy, which satisfied the peasants' land hunger, concluded a very detrimental but speedy peace, and refused to cooperate with the reformers. Kun implemented his conclusions in his own way: (1) refusing to carry out land reform and terrorizing the peasants, (2) making war on everybody, and (3) merging with the Social Democrats. Nevertheless, in the first two months or so the country went along with him because he was ready to stand up against the Czech and Rumanian invaders. In a swift offensive he threw back the Czechs, and the Hungarian Soviet was about to achieve what Kemal attained some years later. But the Entente ordered Kun to stop.

In Hungary the economy was going to pieces. The threat of food requisitions and the socialization of peasant plots led to the first counter-revolutionary disturbances. In the cities of Arad and Szeged, both within the French zone of occupation, the first counterrevolutionary groups, which later became governments, were formed. Another group of counterrevolutionary exiles was organized in Vienna.

Then Kun, an exceedingly cowardly person himself but possessed by the resentful cruelty so characteristic of cowards, resorted to terrorism. His henchman was another Jew, the notorious Tibor Számuelly, who crossed the

---

*Borkenau, *The Communist International*, p. 120. The law was signed by Mátyás Rákosi, whom we shall meet in 1945 as the Communist dictator of Hungary.

unhappy country in an armored train with his "Lenin boys" terrorizing the countryside, his victims being mainly peasants. Of the 342 victims of the Red Terror, 248 were peasants.[18] No one should think that Számuelly or the Communist regime (in whose leadership the Jewish population was over-represented) was in any way favorably disposed to the Jews, a predominantly bourgeois element. According to the statistics presented by the Arrow Cross historian Ödön Málnási, forty-four Jews were killed by Számuelly's terror squads.[19] The Red Terror in Hungary does not match the one perpetuated by the Cheka, but the Kun regime had little time at its disposal.

Amid famine, disillusionment and Red Terror, Kun forces moved against the Rumanians. But under such circumstances the Rumanians finished them off with relative ease. The help expected at the outset from the Russian Soviet never materialized. The Hungarian Red Army disintegrated, and on August 4, 1919, the Rumanian Army entered Budapest just after the Kun government made its disgraceful exit to Vienna. Kun continued to outrage Lenin by committing unspeakable and unnecessary cruelties in the Crimea, where he was sent as political commissar.[20] In 1937 he was purged by Stalin for alleged crimes which, ironically enough, he did not commit.

Meanwhile, a caretaker government was formed in Budapest by the right-wing Social Democrats, Károly Peyer and Gyula Peidl, but after some days this government was overthrown with Rumanian military assistance by István Friedrich.[21] Archduke Joseph was also at hand to play one of his many roles in Hungarian history. He made an abortive attempt in August to grab the reins of power for himself. The Rumanians looted Budapest thoroughly and left in November 1919. On November 16, the counterrevolutionary forces called National Army and headed by Admiral Miklós Horthy entered the capital. The counterrevolution was in place.

9

When the Great War broke out, Rumania remained neutral. Although a member of the alliance system of the Central Powers (a fact known in Rumania only to some few, even among the initiated), public opinion and the opposition of the Liberals under Brătianu made it impossible for old King Carol I to join his kinsmen and his house in its struggle against the Entente. This decision was made at the historic Crown Council on August 4, 1914, at Sinaia, the summer residence of the Rumanian kings in the Transylvanian Alps. Soon after the old King died. With his death, a powerful obstacle was removed from the way of Brătianu's policy, which, like that of Italy, was to enter the war at a decisive moment on the side of the Entente and extract the highest possible price for it. The ultimate goal was the creation of Greater Rumania, which would encompass all Rumanians who lived outside the Old Kingdom.* The new King Ferdinand and his beautiful wife Queen Marie, the

---

Regat, meaning kingdom in Rumanian. The provinces of Wallachia (Munţenia and Oltenia), Moldavia and Dobrogea, which in 1914 encompassed the Kingdom of Rumania, were referred to as such after the Great War.

granddaughter of Queen Victoria and of Tsar Alexander II of Russia, were enthusiastic supporters of the Entente. King Ferdinand seems not to have been influenced in the least by the Hohenzollern blood in his veins; all such sentimental attachments died with King Carol. His nephew was first and last the servant of Rumania, and Brătianu, his prime minister, demanded that the Allies recognize Rumanian claims to Transylvania and Bucovina and did not forget — to the towering fury of the Russian foreign minister, Sazonov — Bessarabia. Yet he hesitated with his declaration of war on the Central Powers. The Germans made a faint attempt to offer concessions in Transylvania to Rumania, an attempt firmly squashed by Tisza, the Hungarian prime minister.

The favorable moment for Rumania came in the summer of 1916 when the great Russian offensive was in full swing, and Cadorna attacked along the Isonzo, pressing the Dual Monarchy hard. Nor was the military situation on the Western front, after the bloody German failure to take Verdun, rosy for the Central Powers, and the Allies urged Bucharest in unmistakable terms to stop temporizing. On August 24, 1916, Brătianu pronounced his famous words at the Crown Council, directed at the few perturbed conservatives of the "German line": "I take the responsibility [for this step] because I trust in our victory."[22] The same evening, the Rumanian envoy in Vienna handed in the Rumanian Declaration of War at the *Ballhausplatz*. Rumanian troops promptly invaded Transylvania.

The war went well for Rumania in the beginning. The weakened Dual Monarchy had no forces to repel the new enemy, and a considerable part of Transylvania was occupied by the Rumanian Army in September. Then the German Balkan Army, under Erich von Falkenhayn and August von Mackensen, struck. Crossing the Danube from Bulgaria, it quickly moved on Bucharest and, after occupying the capital, swept Wallachia clean and drove back the rest of the Rumanian army to Moldavia. King and government fled to Iaşi.

Under the stress of modern warfare, the backwardness of the Rumanian Army's supply and organization was exposed and with it the country's social ills as well (1916-17 being barely a decade since the great peasant rising of 1907). French officers under General Henry Berthelot took care of the first problem: they reorganized the faltering Rumanian Army. The second problem, popular discontent, was handled in a decisive fashion by the King and the ruling class. King Ferdinand told the troops on the front, "Land will be given to you. I, your King, am the first to set the example; and you will also take a larger part in public affairs."[23] The results were immediate and far-reaching. Although neighboring Russia was engulfed in a great revolutionary upheaval for many years, the Russian revolution did not spread to Rumania, despite the similarity of conditions in both countries and despite the close geographical connection. Even after the demoralizing breakdown of discipline among Russian divisions fighting side by side with them on Moldavian soil, the Rumanians, under General Averescu, bravely withstood the German onslaught in the battles of Maraşti and especially of Maraşeşti in August 1917. The front could be stabilized between the Carpathians and the Black Sea.

But it would not have been in Rumanian political tradition to wait in an "all quiet on the Western front" fashion, to bide time until the Entente's victory. The conservative Germanophile politician, Alexandre Marghiloman, remained in Bucharest, where he began negotiations with the Germans and succeeded in concluding a humiliating peace treaty with the Central Powers in May 1918. The King never ratified this political insurance treaty, which he opposed to the end, along with Brătianu and the rest of the Liberals.

Humiliating though the peace treaty was, and though it was a breach of faith with the Entente as Rumania had promised not to conclude a separate peace, it was not wholly disadvantageous for Rumania. The Germans recognized, nay encouraged, Rumanian occupation and annexation of Bessarabia. This province, with its overwhelmingly Rumanian population, formed an autonomous Moldavian Republic, which was to become a part of the Russian Democratic Republic in December 1917. Now its governing *Sfãt* (Council or Soviet), opposing Bolshevik centralization, called in Rumanian troops, which occupied the province in January 1918. After that, the *Sfãt* voted for union with Rumania, with the dual demand of autonomy (never honored) and preservation of the land reform already in effect.*

That was the situation when the Balkan front of the Central Powers collapsed with the capitulation of Bulgaria at the end of September 1918. Mackensen withdrew his troops from the *Südostraum*, and Rumania then made a theatrical "reentry" into the war, a reentry which would later be grudgingly recognized by the Entente. Recognition depended not so much on the intrinsic value of this *opéra-bouffé* as on the services Rumania rendered to the Powers during the turbulent years of 1918-19. The "Versailles system," that is, French foreign policy, had two principal goals in this area: the quest for *securité,* and the maintenance of a *cordon sanitaire* against Bolshevik Russia. Rumania had her place in both schemes.

After the acquisition of Bessarabia and after Rumania's reentry into the war in its last days, Brătianu cashed the promissory notes of the Allies in Bucovina, and ancient part of Moldavia ceded by the Turks to Austria under Maria-Teresa. Although the province was then both historically and ethnically Rumanian, by 1918 almost half its people were Ukranians, and the cities were overwhelmingly Jewish in character. On November 28, 1918, the governing congress "voted," under the pressure of occupying Rumanian troops, for union with Rumania.

But all these acquisitions did not lie as close to Rumanian hearts on either side of the Carpathians as did the union of Transylvania and the *Regat*. With the collapse of the Dual Monarchy, the Hungarian democratic republic of Károlyi adopted a conciliatory attitude toward the nationalities of the Lands to St. Stephen. Professor Jászi, the newly created minister of nationalities, a convinced democrat and a long-standing opponent of the brutal Magyarization policies of Budapest, tried to save what was left to save. He met with Transylvanian leaders in Arad to convince them of the advantages of

*In Bessarabia, as in the rest of Tzarist Russia, peasants seized the land arbitrarily after the outbreak of the revolution.

remaining in Hungary. If anybody was qualified to negotiate with Transylvanian Rumanians, Professor Jászi was. He was a Transylvanian himself, and he meant it when he spoke of transforming Transylvania into an "Eastern Switzerland." But the Rumanians had been mistreated too long to prefer any state under Hungarian leadership, democratic or not, to a union with their kinsmen. On December 1, 1918, the representatives of Transylvanian Rumanians met in the historic capital of Transylvania, Alba-Iulia, and the Governing Council, under the chairmanship of Iuliu Maniu, proclaimed the union of Transylvania with the other Rumanian lands. Their other demands, all of which reflected the spirit of Maniu, were liberty for the nationalities, autonomy for all regions, democracy with universal suffrage, liberty of the press and of association, a radical agrarian reform, and significant improvements for industrial workers.[24]

Iuliu Maniu, who with Ion Brătianu was the architect of Greater Rumania but decidedly the better man, was 45 years old in 1918. Undisputed leader of the Rumanian National party of Transylvania, he exemplified the best qualities of the Transylvania Rumanians, who were much less the product of the Byzantine-Phanariote tradition than their kinsmen in the *Regat*. He was the descendant of the great Semeon Bărnuțiu, and a lawyer by profession, educated at Cluj, Budapest and Vienna. As attorney of the ecclesiastic-cultural center of the Uniate Church in Blaj, which was also the center of Rumanian national consciousness, Maniu became involved in the struggle of the Transylvanian Rumanians at the time of the Memorandum of the 1890s when Transylvanian Rumanians made a desperate attempt to air their grievances to the Dynasty. Later, he was elected to the Hungarian Parliament from one of the electoral districts the Hungarian Nation reserved for Rumanians in order to help maintain the fiction of parliamentarianism. There he courageously and hopelessly fought for his people in the wildest years of Magyarization at the beginning of the century. His struggle earned him the undying hatred of the Hungarians, especially those in Transylvania. His companions in this fight, Vaida-Voevod, the poet Goga, and Văleriu Pop, like many other young Rumanian intellectuals of Transylvania, looked to Vienna for support. Not finding it in the Dynasty, which was committed to Budapest, they found the language and ideas they wanted to hear in the harangues of Lueger, the Christian Socialist Mayor of Vienna and his party against the "Judeo-Magyars." Although these harangues had some influence later in moving the Transylvanian leaders toward fascism and a violent anti-Semitism (some of the most enthusiastic Magyarizers and the most uncompromising zealots of Magyardom in Transylvania were the Jews!), Maniu never wavered in his belief in democracy, decency and due process of law, a belief he had absorbed in the austere, pure atmosphere of Blaj and of Transylvania as a whole, and in the parliament at Budapest.

But such deep faith belonged to another age, another century. It had little in common with the atmosphere of the "Paris of the Balkans," or with the world of the political ethics after 1918, in which this ascetic, incorruptible man was to work for the welfare of his people for the next thirty years. In both contexts, in that of postwar Bucharest and in that of the political world of Hitler and Stalin and Carol II, this greatest son of Transylvania in the twentieth century was hopelessly out of place. All three of the rare "incorruptibles" of Rumanian politics — Maniu, Antonescu and Corneliu Codreanu — perished within a decade, 1938-48. Each sought a different road to salvation for Rumania. Without a doubt the most pathetic figure among them, and the only democrat, was Maniu. Ultimately, the greatest sin attributed to him was that he was unable to live up to the ruthlessness, the atrocious vulgarity and utter unscrupulousness of the politics of his age. To the end, he remained faithful to the three ideals he fought for in his lifetime: (1) constitutional government, (2) Christian conduct of government leaders, and (3) a Rumanian Transylvania. But this was all in the far future on December 1, 1918, that wintry day in Alba-Iulia where Iuliu Maniu experienced the great moment of his life, uniting Transylvania with the rest of Rumania.

The Entente seemed to waver about granting Rumania such great chunks of land. But when Béla Kun established the Hungarian Soviet Republic, there was no time to scrutinize Rumanian performance during the war or how well her claims were founded. Despite the fact that Rumania was encircled by leftist disorder or communism on all sides — in Russia, Bulgaria and Hungary — she remained stable, thanks to the promise of land reform and to national aggrandizement. The sporadic disorders of the Communist elements were handled by the *Siguranţa* (the Rumanian secret police) with ruthless efficiency. Not only did the Rumanian peasant-soldier not revolt, he could be used successfully to crush the Hungarian Soviet Republic. It was these factors which helped to support the immoderate demands of Brătianu at Versailles. The peasant leader Ion Mihalache called the coming land reform "a kind of safety valve" for the ruling class; it served its purpose successfully until the great depression wrecked the economy thoroughly in the 1930s.[25]

After a year and half of *Kuhhandel*, of changes of government, and increased leftist agitation, the ruling class found it expedient to enact the much-vaunted land reform in the *Regat*, after it had been carried out in Bessarabia, Transylvania and Bucovina.* As minister of defense in 1907 Marshall Averescu brutally suppressed the peasant rising, but in 1921, as a hero of the Great War, the head of the popular party, and prime minister, he carried through the land reform in the *Regat*. Altogether, more than six million hectares of land were expropriated in Greater Rumania in this most sweeping of all postwar agrarian reforms in non-Communist Europe.[26] Out of 1,979,083 peasants entitled to land according to the law, 1,368,978 received land until 1927.[27] In 1923, after a fierce political struggle, the Liberal party under Brătianu regained power and fulfilled the last part of the King's promissory note: a democratic constitution was enacted by parliament, granting a wide franchise to men (women were excluded from political rights until 1946). On the surface, as happens so often, things looked more hopeful

---

*In these newly acquired provinces, most of the landlords were not Rumanians, and Rumanian peasants got most of the land—the Rumanian oligarchy of the *Regat* therefore did not object to the land reform.

in this peasant state where as late as 1930, 79.9 percent of the population lived in villages[28] and not all of the remaining 20.1 percent lived in towns deserving the name.

A Greater Rumania beyond the wildest hopes and dreams of the decade before had been established. The *Regat* with its 137,000 square kilometers and its seven million people had blossomed into a state of 294,000 square kilometers and 15.5 million people. Some 30 percent of its population was not Rumanian. Almost a million were Jews. So many Jews were bound to cause difficulties especially if we consider that in 1930 68.2 percent of them lived in towns, and the 31.8 percent living in the villages were rarely engaged in agriculture.[29] The social stratification of Rumanians was just the opposite; 75 percent lived in villages[30] with the result that there was an agrarian over-population of 51 percent.[31] The Jews were not the only nationality in Rumania by far. The more than 1.5 million Hungarians of Transylvania were irreconcilable enemies of the new state. But the country now possessed three great advantages: a democratic constitution and a sweeping agrarian reform supposedly doing justice to the overwhelming majority of Rumanians, the peasants, had been added to economic resources among the richest and best balanced in Europe (Rumania was often referred to as a "beautiful, marriageable girl with a rich dowry"). With the national dream fulfilled, the future looked bright for Greater Rumania.

But in an underdeveloped peasant economy and with the peculiar historical fate of Rumania, sometimes even such a bright prospect is not fulfilled so logically, consistently, and self-evidently as some might expect it to be. Despite the apparent advantages of Greater Rumania with her vast natural resources, radical agrarian reform, and democratic system of government, the Rumania of reality had not changed very much.

10

If the difference between the capital and the countryside in Hungary was great, that between the life of Bucharest and life of four out of five inhabitants of Greater Rumania was even greater. With the exception of some Transylvanian Saxon communities and some German colonies in Bucovina and Bessarabia, the lot of the peasant masses was miserable. Although almost every innovation in the interwar period was supposed to serve their welfare, the peasants in their ideas, way of thinking and civilization were centuries behind modern Rumanian life.

The agrarian reforms liberated them from the bondage and degradations of *de facto* serfdom. But the humiliations inherent in poverty, economic underdevelopment, and a police state remained. The agrarian reform gave land, but no farming equipment, no domestic animals, and no credit to start independent farming. Above all, the agrarian reform did not change the outlook and the lack of education in the villages. The distribution of efficient great estates into individual plots decreased productivity, and many enterprising peasants, who with hard work began to hold their own as masters of their plots of land, were crushed by the great depression of the 1930s. The ideal of transforming Rumanian agriculture into efficient three- to five-hectare holdings was not achieved. On the contrary, as the National Peasant economist Prof. Virgil Madgearu pointed out, after the depression it was the middle-sized peasant properties which showed themselves efficient and grew at the cost of the smaller proprietors, who relapsed increasingly into the growing agricultural proletariat.[32]

Mirrored in the statistics of 1938, the agrarian situation was as follows: Out of 3,978,820 peasant families, 1,002,556 were still living in huts built of plain clay, some 600,000 of them not even possessing a window. About 500,000 peasants lived with their cattle in the same room. Two million peasants did not possess a cow, 600,000 not even a pig, and about 250,000 did not even have a chicken. The average meat consumption of a Rumanian family was seventy pounds a year.[33] Out of 60,855 springs used for water supply, 28,743 were found to be infected with disease germs. This perhaps explains why Rumania, with the record birthrate of Europe (650,000 a year) also held the death record (350,000 infants a year). More than 10 percent of infants died in their first year. These non-European conditions in the countryside receive additional confirmation when we look at the number of doctors per capita: 4.6 per 10,000 inhabitants — but only 1.1 in the rural districts in 1938. The figure coincides with the figure for India in the same year.[34]

As for the workers, they were certainly better off, both in relative and in absolute terms, but Rumania had no working class of importance. With 7.2 percent of the population deriving its livelihood from industry in 1930, Rumania lagged, for example, behind Turkey. The extent of underdevelopment is revealed by the fact that industrial production (the all-important petroleum industry and other mining industries included) was responsible for less than half — in certain years for one-third — of the gross national product in the years preceding World War II.[35]

All this contrasted sharply with the small skyscrapers and the pulsating life of Bucharest. Not without reason did they call it the "Paris of the Balkans." The atmosphere of Dragomir Niculescu or the Confisierie Capşa, the night clubs Alhambra or Albăstru, the worldly sophistication, and the easygoing mélange of Paris and the Orient (with the worst temptations of both well represented) created a corrupting mood (the *douceur* of life in pre-Communist Bucharest was more a mood than anything else). This mood influenced almost everybody, citizen or foreigner, who experienced it for very long. In the mid-nineteenth century, A. Gorchakov complained to N. Giers about the effect of their Bucharest stay on the morals of Russian officials.* Tsar Nicholas II summed up aptly in one of his rare *mots* the essence of the problem: "Rumania — this is not a nation, but a profession! " Field Marshal August von Mackensen, the commander of the German Army,

---

*Barbara Jelavich, *Russia and the Rumanian National Cause 1858-1859* (Bloomington, 1959) p. 34. In a confidential letter Gorchakov wrote as follows: "These Danubian Principalities have been at all times, and with deplorable results, a touchstone for the integrity of our employees."

after a stay of two years, cried out in despair concerning the behavior of his officers, "I came to Bucharest with a troupe of conquering heroes and I leave here with a troupe of gigolos and racketeers!"[36] Even one of the most austere, upright dynasties of Europe, The House of Hohenzollern-Sigmaringen, became utterly corrupted in the one generation between the first and second Carol. But few people worried in Bucharest about that aspect of things. Theirs was a society and way of life that cared neither about the future nor about the past — because it did not have any. So between 1918 and 1944 it made the best of the present.

The superficial and all too speedy adaptation to Western ideas and culture (where Western stands above all for French) had even more terrible consequences in Greater Rumania than it did elsewhere. Such an adaptation could not penetrate deeply or overcome the heritage of many centuries; it gave to life in Rumania only an outwardly Western aspect. European science, ideas and fashions dominated social life in Bucharest. But the real, positive forces of society ought to come from a deeper source: from the moral and cultural bearing of the people. If one looked for these unconscious or subconscious manifestations of the West, one could find none; although one could find many of those of the Orient. But as Rumania was a borderland between the Near East and Central Europe, with her eyes fixed in awe on France and Paris, she no longer trusted her traditional values. The inconsistent nature of the inconclusive, ever-changing imitation of Western forms expressed itself in the atmosphere of Rumanian cities (especially outside of Transylvania), but also in administration, in organization, in every aspect of life. In this cultural borderland, Western intellectual influences had not yet found a modus vivendi with the traditional culture; outside the peasantry, there was no sincere and deeply rooted form of life to be found.

This tension between form and content could be found at every step, but was most apparent in the political life of the country. Despite the fact that there was no open balloting or restricted franchise in existence, as in Hungary, democracy and parliamentarianism served to camouflage the coarse egotism and will to power of parties and individuals whose goal was almost invariably to grow rich quickly at the expense of the state. This led to an unsavory competition between the parties, a competition fought out by means of unscrupulous demagoguery and unabashed promises. The uneducated and politically inexperienced electorate voted for those who were bidding the most. When the new government could not fulfill its impossible promises, it lost its popularity fast, and the naïve electorate turned to a new bidder. Thus, the most popular opposition as a rule became the unpopular government in power. And because they figured time was short, the governing party hacks threw themselves at the pork barrel with two goals: to reimburse themselves for costly electoral campaigns and to secure for themselves the loyalty of "influential supporters."

Under such circumstances there could be no question about taking advantage of the before-mentioned positive aspects of Greater Rumania; no constructive government and no solution of problems is possible in such a political milieu. Political and electoral promises had to be kept at any cost, if not to the masses at least to the "influential supporters," and each successive government gave away as much as the dwindling resources of the state allowed. It was a self-perpetuating process. The misdeeds of the preceeding government could not be exposed, because the vanquished party would have retaliated by exposing the misdeeds of its successor. Judging from the ample instructive, if not every edifying, examples in this vein contained in volumes of Rumanian parliamentary debates of the early 1920s, it would seem that almost all the time and effort of the M.P.'s on the Dealul Spirei* was spent trying to use their influence on their protégés — a practice that seemed more than natural to their constituents, who after all, had elected them for that purpose! The standards of parliamentary life reflected on those pages are among the lowest in recorded history. The real issues were submerged in a flood of petty personal affairs, revindication, slander, invective, "explanation," etc.

There were very few educated Rumanians. As we mentioned before, for good or bad Rumania had no counterpart for the Hungarian Nation. The governing elite it had did not deserve the name. It is no exaggeration to say that in the whole of Europe, the rest of the Balkans included, there was no match for the corruption of all kinds, public and private, which prevailed in the Rumanian upper class and reached as high as the crown.** And yet, some qualifications must be made. Perhaps because of the corruption or because of the long historical experience of Rumania (the task of drawing the line between the two is not an easy one), these people were realists; there were few "enthusiasts" amongst them and no traitors. In matters of foreign policy, their sometimes astounding, almost cynical realism was often employed effectively in the service of their nation.

Internally, in the early 1920s, the consequence of the sparse number of educated leaders and the lack of political experience on the local level produced an extreme centralization of power which extended itself to every possible sphere of life. Balkan liberals always stood for centralization, and the Brătianu government was no exception. Its centralizing policies, which overruled any possible resistance on the local level, were never undone. If there was any opposition, the two time-honored Rumanian means of persuasion or dissuasion were used: bribery and violence.

The electoral campaigns were fought with the free use of the Rumanian gendarmerie (its violence, too, tempered only by corruption), stealing of ballot boxes, and quarantines imposed arbitrarily on any number of districts,

*The hill in Bucharest where the Representatiunea Natională, the Rumanian Parliament, stands.
**For those who did not see and live through the *douce dècadence* of interwar Rumania's ruling classes, some excellent novels by Petru Dumitriu give a good picture. *The Prodigals* (New York, 1963) is especially recommended.

and by crass intimidation of voters.*   These methods reflected not only the rather low educational level of the lower echelons of administration, but also political "necessity." Where demagogic promises did not work, and the direct bribe either was not suitable or there were no financial means available to bribe with, the government had to apply direct pressure in the form of violence. The administrative offical had to go along with all that; his job and daily bread depended on the government that had secured employment for him, and every election brought about a wholesale exchange and replacement of administrative officals. His subservience to the government was augmented by fear that his own shoddy dealings might be exposed. The incredibly low salaries, which often were paid late and sometimes not at all, delivered the whole administration, and also the military, into the arms of corruption. There were honorable exceptions − but they were few and they certainly were not able to change the overall picture. The distinguished Rumanian economist, Prof. Gheorghe Leon, who presented the budget for the year 1934-35, illustrated handily the prevailing corruption when he reported to Parliament that in the last years in the ministries and other administrative organs, 3,567,587,136 lei**had been embezzled by officials. Out of this very considerable sum, the share of the ministry of defense was 2,862,376,868 lei.***These were the officially recognized figures concerning state funds; individual bribes were not included.

*A good illustration of a routine electoral campaign in the elections of 1932 follows: "What may happen during the campaign preceding the polling day reflects the general standard of the country's political life. . . . In the present instance, there have been cases of personal violence and collision between rival parties or between the people and the police. The worst incident is reported from Buzău, where on July 8 a National Peasant municipal councillor, who had distinguished himself for the viciousness of his attacks on his Liberal opponents, was approached by some of the latter in a cafe, for the purpose, it is alleged, of persuading him to abate his electoral violence. A general fracas followed, in the midst of which the National Peasant Councillor was shot and seriously wounded. His assailants hurriedly withdrew to lodge a complaint against him at the police court, but he contrived to arm himself with a revolver and caught them up while they were still in the courtroom. He wounded two of them, one being the head of the local Liberal organization; the latter and the councillor both succumbed to their wounds the following day. . . . To the foreign observer the responsibility would seem to rest with every Rumanian politician who allows the violence of his party passions to outrun his better judgment and with the Rumanian newspapers that exercise no self-control in the discussion of political affairs and in the terms of abuse that they heap on political adversaries." *Near East and India,* July 21, 1932, p. 577.

**Leu (plural lei), Rumanian monetary unit. In 1930, $1 equaled about 167 lei.

***Die Siebenbürgische Frage, (Budapest, 1940), pp. 255-59. Although this pamphlet served very definitely the purposes of Hungarian revisionist propaganda, the figure quoted seems essentially correct, and the writer lacked other sources of substantiation.

34

Greater Rumania made feverish efforts to replace the alien middleman by creating a Rumanian middle class. This change of the guard concerned first and above all the Jewish middle class, but also the Hungarians in Transylvania, and at a later date and to a lesser extent it would reach the Saxons too. Many of the shortcomings that have been described were attributable to the lack of a native Rumanian middle class. In Rumania in 1925, there were 6.8 university students for every 10,000 people compared to 10.7 in Great Britain; by 1932, there were 19.7 in Rumania to 12.1 in Britain.[37] The overwhelming majority of these young men did not take up those professions which Rumania urgently needed — that is, engineering, medicine, technology — but concentrated on law. The number of practicing lawyers searching for a lucrative access to the pork barrel and clamoring for government offices (and when not satisfied, leaning toward the radical right) was proverbial in this period and on the increase.

The unchecked exploitation of the country's resources was the goal not only of the elite and the bureaucracy, but also of this new middle class. If in neobaroque Hungary the common prerequisite for acceptance into the ranks of the Hungarian Nation of recruits from the lower classes was the acceptance of the Szeged Fascist interpretation of its standards, in Rumania the entrance requirements were simpler: the newcomer need only be a Rumanian and adapt himself to the easy-going deceit of the "Paris of the Balkans." The governing circles were willing to extend a helping hand to these badly educated, and more often than not amoral, creatures in order to overcome the Jewish, Hungarian and German minority-group middle classes, and in order to "nationalize" — or as they called it, to "Romanize" — the spiritual and economic life of the country.* In the 1930s there would be a "Romanization" campaign of enterprises owned by the minority middle classes and restrictive measures for the admittance of minorities to universities, but with very different results from those expected by Vaida-Voevod or the other apostles of this course. As in Hungary after the anti-Jewish legislation, in most cases the minorities in Rumania merely featherbedded some comfortable sinecures for the new Rumanian middle class; the real work was done as before by those in inferior positions and those positions were filled mainly by the same minority middle class. Those of the new Rumanian middle class who really did some work did it not in the honorable and more difficult trades or professions, but through political connections they acquired immoral advantages for themselves, and they demanded in the name of the "national idea" that members of their class be preferred to those of the minority middle classes and their frequently inferior services better remunerated.

*The writer remembers a typical conversation in 1939 in Cluj, an overwhelmingly Hungarian-inhabited town, and the capital of Transylvania, when in high Rumanian society somebody remarked that "Mr. X, a high Rumanian official, bought a new house out of bribes." The comment was, "More power to him! One more Rumanian house in Cluj! "

It was the poet Goga himself who pronounced a devastating criticism of the abortive movement to create a Rumanian middle class. After describing these Jacks of all trades who exported and imported every possible article and were everywhere omnipresent, Goga touched upon the essence of the problem:

> These are carnivorous birds who, as if by tacit agreement, prepare the doom of the country. They create a disgusting atmosphere, a pestilential stench of carcasses. . . . Unfortunately, there is for the salvation of these corrupt creatures a theoretical justification, which has already achieved the strength of a dogma — that we should base our national life on this dubious scum of our towns, the well-known policy that we should create quickly and at any cost, a stately bourgeoisie. But because in our great haste we could not wait for the slow process of development, we replaced the citizen with the swindler.[38]

Prophetic words, though how disillusioning that most of the support for Goga came ten years later from precisely those elements whom he condemned in such forceful terms in 1925.

But the government was always hopelessly dependent on a political party, and the political party had insurmountable obligations and indebtedness to the financial interests, both domestic and foreign, which were in turn inseparably bound in a sinister, obscure manner to the system itself. In this disconcerting, vicious circle there could be no question about the balance of privileges and responsibilities. Responsibility is the only guarantee of a democratic government. In the Rumanian sham democracy, the lack of responsibility was the rule. A frightful lack of responsibility toward the public and toward ones fellow man, and utter disregard of the law — both written and moral law — these were the visible results of the adaptation of Western democratic forms in Rumania.

CHAPTER II

The Jews of Hungary and Rumania

You [the Convention] have been told things about Jews, which are extremely exaggerated and do not bear examination. The deficiencies of the Jews have their roots in the degradation in which you forced them to live. The Jews will better themselves as soon as they see that it is advantageous for them to do so. I mean that one must not deprive a single member of the [Jewish category of] people of his Holy Rights, to which he, as a human being, is entitled.

The question is a matter of principle, and must be treated accordingly.

Robespierre, before the French National
Assembly on the question of Jewish Emancipation, 1791

The complete elimination of the Jews from Europe is not a question of morality alone, but the question of the security of nations. The Jew will always act according to his nature and racial instinct. He cannot act otherwise. Exactly as the potato-beetles destroy the potato fields and as they must destroy them [in order to live] so does the Jew destroy nations and peoples. There exists only one remedy against this: the radical elimination of the menace! ...

Dr. Joseph Göbbels, Prague, November 1940

1

In a study of the history of fascism in Hungary and Rumania, the Jewish question deserves a chapter. Professor C. A. Macartney is right when he states that it occupied a position second to none in the history of interwar Hungary,[1] and the same is true of Rumania, so far as Rumanian Fascist movements are concerned.

When Frederick the Great, perhaps in a grave moment of his life, asked his physician Zimmermann of Brugg for proof of the existence of God, the answer was a short one: "The Jews."[2] The strange story of this predestined people has no parallel in the history of the world. At every important turn in the history of Western Civilization they are there — the son of the carpenter of Nazareth, Marx, Trotsky, Einstein, Freud are points in the case. Jewish nationalism is a unique one, of the toughest mold, in which religion and nationhood are not only closely connected, they are exclusively identical. And this nation amidst the nations seems predestined to play a special role in the world, markedly different from the roles of other nations. This is why Jewish nationhood survived the blandishments of Hellenism and the might, the majesty and the terror of Rome, and why it continued to survive in the medieval ghetto, thrived rather than was crushed by the pyres of the

Inquisition, and emerged triumphant from the ovens of Auschwitz. After 2,000 years, the Jews restored the homeland, speaking the same language and worshipping the same God in the same Jerusalem as in time immemorial.

The unusual character of Jewish history has perplexed and fascinated Gentiles throughout the ages, and more often than not a substitute for a rational explanation has been found in charges of ritual murder, alleged desecration of churches, and responsibility for epidemics (a more modern version of the old theme was the "Protocols of the Wisemen of Zion"). When the Romans, tired of incessant insubordination in a minuscule corner of their faraway Syrian province, exiled the Jews from their homeland, the Jews reacted in their own way. They made the scriptures their portable fatherland, evolving from geographical nationhood into spiritual nationhood. Thanks to the exclusiveness of Judaism, it could become the expression of Jewish national consciousness for the coming eighteen centuries. But the medieval *ordo* not being a nationalist one, and being based as it was on Christianity, this peculiar Jewish nationalism, manifesting itself through Judaism, automatically excluded the Jews as full-fledged members of the medieval world. Not having a place among peasants and nobles, the Jews became the oldest middle class of Europe, but not the respectable kind. Max Weber calls their capitalism a "speculative pariah-capitalism"[3] and Professor Jászi, himself a Jew, does not hesitate to call this attitude of the medieval ghetto "parasitism."[4] Barred from the guilds, they were left to make a living in professions which were needed but in which no respectable Christian would engage. These professions, the constant, degrading persecutions and humiliations, massacres and expulsions, products of fanaticism and ignorance both on the Jewish and on the Christian side, developed a Jewish ghetto type, the only type such a situation, which lasted for centuries, could create.

The Jews preferred degradation, persecution and death to giving up their peculiar nationhood. They survived it all, paying a terrible toll in life and property. But for the ghetto Jew, only his God (that is, his nationhood), his income (that is, survival), and his family mattered. Historically, the family was the stronghold in a hostile land. Its honor must not be tarnished. In fact, in the Middle Ages, most Jews obeyed a double standard. Within the family they assiduously demonstrated all the qualities not usually attributed to them by superficial observers. They were reliable, honest, obedient, generous, disciplined and brave. Outside the ghetto, they often felt compelled to employ the wiles of underground fighters in enemy-occupied territory.

In the middle of the fourteenth century, an unprecedented plague, the "Black Death," ravaged Europe and Germany. The numerous Ashkenazic Jews* were blamed for the disease. The ferocity of the massacres in

*In the early Diaspora, the Jews centered mainly in two areas in Europe. Those in Spain, called Sephardic Jews, adopted the Castillian tongue of the Middle Ages called "Ladino." The Jews of the Rhine Valley adopted a medieval German dialect mixed with some Hebrew words called Yiddish, these being the Ashkenazic Jews. The overwhelming majority of Hungarian and Rumanian Jews were of the Ashkenazic group.

Germany knew no bounds. Most of the German Jews (although never all of them) migrated to Poland, where they received a friendly welcome by King Kasimir the Great. They were settled all over historic Poland, which later included Lithuania, White Russia, the Ukraine, and part of Latvia and East Prussia.

The Jews of Poland enjoyed a great deal of autonomy and prosperity during the heyday of the *Reczypoczpolita* (the elective Polish Kingdom), but parallel to the decline of Poland, their lot worsened. When Napoleon's armies swept this area after the French Revolution, these sturdily conservative, nationalistic Jews refused the *Haskala* (enlightenment), their rabbis feeling rightly that it would lead to assimilation and dilution of Jewishness, to the abandonment of the "Jewish mission," and to the eclipse of their power over the superstitious, uneducated masses of the ghetto.

Poland, meanwhile, had ceased to exist as an independent state. Political upheavals rarely meant anything but trouble for the Jews. The new Russian masters restricted the Jews to the area within the former boundaries of Poland — thus, it became the Pale of Settlement for them. Those living in Prussian and Austrian Poland were subject to Prussian and Austrian laws respectively.

During the nineteenth century, therefore, the bulk of world Jewry then residing in this region was not in an enviable position. It lived in a desperately poor environment, amid an ever-increasing agrarian overpopulation, and in an area torn by growing nationalist passions. In addition to all this, there was an unprecedented population explosion among the Jews themselves.* With their movement restricted within Russia and under the impact of grinding poverty, lack of opportunity, cruel laws, and fearful pogroms, many Jews left for overseas. But many others moved to Rumania and Hungary.

The Pale produced no parallel to the treatment of Western European Jews nor to their reaction to emancipation. In Eastern Europe brutal persecution was the rule rather than the exception, with the Jews stubbornly refusing any identification with the nations in which they lived. They made no attempt to become Poles, Russians or Ukranians as their coreligionists eagerly became Frenchmen, Dutch, Englishmen or Italians. The more they were brutalized, the more stubbornly they clung to their religion; that is, to their nationality.

2

During the Middle Ages and up to the nineteenth century, the fate of the Jews in the Lands of St. Stephen was neither better nor worse than in the rest of Europe. There were not a great many of them there, and during the reign

---

*The area of historic Poland counted 617,000 Jews in 1788 (some put it close to 900,000). Within little more than a century, this figure increased roughly tenfold! S.M. Dubnow, *Die neueste Geschichte des Jüdischen Volkes* (Berlin, 1920), I, 90.

of Joseph II their emancipation began. Professionally, they engaged in renting an inn, a butchershop or land from landlords, and trading in cattle or wheat. The towns did not admit them since the predominately German burghers hated them intensely. Nevertheless, the culture of these Jews was predominately German in character.

This situation changed swiftly and radically when the reform generation began the building of a new Hungary based on French ideas of nationhood. The Diet of 1840 removed many medieval Jewish disabilities. The best sons of Hungary championed the cause of Jewish emancipation. Kossuth was cautious at first. He desired, according to the spirit of the age, that the Jews should become Hungarians first, and then he was prepared to grant them the right of citizenship. But the Jewish attitude during the revolution of 1848 removed his doubts and quelled all opposition to Jewish emancipation.

After the French Revolution, the Jews of no country identified themselves so unequivocally with the national and liberal cause as did the Jews of Hungary during 1848-49.* According to Kossuth, out of 180,000 revolutionary soldiers, there were 20,000 Jews fighting.[5] A. Görgey, the commander-in-chief of the Honvéd (Defender of the Fatherland, traditional name of the Hungarian Army), remembered afterward: "In discipline, personal courage, and in stubborn endurance, that is, in all military virtues, they nobly emulated their comrades in arms."[6] In one of the last of its acts, the Diet in 1849 proclaimed full equality for the Jews as a reward for their loyalty to Hungary.

The Austrian commander, General Haynau, demanded a tribute of two million forints from the Jews of Hungary because, as he explained, "With their sentiments and their wicked deeds, the Jews promoted the Revolution, which could never have succeeded to the extent it did without their cooperation."[7] Regardless of the blandishments of the Imperial Edict of Olmütz, during the years of the reestablished Habsburg rule the Jews of Hungary stubbornly adhered to the Hungarian national cause. They went through a rapid process of de-Germanization, assimilation to Hungarian nationhood, and emancipation. The Compromise of 1867 simply codified an established fact: the Hungarian Jews were part of the Hungarian state; they were Hungarians and Hungarians only.

The astounding development of Hungary during the Compromise Era could not have taken place without a middle class in the Western sense. But, as we have seen, the Hungarian Nation frowned on such incongruent professions, and did not welcome the rise of a Hungarian middle class from the ranks of the peasantry. Nevertheless, because a middle class was needed

---

*When in 1938 the Hungarian Parliament discussed anti-Jewish laws, none other than an Arrow Cross deputy, István Balogh, asked exemption for three Jewish families whose forefathers General József Bem cited in his Order of the Day for bravery during Hungary's Fight for Freedom in 1948-49. *Országgyülési Napló-Képviselőház* (Parliamentary Record-Hungarian House of Representatives), May 12, 1938, p. 523. Hereinafter referred to as *O.N.K.*

immediately, the Hungarian Nation encouraged the assimilated Jews to move into these defiling but necessary professions.*

Consequently, the Jews gained a commanding position in the Hungarian economic and cultural life, which they used to further the centralization of the Hungarian state and the oppression of the nationalities. Their Hungarian chauvinistic zeal — that of the neophyte — knew no bounds. It was also the Jewish middle class that was mainly responsible for the establishment of a modern capitalist economy — banking, industry and trade. Along with the benefits of capitalism they brought also its shady side to aristocratic Hungary: vulgarity, exaggerated individualism, and an atmosphere which José Ortega y Gasset calls "The Rebellion of the Masses." But, while in the West this kind of Jewish attitude was only part of the existing standards of the national bourgeoisie, in Hungary the Jews constituted the *only* bourgeoisie, with all the good and bad it represented. Consequently, it became easy to identify them with the negative side of middle class culture, and it is this which later conveniently supplied the Fascist arguments for identifying the Jews with the West.

As for the other middle class, the "middle class of Hungarian gentlemen" — admittedly a very expressive distinction — increased its numbers rapidly

*There was a constant influx of Jews from Galicia (Austrian Poland) to Hungary. There was no restriction of movement within the boundaries of the Dual Monarchy, and many Jews came from the miserable conditions of the Polish center of Jews to Hungary, the "promised land of liberalism." Let's look at the statistics and what this process meant in reality: There were 12,000 Jews in Hungary in 1720 and 93,000 in 1787; by 1848, there were 336,000, by 1869, 542,000, and by 1910, 909,500; roughly 5% of the population.

So far as social structure went, the statistics used here refer to the year 1920; that is, to Trianon Hungary, but these figures are more relevant to our story than the ones relating to the Lands of St. Stephen. Jews constituted a negligible proportion of the working class or agricultural labor. But their proportion in the bourgeoisie and professional groups was extremely high. Of the agricultural laborers, they composed only 0.1%; the dwarf holders of land, 0.2%; miners, 0.4%; industrial workers, 7.3%; transport workers, 2.5%; domestic servants, 1.9%; Army officers, 1.6%. On the other hand, "independent persons engaged in mining," 37.7%; in industry, 12.3%; commerce, 53%; finance, 80%; lawyers, 50.6%; physicians in private practice, 59.9%; authors, 27.3%; journalists (in Budapest 70%), 34.3%; musicians, 23.6%; and actors, 22.7%. Of the salaried employees in mining, 21.3%; in industry, 39.1%; in commerce, 48.2%; and in finance, 43.7%. On the land they provided 16.5% of the 727 owners of properties of 1,000+ hold and 53.7% of persons renting such properties. Macartney, *October Fifteenth* I, 18.

However, these figures are incomplete, because both the village cobbler and the owner of a gigantic metallurgical plant were listed as an "independent person engaged in industry." Also, many Jews converted, or intermarried with the aristocracy, and through this the "Christian" character of the enterprise was assured.

during the latter half of the Compromise Era. The consecutive agrarian crises at the end of the nineteenth century drove thousands of the gentry from the land. The patriarchal Hungarian state was replaced with a modern structure, and the bureaucracy was eighty to ninety percent filled with Hungarians, even in areas where the proportion of nationalities was just the opposite.* The German and Slovak city dwellers went through a rapid denationalization and assimilation process during the Compromise Era. These neo-Hungarians formed, together with the ruined lesser nobles, the other non-Jewish middle class, supplying the bureaucracy and the officer corps to Hungary. This middle class assumed the appearances of an aristocratic way of life, its mannerisms and attitudes, and frowned on the vulgar, upstart Jewish middle class. Until 1919, however, there was enough opportunity for all, and the Hungarian Nation, having a keen political instinct, understood its need for the Jewish middle class, so the silent *Interessengemeinschaft,* as Professor Macartney calls it, worked during the Compromise Era, although the dividing line within the two middle classes was clearly detectable.

But the Hungarian Nation, reinforced by its German (Swabian) recruits, had an infinitely more important reason for feeling challenged by the Jewish middle class than the economic consideration. Although the majority of Jews were middle class oriented both as far as their social status and their sentiments were concerned, it was they who supplied something to the Hungarian scene which had been woefully lacking since the generation of the 1830s — a radical intelligentsia. What is the reason that the Jews were so heavily represented in the leadership of the liberal, leftist, bourgeois-radical and Socialist movements? The Hungarian peasantry, in its dejected state, had little opportunity to adopt Western ideas. On the other hand, this was accomplished with ease by Jews and other foreigners. The Jews engaged in intellectual commerce as they had before in the commerce of goods. Not only the Socialist movement, but every other economic or intellectual cause was fostered by Jews. Indeed, if one were to judge from the participation of Jews in the leadership of these movements, he would get the impression that ninety-five percent of Hungary was inhabited by Jews and not the other way around. Then, too, the idea of championing the masses, democracy, liberalism, social justice, and reform was, as the writer's father and grandfather used to point out, a preoccupation "not fitting to a Hungarian gentleman." But some reactionaries and Fascists found it expedient to put forward a different answer: the Jews are the perpetrators of both the

*In the decade of 1892-1902, when the agrarian crisis was at its peak, the number of administrative posts rose from 60,776 to 97,835—these new openings being largely filled by ruined gentry. Hóman-Szekfü, *Magyar -történet,* V, 528-29. Another interesting statistic: In 1870 Hungary had 23,273 civil servants; in 1900, 125,933; in 1918, 228,975, and Trianon Hungary in 1928 still 120,506. The Budapest Municipality in 1874 employed 215 people; in 1940, 27,000. O.N.K., November, 19, 1940, p. 556.

capitalist scourge and of the Bolshevik menace.* They are the plague bearers, the virus carriers, who infect, disintegrate and destroy the happy, ideal structure of preindustrialist, conservative Hungary. Those ungrateful, self-seeking "infiltrators" (*beszivárgók* — a favorite definition of Jews in Horthy's Hungary), who came there thanks to the Hungarian Nation, now dared to incite the peasant and laboring masses against it, to fill their heads with nonsense about social justice, internationalism and radical ideas.

Had the interests of the Hungarian Nation and those of the Hungarian people been in some preestablished harmony, the accusations leveled against the Jewish radical intelligentsia would have been true. Even then it would have been demagoguery to identify the at that time rather conservative majority of the Hungarian Jews with the radical-minded Jewish intellectuals. But it was not in the interest of the Hungarian Nation, by then a predominantly middle class group, and especially not in the interest of its new recruits from the German minority, to make subtle distinctions. Also, it would seem that almost without exception the radical revolutionary leaders of the world, from Robespierre and Marat through Lenin and Kemal and Sun-Yat-Sen to Nasser and Fidel Castro, have come from the middle class. Hungary had but *one* real middle class — a Jewish one. This is the most important single reason for the disproportion of Jews in the radical movements in Hungary.

The Jewish radicals may have had their failings, but these failings clearly were not derived from the conspiracy of the "Wisemen of Zion." They struck out impartially at feudal landlords and Jewish capitalists; the contemporary speeches of Professor Jászi and the Jewish leaders of the Social Democratic party are proof of that. From the distance of five or six decades, they read like the predictions of Cassandra. At any rate, their views were a definite improvement over the attitudes of the Hungarian Nation, which approached social or national problems in a patriarchal, patronizing fashion at its best, and in a blatantly antisocial, egotistical manner at its worst, and though honorable exceptions do exist, the overwhelming majority of the political nation was thinking on such lines down to 1945. This was the philosophy of those who described themselves as "Liberal-conservatives." — *Conservativism in Central Europe seems invariably to acquire a strong authoritarian touch and their liberalism extended only to the field of economy.*

*Miss Cécile Tormay, as good an interpreter of the opinions of the political nation as anybody, describing the ugly mood in a starving breadline before a Jewish-owned grocery in Budapest during the war, points at a discontented Jew standing at the end of the line, complaining loudly. Miss Tormay draws her conclusions with great ingenuity: "The crowd approved, and failed to notice that the Semitic race was to be found only at the *two ends* of the queue, and not a single representative of it could be seen as a buyer amongst the crowding, the poor and the starving. This was symbolical, a condensed picture of Budapest. The sellers, the agitators were Jews. The buyers and the misguided were the people of the capital." *An Outlaw's Diary* (New York, 1923), p. 45.

The newly created Jewish middle class was interested only in the economics of the status quo, not in its tradition. Thus it was easier for their educated sons to take a look into the future; they were not held back by nostalgia or convention. Moreover, their social status was of the twentieth century; it could be more easily preserved by a democratic transformation than by continuing and safeguarding the way of life the Hungarian Nation so cherished.

3

The Jews of Rumania were almost entirely of the Pale of Settlement kind, and in historic Hungary only the dense Jewish population in Ruthenia bears resemblance to them.

In the Pale of Settlement during the nineteenth and the first half of the twentieth centuries, the term "Jewish overpopulation" would seem appropriate. The demographic pressures of the Jewish population explosion in the area — taking into account the social stratification of the Jews and the existing poverty, social dislocation, underdevelopment, and fierce nationalisms in the No-Man's-Land of Europe — created an anti-Semitism that made life for those desperately poor, wretched Jewish millions increasingly unbearable. If pogroms and discrimination did not help matters much, emigration on a growing scale brought some alleviation.

Until the Treaty of Adrianople (1829), there were few Jews in the Rumanian principalities, these lands being among the most insecure in Europe. After that, their numbers increased rapidly,* their influx maintaining a northeast-to-southwest direction from the Pale, its place of origin, with Bucovina, Bessarabia and northern and central Moldavia receiving the heaviest proportion of the newcomers. That these Jews, being of a primitive, religious-nationalist type, refused any association or solidarity with the new Rumanian state, whose violent, romantic nationalism was inconceivable to them, did not endear them to the local population. Although most were desperately poor and certainly worked for a living, their professions, sometimes consisting of moneylending, usury and shoddy transactions in the village inns they owned, were also more than offensive in the eyes of a primitive peasantry, which still clung to the medieval belief that Jews practiced ritual murder and saw the "despicable Jew" as the one who crucified his Savior. That this detestable creature did not even speak Rumanian decently and dressed in a manner different from the Rumanians,

*Until 1829, the number of Jews was negligible, but after that their number increased rapidly. By 1859, there were 118,000 in Moldavia and only 9,200 in Wallachia, and in 1901, there were 201,000 Jews in Moldavia and 68,000 in Wallachia. A quarter of a million Jews in a population of five million would not seem so great; but they were a predominantly middle class, urban element — of 700,000 urban dwellers two-fifths were Jews. L. S. Stavrianos, *The Balkans Since 1453*, pp. 484-85.

were points in the case against him. That is what the peasant saw in his village. When he went to town on market day or on official business, he saw the towns, Iaşi, Huşi, Botoşani, etc., not only crowded, but inhabited by Jews. And this did not help the Rumanian national cause either.*

According to a Zionist formula, anti-Semitism equals:

$$\frac{\text{Number of Jews} \times \text{Social Dislocations and Misery}}{\text{Assimilation of Jews}}$$

If we accept this formula as a measure of the prevalence of anti-Semitism (before the kind of anti-Semitism which was to develop in Germany, Austria and Hungary during the twentieth century), it is clear that anti-Semitism in Rumania had to reach tremendous proportions. It is interesting to note that the best sons of Rumania, even her liberal leaders, were anti-Semites. For example, Eminescu, the greatest Rumanian poet, Kogălniceanu,** that honest reformer and statesman, Iorga and Xenopol, the two greatest Rumanian historians, and Brătianu, the liberal leader, were among the convinced anti-Semites.

The young Rumanian state, with its inferiority complex, considered the incessant Jewish influx a kind of invasion by an aggressive minority. The brutal measures and treatment meted out to the Jews, on the other hand, did little to accelerate their assimilation and loyalty to an environment they considered inferior. So there seems to be little question about a right or wrong in this case, but rather of two rights; one Jewish, the other Rumanian.

If Hungary's best sons, Kossuth, Deák, Eötvös, championed the cause of the Jews in Hungary, in Rumania they invariably had to look beyond the borders for support — to Crémieux and finally to the Berlin Congress in 1878.*** There, it was Bismarck who exerted enough pressure on the new Rumanian state to grant citizenship to the Jews. The outraged Rumanian Parliament got around it by stipulating that naturalization was to be carried out in every single case by a special act of Parliament. So by 1923 when, again under foreign pressure, Rumania finally granted citizenship rights to her Jews, only a

*When in 1848, the young rebels of Bucharest went to Iaşi to spread the revolt in Moldavia, they did not find the slightest response among the predominantly Jewish inhabitants. These Jews, being relative newcomers, had no interest in provoking the wrath of the local authorities for the sake of the Rumanian nationalist cause. Lukinich-Gáldi, Makkai, *Geschichte der Rumänen*, p. 360. But Rumanian nationalists were not inclined to go very deeply into the intrinsic reasons for the Jewish attitude; they flatly credited the Jews with responsibility for their failure.
**When there was talk about giving the Jews the right of citizenship, Kogălniceanu protested in the spirit of the age: "The Rumanian Jews have nothing in common with the French, English, and German Jews — here they want rights before they become Rumanians." Charlé Claus, *Die Eiserne Garde,* (Berlin-Wien, 1939) p. 87.
***The celebrated speech by Prince A. Gorchakov at the Congress, pointing out the differences between the Western and the Pale of Settlement Jews, was warmly approved in Rumania. Dubnow, *op. cit.,* II, 491.

fraction of Jews had been naturalized; hundreds of thousands were still without citizenship. These foreign interventions on behalf of the Jews only increased mistrust in the new Rumanian state. Local authorities exercised great arbitrariness and brutality in dealing with the disenfranchised Jews — their actions were mitigated only by the prevalent, colossal corruption. Although they had no citizenship rights the Jews had to serve in the Rumanian Army. The intent to make life for the Jews in Rumania so unbearable that they would leave was clear,* with the result that most of the emigrants from the Old Kingdom before 1914 were Jews.**

There were practically no intermarriages between Jews and Christians or conversions of Jews to the Christian faith, both common occurences in Hungary. With most industries, many of the communications media, and the railways owned by foreigners, Rumanian Jews could only occupy the position of middlemen in the growing economy. With the powerful foreign interests enjoying virtual immunity, the wrath of the national inferiority complex descended upon the Jewish middlemen. The Jews were unable even to work out a temporary arrangement with a Rumanian equivalent of the Hungarian Nation — no such thing existed in the Old Kingdom. With a much greater social flexibility than the one which existed in Hungary, the *ciocoi*, the rapidly Romanized Armenians, Greeks, Slavs and in some cases ethnic Germans filled the administrative posts, leaving much of the rest of the middle class terrain to the hated Jews. The resulting insecurity of nationhood, of status, of the economy, of ideas, of the relationships between rulers and ruled — these gave origin to much of the contradiction, emotion and violence that aggravated the life of the new Rumanian state and had a devastating effect on the position of the Jewish minority.

Despite these vicissitudes, the Jews rapidly developed a strong, if not commanding, position in the economy.*** But if their hold on the Rumanian

*Brătianu (the elder) expressed this policy with a Rumanian folk fable, in which the fox, taking advantage of a hole in the fence, sneaked into the orchard, ravaged it, and grew so fat that he could not fit through the same hole anymore and could not leave. Then came the gardener, drew the fox into a corner, and starved him out until he lost weight in order to fit through the hole and also be most desirous to leave. "This is exactly what we are doing with our Jews," said Brătianu. *Ibid.*, III, 275. Rumanian Jews had all the rights and privileges which follow from this analogy.

***In Bucharest in 1938, out of 3,475 lawyers, 1,390 were Jewish; of 14,300 bank clerks, 11,200; in Rumania, out of 258,000 commercial employees, 173,000; in Bucharest between 1925-36, out of 35 billion lei invested in building construction, 29 billion was Jewish capital. 65 percent of the capital investment and 85 percent of the management of 1,015 limited companies in Rumania was Jewish. Out of 1,370 industrial enterprises with a 5.3 billion lei investment, Jews controlled 971 enterprises with a 3.7 billion lei investment. Hector Bolitho, *Rumania under King Carol* (New York, 1940) pp. 39-40.

**By 1910, out of a total of 70,217 emigrants which left the Old Kingdom for the New World, there were 67,301 Jews and only 2,916 Gentiles. Stravrianos, *op. cit.*, p. 491.

economy was in most fields as great as in Hungary, there was little Jewish creativity in Rumanian culture. Although there were numerous Jewish "boulevard journalists," we find no renowned Rumanian poets, writers, composers or artists among them as in Hungary. Only A. Dobrogeanu-Gherea stands out; he was a social critic of Rumanian-Jewish descent, but he stood on the side of the international revolutionary cause.

The apostle of Rumanian anti-Semitism was Professor A. Cuza of Iaşi University. He was delivering his anti-Jewish addresses in the Rumanian Parliament when Hitler was still a child. Because of the unwillingness of Rumanian Jews to become Rumanians, Rumanian nationalism became identical with anti-Semitism at an early date, with strong economic and substantial religious undertones. Professor Cuza was joined in his efforts at the beginning of the century by Professor Iorga, the leading intellectual of Rumania, and by the father of the hero of our story, a high school teacher in Huşi named Ion Zelea (Zelinsky) Codreanu.

By the 1900s, the Rumanian Jews were established enough to press for their emancipation through education, an old, effective Jewish weapon. Resembling the middle class in the closest way and taking into account the traditional Jewish eagerness for learning, they filled the institutions of learning far beyond their proportion to the population as a whole.*

The Jewish intelligentsia that emerged from these institutes was a radical one. The Socialist and later the Communist movements had the Jewish minority well represented in their leadership. But if an educated Jew looked for culture or values to emulate, he looked to France and to Germany, not to the "unspoiled Rumanian peasant" and the romantic nationalism of certain circles within the Rumanian intelligentsia.

Despite the superficially similar economic position of the Hungarian and Rumanian Jews in their respective countries, both of them forming a middle class in the Western sense between an upper class and a backward peasantry,

*The figures presented by Codreanu must be treated with caution. Nevertheless, even if they are only partly true, it is understandable that the ultranationalists and the superpatriots were alarmed to see the future leaders of the country consist of an unassimilated and (according to them) unassimilable minority. Codreanu's figures for 1920 are quoted below:

University of Cernauţi: Summer School — 174 Rumanians, 574 Jews; Law (summer semester) — 237 Orthodox Christians (Rumanians, Ukrainians), 98 Catholics, 26 Lutherans, 21 Other Religions, 506 Jews.

University of Iaşi: Medicine — 546 Rumanians, 831 Jews; Pharmacy — 97 Rumanians, 229 Jews; Philosophy — 1,073 Rumanians, 421 Jews; Law — 1,743 Rumanians, 340 Jews.

Although in the grade schools there is a balance in enrollment between Jews and Rumanians (and other nationalities), there is a glaring imbalance as we get to the lycée, especially to the good, private lycées. In Bucharest, there were 441 Rumanians enrolled in private lycées while there were 781 Jews; in Iaşi, 37 Rumanians and 108 Jews; in Galaţi, 190 Rumanians and 199 Jews. C.Z. Codreanu, *Eiserne Garde*, (Berlin, 1939), pp. 75-76.

the difference between the two is a basic one. The Hungarian Jews, as Professor Macartney put it, "were embarrassingly eager to become Magyars and emphasized their Magyardom to caricature in their mannerisms and utterances."[8] This cannot be said about the Moldavian or even the Bucharest ghetto. The Rumanian Jews remained consciously an alien element, emphasizing always their Jewish nationality and minority status. The dividing line between what Prince Gorchakov called "the Eastern and Western Jews," ran along the Hungaro-Rumanian frontier until 1918.

CHAPTER III

Fascism in Hungary

Fearful are the convulsions of defeat.

Churchill

1

Hungarian fascism, at least the conservative variety, was born with the counterrevolution of 1919.

It is not surprising that such an old, well-established, politically conscious group as the Hungarian Nation should find ways and means to express its protest against an intrusion into its time-honored privilege of running the country unchallenged: the Demo-Liberal-Judeo-Bolshevist ideas* of 1918-19 which were contrary to the Hungarian Nation's concept of the Hungarian way of life. But in the first months after the military collapse the revolutionary euphoria was so great, and the old order so thoroughly discredited, that the faint protests of the ruling class made little impress on the political scene. The Hungarian Nation's elaborate political machine, well established since 1867 with all its checks and balances on the popular will, now was swept away. Compared to the majority in the popular upheaval, their minority was reduced to insignificant proportions. Many of them made overtures to or set up stakes with the new regime. But developments on both the national and the international scene were presently to give the Hungarian Nation another chance — their last chance.

We have seen how at home the impotence and the incapacity of the Károlyi republic and the mistakes and crimes of the antinationalist Kun regime foiled the hopes of the Hungarian people for democracy and reform. The great powers also played their role in this. The success of democracy in Hungary under the existing circumstances depended largely on the interest, sympathy and pressure of the Entente, particularly of France. Both moral and financial help were imperative to that end. And it would have been very helpful if the peace treaty, which was about to be concluded, had demonstrated that the words and deeds of the great Western democracies were in harmony.

The revolutionary mood of the Károlyi republic and the terror of Számuelly excluded the possibility of any successful counterrevolutionary activity in the area under their control. Therefore, the two centers of the counterrevolution were in Szeged, then under French occupation, and in Vienna. The difference between the men gathered in Szeged and those in

*Standard characterization of almost any movement or idea by the ruling class, a characterization which was applied to any idea which was not avowedly conservative or radical right.

49

Vienna characterized a trend and a problem that continued through the whole story of Hungarian fascism.

The Vienna group consisted of conservative, legitimist aristocrats (although they were not strictly legitimist at the moment), Jewish banking and business interests, and some high-ranking officers. The leader of this group was Count István Bethlen, a conservative of the non-democratic, authoritarian, conservative mold, and a politician in the true sense of the word, with great capabilities and vision. His political concept bore close resemblance to that of István Tisza, though Bethlen, being a Transylvanian, was more skeptical and less principled than Tisza, and more flexible and ready to compromise. After all, he was a politician in a postrevolutionary situation. What he did share with Tisza was a profoundly undemocratic attitude, a distrust of the masses (a distrust reinforced by the events of 1918-19 — judging by the way he drew his conclusions from the events of those years), and a conviction that Hungary must rule the Carpathian Basin and that his class must rule Hungary. Beyond this basic core of beliefs, he was ready to make any number of compromises.

The other counterrevolutionary group was installed in Szeged with the benevolent encouragement of the French at a time when the Entente was alarmed by the emergence of a Hungarian Soviet and encouraged its overthrow both from without and from within.

Who were the men of Szeged? It is hard to follow history of the next twenty-five years in Hungary and the conservative variety of Hungarian fascism without at least a brief consideration of the Hungarian Social Association (T.E.Sz. — *Társadalmi Egyesületek Szövetsége*) which at its peak contained about 10,000 social organizations. It operated as a coordinating body, expressing the reactions of the Hungarian Nation to twentieth-century industrial society in general and to the challenges of the lost war and the consequences of that debacle in particular.

These associations were formed in response to the democratic upsurge in the closing phase of the war. They had sections openly known and secret subdivisions that opposed the proposed democratization of Hungary on violently chauvinistic, romantic, racial, and class grounds. Although after the triumph of the counterrevolution they multiplied to the incredible figure of 10,000, two of them were later very important. They were the Association of Awakening Hungarians (É.M.E. — *Ébredő Magyarok Egyesülete*), and most significant, the Association of Hungarian National Defense (M.O.V.E. — *Magyar Országos Véderő Egyesület*). M.O.V.E. had an official department, the Hungarian Scientific Race-Protecting Association, and its infinitely more important secret division, the Etelköz Association (E.K.Sz. — *Etelközi Szövetség*), or simply "X," organized on the framework of the old Magyar tribes before they conquered the Carpathian Basin. The founder and leader of M.O.V.E. was a certain captain on the general staff, Gyula Gömbös. These secret or not secret societies were of different sizes and influence. They had different programs or leaders. But they had one thing in common: they represented and appealed to the Hungarian Nation exclusively. They represented the "middle class of Hungarian gentlemen" in the struggle against the Jewish bourgeoisie and all it stood for.

The secret societies were the starch and brain of the Szeged movement, expressed later in the "Szeged Idea."* The men in the Szeged movement were the lower echelons of the Hungarian Nation, the fixed-income groups, largely of the administration, who suffered most by the general deterioration of the economy. Hit by inflation, they were understandably disgruntled. If a democratic Hungary were established, it would mean the end of their monopoly on administrative posts; much more so in Soviet Hungary. The other group that came to Szeged was made up of the active officers of the K.u.K. Army (Kaiser und Königlich — Imperial and Royal — that is, of the Dual Monarchy), who also rightly feared that the privileged position they enjoyed would be out of place in a Hungarian democratic republic. Many of them had served for professional and patriotic reasons with the Soviet. And there were the refugees from the territories taken over by the Succession States. As we have seen, the entire administration in historic Hungary (with the railroads, utilities, etc., state owned) was almost exclusively manned by Hungarians. Now the Succession States summarily dismissed these people, and expelled a good many of them. The majority of the 300,000 refugees who flooded Hungary after 1918 were former public servants.[1] Thus the bulk of the people who formed the nucleus of the Szeged counterrevolution were more or less dispossessed, or in danger of becoming dispossessed. The wealth was in the hands of the magnates and Jewish financiers, who were in Vienna, and were mainly interested in the restoration of the status quo ante.

The Szeged men, the lower strata of the Hungarian Nation, had less respect for property than those of the Vienna group; consequently, their political program, the Szeged Idea, was radical in comparison with the Vienna group's ideas of restoration. Many Szeged people tried to cooperate with Károlyi or Kun, but for the reasons mentioned before, they were not wanted. The attitude of the Entente toward Hungary helped to diminish their sympathy for democracy, a sympathy in any case never very pronounced. The road for them was wide open toward the radicial right and fascism. Their leader was Gömbös.

Gyula (Julius) Gömbös came from Swabian (German) stock of humble lineage, his family name being originally Knöpfle, corresponding roughly to the meaning of Gömbös in Hungarian. His mother did not even speak Hungarian. But that does not mean that his assimilation to the Hungarians was not sincere. On the contrary, he had all the zeal of the neophyte.**

*Szegedi Gondolat in Hungarian, the always nebulous program of Hungarian conservative fascism.

**Men of foreign origin have often made history in their new countries: Leon Degrelle came from the Meuse region on the quadruple border of Belgium, France, Germany and Luxembourg; Codreanu had a non-Rumanian background of Zelinskys from the Polish-Ukrainian-Rumanian border areas; Hitler came from a town on the Austrian-German border; Fidel Castro's parents came to Cuba from Spain, and Stalin was of Gruzínian stock.

Gömbös may be considered the leader of the conservative Fascists in Hungary, the most significant figure among the Szeged men. He was head of the most important secret society and unalterably committed to that credo of conservative fascism, the Szeged Idea. This idea was later to divide the Hungarian Nation, to break radically with its traditions, to incite with the help of outside pressures high treason and ghastly deeds, and ultimately to assure that the perhaps inevitable doom of little Hungary would be not only tragic but sordid as well.

Few people know about the originality of Gömbös' Fascist ideas or his sometimes unusually keen (although limited) political vision. The idea of a German-Italian alliance came from Gömbös as early as the 1920s. It is he who invented the term Rome-Berlin Axis.[2] He called himself a National Socialist in 1919, years before Hitler did. It is he who was inspired to form a Nationalist International "against the International of gold and the International of Moscow,"[3] both other internationals being according to the age-old concept of his kind, Jewish. His psychology was a complex one. He was of humble lineage and fundamentally hostile to big capital and legitimist aristocratic landowners. He was also the spokesman of the petite bourgeoisie and the military, the two mainstays of the Szeged Idea. Yet he thought it necessary to provide himself with a pedigree — of course, a Hungarian one — which purported to trace his lineage as far back as the seventeenth century, because his national and social inferiority complexes would not permit him to attack the upper classes as an outsider with a rather vulgar background. In other words, he had to establish for himself a nonexistent nobility in order to be able to reject it. We shall deal with his political ideas in detail later when we consider the changes, compromises and "revisions" they went through. Despite them, however, his Hungarian chauvinism, his violent anti-Semitism (so common among Hungarians of German stock), his hostility to democracy in any form, his limited dedication to social justice, and his rejection of the upper strata of the ruling class remained the basis of his thought.

But this picture of Gömbös would not be complete without reference to his mystical, romantic Hungarian nationalism, a nationalism better described in his own words as chauvinism. This overdose of national consciousness with its strong sentimental taint gave him a personal charisma that helped him appeal to the irrational and the intangible in carrying with him on his path many Hungarians who would otherwise have been indifferent if not hostile to him. Lenin defined nationalism as "a stubborn fact;" he learned about it the hard way and took note of it, without being capable of understanding it. Gömbös, his contemporary, understood it, believed in it, and armed himself with it. It gave him his color, his appeal, and the mystique with which he surrounded his cause and imbued his secret societies.

There is little to be said about the military operations of the counter-revolution; there weren't any. When the Szeged and Vienna groups coordinated themselves, a joint mission was sent to Belgrade to ask the blessing of the Entente for their efforts. Gömbös represented the Szeged group and the Marquis György Pallavicini, the Vienna group. After the Hungarian Soviet fell, the so-called National Army, consisting mainly of officers who found their way to Szeged, moved into those parts of Transdanubia which were not occupied by the Rumanian Army. The unfortunate peasants were glad to see the hostile Communists go, and they "let" the National Army come. But Officer Detachments (*Tiszti különítmény*), as they were called, set off a White Terror, a fearful and summary massacre of real or suspected Communists and Socialists and above all, Jews, regardless of political affiliation. They did this, they said, to restore law and order. These conservative guardians of law and order soon exceeded in the numbers of their victims and the bestiality of their exploits the revolutionary terror squads of Számuelly. Their outrages continued unchecked for years. The responsibility for it lies squarely on the new commander in chief of the National Army, Admiral Miklós Horthy.

Horthy joins Bethlen and Gömbös as a key figure in the history of Hungary in the first fifteen years after the war. If Bethlen was the leader of the Vienna group and Gömbös the embodiment of the Szeged Idea, Horthy was the compromise and the link between the two positions, at least in the first decade of the new regime. The wide range of opinion about Horthy, from the most abject flattery to the most indiscriminate abuse, was also influenced by the change which took place in Horthy's position during the twenty-five years he was in power. In 1919, starting out from Szeged with the Szeged men, he backed up his officers with the inflexible *espirit de corps* of the K.u.K. Later, he moved more and more back to conservatism as it is understood in backward societies — conservatism with a strong authoritarian streak.

Unfortunately, his was not a strong character; he never followed up consistently his cherished ideas of medieval chivalry. Ultimately he failed himself and his country, probably against his own intentions. He was, and remained to the end, a K.u.K. admiral of the Austro-Hungarian Navy, a stranger in the twentieth century, a diehard conservative of the Dual Monarchy, whose life's example was the late Emperor Francis Joseph, whom he served for years as aide-de-camp.* If he was not an expert in the politics of the twentieth century, he was much less an expert in its economics. In the first years of his rule, he still had a foot in both the Vienna and the Szeged camps, but later he catered more to the group of conservative magnates, particularly to Count Bethlen.

The influence of Count Bethlen over Horthy from the very beginning of the era to the end of it was remarkably strong. Their conservatism was of the same brand, with the important qualification that while Bethlen had to engage in politics, Horthy could remain aloof to a certain degree. His reason for preferring the older element was rooted mainly in his aversion to modern times, the challenges and the vulgarity of which confused and repelled him. He never really understood what it was all about. So he withdrew to his generation and his kind, who always told him what he wanted to hear. This

---

*Horthy tells in his memoirs that he used to ask himself before every important decision how the late Emperor would have handled the situation. Miklós Horthy, *Ein Leben für Ungarn* (Bonn, 1953), p. 186.

bore the strange consequence that by the Second World War, although he had reasonable insight into world affairs, he had lost touch with Hungarian reality, and when the hour of supreme trial came nobody turned more violently against him than the Szeged element, his personal protégés, in the Officers Corps of his armed forces.

But all this was far away in the hot summer of 1919. Then he was the avenging arm of the Hungarian Nation as it closed ranks for the last time to repel the challenge to its position. When in November 1919 the Entente finally induced the Rumanians to end their pillage and get out of Budapest, Horthy entered the city on his famous white horse at the head of the National Army. There was never any fighting of importance between the counterrevolutionary forces and the Reds.* The "great national upsurge" won, and the new era was born — out of foreign intervention, out of Communist mistakes and crimes, and out of the apathy, however understandable, of the Hungarian people.

2

The Vienna group had no easy task imposing its control over the Szeged men and toning down their embryonic Fascist quest for reform. It was also very difficult to get the economy going and to bring a reasonable amount of order to the land after the upheavals of the past year or so. From 1919 to 1921 there were several short-lived governments that included a fairly broad spectrum of opinion, mainly due to Entente efforts to make the regime as representative as possible. But this was not the aim of the Hungarian Nation, nor of Vienna or Szeged, and the Entente did not press hard enough.

The real masters of the country were the secret societies, which carried out through the Officer Detachments an unbridled campaign of terror well beyond the limited terror carried out by the governments in their official capacity. To make a tentative survey of the White Terror, both official and unofficial, let us consider the figures: About 70,000 people were put into concentration camps under the most objectionable conditions, and 27,000 legal processes were initiated against individuals because of activities under the Károlyi and Kun regimes. There were 329 executions after trial, and some 1200 people were murdered in cold blood. Tens of thousands of Hungarians fled or were in hiding from the White Terror.[4] Nor were the exploits of the Officer Detachments purely anti-Communist or even purely

---

*This is understandable. At the end of its reign, the Hungarian Soviet had at its disposal a force of 284,742 enlisted men and logistics personnel, 14 machine gun companies, 3 armored trains, 280 guns and 9 air force companies; in addition there were many technical groups with all the equipment and ammunition needed. On the other hand, the Szeged counterrevolutionaries could muster only one battalion and about 2,000 refugee officers who recognized Horthy as their commander. There were, in addition, a company of light cavalry and the crew of a battery without guns, an air force squadron and some minor technical personnel. Súlyok, *A magyar tragédia*, p. 253.

54

anti-Semitic. The conservative-Catholic leader, Dezsö Súlyok, describes as an eyewitness their return from one of their routine night expeditions in Budapest, distributing among themselves their loot, wristwatches, jewels, the contents of wallets, etc.[5] The commanders and members of these Officer Detachments often reappeared as the worst perpetuators of Fascist crimes in Hungary. Pál Prónay, László Vannay, László Baky, András Mecsér, Béla Marton, Emil Kovarcz all passed through the preparatory school of the Officer Detachments.

In 1920, the editor of the organ of the Social Democratic party, Béla Somogyi, and another staff member, Béla Bacsó, were kidnapped and assassinated by three members of an Officer Detachment under the command of Lieutenant Emil Kovarcz, later a prominent member of the Arrow Cross. Their mutilated bodies were recovered from the Danube. Horthy personally gave orders to commit the crime.* These and other deeds caused revulsion all over the civilized world. The trade unions of the world proclaimed a boycott against Hungary. The French Socialist leader Léon Blum had intended to speak for Hungary during the peace treaty negotiations, but after the continued unchecked atrocities, he refused to intervene.[6] The international implications forced the government to put some of the most notorious perpetrators of outrages on trial. But it was done much more for the sake of propaganda than for the sake of justice. Heavy jail sentences were pronounced and duly reported in the press. After a few days one might meet the defendants at a fashionable Budapest nightspot, drinking, dancing and flirting. And that is not surprising; the defendants were with monotonous regularity the members of M.O.V.E., É.M.E. and the secret societies. Gömbös took good care of his boys, and Horthy was always ready to take into account the "patriotic motives" behind the crimes. It was he who was their ultimate protector.

Finally, at the prodding of the Entente, elections followed on the basis of the new Friedrich Franchise (named for the prime minister whose government introduced it in 1919), which enfranchised an incredible 39 percent of the population compared with the well below 10 percent of the prewar franchise. For the first time in Hungarian history the balloting was secret. Because of the prevailing White Terror, the Social Democrats did not participate in the elections, which made the convocation of a truly representative assembly impossible. In the elections of January 1920, the right, under the name Christian National Union, gained seventy-seven mandates while the docile left, the United Agrarian Laborers, under István Nagyatádi Szabó gained eighty-seven mandates. Hungary was proclaimed a kingdom again, but the ties with the Habsburgs were severed. In March 1920 Horthy was elected Regent for life. During the balloting, Officer Detachments occupied the Parliament Building. In the spring of 1920, while the negotiations continued for a peace treaty with the Allied Powers, a temporary

*Some years later, when Ödön Benicky, who was minister of interior at the time of the crime, disclosed in a press interview Horthy's role and responsibility in the affair, he got a stiff jail sentence; after his release he committed suicide. *Ibid.*, p. 280.

advance of the Red Army into Poland gave Hungary a chance. France became interested in an alliance with Hungary in case it became necessary to back the Poles. The Millerand note was sent to Budapest to this effect. As a price M. Paléologue promised a revision of the peace treaty provisions to Hungary's benefit.[7] But the Hungarian government did not react fast enough to the French overtures, and the Red Army was soon thrown back by Generals Jozef Pilsudski and Maxime Weygand, and Paris lost interest in the matter.

In June 1920 the Hungarian equivalent of the Versailles Peace Treaty was signed at Trianon Palace, and "Trianon" became a battle cry in Hungary. The Western powers may have had good reasons to fix boundaries and return to "normalcy" as soon as possible; among them, the fear of bolshevism and a Bolshevist revolution were not the least important. But the Trianon Treaty was even more shattering to the cause of democracy in Hungary and contributed incomparably more to the rise of fascism than Versailles undermined the Weimar Republic and aided the rise of Hitler.

Of the 325.00 km.^{2} territory of the Lands of the Holy Crown of St. Stephen (Croatia and Slavonia included), only 92.000 km.^{2} were left under Hungarian control. Some 103.000 km.^{2} went to Rumania, 61.500 km.^{2} to Czechoslavakia, 20.500 km.^{2} to Yugoslavia (in addition to 43.000 km.^{2} of Croatia and Slavonia), and about 4.000 km.^{2} to Austria. Fiume, Hungary's only port, became Italian; even Poland acquired a small piece of Hungarian territory. Of a prewar population of 21 million, Hungary was left with 7.6 million. The right to self-determination was always invoked when a territory could be severed from Hungary, but it was consistently denied when it might have favored the Hungarian cause. More than 3 million Hungarians were forced under foreign domination, in most cases in areas along the newly drawn border, where the arbitrary boundary line ran through a body of overwhelmingly Hungarian-inhabited areas. Many purely Hungarian towns were separated from rump Hungary, towns which were only a few miles away from the new borderline, and which easily could have been included in the new Hungarian entity (e.g., Oradea [Nagyvárad], Satu-Mare [Szatmárnémeti], Košice [Kassa], Subotica [Szabadka], Arad, etc.).

Apart from their disregard of the war aims proclaimed by the Entente and the idea of self-determination, the beneficiaries of Trianon, the very leaders of the Succession States, did not feel excessively happy about their great good fortune at Trianon Palace. Eduard Beneš said once to a friend during his successful negotiations: "I am alarmed when they give me everything I ask for — it is too much."[8] T. G. Masaryk, the grand old man of Czechoslovakia, was of the same opinion. Prof. M. Manoilescu, the Rumanian economist and politician, later a Fascist ideologist, said that Rumania "got just too much at Trianon."[9] This situation was not made easier by the ill treatment meted out by the Succession States to their large, newly acquired Hungarian minorities. If in the past they had just grievances against Hungarian handling of the nationality problem, they now proved that the yoke one suffers does not necessarily make easier the yoke one imposes on others. Rump Hungary also lost most of its raw materials, minerals and forests, but most of the factories remained in the part retained, mainly in Budapest. And in all this, one must keep in mind that Hungarian thought centered much more around historical rights, dating back to a continuity of a thousand years, than around the relatively new and roughly enforced principle of self-determination of peoples. Hungary had one answer for Trianon: "No, no, never!" (*"Nem, nem, soha!"*)

The quest for a revision of Trianon became a cardinal issue of Hungarian life, of politics, of education and of thought. Even though this seems understandable, one cannot help but reflect that if the Hungarians had considered a partial revision on ethnic grounds rather than an integral revision on the basis of the by then dead historical rights, they might have been more successful. Their just claims lost much support because of their quest for the blatantly unjust status quo ante. This intransigence, coupled with France's interest in maintaining the Little Entente, created in 1922 to replace the prewar Russo-French balance against Germany destroyed by the emergence of the Soviet Union, perpetuated the injustices of Trianon. The new regime plastered the walls of Budapest with posters proclaiming menacingly, "The hand should forget its cunning which signs!!! [the Trianon Treaty]." But the Entente powers set the double condition: (1) acceptance of the Trianon Treaty, and (2) permission for the entry of foreign capital in return for leaving the regime in power — and the regime signed it. It is difficult to say what else it could have done under the circumstances. Nevertheless, it was an anticlimax to the thunderous patriotic oratory before, and afterward for the next twenty-five years.

The years 1921-22 were a time of great flux in Hungarian politics. But as time went by, it became evident that it would be the conservative element, the big landowners, the big banking and business interests, which would win the upper hand. Yet, in both the dispute with Austria over the Burgenland issue and at the ill-fated return of King Charles of Habsburg in October 1921, the new regime saw that it was the help of the Szeged men on which it could count. It was the radical right student volunteers, called out by Gömbös, who stopped King Charles in the suburbs of Budapest. Eventually, both internal consolidation and an improvement in foreign relations favored the retirement of the Szeged men from the stage as protagonists.

The Szeged men expressed their dissatisfaction with the turn of events by continuing their terrorist activities.* The flow of excesses, bombings and killings continued well into 1924-25. If the perpetrators were apprehended at

---

*Even at the end of 1921, policemen were murdered by Officer Detachments in the heart of Budapest, because they dared to interfere with the detachments' exploits. And when one of the hotels, their headquarters, was raided by the army in the presence of the prime minister and the minister of defense, the raiders found dozens of ill-treated prisoners in the basement. One of them, for example, an eighty-six-year-old Jewish merchant who was fetched from a railroad terminal of the capital without any apparent reason other than that he was Jewish, was robbed and subsequently brutally beaten by a young member of the Detachment. Endre Szokoly, *És Gömbös Gyula, a kapitány* (Budapest, 1960), p. 154.

all, they got off with light punishment. As in Germany in the same period, the courts dealt severely only with offenses by the left. When the same courts dealt with like or worse offenses by the right, the "extenuating circumstance of patriotic motives" was always taken into consideration. Sentences were pronounced mainly for Entente consumption and were not carried out.

All these antecedents indicated that the time had come for the conservative wing of the Hungarian Nation to take over the government, to consolidate the country in its interest and according to its own creed. Their leader, Bethlen, became premier in 1921, shortly before the unsuccessful return of Charles of Habsburg. His goal was to restore the social, economic and political structure, and the spirit of prewar Hungary, which would lead to the ultimate restoration of its boundaries. Speaking of spiritual restoration, Bethlen, like most of his class, had Tisza in mind. Although never recognizing Trianon, he understood the unfeasibility of revision for the time being. Revision would come after economic recovery, and the first step in that direction was to regain the confidence of domestic and foreign financial circles. To this end, Bethlen had to curtail the anti-Semitic terror, despite his acute personal distaste for the Jews.

During 1922, three political master strokes followed one another. First, Bethlen secured the interests of his own class, the big landowners, whom he considered essential for the maintenance of his Hungary. He was aware of the land hunger among the disinherited peasant masses, especially after the sweeping land reforms carried out in neighboring countries. The leader of the peasantry was Nagyatádi Szabó, an honest weak man, and a peasant himself. But he was not of the militant type, and could never forget while negotiating with Bethlen as an "equal" that he was talking to a count. He would be cajoled, pressured, and lured by appeals to his patriotism, into a completely unsatisfactory land reform with secret articles which were never fulfilled. This reform left the large estates virtually untouched until 1945. Bethlen's second master move was combined with the third. He got rid of the Friedrich Franchise. With 39 percent of the population enfranchised, the Hungarian Nation could not feel comfortable, let alone safe. The assembly had to be transformed into a talking-shop of and for the Hungarian Nation and the Hungarian Nation only. The new franchise, with its elaborate checks and balances, was designed to serve just this end: the percentage of the enfranchised was drastically reduced to 27.3 percent of the population and, except in Budapest proper and a few towns in the country, the open ballot was reintroduced. This made the outcome of the elections, taking into account the electoral terror applied by the notorious Royal Hungarian Gendarmerie, a foregone conclusion; the Government party always won. This party rose from the fusion of the nonlegitimist wing of Bethlen's Christian National Union with the Agrarians of Nagyatádi Szabó. Although the party changed its name in the following decades, the fact that it never changed its content was not lost on the people. Everybody in the country called it the Government party (*Kormánypárt*) regardless of what official designation it took.

At the same time, Bethlen felt the pressure of the workers, who were much less docile than the apathetic peasant masses. Therefore, parallel with his electoral law, he made a concession to them. In his third master stroke he allowed a reasonable freedom for the Social Democratic party with the iron-clad provision, scrupulously observed on both sides, that they restrict their activities to Budapest and some mining and industrial districts, but refrain from entering the rural areas. Thus after establishing the open ballot in the countryside, Bethlen assured the estate owners that their vested interests would not be embarrassed by the attempts of bothersome Socialists to organize their three million *de facto* serfs. Those querulous Jews could pursue their irksome tactics among their coreligionists in mining and industry. The Hungarian Socialists accepted the compromise as the price of survival, with the hope that, surviving, they would be able to do some good. But there were those who considered the compromise a serious handicap to the development of democracy and democratic socialism in Hungary. Not without some justification did both leftist and radical Fascist extremists accuse the Social Democrats of a shameful collaboration with the feudal Bethlenites, of betraying the masses, of such degeneracy and lack of *élan vital* that they could not live without such concessions. Indeed, this compromise seems to have contributed substantially to the Fascist radicalization of the lower classes in Hungary a decade and a half later, especially that of the workers.

After these measures, elections were held which were conducted by Gömbös with the assistance of the gendarmerie. As a result of the new electoral law and the abuses of the Gömbös team, the Government party received its expected majority of 169 seats. The Social Democrats gained twenty-five seats and seventeen went to other moderate leftists. Thirty-five went to the legitimists and to splinter parties of the right. Now Bethlen could pronounce his motto: "The revolution is over." The conservative restoration was accomplished.

3

What did this "neobaroque edifice," as the distinguished Hungarian historian of the period, Gyula Szekfü, called it, look like? As we know, the Baroque is more concerned with form than with content. Members of ruling class families of the author's generation remember a childhood at the end of the era, with gleaming balls, romantic gypsy music, shining uniforms, processions, festivities, fireworks and parades — all displayed against the incomparable backdrop of princely Budapest as it glittered on the banks of the blue Danube.

But for the many, what lay behind this impressive facade? Above all, what did the times hold for the most important single group, the peasantry? In every semideveloped country there is a great difference between town and countryside and between the capital city and the rest of the country. Budapest, if compared with any Hungarian village of the Puszta,* showed a

*Semiarid parts of the great Hungarian plain.

shocking contrast. If one drove twenty or thirty miles beyond Budapest, the Puszta impressed the visitor, despite its romance, more as a Kirghiz steppe than a part of Europe. And little changed there during the neobaroque decades.

In the introductory chapter, the proportion of large and medium estates was noted in relation to the dwarf-holdings and the large masses of landless, agrarian proletariat. In rump Hungary, the situation became even a little worse than it had been in greater Hungary, although the Bethlen-Negyatádi Szabó agrarian reform did not change it to any substantial degree. Out of the four-and-a-half million people engaged in agriculture, more than two-thirds were landless, agrarian proletarians. These made up the famous "three million beggars" of the interwar period in Hungary.[10] In 1930, an average family of five had a daily five cents at its disposal for each member of the family for food, heat, light, clothing and all other needs.[11] Life in the countryside is described by Gyula Illyés, the distinguished writer and one of the "village explorers."*

The face of the native of the "Puszta" is slapped only until the age of 30-35. After that, he is spanked on the back of his nape or neck, usually only once. With the old, bodily punishment should be applied with care. When they are over sixty, they start crying when one lifts his hand to them. Not out of fear, but because of the humiliation. Only by that age does the feeling of human dignity ripen in them.[12]

Illyés says that the infliction of bodily punishment by hand is preferable to the use of sticks, whips, etc., because these people see in a slap or punch a relation between men. When hit by an object they may have unpredicted reactions.[13]

The females of the Puszta were the prey of the landlord, his family, their supervisors, or even of some minor clerks on the estate. Against this there was no appeal; it was a way of life and accepted as such, and was sometimes even considered idyllic.[14] Thanks to its misery, the peasantry imposed on itself a strict birth control long before it became a worldwide issue. Súlyok quoted from a book by Imre Kovács, another of the village explorers, describing the hatred in the village against peasant families with many children. Many times there were even threats to run them out of the village or to burn their houses down.

Parallel with a catastrophic fall in the birthrate, the burgeoning of religious sects ("Devildrivers," "Whitsuntide Waiters," "Fasters," "Tremblers," the "Seedless," etc.) became a widespread phenomenon. There was among the people a kind of moral nihilism, a possessed, holy renunciation of life, a consequence of the fact that they were deprived of a constructive spiritual life. But this atmosphere reflected economic conditions more than moral ones or questions of faith. Wide segments of the Hungarian people reached the point where they gave up hope for the improvement of their economic situation and fell into an all-encompassing lethargy, looking forward quietly to

*A group of young writers of wholly Hungarian descent, mostly of peasant stock, who had a sincere concern for social justice.

inevitable destruction.[15] That was the fate of the peasantry, to which the neobaroque age always referred as the "backbone" or the "mainstay" of Hungary, and which was depicted so attractively in colorful costume on the travel posters of the interwar period.

Disciplinary measures in the village were entrusted to the Royal Hungarian Gendarmerie, which became the Praetorian Guard of the neobaroque regime. They were recruited from peasants who, like the Janissaries, repressed their own kind with a brutality that one German SS man described contemptuously as Asiatic. These gendarmes were stationed in the rural areas only; the towns had a considerably more civilized police force. Together with their brutality went an iron discipline, efficiency and incorruptibility and, like the Janissaries, they obeyed every order without question or remorse. Horthy remembered them with delight, "brave gendarmes, children of Hungarian villages, who knew only how to obey orders...."[16] But by the 1930s this institution slipped out of the hands of the neobaroque regime, its officer corps became thoroughly filled with Fascists, and as an instrument of fascism it committed unspeakable crimes against ten of thousands of innocent citizens.

The workers were in a relatively better position than the peasants. After all, they were in the hands of the "Jewish" Socialists and "Jewish" capitalists. That did not mean much; their wages were miserable compared with those of Western Europe or even Vienna. But wealth is a relative thing. The workers were at least organized, they had a sense of human dignity, and they were aware of their position; consequently, they were in a much more militant mood than the apathetic peasantry. Later in the 1930s, when the radical, revolutionary Fascist movements appeared on the scene, they found many followers among the more radical workers who had grown impatient with the many compromises concluded by leaders of Social Democracy with the Hungarian Nation. There was another factor in addition to revolutionary impatience: nationalism. Many workers could not accept the way the "Fatherland of the Revolution" in general and Stalin in particular interpreted proletarian internationalism — by making the Communist International an instrument of Soviet foreign policy. In the early 1920s, the clandestine Communist party sent some agents from Moscow, but they were quickly apprehended by the secret police and thrown in jail. All this passed without any particular notice among the workers. For them, the 1920s meant a degree of recovery and even a modest prosperity. They had little reason to be dissatisfied with the concessions the Hungarian Nation made to them — until the great depression changed their feelings radically.

As for the Hungarian Nation, after the display of unity in 1919 the early chasm between the higher strata, represented by Bethlen, and the lower strata of the political nation represented by Gömbös, widened steadily. Yet, the gentlemenlike outlook on the world remained a common characteristic of both camps.

An excellent source for understanding the psychology of the Hungarian Nation, its dreams, its concept of life, and its reactions to the challenges of the twentieth century, is Cécile Tormay's *An Outlaw's Diary*.[17] Horthy remembers her leading the reception committee when he entered Budapest in 1919. He was presented with a "beautifully embroidered flag for his troops by Cécile Tormay, the distinguished writer, the president of the Federation of Hungarian Women. . . ."[18] And appropriately so. Nobody ever condensed better into two volumes the outlook of the Hungarian ruling classes.

Regarding the nationality problem, she describes at length the idyllic conditions of the Rumanian peasantry under the rule of Hungarian landlords, the complete freedom which existed for their national development, and their happy, contented, loyal attitude toward their overlords.

> They spoke their tongue, nobody ever harmed them. . . . So was it elsewhere, too. . . . The Hungarians did not oppress their foreign-tongued brethren. . .and yet these people shout now in mad hatred, that everybody who are Hungarians ought to be knocked on their heads. . . .

This puzzling change of heart on the part of the peasants was supposedly only the result of Rumanian nationalistic agitation and the subversion carried out by Károlyi's democratic ideas.[19]

So much for the nationalities. When Károlyi went to Belgrade, the event awakened in Miss Tormay some memories of Serbia in general and Belgrade in particular. After giving due consideration to "Balkan filth," she goes on in her travelogue to describe the *Skuptshina*, the Serbian Parliament:

> When I saw that, I could not help thinking of Hungary's House of Parliament. The two buildings proclaimed both the past and the culture of the two peoples. One is a Gothic blossom with roots in the Danube. When I saw the Serbian Parliament, it was a building like a stable with wooden benches in it, and the walls covered with red, white and blue stuff. Its air was reeking with the scent of onions and sheep, while the windows were obscured with fly marks.[20]

This arrogance after the magnificent war record of Belgrade and Serbia! And this is how unfavorably the representatives of the Serbian peasant-state compared in Miss Tormay's class-oriented mind with the Hungarian upper class Parliament.

The Hungarian Nation was understandably confused about the revolutionary mood after the war, not only about the Hungarian one but the other revolutions, too. After all, what was wrong? Was not everything in an Elysian state of perfection? Miss Tormay looks in despair for a clue and finds it:

> What demonical power, hidden by the fog, prompted these cries? What power cast its spell to lure a haughty, brave nation into shame, cowardice and perdition? Months have passed since I first asked this question, and the obvious answer revolted my conscience, which required time to be convinced. But Calvary has taught me the lesson. Now I seek no longer, I know. It is not an accident that the scourge and the executioner, the law and the lawgiver, the judge and the sentence of the Turanian Hungarians, the Teutonic Bavarians and the Slavic Russians were one and the same. The racial differences of the three peoples are too great to render that mysterious resemblance possible. It is clear that it must originate from the soul of another people, which lives amongst them but not with them, and has triumphed over all three. The demon of the revolution is not an individual, not a party, but a race amongst the races.[21]

After this lucid analysis of the economic, sociological and political roots of the revolution, Miss Tormay discusses the "Jewish Conspiracy" in the style of the "Protocols of the Elders of Zion." (Sample: "How is it that Jewish racial interests are identical in a Ruthenian village and in the heart of New York? ")[22] And the international aspects of the problem receive further illumination in a historical perspective:

> Mirabeau was led towards the Revolution by Moses Mendelsohn and the influence of beautiful Jewesses. They were there in Paris behind every revolution, and they appear in history amongst the leading spirits of the Commune.[23]

After reproaching the Jews for not being sufficiently represented among the martyrs (Leo Frankel and Karl Marx fled after the fall of the Paris Commune), Miss Tormay gives due consideration to the problem in such faraway places as Turkey and Portugal:

> It was during the Turkish Revolution that a Jew said proudly to my father, "We made that. The Young Turks are Jews." I remember at the time of the Portuguese Revolution Marqués Vasconcelos, the Portuguese Minister in Rome, telling me, "The Revolution in Lisbon is instigated by Jews and Freemasons." And today, when the greater half of Europe is in the throes of revolution, the Jews lead everywhere in accordance with their concerted plans.[24]

This and the rest of the story are told with noble sentiment and with great sincerity. But, as Eugene Weber points out so well in his work *Varieties of Fascism*, "Sincerity has no intrinsic value. A sincere fool is still a fool, a sincere Inquisitor still a torturer. A sincere anit-Semite may be any number of things."[25] Miss Tormay expressed the basic ideas and reactions of the political nation in Hungary, repeated *ad nauseam* after the triumph of counter-revolution and summed up in the slogan of the neobaroque edifice: the new regime was to be Christian and national. There is nothing inherently objectionable in the ideal of a state conducted according to the principles of Christianity and its own nationalism. But here "Christian" meant mainly that the state must not be infected by Jewish taint, that is, it must not be democratic, liberal or Judeo-Bolshevist. "National" stood as a euphemism for an implacable — and generously reciprocated — hatred and contempt for the Czechs, Rumanians and Yugoslavs. As for the Government party, it was the instrument by which the conservative wing of the Hungarian Nation imposed its will on the majority of Hungarians. This institution seemed in some ways quite democratic within the framework of the ruling class. In fact if one goes through the parliamentary debates of the era, he may gain the impression that there was genuine freedom of parliamentary life. However, these debates were no real indication of the degree of freedom existing in the country.

The Government party was in effect the executive committee of the ruling classes. It had almost absolute control over the appointment of public servants, local authorities, the *Vármegye*, the police and the gendarmerie. The members of the Government party had to proclaim the basic credo of the regime, Christian and national. Beyond that, they could entertain any number of principles or indulge in any lack thereof so long as they fell in line behind the party leader when the general vote was taken. In his turn, the leader was the representative of the Regent and of the conservative wing of the political nation. There was also a limited opposition tolerated, but it had to be a loyal opposition, to the extent that it could never seriously challenge the rule of the Hungarian Nation. If there was the slightest threat to the equilibrium, either from the right or the left, the apparatus of the political nation went into action with ruthless efficiency. Opposition was restricted mainly to the Parliament, not to achieve results, but rather to give vent to feelings.

It was F. Keresztes-Fischer, one of the more able representatives of the conservatives, who put this long-standing practice into words at the end of the era, in 1943, when there were ominous sounds from the extreme right. Keresztes-Fischer had acted as minister of interior for years. Criticized by the Fascists for some of his measures, he pointed out that "on the basis of long-standing experience, I must proclaim that I had to proceed always in a more radical manner against those parties whose star was rising and could afford more lenience towards those parties whose star was declining."[26] Clear enough.

It was Bethlen who established the principle that the opposition may shout in the Parliament at its discretion — only the streets should remain silent. He was also realistic enough to understand that active anti-Semitism was not feasible for the time being, and it seemed to him very questionable whether it was desirable at all for the ruling class, even in the long run. Not that his class could for a moment have accepted the Jews as equals. Not even in the moment of the neobaroque regime's direst need for the Jewish capitalists did any close personal relation à la Pompidou-Élie Rothschild or Mandel-Clemenceau develop between them in Hungary. A certain amount of anit-Semitism, especially as far as Bethlen was concerned, was an understandable, even a commendable, quality.*

But, as August Bebel defined it, anti-Semitism was also the Socialism of fools, and it was here where the keen instinct of the conservative wing of the political nation detected the potential danger. If once socialism crept in, even in a foolish form, nobody knew where it would stop. A petrified, ultraconservative system could not take chances. In addition to that important consideration, reconstruction after the defeat, chaos, and Trianon could not take place without the participation of the only middle class Hungary had.

But this reconstruction was by no means a healthy process. As a courageous opposition deputy pointed out, the number of monopolies (cartels) had reached 130 by 1928.[27] The landed estates allied themselves with big Jewish capital while tolerating the 95 percent of Jews only with contempt. The unhappy Hungarian people meanwhile reeled under the landowner-capitalist domination. Thus the neobaroque regime, while cruelly persecuting the democratic Jewish intellectual and in their illiteracy identifying Western thought with the Jews, made peace with the capitalists. It was an alliance of aristocratic self-indulgence, laziness and arrogance with the

*Bethlen's definition of the anti-Semite was a person who detested the Jews *more* than necessary.

cynicism, hedonism and amorality of big Jewish finance.[28] The overwhelming majority of Jewish citizens had nothing to do with it.

The Jews were to have a decisive role both in the history of Hungarian fascism and in the history of Hungary in the coming decades. The Szeged Idea and the men of Szeged succeeded in turning the Jewish question into a national obsession, the Jews into a scapegoat, and the whole complex into a prime stumbling block to any rational approach to Hungary's real problems. The Szeged Idea, which had been conceived out of sporadic programs in 1919, came to a brief full triumph only in March 1944, when the Szeged men were able to carry out in concert with their German Nazi allies the main point of their program: "de-Judaization" (*Zsidómentes Magyarországot!*) of Hungary. Some weeks before the end, they succeeded in delivering half a million of their fellow citizens to a horrible death. Then they went themselves to their doom, buried under the blazing ruins of their shattered capital, amid scenes comparable to the advent of the Four Horsemen of the Apocalypse.

Why was there serious anti-Semitism in Hungary with its thoroughly assimilated Jewish community? By 1920, thanks to an aristocratic concept that any work outside the army and the thoroughly feudal civil service was a defilement, the Jews, being the only middle class, had gained a commanding position in Hungary's economy and cultural life. Consequently, the radical elements came from their ranks in the first place. Many of the leaders of the Károlyi and Kun regimes were Jews, although they acted always as Hungarians or as proletarian internationalists. Although the overwhelming majority of Hungarian Jews were diametrically opposed to the Soviet (as the number of Jews murdered by the Red Terror clearly indicates), the Hungarian Nation felt itself directly challenged by the Jews. Because even though the majority of Jews were opposed to communism, that did not mean they were opposed to Károlyi's democratic regime, and democracy was little better than or equivalent to bolshevism in the eyes of the Hungarian Nation. They were ready to accept it in the West but never at home.

We know the kind of primitive anti-Semitism directed against the primitive unassimilated Jewish masses of Eastern Europe, notably those of Rumania. But even in Western Europe, there was a kind of backlash against Jewish emancipation and assimilation, the best manifestation of this being the Dreyfus affair. Not even in the liberal, prosperous, civilized West could people easily accept the "despicable" Jews as equals, working side by side with them in the army, civil service or the professions. France withstood the trial; there were the Clemenceaus, Zolas and Péguys who took care of the matter. Never again did anti-Semitism become a major problem in the West — not even during the German occupation.

But in the beginning of the twentieth century, an entirely new kind of anti-Semitism raised its head in Central Europe, which had nothing to do either with the instinctive aversion of the primitive peasant of Eastern Europe to the kind of Jews living in their midst or with the decreasing social ostracism practiced by the upper classes against the Jews in Western Europe. This new anti-Semitism began in Austria at the turn of the century, in a country where the Jews were completely integrated and useful citizens.* No people can do more than that. But if nevertheless there are political parties in parliament, as there were in Austria, whose representatives can introduce bills that would appropriate a monetary reward for everyone who shoots a Jew or that demand that anyone who kills a Jew should also inherit his property — and if representatives can be elected on such a platform — that is the end of the road.[29] This new kind of anti-Semitism brought an entirely new approach to the Jewish question. It was the kind of anti-Semitism perfected later by a young, unemployed painter named Hitler who sold the newspaper of Lueger and Schönerer on the streets of Vienna, and who got his inspiration and even his oratorical technique from his idols. Because it was he who spread the new credo in Germany and Austria, the whole content of anti-Semitism was a new one.

The Jews of Rumania or Poland did not give their countries a Heine, Börne, Marx, Lasalle, Einstein, Mendelsohn, Ehrlich or Rathenau, or a Freud, Friedjung, Zweig, Adler or Bauer. Anti-Semitism in such countries had to become something infinitely worse than anything the world had seen before. And so it became.

Although that kind of anti-Semitism was unknown in Hungary before 1914, after the war she was the only country in the world to join those two Germanic countries in maintaining a violently hostile attitude toward a completely assimilated, patriotic, useful Jewish citizenry. There is no parallel in the world to German, Austrian and Hungarian anti-Semitism. The responsibility for its development in Hungary lies squarely on the Szeged men and not on the Hungarian people. When Count Pál Teleki spoke at the Peace Conference in 1919 he said:

> The overwhelming majority of the Hungarian Jews have completely assimilated to the Hungarians. They gave us excellent Hungarian writers, artists, and scientists. Because of their assimilation to the Hungarian national soul and spirit one must recognize that, from a social point of view, the Hungarian Jews are not Jews any more but Hungarians.**

*It should be remembered, that Schönerer and Lueger did not come from and did not appeal to Galicia. They came from the Crownlands and appealed above all to Vienna. Schönerer was certainly more radical than Lueger was. Nevertheless, they both incited anti-Semitism against the assimilated Viennese Jews.

**Lévai, *Fekete Könyv a magyar zsidóság szenvedéseiröl*, pp. 48-49. It was Count Teleki who introduced the first anti-Jewish discriminatory bill in Parliament a year later making it practically impossible for a Jew to get a high school or university education. When reminded of his statement above, he curtly answered that it was made for reasons of expediency at the peace conference. And this was not a transitory mood either. Eighteen years later, when he piloted the second anti-Jewish law through Parliament, he prided himself on being the author of the *numerus clausus* and expressed his regret that in Hungary this "eastern" (not assimilated) Jewish community was treated with Western methods. O.N.K., February 22, 1939, pp. 496-500.

Indeed, there was a great deal of cynicism in the position of the Hungarian Nation on the Jewish question. If reminded of this, their first line of defense was always to recall the Jewish leadership of the Commune. But the Hungarian Nation knew very well that in 1919 Kun and his commissars were no more representative of the Hungarian Jews than the Rosenbergs were of the six million American Jews. It would be mistaken to assume that such a thoroughly bourgeois element was interested in war-communism. And the Hungarian Nation could have taken into consideration some other figures and facts. For instance, there were far more Jewish victims of the Commune than there were Jewish commissars. Also, in rump Hungary alone there were 10,000 Jewish war dead to be counted. There was practically no Jewish family which did not lose a member or two in the war. One family had nine sons on the front and 250 families had five sons on the battlefield. Fifty-nine Jews earned the highest distinction in battle (a recognition corresponding roughly to the United States Congressional Medal of Honor), ninety-five Jews earned the Golden Medal and 656 earned very high citations for bravery in the service of Hungary.[30] These figures refer only to Jews living in rump Hungary; if we were to consider as well the Jewish draftees who came from territories then belonging to the Succession States (they comprised half of all Jewish draftees), the figures would be considerably higher.

The Jews of the Succession States, in complete disregard of their economic interests and their time-honored principle as a minority of supporting the government in power, remained strongly Hungarian, and being mostly an urban element, constituted a powerful prop to the survival of Hungarian political parties, press and culture in those areas. That this was the case in anti-Semitic Rumania can be understood. In Yugoslavia, which had no aversion to Jews, the Jewish attitude can be considered unusual. But that it was the case even in Masaryk's democratic, civilized Czechoslavakia (with the exception of some unassimilated Jews of the Ruthenian region) should be considered a yardstick of Jewish loyalty to Hungary. *

Why was all of this to no avail? The Szeged men say, and some of them may also "sincerely" believe it, that it was the role of the Jews in the Hungarian Soviet which turned them against their Jewish fellow citizens. But investigating the question further, we find two crucial factors which are far more important in the anti-Semitism of the Szeged men than Kun and some of his commissars. One is the fact that rump Hungary had practically no nationalities left to assimilate, so that one of the most powerful factors in the acceptance of Jews was gone. The other factor was that most of the administrative posts in the nationality-inhabited areas, formerly filled with Hungarians, were gone and the erstwhile employees were now unemployed refugees in rump Hungary. In addition to that, the universities graduated more students in rump Hungary than they did in historic Hungary (11,000 in 1914 and 12,000 in 1925).[31] These refugees and university graduates broke

*As late as the Munich crisis, Slovak leaders asked the help of Ribbentrop in order to exclude the Jews from a planned plebiscite, because they would vote for Hungary. Macartney, *op. cit.,* I, 299n.

with the aristocratic outlook of the Hungarian Nation and discovered the incentive of the professions and even that of commerce. But the Jews occupied these fields. There occurred a violent conflict of interests, and the response of the Szeged men was an even more violent anti-Semitism. Because of the assimilated, patriotic character of the Jewish community, a racial anti-Semitism had to be introduced into Hungary. This anti-Semitism was at first a strictly middle class and lower middle class phenomenon. Neither the peasants nor the workers had conflicts with the Jews. The landowning artistocracy's alliance with Jewish capital only added fuel to the anti-Semitism of the Szeged men.

This lower stratum of the Hungarian Nation was the one which pressed through the first Jewish law in Europe since 1848, the *numerus clausus*, designed to eliminate Jewish intellectual and professional competition by limiting Jewish enrollment in gymnasiums and universities to 5 percent of total admissions. Although the paragraph concerning the gymnasiums was allowed to lapse, the establishment of a principle was more important in this case than the practical consequences. *When the neobaroque system broke with the general European tradition of toleration, it established a precedent in Hungary.*

What was the response of the Jewish Hungarians? The upper stratum made its terms with Bethlen and grew rich. But the overwhelming majority, the small shopkeepers, the physicians, the bank clerks, the lawyers, felt deeply hurt. They did not seek refuge in Zionism or in communism (as many of the persecuted Polish or Rumanian Jews did), but they thought that there must be some misunderstanding somehow. In order to dissipate it, they became even more fervent and loyal Hungarians, if possible, than before. These unfortunates did not wish to understand that they were in the way of the Szeged Idea in the field of economics and eventually in politics, that the Szeged men were not apt to be exceedingly impressed by any manifestation of Jewish loyalty.

The Jews had, nevertheless, one effective means of checking the Szeged Idea. The Trianon Treaty guaranteed equal rights to all Hungarians, regardless of their creed, race, or nationality. The Rumanian Jews, through their connections abroad, forced the victorious Rumanian state into granting full citizenship to their unassimilated masses — many of them barely able to speak Rumanian — in 1923. The powerful Alliance Israélite now offered its services to the Hungarian Jews. They refused in categorical terms. It was not in Hungarian Jewish tradition to look to foreigners for help against their compatriots. V. Vázsonyi, the leader of the Jewish masses, answered the inquiry of the Alliance in 1924: "The Treaty of Trianon is a sorrow for our nation — it cannot become the source for our rights."[32] Clear enough. But it also showed that the Jews fatally misunderstood those with whom they were dealing. The Paris Alliance drew its own conclusion and broke with the Hungarian Jewish communities, thus excommunicating them from world Jewry. But the Hungarian Jews were undeterred. Vázsonyi, although regretting the move of the Alliance, reiterated the Jewish position in Hungary, "our foreign co-religionists do not understand us either, because we are Hungarians first and above all. We are not Hungarian Jews but Jewish Hungarians."[33] Ultimately the "bad" Rumanian Jews got better treatment as punishment than the "good" Hungarian Jews got as a reward.

4

Bethlen carried out the restoration of prewar Hungary to the extent possible under the circumstances. An ultraconservative spirit prevailed in politics and in the whole life of the state. As far as the economy was concerned, there was a nineteenth-century liberalism. That is why some people prefer to call the neobaroque edifice a "conservative-liberal" structure. But that was not a solution to Hungary's problems. And there were the Szeged men, who clamored for change. They were ready to break with the past and also with the present, in which they had little vested interest.

The refugee civil servants, the disillusioned war veterans, the younger element, and the lower ranks of the officers' corps, all the people whose activities were channeled through the secret societies, were about to be joined in their dissatisfaction by new recruits — the ever-increasing number of university graduates, an appalling number of whom remained unemployed. Employment competition was keen in the ranks of the lower echelon of the Hungarian Nation. Gone were the days when they could hold a monopoly on the administrative and military posts of half a great empire. Not only was Trianon Hungary small after the defeat, it was impoverished.

In the decades between the wars, many of the traditional values of the gentry had been destroyed in this competition, values which made Hungary the beloved political nation in 1848-49, values which drew respect for a man like Tisza from friend and foe alike. A leprosy of conformism, a quagmire of compromise, hypocrisy and ruthless coercion coupled with a panicky shrinking from any responsibility took the place of traditional values in all too many cases, until in 1938 a writer spoke the truth when he said, "No Hungarian generation has counted so many talkative, unrealistic, cowardly, trashy men in its ranks as the present one."[34] He received, of course, a jail sentence for "defaming Hungary." Unfortunately, such jail sentences did not solve the problem.

Compounding the problem of unemployment among intellectuals, Bethlen kept his promise to Nagyatádi Szabó and made high school education for the humble easily accessible. Hungarian high school standards being very high, those who graduated felt themselves to be gentlemen and demanded a desk instead of a tool or the plough. Needless to say, there were not enough desks in a country with the most overexpanded civil service and bureaucracy in Europe. Thirty-nine percent of the yearly budget was spent on administration, with the result that the salary paid in the GS-9 class was six times that paid in the GS-4.[35] Most of the young "baccalaureates" felt themselves part of the Hungarian Nation's Szeged wing, but because they retained reminiscences of their humble origins they were not opposed in principle to some kind of social justice; they were not hardened conservatives.

Finally, articulate youth simply felt out of place in the neobaroque edifice. The natural variance between the older and newer generation widened into a deep chasm, as Prof. Gyula Szekfü points out:

The problem of chasm between generations was accentuated by the neobaroque system, and became an almost insurmountable problem later, because the spiritual development of the middle classes was petrified. This class considered every new move with suspicion, as dangerous to its interests. But it is characteristic of any youth that it adopts attitudes which differ from those of its elders. Consequently, the "conservative" spirit of society banished the youth into a domestic exile.[36]

Also in this group one may count the lower midle class professionals and a group of independent artisans and craftsmen (especially in the region of greater Budapest), most of them of the humblest peasant or worker orgin, who had recently been elevated to a very dubious petit-bourgeois status. These were extreme borderline cases, who felt very insecure. They had no love for the upper classes, and in the interwar period managed to develop a fanatical hatred toward the Jews, who blocked their further advance economically. In another society these groups would have moved to the left. But the Károlyi-Kun experience, Trianon and the Jewish question effectively ruled out not only a Communist but even a democratic solution for this rather complex group. They did not feel at home in the Bethlen system, from which only the loudest and the most articulate could get some crumbs now and then.* Their leader was and remained Gömbös, who favored a Fascist solution. After Bethlen embarked irreversibly on his course, Gömbös broke with him in 1923, leaving the Government party along with six other racist representatives. Together they found the Hungarian National Independence party (*Magyar Nemzeti Függetlenségi Párt*) or simply Party of Racial Defense (*Fajvédő Párt*). The leader of the new party was Gömbös.

This first Fascist-type party hoped above all to awaken the "Hungarian national consciousness" and, according to its program, sought to establish unitary society in the Christian spirit without any contradiction between classes. The party would observe the strict principle of private property, but it favored a just distribution of wealth. The program proclaimed the need of respect for productive labor, denounced "excesses" of capitalism, and foresaw social legislation. After these vague outlines, the more specific and concrete parts of the program follow: sweeping anti-Semitic legislation; the expropriation of practically every Jewish property, commercial or industrial; the replacement of all Jewish professionals until their number decreased to 5 percent of professional employees (this was the proportion of Jews to the population). In order to facilitate this process of Aryanization, the assimilation of Jews was to be undone forcibly; they were to be proclaimed a national minority against their will.

In the populist spirit of Eastern European fascism, the party wished to maintain the agrarian character of Hungary, opposing both capitalist

---

*Bethlen tried to silence the most irritating critics of his system by offering them some "sinecures" in his, for this purpose, extended administration. He, of course, did not apply police methods to these people.

development and economic liberalism. Further, the program advocated more government credit to agricultural development than to industry. The program was hostile toward the magnates and the system of *fideicommissa*, but it proposed the defense of the land of the "historic middle classes." In foreign policy, it opposed the Habsburg restoration or the restoration of the Dual Monarchy in any form, and stood for integral revision and for an unbridled expansion into the Balkans "with the help of the West."

Finally, it wanted to reorganize the obsolete parliamentary system on a corporative basis. There should be, also, more freedom for organizations busy in "racial defense." The Social Democratic trade unions were to be eliminated. The program spoke in the vaguest possible terms about the necessity to improve the lot of agricultural laborers and the workers. It also included such refinements for education as "cleansing the Hungarian racial genius from the worship of Western culture."[37]

After taking a look at the written party program, let us consider what it could mean in action. How was it compatible with the utterances and ideas of its leader? Gömbös was a dynamic, active man. He took the Nationalist International very seriously — up to a point (that point being the Achilles heel of the whole idea, where Gömbös' Hungarian imperialism conflicted with the insatiable imperialism of some other Nationalist Internationalist).

Gömbös, whether in power or in his self-imposed exile, never ceased to scheme and to work in the classical fashion of the Black Hand, whose Col. Dragutin ("Apis") Dimitrjević was one of his idols. As early as 1920, he established his contact with the German right with G. Kahr and the Consul group; with Czarist Russian, Ukranian and Bavarian rightist groups; and with Mussolini's at that time embryonic movement in Milan. The assassins of M. Erzberger and W. Rathenau found friendly asylum at the Gömbös villa and continued their journey to Turkey with the cooperation of the Chief of the Hungarian Police.[38] Gömbös was interested in extending the Nationalist International to Kemal Atatürk's Turkey. But Atatürk was great and farsighted, and Gömbös' overtures never led to tangible results in Ankara.

If he was unsuccessful with Atatürk's nationalism, however, he was drawing closer to adherents of another nationalism — the nationalism of Hitler in his early days. Following up his contacts with the *Freischäre*, he helped to finance the early Nazis and worked out a far-reaching plan with them in 1923 just before the Beerhaus Putsch, which was supposed to escalate into a fantastic plan. The German Putsch was to be followed in Hungary by a similar coup, and after the overthrow of Bethlen, there was to be a Fascist government installed in Hungary, headed by Gömbös. The conspiracy also foresaw a Wittelsbach restoration in Bavaria, and in its later stages the overthrow of Bolshevism in Russia, with a Tzarist restoration to follow in Northern Russia and a Ukraine under German control. Since Gömbös never relaxed his control over M.O.V.E. and a dozen other militant secret societies, and since in addition he controled the semi-Fascist student association, the *Turúl*, he thought he had the necessary paramilitary forces to implement the plan. Through his friends in the Officer Detachments he hoped to take control of the regular Honvéd Army.

71

Bethlen's police were alerted, however; they intercepted the liaison men between Hitler and Gömbös and the whole fantastic plot was exposed. Gömbös protested his innocence, but only Horthy's personal intervention saved him.[39] The rest of the culprits drew light sentences. As usual, their "patriotic motives" were taken into due consideration by the courts, and soon they were set at liberty. After the incident, Bethlen moved in earnest against the Party of Racial Defense. But Gömbös, confident of the protection of high places, continued to harass the alliance of conservative landlords and Jewish financiers.

In September 1925, Gömbös and Tibor Eckhardt organized the World Anti-Semitic Congress in Budapest.* If Gömbös wished by this to embarrass Bethlen, he attained his goal. Ten or fifteen world-renowned anti-Semites came to the banks of the Danube for the occasion.** The congress was brought to a quick end by Bethlen's using the carrot as much as, if not more than, the stick. Gömbös chronically lacked funds. The Archduchess Isabelle, wife of Archduke Frederick, gave him a helping hand. In exchange for a promise that her son Archduke Albrecht would become a Hungarian king, a "national king," she saw to it that Gömbös was lavishly subsidized during his self-imposed political exile.[40]

Bethlen's system finally took care of these activities in a summary but not unusual manner during the elections of 1926; as a result, all of the parliamentary seats of the Party of Racial Defense were eliminated. Only Gömbös kept his mandate, after Horthy personally intervened to assure that his parliamentary election not be opposed by the Government party's electoral machine. Under such circumstances the number of parliamentary seats won in the election was obviously not an accurate reflection of the real Fascist strength or, as a matter of fact, of the real strength of any party. But in the Hungarian parliamentary system any mention of true representation was a mere technicality.

Despite these bickerings within the Hungarian Nation, the controversy was not yet as serious as it became later. Gömbös and the Szeged Idea were not categorically opposed to the "Christian national" spirit of the Bethlen regime. They had too much in common in background, ideas and education, and

---

*Tibor Eckhardt had a colorful career. As a minor refugee official from Transylvania, he became the president of É.M.E., a powerful secret society specializing in anti-Semitic terror. In this capacity, he was personally responsible for the worst outrages, bombings, and murders, and the death of many dozens of innocent people, many of them women. In the meantime, he ambiguously kept very good relations with Jewish financiers.

**It is of some interest that that grand old man of Rumanian anti-Semitism, Professor Cuza, came to Budapest accompanied by the young Ion Moţa. In view of Hungarian-Rumanian relations, the writer considered this fact too incredible until he found it confirmed in Moţa's own correspondence. Once, at least, anti-Semitism made the Nationalist International work. Szokoly, *op. cit.*, p. 234. Also, Ion Moţa, *Correspondenţia cu "Serviciul Mundial,"* Biblioteca Verde, No. 10 (Rome, 1954), p. 46.

many in the two camps were even intermarried. And after all, it was the Szeged men who were the lifeblood of the "Christian Course" (*Kerésztény Kurzus*, another name wherein "Christian" stands much more for anti-Semitism than for Christ). It was they who served the counterrevolution, and it was they who brought the people into submission in the years 1919-20. They had fought for the regime in Burgenland and prevented the return of Charles of Habsburg. Although they were irritated by him once in a while, Bethlen held them ready for any eventuality; he did not burn his bridges. The leading Szeged echelons were still part of the Hungarian Nation. Moreover, even though they vaguely advocated reforms, the sincerity of their radicalism was undeniable only so far as the Jews, the Succession States, France and democracy in any form were concerned. The true character of the Szeged Idea regarding the disinherited popular masses can be measured by some of Gömbös' statements. He thought them "incapable of deciding whether an idea is right or not"; therefore, "the Hungarian people require a patriarchal relationship with their rulers.[41] Such a relationship has to be reestablished. National unity should not be disrupted by destructive teachings."[42] When the regime reestablished corporal punishment after the victory of the counterrevolution, Gömbös always fully approved the measure.

In 1923, Gömbös spoke out vaguely for land reform, mainly for tactical purposes, but he was against the revolutionary spirit that might accompany it. He also gave some technical advice as to how the land reform should be carried out. He preferred to leave 5,000 holds in "racially pure Hungarian" hands, and to expropriate 500 Jewish holds.[43] He scrupulously kept the gentlemen's agreement between landowners and government and never advocated the mechanization or modernization of agriculture, which would have exposed the overpopulation and the incredibly backward state of the Hungarian village.

In 1928, he prepared to make his peace with Bethlen by speaking out violently against agrarian reform, unemployment relief, etc. According to him, one must create employment and not an unemployment relief program.[44]

In regard to foreign policy, he often proclaimed his violent hatred against France. And lest there be too much sympathy for his position because of Trianon, Gömbös set the record straight: "The French do not sympathize with conservative elements, but only with those elements of whom we, the kind of Hungarians who represent a chauvinistic point of view, want no part."[45]

In true romantic fashion, he was for the monarchy, but he firmly opposed Habsburg restoration because he feared that the chauvinistic line would be abandoned. He was worried about the Habsburg instinct for adaptability. Whatever the Habsburgs would have done in the twenties, it is certain there would have been little room for Gömbös' ambitions in their designs. They would have been tolerant on the all-important Jewish issue and would have, by their presence alone, dashed the hopes of a Fascist takeover based on the Szeged Idea.

In his foreign policy, Gömbös planned to establish joint control with Italy and Germany over the whole of Central and Eastern Europe. Hungary was not only to receive the Lands of the Holy Crown of St. Stephen, it was also to dominate most of the Balkan territory as far as the Black Sea! [46] Gömbös really believed that twelve or thirteen million underdeveloped Hungarians, led of course by the Hungarian Nation rejuvenated in the Szeged Idea, could treat on equal terms with seventy million Germans (he considered the *Anschluss* a *fait accompli*) and forty-five million Italians in the framework of a Rome-Berlin axis. This is what the cryptic statement, the "help of the West," referred to in the party program.

Apart from the fact that he had scant hope of extinguishing Rumanian, Serbian or Croatian nationalism in the late 1920s, there was the possibility that both Germany and Italy might have their own ideas about the future of a region so vast and rich, and so important geopolitically. Gömbös never worried seriously about these considerations. All was to work on the "comrades in arms" basis, and on the basis of the Nationalist International. Although one may ask why the Nationalist International was to work only in the western direction and not with the Balkan nationalists also, one can understand that Gömbös violently opposed any form of Danube confederation. But he was enough of a sincere Hungarian chauvinist to wish to "establish a Hungarian fascism and not to imitate Italian fascism blindly."[47]

In the meantime, Bethlen proceeded on his road, unperturbed by the rumblings of the Szeged men, and achieved an impressive success with the Hungarian economy. Far more realistic than Gömbös, he always gave priority to economic prosperity over anti-Semitism or integral revisionism. In 1922 Hungary entered the League of Nations, and by 1924 had received a large loan from the League for purposes of economic recovery, although this was not an unmixed blessing. League control was established over the finances of Hungary, infringing gravely on the dignity of the national sovereignty. But financial stability was achieved, and with the cessation of anti-Semitic terrorism, fugitive Jewish capital was repatriated and there was a great influx of foreign capital. Grain exports soared and industry recovered. Under such circumstances, the currency could be stabilized. A new monetary unit, the pengö, replaced the crown and was established at a rate of 5.1 to the dollar. For years it was one of the world's most stable currencies.

The general economic climate of the twenties and the government apparatus did not allow the Fascists much success. They became only a chronic irritation, nothing more. Gömbös understood this. Yet shortly before his great move, he fired off an interview to the Italian Fascist paper *Lavoro Italia*. Here he once more summed up his views and his dedication to Fascism. He reiterated his intention to develop a Hungarian brand of fascism, but he acknowledged that he had learned and adopted much from Mussolini. Gömbös continued: "We also have Fascist organizations, M.O.V.E., É.M.E., etc. — all these serve a Fascist goal. Soon these will be obliged to wear Black Shirts. The organized Black Shirts of Hungary, the Eagles,* are already operating — they are disrupting the activities of the Socialist organizations."

*The Eagles were an embryonic stormtrooper formation.

Gömbös assured the Italian journalist that many of his partisans were members of the Government party or of the Christian Socialist parties. And "above all, we are anti-Semites." With that he concluded his interview.[48] Bravely spoken. But Gömbös had grasped the realities of 1928. Shortly after that interview, he dissolved his party and reentered the Government party in order to be promoted from captain to lieutenant general and to become secretary and later minister of defense in Bethlen's cabinet.

For the time being, there was little to be heard about Fascism in Hungary. But when the depression came, it gave fascism its great chance not only in Hungary but all over the No-Man's-Land of Europe.

5

Conditions for the rise of fascism in the political and ideological void created by the disappearance of the Habsburg empire were not lacking in Hungary. Both democracy and communism were discredited during 1918-19, from within and without. Wilson's Fourteen Points were as little the basis for the peace treaties in 1919-20 as the Atlantic Charter a generation later was the basis of the Paris peace treaties. Not only was Trianon a blatant injustice, it helped to discredit the ideas of those who imposed it on Hungary. On the other hand, although Hungary had just grievances, she became unreasonable under their impact. National grievances are, as George Bernard Shaw so fittingly ascertained, like a cancer. A suffering nation, like a suffering human being, can think of nothing else until the cancer is removed.

The prewar conservatism of the Hungarian Nation did not really solve the great problems of Hungary. It could create a superficial, temporary semblance of prosperity, but it really benefited only those who had a direct stake in the regime. As far as the great peasant masses and the workers were concerned, they were either forced or bribed into inaction. The Jewish middle class was made responsible for the failure of democracy and communism and even for the loss of the war. Former deference to an esteemed ally turned to scorn for a powerless subject. After 1919, the Jews were only tolerated in Hungary. They were effectively silenced in politics. A Jew found it prudent in the interwar period to keep opposition views to himself. That for 95 percent of the Jewish population.

There was only one group in a position to clamor for change — the Szeged men. Part of the political nation, many of them young, educated nationalists, they would not accept the petrified conservatism of the Bethlen regime as an answer, either for their own future or for that of their country.

The solution in the eyes of these overwhelmingly middle class-oriented people was a Fascist one. There is something curiously elusive about the Szeged Idea — it can be interpreted in many ways. Because it was such a radically new idea within the framework of the Hungarian Nation and such a break with its ultraconservative past, it is hard to find any antecedent that would define it through example or parallel. Count Nándor Zichy's Christian party at the beginning of the century has little relation to it, despite its anti-Semitism. (Note that Christianity there also stood for anti-Semitism rather than for brotherly love.) The lineal descendants of Zichy's party with their violent anti-Semitism were Károly Wolff, the corrupt mayor of Budapest, and his vulgar, corrupt panamist-ridden Christian Course. Their program was fomented in a deplorable fashion by some members of the hierarchy of the Catholic Church in Hungary (Bishop O. Prohászka, for example, who at the same time had an absolutely sincere concern for social justice), and by some Catholic politicians. One thing is sure: the Szeged Idea was an excellent foundation for a Fascist state. The Bethlen regime, even the rich Jews, treated it with sympathy and a conservative reservation. They preferred the neobaroque restoration; they would have liked to keep Hungary and their position in Hungary forever as it was. But if change had to come, and it became increasingly evident that it had to come, they preferred a Fascist way out to anything else. All these ideas were comfortable spiritual exercises in the 1920s, with the relative economic prosperity and with Germany and Russia prostrate. But with the depression and the rise of Hitler and Nazism, the position of the conservatives was challenged in a different manner. The Fascist idea now ceased to be an internal affair of the Hungarian Nation and it brought the disinherited masses on the scene.

Despite Gömbös' claims of originality and his assertions of a need for a Hungarian road to fascism, there was little basic difference between Italian fascism and his interpretation of the Szeged Idea except its all-important violent anti-Semitism of later years. The anti-Semitism of the Szeged men had not only a nationalist or economic character, as it had in Rumania; even before 1933, it acquired a distinctly racist character.

The whole complex of Szeged Fascist ideas was permeated with romantic nationalism. Its followers were "enthusiasts" in the worst sense of the word, in the sense deplored by all the philosophers of the Enlightenment. They could apply a certain amount of realism in internal politics, which they more or less understood, at least as far as their class interests were concerned. But even the semblance of realism deserted them when they entered the field of foreign relations. Here their chauvinist mystique took over, with fatal consequences. And in the region where Hungary is located, one cannot even think about a realistic internal policy without establishing a sound foreign policy — if indeed such a thing is possible in the Danube Basin.

Fascism in Eastern Europe was inseparable from populism. Unfortunately, this populist romanticism did not solve anything for countries tied to the twentieth century. In a country with 22.4 percent agrarian overpopulation in 1930,[19] a carefully considered industrialization seemed to be the answer. To this end a middle class in the Western sense was needed. It was this middle class which Gömbös and the Szeged Idea set out to destroy.

The Szeged Idea was basically a conservative concept. This conservative Fascism was full of contradictions. Its lip service to a very limited agrarian reform and its friendly overtures to workers, provided they join the Fascist camp, were forgotten and contradicted whenever it was expedient. Their goal was summarized in one of the slogans they often used: "Let's have a change of guard! " ("*Örségváltást!* ") They wished to relieve the guard held by the Jewish middle classes. If successful, this would secure them a living for at least a generation. Also, they intended to carry out a "change of guard" in the upper classes. They opposed the ultraconservative older wing of the Bethlen-led Hungarian Nation, who by monopolizing power denied the benefits of power to these mainly young men. Also, because of their alliance with the Jewish industrialists and bankers (these two categories, because of the peculiar character of Hungarian capitalism, encompassed the same group of people), the Bethlen interests denied them the financial advantages to be gained by a posture of anti-Semitism.

The masses were aware of all this and kept far away from the Szeged Idea. There were no serious attempts made from Gömbös' side to appeal to the masses, either. The change of guard was to be very limited. The tragedy of the matter was that even this thoroughly class-oriented, conservative fascism, which could offer more demagoguery than systematic progress for the disinherited masses, was at least in some aspects a step ahead of the immobile Bethlen system. On the positive side it proposed to break the frozen grip of ultraconservatism, to do away with the vicious circle of landowner-capitalist alliance. It would have drastically reshuffled the spectrum of the middle class in Hungary. We can only guess what Hungary could have looked like after that. Taking the place and property of the Jews served as a great incentive to many hundreds of thousands of the ruined "middle class of Hungarian gentlemen" fighting desperately in the postwar period not to slip further. The peasants and workers, even if there is little evidence that their fate would have been substantially improved in a Szeged Fascist state, had little to lose with Gömbös eventual advent to power. This is one of the reasons why it inspired most of the articulate youth and so many members of the petite bourgeoisie.

6

The international position of Hungary during the years 1921-31 — the Bethlen era — was generally favorable for the development of fascism and of Fascist sympathies in Hungary.

A salient fact of this period was that neither Germany nor Russia followed an active foreign policy in the No-Man's-Land of Europe during the Bethlen era. France was supposed to be master of the Continent, with her quest for security-through-alliance systems that supposedly would safeguard the status quo.

Hungary was guided by two cardinal principles in her foreign policy: anti-bolshevism and revisionism.

Anti-bolshevism was the very *raison d'être* of the counterrevolution and one of the main, if not the main, dynamic forces of the regime. As we have seen, it had many qualifications and interpretations, and in many cases it meant acute hostility to democracy and anti-Semitism. But taken in the orthodox sense of the word, communism, although supposedly international, was at that time centered in Russia, and this fact aggravated its menace to Hungarians of all classes. That Russia was the fosterer and patron of

Pan-Slavism, an idea so hostile to Hungarian national aspirations, gave the final touch of monstrosity to the whole problem. At this point it was not the upper class alone, fretting for its comforts and privileges, that stood up against the Russian Bolshevist enemy; it was the overwhelming majority of the Hungarian people. And the more unequivocally Stalin followed a nationalistic policy, the easier it was for the Hungarian, Rumanian and Polish ruling classes to rally their thoroughly patriotic, nationalistic and consequently anti-Russian, masses against the Soviet Union. This anti-Russian feeling was more accentuated in Rumania and Poland because of their more frequent direct contacts with Russia in the past, contacts which were almost uniformly unfavorable. But Hungary remembered 1849 and the Pan-Slavic agitation of the following decades, and she also remembered 1919.

The second cardinal principle was the quest for revision of the Trianon Treaty. Hungary did not even pretend to accept the Trianon peace settlement as permanent or binding. There were differences among Hungarians as to the best methods or timing of revision, but none as far as the principle of revision was concerned: in this the Hungarian people were united from conservatives to right-wing extremists and from liberals to Communists. Nevertheless, temporary concessions had to be made. Hungary needed money, which was available only in the West, and there France, influenced by her allies in the Little Entente whose mission was to oppose Hungarian aspirations, had a great deal to say. It was this reality which toned down Bethlen's quest for revision. Gömbös and his Fascists could easily attack Bethlen from the comfortable position of the opposition for not being revisionist enough, for compromising too much and for selling Hungary's national interest down the drain in order to get money from "Jewish" banks in Paris and London, or through Geneva. After all, it was not Gömbös or Eckhardt who had to face these financial interests at the conference table. Later, when they had acquired responsibilities, when they had to deal with these financiers on the personal, national or international level, Gömbös and Eckhardt and many others of the same brand actually made more unprincipled, far-reaching, and sordid concessions to the same circles than Bethlen had done.

Another fact that imposed a rigid restraint on revisionist effort should have been obvious to Gömbös, M.O.V.E. and its Officer Detachment membership: Hungary was militarily weak. Even given the well-known martial spirit of the Hungarian Honvéd at its traditional best, Hungary could not have put up more than a token resistance against a concerted Little Entente effort. For good or bad, this fact more than any other determined Hungarian policy on the revision question. Nevertheless the "enthusiasts" of the Officer Detachment had their own campaign plans. According to them, "The Only Reliable Army of the Heroes of Europe" would soon reconquer the lost territories. Statements were issued to the effect that on a certain day Kassa (Košice), Pozsony (Bratislava), Nagyvárad (Oradea) etc., would be recaptured. When the day came the people waited fervidly for a reconquest that never came.[50]

Bethlen knew he could not expect any support from the strongest continental power, France, because she was thoroughly committed to the

Little Entente, to security, and as a consequence to the status quo. The Forged Franc Affair* in 1924 did not help Hungarian-French relations either.

England meanwhile was nurturing delusions of a splendid new isolation. She had no vital interests in No-Man's-Land, and despite Lord Rothemere's efforts on behalf of Hungary, the majority of Englishmen were quite indifferent to Hungarian revisionist claims.** The United States was living in the heyday of isolationism, and her influence in Hungary's quest for revision was nil.

The Weimar Republic, like Hungary, had been on the losing side, and the international positions of the two countries had a lot in common. But Weimar showed little aggressive spirit, and by its very democratic nature was antipathetic to the neobaroque system. There was also a great deal of cooperation between Moscow and Berlin in those years. If there were contacts between Hungary and Germany, they were between the Hitler-Ludendorff circle and Gömbös. These rather informal contacts, by no means restricted to Gömbös' entourage as the letter written by Ludendorff to Horthy clearly shows,[51] were expected to help the achievement of integral Hungarian revision.

There were somewhat platonic sympathies between Hungary and Bulgaria and Turkey, but they were of little practical consequence. The traditional Hungarian-Polish friendship, especially strong among the upper classes, was restrained by Polish obligations to Rumania and France.

Austria was prostrate, and until the Socialists of Vienna were gradually pushed back by the Conservative Catholics of I. Seipel, many democratic and Communist exiles made "Red Vienna" the headquarters for their anti-Horthy activities. This, coupled with the Burgenland dispute, strained Austro-Hungarian relations during almost the whole of the Bethlen era.

So the iron ring of Little Entente encirclement prevailed. But if we scrutinize this alliance more closely, it is not difficult to recognize in it in the early 1920s the seeds of its own destruction. Its members had few or no economic ties with one another, and their main national problems were very different, sometimes contradictory. Only one thing held them together, and that a negative one: they all were antirevisionist and anti-Hungarian. Beyond that, the hereditary enemy of Czechoslovakia was Germany, of Rumania, Russia, and of Yugoslavia, Italy. The Bethlen regime's official attitude toward

---

*In 1924, some not very bright Hungarian gentlemen decided the best way to finance revisionist propaganda and anti-Czechoslovak subversion would be to forge French francs on the printing machines of the Hungarian Geographic Society. Both Teleki and Bethlen knew about it but they never thought that the men would go through with their insane plan. When they did, the first attempt to cash the false francs exploded into an international scandal.

**Lord Rothemere, the ultraconservative proprietor of the London *Daily Mail* wrote sympathetic articles in his paper both about the neobaroque system and about Hungarian revisionist claims.

the Succession States, however, was based on the Hungarian need for commerce and foreign loans which would not be facilitated by a perennial disturbance of the peace in the Danube Basin. So a modus vivendi with them had to be found. In this Bethlen was incomparably more responsible and realistic than Gömbös. But Gömbös was in a comfortable opposition, not the head of the government.

To the very end, the neobaroque regime and the Szeged Fascists turned their most implacable hatred on Czechoslovakia, despite the fact that of all the Succession States Masaryk's republic treated its Magyar minority best and despite Czechoslovakia's being the only state which offered even a partial territorial revision, and that as early as 1922-23. Instead, Czechoslovakian democracy, the idea of a democratic republic twenty-five miles from Budapest, was such a red cape in the eyes of both the Christian national system and the Szeged Idea that neither territorial concession nor good treatment meted out to minorities was sufficient to overcome the aversion. Hungarians kept close contact with and financed the Slovak malcontents in Czechoslovakia. Also, the differences between the straightforwardness and impulsiveness of the Hungarian character and the more complex, compromising Czech nature created an antipathy which was and is by no means restricted to the upper classes of either country.

As far as Rumania was concerned, there was no attempt at conciliation from either side (the Transylvania question was not negotiable), nor were the Hungarians in Rumania treated well (although they were not treated worse than the Rumanians by Hungarians for a thousand years). The Hungarians in Cluj (Kolozsvár), for example, were not happy being ruled by those who had been their coachmen and servants some years before. If the neobaroque system or the Szeged Idea had any feeling toward the Rumanians, it was contempt rather than hatred.

There was much less controversy between Hungary and Yugoslavia. Yugoslavia took the least territory from historic Hungary and the smallest number of purely Hungarian population. What is more, the Yugoslav people were anything but contemptible. Their heroism, patriotism and sacrifices were recognized even by Horthy, who made a freindly overture toward them in 1926 at a commemorative festivity of the Battle of Mohács. But this move was not followed up for a decade and a half. The reason was the Hungarian relationship with Italy, which claimed, and even convinced many serious politicians and military experts of the interwar world, that she was a great power indeed.

In 1915 Italy extorted from the hard-pressed Triple Entente an exorbitant price for her intervention, a price which was not justified by Italian military performance. When the exaggerated Italian claims were not gratified at Versailles, the Italian people felt cheated. They could not consider the peace just and did not feel like a victorious nation — which they were not. Besides, Italy, despite its great cultural heritage, was at war's end a backward nation ridden by social ills. A number of internal convulsions followed, and the Italian Fascist movement had its roots in these problems and convulsions and frustrations.

Mussolini was contacted in the embryonic stage of his Fascist movement by a delegation of "Awakening Hungarians" in Milan in 1919, and he promised them he would support Hungarian revisionism if he came to power.[52]

Obviously Mussolini's Italy was the only power that could offer Hungary, if not the breaking of the Little Entente's encirclement, at least an end to her isolation. Connections with Mussolini therefore were looked upon favorably by the Hungarian neobaroque leaders. But, although they preferred fascism as a possible future alternative to democratic reform, they nevertheless preferred their own edifice for the time being. There was too much popular participation and commotion in the Fascist movements for a Horthy, a Bethlen, a Chorin, or a Károlyi. Still, one often heard approvingly during the interwar years in the high society of Budapest, "The iron hand of Mussolini brought order among those Gypsies in the south."* Gömbös and the Szeged Fascists, on the other hand, looked with an indiscriminate enthusiasm to Il Duce in spite of what they regarded as a regrettable lack of anti-Semitism among Latins in general and Italians in particular. So great was the enthusiasm of Gömbös for Italian Fascism that his friends in Hungary addressed him affectionately as Giulio for Gyula (Julius), and his opponents called him derisively "Signor Gömbölini."

But for the first five years or so, Mussolini was disconcertingly reserved in his attitude toward Hungary. The possibility of a Hungarian-Yugoslav rapprochement finally brought him out of his reserve. Bethlen went to Rome in 1927 and signed a treaty of friendship and cooperation between the two countries that was to be the cornerstone of Hungarian foreign policy for the next fifteen years or so. This move made any reconciliation with Yugoslavia impossible, particularly since Hungarians now began to plot common military action with Italy and later with Austria against the South-Slav state. Budapest fostered Croatian disloyalty through its consulate in Zagreb and cooperated with Italy in the reception, harboring and support of Croatian nationalist exiles, a cooperation which led to fateful results in Marseille in October 1934.[53]

However objectionable all this may seem four decades later, it is hard to imagine what else Hungary could have had done under the circumstances. But the Italo-Hungarian alliance, despite common romantic memories from 1848 and the *Risorgimento*, had two weaknesses. One was the *sacro egoismo* of the Italian policy, which left much bitterness among those who fought in World War I. Not even the Szeged Fascists had any illusions about Italian reliability. The second weakness completely escaped the attention of the Hungarians, even the officers: Italy lacked military strength.** It was easy to mistake

*Hungarians are not exactly Nordic. During the centuries they were thoroughly mixed with many neighboring nations. Nevertheless, the Hungarian upper classes often refer to the darker Balkan or Mediterranean types contemptuously as "Gypsies."

**The new Fascist state, reorganized by the "iron hand of Mussolini," was presented by the neobaroque system as a kind of superpower and by the Gömbös Fascists as a living proof of the force of national rebirth. The military parades for military might, especially when they were impressively publicized. And in the mass communications media and education Italy was referred to as "the number one power on earth."

Italy's Hungarian orientation was a realistic foreign policy; it served Mussolini's designs against the Salvs and even Germany, and in the larger sense it also figured in his designs to stir up trouble for France and England. Until the late thirties, Italy had an obedient satellite in Hungary, which she used skillfully as a pawn, along with Austria (what a humiliation for the successors of Metternich!) and Bulgaria in her moves on the Eastern European chessboard. On the other hand, Hungary was mercilessly put in her place when it suited Italian interests to do so.

The price paid by Italy for Hungary's services was ridiculously low. The famous Bismarck maxim, "In every alliance there is a horse and a rider" was rarely so true as in the Hungaro-Italian relationship between 1927-43. In retrospect (especially if one remembers the Marseille murder), it would seem that Hungary paid an exceedingly high price for Mussolini's friendship, that the neobaroque age overrated its value from the point of view of Hungarian national interest. It was the *extent* of the Italian orientation that was excessive, and the reason for this was not so much a political or economic or even a military one. The fault was ideological; it was wishful thinking. This was not so obvious in Bethlen's day, but it became increasingly evident as time went on.

power of the Fascist idea was said to have transformed those "contempt-ible cowards, crooks, and macaroni-eaters into worthy heirs of the Roman Legions."

CHAPTER IV

The Great Crash and Its Aftermath

*Oh! Beware! It is beyond the imagination what
man is capable of when he is hungry.*

The Talmud

1

In October 1929, the "roar" of the 1920s became an anguished shriek in America. The United States had become by far the most important single economic unit in the world. Consequently, the shock wave of the market crash on Wall Street reverberated around the globe.

The full impact of the crisis was not felt in Hungary immediately. World grain prices began to fall almost immediately after Black Friday. But although an acute agrarian crisis had developed throughout the Continent by 1930, Hungary's international credit still stood firm. Even the financial supervision by the League of Nations was suspended, and in 1930 Hungary borrowed more than she had in any single year before. The money came, as almost always before, as short-term loans mostly from private sources.* From such sources, agriculture was heavily subsidized by the government. The price paid for this was a decrease in raw material imports for industry, causing widespread unemployment, dissatisfaction, and even strikes and riots. More than 20 percent of the Hungarian labor force, 224,103 people, were unemployed by 1930, more than 100,000 of them in the Budapest area.[1] (A Communist source set the number at half a million, taking into account the unemployed in every field in 1930.) The majority of the agrarian labor force was only seasonally employed, mostly during the summer months. After the summer, these people, numbering about 800,000, were perennially under-employed.[2] In addition, Hungary had no unemployment relief system whatsoever.

The depression deepened worldwide in 1931, and in Hungary, too, despite the stopgap measures of the Bethlen government. The way out seemed even more difficult for No-Man's-Land as a whole because the new boundaries of Versailles had disrupted the smoothly functioning economic unit of the former Austro-Hungarian Empire. Czechoslovakia renounced its commercial

*To have some idea about the extent of borrowing of Bethlen's system, here are some figures: Hungary's per capita indebtedness by 1932 was the highest in all of No-Man's-Land, if not in the whole of Europe, with $83.10 per inhabitant. Prodigiously indebted Austria was far behind with $69.40. The figure for Rumania is $56.20 and the relatively healthy Czechoslovak economy shows $25.70. Moore, *Economic Demography of Eastern and Southern Europe*, p. 108.

treaty with Hungary. The commercial treaty with Austria was allowed to lapse by 1931. Of all segments of the economy, agriculture suffered the most.

The effects of all this on Hungary were grave. They were reflected in the speeches of the few opposition deputies in Parliament. The worker (if he had work at all) earned 100-120 pengö per month ($20-25). Female help in the textile factories, notoriously underpaid, earned $5-6 per month! The diet of the worker's family consisted of beans, potatoes and sour apples. Then there were the uncontrolled, exorbitant rents of Budapest, among the highest in Europe: a modest dwelling rented for fifty pengös a month ($10).[3] When winter came, the unemployed who were unable to pay rent were mercilessly evicted by the thousands all over Hungary.[4]

To the extent that the countryside regressed during the depression into premonetary barter, it can be said that the economic crisis passed over the heads of the agricultural populace. Unfortunately, however, barter concerned only those who had work. The "agrarian scissors," in the meantime, opened to an incredible angle of 47.3 by 1930 compared with 5.6 in 1928.[5]

The suffering in the countryside was aggravated by the fact that taxes could not be paid in kind but had to be in currency, which was practically nonexistent in the villages. Tax collection was entrusted to the gendarmerie, which carried out its task with its renowned spirit. The concept of inviolability of private homes did not exist in Hungary, and tax-collecting gendarmes entered peasant huts at their discretion. What happened afterward is illustrated in the interpellation of a Socialist deputy who described one incident out of many. The tax-collecting gendarmes confiscated, in lieu of the tax arrears, the last milking goat of an abysmally poor pregnant peasant, the mother of four small children. When she protested, the gendarme put an end to the discussion by striking hard into her belly with the butt of his rifle.[6] In the Transdanubian village of Pacsa, during tax collection routine, the gendarmes found it expedient to fire volleys of bullets into the crowd, killing many peasants.[7] No local doctor dared write a medical report about gendarme-inflicted bruises or wounds. Wages dropped sharply for those still employed, and the salaries and pensions of both government and private employees were cut repeatedly.

But it was the working classes and the lower middle classes which suffered the most. These people were subsequently to be the mainstay of the Fascist upsurge. The apolitical and apathetic peasants were used to all kinds of degradation, and for them suffering would be a less important consideration.

Bethlen negotiated a League of Nations loan and also a French loan (France was the only country on the Continent still financially sound). For this purpose he called elections to demonstrate that he had the country with him. The elections, managed by an aggressive country squire, Sándor Sztranyavszky, brought the expected results; the gendarmes watched carefully that people did not make any mistakes on the open ballot. Supporting the government were 152 Government party deputies and 25 non-party deputies. There was an opposition of 38 deputies: 14 Smallholders, 14 Social Democrats, 7 Liberals, 1 National Radical, and 2 Christian Oppositionals.

And then, in May 1931, the Creditanstalt Bank of Vienna failed. This institution had close ties with Hungarian finance. Short-term loans, especially the German one, were called in, a flight from the pengö started to the tune of five billion.[8] Hungary's international credit collapsed almost overnight.

The government took all the emergency measures it could. Foreign currency exchange restrictions were imposed, the stock exchange was disciplined to a certain extent, a moratorium on debt payments and a bank holiday were declared. All these measures brought little relief.

Bethlen's system, and in a larger sense the whole neobaroque edifice, was on trial. It was clear to many a thinking observer that even if there were important outside reasons for it, the old Hungary had failed twice in thirteen years, in 1918 and in 1931, to cope with the problems of the twentieth-century industrial society and its political implications. The orthodox conservative idea was discredited. Under different circumstances the subsequent soul searching, so common in the Hungary of the 1930s, might have engendered a move to the left. There was indeed some violent leftist agitation in Hungary around 1930-31. Some new recruits, the sorely needed intellectuals graduating from the universities, joined the clandestine Communist party, young men like K. Olt, F. Fejtö and the later so significant László Rajk. There was an attempt by the Social Democratic party to take advantage of the situation and extend its organization to the villages.* But these attempts were met with terror and repression by the regime's still intact and efficient police apparatus. Also, this being the time of the sharp intraparty struggle between Stalinists and Trotskyites, the Stalinists applied their time-honored method for solving political divergencies with their factional enemies by denouncing them to the Hungarian secret police.[9] All this did not enhance the prestige of the Communists or nurture the unfolding of a leftist way out.

The neobaroque system's economy was shattered, but its political framework, the police, gendarmerie and administration was still formidable. Bethlen, to the great surprise of everybody, resigned the premiership in August 1931. His move was motivated more by personal reasons than loss of confidence of the Regent or because of the widespread discontent in the country. In fact, he remained in the background up to the end of the neobaroque age as the powerful political force behind the increasing influence of the Regent, who never failed to consult him before making a decision.

His successor, Count Gyula Károlyi, a relative of the leader of Hungary's democratic upsurge in 1918, Count Michael Károlyi, was of the same school. Indeed the two were probably the most important members of the close inner circle around the Regent that was to become so important later. Károlyi was a *grand seigneur* in the best patriarchal sense of the word. Rigidly honest, simple in his personal habits, he had a great feeling of responsibility toward his peasants and toward the poor in general. It was this patriarchal

*Macartney, *October Fifteenth*, I, p. 99n. In one of the semi-industrial counties, Borsod, in 149 of 202 communes there were Social Democratic circles by 1932.

relationship which he recommended that others emulate as the solution for all the ills of Hungary. Yet, he never felt compelled to make the slightest concession to universal franchise, land reform or labor unions, to what he saw as nothing more than devilish schemes to upset the natural order of things. Like the better representatives of the aristocracy, he felt a genuine responsibility *for* the masses, but he felt no responsibility whatever *to* the masses. All remedies had to come from above and that the remedy should come from "above" was more important than reform itself.

In the meantime, there was growing unrest within the Hungarian Nation. A dissatisfied group of the Government party, mostly former smallholders, seceded under the leadership of Gaszton Gaál and that versatile political turncoat, Eckhardt. It was a measure of the unpopularity of the neobaroque edifice that Eckhardt could in 1932 defeat on an open ballot in a by-election the brother-in-law of the Regent, E. Purgly, the acting minister of agriculture. The rebels formed a heterogeneous new party, the Independent Smallholders, Agricultural and Bourgeois party. The party always had two wings, left and right, representing mostly the well-to-do yeoman farmers (rather than the millions of agrarian proletariat) and the bourgeoisie of the towns. It could channel some of the opposition, but it could never offer a strong, constructive, democratic alternative either to leftist extremism or to the Fascist onslaught.

By 1931 that onslaught had begun in earnest. By the summer of 1931 not only the lower classes, but even those in the political nation who did not have direct stakes in the neobaroque system were clamoring for change. But where were they to go? The road to democracy or to the left was blocked by the discredit of the years 1918-19, by Trianon, and by brutal police methods. And there was an important factor in addition. The left, whether democratic, Socialist or Communist, by its very *raison d'être* not only could not condone anti-Semitism, but had to oppose it with vigor. And anti-Semitism was the very essence of the "social justice" of the Szeged Fascists and their followers in the different strata of the non-Jewish middle classes. By inclination and interest, the rank and file of the Jewish middle class (not the upper stratum, which was fatefully allied with the status quo) could have led a movement toward a democratic solution, but it had been effectively cowed into silence by Eckhardt's terror squads some years earlier. And the neobaroque edifice's being Christian and national had meant a kind of official anti-Semitism since 1919. The Jewish financiers, who became the very backbone of this anti-Semitic system, were not overly devoted to democracy either.

Yet the whole of Hungary was crying for a change, a solution. There was the memory of Béla Kun and Számuelly, and the criminal demogoguery of the Szeged Fascists, who had held the Jewish question before the public since 1919. There was Trianon and the aftermath; there were the soul-destroying activities of 10,000-odd "social associations," the secret societies with their Gömbös control and their avowed Fascist spirit. There were the powerful, ultraconservative, anti-Semitic churches, the semi-Fascist, disorderly student federations (*Turúl, Mefhosz*), the *Vitézi Rend** and the paramilitary *Levente* organization. There was also the example of Italy, the whole spirit of neobaroque education which emphasized a perverted Széchenyi image and slung mud on the ideas of 1848 and Kossuth as "Jewish tainted," and the virtual nonexistence of effective democratic organizations. These factors made sure that if there was to be a change or an unfolding from the economic and social turmoil, it would be in the direction of fascism and not in the direction of democracy. As circumstances deteriorated, Gömbös, risen to lieutenant general and minister of defense in Bethlen's cabinet, carefully started his move toward power. His main tools were his colleagues in the Officers Corps, mostly old cronies of the war and the days of the counterrevolution, but he could also count on the secret societies, M.O.V.E., the all-powerful E.K.Sz. and other organizations in which he had steadily maintained leadership.** In addition, he held firm control of the *Turúl* and other quasi-Fascist, anti-Semitic student organizations, especially of the A.D.O.B.*** Most of those who graduated after 1920 from the "de-Judaized" universities were ardent supporters of the radical right and constituted the backbone of the Fascist intelligentsia of the coming decade. All of them looked to Gömbös to take the lead.

The first plot to overthrow the neobaroque system and install a Fascist dictatorship was foiled in the fall of 1931. Its leaders were General Schill, the former commander of the gendarmerie, and a certain Mayor Vannay, member of secret societies and of one of the cruelest Officer Detachments during the White Terror. Gömbös had sinister connections with this group. He freely admitted in Parliament that he knew about the plot "but warned them to drop it."[10] Considering the system of secret societies under Gömbös' command, one may easily measure his sincerity. It is more plausible to think that he staged the whole thing as a kind of warning in order (1) to draw the attention of the conservatives to the gravity of the situation and (2) to offer his person as a likely alternative. General Schill committed suicide in prison; the rest of the plotters were soon acquitted. The courts, as usual, took account of their patriotic motives.

*Order of Heroes. A characteristic creation of Horthy's, a medieval organization rewarding fealty with land. It claimed to be democratic; anybody could become a member if he served with distinction during World War I in the armed forces — if not Jewish or of Jewish descent. Jewish heroes were refused membership even if they earned the highest decorations for bravery.

**O.N.K., December 16, 1931, pp. 16, 495. In 1931, Gömbös vowed before Parliament on his honor as an officer that he was not a member of any secret societies.

***Á.D.O.B., Committee of Unemployed University Degree Bearers. Because of the gross overproduction of intellectuals by Hungarian universities, the unemployed young intellectuals became a notoriously malcontent, vociferous group, and their organization became a violent anti-Semitic Fascist tool in the skillful hands of Gömbös.

The clamor for a Fascist remodeling of the neobaroque structure continued among officers, civil servants of the administration, and all the non-Jewish middle classes, during the spring of 1932. The "spirit of the age" (*Korszellem*)* was on the march. Dozens of embryonic Fascist circles sprang up in the country. There were ominous rumblings within the Government party itself, and Károlyi faced the almost unprecedented danger of not being able to get a vote of confidence from his usually docile party.

But all these efforts of the right wing of the Hungarian Nation would have been insufficient to shake the well-established grip of the conservative wing on the country had it not been for one of the most shameful developments of Hungarian history in the interwar period. Gömbös needed an apparatus for propaganda and coordination among his partisans in the different dissatisfied segments of Hungarian society. This and other efforts cost money, much money. The Szeged Fascists did not have any, and the landlords were not about to finance their own elimination from power. It was the Jewish financiers who came to the aid of the Szeged Idea and Gömbös. The financiers were especially irked by certain measures that threatened their status in the upper house, which the austere Károlyi, for no anti-Semitic motive whatsoever, deemed incompatible with their vested interests: it is true that they frequently used their position in parliament more to their own benefit than to the benefit of Hungary. Even more outrageous to them was a bill introduced by Károlyi which would have put an end to some of their more obscure stock exchange dealings. All their attempts to dissuade that incorruptible grandee predictably had failed.** But mediocrity, it is said, tends to seek its own level. So the Jewish financiers turned to Gömbös. Here they received a much more favorable reception. Gömbös, who could never bring himself to consider a patriotic, honest Jew even a human being, let alone a Hungarian, found his way only to Jews like a certain Lincoln-Trebitsch*** or one Kenyeres-Kauffmann,**** and in this case to the Jewish financiers. He got what he wanted for his Szeged Idea: the money and

*Invoking the "spirit of the age" served from then on for Hungarian Nazi sympathizers of all brands as slogan, argument, description, explanation, justification and morale.

**Macartney, *op. cit.,* I, 100n. Professor Macartney is worried about a libel suit in case he would write the full truth about this distasteful episode. The writer is less concerned. His father was deeply involved in these dealings through the Gy.O.Sz. (Hungarian equivalent of the N.A.M.) and through the Jewish community of Budapest, is ready to give more details if requested.

***Lincoln-Trebitsch was an international adventurer of Jewish descent, who was involved in Gömbös' connections with Hitler in the early days of the Beerhaus Putsch.

****Kenyeres (alias Kauffmann) was another sinister Jewish crony of Gömbös, who ran under a false name with full gendarme support for Gömbös' party in the election of 1935 against the anti-Fascist deputy, Endre Bajcsy-Zsilinszky. His real identity was later established amid great scandal.

support he acquired were decisive to his advent to power. The Jewish financiers could also sleep more quietly (at least for the time being): the bills introduced by Károlyi, so offensive to their interests, were never mentioned again.

The Jewish-financed Fascist agitation continued through the summer of 1932. There was no substantial force that could oppose it. Károlyi's government was more and more inept at coping with both the economic and political difficulties. Horthy was deeply perturbed. He took counsel with Bethlen, with Károlyi, and with practically everybody of importance.

Meanwhile, the depression, aggravated by a poor harvest, went from bad to worse. The Fascists, with the help of Jewish money, spoke and wrote a lot about the differences between *Helden und Händler* (Werner Sombart's well-known parallel between heroes and merchants) and to the effect that "only heroic methods can save the Hungarian Nation." In October 1932 the Regent finally appointed their hero prime minister. The event did not come as a surprise to anybody in Hungary. It had been decided not in 1932 but in 1918 and 1919 and 1920. Everything that had happened since in every sphere of national life, or to be more exact, everything that had failed to happen, had been a step in that direction.

2

The democratic forces of the country, unimpressed by the fact that Gömbös had dissolved his Party of Racial Defense four years before to take on the protective coloration of the Government party, were deeply worried at his appointment to the premiership. Articulate Fascist public opinion on the other hand looked forward to the advent of a Fascist Hungarian Renaissance under Gömbös. Only the conservative wing of the political nation showed neither apprehension nor anticipation. They and some of the initiated knew that Bethlen, Horthy, and the other leaders of the conservatives* had imposed stiff safeguards on Gömbös before his appointment. He was not to introduce agrarian reform or any radical reform. Nor was he to introduce any anti-Semitic legislation. He was to work with a Government party and Parliament "elected" by Bethlen and imbued with his spirit. Gömbös had specifically pledged not to dissolve Parliament and hold new elections. In addition to all this, he was to be closely supervised by the conservatives — that is, by Bethlen — in every move of importance. Thus, though Bethlen and Horthy had to make the concession of Gömbös' appointment to quell the Fascist clamor, they kept a formidable control for themselves.

Gömbös for his part never for a moment thought of giving up any of his ideals or goals. He was taking one step backward in order to be able to take two or more steps forward in the future, and both internal and external events seemed to justify his restraint. His ideas seemed to have become "the Spirit of the Age." It seemed that he could afford to make concessions for a

---

*Horthy, although he still had some ties with his Szeged men and felt close to the military (a feeling by no means reciprocated), by this time counted definitely among the conservatives.

while in order to consolidate his position both externally and internally. The extent to which he was prepared to conciliate may be measured from the fact that he negotiated an agreement with leaders of the Jewish congregations in Hungary giving them guarantees in exchange for their support for his program.* After that, he announced that he had "reversed his position on the Jewish question."** In the same speech he proclaimed a moderate program, with vague promises of social justice and a secret ballot (but carefully balanced by safeguards which undid the promises or left unlimited elbowroom in which to maneuver). He protested that he did not wish to become a dictator, that he was a capitalist at heart. He wished to establish laissez faire but, typically, "within broad limits." Nationalities were to have complete freedom "unless they develop centrifugal tendencies." He professed impartiality toward both labor and capital, but Social Democracy had to go.[11] His parliamentary programs were repeated in the ninety-five points presented to the Hungarian people as the national program of the Gömbös government. In foreign policy he would strive "incessantly for the revision of the peace treaties by peaceful means." Among the ninety-five points were also some technical emergency measures of an economic nature.[12]

When Gömbös proclaimed his cautious, constitutionally impeccable program, there was but one general reaction in Hungary, that of surprise, pleasant or unpleasant, depending upon who reacted· "It can't be true! " It was not true. Some years later, Bethlen summed it up aptly: "Gömbös had an avowed and an unavowed program."[13] And the unavowed program, the turning of Hungary into a totalitarian Fascist dictatorship, was infinitely the more important one. But for that, with the conservative safeguards imposed on him, he needed time and circumspection. Gömbös never ceased during his four years' tenure in office to work in that direction. He never missed filling a loophole left open by the conservatives with his brand of fascism.

But to the pent-up popular discontent caused by the depression, his compromises and procrastinating methods, and his brand of conservative fascism were no answer. The road to the left being blocked, the revolutionary

*Macartney, op. cit., I, 117n. These gentlemen were bought off by Gömbös by giving them import monopolies on different colonial articles, etc. The Jewish financiers also financed the Government party and Gömbös' cronies.

**In January 1933, Hungarian Jews were still enjoying their "miraculous" accommodation with Gömbös. Two days after the Machtergreifung, Gömbös instructed the Hungarian ambassador in Berlin "to pay a courtesy call on Chancellor Hitler to transmit his felicitations and greetings." More important, the Hungarian ambassador was to remind Hitler of the contacts Gömbös kept with the Nazis in 1923, also "the common principles and common Weltanschauung which he shared with the Nazis." Gömbös told Hitler that if there were any possible controversy between them to discuss "with sincerity what two race-protectors (racists) owe to each other." Allianz: Hitler, Horthy, Mussolini, Dokumente zur Ungarischen Ausenpolitik 1933-1944, (Budapest, 1966), p. 107, hereinafter referred to as Allianz.

outburst broke through in the only direction left open. Many Fascist factions, representing mainly the lower classes, became impatient with Gömbös, his methods, and his kind of fascism. Some months after Gömbös' advent to power, on January 30, 1933, the long torchlight parade passing through the Brandenburg Gate in Berlin heralded the *Machtergreifung*, the advent of Hitler to power in Germany.

About that time, the Hungarian Fascists differentiated themselves into three distinct groups: (1) the conservative Fascists representing the Szeged element of the counterrevolution under Gömbös (later under Béla Imrédy); (2) the broad masses, who did not find an answer for problems accentuated by the depression and who, deprived of a constructive democratic solution, channeled their discontent into radical revolutionary Fascist channels; and (3) the Fascists in the administration, the military and, above all, the Government party. When Gömbös died in 1936, he left unfinished the task of turning the Government party into a single unified Fascist party. His followers in the government and civil service maintained a prudent political ambivalence until 1944, considering it too risky to avow their Fascist sympathies unequivocally after the partial conservative restoration of 1936-37. Perhaps the phrase "fellow travelers of fascism" most accurately places this group in the Hungarian political context for the next decade or so.

One reason for the splits and differentiations in Hungarian fascism lay in the character of the Gömbös administration, the conservative nature and the limited appeal of his fascism, and the checks imposed upon him by the ultraconservatives. These took the starch out of even those few reforms which he, who wished to "underline 25 times the fact that he is a conservative,"[14] would otherwise have been ready to carry out. The other reason was the great depression, which brought immeasurable suffering to the common people for the second time in fifteen years, made them conscious of their unfavorable position, and fostered resentment that could be channeled only in one direction — toward a radical Fascist mass movement.

3

The composition of Gömbös' cabinet reflected in his avowed program, and its announcement was received with the same feeling of anticlimax. Although he prided himself that he was the first prime minister in Hungarian history (with the exception of the Kun regime) who succeeded in forming a cabinet without a single count — no small achievement in the neobaroque age — Bethlenite conservatism was represented heavily. A. Lázár (justice); Miklós Kállay (agriculture); T. Fabinyi (commerce); and one of the best representatives of conservatism with a sincere dedication to social justice, F. Keresztes-Fischer (interior) — all represented the conservative wing of the Hungarian Nation. The minister of foreign affairs, Kálmán Kánya, a career diplomat of the old school, was rather a conservative nationalist also, if one can label him at all. But he had only a Tallyrandian, infinitely circumspect interest in, or perhaps an aversion to, ideas or issues.

Kálmán Darányi, minister of agriculture after Kállay, was of Swabian origin and of illegitimate birth. This latter fact, according to the morality of old Hungary, made him guilty without having sinned, and gave him a nagging inferiority complex. That complex made him attempt to please every faction from ultraconservatives (Jewish financiers included) to radical Fascist reformers, and in this he succeeded to such an extent that he won not only their sympathy but their confidence. It should be no surprise that some years later he became the prime minister of Hungary and the successor of Gömbös.

The minister of finance, Béla Imrédy, was in 1932 relatively young, a talented financier and president of the national bank before his appointment to the cabinet. He represented the most conservative financial orthodoxy in the Gömbös government, and during his cabinet tenure he was able to prevent even a modest agrarian reform.[15] His attitudes won for him the sympathies of both domestic and foreign financial circles, in most cases Jewish ones. He came of Swabian burgher stock, the family name being originally Heinrich, and professed to be a devout Catholic. There was also an unexplained, possibly Jewish, strain in his family which was his nemesis later, but it had certainly not yet been discerned in 1932. Nor could many people then have guessed what unscrupulousness, vindictiveness, limitless ambition and hunger for power hid behind his pale, satanic face. He was like Imre Madách's Lucifer* as the role was interpreted by Major Tamás, the renowned actor of the National Theatre of Budapest. In 1938, in a move that would surprise everybody inside and outside Hungary, Imrédy would take over the leadership of the Szeged fascists, fallen into disarray since Gömbös' death in 1936. He would lead them to a Pyrrhic victory and finally to the doom of 1944. But in 1932, he seemed more of a stumbling block in the way of the Szeged Fascist transformation than its promoter. At that time, he hoped to fulfill his ambitions through and with the Bethlenite wing of the Hungarian Nation.

Unable to fill his first line of officers with Szeged Fascists, from the very outset Gömbös did his best to fill the other important posts which were left to his discretion by Bethlen. Of these posts by far the most important one was the post of secretary-general of the Government party, a post dormant since Tisza had vacated it. It was revived as an act of compromise between Bethlen and Gömbös, and was becoming an increasingly important position in *Gleichschaltung* when Gömbös tried to transform the Government party into a unified Fascist party under his leadership. This post went to Béla Marton, who went through World War I as an officer of the Hussars and through the school of the Officer Detachments during the counterrevolution. He was full of energy and had a talent for organization. He was also as radical-minded as an officer of the Hussars can be, his radicalism expressing itself in a ferocious anti-Semitism. If not exactly intelligent, he was certainly shrewd enough not to side openly with any Fascist group later. He maintained his position as a Fascist fellow traveler within the Government party to the end, although he did more to promote the cause of fascism in Hungary than many full-fledged Fascist leaders.

*Imre Madách, author of the famous play, *The Tragedy of Man*.

92

Another Gömbös man who managed to remain a fellow traveler and serve the conservative Fascist cause from within the Government party was István Antal. Since he is a prototype, he deserves a more thorough consideration. Coming from the very bottom of the Hungarian social spectrum (his father was a village coachman), he managed his education with the help of scholarships. He was one of the rare lower-class recruits to the Hungarian Nation, and loyal recruits from the lower classes were especially welcome in the ranks of Szeged Fascists. Antal had joined Gömbös in the Szeged days and, through his leadership in the student organizations, was the organizer of bloody anti-Semitic disorders in the University of Budapest. More important, on Gömbös' orders, he led the student group that stopped Charles of Habsburg before Budapest in 1921. Endowed with a good intellect and persuasive though demagogic rhetoric, he became Gömbös' speechwriter and also his chief of press and propaganda. In this capacity he gave the Hungarian information media an ugly twist and tone that would be silenced only by the military victory of the United Nations. In this capacity in the next decade, he contributed his share, and a little more than his share, to the formation of an articulate public opinion in Hungary that was neither intelligent nor moral. Personally, he had all the weaknesses of the borderline cases in society. He felt his inferiority and the conditional nature of his acceptance in class-conscious Hungary, and therefore he was ostentatious and a poseur.* He had few moral scruples as far as the sanctity of the word was concerned.** An opportunist, a habitual liar, and a coward in addition, he was a typical product of Hungarian conservative fascism and of the whole unnatural hothouse atmosphere for which the neobaroque edifice was renowned.

His end was an unexpected one. One of his last maneuvers at the time of the Arrow Cross faction's takeover did not succeed, and he was thrown into prison by Ferenc Szálasi's men. Perhaps Antal's fate should be considered with more pity than censure. He had the gifts to do something very different for his dejected people than he did, and in the last analysis his deeds were not fully his own. It was the Hungarian Nation that corrupted Antal as it was the Hungarian Nation that made the historic fall of Hungary much more bitter than it had to be by dint of geopolitical and historical reality.***

These, then, were the most important protagonists of the "reform government," as Gömbös and his partisans liked to call themselves. All

*Col. Gyula Kádár, a leading officer in the Hungarian counterintelligence, described a typical scene when Antal appeared in high society in the evening, spreading out in bad taste on his armchair. Colonel Kádár asked him mockingly, "Pista, are you pretending to be a tired statesman? "

**As minister of justice during the brief Szeged Fascist triumph in 1944, he distinguished himself with repeated lies to Cardinal Mindszenthy about political prisoners. Súlyok, *A Magyar tragédia*, p. 454.

***Nor was this the end. Antal was busy in 1967 writing his "memoirs" for the benefit of the present Communist rulers of Hungary, so the latest news from Budapest indicates. He does his writing while he is derided by the Communist press.

members of the government were members of one or another secret society; most of them were members of the highly important E.K.Sz.

4

Gömbös had two goals when he became prime minister in October 1932. The immediate and avowed one was to combat the catastrophic consequences of the world depression in Hungary in terms of a great reform. The second, and to use Bethlen's famous maxim, the unavowed one, was the introduction of a Fascist system to Hungary. In support of what was called the "Immediacy Program," he introduced several measures that did not amount to much. The program did little to improve the economy, but this was not Gömbös' fault. A minor, underdeveloped economy like Hungary's was fully at the mercy of the world economic situation, and despite all measures, half-measures or omissions, it did not improve significantly until 1937 when the general economic situation all over Europe improved. In the meantime, it remained generally depressed and deteriorating. By 1933, the agrarian scissors opened to an enormous angle: 70.4 percent. Grain prices continued to fall, salaries of state employees and pensions were cut for the third time, and the wages of workers kept falling to reach an all time low in 1935.[16] Nevertheless, a balanced budget was achieved at the cost of tremendous suffering by the people. The ultraconservative economies of Imrédy prevailed, imports were cut, foreign debts were paid, and there was little enthusiasm for Keynesian ideas. All this kept discontent quivering under the surface, among both the "middleclass of Hungarian gentlemen" and the more articulate workers in the lower classes. All this provided an excellent atmosphere for a Fascist mood, although as we shall see it was not necessarily a mood favoring the conservative brand of fascism desired by Gömbös.

If the ultraconservatives thought they had tied Gömbös' hands sufficiently that they could use his name to quell the general clamor for change, they were sorely mistaken. Apart from the mushrooming radical Fascist movements, Gömbös himself did not intend to remain captive in the neobaroque edifice he scheduled for demolition. Not only was the "Spirit of the Age" on his side; there was much terrain left to accommodate Fascist foundations that would make any reversal of his course impossible, even after his departure from the scene.

Even though the Government party was dominated by Bethlen men, this being the most jealously guarded stronghold of conservatism, Gömbös went a long way toward transforming it into one unified Fascist party. He persuaded the Government party to adopt a new name: Party of National Unity (N.E.P. — *Nemzeti Egység Pártja*). When the party executive committee and the position of secretary-general were reestablished, the head of the executive committee was Sztranyavszky and the secretary-general, Marton, both Gömbös men. Many Bethlenites found themselves left out, not only in the executive committee appointments but in other rapidly unfolding transformations.

Marton set to work to establish a gigantic Government party organization all over the countryside, until in less than two years, there was a well-centralized and controlled party machinery in each of the 4,000 villages and towns in Hungary. The staff of these new (and old) Government party centers consisted almost exclusively of Gömbös' Fascists rather than Bethlen men. Every local branch had its Advance Guards (*Élharcosok*), a kind of party militia which by 1935 numbered 60,000 men.[17] The activities of the Advance Guards were manifold. For example, opposition parties complained constantly about the files kept in the ubiquitous party offices. These files contained careful records of the political affiliations of the local inhabitants, their jobs, daily utterances, etc.[18] The guards also ruthlessly broke up meetings not only of democratic and liberal parties, but even those of the radical Fascists.[19] As the years passed, their behavior became more and more arrogant and oppressive.*

There was also an accelerating change within the administrative machinery, so that the Gömbös-controlled Government party became identical with the administration from top to bottom, and imbued with the Szeged Fascist spirit. New appointments and reshufflings were carried out strictly on these lines. Many men of the Officer Detachments, some of them the perpetrators of the worst outrages of the White Terror, found themselves appointed to high administrative positions. Two new, heavily subsidized newpapers expounded the Gömbös ideology. *Függetlenség* was directed at the broad masses and *Új Magyarság* at the Szeged element and the "middleclass of Hungarian gentlemen." Antal installed something closely resembling a tight Fascist censorship. And although police informers were not new in Hungary, their activities were now greatly reinforced, and telephone wire tapping and the violation of private correspondence became commonplace.

On the higher levels in the ministries, Gömbös installed many of the secretaries, undersecretaries, and other appointees who later became Nazi sympathizers. A good number of these people were, like Gömbös, of Swabian origin, although Gömbös insisted that anyone of non-Hungarian origin Magyarize his name if he entered government service.

Then Gömbös turned to the field which was to be his personal undoing — the armed forces. Because he was himself an officer, and because he had received his warmest support from the Officers Corps, it is understandable that by 1935 Gömbös felt himself strong enough to move in this field also.

There had been a long-standing argument on the highest levels of the Hungarian General Staff about the future of the Hungarian Army. Should there be a short-service army based on general draft as proposed by Gömbös (in defiance of the peace treaty but trained surreptitiously), or should there be a continuation of the existing smaller framework of seven brigades until such time as increased troops could be armed? The younger officers, almost all of them ardent Szeged men, supported the Gömbös plan as much for nationalistic reasons as in hope of promotion. Although Horthy sympathized

*Mussolini followed the process of transformation of the Government party into a unified Fascist party "with great joy" and expressed his approval to Gömbös in March 1934. *Allianz, op. cit.*, p. 116.

in 1929 with Gömbös' idea, by 1933-34 he had changed his mind. He was, in the true spirit of Francis Joseph, guarding his role as "supreme warlord" and his control over appointments to army posts.

Gömbös was very careful at first in respect to the army. He had no illusions about Horthy's sensitivity in this respect, so he left the highest echelons of the Officers Corps alone. But he filled the second and third echelons with his men exclusively, and then he made his surprise move. When in connection with the Marseille murder many high-ranking officers were censured by the Hungarian report answering a League of Nations inquiry in January 1935, the officers in question resigned. Inasmuch as they belonged almost exclusively to the Bethlen conservatives, Gömbös gladly accepted their resignations, appointed Szeged men in their places in key positions, and confronted the Regent with a *fait accompli.* Thus he had not only succeeded in imbuing the administration with the "Spirit of the Age," he had made sure that the armed forces were also officered and commanded in their majority by Fascist sympathizers. The Regent was furious. This move displeased him more than anything else Gömbös did, and he decided to remove him from power at the first opportunity.

In Parliament, Gömbös moved in two directions toward the establishment of a broad unitary Fascist front. He established close contact with the extreme anti-Semitic wing of the Christian party, whose leader Károly Wolff, the leader of the Christian Course in the 1920s, now made his most unabashedly anti-Semitic outbursts in a decade in speaking for the interests of the "middleclass of Hungarian gentlemen."[20] Wolff's forces pledged their support unconditionally to the great Fascist design. But far more important was Gömbös' attempt to establish an alliance with Eckhardt. Eckhardt had been head of the Smallholders party since the death of Gaszton Gaál. He and Gömbös understood each other very well. They had identical political ideas and a common Szeged past. They both had organized the anti-Semitic terrorism, and they had plotted together with Hitler in the Beerhaus Putsch days. They belonged to the same set of secret societies, and they had a similar outlook about the future. The trouble was that both had an insatiable lust for power. Gömbös would have liked the support of Eckhardt's Smallholders because there were more bourgeois elements in this party, both urban and rural, than genuine dwarfholders. Eckhardt's support would have closed the lower ranks of the Hungarian Nation against the Jews and the *csáklyások.**
But Eckhardt was not a man to be satisfied with a secondary role for himself and his party. And Gömbös could not and would not abandon his plan to be *Vezér* in the future Fascist state. Therefore, after a hopeful start the negotiations between the two Szeged comrades in arms led to nothing, not for ideological reasons but because of discordant personal ambitions. However, possession is nine points of the law, and Gömbös was in possession. If Eckhardt's price was too high, Gömbös was soon to be in a position to remove him from his path administratively.

*Backwoodsmen is the best English translation for it. Fascists used it to identify Bethlen supporters who shot down reforms.

Meanwhile, in the Gömbös years the Fascist spirit of the age was gaining impetus and penetrating into almost every sphere of Hungarian national life. The secret societies, especially the E.K.Sz. and M.O.V.E., showed a new vigor. Gömbös issued arms (among them 10,000 rifles) to M.O.V.E. for the "just in case" eventuality.[21] Gömbös kept his command over the pro-Fascist student organizations, *Turúl* and *Mefhosz*, which organized violent anti-Semitic and anti-Legitimist disorders under the cloak of their academic immunity. At their meetings, resolutions were passed demanding radical reforms, among other things a land reform that would restrict landholdings to 500 holds. The whole system of education, the mass communications media, and the paramilitary *Levente* organization took an openly Fascist tone. The T.E.Sz., with its 10,000-odd local organizations, was revived from dormancy and began under the leadership of G. Baross a vigorous indoctrination of the population, especially the youth, with Fascist nationalism. By 1935 Gömbös' position seemed strong enough that he could safely seek an open showdown with the Bethlen conservatives. He proclaimed that "we stand at the threshhold of a new world . . ., there are new ideas before the gates of Hungary," and added more significantly, "also all over Europe."[22] When the opposition complained about Antal's high-handed censorship of the press, Gömbös answered, "That country will only become great where there is no criticism." A violent uproar ensued, whereupon he modified his statement to allow "healthy criticism."[23] When the head of the Social Democrats asked him in Parliament to explain the subsidy given to the government press, his casual rejoinder was that he would answer only those questions which he felt disposed to answer.[24]

The mass meetings at which carefully rehearsed crowds greeted him as *Vezér* multiplied. On the front pages of the government paper, his picture appeared always with the caption, "Long Live Our Leader (Vezér) the Hero Gyula Gömbös de Jákfa." During mass rallies, dozens of banners waved around his reviewing stand bearing the symbolic letter "V."* His frequent references to the "*gerstli* democracy"** became more and more contemptuous.

Although in 1933 he went out of his way to reassure the Jewish industrialists, always proclaiming that he did not wish "to apply brutal measures in the economy . . . because the economy is very sensitive and reacts very disagreebly to any use of force,"[25] by 1936 his tone had changed. Slowly but unmistakably, Gömbös turned upon his sponsors. Pressure was put on Jewish businessmen to "change the guard," to dismiss their Jewish employees and hire the Fascist graduates of the universities. Questionnaires were circulated to all enterprises to ascertain the religion of their employees. Gömbös, for good measure, expressed his personal "hope that the desired reapportioning between Jewish and non-Jewish employees will be achieved without the application of pressure."[26] Of course all this had its effect — a

*This cult of Gömbös as "leader" irritated Horthy enormously next only to Gömbös' packing of the armed forces with Szeged Fascists. Macartney, *op. cit.*, I, 173.

**Gerstli* is an ingredient in the famous Jewish dish, *sholet*.

steadily growing, violent anti-Semitism in the non-Jewish middle classes and a Fascist mood all over the country. Gömbös' strongest attack was directed toward the Bethlen men, and in an oblique fashion he used Eckhardt as his spokesman. But Bethlen's influence was still formidable. Seeing that the conservatives had left too much ground open for Gömbös to exploit and that he used his opportunities all too well, Bethlen decided in 1935 "to put him under tutelage."[27]

Bethlen and Gömbös were received by the Regent on February 8, 1935, in a joint audience, and it was Bethlen who prevailed. Gömbös addressed the nation by radio on the fourteenth to denounce Eckhardt and finally to refute Eckhardt's attacks on the Bethlenites (something he had refused to do for more than a year). He also repudiated the Fascist student organizations and their political resolutions. In short, he publicly surrendered entirely to Bethlen.

As events transpired, it became obvious that the surrender was made in the interest of expediency. Some weeks before, Kállay, Imrédy, and other conservative ministers had resigned. In March they were followed by Keresztes-Fischer, the minister of interior. After that, Gömbös carried out a master stroke. With the pretext of "reconstructing his cabinet," he got a carte blanche vote of confidence from the Government party, and by a ruse or an argument that is still a mystery, he gained permission from the Regent to dissolve the Bethlen Parliament — that is, to manage the elections à la Gömbös. The Regent was by nature indecisive and given to sudden changes of mind. Some hours later he would have retracted his decision, but Gömbös informed him that it was impossible. According to another version, Gömbös went into hiding until the decree of dissolution and the authorization of new elections were read to an astonished Parliament.[28] In vain did Bethlen protest later on. The old, shrewd politician had been thoroughly outmaneuvered by a Fascist upstart.

During the electoral campaign, Gömbös gave some taste of what would follow under his brand of fascism. The elections, if one can call them elections, were the most brutally managed of the whole interwar period. In the country, the open ballot was still used. No pretense of liberality was observed, and in one case the gendarmerie even opened fire on the electorate, killing six people. Such methods made the outcome a foregone conclusion. Eckhardt and Gömbös quarreled over their prearranged distribution of seats, but in view of the strong position attained by Gömbös, Eckhardt was now expendable.

That the success of the Government party was formidable was not surprising. It won 170 mandates, about three-quarters of them filled with Gömbös' men. There were twenty-three Smallholders (the number Gömbös offered Eckhardt orginally); two representatives of the Reform Generation (a faction of young right-wing intellectuals supporting Gömbös' policies);* fourteen "Christians," most of them in the Clerical Fascist Wolff-Csilléry group; eleven Social Democrats; seven Liberals; eleven independents (includ-

---

*Of the representatives of the Government party there were 21 non-commissioned officers. Súlyok, *op. cit.*, p. 443.

ing Bethlen); one National Radical; one Christian Opposition; one Legitimist; one National Agrarian Opposition; and finally, two radical Fascists (National Socialists). Reappointed premier by Horthy, Gömbös now had a subservient Parliament and control over the army and administration, over education, propaganda, and youth. A complete conservative Fascist takeover and his personal dictatorship seemed within his reach.* The very articulate spirit of Hungary would be a conservative Fascist one for some time to come, and on an increasing scale, despite the temporary setbacks it suffered in subsequent years at the hand of the Bethlenite conservatives.

5

In the fall of 1935, after securing practically the entire state apparatus for himself, Gömbös resorted to one of his old tactics. He tried to delude the opposition into a false sense of security. He announced a very moderate program designed to excite none of the fears (or hopes) that his actions usually engendered.

This new stance should be considered against the background of his earlier pledge to Hitler and Göring to introduce a full Fascist regime to Hungary within two years and of his other pronouncements at Szeged which were so at variance with moderation.[29] He now promised the creation of a "unitary Hungarian nation" and a "one party, corporate state," and he urged the workers to drop Marxism and come over to the Fascist camp, promising them substantial benefits.** He also announced to friend and foe alike that his hands were not bound any more, and that he considered "null and void the obligations his government had in the past."[30]

Some minor improvements in social policy were also taking place, and by 1936 the world economic crisis in central Europe was abating; consequently Hungary's economic position had improved substantially.

Those forces which opposed fascism in Hungary had little solace when they looked to the future. In the spring of 1936, after their inaction during the Ethiopian crisis, the Western powers stood by while Hitler swept away half of the defenses of France with his occupation of the Rhineland. The extent to which this event affected the whole No-Man's-Land of Europe is difficult to overestimate: the confidence it gave to the Fascists was as great in its dimensions as was the despair it created in the opposite camp.

*Even the pretense of Parliamentarianism was cast aside. Before every session Gömbös summoned the Government party representatives to his office, informed them about a pending measure and instructed them when to applaud, when and how to give vent to their approval, and when to cheer. *O.N.K.*, December 1, 1937, p. 155.

**Marton was busy organizing a Fascist representation for workers, the *Nemzeti Munkaközpont* (National Labor Center), which had some success with segments of labor like those in state-owned enterprises, workers for railroads, post office and public utilities, government employees and agriculture laborers where the Bethlen-Social Democrat pact of 1922 denied to the Social Democratic party the right to organize trade unions.

One intentionally avoids the use of the label "democratic opposition" in describing the opposition to both conservative and radical fascism, because the politics of the time brought together some of the strangest bedfellows imaginable. Because Horthy belonged to their group, the Bethlen conservatives, with the authoritarian conservatism of their class, became by far the most important of all opposition groups. The Smallholders, without any true representation of the great peasant masses, were split. The left wing of the party claimed such true democrats as Ferenc Nagy, while its other extreme was represented by men like the Fascist fellow traveler Mátyás Matolcsy. The cheerfully unprincipled Eckhardt presided over this heterogeneous party: disappointed in his ambition to share the leadership of a Fascist state with Gömbös on equal terms, he had begun to develop a sympathy for democracy — even for Habsburg restoration! The few Legitimists and Liberals also belonged in the opposition camp, as did the Social Democrats. There was also the National Radical Endre Bajcscy Zsilinszky, the future leader of the Smallholders, who after a long period of soul searching and groping was led by ardent patriotism to democracy and a selfless service to his nation. It was a road that would lead him to martyrdom less than a decade later as the only true representative of the virtues of the Hungary the world had learned to admire in 1848. These deviations of his career were never motivated by personal ambition or gain as Eckhardt's were, despite the fact the two had a common background.

The divergent views of the groups comprising the opposition made the establishment of any united front against the Fascists extremely difficult, so for some years there was only a kind of tacit cooperation among them.

With conservative fascism advancing rapidly all over Hungary, Marton felt so emboldened by the spirit of the age that in January 1936 he dared to employ agents to spy upon Bethlenite officials, even cabinet ministers.[31] There was a constant meddling by Gömbös appointees into business still controlled by Bethlen men. In the spring, the pent-up anti-Semitic feeling suddenly but not unexpectedly flared into the open. The fact that this was signalled by student riots excludes the possibility of spontaneity and also points to its origin.

Horthy watched these events with great disquiet. He had come a long way since Szeged, and his remaining ties with the Szeged element were mostly sentimental. He had become an ultraconservative, and he realized how Gömbös had outmaneuvered Bethlen, who was his own confidant and chief adviser. In the spring of 1936 he decided, according to his memoirs, to remove Gömbös from power.[32] Perhaps he could have done it; he hadn't the chance to try. Gömbös fell ill during the summer and died in October, leaving both fascism and its opposition in a state of shock and turmoil.

6

The foreign policy of the Gömbös regime was complementary to its policy at home. It was in foreign affairs that the irreversible damage was done, much more than on the domestic front where the Bethlen conservatives were in a position to exert substantial control and slow down the Fascist advance. Over a policy attached fatefully to a general European trend, they were relatively powerless.

Immediately after his appointment in October 1932, Gömbös rushed down to Rome, where he was duly feted by Mussolini and made effusive pledges to Italy and fascism. This served two purposes: first, he hoped to strengthen his at that time not very strong position at home; and second, he wanted to smash that conservative-legitimist — at any rate, anti-Fascist — school of thought which sought French support for a Habsburg restoration that would shift the French reliance from the Little Entente to a resurrected Austria-Hungary. The logical consequence of such a realignment would have been a partial or integral revision. We shall not go into how much support there was at the Quai d'Orsay for this school of thought; suffice it to say that if there had been any support at all, his visit to Rome finished it, which was exactly what he wanted.

The neobaroque hatred of France and the West in general rested always on two pillars. One, Trianon and the support of the status quo by France, is an understandable one. But the other, the hatred of democracy, liberty, equality, and fraternity, was based on something other than French mistakes or policies. Gömbös did not miss a single opportunity to stir up anti-Western feelings on the second account. He made clear in 1934 that, lest anyone cherish doubts, he had been a National Socialist for a long time, that in his view the "slogans of the French Revolution do not exist in reality. There is no equality in life. Nature itself is against equality. The artificial egalitarianism is communism, and so it is unacceptable for Hungarian individualism."[33]

There were no ties with Germany yet in 1932 — these were the last months of Weimar. But in July 1933, some months after Hitler's advent to power, Gömbös called on him. He was the first foreign statesman to do so. The visit was arranged not through official channels, but through a Hungarian agent of the Nazis, a former member of one of the Officer Detachments, an early acquaintance of Hitler from the Beerhaus Putsch days, a Mr. András Mecsér. Gömbös made clear that his sympathies "do not lie with Weimar, but with the brown Germany." Hitler stood on Bismarckian foundations and was a friend of the Hungarians, Gömbös said, yet he also proclaimed that he was ready to stand up and energetically defend Hungarian interests against the Germans — if it became necessary.[34]

As it proved, Gömbös needed all his energy for this stand, because his encounter with the *Führer* was far from reassuring. Hitler demonstrated great confidence in Gömbös when he told him about his plans in detail, informed him about his intention to start a war, to crush France, to annex Austria, and to destroy Czechoslovakia. He wished to take the Czech lands for himself, but since he did not need Slovakia or Ruthenia, Gömbös could take those territories. For Rumania and Yugoslavia, the *Führer* had his own plans. The order was simple and short: "Hands off! " If Gömbös was prepared to comply, Hitler promised to help him economically and not to stir up the radical Fascists or Swabians against him.[35] The tendency to support the conservative Fascists against the radical ones was a very early Nazi policy, and as we shall see, a very well founded one as far as German national interests were concerned.

The visit was disappointing for Gömbös not only because he was forced to reconcile firm reality with his dreams about the Nationalist International and his grand designs to carve up equally Central and Eastern Europe among Germany, Italy and Hungary; there was a much more painful complication because of Austria. In the 1920s, when there was a Socialist government in Vienna and a danger of Habsburg restoration, Gömbös would have liked to have Austria disappear, the sooner the better. But after the Clerical-Fascists, with the encouragement of Gömbös, had drowned the Socialists in their own blood (signing with the same act their own death warrant), and since Mussolini was firmly for the maintenance of Austrian independence, Gömbös was in a difficult position vis-à-vis Hitler. So, both on the question of revision and on the question of Austria, there was a clear disagreement between the *Führer* and the *Vezér* who, thanks to the *Duce*, revised his position on the *Anschluss.*[36]

It should be emphasized that Gömbös did defy Hitler both on the question of Austria and on the question of revision regarding Rumania and Yugoslavia. In March 1934, the so-called Rome protocols were signed by Italy, Austria and Hungary which, besides establishing substantial economic cooperation, coordinated the foreign policy of the three countries in such a way that it was clearly as much against Germany as against Yugoslavia.

The Hungarian-Italian Entente against Yugoslavia, the subversive activities of the Hungarian counsul in Zagreb, and Hungary's cooperation with Italy in harboring the fascist *Ustaši* refugees from Croatia and Macedonian terrorists had tragic consequences. These developments led in October 1934 to the Marseille murder of King Alexander of Yugoslavia and French Foreign Minister Louis Barthou, who together personified the last hope of setting up an anti-Fascist front in the No-Man's-Land of Europe. Today it is clear that Hungary's guilt was rather that of omission than of commission in the matter, and that the full blame rests upon Mussolini. Yet Mussolini was able to use Hungary as a scapegoat with the help of unscrupulous men like Pierre Laval.

The Marseille affair, coupled with his talk with Hitler, should have opened Gömbös' eyes to the relative weight of Hungary in the future Fascist axis. This did not happen. To the end of his life he insisted that he could treat with Mussolini — nay, even with Hitler — on the basis of equality and the infallibility of his judgment. As late as March 1936, when warned by Representative Súlyok of the dangers of his commitments to Hitler, Gömbös assured him with a superior smile that "he had warned Hitler a long time ago that he should not think of treating Hungary as part of the *Südostraum* because in that case Hungary would treat Germany as *Nordwestraum.*"[37]

Economically, Hjalmar Schacht's concept of using the *Südostraum* to supply raw materials to the Third Reich and buy its industrial products from Germany on the basis of barter, started to gain momentum in 1935. The immediate advantages of this system were obvious. But the long-run suppression of native industries, and the even more onerous dependence on Germany, both economically and politically, which must follow inexorably,

102

did not seem to alarm Gömbös. He happily announced in Parliament that Schacht approved of his economic policy.[38]

By 1935 the Axis was in its formative stage, despite a temporary French-Italian combination to which, if it had solidified, Mussolini would have sacrificed Hungary's revisionist claims without a whisper. During the Ethiopian War, Hungary supported Italy fully. The Hungarian delegate, who always spoke in the League of Nations about the right of self-determination for the Hungarian minorities in the Succession States, thus gave unqualified support to one of the more cynical denials of self-determination in the twentieth century.

After his signal victory in the 1935 elections, Gömbös visited Berlin in September. He felt secure enough to conclude a secret agreement with Göring to introduce a Nazi system in Hungary within two years. Many of the articles of this agreement are still a mystery,[39] but Hitler was supposed to give Gömbös full support in it, and when Hitler annexed Austria, Hungary was to recover Burgenland. In all this Gömbös was helped by the hesitant attitude of the Austrian Clerical-Fascists, whose leader Kurt von Schuschnigg declared that Austria was a "German state" and gave assurance that "Austria will never take part in any anti-German combination." This removed the very *raison d'être* of the Rome protocols. Mussolini understood this.*

The decisive signal to go ahead with these schemings was given by the strange inaction of the West when Hitler occupied the Rhineland. From that time on Gömbös forbade any discussion of foreign policy in Parliament; he tolerated such discussions only in parliamentary committees from which the public and press were excluded.

Despite this unsavory picture, one must give Gömbös credit for trying like the true nationalist he was to work for revision and Hungary's interests. In this he persisted, though by that time he was not at all reassured by cordial German overtures to Rumania and Yugoslavia.** But even here, in the last analysis, he was no more farsighted than the substantial majority of articulate

*The absurdly contradictory nature of Schuschnigg's policy was proven at the meeting of Gömbös, Mussolini, and Schuschnigg in Rome two weeks after Hitler occupied the Rhineland. The Austrian chancellor explained to his partners his position: Austria can never enter into bilateral negotiations with Berlin. Any lasting agreement with Hitler must be based on a multilateral guarantee of Austrian independence. Yet, he would never join any action against Germany, not even sanctions, if the League decided to impose any as a retaliation for the occupation of the Rhineland. In the same breath, he casually announced that he had discontinued the pending economic negotiations with Germany, because the Nazis used an Austrian journalist for distributing funds to Austrian Nazis. *Allianz*, pp. 124-25.

**Hitler advised Döme Sztójay, (the Hungarian ambassador in Berlin) in July 1936, that Hungary should concentrate her revisionist claims on Czechoslovakia — there "he has common aims with the Hungarians." The Germans openly expressed their fear that Hungary, if she felt German support behind her, would start some "adventurous undertaking." *Ibid.*, p. 129.

non-Jewish public opinion.* The Szeged Idea was beginning to bear fruit, and the non-Jewish middle class could not consider any question, whether domestic or foreign, except through the Jewish question. This attitude was complemented by the traditional Hungarian overestimation of Hungary's strength, influence and role in world affairs. The people did not want to see the very concrete dangers that a new world war or, for that matter, a German victory posed as far as Hungary was concerned. They could not even see the danger inherent in a preponderant greater Germany's appearance on Hungary's western borders. All that mattered was that Hitler was an efficient anti-Semite who had carried through the change of guard in Germany, and as Professor Macartney described it so well: "They found it hard to believe, that a so proper thinking man (on the Jewish question) could really fail to be pro-Hungarian on the Revision question or harbor designs on the liberty or integrity of Hungary."[40]

Gömbös liked to repeat *ad nauseam* that "no one can make a policy without Hungary in the Danube Basin."[41] Then again, "I know my race, and I know that it appreciates fantasy very much, because a historical nation and a historical race is worthless without fantasy."[42]

It was Stalin (and there is no evidence to make us believe that Hitler thought differently) who put into perspective this nineteenth-century pretension of the Hungarian Nation, so outdated in the twentieth-century power politics. When displeased with Hungarian behavior during the war, he casually remarked to Dr. Edward Beneš: "The Hungarian question is solely a matter (of the availability) of boxcars!"

*Which does not make the Jewish middle class more farsighted. It was easy for a Jew to be farsighted as far as Hitler went. But as far as Italian fascism was concerned, many a Hungarian Jew toyed with fascist ideas in these years.

The Chief Rabbi of Budapest, Simon Hevesi, called on the *Duce* and after his return from Rome, in his sermon during the High Holidays he was tasteless enough to compare Mussolini with Moses! Jewish middle class families inscribed their sons into the Italian High School in Budapest. The boys paraded with pride in their *Balilla* (Italian Fascist youth) uniforms before their girl friends. The worst of the predominantly Jewish owned and written press of Budapest (*Az Est* papers), looking invariably for the lowest common denominator among men, behaved most scandalously during the conquest of Ethiopia. And this was the style in which the desperate struggle of Ethiopia for her survival was treated:

The Negus sent cannibals into battle. Savage mobs, wrapped in lionskins demand furiously arms from the Negus. This is not a battle but a hunt of beasts of prey.

and T. Kóbor, the distinguished Jewish journalist, wrote about the hopeless struggle of the Ethiopian people in this vein:

The low-flying [Italian] planes bring liberation. Let the bayonet do its ravaging task! The Italian is the only nation in the soul of which tenderness turns into battle. . . . We are patriots, we became soldiers, our character is Roman. . . .

József Major, 25 *év ellenforradalmi sajtó* (Budapest, 1945), pp. 56-57, 68.

When Gömbös dissolved his Party of Racial Defense in 1928 and joined the Government party, he did not even dream of the possibility of establishing fascism in Hungary, much less of turning the Government party into a Fascist One Party. All he wanted to do then was to secure his political and financial future. He never changed his basic ideas and goals despite the revisions he proclaimed as a means to a definite end. He took advantage of the Government party's lack of ideology and filled it with the ideology of Gömbös.

The democratic forces of the country were destroyed, incapacitated and discredited after 1919. The Bethlenite conservative wing harbored the only men who could have opposed Gömbös, and this they did not want to do in 1932. They preferred to use Gömbös for their purposes — or at least they thought so. The Bethlen conservatives thought, because they were not accustomed to thinking otherwise, that as long as the commanding heights were secured they need not worry. They thought to use Gömbös as they used Nagyatádi Szabó or the Jewish financiers. They did not believe in the possibility of a transformation, Fascist or any other, starting from the grassroots.

Reforms could have forestalled Gömbös — necessary and overdue changes wrought by thorough land reform, broad social legislation, curbs on the greed of big capital, and diminished chauvinistic agitation. But Horthy and Bethlen were not the kind of people to initiate such a course. They were confident they could control Gömbös, and before they suspected otherwise, Hungary had a Fascist administration; a thoroughly Szeged Fascist-spirited military; a Parliament with a Szeged Fascist majority; and an educational system, a youth, a press and radio, and an articulate public opinion saturated with the Szeged Fascist spirit and Szeged-style expectations. What is more, all over Europe fascism seemed to be the "Spirit of the Age" and Gömbös had set a foreign policy, a series of commitments, which determined Hungary's course to a bitter end. This was the legacy which Gömbös' partisans inherited after he passed from the scene, and which no effort of the Bethlen-Horthy group could undo later.

Gömbös and his followers were not responsible for the national and international social, economic, and political conditions that surrounded their rise to power in Hungary. What they can and should be blamed for is not their search for redress for Trianon once they had power, but for their perception that it was worthwhile to gamble on a German victory in order to achieve this redress. Was an unconditional Hungarian commitment to a German victory justified? Or would it not seem rather that a full-fledged German preponderance in the Danube Basin was only in the interest of the factions the Szeged Fascists represented? Often, all too often, were the interests of Hungary as a whole and the interests of the Szeged element confused in the next eight years.

Certainly for the Szeged Fascists the most important goal, besides integral revision, was to solve the Jewish question, to preempt as much of the property and position of the Jewish middle class as possible, and Hitler was a great help toward this end. It was Ferenc Rajniss (formerly Rheinisch, an assimilated Swabian), a gifted but thoroughly corrupt, deceitful, journalist-politician of the Szeged Fascist camp, who expressed this idea in Parliament more clearly than anybody ever did: "The Jewish question through the Jewish penetration into the middle classes is primarily a question of the middle class. It is not eight-and-a-half or nine millions of Hungarians who confront 444,000 Jews, but it is 400,000 middle class Hungarians who are confronting 444,000 Jews."[43] Here is the most important single factor behind Hungary's Nazi orientation and also the essence of the social program of the Szeged Fascists.

But this does not fully explain the reasons for that fateful pro-German and pro-Nazi feeling which prevailed among articulate Hungarians. There was also a delusion of grandeur present in the Hungarian ruling classes whether of the Bethlenite or Gömbösite wing. These people did not wish to understand Hungary's tremendously diminished international stature after the disappearance of the Dual Monarchy, which the Hungarian Nation too often could manipulate to its ends and in this manner increase its own importance. It became the political dream of every Szeged Fascist that Hungary and Germany jointly, as equals, should "bring order to East Central Europe." The slogan of Szeged Fascists was from then on: *"Magyar-német sorsközösség"* (The Common Hungarian-German Destiny).

Finally, there was the other fateful delusion of this school of thought — the sincere belief that Hitler was the friend of Hungary. We shall see the extent of Hitler's friendly feelings to Hungary later.

Gömbös, for his part, was a romantic, mystical man possessed of a patriotism which, if it was sometimes oddly expressed, was at any rate far above the "patriotism" of some of his partisans and successors. It is interesting to speculate how he would have acted if confronted with Hitlerian realities and designs toward Hungary in the years 1941-45.

Gömbös brought no alleviation to the condition of the dejected Hungarian masses. Blocked from any constructive way out and victimized by a brutal gendarmerie, their desperation at last vented itself in a radical, revolutionary fascism.

8

Before the great depression, Fascist groups in Hungary were of a Szeged type and a strictly middle-class phenomenon. The various components of the fascism that was the Szeged Idea lined up behind Gömbös in the twenties. There were also several small groups claiming a purely Facist ideology, such as the one led by a certain Perlesz immediately after Mussolini marched on Rome in 1922, or the Wesselényi Reform Club* founded by Miklós Csomós and Béla Szász in the late twenties. But after Gömbös returned to the

*Count Miklós Wesselényi was one of the leaders of the Reform Generation of 1848.

Government party in 1928, there was little future for such movements in the general atmosphere of economic improvement.

All this changed radically with the depression. Although everybody in Hungary was affected, the deepest impression was created in the ranks of the lower middle classes, the borderline strata in the class structure which were aware of their position and were frustrated by it. They were the petite bourgeoisie, and the fixed-income groups made up of public servants, clerks and the like. There were also the young, unemployed intellectuals, in many cases of humble origin, who were graduating from the universities in ever-increasing numbers into a society fostered by nineteenth-century economic liberalism that made no organized attempt to integrate them into the life of the country.

Under any other circumstances these elements would have turned to the left. But that route was closed. They could not yet follow Gömbös in 1931 and 1932 because he was in the midst of "revising" his ideas and making his deals with the Bethlenites and Jewish financiers. So for the next five years there developed a powerful, absolutely spontaneous but disorganized resentment that surged in the only direction not blocked by past or present — radical fascism. The unprecedented proliferation of Fascist parties between 1931 and 1936 was the result of this spontaneity without a true leader. For the first time since 1919, the popular masses re-entered the scene not as leftists but as Fascists, but it would be four or five years before there would be some channeling of these energies into two main groups.

One group would receive the middle classes, which were trying to better their deteriorating position at the cost of the Jewish middle class, and at the cost of the Bethlen conservatives, who were the actual possessors of wealth and power. This Fascist group was hardly more ready to come to terms with the industrial age than the Bethlen system had been and were as much the "displaced persons" of twentieth-century politics (as Prof. E. Weber calls them) as were the lower classes who made up the other group, but for very different reasons. There could be no peace between the Fascist movements of the "middle class of Hungarian gentlemen" and the revolutionary impetus of the lower classes because, as Professor Weber continues, the radical Fascists of the lower classes "were clawing their way upward," while the Szeged Fascists, despite their reformist trappings, proposed little genuine reform and did even less. They only made desperate efforts "not to slip down."[44]

This fundamental conflict, intensified by the clash of personalities and rivalries in the leadership, caused such an implacable hostility between these two Fascist groups in Hungary that not even in the direst emergency was it possible to bring about a united Fascist front in Hungary of the kind that always existed in Germany or Italy. Consequently, by 1931 different groups of the petite bourgeoisie were in full rebellion against the conservative wing of the Hungarian Nation. It would seem that every lawyer, engineer, nurse, or student leader had to publish a brochure stating the program for his own Fascist movement to remedy the ills of Hungary. Organizations multiplied like fungi only to die out some weeks or months afterward and often to reappear later in some other more durable Fascist or Nazi form. The titles of their newspapers are revealing: *Struggle!* *(Harc!)*, *Tocsin!* *(Riadó!)*, *Assault!* *(Támadás!)*, *Endurance!* *(Kitartás!)*, *Courage!* *(Bátorság!)*, *Fist* *(Ököl)*, *Fire!* *(Tüz!)*, *Storm!* *(Roham!)*, *We Shall Conquer!* *(Gyözünk!)*.

In the years 1931-32, from his office in the ministry of defense, Gömbös encouraged these movements, holding them over the heads of the Bethlenites in an "I-told-you-so" fashion and presenting himself as the only man who could offer an assuaging alternative. He felt certain that he could use these forces for his purposes later, but apparently he forgot the message of Goethe's *Zauberlehrling,* in which the wizard's apprentice could not control the spirits he launched. When from 1933-34 on the popular masses increasingly entered the Fascist picture, many of them were exasperated by Gömbös' slow progress toward a Fascist state. While he honored obligations and held back because of his essential conservatism, the radical Fascist movements assumed life of their own. After years of confusion, they found a leader with a certain orginality and charisma, and only those Fascist parties collaborated or fused with the Szeged Idea which had a predominantly bourgeois membership and had no true reform in mind other than the change of guard.

The first Fascist movement to attract popular mass support began in 1931 in the middle Tisza region, which was inhabited by the most miserable of the agrarian proletariat. In their hopelessness, these people since time immemorial had turned for consolation to an array of religious sects. This region was also the home of the celebrated "arsenic women," who in their ignorance and misery and superstition systematically poisoned their husbands.

When the great depression came, these people, who even under normal circumstances were unemployed for nine months a year, suffered tremendously. And at this point, a fanatic (in his own words a "writer, poet, and the leader of the people"), Zoltán Böszörmény, appeared among them. He was the son of a bankrupt landowner, and he was 38 in 1931. He had held many menial jobs before taking up poetry and joining the counterrevolution of 1919. He entered the University of Budapest afterward and became one of the leaders of the Gömbös-controlled Fascist student movements. He claimed to have met Hitler in 1931, although we have no proof of this.* At any rate, in that year he founded the Nazionalsozialistische deutsche Arbeiterpartei's equivalent, the Hungarian National Socialist Worker's party. As party insignia he chose the "Kaszás Kereszt" (Scythe Cross). From the Nazis he also adopted the brown shirt, the Storm Troopers, the greeting *"Heil,* Böszörmény," and the designation of party members as *Néptars,* the equivalent of Volksgenosse.

About his goals, he spoke in poetic phrases fraught with the despair and fervor of one possessed. "This is the fullness of time, and the lonely poet, the Man, who always stood alone, departs to oppose the destructive forces of Money. One man against the whole world." He was the "tribune" who was

---

*Although the recent study of Professor Lackó maintains with certainty that Böszörmény met Hitler personally in December 1931. Miklós Lackó, *Nyilasok, nemzetiszocialisták,* (Budapest, 1966), p. 18.

"ready to caress but also to have hundreds of thousands executed without batting an eyelash."[45]

The Budapest newspapers derided him, but Budapest was immensely far away from the bleak hopelessness and starvation along the Tisza, "the most Hungarian of all rivers." The peasants listened to Böszörmény in awe. When the village explorer, Imre Kovács, asked them what they wanted, their answer was simple, "We have had enough! " or "We fight for an idea." But they could not express in words what the idea was. "They just hated Communists and gentlemen."[46]

Although Böszörmény held the whole region in a ferment for years and had more than 20,000 party members, he could not even run in a parliamentary by-election. Gömbös, with the help of the gendarmerie, made certain that he could not get the necessary recommendations to qualify him for candidacy. The authorities were always particularly sensitive about agrarian unrest. While bourgeois Fascist groups in the towns were left alone, Böszörmény's paper, the *National Socialist*, was repressed; he himself was persistently harassed with lawsuits; his followers bore the brunt of gendarme brutality.[47]

Böszörmény's ideology encompassed a vague mixture of dictatorship, land reform, anti-Semitic and anti-Bolshevist phraseology, anti-Habsburg attitudes, and in general "justice for the poor." In 1935, he issued a "Ten Commandments for the Storm Trooper."[48] All his blood-and-thunder oratory incited no serious consequences until 1936. Then, frustrated by the repression of his cause and the success of Gömbös, Böszörmény planned a fantastic armed insurrection that was to begin in Nagykörös, one of the village-towns of the region. He wanted to seize the public buildings there and march to Kecskemét and Cegléd, and then to repeat this tactic in a snowball movement until his movement gathered enough strength to march against Budapest. After the capture of the capital, he intended to proclaim a military dictatorship.[49] His followers had already bought on the Budapest flea market several used general staff officers' uniforms for the entry to Budapest, the only concrete preparation for the plot.

The "uprising" duly started on the first of May, 1936, with the participation of a few thousand of the agrarian proletariat, but the gendarmes were at hand. They dispersed the quixotic gathering without bloodshed. Seven hundred people were arrested. Several trials followed. Böszörmény got a light sentence of two-and-a-half years. Another eighty-seven of his codefendants got even lighter sentences. "Out of one hundred defendants, ninety-eight owned no land," reports the eyewitness village explorer, Imre Kovács. "They wore torn trousers, miserable short overcoats or old sheepskin vests; none of them wore a shirt." The judge permitted the defendants to return to their misery.[50] And thus, the movement came to an end. After finishing his term, Böszörmény left for Nazi Germany, and in 1945 petitioned the Communist boss Rákosi to allow him to join the Communist party.[51]

The depression also unleashed Fascist movements in the cities, especially in Budapest. From these, the Fascist group led by the Smallholders' deputy, Zoltán Meskó, had risen to some significance and cohesion by 1931. Meskó in the twenties had represented the Christian Course in its most anti-Semitic form. In 1931 he entered Parliament on a Smallholder ticket. Of Slovak origin, he had a maverick personality with the sort of humor that generated humor around him. For about a year, Meskó tried to cooperate with Böszörmény, but the radicalism of the latter made accord between them impossible. On June 16, 1932, he announced in Parliament the formation of the National Socialist Agricultural Laborers and Workers party. In his speech he made the usual statements about the "obsolete dogmas and ingrown financial theories of capitalism," the excesses of which "ruined the society of Europe and beggared the millions of its workers." He announced his program, which called for fearing God, loyalty to the Regent (a rare bourgeois-Fascist quality!), 100 percent revision, the nationalization of banks, placement for the unemployed university graduates, and a policy against the *fideicommissa* with a mild, conditional land reform.[52]

Despite the party's name, most of the program's promised reforms would have benefitted the disgruntled petite bourgeoisie. While there were special demands directed against the Jews, any allegation that Meskó's movement was merely an imitation of foreign (Nazi) practices was vigorously denied.[53] The brown shirt and the swastika in a brown field were nevertheless adopted as party emblems, and Meskó affected a moustache trimmed à la Hitler. Later, when the minister of interior outlawed these symbols as "emblems of foreign power," Meskó exchanged the brown shirt for a green one and the swastika for the crossed arrows that later became significant as the Arrow Cross. By that time (1933) the Csomós-Szász group had joined with Meskó and they called members "brother" *(Testvér)*.[54] After these changes, Meskó changed the Hitler cut of his moustache. The membership of his party was almost completely of the bourgeoisie and "90 percent of its agitation consisted of slander and denigration of Böszörmény."[55]

The basic rule of fascism is that there must be only *one* leader in each country, that there is no room for more. Meskó was not prepared to recognize Böszörmény's pretensions any more than Böszörmény did his. As for Gömbös, he did not recognize even during his "revision" period the right of anyone else to attract Fascist masses or to start a Fascist movement. Meskó saw the writing on the wall. He restricted his movement mainly to Budapest petite bourgeoisie and toned down his criticism of the Gömbös government. Therefore, he often fared much better than Böszörmény at the hand of Gömbös' Advance Guard.[56]

Of the numerous other Fascist parties, the one headed by Count Sándor Festetics was also of some consequence. The count, with his immense landholdings (40,000 holds), was one of the leading magnates in Hungary. His adherence was a rare phenomenon in radical Fascist movements and his financial backing later became important. Count Festetics was minister of defense in the Károlyi cabinet of 1918, and in this capacity clashed with Gömbös, who had also served Károlyi for a while. Later, he joined Bethlen and the Government party, earning fame both in and outside Parliament for his eccentricities. Among other things, he coined impossible and senseless

Hungarian words and phrases which only he understood (for example: "*Darizó mangár*").[57]

In 1933, he became a Fascist and made overtures toward Meskó, but to further his own ambitions he took over the embryonic Fascist movement of a certain Aladár Hehs. This was easy enough, because Hungarian Fascist groups were notoriously in need of cash until the death of Gömbös. Hitler of course did not finance the Hungarian Nazis while he waited for the implementation of the Gömbös-Göring agreement. Festetics' party, the Hungarian National Socialist People's party, issued its program in 1933 as a fairly accurate copy of the N.S.D.A.P. program, with some modifications. According to it, only members of the "Turanian-Aryan Race" could have citizenship rights, there must be social justice, and not Hitler but the Habsburgs represented danger for Hungary. Although monarchist in principle, the program left the question of royal succession open. The heroes of the movement were Hitler, Mussolini, Atatürk, and Pisudski. In the beginning of his pamphlet, we find a familiar apocalyptic admonition: "The tide of multitudes is again rising. After a terrible ebb, a tide is coming. Human soul turned hollow, on the infested bottom of decadence the whiteness of Christ fell into the dust, Purity, Faith, and Honor collapsed."[58]

By dint of the fact that he owned practically the entire Enying district in Transdanubia, Festetics could bring "popular masses" into his movement by his authority alone. He added a green shirt to the dress of the simplest common laborer and, so attired, traveled in his huge limousine all over the country to campaign. In 1935, he ordered his peasants to vote for him, giving them the choice of infuriating either their lord or the gendarmes.

But Festetics was still too much of an aristocrat to be a thoroughgoing Fascist. For one thing he continued to employ Jews on his estates, and this would cost him dearly later.* He even established a school of agriculture on one of his estates, ready to train Jews in the profession if they were willing to emigrate to Palestine.[59] This was not the way to win Fascist favors in Hungary. He also set the record straight in Parliament in the same terms Horthy once used regarding agrarian reform: "We are not land distributors! There are fourteen million holds and nine million people in Hungary! The solution is resettlement! " Whereupon the Social Democratic deputy Kabók interrupted him to suggest that he start this resettlement program on his 40,000-hold estate.[60]

In November 1933, a Nazi party of much more ominous significance was founded by Count Fidél Pálffy. Calling itself the National Socialist party, it adopted a swastika armband, Storm Troopers, an SS, a youth movement on the pattern of the Hitler Jugend, and a program that was an almost unadulterated copy of the one proclaimed by the N.S.D.A.P. During the war, it was the Pálffy party that would form a coalition with the Szeged Fascists under Imrédy, a coalition which acted more openly and was less careful of Hungarian national interests than any other Fascist group. But Gömbös did

---

*He always maintained that "in order to avoid economic disturbances, one should not emphasize the Jewish question." Lackó, *op. cit.*, p. 56n.

not show much understanding toward it. He cracked down in Zala County, the movement's Transdanubian center, and disbanded its Storm Troopers and SS as soon as they were formed.

There was a short-lived unity among the non-Gömbös Fascists in January 1934, when Festetics, Pálffy and Meskó formed a collective leadership of the three movements, all of which adopted the Arrow Cross and the green shirt. Several quarrels followed. Festetics was expelled because of his tolerance toward the Jews, only to ally himself with a certain István Balogh, a well-to-do peasant and leader of a Fascist group in Debrecen called the Hungarian National Socialist Party.*

Pálffy and Meskó continued their collaboration until September 1935, when Pálffy expelled Meskó on personal grounds. Meskó then formed a separate Fascist party which took the same name used by his group in 1932. In the election of 1935, Gömbös blocked administratively both Meskó's and Pálffy's efforts to gain a mandate. Shortly after that, when Gömbös, growing stronger, could adopt a more clear conservative Fascist line, many of Pálffy's petit bourgeois adherents went over to his camp.

This great confusion in the Fascist ranks between 1931 and 1935 was caused mainly by the equivocal position of Gömbös. Considering his past, almost everybody — that is, most of the uninitiated — expected a conservative Fascist milennium. They were disappointed. Meskó expressed this in Parliament in June 1933, when he said that he expected strong anti-Semitic legislation, a Fascist dictatorship and social reform.[61] For the time being Gömbös even had to quell the more vociferous bourgeois Fascists. Answering the leading Fascist journalist István Milotay, he protested that "in seven or eight months it is impossible to bring about a nationalist rebirth such as the Right expected!"[62] Meanwhile he heaped praise on Bethlen and Horthy "as the protectors of conservatism,"[63] publicly denied any connection with Jewish business (which financed him and his party)[64] and, step by step, determinedly prepared his own Fascist takeover. It was to be a Szeged Fascist takeover, and Gömbös was to be *Vezér*. Nobody else. He did not like "the tendency of some of the Nazi movements"[65] (that is, their popular character). On the other hand, he was enough of a Hungarian nationalist to object to the imitative German character of these movements.[66] Both Meskó and Festetics were therefore persecuted, and Festetics had to leave the Government party. The fate of Böszörmény is known.

Gömbös could afford to act this way. The Bethlenites were not likely to protect the Fascist splinter groups, and while Germany became their main supporter after Gömbös' death, during his lifetime all German hopes rested on Gömbös. He had the Germans' promise that they would not conspire with the radical Fascists behind his back or stir up the German minority against him. Later, after the Gömbös-Göring agreement, Hitler paid even less attention to Fascist schismatics in Hungary.

*András Török, *Szálasi álarc nélkül*, p.11. Festetics financed Balogh's election to the Parliament in 1935 in Debrecen, the third largest town in Hungary where the balloting was secret and Gömbös could not avail himself of the services of the gendarmerie.

The other Fascist movements therefore fell into disarray. They lacked a real leader with originality or charisma. Most of all they lacked a sincere social program beyond anti-Semitism, a Hungarian program that was not a slightly altered version or even a plain translation of the N.S.D.A.P. program. The national mystique, one of the primary ingredients of fascism, was missing in borrowed clauses, for no national mystique can be translated from a foreign language. Also, the popular masses somehow felt that the social composition, membership and atmosphere of all these parties, except for the one led by the fantast Böszörmény, was distinctly bourgeois. Consequently, they did not hold the answer for them, and in this the masses were right. Even Macchiavelli, who did not hold the popular masses in very great esteem, had to recognize that sometimes "they have a better judgment than princes do."[67]

Nor did they accept Gömbös. The proliferation of Fascist splinter parties in the early thirties was a clear expression of both the existing revolutionary mood and of the failure of the *Vezér* to rally the whole people behind him. The basically just quest of the Hungarian people for reform was distorted, but they still demanded something more than the social program of the Szeged Idea or an adaptation of N.S.D.A.P. programs.

At last their distorted but just quest for reform found a leader — a man whose ideas were also distorted, even something more than eccentric, but who was honest in his way and patriotic, and above all an original. He does not perhaps deserve the colossal amount of abuse heaped on him from the very first moment he made his debut on the Hungarian political scene.

9

In the late 1940s, by strange coincidence and by even stranger fortune, I visited the Passau-Pocking Displaced Person's Camp in Bavaria, then in the American Zone of Occupation in Germany. On entering one of the barracks, I was struck by the almost religious atmosphere inside. And religious atmosphere it was. The inmates, all of them Hungarians and members of the Arrow Cross party, were commemorating in the cold, damp darkness of the room the anniversary of the "martyrdom" (execution) of Ferenc Szálasi, their former leader. I was about to erupt: It was shortly after 1945, and in addition to possessing a youthful (17) bad temper, I had experienced Fascist persecution and was inclined to look at such Fascist "memorial services" in the U.S. Zone of Germany rather seriously.

But as the "memorial service" concluded and the ill-fed, ill-dressed crowd dispersed, speculating in awed tones about the possible survival of Szálási's son "who will grow up one day to succeed him," murmuring in hurt and indignation about "how Szálasi saved the ungrateful West from communism," as my ear caught snatches of remembered tales about their dead leader, my fury turned to irony. Then as I observed more closely the sincere, ravaged faces of these unfortunate compatriots of mine, I realized that without exception they were the faces of the poorest, lowest, most abysmally miserable agrarian and industrial proletariat of Hungary. There was little in these people to recall the cynical, cruel Aryanizers and changers of the guard of the nouveau riche of 1944. The longer I looked at these simple folk and heard their impotent protests, their inane hopes, and their impossible loyalties, the more my irony dissolved in pity.

10

Ferenc Szálasi, the leader of the only Fascist movement able to rally large, genuinely popular masses in Hungary,* had not a drop of Hungarian blood in his veins. Well-documented investigation discloses that he was not even a Hungarian citizen, according to Hungarian law. On his father's side he came from Armenian ancestors from Transylvania. On his mother's side, he seems to descend from a Ruthenian-Slovak-Hungarian blend, although his mother's family belonged to the Uniate Church which would suggest Ruthenian ancestry rather than Slovak-Hungarian.** His origins were humble enough. He was born in 1891 in Košice, where his father was a noncommissioned officer in the logistics service of the K.u.K. Army. There is ample evidence that he changed his Armenian family name without official authorization from Salosján to Szálasi.[68]

Ferenc Szálasi, like his father, passed through the military academy to become a professional officer. He served thirty-six months as an officer on the front during World War I, but we know nothing of his whereabouts during the turbulent years of revolution and counterrevolution. By 1925, however, he was promoted to the general staff, and in this capacity he started to dabble in political writing, and his work attracted great interest among his colleagues. His essays, and the high distinction he achieved during his examinations at the General Staff College, provoked the interest of Gömbös in this "military revolutionary." Denounced in October 1931 by police agents, he was ordered to see Gömbös, then minister of defense. Gömbös warned him to keep out of politics and ordered his transfer to a remote garrison in the provinces. There he had plenty of free time to meditate and to work out his ideas "for the salvation of Hungary."[69] Trianon, coupled a decade later with effects of the great depression, gave him plenty of food for thought. He met his fiancée, Gizella Lutz, in 1927, but it took another ten years until he found time to marry her — to such an extent was he obsessed with his calling.

It was during those years that his ideology was formed. He read a lot, going through the works of Marx, Trotsky, Bebel, Lenin and Kropotkin so

*Changing the party line radically, this fact is frankly recognized in the new comprehensive history of the Arrow Cross (and that of other Fascist groups) published in Communist Hungary. Lackó, *op. cit., passim.*

**According to Szálasi's own account, his father was the strict, military type. His mother was a religious mystic, who "thoroughly imbued him with faith." *Ibid.,* p. 43.

thoroughly that he memorized whole passages.* These philosophies, the conclusions he drew from them, and their adaptation to Hungarian conditions fused and blended with his own ideas to result in a remarkable concept — Hungarism. It was a long way from the Szeged Idea or the the more or less slavish translations of N.S.D.A.P. programs offered by other Hungarian Fascists.

The opening passage of his ideology as expounded in his *Mein Kampf* entitled *The Way and the Aim* is revealing: "Hungarism is an ideological system. It is the Hungarian practice of the national socialistic view of the world and the spirit of the age. It is neither Hitlerism nor fascism nor anti-Semitism, but Hungarism."[70] This proud exclusiveness follows with a singular inflexibility throughout the history of Szálasi's thought and actions. Describing the ideology of Szálasi is not an easy task, not only because of the lack of sources but also because of Szálasi's inimitable language.**

Apart from the obvious style peculiarity, three things strike the attention of even a superficial reader of Szálasi. First: He was beyond any reasonable doubt sincerely concerned with the welfare of the broad, dispossessed lower classes. Second: He had a rather original plan for maintaining Hungarian supremacy in the Carpathian Basin, which if not entirely his invention is far more conciliatory than any of the policies proposed or practiced by either the Bethlenite or the Szeged Fascist wing of the ruling classes. Third: Szálasi's ideology completely lacked apocalyptic images or a call to violence or terror

*Weber, *Varieties of Fascism* p. 92. According to other sources Szálasi prided himself with "working out his theory all by himself" with the help of textbooks on history, ethnography, geography, Hungarian grammar, also the Old and New Testament, and the *Handwörterbuch der Soziologie*, edited by Vierkandt. (Lackó, *op. cit.*, p. 44) Nevertheless, there is reason to suspect that during the years Szálasi formulated his doctrine, he was under the strong influence of a clairvoyant and dilettante astrologer, an army doctor friend of his named H. Péchy. This gentleman was the fashionable clairvoyant of the higher circles of Hungarian society, having contacts even with Horthy. Doctor Péchy wrote a prophetic world history, based on mathematics, and he predicted the coming wars, revolutions and events in general "with mathematical accuracy." *Ibid.*, p. 62; also, Súlyok, *op. cit.*, pp. 488-89.

**Samples: "Social Nationalism is life's only genuine physics and biology. The true individual forms matter with his soul; his hand is but an instrument. And since this is so, the formed matter is not a value but a ware. Social Nationalism is therefore the nation's biological physics and not its historical materialism." Rogger and Weber, *The European Right, A Historical Profile*, p. 392. Or, some years later on foreign policy: "The East-Westerly orientation of our Fatherland broke down and died away with a shocking suddenness; and without transition it became the border interest-sphere of Europe's Northern and Southern life-sphere." Lackó, *op. cit.*, p. 234. Szálasi was superbly oblivious about such minor details as intelligibility. Speaking before court (during his first trial in 1938), when he was reminded of his chaotic style and theory he dismissed the pretension, retorting, "God, too, created the world out of chaos! " *Ibid.*, p. 111n.

— and ideologically and personally, he was more of an a-Semite than an anti-Semite. In this last he stood far above the majority of the Szeged men, who seemed under Gömbös and unmistakably were under Imrédy, prepared to inflict any amount of humilation, degradation and death to clear their path of middle-class Jews. This readiness was, as we shall see, considered nationalistic policy and the essence of social justice by the Szeged camp. It is an important point to remember, because unfortunately much of the public, both inside and outside Hungary, seemed to believe that such thoughts and deeds were assignable only to the Arrow Cross party and particularly to Szálasi. Even the Jews, who through thousands of years of persecution have developed such a good instinct for recognizing their true enemies, seemed to harbor many a misconception on this account.

Szálasi's Hungary was to encompass the historic Lands of the Holy Crown of St. Stephen, with Croatia, Slavonia, Dalmatia and Bosnia-Herzegovina included as a Croatian unit within the framework of the federation. Within the non-Croatian part, that is, the Carpathian Basin, he wanted to grant to the nationalities autonomous regions only in those areas where their majority was absolute or an overwhelming 80-90 percent (see map). Wherever the population was mixed, for example, Hungarian-Slovak, Slovak-German, Rumanian-Ruthenian or any other, the territory was to be under direct Hungarian control. He called this proposed state "The Great Carpatho-Danubian Fatherland" (K.D.N.H. — Kárpát-Duna-Nagy-Haza), not Hungary. He also liked to call it the "Landscape Land" (*Tájország*), for he would give the Slovaks and the Ruthenes the mountains, the Hungarians, the plains, the Germans, the hills. In the west there was to be a German march in central Burgenland called the March of Hungaria, and Slovakland, Ruthenoland, and Magyarland were to be joined with Croat Slavonland (Dalmatia and Bosnia-Herzegovina included!) to form the new state. In the new state, too, was to be a Transylvanialand within the historic frontiers of the Transylvanian principality. It is not quite clear what rights he was ready to concede to the Rumanian majority of Transylvania. He certainly would not forfeit a predominant position for Hungarians in this much disputed province, which was inhabited in addition by a highly civilized German (Saxon) minority. Nevertheless, he recognized the individual character of Transylvania and refrained from treating it as an integral part of Hungary proper without any qualification or without regard for Transylvania's 70 percent non-Hungarian population.

This association under Hungarian supremacy, which was considered a historical right, was to be a voluntary, brotherly one — as Szálasi explains: "different cut of men from brothers of the same stock." Szálasi, like most other Hungarians, never entertained the slightest doubt about the desire of these nationalities to live under Hungarian supremacy in 1930, 1940, or later. Magyar was to be the official language, and the leaders were to be Magyar. Beyond that, the nationalities were to enjoy the "Pax Hungarica," a wide autonomy of popular education, the use of their native tongue, self-government and justice, and the "self-determination of economic interest

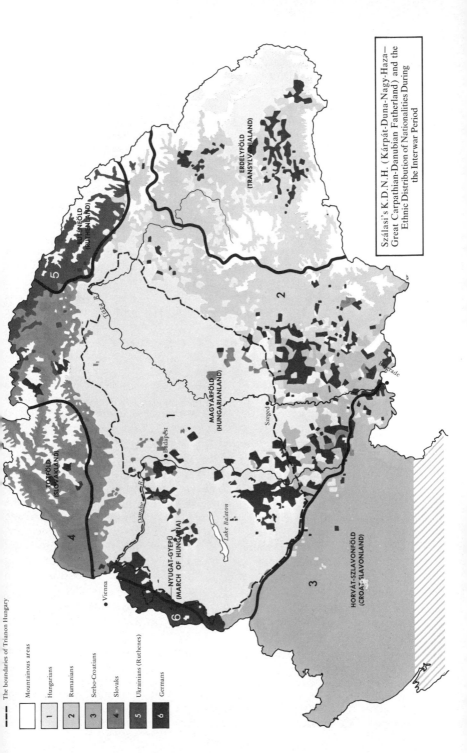

Szálasi's K.D.N.H. (Kárpát-Duna-Nagy-Haza—Great Carpathian-Danubian Fatherland) and the Ethnic Distribution of Nationalities During the Interwar Period

The boundaries of Trianon Hungary

	Mountainous areas
1	Hungarians
2	Rumanians
3	Serbo-Croatians
4	Slovaks
5	Ukrainians (Ruthenes)
6	Germans

ERDÉLYFÖLD
(TRANSYLVANIALAND)

RUTÉNFÖLD
(RUTHENIALAND)

TÓTFÖLD
(SLOVAKLAND)

MAGYARFÖLD
(HUNGARIANLAND)

NYUGAT-GYEPÜ
(MARCH OF HUNGARIA)

HORVÁT-SZLAVONFÖLD
(CROAT-SLAVONLAND)

Tisza R.

Danube R.

Lake Balaton

• Budapest

• Vienna

Szeged

Belgrade

groups." He considered both nationalism and internationalism obsolete; his new system of "co-nationalism" was the solution for the Carpathian Basin.

The new state was to be established by the Hungarian Army, which was to enjoy a commanding position in it in order "to force the nations back to the shaken pillars of Religion, Patriotism, and Discipline." After his K.D.N.H. was established, the inviolability of its borders must be guaranteed by a treaty to be signed by Britain, France, Poland and Russia. Germany is conspicuously absent among the contemplated co-signers.* But this does not mean that Szálasi trusted German intentions or was not ready to protect Hungary against German encroachments. On the contrary: almost to the very end, he prejudiced his own political future in defending his ideas and Hungary's national interests against compromise with Hitler. It was only in the last phase of the war that this consistency, persistence and inflexibility broke down. But during his career, he never ceased to refer to Hungarians in private conversation in his diary, or in correspondence as "this little people, whom the Germans despise, the Hungarian people," through whom "the whole organization of Europe will come about."

His nation would be a working nation and the way of life a "working peace." He intended to build "an industrialized, highly developed peasant state." The society of this Hungary was to be a classless one with three equally important mainstays: (1) the peasants, "who support the nation," (2) the workers, "who build the nation," and (3) the intelligentsia," who lead the nation." Actually, he paid little attention to the peasant's role in his new state. The road to the peasantry led, according to Szálasi, through nature. But the peasants were not an active factor; they accepted and fought for only those things which had already proven themselves. In a word, they were too conservative for him.

The workers, on the other hand, were ready to experiment with new ideas, and when they adopted an ideology they would fight for it — "every ideology has become victorious as soon as it has been embraced by the workers." But Marxism was bankrupt; it did not answer enough of the problems. Although Marxism, Christianity and Hungarism were the three "positive ideologies" of the world, Marxism must be destroyed because of its materialistic tendencies and its strength, but especially because it was directed from Moscow. Liberalism was dismissed by Szálasi with an understandable contempt, if we take into account its performance in the interwar period. He regarded it as both unjust and weak. Because he hoped to build his future society on the workers, it is not surprising that he considered his movement a genuinely proletarian one and contrasted it in derisive terms with the "drawing room

*Not according to Professor Lackó's work. According to him, Germany had to sign and France was left out of the group of cosigners. Later Szálasi widened his concept into a world order, according to which he divided the universe into three orders: (1) the German order, including Western Europe and European Russia; (2) the Japanese order in Asia and possibly in America, and (3) Hungarism in Southeastern Europe. *Ibid.*, p. 59.

radicalism" of other Fascist movements. He proclaimed the "right and duty" of work, and in Szálasi's state strikes were to be outlawed.

His radicalism became even more pronounced when he spoke about the third mainstay of his future society, the intelligentsia, which "is the leader of the nation and guides it." He had no illusions about the state of corruption within the middle classes and the Hungarian intelligentsia of the neobaroque age. He demanded from it self-respect and spiritual rebirth, and he promised to draw freely from the peasantry and workers for a new intelligentsia. This intelligentsia would be the "national general staff" of his new classless society. He openly proclaimed his ultimate goal, which was socialism.

On the all-important Jewish question, he was a moderate among Hungarian Fascists. He did not regard the Jews as a nation "capable of founding a home" or as a race with "roots in the soil" (like the other nationalities of Hungary), but he did not want to humiliate them, persecute them, or kill them; he wanted them to leave Hungary, and he was even ready to let them take their property with them. It is true that he believed in the "Protocols of the Wise Men of Zion" and considered the Jews the chief culprits of both capitalism and Marxism, which he often called Judeo-Bolshevism. But he considered this a question to be solved not according to foreign patterns and not during the war. As far as racism is concerned, he seemed to be a believer in the racial theory but showed remarkable inconsistencies. His racism was by no means as infallible and clear as Hitler's or Alfred Rosenberg's.*

In the matter of religion, he was a devout Catholic. He spoke constantly about a "Christain moral order," but at the same time he believed church and state had to be separated. The guiding Christianity was to be a Turanian one and not, as one of these ideologists—Dr. R. Vágó—put it, a corrupted "Jewish version of Christianity." ** The concept of illegitimate birth was to be

---

*All Hungarian Fascists faced this dilemma. To formulate a Hungarian racist theory in the strictest sense of the word, one faced two insurmountable obstacles: (1) The Hungarian people (especially its middle classes, which professed to be racists) were hopelessly mixed with other peoples (German, Slovakian, Croatian and others); (2) also, because true racism is *uncompromisingly exclusive*, this would have meant an *open, unequivocal proclamation of the oppression of nationalities.* Integral revision, which was, after all, the avowed goal of all Fascist movements in Hungary, would have become in that case rather difficult. Consequently, Hungarian racism was to be a very inconsistent and imperfect one. Called "Turanian-Aryanism," in variance with German Nazism, it was directed *exclusively* against the Jews.

**Although even Szálasi, while professing to be a faithful son of the church, developed his own theory about the origin of Christ. Very much like Hitler, Szálasi, too, found the idea of Jesus being of Jewish descent intolerable. Hitler made an Aryan out of Christ during his table talks. Szálasi improved his days while in prison in 1938 by establishing "with the help of the Bible" the family tree of the Redeemer — arriving at the conclusion that, after all, He is not Jewish! Jesus, according to Szálasi, belonged to the "Godvanian race" (whatever that means), which is related to the Hungarian! Lackó, *op. cit.,* p. 54.

abolished, divorces restricted to cases of "national interest," and only church weddings were to be considered legal. The family was to be the basic unit of society, to be strengthened by all possible means, and every citizen had to belong to a church of his choice.

Besides his sincere devotion to the common Hungarian man and consequently to social justice, there was another tenet basic to his framework of ideas: he insisted inflexibly (and impractically) on legality and the principle that leaders must come to power "by the common will of the Nation and the Head of the State." Although he refused to recognize the electoral abuses and the Parliament elected on the basis of them, he nevertheless recognized Horthy's position as legal. Perhaps this was so because he believed in monarchy and considered Horthy a kind of *homo regius*. In case of free elections, he did not doubt for a moment that the will of Hungarians and of the nationalities would call him to the helm of his dream state (he first named his movement the Party of National Will). After coming constitutionally to power, he would establish a relationship with Horthy like that between Victor Emmanuel III and Mussolini.

These are the main points of Hungarism, the idea that according to Szálasi was perfection itself, the more because "the fall of Hungarism would mean the fall of National Socialism." "Not so much as the dotting of an 'i' could be changed in it." The Arrow Cross party was the body, the flesh only; Hungarism was the spirit. Szálasi had a deep, unshakable faith in his calling as leader — sole leader, of course: "There is but one politician in the state: the leader. The rest are experts." He wished, with the preservation of Horthy's regency, to reestablish the position of the palatine, a position which he reserved for himself and which would entail dictatorial powers. He was a mystic, a spiritualist participating in seances to the very end of his career, and he was indifferent to the practical, worldly aspects of his party program or tactics, and even to the question of membership. He who does not have faith in Hungarism or Szálasi as leader — let him go! Even alone, Szálasi would accomplish everything, "by that secret force" within him. Consequently, "every party member *MUST* accept the ideology of Hungarism and *MUST* accept the Arrow Cross party as the practical instrument for the realization of Hungarism."

During the persecutions, the Arrow Cross party established both secret and legally operating groups, the names of which were adapted from archaic Turanian-Hungarian terminology — almost a must for the nationalistic rightist movements. Szálasi was to be party leader (P.V. — *Pártvezető*) and later, after assuming power, national leader as spiritual leader of the party. Kálmán Hubay was the party president in an administrative capacity. The various departments were the councils for land building, party building, recruitment, industrial recruitment, propaganda, social problems, and ideology.

After 1938, the government banned state employees from politics, mainly in order to keep them out of Fascist extremist parties. Consequently there were secret clan organizations formed where public servants were registered by number rather than by name. Also, the land building council had about

1,500-2,000 secret members besides its legal membership, mostly intellectuals drafting projects for social, economic, military and other reforms, laws and bills for the time when Szálasi would assume power. The party militia was a secret organization which remained inside the party buildings, not daring to appear on the streets until Szálasi took power. There were some attempts in the late thirties to repeat the scenes of Weimar in the streets of Hungary when Arrow Cross toughs came out and organized scuffles in furtherance of what was called (*Eszmevédelem*) "Defense of Ideas", but the stronghanded Bethlenite minister of interior, the terror of the Arrow Cross, Keresztes-Fischer, did not tolerate street fights and scuffles. Szálasi also believed in the corporative system as every good Fascist did.

These were the main trends of the ideology and the organizational framework of the only Fascist mass movement of Hungary.[71] We shall see how the Arrow Cross operated in practice and how many of Szálasi's ideas were realized. So much is already clear: for good or bad his ideas were by no means a copy of Nazism or fascism or any other Fascist movement.

After creating the soul, in 1933-34 Szálasi set about placing it into a body. Following the advice of Napoleon, he was now trying to find bayonets for his idea in order to revolutionize Hungarian life. He first approached the Social Democrats and conferred with Manó Buchinger about the compatibility of the two positions.[72] That the Social Democrats considered him a mixture of fool and *agent provocateur* did not help matters much.[73] He then approached the Fascist wing of the Christian party to negotiate with the Wolff-Csilléry group, with one result — he came away with many new ideas for working out a practical program for the realization of Hungarism. Simultaneously, he published in 1933 a pamphlet excerpted from one of his former studies, *Plan for the Construction of the Hungarian State*,* which got him into serious trouble with his superiors. In 1932, just after he had received a promotion to the rank of major on the general staff, Gömbös transferred him to a provincial garrison.

Gömbös was not happy about his activities. He was having enough trouble getting rid of his own restrictions imposed by Bethlen and making Hungary safe for his own brand of bourgeois fascism with himself as *Vezér*. He tried to get Szálasi to join him, but Szálasi found his conditions incompatible with Hungarism. After a stormy interview, Gömbös warned him that there was "no room in Hungary for more than one politicizing general staff officer, and that the single vacancy was already filled." Yet Gömbös recognized the mystique around the man, because after Szálasi left, he predicted that Szálasi would sit one day in his chair.[74] During the elections of 1935, Gömbös offered a mandate to Szálasi, which predictably was refused.

Finally, Szálasi's situation was made unbearable enough in the army that he resigned his commission (March 1935), and it was after his resignation that he founded the Party of National Will (*Nemzeti Akarat Pártja*), consisting of

*Szálasy, *A Magyar állam felépítésének terve*, (Budapest, 1933). During his earlier career, Szálasi signed his name often with a "y" (suggesting noble Hungarian ancestry) rather than with the humble "i."

him, a certain S. Csia, a typist and two members. The program adopted by this group was called *Aim and Demands*.[75] It explained the doctrine of Hungarism, and had some practical and some impractical propositions for its application.* This program, uniting the "Trinity of Blood and Soil and Work," showed both in its practical and extremely impractical aspects a sincere concern with the common people which went far beyond the usual lip service of other Fascist movements where, usually, only the social justice of anti-Semitism was meant seriously.

During a by-election in April 1936, he polled 942 votes out of 12,051 in a provincial constituency, and he was also defeated during a by-election in October 1935 in Szentendre.[76] Although one deputy, Csoór, who later deserted him, was allowed to enter parliament with a P.N.W. program, Gömbös evidently did not wish to grant Szálasi parliamentary immunity.

After 1935, we see a stagnation in the growth of Szálasi's movement. These were the months of Gömbös' ascendancy, and nobody could foresee how fast he would depart the scene, leaving his work unfinished, his partisans without guidance. Later they were always referred to as "Gömbös' Orphans." (*Gömbös árvák*).

Most of Gömbös' Orphans were left in a thoroughly Szeged Fascist *Gleichgeschaltet* armed forces, where, both because of the *"esprit de corps"* (Szálasi was, after all, a former officer of the general staff) and the Fascist spirit of the military, Szálasi had a strong and valuable support long before he acquired the support of the masses. These officers were sympathizers and helpers rather than devoted Arrow Cross men. Of his two most influential friends, one was General Jenö Ruszkay (Ranzenberger), a Gömbös man, a Swabian who, according to the secretary of the Nazi ambassador, "set the German interests always above the Hungarian."[77] He was an active member of the Officer Detachments, and had specialized in kidnapping Hungarian leftist exiles from Vienna after the triumpth of Horthy.[78] The other was General Jenö Rátz (a Rumanian, originally Răţiu), chief of staff, and later an Imrédist politician, like Ruszkay elevated by Gömbös to a responsible position. Szálasi had many friends among the military even in the entourage of Horthy, and what was more important later, among the Hungarian military attachés abroad. But in order to understand his spectacular rise we must consider the political situation created both inside and outside Hungary by the death of Gömbös.

---

*The program proposes in point six a moratorium on all debts; in point seven, it proposes the state should pay these debts to the debtors; in point eight, it promises a credit financed by the state to all those in need. Török, *op. cit.*, p. 20.

CHAPTER V

La Grande Illusion

Looking over the history of the European peoples I find no example where sincere and devoted dedication to peaceful prosperity appealed more strongly to them than the glory of war, won battles, and conquests . . ..

Bismarck

Oh we shall allow them even sin, they are weak and helpless, and they will love us like children because we allow them to sin. We shall tell them that every sin will be expiated if it's done with our permission.

Dostoevsky

1

Gömbös died at the beginning of October 1936 in a sanatorium near Munich to which he had withdrawn for treatment. This unexpected event threw the whole Szeged Fascist cause in Hungary into disarray and created a wholly new situation and perspective for the radical Fascists.

We have seen how Gömbös fortified his position and how by 1936 he felt the time was ripe for the "revision" of his earlier "revisions." The Bethlen-Horthy wing had been outmaneuvered but not beaten when Gömbös closed his eyes. Horthy even maintains that he realized the extent of Gömbös' machinations and strength by 1936 (in his words, he "came to the conclusion that Gömbös was not a gentleman") and was determined to remove him from power. Only when he saw that Gömbös was a dying man did he desist.[1] But he gave the reins of government to the versatile Kálmán Darányi, who was eager to please everybody and was so good at it that he even succeeded in winning the confidence of every faction, including that of the Gömbös Orphans. It would have been interesting to see how the Szeged Fascist Parliament, administration, articulate public opinion, military, and the well-armed M.O.V.E. detachments would have reacted to any *Csáklyás* attempt to remove their *Vezér* from power. It was a German ambassador who supplied the most probable speculation: when a high-ranking Hungarian official told him after the death of Gömbös that "he was finished anyway," von Mackensen replied, "You would never have got the man out of his position alive."[2]

But possession is nine points of the law. Through the instrument of the Government party with its wide limits for opinion as long as it generally fell in line with that of the party leader, and given Darányi's ability to rise above principle and his impeccable credentials as far as fascism was concerned, Szeged tempers could be kept under control. Rátz and Ruszkay with Marton, Sztranyavszky and Antal made some feeble attempts to install a Fascist

123

dictatorship, and no one can predict what would have happened if a man other than Darányi had been named premier. As it was, these plots and talks came to no consequence.[3] The neobaroque edifice weathered the storm again; it was even able to swing the pendulum back a bit.

The Government party, the time-honored instrument of the ultraconservatives to run Hungary, was the first target of the Bethlenites. This party, thanks to the Gömbös elections, now looked like a unified Fascist party. Szeged mandates could not be taken away, but Marton's and Sztranyavszky's control over the party apparatus was broken. There was an end to the heyday of the Advance Guards and their spying and informing, and provincial files were brought to the Government party center. The youth, women, propaganda and cultural sections, the most telling signs of totalitarianization of the party, were abolished. The premier's role as party leader was reaffirmed. Some very inadequate steps were taken to separate administration from the Government party. The opportunistic Szeged Fascist delegates acknowledged these changes, seething inside, but knowing also on which side their bread was buttered.*

And the pendulum continued its swing toward ultraconservatism. The oddly assorted opposition of Smallholders, Legitimists, Liberals, Christians and Social Democrats, tacitly recognizing Bethlen as their leader in Parliament (he occupied an opposition bench as an independent), combined to try to undo the work of Gömbös. As usual, it was Bethlen who called the tune. He spoke rarely, but what he said was Horthy's position, and it had great weight. He declared that he expected Darányi to liquidate fascism as far as the press, youth and the attacks against private capital went. He significantly added that anti-Semitism was not the only criterion for being a right-wing politician. Then, in the same vein, he observed that "to determine who is a rightist and a leftist is a great and difficult job," because in Hungary the criteria for defining the political right and the political left are very different from those in other countries.[4]

It is not difficult to imagine the German reaction to all this. Hitler had counted heavily on the implementation of the Gömbös-Göring agreement. Now Darányi, who like Horthy and other leaders found out about the agreement only after Gömbös died, had to inform the German ambassador that it was no longer valid. This brought about a complete change in Hitler's attitude toward the Hungarian government. From then on Germany did its best to conspire with the dissatisfied factions of Hungarian Fascists, egged on in its fury by agents like Mecsér and later Baky, and to stir up trouble within the Swabian minority. In addition, thousands of German "tourists" flooded Hungary, visiting even the remotest corners of the country, drawing parallels in conversation between the "progressive" conditions in Nazi Germany and

---

*But the spirit of the Parliament "made by Gömbös" became clear when a Legitimist deputy, Count Széchenyi, spoke about the persecution of Catholics in Nazi Germany. There was an explosion of abuse from all sides of the House. Certainly the Christian National spirit had traveled a long way since 1919. O.N.K., May 26, 1937, p. 712.

the "feudal" atmosphere in Hungary, and especially between the commendable settlement of the Jewish problem in the Reich and the regrettable state of the question in Hungary. Nazi subversion was in full swing.

In March 1937, the Gömbös Orphans (Mecsér, Marton) plotted a *coup d'état* with German help, if not instigation, which was discovered before it could begin. Many police officials and military men were transferred or removed, and some German diplomats were recalled.* Marton's and Baross' denials of the plot to Professor Macartney should not be given much credit as disproof.[5] This abortive coup resulted in the long overdue recovery of guns and ammunition which Gömbös had issued to *M.O.V.E.* The secret societies were disarmed, and the conservatives seemed to retain control.[6] Horthy also removed some high-ranking army officers of Gömbös' nomination, although it was characteristic that he was appallingly ignorant of the mood of the army and for one Szeged Fascist officer he substituted another (Rátz) as chief of staff.

All this should be taken into account when we consider the spectacular rise of the Arrow Cross in 1937. Gömbös could have united the Fascists in so far as they were of the "middle class of Hungarian gentlemen" or the petite bourgeoisie. With nationalistic slogans and aims, with his charisma and dynamism, and with the enactment of some moderate social reforms on one hand and the use of police methods where necessary on the other, he could have carried the lower classes with him. He had also the blessings and possible support of Hitler. But once the Government party's official position became anti-Szeged Fascist, the unity that might have been forged under Gömbös disappeared forever from Hungarian fascism.**The Gömbös Orphans bided their time, trusting the spirit of the age to give them their chance and a new leader, and in the meantime withholding excessive opposition lest it prejudice their jobs in the army or administration or elsewhere. Junior officers, smaller bureaucrats and other minor existences annoyed by the apparent return of conservatism and the ephemeral character of the change of the guard turned radical Fascist. As for the workers and the less apathetic segments of the agrarian proletariat, they grew ever more impatient, and the fact that the Social Democrats and liberals who cooperated with Bethlen did not advocate a very radical social policy did not endear a democratic alternative to the lower classes any more than before.

*Darányi personally had to make apologies in Parliament for "the representative of a friendly power, accredited in our country" who was allegedly involved in the M.O.V.E. plot. *Ibid.*, March 10, 1937, pp. 126-27. Nevertheless, the "representative of the friendly power" von Mackensen, so close to the "Gömbös Orphans," was quickly recalled, and replaced with von Erdmansdorff. Many other members of the German embassy staff were, because of their contacts with the plotters, also recalled.

**János Salló, one of the leaders of the radical right in Hungary, made an interesting statement in December 1937, saying that "the activity of the so-called right radical movements started in earnest only after the death of Gömbös." *Virradat*, December 4, 1937.

The year 1937, however, was a bright year for the lower classes. The economy improved greatly. A few long overdue social measures were enacted (a forty-eight-hour week, paid vacation, Sunday rest, some marginal social protection for agricultural workers), and the Franchise Reform Bill, which finally abolished the open ballot, was passed, although it kept the number of the enfranchised ridiculously low. But by that time, the "revolution of rising expectations" had begun. Such unrest comes rarely at the bottom of an economic and social trough, but rather when improvement begins and is insufficient, or when the course of reform is considered to be endangered. Consequently, a kind of frenzy swept over Hungary and the whole No-Man's-Land of Europe in those years.

There was incessant agitation, everybody felt that change must come, that the peace settlement of Trianon had failed in every respect quite as much as the social system. Everybody was looking forward to a messianic miracle, a panacea. The events in Germany and Spain and the situation in Austria seemed not only to justify this feeling but also to point the way. People were searching for parties through which they could express their sincere desire for social justice; others, in their eagerness to jump on the bandwagon in time, secured three or four "bandwagons" (Fascist parties) for themselves. Anti-Semitism reached a pitch never before known in Hungary, and for the first time in Hungarian history it began to reach the lower classes. By 1937, the middle classes could see no Hungarian problem except that posed by the position of the Jewish middle class in Hungary.* Of course, in that year a well-composed note from Paris or London to Berlin would have helped immeasurably to bring the Fascist "enthusiasts" of Hungary, as well as others, to their senses. But such a note did not come until much later — and then it was too late.

*It was the middle class which steadfastly criticized and opposed the widening of the franchise, and opposed, also violently, the secret ballot. It is to them that Professor Gyula Szekfü addressed his prophetic article entitled "The Middleclasses and the Franchise." "I don't know," he writes, "why are we, those who belong to the middle classes, afraid that if the poor acquire political power, they will be victimized by demagoguery. We see this happening to our middle classes!" This middle class became illiterate, incapable of any realistic evaluation of the situation as far as foreign policy is concerned; they build their revisionist hopes on dreams "which do not even bear examination without discrediting [any Hungarian of common sense]." Professor Szekfü continues by explaining that the Hungarian middle classes (of the present) are devoid of any political or social instinct. "Nowadays we hear in our middle classes plenty of words spoken against large estates and big capital — words translated from foreign languages — [but] the attitude of these middle classes is, nevertheless, determined by such vested interests; if we perpetuate the rule of our present middle classes, the coming of crises can be taken for granted. But the possibility of an internal social disaster, and even of an external political disaster, is by no means excluded." "A középosztály és a választójog," *Korunk Szava* December 15, 1936. Also, Lackó *Nyilasok, nemzetiszocialisták,* pp. 87-88.

126

Into the vacuum left by Gömbös moved Szálasi, much against his own will. Not that he did not want to take power. He simply did not know what spirits he had unleashed, and many of those who gathered around him attributed to him attitudes (excessive anti-Semitism, subservience to Hitler, animosity to Horthy) that were not his. But in such an atmosphere it was much more important what people believed about a Fascist leader than what he really stood for. So although in 1936 few people had heard of Szálasi, by the end of 1937 he was the best known, most loved or feared Fascist leader in Hungary.

What kind of people were the leaders and the rank and file of Szálasi's movement? From the moment of its birth, there had been a serious split in the ranks of the movement between the middle and lower middle class segment and that of the popular masses. This split was clearly visible even in the leading echelons. According to one of Horthy's leading secret police officers, "The extremists [were allowed] to have a constant, invigorating influence [in the Arrow Cross], and the party leadership treated them with deference in order that [the party] should not lose its contact with the masses."[7] One group of Arrow Cross leaders were "activists" (mozgalmisták). Most of them came of the lower middle and the working classes. There were many known Socialists and Communists among them (F. Schallmayer, I. Péntek, etc.). The "activists" specialized in winning the support of the workers, and were very loyal to Szálasi. On the other hand their contempt for those Arrow Cross leaders and members whom they derisively called "Spiessbürgers" (petit-bourgeois) knew no bounds. Open and hidden clashes inside the party between the two groups were an everyday occurrence.[8] It was the activist group that was responsible for the shoddiest Arrow Cross activities and outrages. As one of their worst representatives, Ferenc Omelka, explained: "Szálasi or even Hubay can not do the dirty work. We have to take care of that."[9] It would be mistaken to conclude however, that these people were nothing but criminals and did nothing but engage in criminal activities.

The middle classes were represented in the party leadership by many young officers of the lower ranks. Some young lieutenants and first lieutenants were only sympathizers. Together with the other large middle-class group of the Arrow Cross, the lower echelons of the state white-collar employees, they were later afraid to give vent to their feelings openly. Their names were kept secret following Szálasi's orders.[10] But many high-ranking officers, because of their personal friendship with Szálasi, lent their names and services to the Arrow Cross. When after one of numerous suppressions the Arrow Cross reappeared on the political scene under a new name, almost always some retired high-ranking officers would sponsor it. (Lieutenant General I. Dobó, Colonel D. Mokcsay, Colonel of Hussars A. Bogyay, and many others.[11] There were some lawyers and doctors in the local leadership of the Arrow Cross. The lower middle classes, retired state employees, the petite bourgeoisie, small artisans and craftsmen were well represented in the rank and file. What was conspicuously absent in the Arrow Cross, both in leadership and membership, was an intellectual of good standing. Doctor

Málnási, the chief ideologist of the movement (besides Szálasi), was perhaps the best available, but it would be an unwarranted compliment to consider him a true intellectual.*

What brought the large numbers of workers and, to a lesser extent, the numerous agrarian proletariat to the Arrow Cross?

András Török was a former Socialist who was well versed in Marxism, but considered the Social Democrats to be a group dominated by petit bourgeois bureaucrats.**When he heard Gömbös' 1932 radio address with its ninety-five points, he expected from him a great social transformation, but Gömbös had failed to fulfill these hopes. Török saw that capitalism was breaking down around him and so was liberalism. "Marxism answered many of his questions, but because of its godless, unpatriotic character (because of its internationalism) he could not adopt it without leaving a great void in his soul as in the soul of the majority of the low classes." "So," continues this Hungarian worker, "because the common people desired a new way of life, we saw as a kind of reaction to Marxism the formation of 'modified Socialisms' like the N.S.D.A.P., the Fascists and the Falange."[12]

According to Török, many workers worshipped Szálasi. In their eyes he was the fearless man who would build a "Hungarosocialist Hungary."***He seemed to them a hero out of a legend, one who abandoned without remorse his position, rank and a promising future in order to "help the suffering, toiling millions of Hungarians."[13]

Few people could decipher the inimitable language of Szálasi's program. Fewer cared about Hungarism as such. These downtrodden, rejected people living outside the pale of "decent" Hungarian society felt the transparent sincerity of Szálasi. They did know of his unostentatious, puritan way of life (an extremely rare phenomenon among Hungarian politicians), his concern with the poor, his originality, his inflexibility, and last but not least that important ingredient of Fascism, a nationalist mystique, was also at hand. His

*Dr. Málnasi, a former Socialist, wrote in a "historical work" in 1959 (one year before the Israelis apprehended Eichmann in Argentina) that the Israeli government is hiding Eichmann on Israeli territory [as a kind of gratitude of the "Wisemen of Zion"] for saving the lives and much of the property of Hungarian Jewish capitalists during 1944 through the deals of the SS (see our chapter "1944"). Málnasi, *A magyar nemzet igaz története*, p. 205.

**Török, *Szálasi álarc nélkül*, p. 4. He came from Békéscsaba, an area which was a leftist stronghold since the end of the nineteenth century. Török was in the Böszörmény movement for a while before he became an Arrow Cross activist specializing in organizing the workers. Lackó, *op. cit.*, p. 60n.

***Török, *op. cit.* p. 33. A contemporary police report ascertains the following fact: "Szálasi organizes the workers exclusively. He organizes a labor movement in Budapest, neglects his [party] organizations in the country . . . His middle class following are worried about this. They are preoccupied [about the fact] that [Szálasi] organizes a class movement." Lackó, *op. cit.*, p. 68.

mystique may seem ridiculous to us; it might have seemed ridiculous to the educated, skeptical intellectuals of the Budapest coffee houses in 1937; but it was not ridiculous to the workers or the petite bourgeoisie. When the workers came to the party meetings, the presence of large groups of proletarians reassured them that they were among their own kind.

Szálasi told them over and over "The worker and the peasant are the axis and the foundation of his movement." The P.N.W. issued a paper, the *New Hungarian Worker (Új Magyar Munkás)*, and the titles were like this: "We Accuse the Bourgeois Society! " or "We demand: Rights, Work and Respect! "[14] It was a definite improvement over the Szeged Fascist atmosphere wherein Gömbös "underlined twenty-five times that he was a conservative." Poor people walked on foot for many days to Budapest just to be able to catch a glimpse of Szálasi.[15] The tremendous vitality of the radical Fascist cause was demonstrated by the fact that practically without a penny (the Germans did not start the large subsidies until 1938), men like the peasant writer József Roósz or the house painter Ferenc Szedlár were able to organize tens of thousands of sympathizers — all this despite the demoralizing and absurd quarrels among factions and the hostility of the authorities, whether from the Gömbös administration or the ultraconservatives.

For all his sincerity, idealism, and inflexible principles, Szálasi was too much in the clouds to notice or to care to notice the things that were going on around him. He was not a realist and even less a politician. We know that by 1937 he regularly visited spiritualists and participated in seances.[16] These aspects of Hungarism impinged much more on his mind than such trivial questions as where his party got its financial support, or what were the activities of some of his partisans, or whether certain of his subordinates supported relations with Germany which were incompatible with his own ideas. The fact that he stood up steadfastly when reality finally did get through to him* should not, does not and cannot exempt him from tremendous responsibility for subsequent events consequent on his inattention. He launched spirits, the existence of which he was unwilling or even unable to recognize, let alone to control.

As far as the practical aspects of P.N.W. policy were concerned, in the general confusion after the death of Gömbös, Szálasi succeeded in bringing a memorandum to the Regent's attention in which he proposed a military

---

*The writer remembers a characteristic scene from his boyhood. A prominent Arrow Cross man named Andor Bodolay lived in the same apartment building in Budapest as the writer's family. Once in 1942, Szálasi came to visit Bodolay. As they approached the elevator, a tenant, an elderly Jewish lady, was in the process of getting out of it. Mr. Bodolay pushed her rudely and unceremoniously out of Szálasi's way. Szálasi seemed to be in a state of trance. He could not possibly know offhand that she was Jewish but she was an old lady, and he did not even seem to notice the incident; he continued to gaze into a blue beyond. The writer stood very close to the scene, and he can only reflect, more than two decades later, that this scene was to be repeated later on a much more tragic and larger scale.

takeover and free elections after that — the elections bringing the P.N.W. to power, of course. Szálasi and Horthy would run Hungary the way Mussolini ran Italy, with the king. Szálasi also requested an audience with Horthy.[17] All this led to nothing. The Regent's entourage blocked the request for audience, and Horthy wanted to know only what Szálasi was up to, without any particular sympathy or antipathy toward him.

Szálasi's breakthrough came in the frantic, tense atmosphere of the spring of 1937. Apart from the general political void, a chain reaction of incidents helped him. For one thing, Horthy had shown Darányi Szálasi's memorandum, concealing its real authorship. Darányi found out the authorship through a Szeged Fascist politician, and both the ultraconservatives and the Gömbös Orphans were immediately greatly concerned. Was Horthy toying with the idea of a military dictatorship in cooperation with Szálasi? That would put them, of course, in second place. Szálasi acquired ominous significance in the eyes of the neobaroque edifice; perhaps "there was some higher support behind him."

At about the same time Szálasi began to get the support of the "revolution of rising expectations," and it came not only from the masses. Those who wanted to jump on the bandwagon in time arrived in ever-increasing numbers, thinking that Horthy was behind Szálasi. Szálasi unwittingly encouraged their expectations by flooding Budapest with leaflets: "Our aim is to take power. With the nation — for the nation! Endurance: Szálasi! "* Then came the Gömbös Orphans-inspired plot by M.O.V.E. Szálasi at the same time started his radical *New Hungarian Worker*. That was too much. Eckhardt called him to question in Parliament, quoting radical passages from the newspaper, and Szálasi was promptly arrested on the basis of this and released pending appeal. A whispering campaign said "powerful influences" had got him out of jail. After his release, Szálasi and Csía visited Germany.** The P.N.W. was dissolved amid rumors of the immense strength of its membership, which some claimed had reached as high as 50,000. Yet the confiscated party funds did not even amount to $100. All this persecution and the mysterious, triumphant release increased Szálasi's popularity tremendously. By appealing to his doctrine that the party is only the body and Hungarism the soul, he could keep the Hungarist movement going with neither official organization nor membership.

As the Fascist tide grew both at home and abroad, there was a brief spell of radical Fascist unity. In October 1937, in a mass meeting in Budapest,

*These leaflets were issued in the name of the executive committee of the First Socialnationale, signed by workers "who became disillusioned with communism." Another leaflet of the First Socialnationale "rejects even the idea of participating in the work of the [present] Parliament" because Parliament should be considered "the most massive cheating of the people." Lackó, *op. cit.,* pp. 70-71.

**According to the reports of police informers, Szálasi and Csía visited Germany a year before and twice, not once. Both in August and in October, 1936, they spent several weeks in Berlin, Nürenberg, and Munich. His contacts and activities in Germany are unknown. *Ibid.,* p. 67.

some radical Gömbös Orphans in the National Front led J. Salló and the infamous journalist Rajniss; a remnant of the Böszörmény movement; followers of Balogh and the Race-Protecting Socialist party (whose leader, László Endre, was in the same secret society [*Magyar Élet Szövetsége* – Association of Hungarian Life] as Szálasi);[18] the Irredentist camp; the Pálffy and Festetics groups; and some less significant Fascist splinter parties into the United Hungarian National Socialist party, with Szálasi, Balogh, and Count Lajos Széchenyi on the executive committee.

Szálasi's luck did not hold for long. When the opposition in all its heterogeneity opted for an eventual Habsburg restoration, Balogh saw fit to answer them by announcing the formation of a national kingdom with Horthy as king! This irresponsible step, taken without even consulting Szálasi, let alone the Regent, gave the circle around Horthy an opportunity to turn his mind definitely against Szálasi, despite the fact that (1) Szálasi was not foretold of Balogh's action and that (2) he fanatically insisted on his scheme "to take power by the common will of the Nation and the Head of State." Horthy was convinced that Szálasi was plotting his overthrow and was his most dangerous enemy, and in that conviction he never wavered. Szálasi was arrested again and faced with absurd charges. On November 30, he drew a few months' suspended sentence for "seditious conspiracy."

Yet, the enthusiasts of his following did not become disheartened. They now had a headquarters,* increasing support, the spirit of the age was on their side – and Péchy, the clairvoyant, was prophesying that Szálasi would lead Hungary in 1938 to a victorious revolution and would assume power. On New Year's Eve Szálasi flooded Budapest with leaflets proclaiming: "1938 is ours! – Szálasi, Széchenyi."[19] This, in the atmosphere of the approaching *Anschluss* was more than just publicity. It was a yardstick of success generating rumors of a pending coup.

3

Before continuing the Fascist story in Hungary proper, we must say something about the foreign political situation, because of its general nature on the one hand, and because of the Hitlerian manner of conducting foreign relations in No-Man's-Land on the other. For foreign policy in Hungary had become inseparable from the internal situation, and it had a profound impact on the Hungarian Fascist movements.

It was the irony of Gömbös' fate that he died some weeks before the realization of his long-standing dream; in November 1936 Mussolini proclaimed the Rome-Berlin Axis. But the relationship of the Axis to Hungary was very different from Gömbös' dream. In 1937 there was a great deal of confusion in the eastern part of Central Europe, the direct consequence of French inaction in face of the German occupation of the Rhineland a year

---

*Andrássy Út (street) 60. This building on the famous boulevard of Budapest was the gift of Endre to the Szálasi movement. It was to acquire ominous significance after 1945 as the headquarters of Communist secret police, the dreaded Á.V.H.

earlier. All those countries that had based their policies on expected French support were now hurriedly trying to readjust. Hitler made friendly overtures to the Yugoslavia of Milan Stojadinović, to Poland and even to Rumania, carefully differentiating between official relations and internal support for the Fascist groups. Only the two victims, Austria and Czechoslovakia, clearly did not have a chance. The Little Entente was becoming more amd more meaningless as an instrument of security even against Hungary, let alone against Germany and Italy.

Mussolini was reorienting his policies toward Austria, which he had abandoned by then, and also toward Germany and Yugoslavia. Doing this, he left Hungary out in the cold after he had used her for a decade with a characteristic cheerful pragmatism.

The Western powers, if they cared about the area at all, gave Hungary their usual good advice: Form a united front against Germany with the Little Entente or possibly Austria and forget your difficulties for the time being. This, of course, was a notion that fit nicely into the pattern of wishful thinking current in London and Paris. What it did not satisfy was the Hungarians' need to know what Hungary would derive from such an arrangement.

Under such circumstances, German-Hungarian relations became the most important single factor in the life of Hungary. And these relations after the repudiation of the Gömbös-Göring agreement were very bad indeed. Hitler initiated his double policy, which meant he carried on official relations with the government in power and subversion through the three denominations of fascism in Hungary — the Szeged, the radical and fellow traveling Fascists, and the by now very unreasonable Swabian minority's Nazi movements.*

There began a mutual exchange of insults between the German and Hungarian press, and there were other signs that Germany was displeased and that she was in the position to give substantial expression to her displeasure — the whole course of events pointing to a European, even to a world, war. In November 1937, the halfhearted conservative restoration which followed Gömbös' death sent a Hungarian government delegation to Hitler to iron out difficulties and to take soundings. This delegation arrived some days after the historic meeting known to historians as the Hossbach Conference, which decided the fate of Europe for the twentieth century. Hitler decided to move immediately against Austria and Czechoslovakia.[20]

The Hungarians were left in the dark about Hitler's imminent plans concerning Austria, although by that time the *Anschluss* was seen in Budapest as a foregone conclusion. Responsible conservative circles were not happy

---

*Grave provocations began almost immediately by Swabians after the renunciation of the Gömbös-Göring agreement. The suddenness and intensity of the incidents excluded the possibility of spontaneity. In the town of Elek, for example, a Swabian lowered the Hungarian flag on the main square and ripped it publicly to pieces. When K. von Neurath visited Budapest in June, 1937 and Kánya complained about this and similar incidents, the German foreign minister refused to discuss the matter. *Allianz*, pp. 146-47.

about it: the Bethlenites and the opposition as a whole harbored no illusions as to what could be the effects of Nazi Germany on their border, either with respect to Hungarian national interests or to morale among the Fascist enthusiasts at home. But there was little Hungary could do about it. After the defection of its only member of consequence, Italy, the Rome treaty was dead.[21]

In Czechoslovakia, Hitler stuck to his old plans; he needed Hungarian cooperation in the dismemberment of that country. It is reasonable to assume that he deliberately delayed the visit of Darányi and Kánya until after the Hossbach Conference.[22] It was not military help that Hitler wanted, but to finish the action, to face the world with a *fait accompli*. Therefore, he did not wish to leave the mountainous Slovak part of Czechoslavakia unsecured after he swallowed Bohemia and Moravia. Hungary could have that, "even Pressburg."[23] The Hungarians were pleased and returned to Budapest, but not before offering to have talks on the subject on the general staff level. The offer was politely but firmly refused by the Nazis.[24] In the meantime, the Hungarians played fair toward Austria, never permitting tasteless press attacks of the sort that Virginio Gayda conducted in his *Giornale d'Italia*. Hungary recognized Franco, after a year of praising in the mass media the examples of the Alcázar in Toledo and of Don José Moscardó as symbols of the Fascist spirit so superior to "democratic decadence" and "godless bolshevism." Then, on March 12, 1938, without any previous notice to Budapest, Hitler occupied Austria. It was a development that fundamentally changed Hungary's internal situation and her external position.

By the beginning of 1938, the Szeged Fascists had recovered from the confusion caused by the conservative comeback and the general disarray of the year 1937. Supported by events abroad, they were ready to express their ideas to the government. They chose to do this through a memorandum drawn up by the highest echelon of army officers, men of the temper of Ruszkay and Rátz, for Fascism had become the esprit de corps of the army, which had been taught by Gömbös that it had a holy mission, a Fascist one, to save Hungary. Nobody doubted the imminence of war, but the Bethlenites believed in a long-run axis defeat, and consequently wished to keep Hungary out of it. In this view they clashed with the military, which was convinced of German invincibility and wanted an armament program. The memorandum of the generals to this effect was duly presented to Horthy.

It followed a typical Szeged Fascist pattern for the salvation of Hungary, epitomizing the Szeged spirit. It called for the establishment of a dictatorship because it seemed to be in the spirit of the age and because Hungary could not afford to lag behind. It asked the Regent in the name of the Officers Corps (1) to initiate a nationalist, Christian, popular program which would consist primarily in replacing Jews with Christians in the economy; (2) to exclude Jews from the press, theatre, cinema and cultural life; (3) to implement progressive taxation of big firms; (4) to assure that no more mammoth salaries be paid; (5) to institute measures against nepotism and accumulation of posts; (6) to appoint unemployed intellectuals to the posts they were fitted for; (7) to persecute "mercilessly" all left-wing agitation; (8)

to design a socioeconomic policy to provide for a greater distribution of land; and finally (9) to guarantee more liberty for Fascist organizations.[25] It was clear that such measures could not be piloted through even the Gömbös-made Parliament, so the establishment of a dictatorship was considered imperative.[26] The memorandum proposed little in the military field. But it was drawn up to make possible the armament program — which according to the military politicians would always be blocked by the *csáklyások* and the opposition, and by the demo-liberal, Judeo-Bolshevist Jews until they were eliminated effectively from the life of Hungary. And of course the measures proposed by the memorandum were to serve exactly that purpose. After a change of guard was carried out in the manner proposed by the Szeged Fascists, the rearmament and the securing of Hungary's place under the sun would be easy.

The Regent did not feel enthusiastic about the proposals, to say the least. When Bethlenite minister of finance Fábinyi blocked the rearmament plans on financial grounds (and in a less avowed manner on political grounds), the thwarted Szeged military now had to look for a new tool. They found it in the youthful president of the national bank, Béla Imrédy. After leaving the Gömbös government, Imrédy had been biding his time, following world events attentively. He maintained the best possible relations with the Jewish financiers, especially those in the City of London. In 1938, when he saw the Fascist rainbow rising high, his ambitions rose even higher. Some days before the *Anschluss*, the frustrated Rátz came to see him and presented the memorandum with the Officers Corps' program. He made the proposition that if Imrédy could find the financial means for rearmament,* he would be chosen to work out the political side of the program in place of the obstinate Fábinyi. Imrédy saw opportunity. His insatiable greed for power made him forget his conservative past with astounding speed; he espoused the political side of the program, promising to carry it out if he were put into power and to find the money for rearmament.[27] This agreement reached, Imrédy and Rátz approached the flexible Darányi, who agreed on the secret program with the sole reservation of the dictatorship.

Szálasi, although he had been consulted at the beginning of the Officers Corps action, was now left out of the picture altogether.[28] The resurrected Szeged Idea had no immediate practical need of proletarian Fascist dreamers. At the instigation of his old army crony, Árpád Taby, who served in the entourage of the Regent and László Baky, a major of the gendarmerie (both officers being members of the former counterrevolutionary Officers Detachments), Szálasi now joined in an Arrow Cross plot to seize power. Taby was to keep the army quiet, Baky would mobilize the gendarmerie, and Szálasi would supply the money. The plan, discovered in time, aborted, with the result that Taby was retired from active service and the newly founded United Hungarian National Socialist party was dissolved. Szálasi was put under police supervision.** Baky insured himself against

*The amount needed was 1,000-1,500 million pengös ($250-300 million).

**Taby was a major in Horthy's bodyguards; he was a personal friend and member of the same secret society as Szálasi. He took part in the

possible arrest by doubling his services, he spied on the Arrow Cross for the government's benefit and informed the Arrow Cross about government intentions.[29] Later he tripled his services, adding to his employers the Gestapo and Himmler.[30]

Under Imrédy's influence, Darányi began the old Gömbös tactic of winning over the proletarian enthusiasts — that is the Arrow Cross and Szálasi — to the Szeged Fascists in order to use them and neutralize them at the same time. Meanwhile, Darányi and Imrédy in the greatest secrecy began to work out details of the program. The program was announced in Györ three days before the *Anschluss*, its two most important points being, predictably, anti-Semitic legislation and rearmament. Imrédy duly entered the government as minister of economic coordination. On March 9, two other Szeged Fascists of good standing took over the ministry of justice (anti-Jewish laws) and the ministry of finance (rearmament credits) from the anglophiles.

At that point Hitler entered Vienna, and there was tremendous joy in Fascist ranks in Hungary. In downtown Budapest, crowds of Hungarians unable to see anything but the Jewish question gathered before the German Government Tourist Office (which with its huge Hitler portrait in the window had become a shrine for Hungarian Fascists) to rejoice at the news of German troops reaching the Hungarian border and swallowing Burgenland. The opposition was terrified, not to mention the Jews. Horthy, as usual, was prey to changing moods. Before the *Anschluss* he had made statements to the Nazi ambassador to the effect that he considered the *Anschluss* a foregone conclusion and he approved of it.[31] But as he listened to radio reports of the entry of German troops into Vienna, his Habsburg memories overwhelmed him, and he wept. He now had more to lament than vanished Habsburg glories — much more.

The Germans lost no time establishing a Gestapo office in Vienna for permanent contact with Hungarian Fascists and the Swabian minority. This subdivision, under the able leadership of Dr. Willy Höttl, was set up to coordinate and finance the work of swaying into the pattern of the Nazi *Südostraum* concept the heterogeneous but powerful Hungarian Nazi sympathies.[32]

Without Horthy's authorization, his versatile prime minister Darányi started negotiations with the Arrow Cross to bring it in to the Szeged Fascist fold. Darányi promised to make a place for a number of mandates for the Arrow Cross in the coming elections.[33] It is not without significance that contacts between Darányi and Szálasi were made through a Gömbös Orphan secretary of state, A. Petneházy, and through the chief of the Budapest police, who was supposed to keep Szálasi under police supervision.[34] Szálasi promised not to seek power by illegal means, but that did not seem necessary. In a by-election, with the help of Darányi and German money and trucks

---

founding of P.N.W. When imprisoned in 1938, Szálasi first wanted Taby to become his regent. But Taby chose a different career; it should be considered characteristic of Hungarian politics that during the elections of 1939 Taby was elected as a government party deputy! Lackó, *op. cit.*, p. 44n.

commandeered by the nearby air base's Officers Corps, Kálmán Hubay,* a Szálasi lieutenant, was elected to Parliament on March 27 in Lovasberény.[35]

By that time, it was a frequent occurrence in the officers clubs that Horthy's picture was spat upon and bombarded with leftover food. At a gala performance of the opera, Fascist students and officers taunted Horthy and his wife with shouts of "Rebecca, get out of the castle! " (a reference to the totally unfounded Fascist story that Madame Horthy had Jewish ancestors). Still Horthy had no inkling of the machinations of the trio of Imrédy, Rátz and Darányi. In the beginning of April he made a radio address to Hungary, in which he assailed the Arrow Cross, promised to maintain law and order, tried to calm tempers, and in true Habsburg fashion made a forlorn vow to keep the army out of politics and under his personal control.[36]

In the same month, Darányi piloted through Parliament the first anti-Jewish law, which limited to 20 percent Jewish participation in the press, theatre, law, medicine and in enterprises with more than a few employees. Everyone who had converted to Christianity since the date of the fall of the Kun regime was to be considered a Jew. Veterans and war invalids were exempt; no racial principles applied. This mild Jewish law was as satisfying to the zealots of fascism as a portion of broccoli fed to a tiger.

Meanwhile, Bethlen found out about Darányi's negotiations with Szálasi and that was enough for Horthy. For once, Darányi misapplied his skillful lack of principle, and he was gracefully removed from the premiership.[37]

In complete ignorance of what went on behind the scenes and what went on in the minds of men about him, the Regent on May 13 appointed Imrédy to the premiership because of his good connections with London, his conversatism, and in order to have a Catholic premier during the Eucharistic Congress to be held in Budapest in the summer of 1938.** Imrédy's first task on the agenda as far as Horthy was concerned was to crack down on the Arrow Cross. This Imrédy was all too glad to do, although with a very different motivation from that which Horthy and the rest of the world — which still had illusions about his "anglophile," "Western" sympathies — expected him to have. Imrédy, like Gömbös, wanted to establish his own Fascist dictatorship, not Szálasi's. In addition, he was a conservative Fascist, and had no use for any truly popular program. His professed model was

*Hubay, an opportunistic journalist, was a Gömbös Orphan. He won some notoriety with his paper under the skillful guidance of Antal during the Gömbös era. After he was removed in 1937 from his paper (as a part of the conservative effort to cleanse the press of the Gömbös spirit), he joined Szálasi.

**The non-initiated Szeged Fascist Deputies within the Government party were outraged by the appointment of Imrédy. They considered him the "boy of the banks," an anglophile, and objected "to his connections with Jewish bankers," predicting that "he will represent bank interests only — not agrarian interests." But [according to the same source] some months later the same Szeged Fascist critics gave Imrédy the most unqualified support. . ." Lackó, *op. cit.*, p. 116n.

Salazar's ultraconservative fascism,* which for Hungary, because it was not in the geographical position of Portugal, meant subservience to Germany, violent anti-Semitic measures, and Fascist terror. Imrédy was little worried about this in 1938 and, as we shall see, much less later, when it became clear to him that the Szeged men stood or fell with Nazi fortunes.

In return for these sacrifices, Hungary probably would have enjoyed all the impressive social, economic and political achievements of Salazar's Portugal. That in case of peace. If there were war (and by that time there was a good chance that there would be war), the prospect for Hungary was full of risk. Imrédy knew this, and because he still had some respect for Western strength in May 1938, before the tragic performance of the West at Munich, he moved carefully.

As top priority on his agenda he proceeded with the blessings of the opposition and Horthy to remove Szálasi. First he issued the famous Council Order No. 3400 forbidding employees of the state to enter political parties, a measure directed at the revolutionary Fascists; those few in the state service who had democratic sympathies in the neobaroque age were wise enough to keep it a secret. Then he made a more direct move. Not in vain did Professor Macartney speak about the "spiritual purity" of Imrédy, a man "something more than incorruptible."[38] Imrédy contrived a false leaflet campaign with the Horthyist secret police officer, J. Sombor-Schweinitzer. They flooded Budapest with leaflets, "Long live Szálasi! " written on one side and on the other the by then famous slogan, "Rebecca, get out of the castle! " aimed at infuriating Horthy.[39] Their goal was achieved. Szálasi protested vainly about a "filthy forgery." He was tried for issuing "subversive leaflets" and duly sentenced at the end of August to three years' imprisonment and five years' loss of civil rights. That seemed to leave Imrédy with a clear field. The opposition was happy about his appointment, and so was the West — for a while, at least.

Shortly before his arrest Szálasi, through intermediaries, made his first official contacts with Doctor Höttl, in Vienna. Doctor Höttl confessed to an Arrow Cross representative that although the Reichssicherheits-Hauptamt (R.S.H.A.) sympathized more with the Pálffy-Festetics group than with Szálasi, it was realistic enough to see the greater popular support of Szálasi's movement. Doctor Höttl asked whether Szálasi was ready to subordinate his movement and Hungary to German designs and cede German-inhabited Hungarian territory to Germany. Szálasi refused in uncompromising terms. Nevertheless, from this time on the Germans began to support the Arrow Cross financially. Szálasi wished to get funds from Mussolini also, but the *Duce* did not seem to be interested in anti-Horthy subversion.**Another

*Súlyok, *A Magyar tragédia*, p. 359. During his trial in 1946, Imrédy defined his reformism as a "gentlemen [like] reform policy" ("úri reformpolitika"). Lackó, *op. cit.*, p. 112.

**Macartney, *October Fifteenth*, I, 228-29. Contacts between Szálasi and the *Duce* were made through Szabó, the Hungarian military attaché in Rome, an oldtime friend and comrade in arms of Szálasi. Lackó, *op. cit.*, p. 119n.

interesting contact at this time was made with the Vatican. As always, it was marvelously well informed about the Arrow Cross, but after a short exchange of views, it became clear that Christianity and Hungarism were incompatible.*

Some time before Szálasi's imprisonment, the Bethlenite wing of the Hungarian Nation began in earnest its crackdown on the radical Fascist movements. The Szeged Fascists, being very versatile and conservative, did not suffer. But the Fascist social reformists were confronted with the same law which had been used against the Communists. The traditional way out open to Szeged Fascist pogromist-terrorists and plotters, "taking into account their patriotic motives," was not applied to nationalist reformers. When radical fascism dared to tackle the question of land reform or dared to propose some restrictive measures on the best ally of the landowners, big capital, there could be no allowances made for the mitigating circumstance of patriotism. The trial of Doctor Málnási, Szálasi's historian and ideologist, was a good example of this. Málnási was accused of professing a "subjective" interpretation of Hungarian history. He answered that there was a kind of subjectivity on the part of the 0.6 percent who enjoyed 20 percent of the national income, and there was a 99.4 percent type of subjectivity, the subjectivity, for example, of the 3.7 million Hungarian agrarian proletariat. He preferred to go along with the subjectivity of the 99.4 percent of Hungarians because for him the "nation" was the "people."[40] His statement allegedly established that Málnási exercised an "inadmissible criticism toward the system of large landed estates, which had been the foundation of Hungary for centuries," and "against the capitalist system which supports the state"; therefore, the court could not take into account the "well known unselfish patriotism of the accused."[41] Doctor Málnási was sentenced to a stiff term of imprisonment on the charge that he had criticized the ruling classes in one of his books about Hungarian history.

It was at this time that the neobaroque regime attacked the group known as the Village Explorers. These young writers, journalists and intellectuals of the humblest purely Hungarian origins represented something unprecedented in the interwar period, nay, since 1848: a purely Hungarian interest not of the historic nation but of Hungary as a whole. Above all, they were concerned with the miserable fate of the majority — the peasantry. They were opposed to middle classes of both German and Jewish origin. Although they did not propose any brutal solution for the Swabian and Jewish infiltration problem, they wanted to undo the damage the Hungarian ruling classes had caused by not providing for a Hungarian middle class in the twentieth-century sense of the word. They intended to give Hungary a truly Magyar intelligentsia instead of the assimilated recruits, an intelligentsia which was to come from the mainstay of the Hungarian population, the peasantry. Such ideas had no future in neobaroque Hungary. These young Hungarian

*Lackó op. cit.., p. 119n. Doctor Málnási composed the letter which Szálasi sent to Pope Pius XI. In this letter Szálasi (and Doctor Málnási) maintained that Hungarism was not a "new heathen [teaching]" but its foundations "rest on the Gospel." Ibid., pp. 96-97.

nationalists, the only genuine representatives of the Hungarian people, were exposed to great pressures from the German side and to a lesser extent, from the Jewish side, and when they tackled the tabu subject of agrarian reform, the Hungarian Nation turned upon them in earnest. Some of them were thrown into jail; some of them tried to realize their dreams during the war on the Fascist side, and were duly imprisoned afterward. Others cooperated with fascism, but were nevertheless accepted by the triumphant Communists as fellow travelers after the war. Few of them remained true to democracy to the end. They were uniformly well-meaning, unselfish, Hungarian patriots, whose good intentions were crippled and distorted by the Hungarian ruling classes and frustrated ultimately by the international implications of Hungary's geopolitical position. If they could have prevailed, they might have made great strides in the direction of building a democratic Hungary, a home for all Hungarians. For a beginning, their work was not bad. The ruling classes, applying the famous Law III of 1921 for the first time against non-Communist offenders, took care that this rebirth of the tradition of 1848 should come to an end. The most important members of the group were: Dezső Szabó, Zsigmond Móricz, Géza Féja, Ferenc Erdei, Gyula Illyés, Imre Kovács, Ödön Málnási, Péter Veres, László Németh, Aladár Tóth, György Sárközi and Zoltán Szabó.

In considering Fascist activities in Hungary, one should say a few words about the only considerable nationality of Trianon Hungary, the Swabians (Germans), who in the 1930s numbered about a half a million. They were no better treated than the other nationalities, and their assimilation, especially that of the educated Swabians, was no less vigorously promoted than that of any other nationality before or after Trianon. After assimilation, they could reach the highest posts in administration, church and the military — but as Hungarians. The Swabian peasant masses, on the other hand, lived a rather exclusive, self-segregated life in their clean, efficient villages, mostly in Transdanubia, mixing little with Hungarians. All this changed with Hitler's advent to power. During Gömbös' time, there was little Nazi incitement of Swabians against the government. Hitler, who used the German colonies as pawns in his political game all over the No-Man's-Land of Europe, did not find it necessary to stir up trouble in a Szeged Fascist Hungary which he felt to be in his corner. Moreover Gömbös, although of pure Swabian descent, was an intransigent Hungarian nationalist in this respect and would not tolerate the slightest disloyalty on the part of his Swabian kinsmen. He flatly refused the Nazi doctrine about the *Völkisch* idea of loyalty to Nazi Germany. According to Gömbös, Swabians owed loyalty only to the Hungarian state.[42]

After Gömbös' death, things changed radically. There were many signs of Swabian infatuation with Nazism, and when Hungarians of every political opinion reacted violently, the German press ridiculed Hungarian revisionist claims on the basis of Hungarian intransigence toward their Swabian minority. When the German army appeared on Hungary's western frontiers, the majority of the Swabian population became openly disloyal to the Hungarian state. After 1936, moderate Swabian leaders were pushed aside by Nazi nationalists. Hitler also pressed for the minority rights of his kinsmen, but the Hungarians were adamant for the time being. Szálasi's opinions on the question were stated in the plans about the Great Carpatho-Danubian Fatherland, and that was as far as Szálasi intended to go. It was by no means satisfactory to the Nazis.

The *Dienststelles* of the Gestapo and the SS put forth a very different sort of plan, according to which Hungary and the whole of the *Südostraum* was to be broken up into *Volksgruppen* with national autonomy within the ethnic boundaries, but all territories to be tied to the Reich.* It is easy to see the fateful implications of this plan not only for historic Hungary but, considering the distribution of German-inhabited areas in and around Trianon Hungary, even for rump Hungary.[43] Szálasi, to his credit, never even considered accepting this plan, the realization of which was the main purpose of Doctor Höttl's office in Vienna. Therefore the Germans, never losing sight of their goal, dropped the obvious and easy course of cooperation with the Arrow Cross, the strongest Fascist group with the largest popular backing. They preferred to cooperate with smaller, less scrupulous or patriotic, Hungarian Nazis who were ready to accept the *Volksgruppe* solution, and turned to Szálasi only at the very end, in October 1944, when they had no choice left. The Nationalist International thus suffered a setback again — but then it was Gömbös, not Hitler, who believed in the Nationalist International. Hitler was a more down-to-earth realist. So Doctor Höttl's agents laid down the German line, which was never substantially changed after the spring of 1938: Until the *Volksgruppe* solution could be carried out, there should be general support of Nazi ideas by all the Hungarian Fascist factions and the establishment of a united Fascist front.[44] For this purpose, the daily paper *Magyarság*** was acquired, partly with German funds, and began to propagate openly the *Volksgruppe* solution for the *Südostraum*. Following its instructions from Vienna, however, *Magyarság* did not break with the Arrow Cross. It maintained that despite ideological differences, it still supported the Arrow Cross, "which is subjected to the most brutal treatment by the authorities."[45] Hubay now joined the *Magyarság's* staff, and Baky appeared on its board. Rajniss, in the meantime, found it expedient to re-enter Imrédy's Government party in the summer of 1938. Festetics joined Hubay, and the new union was christened Hungarian National Socialist Party-Hungarist Movement and adopted the green shirt and the Arrow Cross as symbols. Pálffy, for personal reasons, was left out of the new union.

Szálasi's departure to prison brought about the disappearance of the measure of moral restraint he doubtless had exercised. During the fall and

---

*A. Rosenberg, the party ideologist, was quite candid in this respect when he said that "Europe must settle down according to National Socialist principles. What does this mean? This means that Germany will colonize Europe." Gyula Kállai, *A magyar függetlenségi mozgalom (1936-1945)* (Budapest, 1949), p. 16.

**Its editor, Oliver Rupprecht, became the most unabashed and best paid agent of the R.S.H.A. in Hungary, collecting valuable information for his sponsors about the political intrigues in Budapest, and serving as a coordinater between different Fascist groups and the Gestapo.

winter, Hubay, although officially the party leader, played only a secondary role. The gangster Kovarcz* took over the actual leadership of the party and proposed terrorism.[46] He organized the Black Front, a terrorist Arrow Cross group that distinguished itself in February 1939 by throwing a bomb at Jewish worshippers as they left a synagogue on the eve of Sabbath.** A defecting Arrow Cross man revealed the almost unchecked flow of money through Baron von Oberbäck, a high official of the German embassy, from Fascist-led government cooperatives, from the donations of high Hungarian officials wishing to secure the future for themselves, and finally, from the Hungarian-Italian Bank. All these donations arrived in a mysterious account called "Szálasi 100."[47]

As most of these happenings were known only to the initiated, they did not diminish the popularity of the Arrow Cross. On the contrary. Surrounded by the halo of Szálasi's martyrdom, using radical agitation as a method, advocating a radicalism that often acquired the proportions of outright demagoguery, the party flourished as never before.*** During the year following the arrest of Szálasi, the Arrow Cross reached the peak of its popularity. According to a well-documented study by Professor Lackó, in July 1938 when Szálasi was arrested, Arrow Cross membership fluctuated between 10,000 and 20,000. A year later, according to the testimony of Szálasi, there were 200,000 party members, and according to the estimate of Kovarcz, 300,000.[48] The social stratification of the influx, according to the reports of police spies who infiltrated the movements (but whose reports were corroborated by the reports of local Social Democratic party organizations), was the following: The majority of the newcomers were workers in the enterprises and public utilities of the Greater Budapest area; but the hold of the Arrow Cross on the mining regions was also extraordinarily strong. Other industrial areas of Hungary were also well represented and many former Socialists joined the party in those months.****Great support was gained from among the agrarian proletariat of the most depressed rural regions. Many lower middle-class people, such as poorly paid white-collar workers, unemployed or only part-time employed intellectuals, some students, many small artisans, and some old retired people living on meager pensions, were

*Member of the dreaded Officer Detachment of Ostenburg, he was the murderer of Somogyi and Bacsó during the White Terror.

**Népszava, Feburary 4, 1937. Twenty-two people were gravely wounded — among them ten who were over sixty.

***Among other things, the Arrow Cross promised to carry out an agrarian reform which would distribute ten million holds (three-quarters of the cultivated area of Trianon Hungary!), a moratorium on tax arrears for peasants and artisans, also a sixfold pay increase for police officers, "because they perform a dangerous duty." Lackó, *op. cit.*, p. 138.

****Professor Lackó calls them "Socialists." One should keep in mind that the Communist Party was outlawed in Hungary and almost all Communists joined the Socialist party. Many of them went over to the Arrow Cross. Certainly many of them were welcomed back into the Communist party after 1945.

also more than ready to place their hopes in the Arrow Cross.[49] The party did not neglect Hungarians abroad either. Its party cells among the miserable seasonal agricultural workers in Germany recruited 10,000 to 15,000 party members within several months.[50] Hubay aptly called 1938 "the year of the Movement," promising that "in 1939 we shall build our Hungarist state."

In addition to Communists and criminal elements, there was also a strong influx of Swabians into the ranks of the Arrow Cross during the period after Szálasi's arrest. It is difficult not to see this as an attempt by Doctor Höttl to take over the movement from within in the absence of Szálasi. The most important R.S.H.A. infiltration was the entry of Baky into the Arrow Cross in November 1938. The names of the officeholders in the Arrow Cross party did not bear a very strong Turanian imprint either: F. Schréter was head of the Arrow Cross headquarters; Schallmayer, a well-known former Communist, was in charge of the workers organization; Wollyt was the treasurer. L. Gruber, K. Wirth and Wolff were functionaries of importance in addition to Kovarcz himself. One could continue for a long time the names of these Hungarian superpatriots who, in contrast to the neophyte Gömbös and Szálasi, did not feel very warm attachment even to a Fascist platform, if it was a Hungarian one.

The extraordinary increase in Arrow Cross membership did not rest on a firm basis, however. When the cold, efficient Kovarcz tried to organize an "experimental revolt" in order to test the real strength of the party, he was disappointed by the apathy of the neophytes. He concluded that there was a prevalent party mood, a sympathy, but that there was no thoroughly organized support.[51]

The Arrow Cross made an attempt during the fall of 1938 to take over the streets of the capital. Some disorderly mass demonstrations took place, complete with raids on Jewish stores and beatings of Jews, but they were quickly and firmly put down by Minister of the Interior Keresztes-Fischer. These disorders, which never reached major proportions, were used as a pretext for the mass arrest of Arrow Cross militants. Many activists found themselves in concentration camps, where they far outnumbered incarcerated Communists. Hubay saw the writing on the wall. In defiance of activists of the temper of Kovarcz, he decided upon the "legal road to power." But the popular character of the Arrow Cross had been diluted by the influx of middle-class opportunist elements who clashed violently as always with the proletarian membership.[52] When Szálasi was not released from jail as expected, these opportunists saw that they were betting on the wrong horse and stayed away. Only the workers remained faithful.[53]

The most important violation of Szálasi's Hungarist idea in his absence was the obedient parroting by his followers of the *Volksgruppe* idea and the German line.* After all, that was where the money was. Thus neither the Bethlenites nor the Szeged Fascists under Imrédy destroyed the Arrow Cross

*Macartney, *op. cit.*, I, 260. Not in vain did the R.S.H.A. agent Count Pálffy maintain later that "Hubay led the party, after the imprisonment of Szálasi, toward a direction [the line of which] I liked better." Lackó, *op. cit.*, p. 149n.

by imprisoning Szálasi. They only succeeded in removing from it whatever small moral restraint Szálasi's presence provided.

4

Meanwhile, Hitler moved toward carrying through his plans for Czechoslovakia. In these plans, Hungary had a definite role to play; consequently Hitler endorsed this single Hungarian revisionist claim.* But Czechoslovakia had allies: France and Russia. In addition, the ally of France was England, and there was the Little Entente still officially in existence. Also, the Czech frontier was twenty-five miles from Budapest, and Czechoslovakian military strength was not inconsiderable, and for all practical purposes, even in case of a German attack the strength the Czechs could spare for the Hungarian front was more than enough to crush Hungary. The Czechoslovakian Air Force had not even a semblance of opposition in its Hungarian counterpart. These considerations, added to the frantic Hungarian internal situation, made Horthy and Imrédy wary of undertaking obligations when the question came up during Horthy's celebrated visit in Kiel and Berlin in August 1938. They were not averse to participating in the dismemberment of Czechoslovakia as long as they did not have to fight. Ribbentrop at this point spoke his famous mot: "Wer mittaffeln will muss auch mitkochen!"[54]

The visit left Germany with a definitely bad impression of Hungary. Horthy, Imrédy and especially Kánya wanted as much revision for Hungary as possible — but they, like the rest of the world, could scarcely have anticipated what was to follow a month later in Munich. This was especially true in Imrédy's case. Some Fascists were "enthusiasts," others fantasts or ignoramuses; Imrédy was none of these. He was not even a Fascist by conviction, if he had any conviction at all. He was at best the self-appointed savior of Hungary, with the ruthlessness of a messiah whose acts are unrestricted by any law, who used what he believed to be the spirit of the age to further schemes and ambitions which supposedly coincided with Hungary's salvation. But just because he was not a primitive, he did not yet dare to detest the Western powers merely because they had displayed a certain weakness in recent years. He waited for further proof. His whole financial background made him a cold, calculating politician, always able to know the score. But to know the present is not necessarily to foresee the future. Therefore, after his return from Germany, he gave an interview to the London *Daily Telegraph* in which he declared that Hungary would preserve her neutrality in case of a German-Czechoslovak conflict.[55] The German reaction was understandably violent. Imrédy and Kánya visited Hitler again on September 21 — some eight days before Munich — to press Hungary's claim.

It proved to be a crucial point in Imrédy's career. Allegedly, during the meeting Ribbentrop presented confidential documents written by Imrédy to the British Foreign Office, documents which the British had handed over to

---

*The fulfillment of Hungary's claim at the expense of Czechoslovakia, as Hitler notified the Hungarians through Göring, "was to be enough for the present Hungarian generation." *Allianz*, p. 152.

143

the Nazis in order to prove their "disinterestedness in the Danube Basin." And it was this alleged "betrayal" which "made a changed man of Imrédy."*

The Western powers, notably England, committed many omissions and errors in 1938, but not toward Imrédy. Their mistake was committed in Munich eight days after Imrédy's visit with Hitler. The whole alleged affair between Imrédy and Ribbentrop supposedly took place dangerously close to the date of Munich, and it seems quite likely that it was actually the agreement itself that "made a changed man" of Imrédy. It changed radically the balance of power in Europe, especially in the Danube Basin. Such a portentous event could scarcely have escaped the attention of one who had been incubating ambitious Fascist schemes since February.

In Munich, Czechoslovakia was sacrificed to "peace in our time." The goal was laudable, and the sacrifice would not have seemed excessive if by it peace had indeed been effectively assured. As it happened, of course, the immediate and most visible result of the pact was the destruction of the only democracy in No-Man's-Land. With millions of Czechs under German yoke, the prize was even more elusive than before. And the failure of Western policy was now aggravated by dishonor, for the West had simply betrayed an ally. Today we know that Hitler was bluffing, that even if he had started a war before Munich the German General Staff would have tried to overthrow him. But they could not overthrow a victorious leader, one who had just realized such a remarkable diplomatic victory.

For Hungary, the Czechoslovak crisis started in earnest only after Munich. For six weeks or so, Hungarian internal politics calmed down before its

*Súlyok, op. cit., p. 362. Strangely enough, Imrédy never told Horthy or Kánya nor any other Hungarian politician about this "act of perfidy" on the part of Albion. Although two exceptions exist: One is predictably Eckhardt, who found it fitting to his purposes to divulge this "secret" in 1948 in New York. Imrédy told Súlyok, his prosecutor, about it during an intermission at his trial for his war crimes. It is possible to maintain that this claim is ridiculous. As far as Imrédy goes, he embarked on a Szeged Fascist course in a conspiratorial manner with Rátz and the Fascist military long before his alleged tête-à-tête with Ribbentrop. Apart from the rather unusual character of the alleged British act, it is not clear what British interests would have been served with the discrediting of a Hungarian Prime Minister in September 1938, whom London naively believed to be England's friend. Because as late as October 18, 1938, Henderson, the British ambassador in Berlin, reported to London that Imrédy was "not particularly enthusiastic" about Germany and advised caution "lest a worse person will follow." (Kertész, Diplomacy in a Whirlpool, p. 33.) Also, why did Imrédy talk about this "betrayal" to Súlyok only during the intermission of his trial? If he had told it loudly, this would have helped to explain if not to excuse his behavior later! Did he not mention it because he may have been worried that the Soviets would take offense, in 1946, because of his anti-British remarks? Did Imrédy consider during the years of 1938-46 only the immaculate personal integrity and the well-known political consistency of Eckhardt worthy of his confidence?

144

impact. Knowing their military superiority, the Czechs also knew that in a fight with Hungary they could count on the support of Slovak nationalists and Clerical-Fascists. Germany, on the other hand, was not very eager to press Hungarian claims, despite Darányi's conciliatory visit to Hitler after Munich.

Hungary had just claims. If the Trianon peacemakers had not included in the new republic a million Hungarians, most of them living right on the border, there would have been less room for revisionist propaganda, and the unbridled hatred of the Hungarian ruling class against Czechoslovakian democracy likely would have been more apparent. As the Hungarian-Czechoslovak negotiations went on during October, both Neville Chamberlain and Lord Halifax agreed that Hungary had just claims.[56] But no agreement could be reached, mostly because of the stubbornness of Slovak nationalists. In order to avert an armed clash, Germany and Italy were asked to arbitrate. The first Vienna Award returned to Hungary a strip along her northern border of 10,000 square kilometers with about a million people, in the majority Hungarian. The territory was occupied amid much rejoicing during the first week of November.

In the days of Munich, there was a fateful appointment within the military hierarchy which later was to contribute much to the misfortune of Hungary. Henrik Werth, a Swabian who even during the census of 1941 declared himself a German (a rarity among the Swabian middle class), with a German wife, became chief of staff. He was a typical fellow traveler of fascism: he never entered a Fascist party. But he was more convinced of German invincibility and contributed more to Hungary's tragedy than any other military man, and that is to say much. The reasons for his appointment shed light on the neobaroque edifice. One reason was that Lajos Keresztes-Fischer, brother of the Bethlenite minister of interior, as chief of staff had purged the army too vehemently of Arrow Cross influences and his activities had to be balanced. The second reason was that only Werth among the staff officers spoke German well enough to keep close contact with the Wehrmacht.[57]

Meanwhile, Imrédy felt safe enough to move boldly toward his Fascist goal. He knew he had to catch the imagination of the masses in order to carry his scheme through against the opposition of vested interests, liberals and Socialists. These, although fighting in a certain sense for the same ideas as he, did not wish to see them accomplished at the price of fascism. There were two ideas in Hungary in the fall of 1938 which could bring popular support: a true social policy, particularly an agrarian reform, could rally the masses; and anti-Jewish legislation, which pleased the anti-Semitism of the "middle class of Hungarian gentlemen" and the petite bourgeoisie, could also by this time find favor among the lower classes. Imrédy proclaimed his program in two distinctly separate phases — pre-Munich and after-Munich.

Imrédy's Kaposvár speech in early September partly honored promissory notes to Rátz and the military. It proclaimed compulsory military service, with a great extension of the existing military organization in addition to the rearmament that had been announced in the spring. After that came the bombshell — the program for an extensive agrarian reform, a more

145

progressive taxation,* and many other long overdue social measures to exhilarate the masses. In addition, he continued to frighten the vested interests with promises "to transform the social structure," and in the true Gömbös manner he promised that fascism would be realized in Hungary in Hungarian fashion. He made two other points: (1) there was no need for further anti-Semitic legislation; (2) while he would lead, he did not want to be a dictator.[58] But at an intimate dinner after the speech, he openly condemned the parliamentary system, proclaimed his need for dictatorial powers and praised the Nazi and Italian systems.[59] This before Munich.

After Munich the Hungaro-Czechoslovak crisis subdued him for a while, but it did not keep him from forming the "1938 Club" from his supporters (many Gömbös Orphans), and on October 20 he openly refuted in this gathering the idea of integral revision and stood up for Doctor Höttl's *Völkisch* plan. And for the first time, he proclaimed the need for an authoritarian government on the basis of a movement with ideological foundations.[60]

While pocketing all the credit for the Vienna Award, Imrédy transformed his cabinet, strengthening his hand with the new appointments. He then began, in his own words, to "think aloud" about the necessity of a "putsch" to change the constitution in order to override parliamentary opposition to land reform (especially in order to outmaneuver the upper house). Finally, he proclaimed, again in true Gömbös fashion, that his Kaposvár statement about no more anti-Semitic legislation had to be "revised."[61] In addition, one of the Gömbös Orphans, Marton, was gleefully spreading among his cronies that plans were ready for the "reform of the constitution," a euphemism for a Fascist dictatorship.[62]

In the following days, Hungary made an abortive attempt to grab Ruthenia, but both Germany and Italy bade her to respect the Vienna Award, so Horthy's orders were overridden by Hitler in a humiliating fashion. The government resigned in a huff, not daring to give the reasons for its resignation, and Horthy reappointed Imrédy's cabinet, except for the wise old *K.u.K.* diplomat Kánya, who had to be sacrificed to Germany. He resigned and was replaced later by Count István Csáky, a Fascist sympathizer.[63]

Bethlen several times asked Imrédy about his designs, and Imrédy finally felt himself strong enough to be candid. Then Bethlen, the real leader of the opposition, struck. His helper was Sztranyavszky, the former Gömbös lieutenant turned Bethlenite, a position much better fitting this prototype of reactionary country squire than the radical right. These gentlemen were worried specifically about the land reform, something with which the neobaroque edifice never trifled.** According to them, "Imrédy wanted to establish some sort of proletarian Nazi regime."[64] Bethlen acted with

---

*Hungary's system of taxation was a very immoral one. It did not have a gradual income tax, for example.

**It is interesting to note that two days before his downfall, Horthy spent much time warning the leaders of the underground about the dangers of a "hasty" agrarian reform, when Russian troops were less than eighty miles from Budapest! Macartney, *op. cit.*, II, p. 383n.

circumspection. The combined conservative members of the Government party and the opposition Liberals, Socialists and Smallholders who did not wish to see the Fascists accomplish the reform they cherished, brought about an unprecedented feat in the neobaroque age: The government was voted down! *

But the excited expectation of the masses ran strongly against such maneuvers. The majority of the people were with Imrédy, and quite apart from their Fascist sentiments, they rightly suspected a conservative move to foil reforms. The logical conclusion that a parliamentary coalition had been formed from the heterogeneous opposition would have caused a Fascist insurrection inside Hungary and a violent German reaction from abroad. As it was, violent pro-Imrédy demonstrations broke out in Budapest. Some days later, Horthy reappointed the same Imrédy government.** The Fascist quest for reform carried the day — or the mob at least thought so.

Imrédy did not lose time in getting to work. His foreign policy would be, as the new foreign minister Csáky explained, "quite simply the policy of the Rome-Berlin axis all along the line."[65] And leaving the other reforms for the future, Imrédy introduced the Second anti-Jewish Law in Parliament on December 21 as, he said, a "Christmas present" to the Jews.[66] After his reappointment, the servile support of the Government party was a foregone conclusion. But seventy-one representatives of the Bethlenite wing left the party.

The Imrédy anti-Jewish measure was a brutal law. First, the definition of a Jew was a racial one, almost as strict as that set forth in the Nuremberg Laws. The measure victimized 62,000 Christians.[67] It restricted Jewish participation in the different professions to 6 percent as an upper limit which in many cases meant zero percent, thanks to violently anti-Semitic employers. All in all, carried through successively it succeeded in four years in taking away the daily bread of 221,896 Jews (dependents included) or 40 percent of the Jewish population of Hungary.[68] But the "middleclass of Hungarian gentlemen" was happy. Along with the petite bourgeoisie, they started an unsavory competition to change the guard, to "Aryanize" Jewish property

*An eyewitness gives a vivid account of how Imrédy took this event. "After the count of the vote, his face became deformed; he stood up. His fingers — which had a striking resemblance to the claws of carnivorous birds — bent inwards. His eyes started to protrude, his lips moved incessantly and fast. He asked the Speaker to count the votes again; the result remained the same. Then he himself counted them over — to no avail. He fell back into his seat, and his face turned ashen." Súlyok, *op. cit.*, p. 365.

**Some Bethlenites thought that the reappointment of Imrédy was the consequence of German intervention on his behalf. But these hypotheses are contradicted by Keresztes-Fischer and Teleki. It was they, by no means sympathetic either to Imrédy or to his program, who asked the Regent to reappoint him because "if he is not reappointed to the premiership, this will cause the outbreak of a revolution of the extreme right." Lackó, *op. cit.*, pp. 116-17.

and to occupy Jewish positions.* Obviously these people, who represented much of the articulate public opinion, would not be exceedingly interested in the triumph of democracy during the coming war. The demoralization of the Hungarian middle classes that had begun with Trianon moved well apace through this changing of the guard. The interesting feature of Imrédy's anti-Jewish legislation was that while in a few years 40 percent of the Hungarian Jews lost their livelihood, there was no provision made to touch the mammoth enterprises that composed about 90 percent of Hungarian industry and banking and were owned by a dozen Jewish families. The Hungarian Jews were desperate. All their assimilation, loyalty, and patriotism had borne bitter fruit indeed. Those Jews who lived in the former Czechoslovak territories and had returned to Hungary, Jews who did not care for Masaryk's democratic republic because they felt themselves to be Hungarians, now received some, although by far not all, of the reward in store for them. In a falsification of history unprecedented in its cynicism and ingratitude, some of the deputies from the former Czech territories, as for example a Hungarian with the Turanian name of Gürtler, stood up in Parliament and denounced "Jewish disloyalty to Hungary during the Czech rule."[69]

Among others who dared to speak in such a vein was the secretary of the Hungarian party in Czechoslovakia, Andor Jaross.[70] Although his party had professed a pronouncedly democratic program before, Jaross entered the cabinet now as a minister of regained territories, and became the personal friend and closest associate of Imrédy.**

As the "middleclass of Hungarian gentlemen" and the petite bourgeoisie awaited their splendid opportunities, the usually docile Jewish community protested in vain: "Is this what the Hungarian Jews deserve whose only desire for centuries has been to be Hungarian and Hungarian only?" Recalling the many battlefields from 1848 to World War I on which the Jews had fought Hungary's enemies, the proclamation touched upon the essence of the

---

*Even a secret German agent speaks with undisguised contempt about the process, describing how 100 former prostitutes "lacking both brains and capital" acquired Jewish wholesale textile enterprises, winding up his report with the remark that "no German exporter can be expected to take up connections with the questionable Aryan firms described above." Hilberg, *Destruction of the European Jews*, p. 516.

**The rich Jewish industrialists and merchants contributed the lion's share to the budget of the Hungarian party during Czech rule. Jaross accepted Jewish money and Jewish loyalty in his work against the Czechoslovak state. The Jewish population in the towns was the backbone of his articulate support. Now he turned upon them with his cronies (Gürtler included) and blackmailed them out of their property, selling them "protection," which he conveniently disregarded in 1944, when as minister of interior, he organized the transports to Auschwitz. Besides being a profoundly cynical, corrupt man, Jaross was also a vulgar, unprincipled politician, with a tremendous ambition, which he hoped to realize by means of the spirit of the age.

problem: "Permit us to say finally that our faith, honor, and our rights are not the prey of everybody, to the expense of which one may try to resolve problems created by the social ills. Let the honorable legislature pass new laws which oblige everybody to mitigate the social ills. Everybody without distinction to creed."[71] But the Jews were naïve. The point was that the Jewish question was being used as a means of postponing and evading the solution of social ills.

Even all this was not enough for Imrédy. He pressed for a special German secretary of state for the Swabians, but could not carry the motion in the Council of Ministers.[72] The Swabians, nevertheless, were allowed to form their own political party, the *Volksbund,* on Nazi lines. Then in January 1939 Imrédy, with Jaross and his old friend Rátz and the distinguished historian Bálint Hóman (then a fellow traveler of fascism), formed a pseudo-Fascist movement with black uniforms and all other trappings called the Movement of Hungarian Life (*Magyar Élet Mozgalom,* M.É.M.). In Parliament, Imrédy's statements were more and more to the point: "I am not interested . . . in parliamentary arithmetic. . . . I am not giving up my ideas and programs in order to have one or more deputies sitting behind me . . . even if I remain in [a parliamentary] minority."[73]

The Bethlenites, who were the real power within the opposition, were still worried that Imrédy would try for a land reform. Also, although he had left virtually intact the vested interests of their Jewish capitalist allies, his nationalization of certain industries had set dangerous precedents. So the opposition, with Bethlen's leadership, worked out a plan of action for Horthy, and he acted upon Bethlen's advice as he had for twenty-five years.[74]

The pretext for Imrédy's removal was a spectacular if not a very high-minded one; it followed an approach that had already been implemented once in Hungarian politics that year. Neobaroque society had, besides its mania for dueling as a status symbol, another characterstic preoccupation. Long before the Jewish laws, everybody, especially the upstarts and the neophytes, investigated their lineage trying to prove: (1) that they could trace their descent far back and claim noble ancestry; (2) Hungarian descent free from any intermingling with inferior Slavic and Rumanian elements — although it must be stated that Swabian ancestry was not looked upon with much favor either; and (3) most important of all, that they had not even a hint of Jewish ancestry in the family! It is obvious that politicians investigated the lives of one another with meticulous care, because any unfavorable data could be used as a powerful weapon in that sick, hothouse atmosphere. Now Betheln investigated Szálasi's ancestors, and at his request Deputy Súlyok[75] read out the findings in Parliament, hoping thus to discredit this Armenian-Slovak-Ruthenian mixture before the people. There was little reference to what Szálasi stood for; the main count against him was his non-Hungarian lineage. The common people were not much interested; since they found Szálasi representing their plight on an allegedly Magyar platform, they increased their support. In close collaboration with Bethlen, some opposition politicians next found a dubious great grandmother in Imrédy's otherwise pure Swabian lineage, the only data being that she had been baptized at the age of seven, no reference given to her being Jewish. When these politicians visited Imrédy and told him of their findings, offering him the alternatives of resigning quietly or facing exposure, Imrédy took a chance: he refused to resign. At that point, Bethlen took the documents to Horthy, who for obvious reasons wanted to get rid of Imrédy himself. On February 13, 1939, Horthy complained bitterly to Imrédy that by introducing land reform and anti-Semitic legislation without consulting him beforehand he had violated the constitution. This confrontation would have caused any other politician in neobaroque Hungary to offer his resignation forthwith. Not Imrédy, with his aspirations toward a Fascist dictatorship. Seeing this, Horthy produced the documents he had obtained from Bethlen. Imrédy's reaction was undignified. He fainted. When he recovered, he offered his resignation.[76]

The disclosure of Imrédy's allegedly Jewish ancestry had a much more powerful effect on his anti-Semitic middle-class following than the discovery of Szálasi's Armenian ancestry had on the proletarian following of the Arrow Cross. Imrédy was ridiculed and humiliated, and he swore vengeance. His insecure, ruthlessly ambitious, unscrupulous nature was tremendously urged on by his wife, who came from an ambitious Swabian middle-class background and who had been set completely off balance by her position as wife of the prime minister. After talking things over with her, Imrédy announced that he was not retiring from politics. Madame Imrédy dotted the "i's" in case someone did not get the point, speaking up openly in Budapest society: "If the Hungarians don't want my husband, Hitler will bring him back."[77]

5

Count Pál Teleki was appointed by the Regent to succeed Imrédy to the premiership. Doubtless, he was one of the most complex personalities in the politics of Trianon Hungary. He was a *grand seigneur*, a scion of one of the greatest families of Transylvania. A very devout Catholic, though not of the Imrédy type, he was by no means a religious fanatic. He was an aristocrat in the noble sense of the word, who believed in an aristocracy of values rather than an aristocracy of birth. He therefore believed in Western Christian values but refused the middle-class values produced by democratic equalitarianism, mainly because of what he saw as their vulgarity and soul-destroying qualities. Although he loved the Hungarian people, he did not consider them ready for self-government. Although he was a persistent anti-Semite, he could condone only legal restrictions on Jewish influences, not brutality. Although he acted and thought as an aristocrat, he never identified himself with the aristocratic practices of his age in Hungary, which he detested as a perversion of the aristocratic ideal. In his mind aristocracy in 1939 had much more to do with *noblesse oblige* than with privileges or parentage. Of course, these attitudes did not make him very popular in neobaroque society, and he owed his appointment to his close friendship with Horthy. He was also an accomplished scholar of geography, and his popularity among articulate youth (he was both a university professor and director of the Boy Scouts of Hungary) was great.

Although few dared to show more public contempt for the prevailing Byzantinism of the age than Teleki, he radiated a sincere, puritan incorruptibility which earned the respect even of his opponents and was responsible for the fact that he had no real enemies, not even in Berlin. Teleki foresaw a Western victory in the coming conflict, both on moral and material grounds. He appreciated the dangers of a German victory much more keenly than did most of his countrymen. Consequently, although a revisionist himself, he was not eager to achieve revision with Hitler's help. It follows from all this that he was a staunch anti-Nazi and anti-Bolshevik. But all this pointed to his coming failure. The Hungary of the years 1939-41 was not a Hungary in which such individualistic ideas of a better age could prevail. To maintain such a position, a leader would have needed superhuman qualities and a united Hungary standing squarely behind him. Teleki had a somber vision. Years before his end, at the time of his appointment, he said, "We live in a crazy world. The person who cannot adapt himself to it should take his revolver and shoot himself."[78]

Taking over the reins of government from Imrédy, he fused M.É.M. with the Government party and simultaneously dissolved the Arrow Cross. These moves were typical of the Transylvanian character, which counseled that a concession on one side — in this case to Szeged Fascists — must be balanced with a crackdown on the other — the popular Fascist movements.* Teleki made it clear that he not only adopted Imrédy's anti-Jewish laws but he also approved of them. This affirmation was balanced with the watering down of the projected land reform to insignificant proportions.[79] Unfortunately, Teleki's anti-Semitism, although not of an Imrédy type, made it impossible for him to discern that the process brought into motion within the Hungarian middle classes by the "Aryanization" scramble for Jewish property would eventuate in something very different from the purification which he expected as a result of the lawful restriction of the "pernicious" Jewish influence. In addition to that, it was mainly his anti-Semitism which caused him to assess Hungarian fascism in a manifestly erroneous way.**

*Besides these "balancing" considerations, the reason for the dissolution was that by January 1939, the Arrow Cross began to get out of control. Hubay was not a leader who could restrain or discipline the rabble within its ranks. An Arrow Cross "activist" group, simultaneously with the bombing outrage against the synagogue in Budapest, plotted the assassination of strongminded Minister of Interior Keresztes-Fischer, and that of his brother, the former chief of staff. (Lackó, *op. cit.*, p. 156.) After such activities, the party was dissolved on February 24, 1939, and martial law was proclaimed.

**Teleki told some protesting Bethlen politicians "that the Hungarian Fascists are as good Hungarians as they, maybe even better ones, because they see more clearly the most important Hungarian problem" (the Jewish question). Súlyok, *op. cit.*, p. 368.

In March 1939, taking advantage of Hitler's entry into Prague, Hungarian forces fought their way into Ruthenia, in open defiance of that region's right of self-determination. The destruction of Ukranian nationalist irredenta was as much of an asset to Polish interests as it was to Hungarian revision. The only shortlived advantage was a common Hungarian-Polish frontier, duly feted in Budapest and Warsaw. On the other hand, the new Slovak state asked and was granted a German guarantee, and adopted a definitely hostile policy toward Hungary. Hungary found it expedient in these months to join the Anti-Comintern Pact as fourth member with Germany, Italy and Japan. She also quit the League of Nations on German demand.

But all this was insignificant in comparison with Teleki's blunder in May 1939 when, despite grave forebodings, he dissolved Parliament and scheduled elections in the same month. Parliament, "made by Gömbös," was not due for dissolution until 1940. With the European conflict looming on the horizon, its mandate could easily have been prolonged for the duration of the war. As a consequence of tensions, expectations and the prevailing spirit, in addition to the secret ballot — and despite the severely restricted electorate — the elections showed the disheartening Fascist orientation of Hungary as a whole. As the results came in, it became clear that even the Gömbös Parliament would have been something infinitely better than that which came out of these elections with the secret ballot. The Gömbös-made administration could still exercise a powerful influence on the electorate. The Government party won 179 mandates, which along with the thirty-six appointed deputies from Ruthenia and the strip ceded by Czechoslovakia, seemed to give it a comfortable margin. But this was only an appearance. Teleki allowed Imrédy to pick twenty-five or thirty candidates, and among the rest, so many Gömbösites were put up and elected that when all the votes were counted the supporters of Horthy and Bethlen made up no more than one-third of the Government party. Two-thirds were Fascist fellow travelers[80] who were opportunists enough not to avow their true sympathies, biding their time, hoping for some powerful manifestation of the spirit of the age. The Fascist deputy Meskó, threatening these opportunists with exposure, reported without mentioning names that they came up to him in secret after every session of Parliament saying, "Dear Zoltán, go on, continue in this vein, we are with you!"[81] Those Fascists who avowed their ideas openly won forty-nine mandates. Of these, Baky's group won eleven, Meskó, three and Károly Maróthy, two. The Szálasi lieutenants Jenö Szöllösi and Lajos Csoór got in as independent National Socialists, as the bulk of the popular vote went to the Arrow Cross, which had promptly reorganized after its dissolution in February under the name of Arrow Cross party.*

---

*It was the respectable, retired officer friends of Szálasi who lent their names as nominal leaders, in order to make the reorganization of the party possible. But before that, Hubay and Baky gave guarantees to the government that they would seek a "quiet and constitutional" road to power instead of terrorism and insurrection. Lackó, *op. cit.*, p. 158.

The party received millions from Germany for electoral purposes.* Under Hubay, it campaigned surrounded with the halo of Szálasi's martyrdom, and on a very radical social reform program, promising land reform, sometimes showing the miserable peasants the plots of land they would occupy after the Arrow Cross victory.[82] The Arrow Cross won thirty-one mandates all told. It is characteristic of the mentality of the party during Szálasi's absence that many of the mandates were bought as part of the fund-raising campaign.** Its main strength, nevertheless, came from the working class. The industrial belt around Budapest went Arrow Cross, and the great industrial suburb Csepel (also called "Red Csepel") elected two Arrow Cross deputies.*** In the Budapest elections, the Government party received 95,468 votes against 72,835 Fascist ones, and there were only 34,500 votes cast for the Social Democrats.[83] The democratic parties were crushed. Only five Social Democrats and five Liberals were elected. Other bourgeois parties also suffered defeat. The Smallholders were reduced to fourteen mandates. All together the heterogeneous opposition now numbered thirty-two mandates. Taking into account the restricted franchise, the distribution of the popular vote shows an even more dismal picture. Out of 3,928,334 votes, there were something less than 900,000 votes cast for Fascist parties, mainly the Arrow Cross.****

*These funds were acquired either through huge "individual loans" given to leading Arrow Cross men by large German banks, or by buying all available Hungarian currency in Zurich (500,000 pengös) and smuggling it back to Hungary. This feat was brought into the open by Teleki in Parliament. *O.N.K.*, June 14, 1939, p. 522. But after an official Hungarian protest Ribbentrop personally intervened, and the subsidies were temporarily suspended. Macartney, *op. cit.*, I, Appendix.

**Török, *op. cit.*, pp. 88-89. Among the sixty-three Arrow Cross candidates, there were ten landowners, eleven attorneys, eight retired non-commissioned officers, five journalists, six engineers, two Calvinist ministers; the rest were physicians, clerks and high school teachers. There was one worker on the list: Wirth. Lackó, *op. cit.*, p. 166.

***The Communist party ordered its members to vote for the Arrow Cross. Súlyok, *op. cit.*, p. 194.

****New York Times, June 6, 1939. Professor Deák mentions the figure of 750,000 radical right votes out of 2,000,000, but Professor Lackó confirms the figure quoted by the *New York Times:* 900,000. Lackó, *op. cit.*, p. 169. In the industrial suburbs of Budapest, which were called the "Red Belt" before, the extreme right won 65,000 votes (41.7 percent) from which 54,700 were cast for Arrow Cross candidates. The Arrow Cross emerged as the strongest single party not only in the working class suburbs of Budapest but also in the coal mining areas. The increase of Arrow Cross vote was proportional to the decrease of the vote cast in favor of the Social Democratic party. Great was the popularity of the Arrow Cross in the other industrial centers of Hungary, too, and it won a substantial amount of support in rural areas with a radical-minded agrarian proletariat — in Fejér, Veszprém and Vas counties. In Makó, a town famous for its agrarian-socialist traditions, Szálasi's deputy Szöllösi

It was this Parliament and this moral and intellectual standard of the articulate and inarticulate population with which Hungary faced one of the greatest challenges of her thousand-year history. Bethlen saw its inherent dangers and analyzed the situation in an editorial (written but characteristically not signed by him) entitled "The Lessons of the Election." He attacked the Government party for its Imrédist demagoguery, proclaiming that many of its representatives flirted with Fascism. "This is not the way to combat the extreme right." He noted that "part of the bourgeoisie wishes to take power from the aristocracy and the great bourgeoisie." And the remedy was also a characteristically Bethlenite one: "One must restore order and quiet and secure the historical process of development."[84] No wonder the people put their faith in Fascist demogoguery.

When the new Parliament convened, the forty-nine Fascist deputies, following the example of the Nazis in the Reichstag, refused to be seated on the right but occupied the benches on the extreme left. And well they might, especially as far as the Arrow Cross was concerned. For Hungarian Social Democracy with its bureaucratic leadership, the restrictions imposed upon it in organizing workers, the denial of access to the "three million beggars" of the agrarian proletariat, made it a bourgeois party representing mainly privileged, prosperous skilled workers in the labor unions. Wide segments of the government employees and the unorganized working masses had in the years 1939-44 just one defender: the Arrow Cross. A faithful review of the parliamentary debates or the Arrow Cross press of these five fateful years would necessitate a tedious number of quotations. Let it be enough to say that the speeches of Arrow Cross representatives in Parliament in those years were full of demands for improvements for workers, peasants and low-paid intellectuals. They also demanded the redress of injustices, the improvement of working conditions, extension of social services, and so on. In case of refusal, they did not shrink from organizing large-scale strikes, like the Arrow Cross miners strike in the coal mining basin of Pécs in 1940, followed by the sweeping strike in the Salgótarján mining district.* Also, the Arrow Cross

---

won an absolute majority of votes. The Arrow Cross also received an absolute majority in Budapest suburbs where retired old people lived on miserable pensions. Professor Lackó concluded his analysis of the voting pattern as follows: "In those days the influence of the Arrow Cross was much greater than its electoral success would suggest. Partly because of the electoral system: Its restrictions [after abolishing the open ballot] disenfranchised many hundreds of thousands of voters, especially among the rural and urban proletariat; also [because of the fact] that only those over twenty-six could vote." It should also be taken into consideration that the Arrow Cross was running *only in less than half of the electoral districts! Ibid.* pp. 170-76.

*The government, especially the Imrédist "reformist" wing, mobilized the dormant Fascist Trade Unions, led by Marton, the *N.M.K.*, the *E.M.Sz.O.*, and fomented strikes (mostly in Jewish enterprises) in order to balance Arrow Cross radicalism. The Arrow Cross Deputy K. Wirth (the only worker deputy of the Arrow Cross), complained bitterly in Parliament

press of the period is replete with requests for help for starving, suffering individuals. The Social Democratic party, apart from the limitations put upon it by Bethlen, was also, because of its participation in the opposition and its tacit alliance with the conservative wing of the Hungarian Nation, in the unfortunate position of not being able to fulfill a function otherwise its own. Into this vacuum, the Arrow Cross moved successfully. The other Fascist groups of Baky, Pálffy, Meskó and some Christian National Socialists were distinctly bourgeois, never taking their own social programs seriously. This became even more apparent when Baky's National Socialists allied themselves with Imrédy's Szeged Fascists during the war.

Unfortunately, the activity of the Arrow Cross did not consist solely of championing the poor. For the Arrow Cross in the absence of Szálasi resembled Rumania's Iron Guard after the murder of Codreanu. Hubay's regency was always an uneasy one; it was Kovarcz and other criminal elements who dominated party politics, organizing whole series of senseless provocative acts during 1939 and 1940. Great was their frustration, because despite their large popular backing, they were ignored by those in power. Only the minister of interior, Keresztes-Fischer, the scourge of Fascist movements of any denomination, paid them any attention, and that in the form of police persecution. During the German-Polish crisis, they publicly accused the government of organizing a Hungarian Legion to help the Poles.[85] In August 1939 the police arrested thirty members of the Arrow Cross youth because they participated with hundreds of other young men in underground armed training.[86] In October 1939 there was a mass arrest of Arrow Cross men who had organized a "death legion" aiming at an armed uprising to overthrow the government, and incidentally to kill seventeen opposition politicians.[87]

Meanwhile, Europe was rapidly approaching the start of its Peloponnesian War, preceded by the German-Soviet Treaty of Non-Aggression and Friendship. This treaty was a shock to Hungarian articulate public opinion. Both wings of the political nation, the Bethlenites and the Szeged Fascists, were anti-Bolshevist. Both of them also sympathized with Poland which, because of many similarities between the ruling classes and common ties from time

---

about these "artificial" strikes which have but one purpose: "to undermine us" [the workers' support of the Arrow Cross]. Because, as Wirth explained, if the Arrow Cross supported the strikers, the government attacked it on the grounds that as a political party it fomented strikes. If the Arrow Cross stood aloof, the Imrédist "reformists" spread the news among the workers that the Arrow Cross "has abandoned the working class." *O.N.K.,* June 28, 1939. The Arrow Cross answered the schemings of the Gömbös Orphans by establishing a Social Center *(Országos Szociális Központ)* in August, 1939, which was supposed to defend the interests of workers in defiance of Marton and other Szeged Fascists. Simultaneously, an Arrow Cross cooperative, the *Marok,* was also established which worked under the assumption that members of the Arrow Cross were advised to buy in certain stores, owned by Arrow Cross men, who in their turn made increased contributions to the party funds.

155

immemorial, was perhaps the only country in the anti-Nazi camp that still enjoyed pronounced Hungarian sympathies.

Therefore, there was considerable articulate support behind the correct Hungarian attitude toward Poland during the collapse and partition of that unfortunate country. When the Germans asked the Hungarians for the use of some strategic railroads against the Poles, they met with a dignified refusal.[88] But that was the beginning of a tragic process, which was to increase in a snowball fashion. The Gömbös Orphan and German agent Mecsér began to revile the government by spreading rumors that the Hungarian attitude had cost the Germans 60,000 additional casualties[89] (more than all the actual German losses during the entire Polish campaign). The Arrow Cross celebrated the Nazi-Soviet Pact with a noisy demonstration, carrying Hitler's and Stalin's pictures side by side, demanding the release of Szálasi and the revocation of Order No. 3400.* Imrédy was quiet during those months.

In September 1939, Hungary declared her non-belligerency, and during the Phoney War, Germany was not interested in embarrassing Teleki via the Fascists. It was in those months that German policy toward the whole *Südostraum* was established, the policy that would be followed with admirable consistency until 1944. This policy, formulated by the Nazi economics expert H. Neubacher, could be called: "Quiet in the raw material zone!"[90] Any government that would supply Germany with raw materials and maintain order would do for the duration of the war. Rumanian oil was of paramount importance for the German war machine. Second in importance was Yugoslavia; Hungary came third.

This policy was very convenient to the opposition, namely to Horthy, Teleki and Bethlen, who were all convinced of and desired the eventual victory of the Western powers.

Hungary's dependence on Germany was heightened by the constant pressure of the Hungarian military to extend the rearmament program, and armament could be acquired only from Germany. Also, after Germany absorbed Austria and the Czech lands, German-Hungarian trade relations expanded enormously. By 1940, Germany purchased about 50 percent of Hungary's exports and sold her 51 percent of her imports.[91] Politically, the Germans were sensitive about only one thing, namely, that the mass communications media should follow a Fascist line.** Teleki yielded carelessly enough. He summarized his opinion on the subject to Professor Macartney in private, saying that "dictators were childishly sensitive to criticism" and therefore he had adopted the rule that although he would say or publish in the press anything they wanted him to say, in actuality he would do nothing

*Súlyok, *op. cit.*, p. 498. Also the Arrow Cross press was heaping praise on the Nazi-Soviet alliance as a "common front of proletarian states against the plutocracies" (*Magyarság*, August 30, 1939), expecting even more violent anti-Jewish measures in the U.S.S.R. than those taken by Germany. (*Nép*, August 31, 1939).

**Shortly before the outbreak of the war, Wilhelm Frick, the German minister of interior, visited Budapest and asked for this. His request was granted. Súlyok, *op. cit.*, p. 496.

they wanted him to do.[92] In this, as in many other things, Teleki fatefully misunderstood the twentieth century. In the typical *grand seigneur* manner, he dismissed the masses from the picture altogether. For his class, politics always meant that the masses were treated as a kind of anonymous algebraic "x"; one need never worry about their real nature. But twentieth-century history seems to recognize what "x" stands for in the equation.

In Hungary the masses were dejected, but no longer illiterate. Gömbös had begun to subsidize a Fascist press, and most of those whom he put in charge were not removed from their posts after his death. The government papers cost less than one cent per copy and were easily accessible to everybody. In addition, the Germans heavily subsidized the *Magyarság*, and gave free picture material to many other Fascist organs.* By 1939, there were "people's radios" on sale for seven and a half dollars (in fifty-cents-a-month installments). These mass communications media were polluting the minds of the gullible people. Ignorant of the world, they were ready to believe everything they saw in print or heard on the radio, the intellectual capacity and experience of most of them being a mediocre ability to read and write. The results were shattering. Men like Horthy, Teleki or Kállay, above all Bethlen, evaluated the international situation correctly. But when the decisive moment came, they went ahead alone and a deceived, misled people, a polluted and infected public opinion which mirrored the press and radio, did not follow them.

The foremost leaders of the Fascist brainwashing were Milotay and Rajniss. Milotay was an Imrédy man, a gifted journalist who possessed an excellent command of the Hungarian language but an utterly demoralized character. Apart from the shady financial dealings in which he was involved, his wife was a registered licensed prostitute** before marrying this leader of the Szeged Fascist intelligentsia. The photocopy of the license of Madame Milotay was produced several times by the opposition during the Gömbös years to force Milotay to abstain from writing some vituperative Fascist articles. But as time went by, everybody of importance found out about the lady's past, there was no more interest in blackmailing him, and Milotay could go on writing his articles unperturbed. Rajniss, another Imrédy man (born Rheinisch), was an even more unsavory figure. Thoroughly corrupt, he made a luxurious living from the contributions of rich old ladies and German pay. He was in constant close contact with Gestapo agents and was absolutely uninhibited in his anti-American, anti-English, anti-Semitic, and to a much lesser extent, anti-Russian outpourings.[93] Another fascist journalist was Mihály Kolozsváry-Borcsa. Born Mihai Borcea, he usurped according to neobaroque tradition the name Kolozsváry (that is, de Cluj). He was the editor of the big government daily *Függetlenség*. He was a Gömbös Orphan and, according to Horthy, "the right hand of Imrédy."[94] In addition, he was

*Major, *25 év ellenforradalmi sajtó*, p. 68. This material was given especially to Rajniss and his illustrated *Magyar Futár*.

**In Hungary as in many other European countries where prostitution was legal, the prostitutes had to register with the police and receive a permit to engage in the oldest profession.

the head of the journalists' association, which determined without appeal who should engage in the profession and who should not. Among other extracurricular activities, Kolozsváry-Borcsa embezzled the funds of the Revisionist League.[95] These three were the types. The herd of Fascist journalists followed their example. It is no exaggeration to say that such men — Károly Maróthy (Meizler), György Oláh, Ferenc Vajta, Lajos Marschallkó, Pál Szvatkó, Vince Görgey — were, even apart from their political beliefs, the dregs of humanity. Men like these had unrestricted sway over the Hungarian mind during all the war years except for a short interval in 1943, when Kállay was premier.*

*The Hungarian press deserves a footnote. "Hungarian journalism," wrote Milotay, "proudly proclaims that it is worthy of the new world. [This journalism] purified the journalistic profession and the press in time from the kind of spirit which demoralized Hungary [before 1919]."
Új Magyarság, April 12, 1942.
During the dark days of 1940, a delegation of Americans of Hungarian descent called on the Department of State in Washington, D.C., to present a declaration of loyalty. A high ranking official told them: "We collect the inciting and mendacious articles published by the Hungarian press carefully. When the time of reckoning comes, and the judgment on the nations is passed, this material will weigh in against Hungary heavily. It would be a good idea to give a warning to those Hungarian circles whom this may concern . . ." Andor Kún, Berlinből jelentik, (Budapest, 1945), p. 10. Horthy commented to Teleki that "the press makes him vomit," adding that "to forfeit the existing goodwill of the Western powers (because of these vituperations) is criminal." Nevertheless, nothing happened to curb the press and radio, despite repeated protests from the British Foreign Office. Horthy, titkos iratai, pp. 262, 265.
It would be mistaken to think that this propaganda process started with the outbreak of the Second World War. The process of systematic mudslinging began with the triumph of the counterrevolution in 1919. From then on there were, according to the Szeged Idea, only two kinds of newspapers in existence: anti-Semitic ones and those "hired by the Jews." Almost any newspaper with liberal or democratic sympathies was branded as such. Hungarian history before 1919 was systematically besmirched. The Fascists slung mud on Kossuth's memory; the Fight for Freedom in 1848-49 was presented as "the age of Jewish emancipation" and the "age of freedom of thought." During the war, the press attacks against the West were much stronger than those directed against the U.S.S.R. Apart from their mendacious content, with their false "interviews," and falsified photographs which accompanied these reports, it was their style that was significant. It was said that "style is the visible essence of a phenomenon . . . over a period of time it becomes the framework from which no new initiative can emerge without destroying the whole structure. . . . The more original the trend, the more unmistakable the style." The Hungarian Fascist press considered Roosevelt's original name to be "Rosenfeld, which means Redeemer in Hebrew." News from Britain was reported daily under the heading "News from Plutocracy." The Royal Navy and the United States Navy were referred to jointly as the "United Hebrew Armada." American airmen were described as "Chicago gangsters, Texan

During the Phoney War, when Finland was invaded by the U.S.S.R., the Arrow Cross rabble disrupted the pro-Finnish speech of the Social Democratic deputies with noisy outcries like "Old ox!"[96] This support for the "common front of the German, Italian and Soviet labor states," as the Arrow Cross expressed it, was kept up scrupulously by the Arrow Cross but not by the Imrédists. A torture chamber discovered in the Arrow Cross Headquarters in January 1940 provides another example of Arrow Cross irresponsibility. There, in the offices of the Defense of Ideas, some activists under the supervision of Representative Gruber subjected to physical torture Arrow Cross

---

cowboys and the scum of New York's skid row filled with Jewish sadism." Eisenhower became the "No. 2 U. S. general made by advertising" (No. 1 being General MacArthur). Churchill was referred to as a "drunkard," Roosevelt as a "cripple," both being Jewish of course, or at least the "hirelings of International Jewry." According to the Hungarian press, Europe was welcoming the German Army and the SS enthusiastically, Russians, Czechs, Ukrainians and Yugoslavs included. Everybody who thought differently became a Jew automatically, as did Lenin, Stalin, Kerensky, Engels, Anatole France, Erzberger, Sir Stafford Cripps, Lloyd George, even Queen Victoria (she originates from King David!). The most obscene epithets were reserved for Mrs. Eleanor Roosevelt, who became Jewish, too. Although the style of the German Nazis was not exactly serene, nevertheless (if one overlooks the newspapers of the SS or the *Stürmer* of Julius Streicher), in general, Nazi journalism uses a great deal of veracity and restraint if compared with the Hungarian Fascist press.

Naturally, the Fascist press concentrated on the Jewish question. And this was the style — one sample out of thousands — in which these polemics were conducted: A fellow journalist of Jewish faith becomes a "little Hebrew brat, a punk, smelling of goose fat (Jews in Hungary often used goose fat for shortening instead of the non-ritual lard). This filthy creature, who is blabbering away in Yiddish, stinking with the smell of a [chcap] rummage sale, [it is] He, His Highness [who is coming], decorated with his *payes*, (*payes* are locks of hair worn by religious Jews)." *Pesti Újság*, October 12, 1942. No translation could cope with the vulgarity of anti-Semitic polemics in Hungary. This writer assures the reader that the atrociousness of this excerpt is only a pale reflection of the original, which steadfastly ignores style, taste, or the most elementary requirements of decency of reason. The Jews were accused daily of every possible and impossible crime — unleashing both world wars, ritual murders, disloyalty, mistreating their non-Jewish employees, cooperating with the U.S. Air Force and the Royal Air Force during air raids with the help of secret radio transmitters (which was, alas, not true; by and large the Hungarian Jews were too demoralized for such a feat). It was such a press campaign to which the Hungarian people were exposed during one of the most critical periods in their long history. It was such a press and radio which the Bethlenites deemed possible to ignore and tolerate. The obvious question which arises is whether such journalism and propaganda could have any effect on the Hungarian people — to which the answer, unfortunately, is yes, the effects were devastating.

members suspected of disloyalty.[97] Gruber's parliamentary immunity was lifted, and along with other Arrow Cross men involved, he drew a jail sentence. After this, five other deputies left the Arrow Cross, and the flow of Arrow Cross men to the regime's concentration camps continued.

After the Arrow Cross euphoria during the spring and summer of 1939 and during the winter and spring of 1940, an ebb set in. This ebb in the popularity of the movement was not only the consequence of the favoritism Hubay showed toward the bourgeois element in the Arrow Cross (who were derisively called "salon Arrow Cross men" by the proletarian membership). It is true that Hubay carried through several purges of proletarian members who, as he put it, "showed Marxist tendencies."[98] But the chief reason for the recess in Arrow Cross popularity lies in the character of its appeal. The desperate masses, who had been betrayed in their expectations by Communists, Socialists, democrats and their own middle classes, hoped for a quick Arrow Cross revolution, takeover and fulfillment. After this hope too proved to be an ephemeral one, a quick disillusionment set in, as the continuous Arrow Cross defeats in the by-elections during the period clearly show.[99]

The Germans seemed to have lost much of their interest in Hungarian Fascists after the outbreak of the war and changed their attitude about the time of the invasion of Norway and Denmark. Imrédy began to agitate for the necessity of a more complete identification with the spirit of the age, and he suggested that in return Germany should abandon the *Völkisch* solution.* Other Gömbös Orphans began to agitate in a similar vein, and Teleki moved quickly to appoint some Imrédists to important key positions of the Government party. On the other hand, the Germans let the Hungarians know that they would like Teleki to be replaced by a "more pronouncedly pro-German politician," and that "Imrédy himself was regarded a particularly suitable instrument."**

Milotay expressed the line for the Szeged Fascists in clear terms, terms rather better befitting one of his wife's former profession than a Hungarian parliamentary deputy elected on a nationalist platform: "Small nations cannot afford to be choosey as far as boundaries or conditions of friendship go. They must give themselves up to a party stronger than themselves and therefore, must pay any price, even the cost of national pride, in the hope of getting through the difficult times and recovering on another occasion what was lost or abandoned under restraint."[100] The nationalist international certainly had gone a long way since Gömbös' death. General Werth, chief of staff, began his fatal meddling in politics, submitting on May 15 an absurd memorandum to Teleki with utterly fallacious information about an alleged German offer of military cooperation against Rumania with an even more imaginary German promise of giving Slovakia and Transylvania to Hungary.[101] It was during that time that the French front collapsed, and

---

*Imrédy expounded his thesis in the Easter number of Milotay's newspaper. *Új Magyarság*, March 24, 1940.

**Gyula Juhász, *A Teleki kormány külpolitikája, 1939-1941*, (Budapest, 1964), pp. 164-65.

with the Germans on their way to Paris, both Mussolini and the Hungarian Fascists were anxious to jump on the rolling bandwagon before it was too late. Imrédy went into action again at the beginning of June. His following in the unprincipled Government party was increasing by the extent of German advance. They vociferously demanded the dismissal of Bethlenite ministers from Teleki's cabinet. Teleki wanted to resign, but Horthy stood by him. Imrédy demanded a stronger anti-Semitic, pro-Axis policy and social reform.[102] Then, unexpectedly, he relaxed his pressure.

At that point, Hubay and Vágó introduced into Parliament the most controversial point in Hungarism, a nationalities bill providing for the establishment of the Great Carpatho-Danubian Fatherland, demanding autonomy for the nationalities.[103] This gratifying diversion was exploited by the Bethlenites to the utmost. It also sadly proved that the Hungarians were like the Bourbons — they did not learn anything nor did they forget anything. The entire country exploded in a fit of irrationality and intolerance. Patriotic demonstrations followed, and Hubay was excluded even from his Fascist student fraternity because of his "attempt against the thousand-year-old Hungarian state." On June 13, Teleki set into motion the machinery to lift the parliamentary immunity of the "traitors," and soon they were arraigned before a court for championing the least objectionable part of Hungarism. But nobody dared to move against Milotay and the exponents of the infinitely less academic and more dangerous *Völkisch* principle.

An Arrow Cross apology gave a dignified answer to these howls:

One should also mention the chauvinists and those kinds of patriots who confuse in their exaggerations the interest of the nation with the interest of those who rule, and who enjoy the benefits of the system. It is these who cause the ethnic and religious clashes, who forcibly Magyarize and who exclude the class-conscious workers from the nation. These blind ideas make peace in the Carpathian Basin impossible.*

Meanwhile, to paraphrase Roosevelt, Mussolini's hand that held the dagger stuck it — into the back of his neighbor. And four days later, crack SS divisions were goose-stepping past the eternal flame under the Arc de Triomphe. It was a sad day of humiliation, indignity and disgrace for the Christian West. Teleki saw it otherwise. Observing the occasion in Parliament, he remembered Trianon, and "with solemnity" he sent "his greetings to the German Army and its commander."[104] Deputations of Government party M.P.'s waited on the German and Italian ambassadors, and the "middle class

*Rudolf Kékessy, *Vádak és valóság*, (Budapest, 1941). Despite the good intentions of Szálasi, it would seem that in No-Man's-Land, each nationality prefers its *own* extremist nationalist movement. When during the summer of 1940, the Arrow Cross tried to implement the nationality policy of Hungarism by forming a Slovakian section of the party in the territories which returned from Czechoslovakia a year before, the Slovaks answered this attempt with positive hostility. They refused to have anything to do with any Hungarian party, the Arrow Cross included. L. Olexa and V. Vipler, A *nyilaskereszt árnyékában*, (Bratislava, 1959), p. 59.

of Hungarian gentlemen" remembered only one man — Gömbös. Teleki deposited a wreath on his tomb, proclaiming that "his dream of a New Europe has come true."[105]

Nor were these grovelings and rejoicings at the fall of France and, as the "middle class of Hungarian gentlemen" wishfully saw it in June 1940, the fall of Western democracy due solely to their resentment over Trianon.* As in the case of Czechoslovakia, the Hungarian ruling classes harbored an unfeigned antipathy to everything that had happened in France since 1789. They were grateful to Hitler that he had removed this "bad example," which so impudently questioned their time-honored privileges. The France of Pétain and of the *Action Française* was much more to the liking of Horthy and Imrédy — they differed on many things but not on that account.

But on that Good Friday of the Christian West there were people at the helm other than Bonnet, Laval or Pétain. In England, Churchill replaced Chamberlain, and in the great drama he was destined to become the greatest actor. An unknown undersecretary of war, Charles de Gaulle, raised high the Cross of Lorraine which was also the Cross of Saint Joan and, following in her footsteps, "assumed the burden of France" to reverse the verdict of history and to wash her stains clean. And Roosevelt was carefully piloting his nation toward a war he considered inevitable, and which, if won by the Axis, would have meant disaster for his country.

In short, the rejoicing in Budapest not only came too soon; it was also stupid. The more so because the joke current in Italy in those days fit Hungary's position even more: "If England wins, we will lose, but if Germany wins, we are lost."

The very next day after Hitler danced his jig at Compiègne, Russia moved against Rumania. Neobaroque Hungary, which never dared to assert her just revisionist claims alone, moved in the wake of the U.S.S.R. to reclaim Transylvania from Rumania. Hitler was less than enthusiastic, because all this could endanger not only the quiet in the raw material zone, but through its implications, the raw material zone itself.** Horthy tried every means, even some not exactly "gentlemanlike" ones which throw an edifying light on his

---

*All over Hungary the "middle class of Hungarian gentlemen" repeated the editorial of the Nazi party organ which so aptly expressed its mood: "Paris was a city of frivolity and corruption — of democracy and capitalism [where] Jews had entry to the court and Negroes to the salons . . . That Paris will never rise [again]!" *Völkischer Beobachter*, June 14, 1940.

**He said so in unequivocal terms in his letter to Teleki. (See *Allianz*, pp. 263-65.) As the Hungaro-Rumanian conflict deepened, the Germans sent a stiff note to Budapest. "In order to clear up any possible misunderstandings," Ribbentrop warned Hungary that in an ensuing conflict, she could not count on German support against Rumania, adding ominously, "one can see the beginning [phase] of such a war, but not the course it might take," concluding that it would be Hungary alone who would have to bear the consequences of her conduct. *Ibid.*

alleged pro-Jewish sympathies, to convince Hitler of the righteousness of Hungarian claims.*

But the Hungarians had mobilized an army of 400,000 and Hitler saw that he could not maintain the status quo. He had gained an important advantage out of the Second Vienna Award when the Hungarian-Rumanian dispute was submitted to Germany and Italy for arbitration. He used it on August 30, 1940, when he split Transylvania. It was a solution that did not satisfy anyone. Hungary acquired 43.591 square kilometers with a population of roughly 2,500,000 people. Of these, Hungarians were in slight majority only if the Jews were considered Hungarians; otherwise, the Rumanians and the traditionally anti-Hungarian Transylvanian Saxons outweighed them. In the next years Hitler skillfully exploited the situation he had created to rally Rumanian and Hungarian loyalty, promising to Antonescu (or to the Hungarians) the other half of Transylvania in exchange for support. He also used the "favorable" Vienna Award in order to extract from Teleki a state-within-the-state status for Hungary's by then completley Nazi German minority, and the promise to ease the pressure on Hungarian Fascists.**

During the Transylvania crisis, Imrédy suspended his pressure on Teleki. He was drafted into the army, and his cronies in the mass communications media made good propaganda for him, photographing him in uniform for newsreels, magazines and newspapers, always in the forefront of the Hungarian Army advancing into Transylvania — to the great disgust of the Bethlenite conservatives.[106]

In August another fantastic Arrow Cross plot blew sky high. The gangster Kovarcz, now a representative in Parliament, and another Arrow Cross representative, Wirth, organized an Arrow Cross group, mostly of proletarians, who were to kidnap Horthy, to liberate Szálasi from jail and force Horthy to appoint him premier, to proclaim a Hungarist State, and in case of reluctance, to kill Horthy. As an accompaniment to all this, a considerable

*Horthy wrote a letter to Hitler about Transylvania, in which he deemed it proper to describe the Transylvanian Jews in the following vein: "The Transylvanian Jews were content with Rumanian rule, because they found out quickly how much money they need to bribe, how much profit the transaction will bring in, and whether it is worth it to undertake the trip to Bucharest." (Horthy, *titkos iratai*, p. 221). The ardent Hungarian patriotism of the Transylvanian Jews in the meantime was well known in Budapest and elsewhere, and was counted upon in every Magyar political move inside or outside of Transylvania. The report of an avowedly pro-Rumanian U. S. correspondent, who visited Transylvania during these months of crisis, makes melancholy reading: "The Jews, having been the backbone of pro-Magyar sympathies for twenty years, now figured that Hungarian anti-Semitism would never be as hard as Rumanian anti-Semitism." (Waldeck, *Athene Palace*, pp. 143-44.) Little the Transylvania Jews knew about the Szeged Idea after their twenty years of seclusion.

**Hitler and Ribbentrop presented the bill for Transylvania in an unabashed fashion to Sztójay — even before the Hungarians fully occupied the territory awarded to them. *Allianz*, pp. 282-88.

number of terroristic outrages were planned. The plotters sent an emissary to secure the approval of Rudolph Hess before being denounced by an agent to the police.* Kovarcz and Wirth could not be arrested while they retained parliamentary immunity. In response to motions in Parliament that this immunity be suspended, the Arrow Cross representatives were outraged at the suggestion that a "major of the army with an excellent record like his" (Kovarcz') might try to escape. They protested that it was shameful to put such a man under preliminary arrest when every Jew involved in shady financial dealings might defend himself on bail. They offered as guarantee for Kovarcz the whole Arrow Cross party.[107] The offer was accepted and Kovarcz took the next train to Berlin. There he enlisted in the SS, retaining his rank; when he returned to Hungary it was with the German army in 1944. The rest of the defendants, who had fewer connections or less skill, drew sentences of up to fifteen years' imprisonment.

The other important development at the end of July was the formation of the Hungarian National Socialist party under the leadership of Pálffy and Baky. This group had eleven representatives in Parliament and was a distinctly bourgeois Fascist group despite some peasant following in Transdanubia. Accepting the *Völkisch* idea, they got the full backing of the German subsidized paper *Magyarság* and became, as Professor Macartney aptly put it, the "contractual agent of Germany" in Hungary.[108] General Ruszkay was elected party leader and it was not surprising that the group fused with Imrédy a year later. As the *Magyarság* explained later, the paper (that is, the R.S.H.A.) would have preferred to cooperate with the Arrow Cross, but it was too intransigent toward the *Völkisch* idea.[109]

In September, when the Germans presented the bill for the Vienna Award, in addition to Swabian autonomy they demanded the repeal of Order No. 3400, more anti-Jewish legislation, the release of Szálasi, liberties for the extreme right, social reforms, more economic help for the German war effort, and a more pronouncedly Fascist regime on the order of the Iron Guard regime prevailing in Rumania. The German demands were conveyed by the Hungarian ambassador in Berlin, General Döme Sztójay (originally Stojaković, a Serb from the Vojvodina), who had been appointed by Gömbös. He was a typical Fascist fellow traveler. He was convinced of German invincibility, and he represented this view with such dedication that it was often said in Budapest that it was not the Hungarians who had an ambassador in Berlin, but Hitler who had an ambassador in Budapest. He was not a corrupt or violent man, but neither was he very bright, and it was because of this insufficiency rather than through any evil or treacherous intentions that he contributed more than his share to the damage suffered by Hungary in World War II.**

*Horthy, *titkos iratai,* p. 225. Although the plot was discovered in August, because of "diplomatic reasons" it was kept a secret until November. Lackó, *op. cit.,* pp. 228-29.

**The reports and exhortations of Sztójay are now available to the public. It seems unbelievable that Hungary did not find a more deserving diplomat for the key post in Berlin. See *Allianz, passim.*

Order No. 3400 was duly revoked, Teleki began the preparation of a new anti-Jewish bill, and at the end of September Szálasi was released from jail. He was openly contemptuous of the fact that it had been German pressure which secured his release. He told Teleki some weeks later that if it was truly German influence that freed him, he would prefer to go back to his cell. He set about reorganizing his ramshackle, demoralized party, purging some and readmitting others into the fold. It is interesting to note that this mystic, by God knows what intuition, considered his release to be but "a suspension of his sentence for five years,"* which turned out to be the case.

The Germans, as always, promoted Fascist unity and the acceptance of the *Völkisch* solution. In the first joy over Szálasi's release, and because of his close personal relations with Ruszkay, things looked bright. Ruszkay and Szálasi fused their two parties on September 29 under the name Arrow Cross party with a mixed executive board and Szálasi as leader. The action seems to have been occasioned more by enthusiasm than by any mutual hope of coordinating party programs, because Szálasi stood as far from *Volksgruppe* solutions and as inflexibly on Hungarism as ever. Now Ruszkay pressed for a union with Imrédy, who claimed to have 120 to 160 Government party delegates behind him. Szálasi's conditions were unyielding: if Imrédy wanted to join, let him accept Hungarism and let him submit to Szálasi's leadership. Imrédy refused.[110] Much more formidable was the clash between Szálasi and the Germans. By that time, the Germans had gone much beyond the *Völkisch* idea. They wanted to turn the whole Danube into a "German river," to resettle the Hungarians living in the area and bring in Germans in their place. Officially, however, they still backed the *Völkisch* principle so incompatible with Hungarism.[111] So the Germans abandoned further negotiations with the intractable Szálasi and never seriously resumed cooperation with him until the twelfth hour struck. Szálasi soon developed another clash with the new Swabian autonomous organization, the *Volksbund*, whose leader Franz Basch asked him to stop Arrow Cross recruitment activities among the Swabians. Szálasi refused, because he considered that the Swabians were Hungarian citizens and therefore eligible for membership. One can well imagine the fury of the R.S.H.A. over such blatant defiance of the *Ein Volk, ein Reich, ein Führer* principle.**

Imrédy was in truth a much more "suitable instrument." He moved against Teleki in mid-October within the framework of the Government party. But Teleki had assured himself a majority with the new Transylvania delegates, around fifty in number, who were "called in" and not elected (there were

---

*Macartney, *op. cit.*, I, 433. Immediately after his release, Szálasi visited the Arrow Cross organization of his own precinct and he fetched an Arrow Cross party card for himself, indicating his profession as a "weaver." Lackó, *op. cit.*, p. 230.

**Macartney, *op. cit.*, I, 457. Basch's fury is understandable if one takes into account the popularity of the Arrow Cross among the Swabians. During the election of 1939, the Arrow Cross won sweeping victories in the Swabian-inhabited suburbs of Budapest and in many Swabian mining communities. Lackó, *op. cit.*, p. 170n.

"called in" deputies from the former Czechoslovak territories also, not elected ones). It was possible for Teleki to call in from his native Transylvania representatives of his ideas, his clan, in many cases his family. With the help of these and with the all-important support of Horthy, he was able to inform the followers of Imrédy that they could leave the Government party if they did not like his policy. Once again the characterless vacillation of the fellow travelers of fascism was proven: out of 120 to 160 sympathizers of the spirit of the age, only eighteen of the most avowed Szeged Fascists in Parliament left with Imrédy. On October 18, the Government party formed the Party of Hungarian Renewal *(Magyar Megújulás Pártja)*, which represented the who's who of Szeged fascism: Imrédy, Jaross, Rátz, Antal Kunder, Milotay and Rajniss, to mention only a few. Party leaders were to be Imrédy, Rátz, and Jaross. Their announced program called for a complete Axis line in foreign and domestic policy, proposed "the solution of the Jewish question, especially the economic aspects of it [meaning the increase of the profitable Aryanization]," also a Fascist constitution (a corporative system), and the nationalization of banking and heavy industry (which was Jewish). It spoke in the vaguest possible terms about an agrarian reform, which would have violated the interests of some of Imrédy's partisans, and it pledged ill-defined support to "social reform."[112] Imrédy made violent outbursts against the members of the Arrow Cross, whom he called "police characters" who are "only inspired by the desperation of those who are trampled upon."[113] Jaross put things much more deliberately: "He who derives his political creed from Szeged must avow the Szeged Idea, which has matured through the last 20-22 years into a Hungarian National Socialism."[114] Also: "This flame was kindled in the political sense by Gömbös, and it was Imrédy who redefined it more thoroughly."[115]

Szálasi had the lowest possible opinion of Imrédy's new party, calling it the "Party of the Right Honourables, the Stellenbosched Ministers, the Old School Ties and the Place Hunters," and a "mule which is tough, treacherous, false, and untrustworthy."[116] Not a pleasant picture but not a bit exaggerated. The indefatigable Ruszkay brought about a meeting between the two rival Fascist leaders in November. Imrédy asked how Szálasi had "enjoyed prison" where Imrédy's treacherous provocation had sent him; whereupon Szálasi showed the holes where his teeth had been kicked out while there. Finally, because of Imrédy's cynical attitude and Szálasi's inflexibility the meeting ended in mutual discord.[117]

Horthy was furious about the Fascist commotion, no matter whether Szeged Fascist or Arrow Cross, and taking into account the Kovarcz-Wirth activities, this is not surprising. In addition, during October the Arrow Cross organized a sweeping strike in the coal mines. All mines joined unanimously, and by the end of the month 40,000 miners were idle in the greatest strike of the interwar period in Hungary. Szálasi next planned a general strike — the coal mines were to be only the beginning. When the Honvéd was ordered to repress the strikers, some commanding generals refused to use force against the miners. All this was kept secret from the public; the mining areas were sealed off by the army from the rest of the country. By the end of the month, however, the government, with the help of violence and concessions, had mastered the situation.[118] Horthy proposed to Teleki the reimprisonment of Szálasi and the mass execution and arrest of Arrow Cross men as an example to others.[119]

To those for whom the world consisted of the Danube Basin, the Spirit of the Age seemed on the march. Even Teleki was bitten by the bug. On November 13, he presented to Horthy in great secrecy and very reluctantly a project that would have turned Hungary into a Fascist corporate state. It made careful provision for the preservation of the old regime and eliminated by intricate devices the Liberals, Social Democrats, and the Arrow Cross,[120] but it did not advance beyond the planning stage.

Also in the winter of 1940, Hungary concluded two significant treaties. In November, she became the first country to adhere to the Tripartite Pact concluded among Germany, Italy and Japan against the United States. There was no special prodding from the German side for Hungarian adherence. Both Ruszkay and Szálasi felt that as a secret corollary to the Tripartite Pact, Germany (probably smarting under the impact of Iron Guard misrule in Rumania) had reverted to her former attitude: Any stable government assuring order in the *Südostraum* would do. And in the months after Hungary's adherence to the pact, Germany greatly reduced contacts and encouragements to Fascists.[121] At the same time, German troops passed through Hungary without opposition or fanfare on their way to Rumania to protect the oil fields against Russia or England. After the Tripartite Pact, Hungary in December concluded a Treaty of Eternal Friendship and Nonaggression with Yugoslavia without first settling outstanding territorial claims or setting forth terms for the treaty's renunciation.

Meanwhile, Horthy and Bethlen made an attempt to send a representative of the opposition to the West in order to establish a Hungarian Committee, or to prepare for the eventual exodus of Horthy and the chief representatives of the opposition to London to form a government in exile. Instead of the logical choice, Bethlen, they sent the charlatan leader of the Smallholders, the turncoat Eckhardt, who with his inconsistent record and his hands stained with Jewish blood from the White Terror, could accomplish nothing. He left Hungary in the spring of 1941 for the United States, amid the catcalls of the Fascists. Milotay, referring both to Eckhardt's past and to his intentions, styled him "Coriolanus."

These were the days of the Battle of Britain. The English showed beyond reasonable doubt that far from being "corrupted completely by the Jews," as Hungarian Fascists of all denominations believed it to be, their decadent democracy apparently gave them plenty of things worth fighting for. Ilya Ehrenburg, by no means a friend of England or the West, expressed the significance of the Battle of Britain thus: "It was the first victory of human dignity over the barbarity of Fascism."*

*Gleb Struve, *25 Years of Soviet Russian Literature*, (Norman, Okla., 1951), p. 316. During the Battle of Britain, most of the Hungarian press rejoiced at the agony of London, Bristol, Coventry, etc. When a liberal paper reproached them for their sadistic glee, the government daily gave a

167

Italy, Hungary's chief ally, made an ignominious martial showing. She was defeated on the ground, on the sea and in the air by the British, and effectively checked and humiliated by little Greece. But this did not dishearten the Hungarian Fascists, because since 1933 they had looked for inspiration to anti-Semitic Berlin rather than to Rome. It was the conservatives who tried desperately and unsuccessfully to break through the wall of *sacro egoismo* to get some support from Mussolini against Germany. They could not, or did not wish to, understand that to Mussolini Hungary was just what he had said — a "pawn," nothing more.[122]

Now Hitler came to Mussolini's aid. In March, he sent troops to Bulgaria, and on March 25 Yugoslavia's government, belying the country's past and in open disregard of the wishes of the people, adhered to the Tripartite Pact. The Nazis promised them Salonika as a reward for stabbing Greece in the back. The Hungarian press exulted: "It can now truly be said that peace in the *Südostraum* is assured. . . . After the imminent liquidation of the regrettable Greek episode [*sic!*], peace in this part of Europe seems 100 percent assured for as long as can be seen."[123] Little did the Fascists or the opportunist fellow travelers of Fascism know the spirit of the Serbian people.

Because the next morning, March 27, 1941, as Churchill so eloquently said, "Yugoslavia found her soul." The people rebelled, sounding a wild, thrilling refusal through the streets of Belgrade. Every thinking European and Westerner was with them. Their deed was a bell in the dark night, promising the coming of the dawn.* But the most moving tribute of all took place on the Canebière of Marseille. "Suddenly men and women bearing flowers appeared at the street where King Alexander and Barthou were assassinated in 1934. Soon the street was covered with flowers." When the Vichy police tried to break up the demonstration, the Marseillais bought streetcar tickets and

---

swift retort: "They say that one should contemplate the destroyed cities [of England] with compassion . . . with the kind of deep compassion, perhaps, to which only a democratic heart of the Lipótváros is capable — if the ammunition works owned by another Jew [in England] is destroyed [by German bombs]." The Lipótváros is a predominantly Jewish middle class district of Budapest. *Függetlenség,* January 6, 1941.

*The writer remembers that day with an almost religious emotion. The Yugoslavian radio announcer's voice trembled as he cried, "Radio Beograd! " and the shouts and the cheers of the crowds could be heard, the proud, wild declaration: "Bolje rat njego pakt! " and "Bolje grob njego rob!" "(We) prefer war to that treaty! (We) prefer to die rather than to be slaves!" The brave, old, martial songs "Spremte-se, spremte-se, četnici," "Oj Sokole," and "Oj Srbijo" filled the air, songs which sounded to youthful ears like a prayer or a benediction. Finally, there was a little Balkan nation without *Kultur* which cared nothing for the "New Order" or the "Spirit of the Age" and prepared itself with a wild, enthusiastic bravery for the ultimate sacrifice and its reward: resurrection. It seemed as if Marko Kraljević were leading the crowds of Belgrade that day, and that Colonel Dragutin Dimitrjević had risen up to assist General Dušan Simović and his friends.

dropped the flowers out of the car windows. When the police closed the flower shops, the people dropped paper flowers.[124]

Hitler decided to destroy Yugoslavia. To do so he needed Hungarian cooperation. When Horthy discovered Hitler's intentions, he was entering one of those unpredictable "enthusiastic" moods of his. He suddenly saw revision coupled with the possibility of Hungarian access to the Adriatic, the romantic vision of his youth. These considerations outweighed any others, moral or political. When Teleki reminded him, "We cannot stab in the back those people to whom we have sworn friendship," Horthy made the remarkable reply: "Yes, but the people to whom we swore friendship are no longer there."[125] A strange answer from someone who professed as much faith in legitimacy as he did; the dynasty, the king, was still there, the legitimate ruler who had appointed the new government. It would have been futile for Teleki to mention that Hungary had concluded a treaty with Yugoslavia rather than with a particular government, because popular sovereignty did not impinge upon Horthy. With Teleki thus left alone in that shameful moment of Hungarian history, Werth, the Swabian chief of staff, made irreversible and unauthorized commitments to General F. Paulus, who came to Budapest as the representative of the O.K.W. Werth promised full Hungarian military participation in the German campaign.[126] In exchange Hungary was promised the whole Vojvodina, and at first even Croatia. Sztójay also helped to force the hand of the government toward intervention.[127] The die was cast.

Teleki felt that everything was crumbling away around him, and he also saw the consequences. On the evening of April 3, after attending church, he withdrew to his home. He knew that he could command no support — his friend the Regent had deserted him, and his chief of staff had betrayed him. As a politician, Teleki may have committed errors, but in that hour at the dawn of his eternity it was the good and the noble that won an absolute victory in him. He cast out from himself everything that was calculating or worldly, and looking deep and far into the future, he wrote the following letter to Horthy:

Your Serene Highness,

We have become the breakers of our word — out of cowardice — contrary to the Treaty of Eternal Friendship — based on [your] speech at Mohács.[128] The nation feels it — and we sacrificed its honor.

We allied ourselves with scoundrels — because there is not a word of truth in the stories about atrocities.* Not even against Germans, let alone against Hungarians! We shall become robbers of corpses! The most abominable of nations!

I did not hold you back. I am guilty.[129]

---

*Atrocity stories were duly spread by the Hungarian press — allegedly committed by Yugoslavs against the Hungarian minorities — stories which were pure (or rather impure) inventions, serving one purpose only — to prepare the public for the breach of faith.

Perhaps with my voluntary death I can render a service to my nation.*

After finishing the letter, Teleki took his own life. But he could not render through his death the service to Hungary he sought to. The people reacted numbly to it, as they reacted numbly to the arrival of German armored columns some hours later — and as they reacted numbly some years later when they saw on their Jewish fellow citizens the yellow stars that marked them for Auschwitz. Yet despite its failure as far as concrete results are concerned, Teleki's deed was nevertheless great. It proved the existence of another Hungary, a Hungary vastly different from the one of Imrédy, Baky, Milotay or Kovarcz, even from that of Bárdossy.

*Macartney, *op. cit.*, I, 489. This version differs slightly from the Communist one.

CHAPTER VI

"The Common Hungarian-German Destiny"*

In every alliance there is a horse and there is a rider.

Bismarck

1

The day of Teleki's suicide, Horthy appointed Foreign Minister László Bárdossy to the premiership. The eleven months of Bárdossy's term were extremely rich in events. The treacherous Hungarian attack on Yugoslavia took place as a beginning, the Third Anti-Jewish Law was passed, Hungary went to war with the U.S.S.R., and tens of thousands of Jews were forced across the eastern border into the hands of German extermination commandos. Some months later, England declared war on Hungary, and Hungary subsequently declared war on the United States. It was also under Bárdossy that the ghastly Újvidék massacres, in which Hungarian gendarmes exterminated thousands of civilians, took place. Bárdossy violated the constitution several times, and by the end of his eleven-month rule he was hoping for an all-out Fascist Hungarian government and thinking of deporting all the Jews.[1] All these events cannot be ascribed solely to Bárdossy. Only the most fatal one, the declaration of war on the U.S.S.R., was entirely his doing.

Bárdossy was a man with great abilities which contributed to an intellectual arrogance that was his undoing — and what is much more important, his country's undoing. He came from a respectable Hungarian middle-class background in Szombathely in Transdanubia. He was by far the most gifted and brilliant officer in the foreign service during the neobaroque age, but because of the existing caste system in Hungarian society, he could not rise as high as he thought he should on the basis of his merits. This and his constant gastric troubles gave him much bitterness. As for his political connections, he was a convinced conservative. As a diplomat, however, he was flexible — very flexible. Although by no means an enemy of the West, he established close contacts with Hitler as early as 1939.[2] Believing firmly that the West could not and would not help Hungary in seeking redress for Trianon, he sought help in Berlin and Rome. In order to gain Hitler's favor, he was ready to eliminate with a singular ruthlessness everything that would block it. Up to this point one may follow his logic. What is objectionable is that he so completely committed himself to a pro-German position without even being convinced of the certainty of German victory let alone its desirability for Hungary. And he maintained this position even after he was

*Magyar német sorsközösség, the favorite slogan of the Fascists in Hungary during the Second World War.

171

convinced of German defeat, simply because he did not have the integrity to proclaim that he was wrong. He was the typical Fascist fellow traveler, and except for Imrédy and Werth no one harmed Hungary as much as he. When after the war he was led to execution, he cried out, "God deliver Hungary from these rascals! " and most of the former beneficiaries of the neobaroque edifice proclaimed him holy. Why did Bárdossy not cry out in 1944? His martyrdom is that of the riverboat gambler who loses his wager. Hungary reeled for a long time under the consequences of the miscalculations, ruthlessness and irresponsibility of his policies. As did so many others like him, Bárdossy confused the welfare of the Hungarian people with that of his class.

2

The German attack on Yugoslavia started at daybreak on Palm Sunday. Swarms of German divebombers descended without a declaration of war upon the defenseless city of Belgrade, previously declared an open city, killing tens of thousands of civilians. Four days later on April 10, Hungarian troops marched into the Vojvodina, coupling breach of faith with the killing of thousands of Serbs and the deportation of tens of thousands of others.[3] For many months they maintained a brutal military misrule that inflicted great suffering on a heroic people, a people whom neobaroque Hungary had never dared to challenge in open battle. But all these deeds failed to secure for Hungary the prize she had been promised. For Antonescu vetoed effectively the reannexation of the Banat — where the hostile and antagonized Swabian majority had in any case no desire to be returned to Hungarian rule.

In May, the Third Anti-Jewish Law was passed, bringing Hungarian anti-Jewish legislation up to the full Nuremberg racist level, in many aspects even exceeding it.[4] The Szeged designation "Christian national" no longer defined the regime; it had yielded to the Fascists' newly coined definition: ancient Christian (that is, not Jewish convert)-racially Hungarian (Őskeresztény-Fajmagyar).

When Hitler planned his Operation Barbarossa he foresaw a role in it for Finland and Rumania, but he did not envisage any role for Hungary. Consequently, although Werth had some considerable knowledge through unofficial military channels about what was coming,* the Hungarian government did not find out officially about the invasion of the U.S.S.R. until the morning of June 22, 1941. And during the next four days, a tragic but characteristic sequence of events decided Hungary's future for the rest of the century.

Werth, that sinister figure, was meddling in politics in a manner reminiscent of the "holy mission" with which Gömbös had indoctrinated the army. Submitting one memorandum after the other about the desirability of Hungarian participation in the war, he gave explicit assurances of Soviet defeat "by harvest time" (that is, in two or three weeks), with hints that

*Allianz, pp. 307-13. Sztójay, too, sent reports to Budapest to this effect.

Hitler might give Transylvania to Rumania in case of Hungarian reluctance. In reality, the Germans demanded only the breaking of diplomatic relations with Moscow, no more. Molotov showed the greatest understanding of the situation, offering Hungary in return for nonaggression the whole of Transylvania after the war. He also tried his utmost to enlighten the Hungarian ambassador J. Kristóffy as to the difference between the sublime and the ridiculous.[5] Kristóffy communicated Molotov's message to Budapest where, according to Horthy's version, it was concealed from him. According to Bárdossy, Horthy read Kristóffy's telegram and commented that "his face would burn in shame if he could not participate in this war."[6] According to German sources, Horthy sent a reproachful message to Hitler on the twenty-second, "regretting sincerely" that he was not called upon to do his share in Germany's struggle against Communism.[7]*

During the first three days, Bárdossy was still opposed to Hungarian entry into the war, and then on June 25, one of the mysteries of World War II occurred. Košice was bombed by aircraft, supposedly Russian, but identified by the Hungarian military at the Košice airbase as German. It will probably never be known for certain which side did the bombing. It is not even important. Air attacks on border towns occurred many times during the war — the Americans bombed Basle and Schaffhausen, the Italians Bitolj, the Russians Harparanda on the Swedish-Finnish frontier, and so forth. One thing is certain: The U.S.S.R. was ready at that point to go to any length to keep Hungary neutral, and it is therefore reasonable to assume that the Soviets were not interested in provoking incidents. Also, such minor incidents could have been easily settled.

Bárdossy's intellect, which he considered infallible, led him to different conclusions. According to his own account, he was convinced by that time that Hitler wanted to drag Hungary into the war sooner or later; the military and Horthy also wanted war, so it was better not to ask, "What do you want? " but to make a voluntary offer.[8] He acted swiftly. He threatened the military witnesses of the Košice raid with dire consequences if they mentioned that the attacking planes were German, as he was personally firmly convinced they were, and the next day, in violation of the constitution, he declared war without consulting Parliament.[9]** Molotov tried

---

*Horthy, *titkos iratai*, p. 296. Understandably, it became the axiom of Hungarian Communist historians that Molotov did not make any offer concerning Transylvania at that point. To this effect even an "original" Kristóffy telegram was produced, which looks as if it has been edited—to say the least. According to this document, Molotov "did not say anything [to the effect] that Hungarian demands could be satisfied at the cost of Rumania." After that, Kristóffy "assures" everybody concerned, that "he (Molotov) will say nothing [about Transylvania] in the future either." *Allianz, op. cit.*, p. 314.

**After Bárdossy's portentous announcement, the house continued to discuss the really important thing: how to take away some lucrative law offices from some Jewish attorneys — as if nothing had happened. *O.N.K.*, June 27, 1941, pp. 305-28.

to conciliate to the end. Even when Kristóffy handed him the declaration of war, he was told to "take back that bit of paper" or to wait a little.[10] It was no use. Two days later, on June 28, a small Hungarian armed force crossed the Hungarian-Soviet frontier to begin one of the most senseless and disastrous adventures in Hungarian history.

3

Professor Macartney weighs well the meaning of Bárdossy's step:

In the larger sense it is unfair to single out any one point in a continuous curve as marking a turning-point, or any one step made in a march which is always consistent in direction and even in pace, as more fateful than any other. Yet the decision which Bárdossy had taken on that June afternoon can truly be described as decisive, since it had carried Hungary past that all-important dividing-line which separates the State technically at peace, and thus entitled by international convention to be treated as intangible even by those who hate it, from the belligerent, which, if defeated, can be dealt with by the conquerors at its mercy. Hungary was now committed, as a belligerent, to one of the two parties in the world struggle, and committed irrevocably; for although Bárdossy had not promised Hitler not to make a separate peace, the country's geographical position alone, not to mention her situation in respect of armaments, was such that — as Kállay was subsequently to discover — once fitted into Germany's operational machine she could not possibly be extricated, or extricate herself, until that machine had ceased to function. She had therefore to reckon with all the consequences of defeat if defeat came to her party in the war; which consequences, incidentally, were bound in the circumstances to include not only the imposition of whatever territorial terms the victors cared to dictate, but also the annihilation of her entire ruling class. This followed, if from nothing else, from the fact that in default of any other serious pretext (the Košice incident could easily have been settled without war, even if the Russians were really to blame) she had chosen to announce as the motive for her action her desire to take part in a crusade against Bolshevism, thus leaving the U.S.S.R. no choice — if it wanted one — but to retort in kind and see whose arm was the longer. The stirring up of revolutionary feeling against a regime which had itself chosen an ideological battleground was now a natural and legitimate weapon for the Soviets to use, and if and when in a position to do so, they would inevitably extirpate their challengers.

Finally, although Bárdossy's declaration of hostilities was confined to the U.S.S.R., so that in theory it did not affect Hungary's relations with the Western Powers, it was, again in the circumstances, impossible that that situation could be long maintained. Germany's opponents were bound to end by uniting not only against Germany but also against her allies and satellites. War with Russia must sooner or later lead on to war with Britain and the U.S.A.[11]

There was little enthusiasm in Hungary for the war effort, and very few people understood at that time the implications of the step taken by Bárdossy. Not even the Hungarian Nation wanted war. What they desired were the fruits of war, and the removal of that ugly abscess in Moscow which, like the ones in Prague and Paris, seemed to challenge their privileges so insolently. Those of the political nation who had condemned the Nazi-Soviet pact two years earlier felt a great relief; they could be pro-Nazi without reservation again.

Bárdossy was just as conservative in internal affairs. When the Imrédists rebuked him for "stagnating and not moving with the times," he declared that he refused to "indulge in experiments or projects during the war."[12] However, one rather bloody experiment was undertaken right after the beginning of the Soviet campaign: 12,000-30,000 Jews* who were not Hungarian nationals were driven across the border into Galicia and swiftly exterminated by the waiting SS *Einsatzkommandos*. It was the Hungarian military that proposed the deportation, and in some places, such as Kamenec-Podolsk, the Hungarian Army also participated in the massacres.[13] But at that point in July 1941, few people in the general public or the government knew about the exterminations. Even Bárdossy did not know yet. And as far as the overwhelming majority of Jews with Hungarian citizenship were concerned, their lives were still safe at that point.

4

Thanks to Bárdossy's obliging attitude, the German government did not find it necessary for the time being to conspire with the Hungarian Fascists. The R.S.H.A., on the other hand, did continue its schemings. Its main goals were as always: right-wing unity; union of the "head" with the "body" of the Fascist movement, that is, of Imrédy with the mass support of the Arrow Cross; unreserved Hungarian acceptance of the *Völkisch* solution; and subservience to the Reich. Imrédy did not cause any particular difficulty, and the R.S.H.A. cleared him for a political future in the new order by declaring that all documents supporting allegations about his Jewish ancestry were forgeries.[14] Then Szálasi was approached by Ruszkay to reconcile his differences with Imrédy. But, Szálasi, of course, would not abandon an iota of Hungarism.

At that point a new personality entered Fascist intrigue: Archduke Albrecht of Habsburg. He had figured in Fascist designs in the early twenties when Gömbös wanted to make him King of Hungary. Albrecht had recently repossessed large family estates in the newly won Yugoslav territories and hoped for the return of even larger family estates in the Czech part of Silesia, then under German rule. In return he pledged to the Nazis that if they supported his candidacy for the Regency, he would introduce a Nazi regime to Hungary based on the *Völkisch* idea, unconditionally subservient to Hitler.[15] Imrédy's party was agreeable, but Szálasi brusquely rejected Albrecht's feelers as contrary to three important points of Hungarism: (1) power must be achieved with the consent of the Regent and the nation; (2) the Arrow Cross must continue to admit Swabians; and (3) the *Völkisch* idea

---

*Hilberg, *Destruction of the European Jews*, p. 520, puts the number at 12,000; Macartney, up to 30,000. *October Fifteenth*, II, 37-38.

contradicted Hungarism.[16] Baky and Pálffy then broke their year-old uneasy alliance with Szálasi. They could not change his determination, so there was no reason for a continuation of this grotesque alliance of self-seeking, Szeged Fascist, bourgeois elements with a patriotic, proletarian, Fascist movement.* In September 1941, Baky and Pálffy founded the Hungarian National Socialist party, and the *Magyarság* duly repudiated Szálasi and endorsed the new party, proclaiming that the new party structure accepted "not merely friendship with Germany but also German leadership."[17] Even more clear was Pálffy's statement reflecting the acute German disappointment over the failure of the Iron Guard in Rumania some months earlier and the Third Reich's determination not to allow anything more to upset the quiet in the raw material zone: "Such a disturbance and the upheaval which would follow it would not be in the interest of that power which defends the whole of Europe from bolshevism with a struggle demanding such a bloody sacrifice. Even an interruption for a week may cause immeasurable damage to production. Therefore, we do not see any other way than the constitutional solution."[18] The program of the Baky-Pálffy group was consequently extremely conservative.[19] On September 24, 1941, Imrédy concluded a parliamentary alliance with the Gestapo agency, pledging allegiance to its *Völkisch* goals; in turn the Nazi agents pledged not to raise any question of reform, to abandon their "dynamic policy" and to "renounce revolution." The new alliance was called Party Alliance of the Party of Hungarian Renewal and National Socialists (*Magyar Megújulás Pártja Nemzetiszocialista Pártszövetség*). The mixed executive committee, consisting of five Imrédists and four National Socialists, was a gruesome mixture of corruption and treason; almost all of its members derived their past from Gömbös: László Baky, Béla Imrédy, Fidél Pálffy, Antal Incze, Andor Jaross, János Lill, Ferenc Rajniss, Jenö Rátz, Olivér Rupprecht. Imrédy's words in Parliament put the final seal on this new alliance, demonstrating both his creed and his insight into the future: "The era of revolution had passed in all Europe!"[20]

Szálasi was weakened by these events, but not broken. Some deputies left him, partly because of opportunism (they believed Szálasi's inflexible devotion to Hungarism spoiled their chances for a bright future), partly because of personal motives. As everywhere in Europe, after the attack on the U.S.S.R., the crypto-Communists dropped their masquerade and seceded from the Arrow Cross to rejoin the clandestine Communist party. Szálasi welcomed these changes and even increased the purges himself.[21] As usual, he was never susceptible to practical considerations, despite the fact that after the Bakyist-Imrédist union, a ferocious struggle started in the ranks of his

---

*Dr Höttl came personally to Budapest in September to make arrangements for this. Afterward, Baky gathered the Arrow Cross representatives, and told them in a matter-of-fact tone that "the instructions from Berlin arrived, and that we must form with Imrédy a rightist government and whoever did not come (with him) would miss the bus." He (Baky) "would not wait anymore; he would leave [the Arrow Cross] right away." Lackó, *Nyilasok, nemzetiszocialisták*, p. 266.

supporters. It is in reality but a renewed manifestation of the internal conflict that had plagued the movement from its birth, raging between the bourgeois and proletarian elements.

When the membership was polled about a possible union with the Imrédists, according to the police spies, "the workers oppose it and the middle class intellectuals press for it vigorously," and again, "All letters which arrive announcing the abandonment of the Arrow Cross are written without exception by members who belong to the middle classes"; finally, "the workers will stick with Szálasi . . ."; "they consider Imrédy [somebody with] a too-bourgeois mentality . . ."; "they hope to accomplish the violent changes they desire with the help of Szálasi."[22] So, despite the fusion of Imrédists with the R.S.H.A. agency, there could be no question of a united Fascist front. With the fusion of the Pálffy-Baky and Imrédy groups only Szeged Fascist unity was achieved, not complete Fascist unity.

The only step taken in the right direction during these months, and then, like many correct moves during the neobaroque age, taken when it was already very late, was the dismissal of the meddling Werth as chief of staff. He infuriated not only Teleki but also Bárdossy[23] with his incessant memoranda, which meddled into business which was not his. He was replaced with another Swabian, General Ferenc Szombathelyi (Knauss), but Szombathelyi was a loyal Hungarian.

5

Meanwhile, "General Winter" arrived in the Soviet Union. The Russians had recovered from the first blows of the blitz; they had also found out what the Herrenvolk had in store for the "inferior" Slavs, and their traditional and passionate love for Mother Russia was greater than their hatred for the Politburo. A holy nationalism stiffened the resistance before Moscow and elsewhere. The Russian engagement in Europe increased Japanese appetites, and Japan provoked the United States at Pearl Harbor. Three days later, Hitler, in complete underestimation of the realities of the world, declared war on the United States. So at the first failure Germany suffered in the war, an uncommonly strong new enemy of the Axis entered the arena: the United States. Just a day before Pearl Harbor, Britain, pressed hard by Stalin, declared war on Hungary, Rumania and Finland.

When the Axis declared war on the United States, Bárdossy, under German and Italian pressure and under even stronger pressure from Sztójay, followed suit. The United States was sympathetic. Herbert C. Pell, the United States minister, made a gesture of understanding to Bárdossy: "I suppose you are doing this under heavy pressure from Germany and that the declaration reflects no hostility on the part of the Hungarian people towards the people of the United States?" But Bárdossy did not like his decisions questioned. Once the dice were cast he did not even consider it important to be civil to the United States. He answered accordingly, "Hungary is a sovereign and independent state and makes this intimation as such. Her Government and people are entirely one."[24] Thus, one way or the other, during the first six months of Bárdossy's government, little Hungary became involved in war with three of the strongest powers on earth.

At the beginning of January 1942, Ribbentrop and Keitel visited Budapest and pressured the Hungarians to send the Second Hungarian Army (about 200,000 men) to the Russian front for the anticipated great attack which was supposed to crush the recalcitrant Russians in the coming summer. The Hungarians were reluctant to commit themselves, but Sztójay wired, phoned and intervened, purveying the usual admonition that in case of refusal Transylvania would be lost.[25]

At the end of January, a memorable event occurred in Novi Sad (Újvidék), where a small band of Yugoslav partisans (if they were Yugoslavs at all) began a guerilla action. There are strong reasons to believe that there was German provocation involved,[26] because of all occupied areas of Yugoslavia, it was Hungarian-occupied Vojvodina that before these incidents and afterward was the calmest. The authorities first deputized the Hungarian inhabitants of this mixed region, and with the help of the civilians, they summarily murdered 1,800 innocent Serbians and Jews (many women and children) in the villages surrounding Novi Sad. But all this was not enough for the military and the gendarmerie. The military commander Ferenc Feketehalmi-Czeydner wanted to show off. He threw a cordon around Novi Sad (population 61,000). A curfew was ordered. The Royal Hungarian Gendarmerie, which carried out this feat, was issued generous portions of rum before undertaking the task. In a savage frenzy, they dragged about 3,300 persons (147 children and 299 old people among them) to the frozen banks of the Danube and to the local cemetary, stripping, robbing, mutilating and murdering them there, throwing their bodies under the ice of the river. Most of the people killed were Serbs, but almost the entire Jewish population of about 700 (most of them patriotic Hungarians under Yugoslav rule) was also exterminated. The gendarmes and the Honvéd pillaged for three days in Novi Sad, uninhibited by their superiors. Germans, Hungarians and Croats were also shot by drunken gendarmes.*   This was too much even for neobaroque society. The

*Macartney, op. cit., II, 69-73; also Allianz, pp. 320-35. The minutes of the Hungarian investigation following Novi Sad are available. Because they are symptomatic of the spirit of the gendarmerie and of many members of the Gömbös-appointed Officers Corps, here are some details: a captain of the gendarmerie, M. Zöldi, "staged a fake clash between civilians and gendarmes" in order to justify the massacres. His colleague, first lieutenant of the gendarmerie, Fóthy, "ordered his gendarmes to place guns in the hands of the murdered civilians and to fill their pockets with hand grenades in order to justify the massacre posthumously." In the meantime, Fóthy quickly sent eight valuable furcoats, which he took from the dead bodies of his victims, to Budapest to sell them. Another gendarme officer bandaged his gendarmes to pretend they were wounded in order to justify new massacres. A high-ranking Hungarian officer, when asked by desperate civilians to come and check up on the senseless outrages, answered that "as long as the shooting continues [outside] he has no intention of leaving [the safety of the room]." He was accused of cowardice by the military tribunal later.

opposition protested. But the entire Fascist camp, with the generous help of the many Fascist fellow travelers in the Government party, abused the champion of the victims of Novi Sad and of Hungary's honor, Smallholders leader Endre Bajcsy-Zsilinszky, for "impugning the honor of the army." And in the *K.u.K.* tradition, the question of "honor" was a tabu. The officers involved used this tabu effectively to their purposes, lying and deceiving Horthy,[27] Bárdossy, even their own superiors.[28] In neobaroque Hungary the word of an officer closed the case. It was not the last time that the conservatives were to suspect that the true *K.u.K.* spirit might differ vastly from that spirit with which Gömbös inspired the Hungarian Officers Corps. But for the time being, Horthy personally reassured Feketehalmi-Czeydner, that although he had been "strongly attacked in Jewish circles," nothing would happen to him, "because he was a good soldier and good patriot."[29] Indeed, a man with the integrity of Kállay had to come along, and what was more important, the military situation had to change decisively, before this shame could be scoured from the name of Hungary.

When a year later Bajcsy-Zsilinszky brought up the case in Parliament, it gave occasion to one of the most degrading sessions in Hungarian parliamentary history. Imrédy's party made the arrangements for the performance, generously supported by the Fascist fellow travelers of the Government party and the Arrow Cross. Bajcsy-Zsilinszky could not even complete a sentence over the noise of Imrédists and other Fascists. When he began his address, Rajniss (Imrédist) began to shout: "They killed Hungarian gendarmes! " "Tell it to the English! Because you are speaking to them now anyhow! " As the roar increased and some Fascists left the chamber in protest, Jaross, (Imrédist) banged on the table: "Do not leave! " Pacolay: (Fascist fellow traveler, Government party) "Treason! "

Bajcsy-Zsilinszky tried to continue his speech, quoting figures and facts about Novi Sad, whereupon in the general roar J. Piukevich (Fascist fellow traveler, Government party) cried, "All this has an American line! "

By that time, the alarm bell was sounding, only to be drowned out by the deafening noise, and Speaker András Tasnádi-Nagy, a Fascist fellow traveler, threatened to silence Bajcsy-Zsilinszky. Jaross: "Deny him the right to speak! " K. Mosonyi (Imrédist): "Go to America! " "Deprive him of his immunity! " Others: "Are you Hungarian? " "Let's throw him out! " "It is sad that you bring such things up! " "How can one speak like that in a Hungarian Parliament? "

The speaker warned Bajcsy-Zsilinszky again that he spoke "against the public interest," and that he would deny him the right to speak. Imrédist interruptions: "He speaks in order to endear himself to America! " Piukevich: "They listen to him in London and in America! " By that time Bajcsy-Zsilinszky lost patience and said, "There will be a time when you will speak otherwise! " Whereupon Rajniss: "We are ready to die for our convictions! "* In the general noise and heckling, Bajcsy-Zsilinszky cried

*When in 1946 Rajniss got his chance to do so, he showed a singular lack of willingness and dignity.

out in despair: "Only my Hungarian conscience was speaking out!" At that point, amid general abuse and hollering, the speaker silenced him. As the noise was dying away one last Fascist remark: "There is no need for such Hungarians!"[30]

This session shows not only the morale of the first Parliament elected under the secret ballot but especially the morale of the Szeged Fascists, the Imrédists. Another peculiar feature is that all the hatred and abuse were directed exclusively at the West — none at the U.S.S.R. This session explains the events of 1944 in Hungary. The Szeged men were responsible for both.

In February 1942, Horthy made an attempt to perpetuate the rule of his family by electing his son as Deputy Regent and his successor. His son István, if not the "incomparable genius" Horthy described to Szálasi,[31] was more liberal, less anti-Semitic, and as anti-Nazi as his father. He himself did not wish to become Deputy Regent, according to Kállay, but his father forced him into it.* The entire Fascist camp was opposed, although on various grounds, to this perpetuation of the neobaroque regime. Szálasi opposed it on the grounds that it would perpetuate the Regency, which was meant to be provisional, and because young Horthy would be elected by a Parliament that did not represent the Hungarian people's will. The Germans were also violently opposed; consequently in Parliament Imrédy made an unprecedented personal attack on the Regent. Ruszkay, and with him the Archduke Albrecht, who had the most to lose in the affair, were desperately spreading slander about young Horthy, especially in Berlin. They tried to win over Szálasi for the Imrédy opposition front, but Szálasi dismissed the young Habsburg contemptuously as "an agent of German imperialism."** But young Deputy Regent Horthy was duly elected by a servile Government party in alliance with the opposition. Some days later, Szálasi expelled the rather unprincipled Hubay and the Nazi agent Ruszkay from his party. Both Hubay and Ruszkay joined Baky's R.S.H.A. agency's party, which was allied closely with Imrédy. With this and other desertions and expulsions, the Arrow Cross representation in Parliament sank to twenty. Out of these, fourteen were reliable Szálasi men, six unreliable.[32] Archduke Albrecht condemned the election of young Horthy in strong terms in a personal letter written to the Regent himself.[33]

By that time, February 1942, the attitude of Horthy and his circle was maturing. Horthy never desired or believed in German victory, although he

*Súlyok, A Magyar tragédia, p. 483. More likely it was the "female camarilla," which pressed the issue: the Regent's wife, István's wife (Countess Edelsheim-Gyulai), his mother-in-law and some other female members of the family. Karsai, A budai vártól a gyepüig, p. 124.

**Macartney, op. cit., II, 76-78. But at the same time Arrow Cross "activists" flooded Budapest with leaflets attacking young Horthy in terms so vulgar only somebody of the stature of Omelka could have thought of them. He got his reward for his poetic imagination from Minister of Interior Keresztes-Fischer. The whole group which conceived and distributed the leaflets received severe jail sentences. Lackó, op. cit., p. 277.

was sometimes carried away into raptures of "enthusiasm," but the entrance of the United States into the war dissipated the slightest doubt in his mind about the outcome. Also, the British-American bloc seemed enough of a guarantee to the Bethlenites that Soviet designs on Central Europe would be checked. Bárdossy, on the other hand, decided that Hungary had to stick for good or ill with Germany as her only chance for survival; consequently, the best thing she could do was to please the Germans. Willing to be consistent, Bárdossy asked the Regent to dismiss the Bethlenite ministers from the cabinet (above all Keresztes-Fischer, the iron-handed minister of interior) and to replace them with pro-Germans to further anti-Jewish legislation and the deportation of the Jews.[34] Horthy was already annoyed at the way Bárdossy had defied him on the issue of granting his son not only the Deputy Regency but also the stipulation, "*cum jure successionis*" (right of succession).[35] And as the Regent wished to disengage Hungary from the Axis, he saw that Bárdossy with his openly contemptuous, intellectual arrogance was not the man to carry out such a policy.

6

Miklós Kállay replaced Bárdossy on the 9th of March. Kállay was a Bethlenite with all his heart. Frankly conservative in the Hungarian and not in the Western sense of the word, he was hostile to any popular movement, consequently to Nazism, also. He sympathized with Italian fascism but from a distance — as far as Szaboles county (which his family had ruled for centuries) was from Rome. He would have liked to have kept Hungary as it was. He stood on the foundation of the Crown of St. Stephen, because he saw in it a guarantee that his class would continue to rule Hungary as it had for a thousand years. On the all-important Jewish question he was much more open-minded than Bethlen or Horthy, who merely tolerated the Jews because they needed them as auxiliaries for their class rule, never going beyond that *Interessengemeinschaft*. Although Kállay believed basically as they did, he went beyond it. He was ready to consider the Jews human beings and to make allowances for their tragic past in evaluating their present. Kállay was a good politician and a realist without even a grain of Fascist enthusiasm, and he was as flexible as Bethlen could be — a long line of ancestors had bequeathed upon him these talents. But flexibility in his case did not mean cynicism or immorality, only that he was ready to take one step backward in order to take two steps forward later — and he never lost sight of his goal, whether advancing or retreating. This goal was simple: to save Hungary and the equivalent in his mind, his class, the Hungarian Nation. He was convinced from the outset of ultimate Axis defeat, yet he knew that the Germans were still strong enough to inflict disaster on Hungary. Therefore, he had to proceed carefully in his plans to disassociate Hungary from Hitler and bring it eventually under British and not Soviet control. He, like Horthy, was convinced that the Western powers (now that France was gone) were interested in a conservative Hungary.

Churchill called the first half of 1942 the "Hinge of Fate." Kállay's pro-German and anti-Jewish utterances of those days caused no little consternation in democratic circles.* Unfortunately, no one else was misled as to Kállay's real intentions—neither Imrédy, who received Kállay's appointment and pro-Nazi statements with a skeptical Goethe quotation, *Die Botschaft hör ich wohl allein mir fehlt der Glaube*, and promised to be a "consistent and determined opponent" of Kállay,[36] nor the Arrow Cross, whose spokesman "did not even give the benefit of doubt" to Kállay,[37] nor Göbbels, who sardonically commented at the appointment of Kállay that he "never had any illusions about Hungary so he was not undergoing disillusionment."[38]

But as spring came, all internal political struggle subsided for several months when the Second Army went to its doom in Russia. Many members of Parliament, among them Imrédy, enlisted for "service at the front" — that is, office work behind it — although Imrédy was not so fortunate. On the orders of Horthy, he had to serve on the frontline. The Regent's son did not hide out in a comfortable office either. He flew several combat missions, and on his saint's day, August 20, the day of St. Stephen, he crashed in his fighter plane and died.

After that, the "female camarilla" wanted to carry out a coup to crown young Horthy's infant son with the Crown of St. Stephen as Apostolic King of Hungary — and thus found the Horthy dynasty. It was only after the resolute personal intervention of Cardinal Justinián Serédi, the Primate of Hungary, who did not wish to see "a Calvinist baby" on the throne of Hungary that the Regent abandoned the plan.[39]

It was at this time that the horrors of the Jewish labor battalions began. Bárdossy enacted the law that excluded Jews from service in the armed forces. Labor battalions were formed in which people of Jewish faith wore yellow and those "racially" Jewish but baptized wore white armbands. As the Second Army was being organized, the Jews with little regard to age (up to forty-five and fifty) were called up also. These unfortunates fell into the hands of the Szeged Fascist military, who were unrestrained by any civilian interference. The consequences were disastrous. Lawyers, doctors and other intellectuals were called up often on the basis of denunciation by their enemies and with no regard for their age. The commanders of these battalions were in many cases seasoned Fascist sadists. Their activities were blessed by most of their superiors. Some officers were confidentially ordered to "bring their battalion home in an attaché case," that is, the card index only.[40] These officers went to work to carry out orders. Former Jewish officers, veterans and heroes of the great war, were beaten, humiliated, frozen and starved to

*Súlyok, *op. cit.*, p. 477. Also, Colonel Gyula Kádár told the writer that when he organized a too enthusiastic farewell ceremony for a Hungarian division leaving for the front, Kállay was very dissatisfied. He told Colonel Kádár that they *had* to go, but there was no reason even for rejoicing, much less for making noise.

death, driven out to clear Russian mine fields without any advance training.* In addition to the effects of hunger and maltreatment, they were ravaged by an appalling typhoid epidemic. They were left alone in most cases to die. In the village of Doroshich, there was a barracks full of Jewish labor battalion typhoid cases. The barracks was set afire by the Hungarian military, and those who tried to escape were shot. About 400 Jews perished there.[41] Drunken officers occasionally forced the Jews to climb trees and made them jump from branch to branch as they shot at them, playing "hunt". It is in this way that Atilla Petschauer, who had won the world fencing championship for Hungary during the Olympic Games, perished.[42] Professor Macartney writes that Jewish losses in Russia were proportionately not higher than non-Jewish ones.[43] This is true. What Professor Macartney failed to notice was that the labor battalions were not engaged in combat, were in most cases hundreds of miles from the front, and suffered their losses not from the enemy but from Hungarian "military" activity. Out of 37,200 Jews sent to Russia, there were, according to official Hungarian figures, 25,456 killed, wounded, or missing between January 1942 and January 1944.[44]

In September 1942, Kállay tried to stop this nightmare by replacing the Szeged Fascist minister of defense, Károly Bartha, who had refused to do so much as lift a finger against it, with General Vilmos Nagy, a friend of the Jews. But Nagy's humanitarian instructions were sabotaged in most cases by the clannish, closed Szeged Fascist military establishment. Imrédy's party could not tolerate Nagy's humanitarian policy, and in less than a year he was blackmailed into resignation.[45]

7

By January 1942, Hitler had decided to destroy European Jewry before the end of the war. In January, the famous Wannsee conference took place, the Final Solution was decided upon and Eichmann went to work. The German task was an easy one in areas under direct German occupation, but in their satellites they had to deal with the governments. The Croat and Slovak Clero-Fascists did not cause any difficulty, although Jozef Tišo had some second thoughts when the Vatican intervened. Bulgaria enacted some superficial anti-Jewish measures, but balked at the crucial deportation demand.[46] Antonescu seemed first to agree to deportation, then (apparently he discovered the real nature of "resettlement") abruptly changed his mind.[47] Despite the onerous anti-Jewish laws, the military's brutalities in Novi Sad and with the labor battalions, and the expulsion and extermination of Jews with no Hungarian citizenship, the bulk of Jewry, about 800,000, were still alive in Hungary in 1942, many of them still prosperous. Kállay was

---

*As an instructive parallel, the men of the German officers corps — even those in the SS — had great psychological problems in fulfilling orders they knew would lead to the mistreatment of their Jewish war veterans. Hilberg, *op. cit.*, p. 278.

determined to keep it that way. But he was soon subjected to pressures from the Imrédists, the Jew-hating, non-Jewish middle class (in close concert with the Germans), to bring destruction to these 800,000 human beings.

When in October 1942 the Jewish expert of the SS, Dieter Wisliceny, came to Budapest for a private visit, the Imrédist (although a Fascist fellow traveler in the Government party) secretary of state, Baron Miklós Vay,* sought him out and offered him the "resettlement" of Hungarian Jews *sua sponte*. The perplexed Wisliceny pleaded that he had no authority to discuss the matter.

Authority was not long in coming. On the seventeenth, Sztójay transmitted the official German demand to mark the Jews with a yellow star and to "resettle" them "in the East [Auschwitz]." Sztójay, as always, did his best to champion German demands to the utmost. Nor was Sztójay ignorant of the nature of the resettlement: being a confidant of the Nazi hierachy, he had flatly told György Ottlik, the editor of the semiofficial *Pester Lloyd*, during the latter's visit in Berlin some weeks before (summer, 1942) that he was aware that resettlement meant extermination. Ottlik reported his conversation with Sztójay to the Foreign Ministry in Budapest on October 10, 1942.[48] Kállay flatly refused to obey the demand. He had no illusions about what was going to happen to the Jews. Even without Ottlik's memorandum, the mass extermination of Jews in 1941 all over the occupied U.S.S.R. had been witnessed by thousands of Hungarian soldiers and officers, and it did not require a great deal of imagination on Kállay's part. It is ridiculous and contemptible for anybody who served on the Russian front and passed through Poland and the occupied U.S.S.R., an area inhabited before by six million Jews and by then devoid of Jews, to maintain that he did not know what was going to happen to the Jews when they were deported. Kállay was not that kind.

But other Hungarians were. There was the Archduke Albrecht, for example. He visited Berlin in December and suggested to Himmler through an intermediary that he "exert pressure on Horthy and Kállay through Hitler" in order to bring about the Final Solution.[49] But to no avail. Kállay stood like a rock, and Horthy and the whole Bethlenite wing supported him against the Germans — and more important, against the Szeged Fascists under Imrédy at home. Szálasi, contrary to the myths, never supported the deportations, and when they came about under Imrédist rule in 1944, he was opposed to them.[50] How can Horthy be explained, the man who wrote in a personal letter to his friend Teleki as late as October 1940: "I was all my life an anti-Semite and never entertained personal relations with Jews. It is I who first preached anti-Semitism loudly in Europe." But, as he added, he could not tolerate inhumane, sadistic anti-Semitic action "while we still need them."[51] And Bethlen and many other ultraconservatives who thought in the same vein were the protectors of the Jews during the war. If it had been up to

---

*Prof. Hilberg calls him "Fay" but this is German misspelling. The person in question is the Imrédist Government party representative, Baron László Vay. Hilberg, *op. cit.*, pp. 522-23.

them, would the Hungarian Jews have survived? When we consider this seemingly inconsistent phenomenon more closely, we can offer the following explanation:

First, the Jews were not challenging the ultraconservatives and not blocking their economic future — in many cases they were their allies. The "middle class of Hungarian gentlemen," on the other hand, and the borderline cases of the petite bourgeoisie, the military, all the elements rallying behind Imrédy, those in the Arrow Cross to a lesser degree, and the fellow travelers had everything to gain through the spoilation and extermination of the Jewish middle classes. They ardently wished also to remove the *csáklyások* from the helm of state and to take their place — believing that they were far more capable of fulfilling the demands of the spirit of the age than those "reactionaries."

Secondly, Horthy and the Bethlenites believed in and desired an Allied victory with an Anglo-Saxon influence in the Danube Basin. They knew well that they would then be called to account for the fate of the Jews. In a way, they believed too much in their own allegations about Churchill's, and especially Roosevelt's, being the tool of Jewish financiers, and they were inclined to credit the Jews in America and elsewhere with exaggerated influence, which even if not true made them wary of delivering the Jews to their death. *Because by 1943 the question was not whether to enact one or two anti-Jewish ordinances, more or less — but whether the Jews should live or die.* The Fascist middle classes on the other hand did not believe in and had no desire for an Allied victory that would have brought democracy to Hungary, and with it the odious system of free competition in which the job qualifications are not decided upon the basis of baptismal certificate or racial background. Until 1945, the Jewish middle classes were much more identified with Britain and America in Hungarian Fascist minds than with bolshevism. It was for that reason that these groups hated the Western Allies much more than bolshevism.

The third reason for conservative tolerance was explained by Kállay, who frankly and correctly expounded the old Bethlenite concept of the early twenties when he stated that the demands on the Jewish issue, once fulfilled, would have been followed by others directed "against the whole Hungarian 'elite.' "[52] Both Hungarian and German Nazis were eager to destroy this elite (that is, the ruling Bethlen-Horthy ultraconservatives). To remove the pillar on which they rested, the Jewish capitalist, would have been a decisive step in that direction.

Finally, the ultraconservatives, although many of them looked down upon the "despicable Jew" with a medieval aristocratic contempt, retained too much noble Christian sentiment to hand over those 800,000 unfortunates to wholesale destruction. On the other hand, moral and Christian considerations were nonexistent beyond a nauseating lip service among those classes in which Imredy represented Catholicism and Jaross represented nationalist integrity, the butchers of Novi Sad, the Officers Corps, and the "honor" of the army, and Milotay was the intellect, and in which men like Baky and Rajniss put forward their R.S.H.A. brand of Hungarian patriotism while cashing Gestapo paychecks. For them to destroy the Jews was to secure their own economic and political future. To this end they were willing to sacrifice even Hungary, not only the hated Jews. Kállay's minor anti-Jewish bills, enacted as a camouflage move, had not imperiled even the economic existence of Jewish majority let alone their lives. They were met with derision by the Fascists. In their *nouveau riche* circles, they kept the Jewish question constantly and consistently to the fore. These circles, well-entrenched in administrative and military posts thanks to Gömbös, did not wait for official guidance. At Budapest University, for example, as early as 1941, the few Jewish students were forced by their colleagues to wear distinctive marks. As the Imrédist leader, Antal Incze, explained in Parliament, "The students decided to call upon the Jews to confess openly their Judaism. There is nothing illegal in this, and nothing else happened, except that the students prepared at their own cost extremely tasteful Jewish stars for them and called upon them to wear them."[53] Prince Felix Schwarzenberg, though not speaking of Jews, summed up well the attitude of Hungarian Fascists toward the Jews: "To degrade first and then — destroy! " Beneath their opportunistic surface, the Fascists were seething against Kállay because of his protection of Jews, his Anglo-Saxon orientation, because he had curbed for the first time since 1938 the voice of the Fascist press in its anti-Western, anti-Jewish outpourings. These "ancient Christian and racially Hungarian" circles were incapable of looking at any Hungarian problem apart from the Jewish issue — that is, their own economic and political future. When the tide turned so suddenly and unexpectedly against them in the winter of 1942-43 at Stalingrad, El Alamein and French North Africa, coupled with the shattering defeat of the Hungarian Second Army at the Don River, their hatred was suffused with alarm. Being also "enthusiasts," unwilling and unable to evaluate realities, they drew their conclusions in their own way.

8

Kállay by that time had put into effect his plan to extricate Hungary from the Axis camp. Hungarian diplomats in neutral countries, especially in Turkey but also in Switzerland, Sweden, Portugal and Spain and at the Vatican, began complicated negotiations with England and the United States. He also established close contact with the opposition and its democratic wing, the Hungarian National Independence Front (*Magyar Nemzeti Függetlenségi Front*), the backbone of which was the Alliance of Smallholders, now purged of Eckhardt's reactionary, opportunistic spirit and under the leadership of Bajcsy-Zsilinszky and the Social Democrats. On the other hand, the Communists were persecuted as they had not been since 1919.

The Germans, through their agents in every parliamentary committee, mostly Imrédists, were well aware of all these activities.* When Horthy visited Hitler in April 1943, Hitler reproached him for Kállay's contacts with the Allies and his lenience toward the Jews. When Horthy answered that he could not kill the Jews, Hitler pointed out that they had to be treated like rabbits or tuberculosis bacilli.[54]

The Germans then began to conspire with the Hungarian Fascists in earnest. And this time it was not the R.S.H.A. alone but also the Wilhelmstrasse that made the contacts. The main German troubleshooter in the area, Edmund Veesenmayer, came to Budapest for the first time in the spring, traveling as the representative of Standard Electrical Appliances. In his report, he quickly discarded Szálasi as the leader of a movement "which had become degenerated" and was unimportant,[55] and after dismissing other Fascist groups he recommended Bárdossy and Imrédy as the prospective heads of a national government which would bring about a pro-Axis course.[56] Consequently, Imrédy moved. His party was about to ask Kállay in Parliament a series of embarrassing questions concerning his negotiations with the West and about his contacts with the democratic opposition. As Imrédy openly proclaimed, his purpose was to bring the Kállay government down. Reason: the "common Hungarian-German destiny." Hungary was to conquer or die with Germany and Germany would never be fully defeated. She was Hungary's only friend. Kállay was a defeatist; he had to go.[57]

In order to prevent this move, Kállay obtained from the Regent a decree to prorogue Parliament for six months. This clever tactical move was greeted in Parliament with a predictably angry, disorderly demonstration by the Fascists. But this unfortunately did not disrupt the Imrédists' connection with the Germans. Even Mussolini's ambassador, a Fascist himself, reported that "Imrédy is at the order of the Germans," and that "the policy followed by him is mediocre."[58]

That the Imrédist policy was a mediocre one was true. But those 400,000 Hungarians which this policy served *had* to gamble on German victory — they had in 1943 no other hope for realizing their ambitions. This explains their unconditional subservience to Germany, to any Nazi design or order concerning Hungary. And this alone was what mattered for the Germans, especially after Mussolini's fall and the Italian capitulation. These impressive turns of events did not impress the Hungarian Fascists or their fellow travelers. They had long ago looked to Hitler for guidance rather than to Rome. But the effect of these events on the Bethlenites, who considered Italy

*Kállay, *Hungarian Premier*, pp. 184-85. Kállay even succeeded in stealing through a Croatian agent of his a report Baky prepared about the proceedings for German use. The treasonable connections with the Germans were not restricted to Baky. Imrédy, Rajniss and Jaross were also prominent in this along with one of the worst representatives of the Arrow Cross, G. Vajna.

their only friend, was extraordinary. German economic demands were refused by Kállay, together with every other possible German demand. American and British war planes flying over Hungary almost daily in these months were not interfered with — remarkable if we consider that Allied aviation suffered heavy losses when violating the air space of Switzerland, for example.

But the Italian example and the constantly approaching Red Army convinced Hitler that something had to be done about Hungary.

While Kállay continued his negotiations with the Allies, the Anglo-American forces did not advance as fast in Italy as everybody expected they would. Gen. Alfred Jodl considered their advance timid and not corresponding to their potential. Imrédy expressed pleased surprise over the fact that "after the Italian betrayal" the English "did not have guts to invade Dalmatia."[59] Imrédy's party continued its activity on the same lines as before. The most revealing document is a report by the chief of Horthy's secret police, Sombor (Schweinitzer) about a conversation dating from this period with an Imrédist politician, who explained to Sombor's informant that Imrédy was not "chasing rainbows" with his hopes to take power. Then he continued that "the Germans will ultimately tolerate only such government in Hungary which will not weigh the chances of the outcome of the war but will serve without reservation the interest of the Reich."[60] To make his point, the Imrédist cited several Europeans, like Quisling, Mussert, Clausen, Laval, Déat, and a host of others, as examples of the kind of men who had displayed by their actions the desired attitude. He added that because Kállay's government was not such a government, its days were numbered. The Imrédists "do not miss a single opportunity to let the Germans know how much they disapprove of Kállay's policy." When the cup overflowed, it would be they who would be called to form a government to serve the Germans, not the "lunatic Arrow Cross."[61]

This incredible document correctly analyzed both the German intentions and requirements for collaboration and also the Imrédist position. The cardinal omission in this basely concocted analysis was: "What if Germany does not win after all? " Regarding that possibility, the Imrédists refused to be sobered up — on the contrary, they saw opportunity in the catastrophic German setbacks. It was in similar vein but not in such a candid manner that they addressed a memorandum to Horthy himself in May 1943,[62] after the prorogation of Parliament. Imrédy formed a party guard of his K.A.B.Sz. (*Keleti Arcvonal Bajtársi Szövetség* — Alliance of the Veterans of the Eastern Front). After his ephemeral service at the front, he always pretended to be a guardian of these veterans. In November, Veesenmayer visited Budapest again. Mecsér chaperoned him through political circles. His task was to prepare the maturing German intervention politically, to establish a kind of Fascist unity which was compatible with German designs in case of the occupation. Because of this, he ignored Szálasi completely. This "nitwit," as he called him, "had to be excluded from any future combination."[63] His main contacts were the Imrédists.

The decisive meeting between Veesenmayer and Imrédy, Rátz, Ruszkay, Hubay, and a host of other Fascists amenable to fulfilling German orders without a question, took place in Budapest, in the apartment of a businessman called Félix Szentirmay. According to his own confession, Imrédy explained to Veesenmayer that a Fascist advent to power could not be expected from Hungarian internal forces alone. On the other hand, Hungary under Kállay represented a serious risk for Germany. Horthy, continued Imrédy, must be brought into a situation in which he would be forced to appoint a Fascist government. Allusions were made to E. Hácha's example, and there was some reference to a possible German occupation of Hungary. To Veesenmayer's inquiry whether in that case Imrédy would be ready to form a government, he answered in the affirmative.[64] With this assurance Veesenmayer left for Berlin and reported to his superiors. His memorandum is full of contempt toward Hungary and Hungarian people. For good measure, he certainly did not intend to be grateful to the Szeged Fascists for their cooperation. He concluded his report with the suggestion that, although for the present time Imrédy and his followers seemed to be the best bet for collaboration in Hungary, in the event of victory "they can and should be put in their place effectively."[65] If he could not unite the Fascist "head" with the Fascist "body," at least he could secure the head and the German Army, which was as good a substitute for the "body" as anything Hitler could think of in 1944. The Wehrmacht and the SS, coupled with the R.S.H.A., could secure for Imrédy an absolute working majority.

Meanwhile, Kállay continued his policy unperturbed despite the fact that the Western Allies referred him more and more to Moscow. He put the butchers of Novi Sad on trial, though they were not arrested before the verdict — nobody dared to question the honor of an officer. The example of Kovarcz had not shaken this axiom of faith. So they saw their opportunity and took it. Archduke Albrecht smuggled them in his car to Austria, where they were given asylum and enlisted with their full rank in the SS.[66] Such was the extent of German dissatisfaction with Kállay.

In November (after the departure of Veesenmayer), in the reconvened Parliament, Imrédy had made a savage attack on Kállay's policy, prophesying the bolshevization of Europe and refusing an "Anglo-Saxon solution." By that time Imrédy was openly referred to as *Labanc*, a charge he virtuously repudiated.*

Kállay was by no means secure within the framework of his own Government party either, the majority being Fascist fellow travelers, only opportunistic considerations preventing them from avowing their disapproval of Kállay's policy. When in February the Russians were not more than 100 miles from Hungary, they expressed their opinion in a memorandum to

*O.N.K., November 15, 1943, p. 176. "Labanc" were the Hungarian traitors who fought against Rákóczi on the Austrian side in the rebellion of 1703-11.

Kállay, signed by only thirty deputies (the majority were too cowardly to sign), which repeated the Imrédist line calling for "a hard militant right-wing policy based on the Szeged Idea at home," with measures against the democratic elements, and "new and effective measures against the Jews."[67] They also demanded the lifting of the ban on anti-Semitic press campaigns imposed by Kállay in order to prevent "the rehabilitation of the Jews in the eyes of Hungarian public opinion."[68] It also demanded a more pronouncedly pro-German press. As far as foreign policy was concerned, it demanded the continuation of the policy of "staking everything on one card ("the common Hungarian-German destiny")."[69] The other alternative was bolshevism. How small Hungary could have prevented a Bolshevik takeover of Eastern Europe when the mighty Reich was unable to do much about it, only the fellow traveling enthusiasts of the Government party knew. Kállay ignored the memorandum. And the Government party, true to its traditions, gave him two resounding votes of confidence on the second and ninth of March 1944.

Horthy wrote a letter to Hitler in February asking the surviving defeated Hungarian troops be released to defend Hungary, a euphemism for bringing them home.[70] Hitler did not answer. He sent a message to Horthy that he had the flu and that germs in his letter might infect the Regent.[71] Hitler did have an answer for Horthy nevertheless: Operation Margarethe, the cover name for the plan to "secure" (the occupation of) Hungary, a plan carefully worked out in concert with Nazi agents in Hungary, especially those like Baky and Rajniss in Imrédy's party.

10

No other Hungarian class or political group was bound so close to the fate of Nazi Germany as the Szeged Fascists. There was not, there could not be, any common destiny between Hungary and Nazi Germany. There was thus a Szeged Fascist-Nazi common destiny rather than a Hungarian-German one. Imrédy took the consequences. It was a sad result of twenty-five years of the Szeged Idea that the Hungarian people were not in a position to make clear to Imrédy and his partisans that the fate of Szeged fascism and the fate of Hungary ought not to be one and the same. But the Bethlenite conservatives were not in the habit of calling on the people for support. In order to gain their support and to awaken the people from their apathy, they would have had to offer the reforms they had refused for twenty-five years. As far as the democratic opposition was concerned, by 1944 they owed their existence to the Bethlenites. And because the same Bethlenites had paralyzed them for the last twenty-five years, they most certainly were not in any position to preach a democratic mass uprising of any kind.

Under such circumstances the balance was with Germany, at least for 1944. There were two German policies concerning the *Südostraum*. One was the official one which was that of the Wilhelmstrasse, and the second, which was elaborated and upheld in the far more important schemings of the R.S.H.A., revealed ultimate German intentions after the victory.* Hitler served in most cases as an arbiter, and was not necessarily always in agreement with the R.S.H.A. zealots. His maxim was: "Quiet in the raw material zone." The Germans were ready even to defer removal of Kállay because of the military situation. For a time, it is true, they had hoped for a large-scale Fascist upheaval and had fostered a broad fascist united front. But by 1943 they were convinced of the utter impossibility of a union between bourgeois and proletarian fascism.**

The Germans never spoke of a Nationalist International. They were never especially interested in a social revolution and social justice in Hungary. In this, they heartily concurred with the Szeged Fascists under Imrédy. What the Germans in 1944 needed was unconditional collaboration. Imrédy was ready for this; Szálasi was not. The Imrédist and Fascist fellow traveler "head" with an SS and Wehrmacht "body" seemed to serve the purpose. "The seeds of Szeged" — as Jaross and other Imrédists used to say — "ripened into national socialism" indeed.[72] It was against this background that on March 19, 1944, this monstrous cultivation was about to bear fruit. It was against this background that a silent, abandoned, misled, and betrayed Hungarian people faced one of the greatest trials of their thousand-year-long history.

---

*When preparing Operation Margarethe, the R.S.H.A. memorandum again and again emphasized the idea that Hungary belonged always to the Habsburg Empire, and "for the long run its absorption into the (framework of the) Reich is inevitable." Karsai, *op. cit.*, p. 422.

**The impression Pálffy and Baky created in proletarian Arrow Cross members was expressed by one of the activists after their secession: "Pálffy and Baky were completely insensitive and incomprehensive toward the workers. They speak about social reforms but those reforms are (supposed) to serve only the bourgeoisie and the intelligentisia alone . . . They are against any organization of workers — even [within the framework] of the Arrow Cross." Lackó, *op. cit.*, p. 270.

CHAPTER VII

1944

The Hungarians have always been poseurs . . . they all wear swords but have none of the earnest chivalry which the bearing of the sword should imply.

Adolf Hitler

1

The somber memory of 1944 still haunts the Hungarian scene. The consequences will embitter for a long time to come the lives of those who were even remotely connected with it. That year, all the long-pent-up fury of Fascist emotions had free reign over Hungary, setting in motion a pendulum which, when it swung back, brought retribution without peace.

As we have seen, Hitler decided at the end of February to "secure" Hungary. Operation Margarethe was about to begin. In the original plan, the troops of the Fascist Little Entente, those of Antonescu, Tišo, and Pavelić, were also supposed to participate, but Doctor Höttl at the last moment succeeded in convincing Berlin how embarrassing such a move would be for the mighty Fascist Fifth Column in Hungary.[1]

Zero hour was approaching. On March 15, the Germans carried through an important part of their plan by getting Horthy out of Hungary, as his presence when the occupation occurred might cause unnecessary complications. Hitler invited him to Klessheim Castle near Salzburg for a discussion. Horthy arrived at Klessheim on the eighteenth of March. Here he was to find out that, unfortunately, Hitler's wars were not conducted like climbing parties in the Tyrolean Alps, where those who get tired or dizzy can wait in a rest house halfway up while the hardier climbers go on to the peak. Hitler flatly told him about Kállay's negotiations, adding that Italy's treachery had taught Germany a lesson, and that therefore he had given orders to German troops to occupy Hungary. Horthy protested against the accusation of treachery.* He also expressed his wish to return to Hungary immediately. But some carefully timed false air raid warnings served to keep him in Germany until the occupation was carried through. Hitler also persuaded Horthy not to abdicate, and Horthy, as he liked to say, remained "on the bridge of the ship" to "save what could be saved." Many things can be

---

*A memorable clash occurred at that point. Horthy, in the true medieval fashion, offered to commit an honorable suicide as a guarantee in case of Hungary's treachery. Retorted the earthy proletarian of the twentieth century, "I won't get anything out of that! " Horthy, *titkos iratai*, p. 435.

explained with beautiful words and plausible reasons. But the only real service Horthy could have rendered to Hungary on March 19, 1944, would have been to abdicate.

In Hungary, things went smoothly for the German Army. If they expected resistance, they were pleasantly surprised after crossing the border in the small hours of Sunday, March 19. Even Eichmann, entering Hungary with the first SS formations, was pleasantly surprised at the quiet, friendly reception his men got everywhere.

When the first news of the German border crossing was reported to Kállay, he called on the commanding officers of the Hungarian Army to explore the possibility of offering a symbolic, token resistance, even though effective resistance was not feasible. Kállay fully understood the meaning of such a gesture for Hungary's future. But he ought not even have tried with Gömbös' Szeged Fascist military. Most of the officers arrived at the conference, at a time when every minute counted, after a deliberate delay of hours, and then they told Kállay that they would not take orders from him, but only from the Regent, who was of course in Germany.[2] So the German occupation was carried out during the night without incident and when the sun rose, Hungary and Budapest were firmly in German hands.

The Fascist fifth column was waiting. A Gestapo agent in Budapest notified Rajniss and through him the Imrédists about the coming of the Germans.[3] Baky was ready with his lists and gendarmes to go into action.[4] In the early hours of March 19, 1944, they set forth with the Gestapo to arrest every Bethlenite and opposition politician they could find.

On the same day, as in the case of Teleki's suicide, another Hungarian staged a strictly one-man show. When the Baky-Gestapo group tried to seize the opposition leader Bajcsy-Zsilinszky, he opened fire upon them and resisted until he emptied his last bullet into the gendarme-Gestapo gang. They captured him wounded and bleeding — the only Hungarian who resisted, the only casualty, the only one whose blood was spilled on that shameful day.

Meanwhile, Horthy's train was approaching Budapest. The Germans found it expedient to organize additional delays on the way. There was the usual controversy between the SS and the Wilhelmstrasse about the character of the future Hungarian administration. This controversy raged even on Horthy's train when, to his great surprise, Edmund Veesenmayer, the German agent of the previous year, was presented to him as the new German ambassador. Horthy had an even greater surprise when he found out that the Hungarian-Swabian police officer, Peter Hain, in charge of his personal security for many years and absolutely trusted, had been a paid Gestapo agent since 1938 and had just been nominated by Ernst Kaltenbrunner, also on the train, as the head of the Budapest political police.[5] Veesenmayer and Kaltenbrunner had a sharp exchange about the composition of the new Hungarian regime. Vessenmayer favored an Imrédy cabinet with some Fascist fellow travelers from the Government party. Kaltenbrunner considered putting into power the contractual agents of the Hungarian National Socialist party (Baky-Pálffy group) to be the best solution. The R.S.H.A. abhorred Imrédy as a Jew, and considered a government of its paid agents the most effective means of ensuring the interests of the Reich in general and the SS in particular. Horthy was adamant about Imrédy personally: he would never appoint him prime minister. So for the next two or three days Veesenmayer, whose official title was significantly not only German minister but also ambassador plenipotentiary of the Reich in Hungary, had to devote all his time to trying to form a cabinet of collaborators acceptable to Horthy, the Wilhelmstrasse and the SS, and to the jealousies and greed for power of the Hungarian Fascists. He was ready to include every Fascist and fellow traveler group in his plans except the Arrow Cross. And with good reason.

Because of the relative wartime prosperity of the lower classes, because of the police terror which Kállay and Keresztes–Fischer exercised toward the Arrow Cross,* and last but not least because of Szálasi's principled devotion to Hungarism and his refusal to adopt R.S.H.A. schemes, the Arrow Cross was on the decline. It was constantly plagued by desertions and defections. Even Szálasi's appointed successor Málnási had to be purged because of his opportunistic deviations in the direction of the Baky group and the Germans.** Party membership sank to 127,000. In Debrecen, compared with 18,536 members in 1939, there were 939 left in 1943.[6] The defection of the bourgeois element in the Arrow Cross to the Baky-Imrédy coalition had continued apace during 1942 and 1943. Some Arrow Cross leaders welcomed this exodus, claiming that it gave them a good chance "to emphasize the proletarian character of the party," adding that "the petite bourgeoisie and the white collar [membership] just would not budge from their insipidity."[7] By the fall of 1942, the former communist Kassai-Schallmayer could proudly proclaim that he had won Szálasi over to the idea of placing the Arrow Cross entirely on proletarian foundations. Worker and peasant "great councils" were formed simultaneously, and Szálasi had explained to them "the paramount role which workers will play in the coming Hungarist state."***

*In March, 1943, mainly because of its base attacks on the Western Allies (which were continued in open defiance to Kállay's instructions) even the party's daily, perhaps the most vulgar of Fascist newspapers, *Pesti-Ujság,* was suppressed only to reappear some months later under the title *Összetartás,* a newspaper which proved itself by no means superior to its predecessor.

**Doctor Málnási did his best to convince Szálasi to cooperate with the R.S.H.A., an effort which led to his expulsion from the Arrow Cross. After that, he established sinister connections with the Gestapo, writing psychoanalytical studies of Szálasi for the R.S.H.A., even sending a copy of his work to Keresztes-Fischer. He was rewarded by the SS with the position of director of the Gestapo-subsidized paper of the Bakyists, *Magyarság.* Lackó, *Nyilasók, nemzetiszocialisták,* pp. 123, 259, 268-69.

***Ibid., p. 258. Which does not mean that the Arrow Cross did not cooperate with the authorities against Communists. In the factories, Arrow Cross cells were instructed by the party to inform the authorities about the slightest Communist commotion. (*Ibid.,* pp. 290-91.) Arrow Cross papers published the autobiographical notes of former Communists

Szálasi continued to make his routine "trips around the realm," but despite the obvious unequivocal radicalization process within the Arrow Cross, he was met everywhere with apathy. He also visited Transylvania and attempted to implement the "co-nationalist" program of Hungarism among Rumanians — without the slightest Rumanian response. The Arrow Cross tried to organize mixed Hungarian-Rumanian party organizations. The attempt not only did not attract Rumanians, it infuriated the chauvinistic Hungarian bourgeoisie of Transylvania, which with its keen political instinct quickly identified the Arrow Cross with the detested Iron Guard. They joined the Imrédists in great numbers instead of the Arrow Cross.[8] But Szálasi did not flinch or waver. He continued to work on his plans for a Hungarist Corporative State, planning to make obligatory for all officials an anthropological examination, complete with such refinements as comparative skull measurements.* There was not the slightest hope of reconciliation between him and Imrédy, as we have seen. Vajna and some other questionable Arrow Cross representatives tried to ingratiate themselves to the Germans but were not successful.

On March 31, 1943, the Arrow Cross handed a memorandum to Horthy, in which, after expounding their criticism of the existing government policy and social order, they repeated their request for granting a Hindenburg-Victor Emmanuel III type of power to Szálasi and begged in abject terms for an audience, which was as a routine refused.[9] Kállay received Szálasi for two hours, and after reading his memorandum advised him that it was "both in thought and composition" un-Hungarian and, therefore, incomprehensible to him."[10]

Things looked even worse for Szálasi at the beginning of 1944. According to his own notes, party membership had sunk well below 100,000; there was

under the revealing title "Marxists in the Arrow Cross," arriving at the conclusion that "only the Arrow Cross can offer an alternative to cosmopolitan, Jewish Marxism," adding, "By now everything is clear . . . The Soviets betrayed the working class — they shook hands with the bankers of the City of London within the walls of the Kremlin." *Ibid.*, p. 309.

*The project of the new Hungarist Corporative State included an outline for a new constitution which, according to Doctor Vágó, "was similar to the constitutional reform accomplished by the wise Portuguese statesman, Salazar, with such beneficial results [for Portugal]." Arrow Cross radicalism and the championing of the proletariat bears as little semblance to Salazarism as the "Turanian" Catholicism of Doctor Vágó does. According to Doctor Vágó, Arrow Cross bureaucrats and army officers worked on the project of the new constitution "independently of each other" and arrived at the conclusion that administration should be decentralized. The decentralization should follow the pattern of the seven military districts of Hungary, "which in their turn, led back miraculously to the original system of the seven tribes of Hungarians which conquered Hungary." Lackó, *op. cit.*, p. 303; also, Macartney, *October Fifteenth*, II, 103-4.

no leadership worthy of the name, and both rank and file and the party hierarchy were apathetic.[11] Still Szálasi was unperturbed. What he really cared about was organizing his Institute of Racial Biology and arranging for an audience with Horthy which would, according to him, eventuate in his assuming power "through the common will of the Nation and the Head of State."[12]

Ignored completely by the Germans, who were dealing with Imrédy and Baky on much easier terms, the Arrow Cross, when the German occupation occurred, was the only political party that scattered protest leaflets all over Budapest.[13] Szálasi objected in sardonic terms to Veesenmayer's title "plenipotentiary." But all the Arrow Cross commotion did nothing to move either the Germans or their Szeged Fascist collaborators; they were ready to ignore Szálasi for a long time to come.

2

By the twenty-second of March, the efforts of Veesenmayer were successful. A collaboration government was formed under the chairmanship of General Döme Sztójay, the Hungarian ambassador in Berlin, whom Gömbös had appointed. There simply could not have been a more uncritical servant of Nazi Germany leading a Hungarian government than he. Besides this, he was not very bright, to say the least. In addition to Sztójay, the new government was pronouncedly Imrédist, Szeged Fascist in character with some Gömbös Orphan, Fascist fellow travelers of the Government party like István Antal, Béla Jurcsek, Lajos Reményi-Schneller included.* The Baky group, nominally the ally of Imrédy but now quite openly committed to standing or falling with its sponsors, the R.S.H.A., suffered a setback. Imrédy himself did not enter the government until May but remained its directing spirit from the outside.

By the end of March the Red Army had captured the Bukovina and penetrated deep into Rumania. Their spearheads were now thirty to thirty-five miles from the Hungarian border. The Szeged Idea had no time to waste: they had to make themselves memorable in the history of Hungary and the world. They succeeded to a remarkable degree, although because of the ensuing confusion they have not received due credit for their accomplishments from historians.

A very considerable portion of the non-Jewish middle classes and the petite bourgeoisie exulted at the fall of Kállay and expected that the new government would "put an end to the Jewish underground, the trifling with our honorable ally, and the betrayal of Hungary's interests and Hungary's honor."[15]

*Sztójay notified all Hungarian diplomatic representatives in a circular that "the new government, as far as the internal policy of Hungary is concerned, will pursue and accomplish the aims of Gyula Gömbös." In foreign policy, Sztójay promised full-fledged collaboration, exhorting Hungarian diplomats abroad to conduct themselves accordingly. *Allianz*, p. 382.

The program of the new government was to carry out a thorough social and national revival based on the Szeged Idea, to bring about full cooperation with Germany, to increase to the utmost Hungary's participation in the war and her economic help to Germany, and last, to solve the "Jewish question." It can safely be said that this last was the main point of their program, and it was the one for which the Szeged Fascists had considerable support and great success; to all other points they offered only a token loyalty, no more.

In the next fifteen or twenty days, Hungary's face, which did not even bear the semblance of war and had not been exposed even to air attacks, thanks to Kállay's policy, changed completely. The Americans and the British commenced heavy air attacks, sometimes involving more than a thousand bombers, against military targets in Budapest and other towns now crowded with the German war machine. The new government dissolved all political parties except the Fascist ones. The Government party duly endorsed the new program, perhaps with more enthusiasm than it had displayed three weeks earlier when it endorsed the policy of Kállay. Social Democratic, Smallholder, legitimist, Christian, and liberal parties were outlawed and trade unions dissolved, their headquarters occupied, their property confiscated. Mass arrest of opposition leaders by a Gestapo-Baky team followed. The anti-Fascist minister of interior, Keresztes-Fischer, most of the democratic politicians, even the Bethlenite conservatives and legitimist members of Parliament were dragged to Mauthausen. Milotay found it proper to write an editorial in his Imrédist *Új Magyarság* under the title "Martyrs," insulting and besmearing one by one the now defenseless ministers and M.P.'s who had been arrested.[16]

Any organization not expressedly of a Fascist character was either dissolved or had to go through a thorough *Gleichschaltung*.* The military guilty of the massacres of Novi Sad returned triumphantly from their exile, and Hitler insisted personally that they be not only rehabilitated but reinstated into the Hungarian Army. Bethlen escaped detention with the help of Horthy and was in hiding; Kállay took refuge in the Turkish Embassy. The whole administration was purged of Bethlenite conservatives in the commanding positions; they were to be replaced with Imrédists all along the line. Here, as in the military, the *Gleichschaltung* was not difficult at all. After twenty-five years of the Szeged Idea, the changes of the nineteenth of March were more than welcomed and by no means opposed.

The protection which Kállay extended to refugees and Allied prisoners of war was brought to an end. General Kollontay of Poland was apprehended by the Gestapo and shot. Subsidies to Polish schools were stopped; Imrédists did not consider it appropriate to anger their German masters with the "two-faced, defeatist" attitudes implicit in aid to Poles or other Allied nationals. All the non-Fascist press was suppressed, and the government press was brought into line by the new press dictator, Mihály Kolozsváry-Borcsa, who was a close collaborator of Imrédy. In April in Budapest, Kolozsváry-Borcsa, inspired by the example of Göbbels, carried out the Fascist must; a

*The Pen Club and Rotary Club were dissolved.

ceremonial destruction of books by Jewish authors and other authors the Imrédists did not like (for example, the works of André Malraux and the works of many non-Jewish Western writers). Listening to non-Axis broadcasts was forbidden under threat of severe penalty. The controls imposed by Kállay on the Fascist press, and so hotly resented by it, were now removed. An unprecedented flow of invective and lies followed, directed in most cases against Jews and their "allies," the Western powers. The uninformed, highly emotional and gullible Hungarian masses were thus exposed to an uninhibited Fascist outflow precisely at a time when they needed more than ever a clear picture of the state of things. A paper called *Harc* (*Struggle* — the Hungarian equivalent of Streicher's *Stürmer*) began publication as the organ of the newly formed Institute of Research on the Jewish Question (*Zsidókutató Intézet*), adding its own highly concentrated heat to the flames of hatred incited by dozens of Fascist papers.

One of the ugliest aspects of this campaign was the incitement of the population against the Allied, more specifically American, aviators who bailed out during the bombings. The population was fed day by day with reports about the "Texas and Chicago air gangsters who dropped explosive toys and poisoned chocolate in order to victimize innocent Hungarian children."* But the press alone was not considered sufficient to incite the populace against the United States Air Force. The walls of Budapest and of all Hungary were splashed with posters depicting a child, covered with blood (the Imrédist

*Here are some excerpts, out of hundreds, in order to illustrate what this campaign was like:

"During the air attack against Debrecen, it was the scum of American latrines who came [to Hungary] in order to murder Hungarians. These dastardly beings, filled with Jewish sadism, came to carry out the devilish, sinister vengeance of Jewry, which feels offended [by the "Fascist Renaissance" in Hungary]." By Dr. K. B. in *Összetartás*, June 29, 1944.

And Vince Görgey, the Bakyist agent, described captured U.S. airmen, with whom they arranged an "interview," in the following vein:

"Are these shaggy looking creatures, whom to call semi-intelligent would be a flattery, the ones who would represent the Officers Corps of the U. S. Air Force? I see sneaky looks all around me. The terror pilots stand with their hands in their pockets; they throw glances at each other. In the middle [of the group] there stands a redskinned Indian, with harelips . . . The faces of two lieutenants bear strikingly Jewish features — and as it turned out they are indeed Jewish. . ."

Görgey reports further, that the Indian [airmen] hates only the whites — but not the Hungarian or German whites! Only the Anglo-Saxon whites "who corrupted and killed his parents." After the Karl May atmosphere, Görgey continues in this fashion (the 1944 version of *Uncle Tom's Cabin*): The American Negro airmen get 10,000 dollars premium after each flight — Görgey saw the wallets of the U. S. Negroes bulging with 10,000 dollars! Görgey arrives at his conclusion: Texan cowboys, and the unemployed of New York and also some Chicago boxers came over to kill Hungarian children. *Új Magyarság*, April 21, 1944.

theatre-artist, Antal Páger, obligingly put the picture of his little daughter, Juliet, at the disposal of Fascist propaganda),* raising her mutilated, bleeding chunk of hand accusingly to the sky with the inscription, "Am I also a military target? "**

These base incitements, which like so many events of 1944 in Hungary had nothing to do with German initiative, brought rich results. There were investigators attached to the United States military mission in Hungary after the war looking into the bestial murders of United States airmen, and more than one of the perpetrators was tried and sentenced for his exploits. The Hungarian authorities, notably the gendarmerie, showed as a rule great understanding toward these and other "manifestations of patriotic anger" against the American "hirelings of international Jewry." Only a few of the Allied airmen forced to bail out over the Hungary of 1944 were fortunate enough to be discovered by Bethlenite aristocrats willing to hide them on their estates. All these acts and much more occurred in less than a month. Justification: the old Imrédist, Szeged Fascist line: Hungary stands or falls with Nazi victory — the "common Hungarian-German destiny."

In view of what happened later, after the Communist takeover, there was no lack of apology and justification for the anti-Western policy of the Hungarian Fascists, whether Imrédists, Arrow Cross, or the fellow travelers of the Government party. They were posthumously endowed with superhuman wisdom, foresight, and patriotism.

Suffice it to say that in 1943, in 1944, or even in the first part of 1945, it would seem that not even Stalin knew what kind of policy he would follow in No-Man's-Land. Otherwise, permission to hold free elections in Austria, Hungary and Czechoslovakia (but never in Poland, Rumania or Bulgaria), and the awarding of the highest Soviet Order to King Michael, would seem extravagantly and unnecessarily devious dispensations on the part of the Soviets. Similarly, those in the camp of European Fascism, whether Clausen, Quisling, Mussert, Déat, or Doriot and the vast Nazi camp in Austria, proved also to be prophets of doom, foretelling for their respective countries with the same clairvoyance as Imrédy, Milotay or Szálasi the coming "Anglo-Saxon betrayal," and the inevitability of communism. In view of what happened later, it is important to point this out because sometimes even such serious scholars as Professor Macartney indulge in factitious justifications of Imrédy's or Bárdossy's concepts.

It is well in that regard to take a closer look at the alternative they

*Páger, a gifted actor and a very active Imrédist, was welcomed after the war in Perón's Argentina, but in 1956 he returned to Communist Hungary, where he is the protagonist of many "socialist-realist" plays.

**The fifteen or twenty air raids against Budapest compare very favorably with those directed against Vienna during the same period, even with the bombings of Bucharest and Belgrade. In Sofia, the devastation in residential areas was incomparably greater than in Budapest — and as far as the damage in the residential areas of the cities in the Reich are concerned, there is simply no room for comparison.

supported. The Imrédists-Bakyists, without the slightest reservation, risked Hungary's future on a Nazi victory. Apart from the fact that in March 1944 such a victory was highly improbable, was such a victory desirable for Hungary? During the war, Hitler could not show his real intentions toward Hungary, or his real feelings. Göbbels expressed this attitude in his diary when he wrote that there was no necessity for solving every outstanding problem with Hungary during the war; it was better to leave things for after the war. And here Hitler's secret conversations provide a good inkling of what was in store for Hungary. The *Völkisch* solution alone, accepted by the Imrédists and Bakyists, would have destroyed Hungary as an independent sovereign unit. The country would have been carved up and tied to the Reich in a form little better than that of the Czech protectorate. This policy, as we have seen, was reaffirmed just before the Germans marched into Hungary.

But beyond political considerations, one cannot but feel the intense antipathy the whole Nazi leadership, Göbbels, Ribbentrop and Hitler, felt toward Hungary. There is little reason to believe that Imrédy's or Baky's subservience would have changed this basic attitude. As for Hitler himself, he considered the Hungarians on the same level as the Russians — "lazy . . . by nature the man of the steppe."[17] He never concealed his opinion that he considered the Rumanian peasantry incomparably superior to that of Hungary.[18] He was somewhat more than contemptuous of Hungarian martial qualities. Not only as on the Russian front, but in case of a Hungarian-Rumanian conflict, he foretold a resounding Hungarian defeat.[19] More ominous than these observations were the plans to "turn the Danube into a German river." In order to save the German minorities from the "wild nationalism of Hungarians," Hitler thought of "taking control of the state" in Hungary. He thought of resettling all German minorities from southeast Europe along the Danube.[20] He fully approved of the Viennese idea that Hungary was always part of the Habsburg Empire.[21] He looked forward to the day when Hungary would be taken over, and in that way "order will be restored there."[22] If there were any doubt about the justice of his position, Hitler removed it by saying that he would only be "repaying the Hungarians in their own coin, once the war is over, for having everywhere and so promptly taken advantage of circumstances and pulled their chestnuts out of the fire."[23] There is little doubt that Hitler, in the event of a German victory, would have been in a position to translate his feelings into policy. This was the reality as far as the "common Hungarian-German destiny" was concerned. Yet it is this one card on which Hungarian Fascists staked Hungary's future and honor in 1944, when only lunatics believed in a German victory.

Inside Hungary, the Germans, notably Veesenmayer, continued to work for the much-vaunted unity of Fascist parties, a persistently expressed German goal that was never to be achieved. We shall discuss the Arrow Cross later because it stands at this point salutarily apart from the unsavory scramble for power so characteristic of the other groups.

The Baky-Pálffy National Socialists under the protection of Himmler, and the Imrédists, the choice of Veesenmayer who favored the more conservative elements as opposed to those favored by the SS, were soon at loggerheads. Veesenmayer tried through another pet choice of his, Bárdossy, to give a broad, conservative Fascist character to this grand design of Fascist unity. The Government party was more than willing to go along. At the end of May, Imrédy was appointed minister of economic coordination. His appointment came after veiled threats to Horthy concerning what would happen to him if he refused to appoint Imrédy. At that point, the uneasy alliance between the Imrédists and the Baky-Pálffy-R.S.H.A. agency broke down. The Bakyists began a campaign against Imrédy, flooding Budapest with leaflets about his allegedly Jewish origin, complete with illustrated family tree. Whereupon the German antagonists of the R.S.H.A. secured a statement from Hans Fritsche, with the signature of five other bona fide anti-Semites, that the original documents concerning Imrédy's Jewish ancestry were forged. It is hard to discern even the semblance of principle on the part of those involved in this scramble for power between Imrédists and Baky-Pálffyists. Both sides were ready to serve the Germans, and each of them tried to enlist German support by trying to convince their sponsors (Veesenmayer and Himmler respectively) that it was they who were the real and most unreserved collaborators. Their struggle reflected the struggle in the German hierarchy — that is, the SS and Gestapo versus the Wilhelmstrasse. Accordingly, Veesenmayer, by inclination more in sympathy with the conservative Bárdossy and Imrédy, was opposed by the radicalism of Himmler, Kaltenbrunner and the R.S.H.A. with their contractual agents, Baky, Pálffy and their group. Needless to say, under such circumstances no semblance of the Fascist unity so dear to Veesenmayer's heart could be achieved. There was a name for the proleptic child of Veesenmayer as early as April 5: Party of National Coalescence (*Nemzeti Összefogás Pártja*).[24]

As far as the Arrow Cross was concerned, it was equally hated by the Imrédists, the Baky-Pálffy group and the Fascist fellow travelers. And no wonder. Szálasi protested the German occupation, ordered his followers to demonstrate against it, inflexibly stuck to Hungarism, and denounced the new government as "petit bourgeois," unworthy of the confidence of the nation. In his meeting with Veesenmayer, he insisted on Hungarism and made the impression on the German of a "buffoon who alternately swaggered and groveled" and whose followers were a "gang of fantasts." Veesenmayer did not want to have anything to do with him. He did, however, arrange the desideratum No. 1 on Szálasi's agenda, an interview with Horthy on the third of May, which despite Szálasi's hopes only fortified Horthy's intention never to appoint Szálasi to office.[25] But whatever the opinion of its leader in government circles, the Arrow Cross was nevertheless a bona fide Fascist party, and the right to organize could not be denied it. Apart from all this, Szálasi, foreseeing that Imrédy would eventually compromise himself, concentrated his attention on the really important thing — a plan to reorganize Europe into tribes, with Hitler as supreme tribal leader, Mussolini as deputy tribal leader, himself as tribal leader for Hungary (with Horthy as head of state) — and duly forwarded the plan to Hitler in mid-June.[26]

The workers and the masses continued to be drawn to Szálasi and not to the Szeged Fascists, despite their revived blandishments of the Fascist trade unions under Marton, who even went to the length of cooperating with some Social Democratic leaders, some of whom were contacted in underground hideouts, one of them fetched back from Mauthausen in order to ensure labor discipline.[27] In April, that efficient gangster Kovarcz returned from his German exile and assumed the leadership of organizational work within the Arrow Cross.[28] Under his able leadership many dormant Arrow Cross party organizaions assumed a new life and new Arrow Cross organizations even rose in localities where there were none before. Concentrating its organizational efforts on the working class, the Arrow Cross remained, in the words of Professor Lackó, "the strongest faction of the extreme right."*

3

On the very first day of the Szeged Fascists' advent to effective power, Hungary was turned into one huge torture chamber as in close cooperation with their German friends, the Fascists began the realization of the most important point of their program: the Final Solution of the Jewish question. Up to March 1944, about 800,000 Jews in Hungary lived in relative safety while Jewish communities around them were engulfed by the holocaust. One man had stood between them and their destruction: Kállay. Now the Szeged Fascists, with the overwhelming approbation of the administration and the support and sympathy of the non-Jewish middle classes, set to work with dazzling speed to accomplish in several weeks as much as and more than the Germans accomplished in other countries in five years. Eichmann got every possible assistance in his work; as he remembered during his trial in Jerusalem: "Hungary was the only country where we were not quick enough for them. They turned their Jews over to us like turning over sour beer."[29] The Imrédists had reason to hurry. In a few months the Red Army might occupy Hungary and save the lives of those unfortunates. When the Eichmann-Imrédy team (Szálasi opposed the measures to the very end) assumed charge of these affairs, the Russian spearheads stood thirty miles from the most heavily Jewish-inhabited region of Hungary, Ruthenia.

Base emotions and the greed of Szeged Fascists for Jewish property combined to produce a situation in which the unspeakable, the ultimate in horror, torment, and degradation for the first time in Hungarian history was the fate not of individuals but of masses. The spiritual concepts of the Szeged Idea and the twenty-five years of its proliferation bore ample fruit in these months in the spring of 1944. So did the lamentable widespread apathy of the Hungarian masses.

*Lackó, op. cit., pp. 314-16. Professor Deák's sources, although not in a categorical statement, estimated the Arrow Cross membership around 500,000 in September, 1944. Rogger and Webber, The European Right, p. 396. On the basis of the evidence given by Szálasi and Kovarcz, who at the height of Arrow Cross popularity during the spring of 1939 considered the movement as 250,000-300,000 strong, the Deák figure seems very exaggerated.

The regular Hungarian Fascist excuse (like that of Austria and Germany) was that no one realized what was going to happen to the Jews. Everyone thought that the measures meant "only" deportation, humiliation, spoilation, incarceration in ghettoes and maybe incidental small-scale murder here and there, and that "the Jews were going to work."

How far can the Imrédist leadership or the "middle class of Hungarian gentlemen" claim ignorance concerning the fate of Jews delivered into German hands? We remember Sztójay's statement to Ottlik in 1942. Now Sztójay was the prime minister of a government which enacted these measures of "resettlement." Moreover, tens of thousands of Hungarian soldiers and officers passed through Poland and Russia, and many of them knew of or had even witnessed the "resettlement" — the mass extermination — of Jews there. By 1942-43, in an area where there had been about six million Jews before, there was not a single Jew to be found. No, for those who were on the eastern front there could be no reasonable doubt as to what was in the making. Above all, the patrons of the Veterans of the Eastern Front (K.A.B.Sz.), Imrédy and his party, could not have remained ignorant.

The Imrédist actress Sári Fedák, divorced wife of the distinguished Hungarian Jewish writer Ferenc Molnár, visiting the Hungarian forces in Russia with the Hungarian equivalent of the U.S.O., saw the charred ruins of the Jewish district in the city of Proskurov in the Ukraine, and when told of the fate of its 20,000 inhabitants commented, "It is about time to take similar steps in Budapest! " BBC and Voice of America broadcasts on the subject could be dismissed as Jewish lies, reliable eyewitness accounts cannot. Even to Horthy, Hitler referred to Jews as "tuberculosis bacilli," "harmful insects," "rabbits," etc., who must be treated accordingly. Horthy himself complained after his return from Klessheim in March 1944, "I am charged with not having permitted the Jews to be massacred."[30]

So much for general articulate and inarticulate public opinion. The government enacting these measures had explicit warnings and knowledge about Auschwitz, which was to be the graveyard of Hungarian Jewry. Even greater was the responsibility of the Jewish leadership of Hungary, the most spineless, the most servile and, with that of Vienna and Germany, the most contemptible in all of Europe.* We shall see how it was possible, with Allied bombings increasing and the front a dozen miles from Hungary, to mark, concentrate and deport to Auschwitz so large a number of Jews. Because the main requirement of this monstrous campaign was speed, an almost incredible speed, and because its achievement was assured by eager Hungarian cooperation, most of it was over before the world could take note of it.

From the very first day of German occupation, Eichmann had assumed the direction of the anti-Jewish measures. But to carry out such a great operation in such a short time, Eichmann needed the cooperation of the Jewish leaders, too. He succeeded in forming a *Judenrat,* a Jewish Council, an indispensable

*During the Eichmann trial, the surviving Jewish leaders of Hungary were confronted with the shameful burden of their guilt. When Chief Justice Gideon Hausner thundered his accusations at Baron Óbudai Freudiger, he cried in public.

element in the Nazi destruction process, which thanks to Eichmann's charm and his promises that "business will go on as usual," became an obedient tool in German hands.[31] The Hungarian minister of interior, Jaross, was Imrédy's second in command and perhaps the worst representative of his party. He had two secretaries of state for Jewish affairs at his disposal, László Endre, one of the most pathological Jew-haters in Hungary, and László Baky, who was to secure the gendarmerie, another indispensable tool in this operation.

The population began its anti-Jewish outbursts right after the entry of the Germans.* In no time at all, about 35,000 denunciations had been made against Jews and democratic elements.[32] Jews were dragged away from their apartments according to lists sometimes compiled from the Budapest telephone directory. When the Germans demanded further "hostages" by the hundreds, the Jewish Council was ready to cooperate by "calling in" new victims.[33]

By the end of March the anti-Jewish ordinances began to pour out. First, the Jews were ordered to wear distinctive badges. The definition of a Jew differed little from that set forth in the Nürenberg Laws. Initially, seventy-five percent of the war invalids and the war widows and orphans of the Second World War (but not of the first) were to be exempted. (Later this was modified because it would have included the families of the many thousands of Jews who perished in the labor services in Russia.) Also, supposedly those Jews who had been faithful to Hungary under Czech, Rumanian and Yugoslav rule were to be exempted. We shall see later how these exemptions were honored.

It became important to emphasize the wearing of the yellow star, because all other measures were applicable to persons who had to wear it — that is, the more than 99 percent of Hungarian Jewry, including the 62,000 Christians. In the next five weeks or so, by orders of ministerial council, Jews were dismissed from all gainful, salaried employment, their businesses (in Budapest alone, 18,000 out of 30,000 shops were Jewish) were confiscated; they were to be expelled from every profession; they were forbidden to travel except by special permit; their food rations were drastically reduced; and they had to surrender all the cash they had with the exception of a sum of 3,000 pengö ($100-$150 at that time) per person. Also, they had to surrender their bicycles, vehicles, radio sets, telephones and jewelry. They were forbidden to patronize cafés, restaurants, hotels, movie theaters, museums, parks or baths, and were allowed to leave their homes only during specified hours. Jews were expelled from the Association of War Veterans and practically all other associations save purely Jewish ones. The Hungarian authorities had their own methods of going far beyond these regulations. One of their favorite methods was to check whether the yellow star was sewn firmly enough on the dress or coat. They pushed a pencil under the Star and

*How far some Hungarians were ready to go is illustrated in the letter written by the "Catholic prostitutes" to the minister of justice (Antal), asking him to remove their Jewish fellow workers. Macartney, *op. cit.*, II, 276n.

if it fit under the sewing that meant a premature deportation to Auschwitz.[34]

Immediately after the first American air attack, two Imrédist ministers went to see Veesenmayer and told him that "revolution threatened unless something drastic could be done right away against the Jews."[35] Endre could report to the press with deep satisfaction that "Hungarian anti-Semitism is no imitation."[36] All this would not have mattered very much in view of the coming allied victory. The lives of Jews were not officially endangered by these measures, and that was what mattered. But the Final Solution was directed precisely at the lives of Jews.

The Council of Ministers decided on April 7, 1944, "to cleanse the territory of the country of Jews" (Order of the Council of Ministers No. 6163/1944 res.),[37] although this measure was apparently decided upon five weeks before the deportations actually began. The excuse given for the mass deportation to Auschwitz was the proximity of the Red Army to the Carpathians. The German military, for security reasons, demanded the removal of Jews from the rural districts and their concentration in ghettoes in the towns. Because this concentration was done in the most inhumane manner, and because of the overcrowding and total lack of accommodation and sanitation, very soon epidemics of typhoid and other contagious diseases broke out.[38]

After that, the Hungarians asked the Germans to "take over" the Jews. The fateful request was transmitted on April 20 at 4:00 p.m. Eichmann was willing to oblige.[39] With the help of Hungarian gendarmerie and administration, this task was carried out with such speed that by the end of the period of May 15 to July 1 the only Jews left in Hungary were in Budapest. Only eight German officers and forty SS enlisted men helped the 20,000 Hungarian gendarmes in these operations.[40]

The deportations were indiscriminate. Secret directives were issued by Endre that "the existing exemptions have to be declared false. In case of Jewish protests it should be pointed out that at the border the Germans will check these exemptions again."[41] Before the roundup, the gendarmes were enlightened by their superiors that "none of them would be held responsible for one or two atrocities committed during the deportations."[42]

The parliamentary representative of Mukačevo, Aladár Vozáry, reported what he saw in his constituency during those days. The pattern of what happened there was repeated with monotonous uniformity by the gendarmes and the population all over Hungary, with no effort made to conceal acts of savagery; indeed, one could almost believe that the gendarmerie and the government made a point of displaying those proceedings before Hungary and the world. All the while, they denied the outrages categorically with a remarkable consistency and a sickening hypocrisy.

Representative Vozáry reports his experience:

> On the day of Passover the collecting of Jews from the rural areas of Ruthenia begins. The gendarmes go from home to home, they give several minutes for gathering some clothes and food, then they drive the Jews into their temples. They rob them of their cash, valuables, and jewels. The

abandoned houses are not locked, so the free plunder starts right away. Also the livestock from the Jewish barns disappears. The collected Jews have to walk from the villages on foot to Mukačevo, Užhorod, and Berehovo, (30-40 miles away!). General Álgya Papp, who objects to the abuses of the gendarmerie, is removed in 48 hours by wire from his post. He is replaced by General Fehér (Weiss), who adopts a strong line in Jewish affairs. Those Jews who were dragged to Mukačevo, for example, are quartered in two brick factories. It would be possible to put up 200-300 people there at the most — but the general masses up 14,000 people there. The brick ovens become jails. The Jews suspected to be "Communists" or "Zionists" are put in these ovens. One can only stand in them. There is a rain pouring down for days, and there is no roof over the great masses who have to stay in the open. The two brick factories are surrounded with fences. Food of the inmates: From the Jewish Council in Mukačevo, they bring in a bathtub a potato soup, about one spoonful per person. This is their daily food. All kinds of contagious diseases erupt among them, dysentery, typhoid, smallpox. The isolation is increasing. Any medical treatment, sanitation, disinfection is impossible. Inside the fence there is a Jewish guard; outside gendarmes, police and the Gestapo watch.

On the eighteenth of April the Jews of Mukačevo, that is, 13,000 people, are notified that by 6:00 p.m. next evening they have to move into a part of the city designed as a ghetto. One may well imagine the havoc. The transfer is carried through, nevertheless. By night most of the abandoned Jewish apartments are broken into [by the Hungarian population] and the pillage goes on until there is nothing left to rob. When, after a month, the official inventory in the Jewish apartments is taken, they find in most places only empty walls.

The massacres of Mukačevo start in the coming days. The Jews, who have been starved for more than two weeks in the brick factory camps, are driven to work. They are so worn down that they can barely drag themselves along. On the main square of Mukačevo [the gendarmes] attack them with blackjacks. They are scared and begin to run; at that point they open fire upon them. Result: countless dead and wounded. The others stop, they are cruelly beaten [by the gendarmes], and then they give them rods in order to start the work assignment. They have to destroy the inside of the great Jewish temple of Mukačevo! All their work has to be done on the day of Sabbath by the very religious Jews of Ruthenia. Then the territory of the ghetto has to be restricted. Within an hour on two separate occasions, two or three streets have to be evacuated. In some houses already twenty-five to thirty-five people are congested into one room.

On April 26, there is a secret conference at city hall. Professors, teachers, public servants are given short courses on how to carry out the search of Jews in the ghetto, both as far as their persons and their homes are concerned. Next day these trainees in groups of three enter the ghetto and gather everything of value. The result of these exploits is taken from the ghetto in wagon trains and much Jewish property is plundered. German soldiers are billeted in the empty Jewish homes. They empty the available property [furniture, too] into boxcars and send it to Germany. Inscription on the boxcars: "Gift of the Hungarian Nation to the Germans who suffered from the bombings."[43]

Reported Endre after his inspection of Jewish ghettoes: "The provincial ghettoes had the character of sanatoria. At last the Jews had taken up an open-air life, and exchanged their former way of life for a healthier one."[44] Jaross, the Imrédist minister of interior who once made a living from the contributions of rich Jews, recorded with satisfied racial self-consciousness in Nagyvárd (Oradea), a town which the 30,000 Jews, more than anybody else, kept Hungarian during twenty-two years of Rumanian rule, "I saw a new Nagyvárad open up [before my eyes] in the sunshine of May. I saw a new nationalist Nagyvárad where there were no Jews on the streets. Every contagious substance, every possibility of infection, must be removed from the body of the nation. In this matter the government will proceed further; I do not want to speak about this in detail. Watch the coming events carefully."[45]

There was good reason to watch the coming events carefully, because all these horrors did not satisfy the Szeged Fascists. After several days, the deportations to Auschwitz began. It was at this time that Col. L. Ferenczy of the gendarmerie, in command of these gruesome operations, reported the ultimate goal of the deportations to the ministry of interior, "Extermination by selection."[46] The Final Solution was truly under way.

Before the Jews were carted away to Auschwitz, every care was taken that their departure and death would result in no misplaced property. Everywhere the gendarmerie and civilian volunteers "urged" them to reveal the whereabouts of their hidden valuables. One typical report of the Jewish Council out of hundreds about these proceedings:

> Before the husband, the wife is beaten, and if this does not bring the desired results, the children are tortured. Blackjack, cattle prods, terrible beating of palms and soles with sticks, punches, kicks, fingernails torn off, were the methods of Hungarian gendarmes to make these unfortunates confess. The most unlucky ones were those who had honestly confessed and surrendered their assets before. In vain did they torture them, they could not hand over anything more.[47]

After 20,000 gendarmes had reduced tens of thousands of Jews, men, women, children to a bloody pulp by starving and beating, they drove them to the trains.* Reported Representative Vozáry from Mukačevo:

> The evacuation of the Mukačevo ghetto was carried through with whips, blackjacks, gun butts, tommyguns. The 12,000 Jews of Mukačevo were beaten, kicked and forced to run from the ghetto to the brick factory. Here they had to put down what belongings were left to them; they had to undress naked, men, women, old people, children, all of them. Denuded, they were forced to step back, and civilian women, gendarmes, policemen, and Gestapo workers searched and tore their clothes to see whether there was something sewn up in them. Those who did not undress

---

*In Oradea 20,000 Jews were tortured by the gendarmes in one great sweep to reveal their hidden wealth. One of the reinstated butchers of Novi Sad, Márton Zöldi, conducted the proceedings. Hilberg, *Destruction of the European Jews*, p. 541.

fast enough were punched. Most of the people were bleeding by then, and they stood in mortal silence, naked. In contrast to them the searchers were bellowing loudly. They returned the clothes, tore up the I.D. cards, all the Jews became "unpersons." Then they drove them with blackjacks and gun butts to dress. The congestion and hustle was terrible. They forced ninety people into one boxcar;* apparently there were too few boxcars and too many Jews! There was one barrel of water and an empty one for other needs in each of them. The echelon was left standing under the burning sun; it would move only next day. By that time many people went insane, even more died, because they threw all the Jewish sick from the hospitals into the boxcars. They did not open the boxcars before the train started, they opened them in Čop [twenty miles from Mukačevo]. There the dead were removed and the insane shot.[48]

After such proceedings it was time for Imrédy to congratulate himself: "This was a resolute operation! Contrary to the false rumors spread abroad, I can state that not a drop of Jewish blood is staining the hands either of the Hungarian authorities or of a single Hungarian."[49] This is the man to whom Professor Macartney attributes "idealism . . . spiritual purity" and an "absolutely sincere and deep religious devotion."[50]

Fortunately the world did not accept these oversimplified accounts of the Final Solution. The "false rumors" about the horrors in Hungary were multiplying. Besides the unnecessary and purely Hungarian brutality, there was the incredible speed which characterized those operations. The Germans offered two forty-five boxcar trains daily — the Hungarians pressed for six![51] Within six weeks, all Hungarian Jews outside of Budapest were taken to Auschwitz.

There is simply nothing comparable in the annals of the Final Solution in Europe. And all this in the year 1944, with the front on Hungary's borders and the entire country under constant air attacks!

Communications often go slowly in wartime, when they must filter through warring factions, neutrals and fronts, but when the Christian West finally grasped the extent of the Szeged Fascist-Nazi challenge, it reacted in an unprecedented manner. It was inconceivable for mankind that in the late spring of 1944 at the time of the American entry into Rome and of D-Day in Normandy, the Hungarian and to a lesser extent the German Nazi desperadoes should dare to affront humanity with such audacity in the very heart of Europe.

Contrary to Rolf Hochhuth's *Deputy*, it was the Vatican which moved first and most persistently. The Church had received positive knowledge through its well organized intelligence in Catholic Poland about the gas chambers of Auschwitz. Knowing the professed Christian morality of Imrédy and his cronies and being convinced of a coming allied victory, the Vatican did not move until the Jews' very lives were in danger, that is, when the deportations started. *But on the very day* when the first train left Hungary

*The boxcars used were the sixteen-ton European type, not the usual American type of sixty to seventy tons.

for Auschwitz, the papal nuncio, the dean of the Budapest diplomatic corps, the beloved Angelo Rotta, went to Sztójay and handed a stiff note of protest pointing out in unequivocal terms: "The whole world knows what the deportations mean in practice." He demanded an end to the deportation, threatening the protests of the Holy See.[52] But this did not impress the Szeged Fascists — after all, the nuncio did not tell them anything about the fate of the Jews that Sztójay had not known for a long time, or that the cabinet did not know from Colonel Ferenczi of the gendarmerie. The savage, wanton, indiscriminate deportation went on unchecked, delivering its daily freight to the ovens of Auschwitz.

One must draw a line between the Vatican, which had rejected anti-Semitism a long time before, and the Hungarian, Polish, and Slovak Catholic Church. Hungarian Catholicism was for a long time the very motivating force of anti-Semitism, seeing in the Jews the embodiment of radical, democratic ideas. But the clergy did not want to exterminate. They wanted to convert both ideologically and in religious terms. Their anti-Semitism was a medieval one, not the twentieth-century, German-Hungarian-Austrian anti-Semitism. Unfortunately, their flock did not distinguish so delicately, and many Hungarian churchmen were shocked at the spectacle of 1944, both on humanitarian grounds and also because they must have felt their partial responsibility for it.

Cardinal Serédi was of this type; Bishops Apor, Márton, and Virág were rather of the Vatican mold. Bishop Apor of Győr, the noblest figure in the Hungarian Church hierarchy, tried his best to prod Cardinal Serédi, the Primate of Hungary, into action.* When he protested vehemently to Jaross about gendarme atrocities in the Győr ghetto, Jaross let him know that "if he did not shut up, and dared to criticize or interfere with his measures, he would throw Bishop Apor into a concentration camp."[53]

Finally, Pope Pius XII personally sent a note full of pain: "Hungary is the Land of St. Stephen and of the Virgin Mary (Regnum Marianum). The treatment meted out to the Jews is an eternal stain on her honor."[54] After that Pope Pius instructed Cardinal Serédi to protest. Cardinal Serédi was a true representative of Hungarian Catholicism, and being both a moderate anti-Semite and a skeptic, knowing the Szeged Fascists well, he undertook the task without hope of success.

The pastoral letter he issued is a curious document. It begins by discussing wages and hours, pays attention to American air attacks during which "the disabling of innocent children by means of explosive toys scattered by airplanes" takes place. Then it touches upon the Jewish question. It mentions "a number of Jews who have executed a wickedly destructive influence on the Hungarian economic, social and moral life," elaborating further that those lawful means which restrain or eliminate Jewish influence were welcomed. Yet, the deportations and the horrors which accompanied them are

---

*Hilberg, *op cit.*, p. 539. He died the martyr's death some months later when marauding Russian soldiers shot him while he was trying to protect the honor of some unfortunate women.

condemned in forceful terms. The pastoral letter also states that all efforts by the Church to alleviate and stop these abuses had been unsuccessful, and ends in a solemn warning to the faithful not to associate themselves or get involved with the deportations and the horrors which accompanied them.[55]

The government found out what was afoot, forbade the postal authorities to forward the pastoral letter, and the "Catholic" ministers, Imrédy, Kunder, Antal, and Sztójay, hastened to the Primate to give assurances that the worst abuses would cease.[56] These blatantly false assurances, which Cardinal Serédi did not believe, were considered ameliorative enough for the Primate to suppress the letter, so that it was never read from the pulpit.[57] Bishop Apor of Györ expressed his grave doubts both as to the assurances of the Imrédists and also as to the fulfillment of the moral duty of the Church, demanding the publication of the pastoral letter, but Cardinal Serédi had already achieved his vaunted compromise. He could not be moved further.[58] Nevertheless, in the coming month thousands of Jews would convert to Christianity in hope of protection, because Church protection was understandably always stronger for the baptized Jews than for those who adhered to Judaism.

Yet the process of destruction continued during the last week of June and the first week of July when these events took place.

Incredible as it may seem, the great prize, the quarter of a million Jews of Budapest, even in the middle of June still had some illusions. In order to dissipate suspicion, a special SS courier brought to Budapest bundles of postcards written by the deportees from Waldsee (a cover name for Auschwitz), which were distributed by the Jewish Council.[59] But the relatives read these postcards with increasing foreboding. Why did they always speak in first person singular? Why was there never a word about wives, husbands, or children? Why was it that only young men and women wrote? The breath of an unspeakable tragedy struck the Jews of Budapest — and the deportations continued. In Pécs, the Jews, bleeding and broken after the gendarmes' search for valuables, were forced to stand at attention in the sports stadium while Endre reviewed them, asking: "Why does not your famous God Jehovah work a miracle for you now?"[60]

It was at that time that the conscience of the Christian world awoke in the West. Swiss and Swedish papers wrote detailed accounts of the horrors in Kosiče, Nyiregyháza, Mukačevo, Székesfehérvár, Oradea, etc. Such reputable organs as the conservative *Neue Züricher Zeitung* and *Die Nation* wrote detailed daily reports about the events under the title, "Diary of Horrors". American Quakers protested. The *Gazette de Laussane* carried editorial after editorial describing the gruesome details, ending an article under the signature of editor Georges Rigassi: "This is what the chivalrous and Christian Hungarian Nation did with the Jews." The *Journal de Genève* wrote a violent series of articles. All the neutral embassies in Budapest protested vehemently, with the Swedish, the Swiss, and particularly the Vatican representatives the chief protagonists. The International Red Cross presented specific demands. The nuncio prodded the neutral ambassadors into protest after protest, almost a daily occurrence. It should be remembered that one of the most enthusiastic champions of the Jewish cause was Miguel Sans-Briz, the chargé d'affaires of Franco Spain.[61]

But not only the neutrals and Franco were revolted. Antonescu's Rumania offered transit facilities and transportation for 30,000 Jews through the port of Constanța.[62] Few Jews actually escaped to Rumania, however, although it would have been easy, especially for the Jews in Transylvania. For one thing, when the anti-Jewish excesses started, the Hungarian press took the precaution to publish a false report that Hungarian Jewish refugees were being shot on the spot upon their arrival in Rumania. Endre was deeply perturbed that Rumania "made it possible for the Jews to infiltrate — they want to ingratiate themselves with the English."*

The Hungarian Fascists themselves were certainly above attempting to ingratiate themselves with the West — before 1945 at least. When the foreign ministry reported to the Ministerial Council on the wave of indignation sweeping the world and presented the demands of the International Red Cross, Imrédy, Jaross, and the Fascist fellow traveler ministers of the Government party flatly opposed the cessation of deportation or any measures of alleviation. They repeatedly warned the foreign ministry not to meddle with the affairs of the ministry of interior.[63] The Imrédy party ministers expressed their indignation over the fact that "the foreign ministry considers the question only from the point of view of the neutrals and the enemy but the German point of view does not matter to them." Imrédy, with his "absolutely sincere and deep religious devotion," had some afterthought saying, "It pays to preserve good relations with the Vatican because we may need them at the peace conference — although the nuncio should worry about Hungarians rather than Jews."[64]

Finally, after one stormy session, they arrived at a new conclusion: It was the Allies who were really guilty of brutality! Let them stop the bombings, then the Hungarians might consider doing something about the Jews.[65] They were flatly opposed to accepting any foreign offer of emigration, protection or asylum for Jews. Jaross threatened to resign if these offers were ever so much as considered.[66]

The Allies did not cease their bombings, and ultimately their air attacks were to be the salvation of the Budapest Jews. Horthy, after proclaiming it

*Lévai, *Fekere könyv a magyar zsidóság szenvedéseiről*, p. 288. Nor did the Szeged Fascists leave it at that. The Hungarian government complained to Veesenmayer about "the different treatment of the Jewish question in Rumania to the treatment Hungarians mete out to Jews," and on July 11, the Hungarian Foreign Ministry complained to Veesenmayer with great indignation that there are regularly 20 per cent Hungarian Jews among the transports of Jews which leave Constanța for Palestine! Veesenmayer immediately contacted his colleague in Bucharest, but all that von Killinger could do — the time being July, 1944 — was to agree that the Hungarian statements "were essentially correct." This is how far the Szeged Fascists were ready to go in their extermination campaign! Andreas Hillgruber, *Hitler, König Carol und Marschall Antonescu*, (Wiesbaden, 1954), p. 245.

his duty "to remain on the bridge of the ship," dropped out of the political equation until the end of June, surrendering himself alternately to reminiscence of receding glories and sessions of weeping. After the beginning of German and Hungarian Fascist outrages, Kállay sent him a letter from his hideout, the Turkish Embassy, urging him to abdicate immediately — but to no avail.[67] Although Horthy's intervention on behalf of the Budapest Jews was decisive, at the beginning of the deportations his position was more than equivocal, and it was ominously like his position during the two other decisive moments for Hungary during the Second World War, the Yugoslav crisis and the attack on the U.S.S.R. Apart from his complete failure to comprehend twentieth-century economics, politics and life, Horthy was and remained a revisionist, anti-Communist and anti-Semite. Nevertheless, he did not desire, and by 1944, he did not hold possible, a German victory. He also had the Christian humanistic values of his class, limited but far superior to those of Imrédy, Endre, Baky and their German bosses.

So, keeping this in mind, we may recall that in a fit of "enthusiasm" he rode roughshod for revision's sake over the Hungaro-Yugoslavian Treaty of Eternal Friendship, only to regret it later. He felt personally insulted that Hitler did not let him participate in the "crusade against bolshevism," only to be very, very sorry when the fatal effects of the unnecessary and unsolicited Hungarian intervention became clear to him. When the deportations started, he felt similarly "enthusiastic" that the Szeged dream of "Hungary without Jews" might be fulfilled. Speaking to Baky, he recalled that Baky, being an old officer of his from Szeged, must know how much he, Horthy, hated Jews and Communists — "out with them from the country! " But, continued Horthy, Baky must understand that some of the big Jewish capitalists must be saved.[68] He spoke to Veesenmayer in the same vein, expressing an interest in saving only the "economically valuable Budapest Jews, those who are well off." As to the remaining Jewry — and here he used a very ugly term — he had no interest in them, and he was quite prepared to have them go to the Reich or elsewhere for labor.[69] Finally, speaking to Endre, Horthy said that he had no objection to the deportations in the hope that if they were speedily concluded the Germans would leave Hungary.[70]

What was more ominous, on March 29 Horthy gave a "free hand to the government [under Sztójay]" and expressed his intention of "abstaining from any interference concerning the anti-Jewish measures taken by the government."*

Then the storm in the West broke, and reality awakened Horthy from his "enthusiastic" moods as it had before in the cases of Yugoslavia and the U.S.S.R. When the Pope protested it was bad enough, but when at the end of June two other "impeccable gentlemen," the King of Sweden and the King of England, wrote personally to Horthy in regard to the deportation horrors, Horthy understood that something had to be done. But what?

*György Ránki, *1944 március 19* (Budapest, 1967), p. 159. In the typical form-without-content manner, Horthy considered it enough to dissociate himself from the horrors if he did not *sign* the ordinances.

Finally, the West acted. President Roosevelt, shortly after the Archbishop of Canterbury's address on the subject at the end of March, asked Hungary in the name of Christianity not to persecute the Jews. But with the situation unchanged by the end of June, Roosevelt had had enough. He sent a stern note letting Hungary know that he was not relying on Christianity and humanitarian principles alone to back up his demands, but also on the force of arms.[71] He was as good as his word: in less than a week, thousands of American bombers clouded the skies over Hungary to warn the tyrant and give hope to the oppressed.* Simultaneously, Anthony Eden, while expressing British disgust over the actions of the Hungarian government, warned them that the Red Army was approaching, and that retribution would be taken in due time.[72]

All these protests, bombings, threats and horrors somehow converged in that last hectic week of June. On June 26, Horthy called a Crown Council and gave explicit orders that the Budapest Jews were not to be deported.[73] (Incidentally, on the same day Cordell Hull repeated Roosevelt's warnings.) Horthy's order did not stop the deportation of Jews from the countryside to Auschwitz, not even those in the suburbs of Budapest, which meant that another 64,000 Jews went to the ovens.[74] Jaross prided himself later with sending them surreptitiously to Auschwitz against the will of Horthy.[75]

But all along the fat prize so coveted by the Szeged Fascists had been the rich, thoroughly assimilated Jewish community of Budapest. For twenty-five years their hatred for these representatives of the West had exceeded all bounds. When the deportations began, the Hungarians had wished to begin with Budapest and had clashed with Eichmann over his decision to clear the countryside first.[76] Now, just as they hoped to bring the whole operation to a close with a great flourish, this great prize with its almost limitless possibilities for loot was slipping away. The Szeged Fascists were not prepared to take this reversal, and they took their countermeasures.

The deportation of a quarter of a million Jews from Budapest had never been envisioned as a simple matter by the Germans and the gendarmerie. The 20,000 gendarmes were not considered enough for it; the notoriously Fascist public servants in Budapest, the mailmen, public transportation conductors, chimney sweeps and so on, were to act as pilots. Streetcar and bus traffic was to be halted and a false air raid warning was to be the signal to start the action. There was to be a simultaneous "discovery" of explosives in synagogues and of plots and attacks on police, illegal currency transactions

---

*Racism has exigencies which are unknown to nature. The writer, commandeered in those days with other Jewish youngsters to put out fires caused by U.S. bombs in the great *Mávag* factory in Budapest, worked hard in the heat, half-naked. Suddenly, Imrédy appeared with his escort to inspect the damage. He walked up to us, warmly congratulated the Jewish boys "for their exemplary Hungarian patriotism." Working half-naked, we did not wear Jewish distinctive marks. At that point, one of his escorts informed him that we were Jews. Imrédy's face turned gloomy, and he quickly abandoned the "exemplary Hungarian patriots."

and sabotage, suggested by Veesenmayer to forestall atrocity propaganda.[77] Zero hour had been set for June 30.

Now Horthy had vetoed their plans. At this point, the Baky group, the most frustrated of all (because of all their R.S.H.A. support they were still out of power), acted. They wanted to combine the deportation of Budapest Jews with a *coup d'état*. Their fantastic plan was to send a Bakyist journalist, V. Görgey, with a small group to assassinate the chief of protocol, István Bárczy, a close friend of the Regent, and to take from him the keys to the secret entrance to the palace. They were then to enter the palace and browbeat Horthy into appointing a Bakyist government, or in case of reluctance, to kidnap him. Meanwhile, during the weekend, strong formations of Baky's gendarmes were closing in on Budapest in order to back the coup and carry out the deportations. The coup did not succeed. Barczy was not assassinated, and Horthy was warned of the plot by a variety of people ranging from the Jewish Council to the Arrow Cross. He ordered loyal troops to Budapest and Baky's gendarmes withdrew. On July 6, Imrédy denounced his former ally in forceful terms, but no measures were taken, either against Baky or against the would-be assassins of Barczy.[78]

Horthy's return to politics made itself felt, however. There was a change of personnel in the leadership of police, army and gendarmerie, and it was proven conclusively that without Hungarian help no deportations of Jews could be carried out. Eichmann made several attempts in vain; in vain did Hitler write the most threatening letters on the subject; in vain did Ribbentrop and Veesenmayer make almost daily presentations. The matter came to a standstill until October, when there was a Hungarian government which again gave Hungarian help and cooperation to much more limited anti-Jewish measures.

Rarely in history has the Jewish question occupied such a central position as it did in the history of Hungary in 1944, when it served as a measure, a barometer registering the excesses in good and bad. By way of illustration, there are two other characteristic episodes which deserve mention.

One was the R.S.H.A. action in May 1944 to acquire in one sweeping transaction from the Jewish owners (in German concentration camps) most of Hungary's heavy industry, mining and banking in exchange for letting them emigrate to Portugal with a quantity of jewels the like of which customs officials in Lisbon declared they had never seen before.[79] Imrédy, although he was very unhappy about the transaction, as minister of economic coordination sanctioned the action in an agreement with Veesenmayer on June 2.[80]

The other celebrated event was the Kastner affair. In May 1944, when the deportations started, a Zionist leader from Transylvania, R. Kastner, one of the Jewish leaders who knew about the Auschwitz gas chambers, tried to conclude a deal with Eichmann exchanging one million Jews for war materials (among which there were to be no fewer than 10,000 trucks) to be delivered by the Western Allies to the SS for use "exclusively on the Russian front." Eichmann and the R.S.H.A. promised to suspend the killing of the Jews until agreement was reached, and to deliver the Jews thereafter. As Eichmann put it, "Blood for goods — goods for blood."[81] Since then, an incessant flood of Jewish reproach has been directed at the wartime Allied leadership because of the Allies' failure to accept the offer. However, two things must be pointed out which may serve as a yardstick of Nazi sincerity in their offer. First, the Allied refusal was not given before the beginning of July; the deportations and the worst mass exterminations took place between May 15 and July 9. Contrary to the solemn promises of Eichmann and Himmler, the SS did not suspend the killing for a moment. From Hungary alone, about 450,000 people reached Auschwitz during those seven weeks.[82] So the Nazis steadily destroyed their "merchandise." Secondly, the real Nazi intention is obvious from their promise to use the war materials exclusively against the Soviet Union. One can only guess what effect the acceptance of this offer by the West would have had on the very strained Allied-Soviet relations in the spring of 1944. It would rather seem that by this devilish maneuver, which the SS did not even pretend to live up to,* the Nazis hoped to use the humanitarian feelings of Western Christendom to embarrass or to split the anti-Nazi coalition.

Kastner would have done a much greater service to Hungarian Jewry if, instead of hatching patently unworkable plans with Himmler and Eichmann, he had informed not only a charmed circle of egotistic and unscrupulous Jewish leaders about the realities of Auschwitz, but also the three-quarters of a million Jews who lived in a fantastic illusion about their fate to the very end. If he had, there is some possibility that in 1944 they would not have so obediently walked to their doom. But he and his circle in Cluj kept the information to themselves and saved only themselves. The verdict on Kastner was returned in 1954 in Israel. He was shot by an enraged Jew on the steps of his house, after he was acquitted by an Israeli court.

The Western Allies can be exonerated for not walking into the trap that the SS had set for them; but on the debit side, despite repeated requests by Hungarian Jewish leaders, the Allies did not target-bomb the railroads leading to Auschwitz or the involved agencies, such as the gendarmerie installations, during the speedy deportation process.[83]

4

Horthy's return to active politics occurred during those hectic days at the end of June 1944, amid anti-Jewish horrors, retaliatory bombings, floods of foreign protests, hypocritical denials, plots and counterplots. The signal for his return was given by Bethlen more than by anybody else. For the last time, but as decisively as ever, Bethlen defined for Horthy the existing situation and showed the way out of it. As he had for twenty-five years, Horthy followed meticulously the line laid down by Bethlen.

In the memorandum Bethlen sent Horthy from hiding at the end of June, he violently condemned the government for unreservedly selling out

---

*Never was Auschwitz working in such a full swing as during the promised suspension period of May 15 to July 7.

Hungary's interests to Germany. He saw the Jewish horrors as measures that "irreparably soiled the name of Hungary before the world." Moreover, he perceived what effect the free plunder of hundreds of millions of dollars worth of Jewish property had on the morals of the people: "It has become the source of the most atrocious corruption, robbery and theft in which, alas, very considerable portions of the Hungarian intelligentsia are also involved." He wanted Horthy to put a speedy end to such outrages, because if he did not, "the whole Christian Hungarian society will be soon contaminated irreversibly." He saw that with the anti-Jewish measures "the most unbelievable moral degradation and corruption is spreading among Christians, too" and with this, moral resistance would be destroyed, and bolshevism would be the consequence. Bethlen had no illusions about Germany's chances to win the war, and he wanted to extricate Hungary from it before it was too late. In order to achieve this, he proposed to Horthy the establishment of a coalition government consisting of military loyal to Horthy and of Bethlenite conservatives, the dissolution of all political parties (only Fascist parties were left), and the replacement of Szeged Fascists in the administration by Bethlenites. He named many probable candidates and made suggestions about how to carry this change of the guard through while avoiding German intervention.[84] As we shall see, Horthy followed point by point Bethlen's advice and instructions.

Horthy wanted to appoint the government suggested by Bethlen under Gen. Béla Lakatos in the first week of July, but the Germans, who had been informed of Bethlen's memorandum and Horthy's intent by Hungarian Fascists, were able to pressure Horthy into postponing his plans. They next demanded the inclusion of Ruszkay and Endre in the government and the deportation of Budapest Jews. Horthy flatly and successfully refused on both counts, and there was a lot of talk in Hitler's notes and among Hungarian Fascists about removing the palace clique (i.e. Bethlen).[85]

At that point, at the end of July and the beginning of August, an intense political struggle erupted between the Wilhelmstrasse and the R.S.H.A. about the kind of Hungarian government that ought to emerge from the shakeup of the hectic days of June. Veesenmayer, as always, favored a government of Fascist unity, which would include the Fascist fellow travelers of the Government party, the Baky-Pálffy group, the Imrédists, even the Arrow Cross. The SS under Gen. Otto Winckelmann thought it time for their agents Baky and Pálffy to form a government that would establish integral National Socialism. Szálasi insisted on Hungarism and full equality with Germany before he would join the unified Fascists. His radical social program alienated the Szeged Fascists and his integral nationalism the Germans. But as Szálasi's strength among the still-neglected popular masses had increased in the last months, even Veesenmayer could not dismiss him as contemptuously as he had in March. Winckelmann, on the other hand, was relieved that this difficult man need not be included in the schemings.

Veesenmayer saw that his pet candidate Imrédy had outlived his usefulness and was in the way of a coalition between the Gömbös Orphans Jurcsek and

Reményi-Schneller and the Baky-Pálffy group, this being all that could be salvaged in the direction of Fascist unity. So the Baky-Pálffy group, with the help of the SS, got a confirmation from Berlin that Fritsche's affidavit about Imrédy's racial purity was a false one, and that he was not only 12.5 percent but maybe even 37 percent Jewish after all. Jurcsek and L. Szász refused to serve with such a dirty Jew in the same government. Veesenmayer deemed the Szeged Fascists of the Government party more valuable than Imrédy, Kunder, Rátz, and Jarros in a possible coalition with the Baky-Pálffy group, and hence the Imrédists retired from government and political life for good. Imrédy withdrew to West Hungary, where little was heard of him until 1946 when he faced the fate to which he had delivered so many tens of thousands of better and braver Hungarians than he. Some of his followers, such as Rajniss and the head of K.A.B.Sz., K. Ney, worked directly with the R.S.H.A. from then on. At any rate, in August the crisis temporarily subsided without Fascist unity, and once again the most diverting topic of public discussion was the old favorite: Imrédy's Jewish ancestry.[86]

The Fascist administration was understandably chagrined by the temporary obstacles which prevented it from carrying the Final Solution of the Jewish question to a satisfactory conclusion. It consoled itself meanwhile with unleashing a not less savage campaign against the Hungarian Gypsies. This almost idyllic status quo could not be shaken even by the shattering effect of Stauffenberg's bomb on July 20, or the thunder of Russian guns which by then had reached both Warsaw and Hungary's eastern border. In another two weeks, De Gaulle and Eisenhower were reviewing the triumphal parade of Allied armies on the Champs Elysées — Paris, that shining monument of the Christian West, was once again free.

5

After Russian troops captured Iaşi on August 23, King Michael proclaimed Rumania's capitulation, and as a reward he was allowed to reannex Transylvania. In that country for which neobaroque Hungary reserved her most contemptuous epithets, the people, from the Communists to the conservatives, united under their brave young king to save what could be saved. There was not a single informer or traitor among them, and the Germans with their twenty-one divisions had been taken completely by surprise. They were deprived of the chance to turn Rumania into a battlefield, a rearguard action arena. The Officers Corps remained faithful to its oath and followed as one man the orders of its supreme commander, King Michael. The risks inherent in Rumania's capitulation to the hereditary enemy were tremendous, by all means greater than for Hungary, yet because the nation's leaders knew there was no choice, sober realism prevailed. The appeals of the hastily formed Sima government in Vienna were of no consequence; they did not succeed in controlling so much as a square inch of Rumanian territory.

The show put up by Hungary was something very different. The Rumanian capitulation brought home to most Hungarians what five years of war and all the bombings of 1944 and the anti-Jewish horrors had not — that Hungary might become a battlefield and Germany might lose the war. The broad masses were as apathetic as ever, but there was a violent controversy within the Hungarian Nation about how to draw conclusions from the happenings.

After the Rumanian capitulation, Horthy's circle got their chance to carry through Bethlen's plan. Political parties (all Fascist by then) were dissolved in the next few days. The day after Rumania's defection, Horthy forced Sztójay to resign, and the military-conservative-Bethlenite government under General Béla Lakatos was formed. The Germans had their hands full both in the East and West and, expecting worse, they acquiesced to the changes — but not before forcing upon the new cabinet two Gömbös Orphan ministers, Béla Jurcsek and Lajos Reményi-Schneller. These two were the eyes and ears of Veesenmayer, promptly and faithfully informing him about every minute detail of Horthy's attempts to extricate Hungary from the war. This, and Horthy's declared intention to continue the fight against bolshevism, reassured the badly shaken Germans in those uneasy days. Horthy also decided irrevocably to conclude an armistice with the Western powers, to assure Western occupation of Hungary and then hold out in the east against the Soviets, and to preserve as much reannexed territory as possible. He really believed this to be a feasible policy even after the military and political showing Hungary had made in the recent past. In this and in any policy he had the full support of the Bethlenite wing of the political nation.

Despite the existing realities, one must have an understanding for Horthy's reluctance to capitulate to a Soviet-Rumanian force and to Soviet occupation. His whole past protested against it. And for good or bad, Horthy and his circle were of a very different mold than their opposite numbers in Bucharest.

The Lakatos government did its best to purge the most important administrative posts of the Szeged Fascists — the March Men, as they were called. Every single one of them was removed unless his continued presence was absolutely demanded by the Germans. Endre, Baky, Antal, Szász, Kolozsváry-Borcsa and many others were dismissed. The trouble was that in both the army and the administration there were thousands of unreliable and unprincipled fellow travelers left, who had become in one way or another accomplices in the wholesale robbery of Jewish property, or who were responsible for atrocities and offenses against the Jews. They desired to maintain the status quo, still hoping for a miracle, or the "secret weapon," or anything that would forestall the reckoning. This considerable portion of public opinion was ready to stake everything on the most hopeless card of all — German victory. And then there were the "enthusiasts" of the Fascist right, those who were neither willing nor able to understand reality, and who always in every situation saw only themselves. For them the Rumanian capitulation meant one thing; they must rally the nation under their leadership to a struggle, which (they believed this in August 1944!) would end in an Axis victory.

It is in this vein that, on the morning of August 24, the Arrow Cross men stormed into the German Embassy and called upon Veesenmayer to bring them to power. Veesenmayer politely refused them, preferring to deal with Horthy. But he could no longer dismiss Szálasi in the contemptuous way that he had before. He knew that if every other possible Fascist party and Fascist combination failed, he might have to appeal to Szálasi, even if it disgusted him.[87] He fulfilled Szálasi's pet request: he arranged another audience with Horthy. This one proved to be decisive. Even the extremely wishful thinking of Szálasi could not misinterpret Horthy's contemptuous condescension or his determiniation to extricate Hungary from the war. He did not even answer Szálasi's usual suggestion that he appoint him prime minister of a cabinet of Fascist unity. After this audience, which took place on August 29, Szálasi gave up the thesis that he had to "assume power with the agreement of the Nation and the Head of State." He decided that "Horthy no longer believed in German victory and was a puppet in the hand of Bethlen and the Anglo-Jewish gang."[88] From that time on, Szálasi almost unreservedly (because his reservations remained only theoretical) collaborated with the Germans. It is interesting to note that in the very moment when Szálasi turned realistic, even that little good which existed in his movement disappeared; only a greed for power and a lunatic Fascist enthusiasm remained. Consequently, Szálasi began to urge Veesenmayer and even the SS to help him take power. Arrow Cross and German representatives met to take soundings of each other. The Germans flatly refused to help Szálasi to power. Szálasi withdrew to the country to draw up imaginary cabinets, because after the dissolution of all political parties there was little else for him to do.

Horthy tried to establish contact with the Allies in Italy and through the old Kállay lines, both through direct contacts and dissident ambassadors in neutral countries, mainly in Switzerland. From the beginning of September until the fifteenth of October, a mad race took place between Horthy on one hand and the Germans and the Hungarian Fascists on the other. Horthy tried to keep the Russians out of the country and conclude a Western-oriented armistice. He met an unequivocal refusal from the Allies, who advised him to turn to Moscow. It should be considered the greatest credit to Horthy that he now was able to overcome his understandable disgust for communism and to triumph over himself and his past in the interest of his country and people. Never did the old Regent during the twenty-five years of his reign become so united with the fate of his people as in the tragic and humilating hour at the beginning of October when he sent a personal letter to Stalin through the Hungarian delegation asking for an armistice.

The Germans worked on many points through their usual system of Wilhelmstrasse channels, that is Veesenmayer and the R.S.H.A. through the SS. They maintained their relations with the Lakatos government, sending Heinz Guderian to Budapest to encourage resistance against Russia. They kept the Arrow Cross waiting, using them as only one pawn in their race for time. Despite their solemn promise to deal with the Arrow Cross only, they kept close contact with the Szeged Fascist Hungarian General Staff and with other splinter Fascist groups inside and outside the Government party, ever ready to drop Szálasi if a more convenient solution was found. They got immeasurable intelligence help from every possible Hungarian Fascist group. It may safely be said that in these decisive weeks the Germans were informed about every word, every move planned or executed by Horthy's partisans, and this is the most important single reason why Hungary was the only country among Hitler's satellites whose attempts to extricate itself from the Nazi grip resulted in total failure.

In the first week of September, the Russians crossed the mountain passes of southern Transylvania in strength, and any resistance to their armored columns on the plains was not only hopeless but suicidal. Horthy decided suddenly on September 7 to ask for an armistice. But he considered it a point of honor not to betray the Germans, so he asked for five German armored divisions for reinforcements, hoping the Germans would be unable to fulfill the request. He was mistaken. The Germans did find a scratch force, which they sent to Budapest rather than to the front in order to secure Hungary's capital. It was easy for them to manipulate in this way; they knew every word spoken and every plan made in the meetings of the palace clique.

Horthy's chief adviser and mentor was, as always, Bethlen.* Szálasi also had his sympathizers everywhere, who reported faithfully to him, too.[89] The general staff was ready to break its oath to the "supreme warlord" without a twinge of conscience and to "answer any compromise with sabotage and armed resistance."[90] Gömbös' son proved to be an excellent source of intelligence. Having many acquaintances among the Officers Corps through his father, he moved on his own to find out who was opposed to ending the war and supplied Szálasi with valuable information, for which he was to be duly rewarded later.[91]

Such was the situation on September 13 when the Hungarian Army in a preventive move went into Arad in Rumania, where there were some Jews foolish enough to wait for them. Although the military situation was something more than desperate, the Hungarian Officers Corps could not sit still while Jews were living in peace in a town dominated by the Hungarian Army. Some hours after their arrival, the distinctive yellow stars appeared, terror was unleashed, and only the speedy reconquest of Arad by Soviet and Rumanian forces prevented worse outrages. The spontaneity of this seemingly minor incident, which occurred under the Lakatos government, which was opposed to anti-Semitic measures and had nothing to do with German demands, illustrates the attitude of an all too large segment of the Hungarian Officers Corps.

On September 8, when Szálasi found out about the ill-fated decision by the Regent and the palace clique to seek an armistice with the advancing Russians, he considered that Horthy had acted "unconstitutionally," and he abandoned the few scruples he still had. He proposed an immediate seizure of

*Macartney, op. cit., II, 343n. The minutes of both important cabinet meetings, on August 25 and on September 8 respectively, are available now in Allianz, pp. 386-400.

power by the Germans and his men, although he still felt some inhibitions about putting his need and desire for German help into clear terms. He made a wise move when he gave Kovarcz plenipotentiary powers and put him in charge of organizing the Arrow Cross armed forces. Kovarcz made a stipulation that the Germans were not to cooperate with any other Fascist group except the Arrow Cross, which the Germans promised and ignored at convenience. The SS cooperated and under its protection hid both Kovarcz and the K.A.B.Sz. under Ney. The SS also maintained close contact with their agent Baky, who was organizing the gendarmes for zero hour. Finally, the Germans reached understanding on an individual basis with many senior Hungarian officers. Regarding the traditional controversy between Winckel- mann in command of the SS and Veesenmayer, it seems that at this hour of danger, despite their deep personal dislike for each other, they stopped playing on the jealousies of Hungarian Fascists and pulled together to accept any help they could get.[92]

Hitler had his own ideas about the action to prevent Hungary's defection. He sent his trusted countryman, the Viennese Otto Skorzeny, the liberator of the *Duce,* to Budapest with a plan of the underground passages of Buda castle. Skorzeny was to organize the seizure of Castle Hill, where most of the government offices were, with a combined kidnapping of various persons, including Horthy. Skorzeny duly arrived in Budapest on the seventeenth of September, checked in under a false name, and started to spread his web with the help of many high-ranking Arrow Cross men and other Hungarian Fascists.[93]

In the middle of September, heavy Allied and Russian air attacks disrupted life in Hungary. The Hungarian authorities started a hunt for Arrow Cross and Baky partisans, but all of the important ones were living under German protection by that time. No arrests of importance were made.

Parliament reconvened for the last time in neobaroque Hungary on September 21. Lakatos made a long speech refuting accusations of "so-called class rule," making overtures toward the Western Allies, and asking for favorable armistice conditions. It was a speech that could have been written by Kállay.[94] The trouble was that a lot of things had happened since March. In responding to the speech, the Arrow Cross representative Szöllösi explained bluntly to Lakatos that the "fate of Hungary will be decided in London, in Berlin, or in Moscow," and the Arrow Cross "expects relief from Berlin." He also demanded that "in case of armistice negotiations, Parliament should be informed beforehand."[95]

With the arrival of the Soviet Army in Hungary during the last week of September, we enter upon one of the most unhappy chapters of our story.

Nobody will deny that Russia was invaded and that whatever one has sown, one will also reap. No one could forget or forgive the singular ruthlessness which the Axis displayed in the time of its victorious march through Europe, especially in Russia. And of course no army in the world consists of saints. Nevertheless, in the history of the twentieth century, the rape, the pillage, the altogether unbridled behavior of the Red Army in Hungary and elsewhere is almost without precedent. It would have been much better for the Allied image (especially for the Soviet one) had the Russian armies, with the memory of their twenty million dead compatriots still so green, adopted an attitude of cold, contemptuous aloofness toward the populace while concentrating their savagery on those who were guilty of Fascist crimes. But were those twenty millions avenged through the sordid rapine of 1944-45? And was this even vengeance? Because the same outrages — although to a lesser extent — were committed in anti-Fascist, brotherly and much-tried Yugoslavia, as well as in Bulgaria and Czechoslovakia and the Danish island of Bornholm in the Baltic Sea. They were repeated everywhere the Red Army set foot, with one notable exception: Poland. Here Stalin's realism took into account the existing high tension in Polish-Russian relations, and here he enforced an iron discipline, proving that all along it was he who permitted, nay, encouraged, the base rampage from anti-Fascist Serbia to Nazi Austria.*

In Hungary, in the crucial weeks of the early fall of 1944, the consequences of the Fascist press's playing up the experiences of the first town "liberated" by the Red Army were disastrous. If it gave a measure of righteous satisfaction to Fascists who were themselves guilty of much worse crimes, it struck fear and doubt into the hearts of honest Hungarians. Even the Jews of Budapest, living in the antechamber of Auschwitz, trembling for their lives and waiting for deliverance, knew fresh fear. But they had no choice; they could only wait. Those non-Jewish Hungarians who had a choice other than Auschwitz or the tender mercies of Stalin's armies had second thoughts, which were exploited to the utmost by the Hungarian Fascists, who knew that their crimes were too great to be forgiven, and that they had to face a retribution very different from the transitory rampage of semi-barbarous Russian hordes.

The race between the Bethlenite attempts at armistice and the German attempts, with the help of their Szeged Fascist and Arrow Cross allies, to forestall it continued, entering its decisive phase in the fourth week of September. Veesenmayer still had many irons in the fire; he had not ruled out even another accommodation with Horthy. His conservative aversion to Szálasi's Hungarism led him to appeal to the Arrow Cross only in the direst emergency, and then he would lie and doublecross if it fit his ends.

Veesenmayer and Winckelmann were ordered to see Hitler on September 21. Before the meeting, Veesenmayer asked Szálasi to forward his proposals for the future. Szálasi was ready to assume power with or without Horthy's consent, substituting the mystery of the Holy Crown of St. Stephen for the legality he had insisted upon so staunchly before. He made the condition that Hungary be defended like Germany, demanded the delivery of arms, and

*Milovan Djilas, *Conversations with Stalin* (New York, 1962), p. 109-111. Of course, many individual Russian soldiers showed the generosity, magnanimity and goodness for which the great Russian people are renowned. They were uniformly very kind to children, and rarely did they kill civilians. They "only" raped and plundered them.

made it clear that German power must be used to avoid the "repetition of the fate of the Iron Guard," a spectre constantly haunting the Arrow Cross in those days. And he did not like the other parallel with the Iron Guard either, the possibility of sharing the fate of Sima, of heading a Fascist government in exile.[96] When Szálasi was asked what kind of cabinet he intended to form, his answer reflected the changes that had taken place in his thinking. He mentioned the names Rajniss, Ruszkay, Jaross, Pálffy, Jurcsek, Reményi-Schneller, Szász. This was a purely Szeged Fascist list of the most unquestioning and unscrupulous servants of the Germans (some of them R.S.H.A. informers and contractual agents), none of them sympathetic to any social reform deserving the name. Finally Szálasi moved into German premises for protection.[97]

Then Veesenmayer left for the *Führerhauptquartier*. He had succeeded in accomplishing a de facto Fascist unity after all, although the only cement holding the divergent, jealous, heterogeneous elements together was German power coupled with the extreme emergency situation.

Szálasi was cut off from most of his contacts in his protective custody, but he was not idle. He worked out an act of abdication for Horthy by which the Regent was to retire because of his "shattered health" and call down the blessings of heaven on Szálasi's policy. Szálasi worked out in his inimitable language a proclamation, an "order of the day to the nation in arms" (*Hadparancs a fegyveres nemzethez!*) with which he later assumed power. All kinds of other constitutional amenities and refinements followed to justify his action.

One of the most important parts of his task was to work out — with Russian troops fifty to sixty miles from Budapest and the Allies on the western borders of the Reich — an elaborate project which was to establish Hungarism in Hungary by the first of January, 1945! He meant to govern constitutionally through Parliament, but parliamentary activities were not to interfere "with the nation's will to live." The nation was to be organized into corporations, the whole administration was to be reorganized and centralized mines and power stations were to be nationalized, and big industry and trade put under state control; agriculture was to be mechanized and its indebtedness to capitalism ended; new legal and educational systems were to be established, both permeated with Hungarism. Foreign policy was to be reassessed in order "to fit Hungary into the future National Socialist community of Europe." Although the definition of the Jew was racial, Szálasi, as ever, flatly overruled deportations. Jews were to work in Hungary until the end of the war and then be resettled elsewhere, pending an international agreement concerning their status. Also, he did his best in his plans to bring about a total mobilization in order to achieve victory.[98]

Meanwhile Rajniss moved along Szeged Fascist lines to organize in Parliament a National Alliance (*Nemzeti Szövetség*) of Fascist and Fascist fellow traveler deputies in order to force Horthy constitutionally to appoint a Fascist government. The roots of this organization go back to July 1944; it was formed in the hectic days when the March Men suffered their first setback, thanks to national and international revulsion against them. This group proved to be somewhat close to the much-vaunted Fascist unity. Although Rajniss wanted to give an unequivocally Nazi twist to their declaration, and it could be used as a tool to bring Szálasi legally to power, the majority of deputies found it expedient in the interests of conservatism to water down the more radical references to Nazism. The fascist fellow travelers of the Government party, knowing about Horthy's moves, even about the departure of the Hungarian delegation to Moscow, tore off their masks. In the shortest time 138 deputies in the lower house joined the National Alliance. It is illustrative of the composition of Hungarian fascism that a similar move failed completely in the upper house, with the notable exception of Archduke Joseph, who after a tortuous career had become an ardent Arrow Cross supporter.[99]

Veesenmayer returned on October 2 from his meeting with Hitler. He brought explicit instructions to give Horthy a last chance. Szálasi and Kovarcz were not of a mind to wait. They pressed the Germans for three things: (1) an immediate Arrow Cross takeover with German help; (2) guarantees for Hungarian sovereignty and effective German defense of it; and (3) assurance of no German cooperation with any other group besides the Arrow Cross. Veesenmayer would have given a negative answer to all the three demands, but he could no longer afford to treat the Arrow Cross with total disdain. So he procrastinated, using the most improbable excuses for delay, among which the one "to wait until the outcome of the American presidential election" was the most incredible. This, of course, infuriated Szálasi, who was in one of his most unrealistic and "enthusiastic" moods — the long coveted power was in sight! Finally, despite Veesenmayer's other engagements and plans, the list of government officials over whom Szálasi was to preside two weeks later was drawn up. The interesting feature in this list was that it included two Gömbös Orphans, Jurcsek and Reményi-Schneller, still members of the Lakatos government, who accepted a portfolio in a future Szálasi government.[100] The last days of neobaroque Hungary passed in anguish, disgrace, treason, disunity and confusion. The Bethlenites and Horthy tried to serve the nation sincerely, but twenty-five years of mistakes and omissions made themselves felt. They went forward alone; no one followed them.

On the sixth of October, the eighth anniversary of Gömbös' death, an explosion shattered the quiet of the evening in Buda. The Resistance Movement, so weak and inept otherwise, carried out its great feat. Choosing the right symbol, it blew up the statue of Gömbös. The vast Fascist camp understood the message. Press and radio erupted in an unprecedented barrage, with the Imrédist paper sounding the *Leitmotiv* in its editorial: "On Guard, Hungarians!"[101]

Horthy's group made some attempts to prepare for the armistice militarily. Although it is perfectly true that Horthy did not prepare for the armistice in a satisfactory manner, this was not done intentionally but through his fatally mistaken faith in the loyalty and decency of the Hungarian Officers Corps. And while Horthy and his entourage have been widely condemned for this failure on the grounds that it was the proximate cause of Hungary's complete failure to redeem herself from the Nazi alliance, little attention is paid to the almost complete lack of popular support for Horthy's efforts. As far as the majority of the administration and above all the army were concerned, they were positively hostile to the idea of abandoning Nazi Germany. While the Fascist camp organized in secrecy and safety under German protection for the zero hour, they and the Germans knew every move Horthy and the palace clique made or were about to make, and took their countermeasures accordingly. The game was a very one-sided one.

The K.A.B.Sz. was dissolved when it made a premature attempt to seize Budapest. On October 11, the R.S.H.A. removed by kidnapping the loyal commander of the Budapest garrison, General Szilárd Bakay. New German troops arrived in Budapest, and Hungarian troops were prevented from moving toward the capital. Even if they had arrived, it is doubtful whether their Szeged Fascist or Arrow Cross Officers Corps would have obeyed Horthy's orders with any greater dedication than it did 50-200 miles from Budapest. Horthy established contact with the Resistance Movement; four days before his downfall he received its leaders, whom he lectured about the dangers of an agrarian reform. Outside the palace, German planes showered Budapest with leaflets bearing the slogan of the Hungarian united Fascist front: "Either we destroy or we will be destroyed (*Vagy megsemmisítünk, vagy megsemmisülünk!*)." That the latter would be the outcome seemed indicated by the course of succeeding events.

On October 6 the Russians broke through the Hungarian-German defenses on a front of 117 kilometers and their tanks swept across the Hungarian plain, conquering in four days about one-fourth of Trianon Hungary. On October 11 the Hungaro-Soviet armistice was signed in Moscow with the provisions that it go into effect at an unspecified date in the near future. In accommodation of a request from Horthy, the Soviet High Command halted its advance sixty miles from Budapest in order not to interfere with and confuse the Hungarian action.[102] On October 12 the National Alliance protested in forceful terms to Lakatos about the pending armistice. Jaross distinguished himself during this interview with his usual vulgarity. The same day, the Fascist fellow traveler and speaker of Parliament, Tasnádi-Nagy, warned Horthy personally that he had to consult Parliament before concluding an armistice.

Meanwhile Szálasi had concluded a written agreement with Veesenmayer on the eleventh in which Veesenmayer, in the name of the *Führer*, recognized him as "the only responsible man in Hungary" and promised to treat Hungary under him as an equal, and to defend her as German soil would be defended.[103] One may have some idea of Veesenmayer's good faith if one recalls that the next day he made serious efforts to mend relations with the Regent and Lakatos.[104]

Winckelmann and the SS worked out their own plan, which was to take the National Alliance to Esztergom, the seat of the Primate of Hungary, a town thirty-five miles from Budapest, there to proclaim the deposition of

Horthy by the rump Parliament and his succession by Szálasi. Any resistance to this was to be broken by German-Hungarian Fascist military action.

The Russians grew impatient and demanded the proclamation of the armistice, which Horthy's entourage decided to do on Sunday, October 15.

6

The fifteenth of October, 1944, brought the supreme trial of the twenty-five-year-old neobaroque system. Horthy did not see it coming. The tragic illusion and error of an old man was exposed on that dark day. Horthy was convinced that with the 10,000 social organizations, his gendarmerie, the "Order of Heroes" and especially his army and its Officers Corps whom he as supreme warlord had pampered and defended for so long, all Hungary was marching firmly behind him. On that day he found out that even in his own closest circle very few took seriously their oath of allegiance to him.

We shall consider only the most important aspects of the Fascist *coup d'état*. On the morning of that hectic Sunday, the situation was this: Strong Russian forces stood sixty to seventy miles from Budapest — four or five times closer than they were to Bucharest at the time of King Michael's action. The "loyal" Hungarian troops did not arrive in Budapest (although subsequent events made it doubtful that Hungarian troops commanded by Gömbös' Officers Corps could or would act loyally anywhere except by accident). Yet there were more Hungarian troops in the capital than German ones; the available German forces in and around Budapest were not strong. Horthy's contacts with the weak forces of the democratic resistance were recent and badly organized and coordinated. The understanding with Marshall Rodom Malinovski's headquarters was the worst possible. But the Arrow Cross, K.A.B.Sz. and Baky's gendarmes were ready, and far more important, the high-ranking officers of the Hungarian General Staff were also ready, for treason.

In the early morning hours young Miklós Horthy, the only surviving child of the Regent, who in the last weeks participated in his father's work in good faith but rather clumsily, was lured by Skorzeny's agents with the help of a Hungarian police official, J. Marty,* a Gestapo agent, into a purported meeting with "emissaries of Tito." After a brief scuffle, young Horthy was kidnapped.

It was after that event that Horthy, who had been understandably upset about the fate of his last remaining child, met Veesenmayer. It is typical of the neobaroque age that the "form without content" philosophy was to be maintained to the end. Horthy always insisted, even while dealing with Germans of the moral stature of Hitler, Himmler, Ribbentrop, Veesenmayer and Eichmann, on giving "advance notice" before defecting. But the intrinsic value of this senseless "advance notice" was not preserved, just the form, because Horthy's proclamation was to go out literally at the very moment

*The writer knew this repulsive creature well from his Siberian imprisonment; there he worked as an informer for the M.V.D.

when he announced his intention to Veesenmayer,[105] not giving him any time to disengage German troops honorably or protect them. Apart from the absurdity of dealing with Nazis in such a fashion, Horthy owed much more to Hungary than to such formalities, and he missed many opportunities because of empty form.

The proclamation itself, broadcast to the nation at 1:00 p.m., was an honest, reasonable, patriotic document. One feels disposed to forgive him much for it. After twenty-five years of misrule, he could achieve finally that greatest of triumphs, the triumph over self, and become one with the interests of his people. He said:

> Today it is clear to any sober, thinking person that the German Reich has lost the war. All those governments who feel themselves responsible for the destiny of their countries, must draw pertinent conclusions from this fact, for as the great German statesman Bismarck once said: No nation ought to sacrifice itself on the altar of an alliance. In full awareness of my historical responsibility, I have the duty to undertake every step in order to prevent further unnecessary bloodshed. A nation that would allow the land of its forefathers to be turned into a theater of rearguard action in a war already lost, defending in a servile spirit alien interests, would lose the respect of public opinion throughout the world.[106]

But the Hungarian Fascists of all factions and denominations, united for the first and last time, were about to do precisely what Horthy had said must not be done. As for the population, it received the Regent's appeal with its usual, almost impressive, indifference and apathy, but in some cases with positive hostility. The Fascist opposition went into motion. Kovarcz's men promptly took over the radio station (not even for this vital nerve center was adequate defense provided).[107] The undignified panic among the Szeged Fascists in the government, on the other hand, was indescribable. The ministers Jurcsek and Reményi-Schneller, after endorsing the armistice, went from Horthy straight to the German Embassy to ask asylum. They found Rajniss, Szász and many others already there. Some Arrow Cross leaders, Szöllösi for one, ran away to western Hungary. But the democratic resistance on that day behaved in a manner fully as cowardly as did their Fascist counterparts.[108] Szálasi was sealed off by the Germans altogether. Even his proclamation, already prepared, was to be read on the radio later without his authorization.

The German Embassy would have been as little protection as the one in Bucharest (where the desperate German ambassador, von Killinger, committed suicide) but for the intrusion of a decisive and shameful factor. Horthy's efforts on this day were foiled not by the bands of Kovarcz or the Imrédist K.A.B.Sz., or even by the German SS or by Skorzeny, but solely by the Hungarian Army Officers Corps. Senior officers with Veesenmayer terrorized Chief of Staff János Vörös, and issued in his name false proclamations contradicting the Regent. Subordinates arrested their commanding officers who remained loyal to Horthy,[109] the most decisive of these acts being the arrest of General B. Aggteleki, commander of the all-important Budapest garrison, by his subordinate, General Iván Hindy. That arrest paralyzed all Horthyite activity in the capital. By 5:00 p.m. everything was decided. Horthy's attempt to extricate Hungary from the German *Götterdämmerung* had failed miserably.*

By evening, with the help of the Hungarian Army, the whole country and the capital city had been delivered into German-Arrow Cross hands without the slightest resistance. At 8:21 p.m., the Budapest radio broadcasted Szálasi's lunatic "Order of the Day for the Armed Nation." A statement was read later by the chief of staff (or in his name) about "the shameful treason of the Regent," exhorting the Hungarian Army to keep fighting. Arrow Cross, K.A.B.Sz. and other Fascist statements in the same vein followed.

Horthy and the very few who remained loyal to him were as isolated as ever on Castle Hill in Buda. The bodyguard with some "loyal" Hungarian troops tried to put up resistance, mining the access streets to the castle. But Arrow Cross soldiers had taken the detonating devices out of the mines.[110]

At dawn on the sixteenth, Veesenmayer came to Horthy and politely arrested him.[111] The bodyguard fired a few protest shots, but Horthy, seeing the futility of resistance, ordered a cease-fire.[112]

Because of Szálasi's fanatical insistence on legality, the whole of October 16 was passed with attempts to bring Horthy to appoint Szálasi legally as prime minister and his successor. Szálasi personally asked him twice during the day. Horthy advised him to get himself appointed by the Germans, and threw him out.[113] Through Veesenmayer, Hitler demanded from Horthy (1) abdication; (2) appointment of Szálasi; (3) revocation of his proclamation. In exchange Horthy was to be guaranteed "treatment due a person of sovereign rank."[114] Horthy still wavered. Then the Germans came forward with their most persuasive argument.

Horthy was standing in the bathroom of his apartments in the royal palace, when Veesenmayer came forward and pushed under his nose a dirty sheet of paper with a text typewritten in German saying Horthy was abdicating and appointing Szálasi in his place.** With him he brought the loyal General Lakatos. Veesenmayer let Horthy know that the price for his

---

*The greatest burden of guilt rests with the following commanding officers of the Honvéd: Hindy, Ruszkay, Adday, Nádas, Kapitánffy, László, Bereggffy, Zákó, Heszlényi, besides many, many others, the majority of them coming from Swabian (German) stock.

**The original document was lost, although the text was reprinted in *Pesti Hírlap*, according to which there were two documents issued by Horthy. One made an appeal to the Honvéd declaring the proclamation of the previous day null and void and exhorting the Honvéd to continue the struggle. The second document was addressed to both houses of Parliament. In it Horthy made it known that "in order to preserve the unity of the nation and to assure the successful continuation of the war effort," he resigned from his functions as Regent. "Simultaneously, I entrust Ferenc Szálasi with the formation of a government of national unity. Budapest, 16th of October, 1944. Horthy." *Pesti Hírlap*, October 18, 1944; also, *Allianz*, p. 403.

recalcitrance would be young Horthy's life; on the other hand, if Horthy signed, his son might join the family in an honorable exile.* Veesenmayer gave his word of honor to this condition, whereupon Horthy signed, sealing the fate of neobaroque Hungary in the bathroom between the toilet and the basin.**

Nobody would condemn the deservedly famous ties of loyalty and affection that existed in the Horthy family. But the head of state, or for that matter any person in a position of public responsibility, has other than mere family obligations. Horthy had remained at his post in March when only by his abdication could he have served his nation; now he was abdicating for his son's sake when, as his efforts collapsed, only his refusal to legalize Szálasi's Fascist-German coup could have helped his nation. Is it too much to ask of a head of state that he be the servant of his nation first? The code of honor professed by Horthy and his circle for twenty-five years (and before and after) did not leave any doubt about how one should act in such a case. But, like most of their other codes, this one too proved to be form without content, failing miserably before the realities of the twentieth century in Hungary.***

*This promise was never honored. Young Horthy was by that time in the concentration camp Mauthausen and was transferred later to Dachau, where he stayed to the end.

**Horthy, *Ein Leben für Ungarn*, pp. 293-94. It seems, according to the triple account of Veesenmayer, R. Rahn, Hitler's special envoy, and the high SS functionary H. Kienast, that Horthy collapsed under the threat to his son's life earlier in an even more undignified fashion. According to Rahn, Horthy cried like a little child, held Rahn's hand, promised to annul everything, ran to the phone — without calling anyone however — and in general appeared to be totally deranged. Hilberg, *op. cit.*, p. 552.

***A relevant example of heroism, taught and exemplified ad nauseam both by conservatives and Fascists in Hungary:
Against the incomparable backdrop of Toledo rise the towers and ramparts of the Alcázar of Toledo. Within it, in a little room, the commander, Colonel José Moscardó, is on the phone. The Communist Jefe de Milicias has just told him that if he does not surrender the Alcázar within ten minutes, he will execute his son who is in his hands. And to underline his threat he gives the receiver to young Luís Moscardó:
Luís Moscardó: "Father!"
Colonel Moscardó: "What's new, son?"
Luís Moscardó: "Nothing. They say that they will shoot me if you do not surrender the Alcázar."
Whereupon Colonel Moscardó answers: "Commit your soul to God, and cry out, 'Long live Spain!' and die as a patriot!" Then turning to the Jefe de Milicias, "You may as well keep the ten minutes you offered me, because the Alcázar will never surrender." A few days later young Luís was shot. *Alcázar de Toledo*, El Conde de Peromoro, ed. (Toledo, 1956), pp. 17-18.

CHAPTER VIII

The Hungarist Empire*

Du sublime au ridicule il n'y a qu' un pas.

Napoleon

1

About that which followed Horthy's abdication, one might repeat the words of Euripides: "Whom the gods would destroy, they first make mad." Finally, the *enthusiasts* of the Arrow Cross came to power, and while about half of Hungary was already in Russian and Rumanian hands, they set to work to transform the fast-dwindling remainder into a Hungarist state. Feeling vaguely the absurdity of their efforts, they plastered the public walls with posters showing Christ in the storm on the Sea of Galilee addressing the people of Hungary: "Why are you afraid, O men of little faith?"

As for more tangible things, the Arrow Cross began its regime in the early hours of October 16 with a bloody pogrom. The hooligans of the Arrow Cross Militia *(Fegyveres Pártszolgálat)*, which was to acquire an ominous significance in the ensuing months, broke into Jewish houses in Budapest and massacred in cold blood two to three hundred Jews, mostly women and children. German tanks participated in the outrage, shelling the buildings. The absurd and mendacious accusation was that the Jews had fired shots upon them. Unfortunately, most of the Budapest Jews had neither weapons nor the courage to fire them.

This was the first pogrom Budapest had ever witnessed. About 7,000 to 8,000 Jews were driven the same day to the racetracks. Many were shot on the way.** The red-light district of Budapest being only two or three blocks away from the incident, the prostitutes decided to improve the occasion. They stormed out of their houses and insulted, attacked and robbed the hapless victims. After the Jews had spent three days on the racetrack without

---

*Sometimes Arrow Cross leaders referred to the territories (consisting of several counties) which they nominally controlled as the Hungarist Empire *(Hungarista Birodalom)*.

**Many survivors have told the writer the story of those days. Out of the many gruesome incidents, perhaps one should be recorded because of its symptomatic nature. As the lines of Jews were driven in the drizzling rain through the streets of the capital toward the racetracks amid the abuse of their fellow citizens, a little girl of four whose parents had been previously shot strayed away from the column. An Arrow Cross man grabbed the little thing and threw her back into the line with such vigor that she landed with her face on the muddy pavement, lacerating her skin. The onlooking crowd greeted this feat with laughter, roaring its approval.

food or shelter, Szálasi personally ordered an end to the outrage. A tragicomic aspect of the affair was that when the Jews found out about Szálasi's order that they might return to their homes, they broke out in cheers, "Long Live Szálasi!"

Indeed, as always, there was an immense abyss between Szálasi's morality and that of his followers. The same may be said for the government he formed while still in the German legation. It represented the much-sought Fascist unity, which only mortal danger was able to bring about. It was a strange mixture of Szeged men who since 1919 had dispersed in all shades of Fascist movements, men like Kovarcz, Jurcsek, Szász, Reményi-Schneller, Rajniss, and Emil Szakváry; disloyal soldiers like Károly Beregffy and Vilmos Hellebronth; the R.S.H.A. was represented with Pálffy, and a dissident Trotskyite, Ferenc Kassai-Schallmayer, was also included. Kassai liked to brag that he knew Lenin personally. That sinister figure Endre, Szálasi's close friend from their secret society, the *Életszöveség*, appeared as commissar for the operational zones. The prime minister was Szálasi himself. His government was a coalition of the National Alliance with the Szeged Fascist military and the Arrow Cross. Imrédy and his party, with the exception of Rajniss, held aloof, their mutual hatred of Szálasi being insurmountable.

Szálasi quickly legalized his position. He had dreamed of becoming palatine in the old Hungarian tradition, but conservative circles were opposed to that, so he created for himself a new title: National Leader (*Nemzetvezetö*). Then, summoning a Council of Regency, he legalized the position of National Leader on the basis of the abdication extorted from Horthy. On November 3, Parliament met (55 deputies out of 370) and unanimously adopted the new arrangement. The same day Szálasi swore amid full pomp and circumstance in the royal palace, before the Holy Crown of St. Stephen, to uphold Hungarian laws and to ensure Hungary's welfare and glory. The same evening, the Red Army reached the suburbs of Budapest. Despite that minor inconvenience, the administration and the military swore allegiance to Szálasi in the next few days without incident or difficulty.

There was an almost complete change of guard. Every possible higher administrative post was filled with Arrow Cross men, mostly of lower middle-class origin. All the official posts in Russian-occupied Transylvania, Ruthenia, and Vojvodina and eastern Hungary, referred to by the Arrow Cross as "temporarily occupied territories," were also filled with Arrow Cross men. But, since by that time there were no nationalities left under their control, Hungarism's least unattractive aspect, its nationality policy, could not be applied; there was never any attempt made to do anything about it, with the exception of giving full jurisdiction to the SS over the Swabians of Transdanubia.

The de facto Fascist unity became de jure when on November 16 Ney and Pálffy entered the Arrow Cross with the K.A.B.Sz. and fused the National Socialist R.S.H.A. agency with the Arrow Cross, inviting their membership to follow them. Baky, who harbored personal ambitions and heartily detested Szálasi (a feeling generously reciprocated), hesitated for several weeks, but on

December 4 he made his ceremonial entry, getting a secretary of stateship without portfolio. There seems also to have been a rush of more humble members, mostly workers, into the new party. The Government party and the Imrédists, although collaborating, did not fuse with the new party.[1]

Then, with the rumble of the heavy Soviet artillery in their ears, the rump Parliament, consisting mainly of the National Alliance and the government, set to work. The same Parliament retroactively legalized the actions of the Arrow Cross since October 16. But when the issue of the Plan of National Reconstruction (which was to transform Hungary into a Hungarist Corporative State by March 1, 1945) came up, it opened the familiar chasm in the Fascist ranks. The Corporate Order of the Working Nation, referred to by its Hungarian initials D.N.H.R. (*Dolgozó Namzet Hivatásrendje*), was to consist of fourteen corporations: (1) soldiers, (2) clergy, (3) mothers, (4) teachers, (5) medical services, (6) civil servants, (7) free professions, (8) peasants, (9) miners, (10) factory workers, (11) artisans, (12) transport workers, (13) traders and (14) bankers. There is some indication of the Hungarist concept of social values in the hierarchy of numbers of these corporations. This basic Hungarist concept was brought before the rump Parliament in the early days of December in Sopron, where the governing body had moved when the Russian advance menaced Budapest. Both the Szeged Fascists (consisting of the Imrédists and the Government party — Fascist fellow travelers and the Baky-Pálffy group united with the National Alliance) opposed the measure. As Rajniss put it: "About such sweeping measures, which would transform the whole social structure of the country, only Parliament is competent to take action." Szálasi had no illusions about the nature of action to be expected from the Szeged Fascist majority. He promulgated the D.N.H.R. simply by decree next day, and the Szeged Fascists read about it in the *Official Gazette (Budapesti Közlöny)*. But the appearance of Fascist unity was preserved, despite other ominous rumblings under the surface. The Arrow Cross deputies contemptuously ignored the sessions of the rump Parliament and did not wish even to be seen with Imrédy, Jaross and Hóman. Imrédy and Jaross bitterly complained. "It would seem," observed Jaross, "as if there are two separate groups: the National Alliance and the Arrow Cross. This is not right. The Arrow Cross is also part of the National Alliance. We shall clarify the situation." But the Arrow Cross was more than it had been during previous years. The only Imrédist who was a member of the Szálasi government, Rajniss, had submitted his resignation by March 1945, a resignation which Szálasi accepted.[2] None of the plans or designs of the Arrow Cross were carried into effect, nor did the struggle within the Fascist camp have any consequences, because of the swift Russian advance. Few of the ministries had any affairs to administer, with the exception of the defense ministry, the new ministry of total mobilization under Kovarcz, and above all, the ministry of interior under one of the worst representatives of the Arrow Cross, Gábor Vajna.

With only the Budapest Jews left, and with Russians in the suburbs, Vajna set to work. On his first day in office this brutal, ignorant man caused an international incident by declaring that he would not respect exemptions of Jews of foreign nationality. Vajna also declared all other exemptions of Jews void. There were only Jews, period. All Jews were under his jurisdiction. The even more ignorant Arrow Cross foreign minister, Baron Gábor Kemény, concurred with Vajna in the new Arrow Cross doctrine of international law. Arrow Cross Militia hooligans took this seriously, molested several Jews of foreign nationality, stormed into the apartment of one of the heroes of World War I, Captain Bienenstock, who because he was 75 percent disabled had been exempted from anti-Jewish measures. They beat him up, tore his medals from his chest, dragged him to the Danube, and shot him. After this and similar acts, the foreign ambassadors protested violently, threatening to sever diplomatic relations. Kemény and Vajna backed down, pleading plausibly that they did not know about the existing international regulations concerning Jews of foreign nationality.[3]

At the end of October, the foreign diplomats intervened with Szálasi for the Jews' sake. He reiterated his well-known position that there would be no deportations. He recognized the foreign nationality of Jews, also the Jews under foreign protection. Those who had no exemption were supposed to move into a ghetto, which, according to Szálasi's orders, was supposed to have "four gates directed toward the four cardinal points."[4] Count Miklós Serényi* was appointed head of the "section of the Arrow Cross dealing with the elimination of Jews,"[5] by which Szálasi did not mean extermination. Csaba Gál was the head of the "anthropological" section of the Arrow Cross, checking whether the Arrow Cross men had Jewish features or Jewish blood in their veins.[6] Able-bodied Jews were supposed to work inside Hungary.

So much for the theory. The practice, as always in the case of the Arrow Cross, turned out to be somewhat different. Jews by the tens of thousands were driven on foot in autumn gales toward Austria to work in German factories. Eichmann reappeared at the end of October for his prey. Thousands perished on the way and after arrival in Austria. Kovarcz seems to have carried out the total mobilization of Jews only, not of the entire country. The Germans, exactly as in March, asked only for Jews capable of work and not the old and sick and children. This time, there were no Imrédists around "to cleanse the territory of the country of the Jews" (to use the words of Order No. 6164/1944 res. of the Ministerial Council), and to hand over indiscriminately all the Jews.[7] But as public order broke down, Arrow Cross hooligans robbed and butchered the Jews inside and outside Budapest at their discretion.[8]

The neutrals, mainly the Swiss, Swedish and Vatican Embassies, but also the Spanish and Portuguese representatives, issued a limited number of protective letters for Jews. The Jews falsified the letters, especially the Swiss ones, in order to save as many people as possible (this was the only substantial Jewish manifestation of overt resistance and rescue during the

*He came to the United States in 1956 as a Hungarian Freedom Fighter and was duly deported in no time.

entire war)* whereupon the Arrow Cross began to disregard them. The Swiss ambassador Lutz and his Swedish colleague, Danielssen, protested vigorously the Arrow Cross action.

And one should not forget the noblest martyr of them all: Raoul Wallenberg. This young, American-educated (University of Michigan) Swedish nobleman and diplomat came to Budapest at the request of the War Refugee Board created by President Roosevelt to coordinate and step up the rescue operations for Jews in Nazi-dominated territories. Wallenberg arrived in Hungary in the chaotic days of June 1944. He did his best, and many thousands are living today solely because of him. He brought people back to life by the hundreds, reaching them on their infamous "death march" on Highway No. 2 from Budapest to Vienna. He was rewarded with insults and kicks by Hungarian Fascists. He took the beatings and was happy if he could save some unfortunates. He stayed in besieged Budapest to continue his work. Finally, the Russians dragged him away, and for ten years denied any knowledge concerning his fate, alternately accusing "Szálasi's bandits" of his murder, and upbraiding the West for "trying to make cold-war propaganda out of the Wallenberg case." Finally, as a gesture of de-Stalinization in 1956, they apologized to the Swedes for the "misunderstanding" and notified them that Wallenberg died in 1948 in a Russian jail. In Budapest there is a street named after Raoul Wallenberg, in the very area of his activities, and he will be remembered in Budapest as long as Jews live there.**

By the end of November, the horrors of the treks to Vienna somehow impinged on Szálasi's consciousness, and he cancelled all further foot marches because of the death rate of Jewish women.[9] The horrors in Budapest proper continued, the driving of Jews from the protected international ghetto to the regular ghetto, the wholesale pillage of Jewish property by fellow citizens and Arrow Cross men, and the dragging, shooting, starving and tormenting of Jews. The Russians were only five miles away.

By the beginning of December 1944, Szálasi was no longer in Budapest. The events there did not get through to him, nor did the reality of the

*Even this action was organized by Zionists and originated in Palestine. A brave young Jewish girl of Hungarian descent, the legendary Anne (Chana) Szenes, was parachuted by the R.A.F. into the Hungary of 1944 in order to organize Jewish resistance to the Final Solution. Although she wore a British uniform, after she was intercepted by the gendarmes and Arrow Cross hooligans, she was nevertheless subjected to hysterical orgies, dishonored, tortured, mutilated, and after a mock trial, executed.

**President Truman, Eleanor Roosevelt, Dean Acheson and Senator Arthur Vanderberg, together with the Swedish government, tried in vain to intervene with the Soviets on Wallenberg's behalf. G. B. Freed, *Humanitarianism vs. Totalitarianism: The Strange Case of Raoul Wallenberg* (Ann Arbor, 1961) XLVI, 504-7, 515-16, 521-28. Raoul Wallenberg's mother, like many others, does not consider the case closed. As she expressed in September, 1967, in a heartbreaking personal letter to the writer, she still hopes that her son is alive in a Russian prison.

military situation. Only Budapest proper and one-half of Transdanubia remained in Hungarian and German hands.

Still the Arrow Cross zealots continued in deadly earnest their actions directed toward a complete Hungarist transformation of Hungary. The Hungarist greeting, "Endurance! Long Live Szálasi! (*Kitartás! Éljen Szálasi!*)" was introduced as obligatory. The authorities arrested as many Bethlenites, or "reactionaries" as they called them, as they could lay their hands on, Kálmán Kánya, Count Moric Eszterházy, General Lakatos, General Gusztáv Hennyey, and the former chief of staff Ferenc Szombathelyi being the most important ones. The great prize, Bethlen, eluded them in hiding. But they got their hands on Kállay: the Arrow Cross foreign minister, Baron Kemény, under dire threat of invading the embassy with Arrow Cross men and the Gestapo, forced the Turkish ambassador to surrender this chief architect of a reasonable and truly Hungarian foreign policy. Kállay was dragged away and handed over later to the Germans, who imprisoned him in Dachau.[10] That evil spirit of the Gömbös Orphans, Antal, could not this time shift his allegiance to the winning side quickly enough. He had irritated the Arrow Cross for too long in the ranks of Szeged Fascists; he also was promptly arrested.

The Church handed a dignified, patriotic memorandum to Szálasi at the end of October, urging him to spare Hungary the trial and destruction of further fighting in a war already lost. The Bishop of Veszprém, later Cardinal József Mindszenty, was the spiritual father of the document, which led to his first arrest, that being the only tangible result of the plea.[11] This plea of the Church was an occasion for refreshing old memories. Two other bishops who protested against gendarme atrocities during the Jewish deportations of the past spring were also arrested.[12]

As for the people as a whole, the traditionally apolitical Transdubian peasantry held commendably aloof from the Arrow Cross. Not so the workers, the real strength of Szálasi's movement. He had plenty of support among them in addition to the petite bourgeoisie and the nouveau riche, who feared free competition with the surviving Jewish bourgeoisie in the event of change.

As far as active resistance was concerned, only the lonely patriot Bajcsy-Zsilinszky, who was returned by the Germans in early September to Hungarian jurisdiction, tried with several loyal, progressive-minded Hungarian officers to organize an armed uprising to save Budapest. Denounced by informers planted in the group, they were tried and executed on Christmas Eve of 1944. It must have been a great satisfaction for General Feketehalmy-Czeydner, now the first deputy of the minister of defense, who was a fellow Swabian, to have the privilege of making the arrangements for Bajcsy-Zsilinszky's trial.[13] Before Bajcsy-Zsilinszky died, he left a testament to the Hungarian people in which he called upon them "to show more backbone in the future."[14] "I will be present at the peace conference!" were his last words.[15] It is not the least of the stains on Szálasi's record that he did not use his right to commute the sentences of these true Hungarians. But resistance and sabotage were positively on the increase, although the most common form of protest was desertion from the ranks of the Hungarian Army. Baky reorganized a monstrous field gendarmerie unit to combat this trend. The blood court of the Arrow Cross party, the Chair of National Retribution, *(Nemzeti Számonkérö Szék)* was at work everywhere in the ever-dwindling Arrow Cross territory. The most merciless of provost marshals was the Arrow Cross captain, Domnics, the man who conducted the interrogation of Bajcsy-Zsilinszky.

Meanwhile, Moscow had to make arrangements for the future of Hungary. Horthy's failure precluded any Finnish, Rumanian, Italian, or Bulgarian solution. In order to avoid the otherwise logical outcome, that is, to identify Hungary as she had identified herself and thus carry the "common Hungarian-German destiny" to its conclusion, and in order to forestall a possible Austrian or German type of four-power control, the Russians swiftly formed a "democratic government" from the available Hungarians. These were the members of Horthy's armistice delegation, some Hungarian officers who had defected to the Soviets to avoid arrest for their loyalty to Horthy, and a sprinkling of Hungarian Communist émigrés in Moscow. The government was established in Debrecen on December 22 under Russian occupation. Now this government, having no Hungarian troops under its command whatsoever, was induced to ask for an armistice from the United Nations (that is, the U.S.S.R.), and this request was gracefully granted by Moscow. On January 21, 1945, Hungary's position was separated in this rather artificial manner from that of Nazi Germany and Austria, and the "common destiny" came to an end when it could for once have done some good for Hungary. An Allied Control Commission was established on the Rumanian rather than on the Austrian model; that is, with a Soviet chairman and pro forma United States and British members. That it was an important personage like Marshal K. E. Voroshilov who was appointed chairman stresses the absolute character of Soviet supremacy in the commission. And yet, although they never abandoned the commanding heights, it was certainly not clear at the time to the Russians themselves what they were going to do about Hungary.

Szálasi, in the meantime, visited Hitler on December 4, accompanied by Foreign Minister Kemény, and Minister of Defense Károly Beregffy. Mecsér, who was then Hungarian ambassador in Berlin, was also present at this meeting. Hitler refused to see his puppets at first, but Szálasi threatened that if he did not, he would not give Hitler more soldiers. Szálasi tried to save Budapest from the coming horrors, but Hitler did not want to hear about such a concession. Budapest was to be held at all costs. He promised Szálasi that he would drive out the Russians with "secret weapons"* soon, and made the curious statement that when Rumania defected, he had wanted to

---

*The Hungarian Fascists could not possibly lag behind. The Arrow Cross military journal *Hungarian Sentinel* (*Magyar Orszem*) reported on December 13, 1944, that the new Hungarian weapon the "lidérc" (hobgloblin or demon) had been invented! This new weapon is not to be confused with another Arrow Cross secret weapon, the "Szálasi rocket." The military journal explains further, that "according to the very serious

restore the whole of Transylvania to Hungary, but Horthy's attempt at defection spoiled Hungary's chances. Hungarian refugees and materiel were to be allowed to enter Reich territory, and in addition to the two Hungarian SS divisions in existence, four others were to be formed, and to swear an oath of allegiance to Hitler. These divisions were to be named after the heroes of Hungary's Fight for Freedom in 1848-49 — Kossuth, Petöfi, Klapka, and Görgey.[16] Most certainly Hungarism's "Socialnationale," like Gömbös' Nationalist International, had come a long way. But Szálasi had something else in mind, too. Possibly chagrined by the fact that he had no "head of state," with his unfailing talent for choosing the contemptible he now offered the Holy Crown of St. Stephen to Göring! The Reichsmarshal, although greatly flattered by the offer, explained that he had to have the Führer's approval before he could give a definite answer, and that the "military situation has to change in the favor of the Axis" before the coronation could take place. Nevertheless, Arrow Cross experts went to work to establish kinship between the Göring family and the House of Árpád, and to forge a coat of arms and other appropriate credentials to endow the newest Apostolic King of Hungary with the proper noble aura.*

By December 10 all government installations, Arrow Cross party members and ministries were evacuated from Budapest to Szombathely and Sopron, two-and-a-half miles from the German border. Parliament held its sessions in Sopron, and Szálasi withdrew into his fantasies on an estate in the little village of Velem near Kőszeg, on the German (Austrian) border, but not before declaring the coming Christmas the "Christmas of hope," to be celebrated forever in Hungarist Hungary.[17]

In the meantime, the Arrow Cross Militia was terrorizing the population. In Budapest, which had been completely encircled by Christmas, about 100,000 German and Hungarian troops cut off from the main forces were contributing to the mounting terror.

On December 24, Budapest was still practically untouched by war except for some industrial suburbs and the area around the marshalling yards. Damage was notably slight in the beautiful historic Buda district and in the fashionable downtown areas. But when the Swedish ambassador and the nuncio offered to mediate with the Soviets to forestall the holocaust, they were arrested by the gendarmerie.[18] On December 29, the Soviets themselves had two representatives driven to the Fascist positions on two different points to try to negotiate a settlement that would prevent the senseless and hopeless siege. The men were murdered, despite previous notification of their coming broadcast on loudspeakers, and despite white flags displayed. Their simultaneous murder in two different places precludes accident.

---

opinion of military experts, this new weapon will decide the issue of the war." Karsai, *A budai vártól a gyepüig*, p. 613.

*Der Spiegel, March 18, 1968, p. 164. The Hungarian equivalent of the *College of Heralds*, printed in exile, still prints the coat of arms of the "Göring-Árpád House," despite the violent protests directed against such malignancies by Hungarian aristocracy living in exile.

After that, the destruction of Budapest began in earnest. The Arrow Cross appointed Ernö Vajna as the party representative for the defense of the city. The commander of the Hungarian garrison was none other than Hindy, who had paralyzed Horthy's action in Budapest. The German commander was SS General Pfeifer-Wildenbruch, who would have exterminated the Jews left in the encircled city had he not been prevented from doing so by Hindy.[19] But the Arrow Cross Militia was doing its best to kill Jews individually, to organize hunts for Jews hiding in Christian homes. The bodies of slain Jews were thrown into the icy Danube. One of the most vicious Arrow Cross killers was a defrocked Franciscan monk, Father András Kún. He wore his cassock with the Arrow Cross insignia, and carried a pistol. He raped many Jewish women before he killed them. His order to open fire upon his victims was always "In the Holy Name of Christ, fire! "

All German attempts to relieve the siege failed. On January 18, Russian and Rumanian troops cleared the Pest side of the city, while the defenders blew up the majestic Danube bridges before withdrawing to Buda. Four weeks of havoc followed. On February 13, silence fell over the shattered gothic cathedrals and the blazing baroque and rococo palaces of Buda. Budapest had fallen. One of the most beautiful cities of the world was destroyed in a delirium of Fascist "enthusiasm."

All this was not enough to bring the Fascists, bottled up in the western corner of Hungary, to their senses. Szálasi by that time had retired completely into the clouds. In January, nevertheless, he resumed his traditional "trips around the realm."[20] In his last public appearance on January 20, he promised full compensation for every penny people had lost in the war and threatened death to anyone who did not believe in the coming victory.[21] He commandeered the press for weeks to print Arrow Cross ideology, and the Szálasi radio kept referring to Hungary in February 1945 as the Hungarist Empire. Szálasi would not receive high administrative officials who wished to discuss important current problems because he was busy writing his memoirs. They were to consist of seven volumes: *My Struggle (Harcom)*, *My Imprisonment (Bebörtönzésem)*, *In the Csillag-Prison (A Csillag börtönben)*, *Free Again (Ujra szabadon)*, *The Struggle for Power (Harc a hatalomért)*, *In Power (A hatalom birtokában)* and *Hungarism Triumphant (A gyöztes Hungarizmus)*. All newlyweds were to receive this septet as a wedding gift from the Hungarist State.[22] Being a spiritist, he spent much of his time at seances, where he made frequent contact with a departed Scot named John Campbell. This communicant foresaw the downfall of the Western powers.[23]

The Arrow Cross prolonged the agony and increased the destruction of Hungary to colossal proportions.* They set to work to evacuate both men

---

*Altogether about 40 percent of Hungarian national wealth was destroyed in these months. *Allianz*, p. 104. (The Communist figure includes all the damage since March 19, 1944. However, the most appalling destruction occurred after October 15, above all, during the senseless defense of Budapest.)

and material possessions to Germany and to destroy even that little which escaped the fury of German rearguard action. This was pursuant to the famous Veesenmayer-Szakváry agreement, concluded between the plenipotentiary of the Reich and the Gömbös Orphan minister of industries in the Szálasi cabinet, Emil Szakváry (Löffler).[24] First, the Arrow Cross wanted to evacuate the whole Hungarian population "for the winter," to come back in the spring after the secret weapon defeated the Russians.[25] But the Hungarian people resisted this senseless uprooting process, as did the churches. The Germans dropped even the pretense of respecting Hungarian ownership of property. High-ranking Hungarian officers and officials entering German territory with their cars were ordered to surrender their vehicles, and Hungarian material goods were to be utilized regardless of whether they were state or private property. The wholesale robbery of Hungarian national wealth and the wholesale indignity meted out to Hungarians upon their arrival in Austria[26] did not even draw an appreciable protest from the Hungarian Fascists.*

They had more important things to do. The Arrow Cross held its annual meeting on February 2. Baron Kemény, the foreign minister, traveled to Zagreb and concluded an agreement with Ante Pavelić on "the conception of the fight waged by the two countries under the leadership of Greater Germany."[27] After that, the greatest of Arrow Cross achievements was accomplished: Kemény met Prince Mihai Sturdza, Sima's foreign minister, in Vienna, and they found a "just and satisfactory settlement of the Transylvania problem."[28] One may only repeat the words of Professor Macartney: "It is a pity that he [Kemény] never divulged what this was." A new Arrow Cross paper was started for the Hungarian minority in Slovakia, and the old Arrow Cross daily made a last violent attack (after the dismissal of Rajniss) on the Szeged Fascist reactionaries: "There is no significance to be attributed to their meetings, where mummies left over from the political world of Bethlen, Kállay and Teleki meet and cry over their lost positions and over the remembered ministerial armchairs."[29] Parliament met on March 22, the speaker still explaining the position of civil servants in the corporative

*Between October 31, 1944, and March 31, 1945, the Germans took out of Hungary by rail or by barge (army wagons and trucks not counted) 45,383 tons of bread grains, 11,203 tons of lubricating oil, 7,905 tons of sugar, 3,045 tons of medicines and chemicals, 189,753 tons of machinery, 100,000 head of livestock and unspecified quantities of other stock like 900 100-axle train loads, not counting what went by road and boat, 1,150 other train loads and 314 tug loads. Besides that, 43.6 percent of Hungary's total park of locomotives, 37.4 percent of her diesel trains, 61.9 percent of her passenger coaches, 74 percent of her trucks, 487 out of 489 units of her river fleet. Of what was left behind, the larger part was damaged. In 1945 only 10 percent of the locomotive parts and 18 percent of passenger coaches were intact, left probably in areas which were occupied before Szálasi's advent to power. *Demokrácia*, February 10, 1946. It must be emphasized that these figures are by no means complete.

system of the D.N.H.R., and on the following day Jurcsek introduced a new brand of unscented soap.[30] Anthropological examinations for Arrow Cross members to establish the degree of their racial purity continued apace.[31]

About the same time the Russians attacked in strength and in less than two weeks, by April 4, they swept Szálasi and the Germans from Hungary, proving once again the maxim of Maurras: *La bêtise est sans honneur!*

2

The year 1944 marks the culmination of our story and one of the greatest trials of Hungarian history. So great a year was it that its consequences and the transformations that took place after 1944 can be only partly evaluated as of this day.

The ordeal Hungary had to undergo would have tried severely a much healthier society than that of neobaroque Hungary. Thus it was not Hungary's failure but the *extent* of that failure that was shocking. In 1944, only the most negative forces, the Szeged Fascists and the Germans, seem to have fulfilled their role on Hungarian soil. About those segments of society which professed devotion to Christian Western ideals, the terrible words of the Scriptures might be said: "Thou art weighed in the balance and found wanting."

The Bethlenite conservatives, who were at one point in the position to do what their opposite numbers in Rumania did, failed. They failed because they could have succeeded only in cooperation with the Hungarian people, and it was not in the Bethlenite tradition to call upon the people for support. They did not comprehend the extent to which Fascist radicalization had been effected in the country, and when Horthy, Kállay, and others tried to move forward, nobody followed them. Their call was an ambiguous, uncertain one, and if Horthy ultimately could discern the sacrifice that he ought to make for his country's sake, one may only add: The spirit was willing but the flesh was weak. Weak and lonely was the old Regent on October 15, 1944.

His isolation was due in part to the failure of the Hungarian Army. The Szeged-dominated Officers Corps could have behaved only as it did in 1944. Consisting mostly of non-Hungarians, it equated its own interest with that of Hungary and acted accordingly. What followed was high treason, insubordination, dabbling in politics, and poor military performance.

The Church also failed to lead its flock; its hesitant, equivocal stand was the clearest on the all-important Jewish question, a far cry from the instruction of the gospel: *Docete omnes gentes..*

The Hungarian people, without leaders deserving the name, failed to save what was left to save of their homeland and honor mostly through apathy. Of all the failures, theirs is the most excusable. But excuses do not diminish the extent of the tragedy that befell Hungary in 1944.

The Jewish leadership failed utterly. Although by May 1944 they knew every detail about Auschwitz, they failed to inform the hundreds of thousands of prospective victims about the fate that awaited them. The

Jewish leaders of Budapest especially feared the consequences of jeopardizing their own privileged position. It was a repulsive sight to see those collaborating creatures running about their headquarters, wearing their yellow badges, and threatening their fellow Jews with the Gestapo in case of disobedience. S. Stern, the chairman of the Jewish Council, insisted on the title *Hofrat* and was the worst of the collaborators, but not the only one by far. Their work contributed greatly to the efficiency of the Final Solution just a few weeks before liberation. Only one exception should be made: Lajos Stöckler refused all exemptions, and did his best for the Jewish masses.* The Jewish Council went to the extreme in collaboration. When in May 1944 the deportations to Auschwitz began, the Jewish Council wrote to the minister of interior: "We emphatically declare that we do not seek to lodge complaints about the merit of the measures adopted, but merely ask that they be carried out in a humane spirit."[32] In other words, they did not object to Auschwitz (the fate of Jews delivered there was well known to them by then), they just wanted it all done nicely, in a humane way.

How different the answer of the French war veterans, who were at once exempt from the anti-Jewish legislation of Vichy: "Would the general commissar for Jewish affairs consider subversive a statement: We solemnly declare that we renounce any exceptional benefits we may derive from our status as ex-servicemen." That proud, dignified statement was presented to the Vichy authorities by the Jewish inspector general of the French artillery, General André Boris.[33] As Léon Gambetta said in his famous essay, "The true democrat does not merely recognize equals — he creates them!"

From this, as from many other points of view, the assimilation of Hungarian, Austrian and German Jews was a dismal failure. Perhaps because of the very nature of the process, such a thing is possible only in a true democracy. The former Central Powers have been far short of that at any time in their history. That is why the groveling, cringing, self-seeking Jewish leaders of Budapest were as they were, and why they added to the long series of failures of their native land. As for the Jewish masses, the atmosphere of Hungary after 1919 was certainly not one to breed dignified Jewish heroes, so there was more compliance and less Jewish resistance there than elsewhere in Europe. These unfortunates were even worse off psychologically than their unassimilated brethren in Eastern Europe. Most of them were not Jews any more, but they were refused by the host nation.

Only the 400,000 Hungarians of the "middle class of Hungarian gentlemen" who, as Rajniss so aptly stated, were opposed to 434,000 (later about 800,000) predominantly middle-class Jews, fulfilled their role. The Szeged Fascists did their best to maintain their position even at the price of treason and the ruin of Hungary. They did their best to make any attempt to extract Hungary from disaster impossible. They did their best to remove once

*Lévai, *Fekete könyv a magyar zsidóság szenvedéseiröl*, p. 204. Stöckler took over the leadership of the Jewish community during the glorious days of the Hungarian Revolution in 1956 and was thrown into jail after the return of the Russians.

and for all their rivals, the Jewish middle class, from the scene. In 1944, for their personal and class interest, they staked everything on the by then absurd possibility of German victory, which even if achieved would have meant the destruction of Hungary as a national unit.* Let us repeat it again: Whatever great plans Imrédy and the heterogeneous, disunited, conservative Fascist camp had for the salvation of Hungary, one can see only two things realized from their program from March 19 to July 1944 — the time they reigned supreme in Hungary with their German masters: (1) A collaboration which did not stop at anything, and which was as much anti-Western as it was anti-Soviet, and (2) the Final Solution of the Jewish question.

It is the anti-Jewish measures for which Imrédy and his cronies carry the greatest responsibility, a responsibility which extends far beyond them. Through the plundering of many hundreds of millions of dollars worth of Jewish property, they made broad segments of the population, especially among the non-Jewish middle classes, their accomplices, and even more important, through carrying out much of the anti-Jewish horror, they made many in the administration their accomplices, too.**

Of the 825,000 Jews living in Hungary in 1941 (both the baptized and the Mosaic ones), 255,000 Jews survived. About 570,000 perished in the last months of the war, that is, 70 percent of the total. Even this number is deceptive, because most of those who survived were in Budapest where there was no mass deportation. Out of those deported, 82 percent perished.[34] It is important to state these figures clearly, because they have at times been manipulated in ways that are highly misleading. Some Hungarian émigrés like to take responsibility only for the 261,000 Jews (or less) who perished out of the 481,000 Jews of Trianon — that is, present — Hungary. But it was not Beneš, Tito, or even Antonescu who was responsible for the 309,000 Jewish deaths in the territories "returned" to Hungary after 1938.*** The figure of Imrédist responsibility is 570,000 dead. Let us also remember that Eichmann and the Germans always asked for Jews capable of work, and that they asked for a modest 50,000! [35] When the Szeged Fascists handed over the whole Jewish population, there was little doubt that the SS would not feed Jews they could not use for work. In Nüremberg, Veesenmayer aptly summed up

---

*Communist historians always pay compliments to Imrédy's "logic," his "logical trend of thought," Horthy, *titkos iratai, op. cit.,* p. 442.

**Perhaps the government daily paper did justice to the popular mood when it editorialized on July 10, 1944, at a date when death enveloped the majority of Hungarian Jews in Auschwitz: "Rarely did the legal government [of Hungary] take a measure which would have been greeted by the population at large with such joy as the restriction of the rights of the Jews." *Magyarország,* July 10, 1944, p. 1.

***It is a part of this unsavory manipulation of the figures that Horthy permits himself in his memoirs to quote a figure of 110,000 Jews in hiding "with their Hungarian friends"! Horthy, *Ein Leben für Ungarn,* p. 272. About 6,000-8,000 is closer to the truth.

Hungarian responsibility for the extraordinary fact that in 1944 such a feat could be carried out:

> If the Hungarians had refused the German demands regarding the Jews with an iron consistence, there was nothing the Germans could have done about it on their own. There would have been pressure, but 1944 was already a 'crisis year' — there would have been no way to mark, concentrate and deport a million people. Such a task is a police task of tremendous nature, the accomplishment of which in three months was made possible only through the enthusiastic help of the Hungarian police and authorities. There was no way to bring help for this task from the outside — such a task could be carried out only by those who knew the land and the people. Eichmann had only a small staff. Such speed and smooth work was only possible with the full help of the Hungarian government.[36]

Veesenmayer's statement was corroborated by the fact that when Horthy, under the pressure of foreign intervention, stopped the deportations, the Germans were never again in a position to resume them on their own. And no amount of threat or demand from Hitler changed this. Had Horthy acted earlier, with every week he could have saved the lives of 100,000 people. But the deportations were not the work of Szálasi, but of Imrédy and his cronies. Horthy correctly summed up the activities of the Szeged Fascist Imrédists in a letter to Hitler after he dismissed the March Men: "The resigned government employed [in the Jewish question] such methods which no other nation ever used, and which provoked even the disapproving criticism of German authorities [in Hungary]."[37]

The memorandum of Imrédy's party, handed to Horthy, stated as early as May 1943 that "after cold consideration we see clearly that Hungarian and Jewish interests [and paths] part from each other irrevocably."[38] That was true in 1943 only as far as the 400,000 Szeged Fascists were concerned. The Szeged Fascists in 1944 made sure that the validity of their maxim should be sealed with the blood of 570,000 Jews, leaving a legacy of bitterness and hatred between Hungarians and Jews which shocks even the inattentive foreigner who runs across it, and which promises, contrary to pious or hypocritical statements, little good for the immediate future. This was the greatest single accomplishment of the Szeged Idea.

If the Szeged Fascists did their utmost for their flock of 400,000 with "cold consideration," Szálasi did what he did with a warm if idiotic heart. And although he lost most of his integrity at his first touch with reality in September 1944, he did not grow more realistic. He was so much infatuated with power and so much taken with his moods of Fascist enthusiasm that his positive qualities — his Hungarian patriotism and his insistence on Hungarism — all but vanished when he actually attained power. And although he had correctly evaluated German intentions while he was still in opposition, once the Germans had helped him to power, Szálasi was neither willing nor able to realize his, or for that matter Hungary's, real importance in German eyes. There can be no reasonable doubt that the Germans resorted to Szálasi only in dire emergency and even then viewed him with an attitude of contemptuous toleration. Hungary was only one cog in a German war machine that stretched from Narvik Bay through Europe to the Vistula River. There is no question about what the Germans would have done to Hungarism in the case of a German victory.* For such an eventuality, the genius of an Imrédy or a Baky was much better adapted for cooperation than Szálasi's. This was well proven in December 1944: despite all his pledges to fend off bolshevism, Hitler made his last great effort on the Western front against the Americans in the Battle of the Bulge, while during those same days the Russians quietly encircled, destroyed and captured Budapest.

Little can be said about the Hungarist idea in action. It would be extremely interesting for the historian if Szálasi had had the chance to put Hungarism into practice, but as it happened, it was but an untested theory. The Szeged Fascist experiment of six months cost Hungary more in terms of human life, property and national honor than all the preceding years of World War II combined. Szálasi's six months' rule over an ever-dwindling territory resulted in the destruction of Budapest. These sacrifices achieved nothing for Hungary. Because the Arrow Cross depended for its existence exclusively on the mystique that surrounded the personality of Szálasi, whatever his intentions might have been the brunt of responsibility for the events after October 15 rests on him. Even if we take into account the exceptionally unfortunate geopolitical realities of the Carpathian Basin and the fact that Hungary is a small nation, both the anti-Jewish horrors and their consequences and the destruction caused by the German rearguard action could have been avoided. Perhaps a somewhat better postwar start could have been made if the non-Szeged Fascist Hungarian leadership had not been completely discredited, with German help, by Imrédy, Baky and company after March 1944, and if Szálasi had not assumed power in October. The Russians were by no means sure in 1944 what they would do in Hungary. Unlike Hitler, they had a greater affinity for Hungary than for Rumania, both emotionally and with respect to national interest. Judging from their conduct in late 1944 and the early months of 1945, if the Hungarians had not acted as they did in 1944 it is almost certain that a part of Transylvania could have been saved for Hungary. Perhaps even an Austrian type of solution would have been possible. But if that was even a vague possibility, events after the nineteenth of March and the fifteenth of October finished it.

The full responsibility for the year 1944 lies with the Szeged Idea — the line that can be traced from Gömbös straight to Imrédy. Most of the protagonists of 1944 also came from Szeged. The Arrow Cross followers and Szálasi, those whom Horthy called "the scum and the nitwit who leads them on," were but the by-product and the yardstick of Hungarian ruling class —

*Veesenmayer stated later that "when the Imrédists, with whom I sympathized, left the government . . ." he considered "Szálasi and his party the best possible guarantee [left] for safeguarding German interests — *for the duration of the war*." Lackó, *Nyilasok, nemzetiszocialisták*, p. 327. (Italics are the writer's.)

whether of Szeged or Bethlen mold — failure to cope with the challenges of the twentieth century. The Hungarian nation not only abdicated its responsibility to carry out reform; it also murdered, imprisoned, exiled or effectively cowed into silence those who could have offered a constructive alternative to its class-oriented rule. The common Hungarian people were not scum; Szálasi and the Arrow Cross personified and gave voice to their despair.

CHAPTER IX

The Emissary of the Archangel

*It is a fine thing to be honest — but it is also
a very important thing to be right.*

(Winston Churchill, speaking about Stanley Baldwin)

1

Disillusioned by the [promises] of the clichés of *Politicânismul*, fed up
with promises and programs, those masses of citizens which are pure in
their soul wish one to rule over them. The people ask for a master. For
them this does not mean the fist or the sword, neither does it mean
contempt for the masses — but [it means] a lofty moral height, which is
above questioning or doubt, [it means] order and security. . . . What will
emerge from this sinister confusion which seems to forecast the storm?
What surprises and changes will come out of it? Will there come a man
who will be capable of uniting all this yearning [for a better future] into a
single creative current that will replace the apathy of millions with a newly
[found] strength? *

When Goga wrote these words in 1925, there existed in its formative stage
a movement whose leader would become the leader of millions, and indeed
the nemesis of all that stood for superficial adaptation of Western ideas in
Rumania and for the form without content of Rumanian life. His name was
Corneliu Zelea Codreanu.

2

*Though very young at the time, the writer remembers well the turbulent
days of the autumn of 1937, when the most hotly contested elections of the
interwar period were being fought in Transylvania. As a child of eight, I
visited with my parents some relatives and family friends in a village deep in
the Apuşeni Mountains, the heart of Rumanian Transylvania, home of the
Moţi and birthplace of the legendary Avram Iancu. In the evening, when the
intelligentsia gathered in the salon of the owner of the local sawmill (a
Hungarian Jew), the venerable dowager duchesses of village society discussed
but one thing: the coming visit of Codreanu, the dreaded captain of the Iron
Guard, next day. There was simply no limit to the abuse these ladies and
gentlemen, Hungarians of the Christian and Jewish faith, heaped on him. One*

*Goga, *Mustul care fierbe*, p. 28. "Politicânismul" (sometimes "Polici-
ânismul") political demagoguery and/or government by police brutality
— these were the derogative terms applied by its enemies to the realities
of Rumanian Parliamentarism.

246

of the ladies, who had seen him in Târgu-Mureş the year before, spoke of him as if she had seen the monster's head but dared not describe it.

Something of an adventurer by nature, I decided I must take a closer look at this fabulous being, whatever the cost. Next day I proceeded to carry out my decision. My best friend, the son of the local Orthodox priest and older than I by four years, provided some pieces of peasant costume, and the two conspirators headed toward the churchyard where the Legionary meeting was to take place.

The little square before the church teemed with peasants dressed in their colorful Sunday best. Many of them had walked dozens of miles to get there. And there were many, too many, gendarmes from the local gendarme station. The prefect of the district of Turda had, as officials of inefficient, corrupt régimes often do, administered a pinprick to exasperate rather than a blow to crush; he had forbidden Codreanu to speak but had not outlawed the meeting itself. And the crowd of simple, miserable peasants swelled until the churchyard could hold no more.

There was suddenly a hush in the crowd. A tall, darkly handsome man dressed in the white costume of a Rumanian peasant rode into the yard on a white horse. He halted close to me, and I could see nothing monstrous or evil in him. On the contrary. His childlike, sincere smile radiated over the miserable crowd, and he seemed to be with it yet mysteriously apart from it. Charisma is an inadequate word to define the strange force that emanated from this man. He was more aptly simply part of the forests, of the mountains, of the storms on the snow-covered peaks of the Carpathians, and of the lakes and rivers. And so he stood amid the crowd, silently. He had no need to speak. His silence was eloquent; it seemed to be stronger than we, stronger than the order of the prefect who denied him speech. An old, whitehaired peasant woman made the sign of the cross on her breast and whispered to us, "The emissary of the Archangel Michael!" Then the sad little church bell began to toll, and the service which invariably preceded Legionary meetings began. Deep impressions created in the soul of a child die hard. In more than a quarter of a century I have never forgotten my meeting with Corneliu Zelea Codreanu.

3

There can be no understanding of the Iron Guard without a thorough understanding of Codreanu. The movement was created by Codreanu, inspired and led by him, and no movement was more dominated by its creator even after his death than this one. And to understand Codreanu, we must understand something about the nature of Rumanian nationalism.

As in every country that achieved nationhood at a relatively late date, nationalist feelings in Rumania even before World War I were rather overdeveloped. But because of additional specific Rumanian circumstances — the absence of a Rumanian middle class, almost complete foreign domination of the economy, the precarious international position of the new state between the giant Russian Empire and the formidable Dual Monarchy (with irredentas in both cases), the backwardness of the country, the people's almost Oriental indolence, and the refusal of the upper classes to have anything to do with Rumanian values (because that would have meant peasant values), preferring to import Paris instead — all those factors made certain that Rumanian nationalism would manifest itself in a national inferiority complex. In Rumania, before and after the great war, everybody was a nationalist. The ruling classes, especially the liberals, "loved Rumania like a prey," as Professor Weber put it.[1] It is in this sense that we can call them patriotic or even nationalistic.

One form this nationalism had taken was hostility to the "foreigners" inside Rumania, because it would have been a risky enterprise to assault enemies beyond the borders of the country in the years before the great war. In the category of "foreigners" to be fought, one should not include the great foreign financial interests that dominated the Rumanian economy. They were untouchable, because they were closely tied to the ruling elite, especially the liberals. But Greeks and Armenians were another matter; and incomparably more offensive to nationalists, both for their large number and their lack of will or ability to assimilate, were the Jews. All great and honest Rumanians without exception were anti-Semites, as every great Hungarian of the nineteenth century was ready to accept the very different kind of Jew living in Hungary as Hungarian.

At the beginning of the twentieth century, Rumania produced her first scholar and intellectual of international stature, Nicolae Iorga, professor of history at the University of Bucharest, a true Goethean *Tatmensch*, and an assimilated Greek. After a riotous student protest against the performance of an almost exclusively French program of plays for Bucharest high society, Iorga started a conscientious new nationalistic movement and a newspaper, the *Neamul Romanesc* (*Rumanian Nation*). Yet, there was no deep response among the people. Iorga did not offer any sweeping social program; he urged a campaign against Jews and foreign concessions, and he demanded a better organization of national and economic life, moral uplift (fight against alcoholism), and better education. In the field of education, at least, Iorga did much — for the élite. His schools in Valenii-de-Munte, and later in Venice and in France, educated scores of Rumanian leaders, among them the future King Carol and the peasant leader Ion Mihalache.

The same era also produced Alexander Cuza, a former atheist and socialist who managed through populism and economic nationalism to find his way back to tradition. He became a *Junimist* (the young neoconservatives of Rumania) and saw the solution to almost every Rumanian problem in a violent anti-Semitism. Professor of political economy at the University of Iaşi, Cuza joined Iorga in founding the National Democratic party in 1909. Most Rumanian democrats and liberals, even elevated spirits and humanists, never found rabid anti-Semitism incompatible with their own ideas or with their worship of France and the West, because their anti-Semitism had little in the way of social or religious origin but was mostly of an economic, nationalistic kind. French and Western criticism of Rumanian anti-Semitism did not change their minds. They yielded to Western pressure when and as much as they had to — with the irritation of a person who talks common sense and reality when confronted by others with pure abstractions. But all these nationalistic movements did not even scratch the surface of the great problems: the huge peasant majority and the lack of personal and governmental responsibility in every sphere of national life.

Marxian socialism, in its antipeasant and antinationalist form, had little appeal in a country with a miniscule working class even before the great war when it was not yet identified with the hereditary enemy, Russia. After the formation of the U.S.S.R., communism became the byword for high treason. Such a state of affairs was not the fault of the Rumanian Communists. In the 1920s, Lenin of course subordinated all Communist parties to the Third International. Subsequently, Stalin subordinated the Third International to Soviet foreign policy, which in its turn became increasingly synonymous with Russian national interest. Under such circumstances the Rumanian Communist party was forced to adopt very much against its will a plank which would have severed Transylvania, Bessarabia, Dobrogea and Bucovina from the Rumanian state in the interest of "self-determination of nationalities." It is not surprising that communism never appealed to anybody of consequence among the Rumanians. Most of the few Communists in Rumania came from the hostile national minorities, Jews, Hungarians and Ukranians, who had some interest in the realization of such an impossible and un-Rumanian platform.

But there was a Socialist current in Rumania which was not incompatible with the nationalist interest, and which concerned itself with the majority of Rumanians, the peasantry: populism. Populist ideas can be found in every Fascist movement, even in the highly industrial N.S.D.A.P. But in Eastern Europe, where the people and the peasantry were virtually identical, the Fascist currents had an extremely strong Populist content.

In its ideological content, *poporanismul* (populism) was strikingly similar to that in Russia; it was no coincidence that its chief exponent was a Bessarabian Rumanian, Constantin Stere. The conditions and the problems in the *Regat* before the war were almost the same as those that gave birth to the Populist movement in Tsarist Russia. Stere was against industrialization and wanted to base the whole Rumanian economy and consequently the nation's cultural and political life on the peasantry. He denounced Westernization and the "Golgotha of capitalist development" and like most Rumanian intellectuals, he was against the Jews. He considered them "foreigners" and "representatives of vagabond capital," and although he deplored "vulgar and ferocious" anti-Semitism, he considered the Jews disruptive to a desirable Rumanian national development based on the peasantry.[2] It is to Stere and to his ideas that the Iron Guard owed its first debt.

Another nationalistic mystique with a strong social strain and a ferocious xenophobia was expressed on a lyrical level by the country's greatest poet, Mihai Eminescu (originally Eminovich), whom the Legionary intelligentsia persistently called "the great forerunner of the Legionary movement."

But the anti-Semitism of Eminescu and Stere did not answer the needs of the new nationalism of Greater Rumania, whose Jewish population had been tripled at Versailles. Both because of its "ferocious and vulgar anti-Semitism" and because of the personal contacts between Codreanu and Cuza, the third formidable influence on the formation of Legionary ideas came from Iaşi and the Cuzist movement. These influences and precursors can be detected on the political and ideological levels of the Iron Guard.

An even more important influence, however, and one that positively permeated the history and ideology of the Iron Guard, was a mystical, religious one that derived from the role of the Rumanian Orthodox Church in the Rumanian state and in Rumanian nationalism. Although the elite of the nation showed a worldly indifference to religion, the peasant masses remained deeply devout, mystical, and often superstitious, thus widening even further the gulf between rulers and ruled. But the Church, which after the secularization and expropriations by Prince Cuza in 1864 was dependent on the state, could not give any guidance deserving the name. The positive aspects of Christianity had withered away and were not replaced by secular culture. The Church restricted its activity to the magnificent ceremonies so characteristic of Orthodoxy (again more form than content), and to the proclamation of time-honored and somewhat time-worn moral principles. While the Orthodox Church was an embellishment of the state apparatus and nothing more, the common people were given over to their superstitions and the Bucharest elite to its French philosophy.

But this was true only of the older generation. The younger generation could see that the achievement of a long-cherished dream — the unification of all Rumanians — might, so far from solving all of Rumania's problems, actually emphasize the old problems while creating new ones simultaneously. So while in the 1920s the older generation of the articulate public, dizzy with victory, was thrashing over the old slogans of nationalism, the younger generation was looking for a new meaning to life and to politics.

Orthodox Christianity may be universal in theory, but in practice it considers not only the individual alone but also the nation as a natural personality, and it is convinced that, as Iron Guardist ideologue Nichifor Crainic said, the natural entities of the nations as such participate in the hierarchical order of the Christian spirit. In the Western Christian concept, the state, the church, and the nation are separate entities, and their inter-relation is determined by moral and rational rules on the basis of free accord; in the Orthodox country, the state, the church and the nation form a collective entity which has a will superior to that of the individual.* This sense of collectivity, reinforced by Orthodoxy, was the main impulse of the Iron Guard. The Orthodox Christian, unlike the Catholic or Protestant, does not fight an individual battle for his own salvation against sin and temptation. Personal ethics are consequently of lesser importance. For him the blessing of

*One is reminded of the slogan of Nicholas I's Russian "official nationality."

immortality can be attained here on earth, too — in an impersonal unity with divinity achieved through fasting, deep contemplative prayer, and sometimes a rather mechanical exercise of his religion. Under such circumstances, the individual may be strongly tempted to join the institutions of the Church and let himself be carried along by the mystical current of Orthodoxy rather than to struggle against sin on a day-by-day individual basis. The philosophy of life for the majority of Rumanians, the peasantry, was deeply rooted in Orthodoxy. To the peasants, Orthodoxy was more than just a form, it was a way of life. Its concepts shaped their values, their thoughts, their behavior. It also shaped their ideas about relations between state, church, and nation. For them, form and content were in equilibrium. But this rural Orthodox Christianity had little in common with the superficial, rather Byzantine Christianity and relationship which the Church hierarchy entertained with the Rumanian state.

If the young generation of nationalists were looking for a solid basis from which they could undertake the gigantic task of bridging the abyss between form and content in Greater Rumania, and if they were looking for proven values which were thoroughly Rumanian and still commendable, they had to arrive at those peasant values which were synonymous with Orthodox Christianity. The nationalist movement, which received its inspiration from and tried to build its foundations on such ground, thus had to bear a very strong Orthodox imprint. Not only did Rumanian peasant Orthodoxy strongly influence the ideology of the Legion, but it became synonymous with it. In its turn, the success of such a nationalist revival had to bring into motion a religious revival. Wrote Vasile Marin, the comrade in arms of Moţa:

> Through the national mystique a man is born who will be divorced from the prevailing materialism of the present age — instead, he will pass through a school of heroism. He will become a man of cardinal virtues, a hero, a priest, an ascetic and a pure, virtuous knight.[3]

4

Corneliu Zelea Codreanu was born in 1899 in the town of Huşi in the northern part of Moldavia, a town where Jews were in the majority. His father, a teacher in the local gymnasium, was a newcomer on Rumanian soil. Shortly before the birth of Corneliu, Ion Zelea Codreanu came to Huşi from Austrian Bucovina (where he bore the name Zelinski) with his Bucovina-German wife, Elisabeth Brunner. He became a fervent Rumanian nationalist, Romanized his name to Zelea and added Codreanu to it, the name of the profession of his ancestors (forester, *codru* meaning forest in Rumanian). His children bore the names of Rumanian or Dacian heroes — his daughter was named Irredenta, two of his sons, Horia and Decebal, and his oldest son, Corneliu, was named for the Roman centurion converted to Christianity.

The elder Codreanu threw himself into Rumanian nationalist movements with all the zeal of the neophyte. He became a close friend of Professor Cuza, who with Professor Iorga was an active leader of the National Democratic party. Ion Codreanu and Professor Cuza proudly displayed the swastika, the symbol of the international anti-Semitic movement, about two decades before the rise of Hitler.

In such a home did Corneliu grow up. He got his first taste of formal education in the austere atmosphere of the Mănăstire Dealului, a former monastery transformed into a military school. He himself maintained later that he was imbued there "with a healthy faith in his own strength," and that the "military education . . . inspired him for the rest of his life."[4]

When Rumania entered World War I, Codreanu, then seventeen, ran away from home to join his father, who was captain of a company advancing into Transylvania. But young Corneliu, to his grief, was returned home because of his youth.[5] He continued his high school years in an infantry school in Botoşani in order to be able to get back to the front, but the war ended before he had a chance to fight.

In the months after the war, leftist disorders and the menace of bolshevism were especially acute in Moldavia — battles were going on with the Bolsheviks in the north, east and west, and across the Pruth; Bessarabia was by no means pacified. In this hectic atmosphere in March 1919, young Corneliu gathered some youthful friends in the Dobrina forest outside of Huşi, and they swore that they would resist in case of a Bolshevik attack, and they would continue to fight as guerrillas in case of occupation.[6]

But Rumania remained surprisingly stable, and she was even instrumental in crushing the Hungarian Soviet regime some months later. Codreanu, with the frustration of a fervent nationalist unable to find an outlet for his zeal, went to Iaşi to study at the faculty of law of the university. The capital of Moldavia, the holy land of Rumanian nationalism, the town of Bogdan Petriceicu Haşdeu, Eminescu, Vasile Alecsandri, Iacob Negruzzi, Kogalniceanu, Iorga, Semeon Bărnuţiu and many other apostles of Rumanian nationalism, Iaşi represented a different kind of Rumanian nationalism than that of Bucharest and Wallachia. It was more conservative and respectful of Rumanian traditions, and French influence was less evident. Iaşi was also flooded with Jews — more than half its population consisted of unassimilated, primitive Jews from the Pale of Settlement. Their number, thanks to bloody events within the Pale and the formidable corruption of the Rumanian authorities who admitted herds of Jews for a small bribe, was on the sharp increase after 1918.

In this Iaşi Cuza had preached his anti-Semitism for a quarter of a century. Codreanu was received cordially by the old comrade-in-arms of Cuza, and père. Iaşi provided a fertile field for Corneliu's zeal in the years 1919 and 1920. Although the government and the *Siguranţa* maintained a firm grip on the country, the general leftist turmoil could be felt in Iaşi, too. Strikes, disorders, leftist agitation, Soviet power just across the Dniester — all this kept the town in a ferment.

Two central ideas inspired Codreanu in those days: (1) Rumania for the Rumanians, for all the Rumanians and only for the Rumanians of Professor Iorga, and (2) nationalism is the creative force of human culture — and culture is the creative force of (Professor Cuza's) nationalism.[7]

Codreanu found his way to the non-Communist workers. With Constantin Pancu, an electrician, he became the moving spirit of a rapidly growing group, the Guard of National Consciousness. Codreanu saw that "it is not enough to defeat Communism, but one must also fight for the rights of the workers. They have a right to bread and dignity."[8] He proposed nationalist trade unions and a struggle against the parties so that "the workers should get their rights within the framework of the nation and not against it."[9] With this small but growing group, Codreanu acted spontaneously in the style of Mussolini's *fasci di combattimento*. Whenever there was a strike, his group appeared, tore down the red flag from the factory or workshop and substituted the Rumanian one. Strike-breaking workers were also organized who, when the bourgeoisie timidly withdrew, went out and took direct action, borrowing unconsciously from Mussolini who was doing the same thing in Italy. For Codreanu's workers also, "the most important thing was to act."[10] This was not the action of the ruling classes, for in these counterviolence groups there were mostly workers and student volunteers.[11] It was in those days that Codreanu began to dream about a national and Christian socialism and nationalist trade unions.[12]

But when land reform was enacted by Marshal Averescu in the *Regat,* the leftist rumblings calmed down, and Codreanu concentrated his activities on the student body. There were two currents among the students, one liberal democratic and the other nationalist. The latter paraded a ferocious anti-Semitism and an equally zealous anticommunism. The government at that time could not and would not enact a *numerus clausus* against the Jews, who were represented in the student body sometimes ten or twelve times their proportion in the population. The Rumanian students, unable to force the hand of the government in the matter of anti-Semitic legislation, acted on their own by excluding Jews from student organizations. Codreanu contributed his share, perhaps more than his share, to this decision, arrived at by the all-Rumanian Student Congress in Cluj in September 1920.[13] The new spirit spread quickly to other universities, especially those like Cernauţi with a heavy Jewish attendance. Emboldened by success, Codreanu and his companions demanded in the fall semester of 1920 that the authorities permit the opening of the academic year with a religious service.[14] By that time, Codreanu had drawn a small, tight-knit group of nationalistic, religious students around him, and this group succeeded in forcing its way with the apathetic, disorganized majority because of its readiness to apply terror through direct action and to accept the risk and the odium of such behavior. They attacked liberal and leftist students, defied the dean and, when the local press took unpleasant note of their behavior, destroyed the offices of offending papers.

Finally, the authorities acted. Codreanu, the moving spirit of the disturbances (all of which bore a strong anti-Semitic taint), was excluded from the university. Professor Cuza hurried to the aid of his protegé, and Codreanu was reinstated in the school of law and graduated in the summer of 1922, although he was never allowed to graduate from the University of Iaşi.[15]

In the summer of 1922, a Jewish theater group visited Iaşi. Codreanu considered the performance of plays in Yiddish a much more evil challenge than the performance of French plays had been considered by the students of Bucharest a decade and a half before. "Direct action" followed. Codreanu's group entered the theater and, "hurling everything they could lay their hands upon,"[16] drove the actors from the stage. Codreanu agreed that "this might seem uncivilized," but he explained that Jews who brought bolshevism into the world with all its hideous consequences were not all that civilized either.[17] "We caused disturbances, that's true. But these disturbances were [aimed] at preventing other, much more dangerous and irreparable disturbances which were prepared by the hirelings of the Communist revolution in this country."[18]

In the fall of 1922, Codreanu went to Berlin to study for a year. He did not find the atmosphere of Weimar Germany attractive; the lack of anti-Semitic consciousness among German students irritated him. But three important events occurred during his stay in Berlin and Jena. He saw at first hand the ravages of inflation in postwar Germany, and he heard for the first time of Hitler, "who is organizing an anti-Semitic movement in Munich." Characteristically, this first news came to him from a German worker friend of his, and it was in Germany that he got the news of the triumph of "the hero Mussolini, who crushed the head of the poisonous dragon with his foot." The lack of anti-Semitism in Mussolini's teachings did not seem to bother Codreanu. He was convinced that "if Mussolini lived in Rumania, he would be by all means an anti-Semite."[19] Mussolini's victory convinced Codreanu of "the possibility of defeating the Hydra."[20]

It was in Jena that Codreanu heard the news of the general strike of students all over Rumania, proclaimed on December 10, 1922, against the contemplated new constitution, which was to grant citizenshp rights to Rumanian Jews. The students demanded a *numerus clausus*. Codreanu returned without delay to Iaşi to assume the leadership of the movement.[21]

5

A look at Rumanian politics and economics in the 1920s does much to enhance an understanding of the context and atmosphere in which Codreanu founded his Legion of the Archangel Michael.

In January 1922, General Averescu, after enacting agrarian reform, yielded power to the Liberal party, or more precisely to Ion Brătianu and his class. By this time, the traditional conservatives, with their mainstay of the great landed estates gone, were fading away from politics. It was the Liberals, one great Rumanian party of the "traditional parties," with their heavy representation of banking and industry (the grande bourgeoisie), who were to be the conservative force in Rumanian politics. The Rumanian National party of Tranyslvania would unite with the Peasant party of the *Regat* to establish a more progressively minded democratic party that was closer to the peasant masses.

Ion Brătianu, the son of the founder of modern Rumania, was as dominant a personality as his father had been. If the father put Rumania on the map, it was by large extent the merit of his son that Greater Rumania appeared on it. A forceful, shrewd politician with a temperament incompatible with the democratic process, he was the undisputed boss of the Liberal party and the whole liberal system, which did not outlive him for long.

Although liberal politics had a distinctly Phanariotic flavor, it was by no means unprincipled. It tried to centralize the rather new heterogeneous state as much as possible, both in administration and in the economy, and to industrialize Rumania without the help of foreign capital. Liberal suspicion of foreign capital becomes understandable if we consider some figures. During the interwar period, 91 percent of the petroleum industry, 74 percent of metallurgy, 72 percent of the chemical industry, 70 percent of the industry connected with forestry, 95 percent of electricity and gas production, 17 banks with one-third of all capital to be found in Rumanian banks, and 70 percent of all insurance business were foreign-owned.[22] And these figures by no means take into account all foreign influence in Rumanian economics. When another member of the Brătianu clan, Vîntila Brătianu, gave a new slogan to the liberal policy of economic autarchy: "We shall do it by ourselves," he summed up the Liberal economic policy.

This process of industrialization and centralization provoked great discontent among the peasant masses and in other classes as well. It can be safely said that the Liberals did not find any substantial support in the population at large apart from the administration and army, which depended on the system, and the grand bourgeoisie, which profited from it. Like any forced industrialization, this one laid extraordinarily heavy burdens on the peasantry. Discontent was handled by the gendarmerie, the police and the extremely brutal Siguranţa, which achieved a notoriety it had never known before.* But the Liberals were not worried about that aspect of things. Their quasi-Marxist approach found a quasi-Marxist justification in the thinking of the brilliant Liberal ideologist, Stefan Zeletin, who readily admitted that the peasantry was to play a secondary role in social movements and none at all in politics. The unhappy condition of the peasantry was considered a necessary price to be paid for the building of capitalism in Rumania. Zeletin easily dismissed the Socialist movements. Since Rumanian capitalism was in the process of formation and had a revolutionary character, "a proletariat pursuing its own revolutionary goals [was] nonsense."[23]

Despite the obstruction of the opposition, the Liberals rammed a new constitution through Parliament in 1923. In addition to the recognition of the civil rights of Jewish citizens, it upheld the strong royal prerogative of the Constitution of 1866 (King Ferdinand was on good terms with Ion Brătianu). The new constitution declared that all mineral wealth of the subsoil was the

*A good insight into these police methods is the account of C.G. Costa-Foru, *Aus den Folterkammern Rumäniens* (Vienna, 1925).

property of the state, and last, but not least, it declared that the constitution could be suspended "either in the whole or in part," and "in an event of danger to the state," it provided for martial law.[24] These provisions made it possible during much of the interwar period for Rumania to be kept under martial law, censorship and unlimited police brutality.

Even more important than the constitution was the new electoral law, inspired by a similar law in Fascist Italy, which gave 70 percent of the seats in Parliament to the party that won 40 percent of the votes cast. The remaining seats were to be distributed proportionately among the other parties. Those which gained less than 2 percent of the vote obtained no seats at all. In theory, this law would have simplified Rumanian politics with its numerous parties. In practice, it immeasurably aided the party in power (this also meaning the administrative help) in controlling elections. The Liberals made good use of this effect.

Popular discontent was growing. The general recovery of the twenties made itself felt but little in Rumania because the forcible industrialization efforts were exacting such a toll on agriculture.* In 1926 the two strongest parties of the opposition, the Rumanian National party of Transylvania and the Peasant party of the *Regat*, after many unsuccessful attempts, finally united in the National Peasant party under the leadership of Iuliu Maniu and Mihalache. Despite police error, the party won some by-elections in the countryside, and when in 1927 both the King and Brătianu died, the road was open for change. Even before that, there had been two transition governments, those of Marshal Averescu and Prince Barbu Stirbey, while Brătianu held the real power and enjoyed the support of the King.

Vîntila Brătianu was not able to replace Ion, and Maniu increased pressure on many fronts; he embarrassed the government when it tried to obtain a foreign loan and organized a grandiose protest meeting in May 1928 in Alba-Iulia with the participation of tens of thousands of peasants. The Regents (Prince Nicholas, the brother of the future King Carol II, the Patriarch Miron Cristea and the chief justice of the court of cassation, Gh. Buzdugan)** on November 9, 1928, finally entrusted Maniu with the formation of a cabinet. The Liberals had failed in their otherwise commendable attempt to industrialize because they lacked both a concerted plan and capital. When they tried to obtain the capital at home, they could not do so despite their police apparatus. To carry out an openly antipeasant policy in a peasant state with the profits going to a tiny minority — the upper bourgeoisie and the party hacks — was not possible in the face of the criticism

---

*A revealing item: In one of the better years for agriculture, in 1923-24, the government spent 600 million lei on the all-important cooperative movement — the success of which could have largely decided the issue of agrarian reform, while private bankers received 7.5 billions for the same period. Roberts, *Rumania: Political Problems of an Agarian State*, p. 127.

**King Ferdinand was succeeded by his grandson, Michael, 7. His son, Carol, was excluded from the succession by Ferdinand with the agreement and instigation of Brătianu.

directed against it. The very democratic institutions with which Brătianu endowed the country prevented him from using his repressive apparatus to the extent necessary to silence the opposition completely.

6

Our picture of interwar Rumania would not be complete without a few words about Rumanian foreign policy. This foreign policy was the same from 1918 until the fall of France: to maintain the status quo. As this was also the goal of France, it fulfilled Professor Iorga's definition of what Rumanian foreign policy was to be: "Rumania never conducted an independent foreign policy — her foreign policy was always identical with that conducted by her strongest ally."[25] As long as Rumania's strongest ally was France, the preservation of the status quo seemed best secured within the framework of the League of Nations, the Little Entente* along with Czechoslovakia and Yugoslavia, and an alliance with Poland.

The leader of Rumanian foreign policy right after the war was a forceful personality, Take Ionescu. After Ionescu's death in 1922, for almost fifteen years — until the late 1930s — Nicolae Titulescu conducted the policy for the preservation of the status quo. This corrupt, unusually tall and ugly man was an excellent orator and a staunch friend of the West. With rare foresight, he tried to bring about a rapprochement with Russia because, of all the three irredentas menacing Rumania, the Russian interest in Bessarabia was the most dangerous. Hungary was well taken care of by the Little Entente, and Bulgaria by the Balkan Entente, but the U.S.S.R. was a different matter. In 1920, it seemed for a short while that the hard-pressed Soviets would recognize the reannexation of Bessarabia by Rumania through an exchange of notes between Chicherin and Vaida-Voevod. But Vaida-Voevod fell from power and the negotiations were discontinued.[26] From that time on, with the U.S.S.R. more firmly established, she did not find it necessary to recognize Rumanian rule across the Dniester.

The Rumanian administration installed in Bessarabia was the worst in Rumania. It might even be safey said that the consecutive Rumanian administrations there succeeded with incredible stupidity in turning this most dangerous irredenta into the most misruled province of Europe. In 1924, the pent-up discontent burst forth in the armed insurrection of Tătăr-Bunar, which was put down by the Liberal government with great cruelty. As a result of this and other experiences added to it, communism in Rumania came to be considered high treason.

In the 1930s, Titulescu cooperated closely with Barthou and King Alexander in France's only serious effort to block fascism and Nazism in East Central Europe. The Marseille murder, coupled with the constant weakness shown by the West in general and that of France in particular, shook the

*Incidentally, the name of the alliance, Little Entente, originated from a malicious comment in the Budapest press in the spring of 1920. Beneš liked the name and popularized it.

Little Entente to its foundations, and Munich put an end to it. Yet even in the spring of 1939 Rumania accepted an English guarantee, and it was only after the fall of France, and by no means of her own choice, that she abandoned the Western line. As a matter of fact, Greater Rumania survived the fall of her principal ally and idol only by a few days.

7

The uproar of the Rumanian student population on December 10, 1922, and the ferment, strife and disorder at the Rumanian universities that followed were centered on the Jewish question. The immediate cause was the coming new constitution, which after more than half a century of discrimination against Jews in Rumania finally granted them (at least on paper) citizenship and rights as citizens.

If the Jews of the *Regat* had successfully restrained their Rumanian chauvinism in the past, the more than half a million new Jewish subjects found the attractions offered by the romantic Rumanian nationalism even more resistible. It can be safely said that they were in the majority positively hostile to the new Rumanian state.*

*In this uncompromising hostility, it was the 300,000 Jews of Transylvania who were the leaders — but few of them on a Jewish-Chasidic platform! In the forefront of Magyarization for decades and considering themselves Hungarians first and last, they were isolated after the war in a salutary way from the Szeged Fascist movement in Hungary and from the pogroms organized by Gömbös and Eckhardt. Their minds were not able to conceive that the new Hungarian anti-Semitism was of a racial kind and infinitely more dangerous than the "old style" Rumanian one! Living in the memories of the past, they had no use for Rumanian anti-Semitism and corruption and having very considerable economic power, they greatly impeded the main Rumanian effort to Romanize the towns of Transylvania by maintaining Hungarian schools, newspapers, language and organizations in the towns, thus justifying the Rumanian nationalist claim that a Jew, one way or the other, is an enemy of Romanism.

The large number (250,000) of Jews in Bessarabia, of the classical Pale of Settlement type, were most unhappy with the mixture of Rumanian anti-Semitism, misrule, and corruption. Rumanian rule did not inspire the poverty stricken, staunchly Jewish nationalist, unassimilated masses any more than Tzarist Russia did with Purishkevich and Khrushevan's Black Hundreds, who originated here. If the Jews in Bessarabia looked for ideas, they certainly preferred communism or Zionism to Rumanian nationalism — let alone to Rumanian romantic nationalism — a position utterly inconceivable to the Pale of Settlement Jews.

The heavy Jewish population in Bucovina, concentrated for the most part in Cernăuți, was certainly unhappy about the departure of the honest, not anti-Semitic, civilized Austrian administration and the arrival of the corrupt Jew-baiters from the *Regat*. If the Habsburgs had unreservedly loyal subjects anywhere in the Empire, the Jews of Bucovina, especially those in Cernăuți, were they. Their culture was German; the culture and language of the Transylvanian Jews was

The Eastern Europe ghetto had, naturally enough, little or no contact with the traditional spirit of the country. Here Christianity and Judaism were both vehicles of nationalism more than anything else, and here they were much more at loggerheads than in Western Europe. For reasons not entirely attributable to its inhabitants, the East European ghetto was not a character-building school for Bayards, Cids or Parsifals. The problem there was to survive both physically and ethnically through the practice of Judaism, and there was little time or concern for anything else. To make matters worse, too many of the Jews dressed in their Chasidic gabardines spoke very bad Rumanian, and in most cases had their own Yiddish-Hebrew schools. When they did come into contact with village dwellers in Eastern Europe, their single-minded struggle for survival did not endear them either to the peasants or to the town-dwelling nationalists.

That the Allied Powers enforced their civil rights in 1923, thanks to the intervention of the all-powerful *Alliance Israèlite* on their behalf (an intervention the Hungarian Jews under Vázsonyi proudly refused), only weakened their position in the eyes of the nationalists. The subsequent brutal treatment of the Jews in Rumania, on the other hand, did not accelerate assimilation or enhance its desirability in the eyes of the Jewish community.

Hungary's racial anti-Semitism was a product of the inability of the lower echelons of a small ruling class (400,000) to make a comfortable living any longer from their monopoly on the bureaucratic and administrative jobs. In Rumania, anti-Semitism was of a different, infinitely more complex nature. For Codreanu and the Iron Guard, it was not a racial nor even a religious problem.* It had been Professor Cuza who periodically broke out against the Jews "for crucifying our Savior." Codreanu, for his part, said little or nothing in his writings against the Jewish race or religion as such. On the contrary, he considered them dangerous "because of the impossibility of assimilating them."**

Hungarian and that of Bessarabian Jews was Yiddish or Jewish — anything but Rumanian. And the *Regat* Jews, though by far not so disloyal as the newcomers, they, too, looked rather to Paris and (until 1933) to Berlin for inspiration and culture than to the "unspoiled Rumanian peasant."

*There is more than ample evidence on that account. Ion Moţa braved the international anti-Semitic center in Weimar in 1936 in a letter, flatly refusing the racial concept as an answer to everything, and especially opposing the religious concepts. Biblioteca Verde No. 10, p. 3, Ion Moţa, *Corespondenţia cu "Serviciul Mundial,"* (Rome, 1954). Ion Banea, the Legionary leader who resembled Codreanu the most, put it in ever clearer terms: "The Jews . . . can not be persecuted on a racial or religious basis — only on the basis of the danger they represent to the state." *Rânduri către generaţia noastra* (Omul Nou, November, 1951), pp. 14-15.

**Claus Charlé, *Die Eiserne Garde*, (Berlin-Wien, 1939), p. 87. In his Codreanu biography, Charlé thought it a heresy that Codreanu even considered such a possibility and did his best to explain that Codreanu never really thought of it.

But if Codreanu's nationalistic and economic arguments against the Jews were partly justifiable, his anti-Semitism was so extreme as to be considered pathological. He had none of the calculating, murderous cynicism of an Imrédy or a Jaross; rather his anti-Semitism had all the fanatical characteristics of that of Endre or Hitler without the racist trappings. Codreanu tended to see everything in a chiaroscuro projection. Despite his realism in local politics, the problem for him was always the clash between light and darkness, good and evil. For him the light and the good were in the unspoiled peasant, and in loving and in faith, rather than in knowing and possessing. And the Jew represented the incarnation of evil on earth, the flesh and spirit of all he sought to refute in the twentieth century, the antithesis of his ideal romantic world and the romantic nationalism he derived from it. Communism, which outraged him with its rational approach to things he considered sacred and dared to approach only through mystical love, was equated in his mind with the Jews, and so was freemasonry. "The Jewish press attacks the religious feelings in us, weakens the moral resistance in men, and attempts to destroy [our] tie with Eternity. It spreads antinationalistic theories, weakens the faith of the people and estranges it from the soil. [The Jews] take from us our love for Him, [the love] which gave us always inspiration for our struggle."[27]

Codreanu saw the capitalistic exploitation of the Carpathian forests as a Jewish plot to rob the mountains of their magnificent coniferous forest cover for pennies. The plot was carried out through, by, and with the help of corrupt Rumanian officials. The corrupting of politicians and officials was in turn considered an almost purely Jewish act — as much a means as an end of Jewry in Rumania.[28] Codreanu sounded much more reasonable when he spoke about the Judaization of Rumanian towns, an especially offensive phenomenon to nationalists in his native area. Codreanu asked in horror, "Will we have an intelligentsia from this alien element in fifteen or twenty years? " In the same vein, he questioned the preponderance of Jews in the universities of Rumania. But he also arrived at the anti-Semitic maxim of conservative Eastern Europeans: All progressive thought, capitalism, socialism, the industrial revolution and all its evils, consequently everything that differed from nationalism based on religious mysticism and the unspoiled peasant or student idealism, were purely Jewish phenomena.[29] He did not confine his hatred to the unassimilated Jews of Iaşi or Huşi; when he visited Strasbourg, he "could not find the slightest difference [between the highly cultivated Jews of the Alsace] and those of the marketplace of Iaşi . . . the same creatures, the same behavior, the same intonation of speech, the same devilish eyes, with the smiling lips in which one could read only naked greed." And the Jews of Grenoble were the same.[30]

Religious mysticism and romantic nationalism had even less to do with economics or social sciences than they had with reason: Codreanu strayed off completely when he maintained that there were actually two to two-and-one-half millions of Jews in Rumania, that the numbers had been deliberately cut by a corrupt government to hide the truth.[31] He believed in an ultimate

Jewish goal to proclaim a "New Palestine" in the Jewish-inhabited area of Moldavia, Bessarabia and Bucovina and to establish a contact through the sea with old Palestine.[32]

8

When Codreanu returned from Germany, he was in high spirits. The unexpectedly violent anti-Semitic reaction of the Rumanian students to the planned constitutional amendment had aroused great hopes in him, and he joined the movement, enthusiastically organizing the student protests in Bucharest, Cluj, Iaşi and Cernauţi during the winter of 1922-23. But by March 1923 it was clear that the Liberal apparatus was neither willing nor able to change its mind on the question of Jewish civil rights, and that consequently it would not agree to the quota system so much desired by the campus would-be intellectuals who feared Jewish professional competition.

Finally, on March 4, 1923, when the promulgation of the new constitution seemed imminent, the League of National Christian Defense (*Liga Apărării Naţionăle Creştine*) was formed under the leadership of Professor Cuza. Its program consisted of anti-Semitism in a singularly sterile form. It proposed the restriction of Jews in the universities and in the professions, commensurate to their proportion in the population, that is, to 5 percent. It proposed little else.[33] Solemn religious services marked the founding of the league, and the L.A.N.C. banner, Rumanian national colors with the swastika in the middle,* was paraded through the streets of Iaşi. Under Professor Cuza, Codreanu was assigned the task of organizing the League nationwide, with special attention to student affairs.[34]

In 1925, some minor Fascist groups joined the L.A.N.C. One of them was the *Făscia Nationălă Romăna*, founded in Bucharest in 1923 under the leadership of Lungulescu and Bagulescu. Its Fascist, corporatist program had two local refinements: (1) violent Populist anti-industrialism and the desire to preserve Rumania's agrarian character (industrial countries were not happy and had social upheavals) and (2) violent anti-Semitism, with detailed plans as to how to rid Rumania of Jews. Its economics were childish — no imports without twice as many exports.[35] Professor Henry Roberts is surely right in saying that the only original plank in this Fascist program was to transform the clubhouses of the dissolved political parties into state-supervised brothels.[36] The other group that joined the L.A.N.C. was Rumanian Action (*Acţiunea Romaneasca*), which consisted of students and professors of the University of Cluj. This group, with its Maurrasian leanings and inspirations, brought an all-important recruit with it — Ion Moţa, whose importance as an ideologist of the Iron Guard was second only to Codreanu himself. Moţa had just finished the translation of the Protocols of the Elders of Zion into Rumanian. He was the son of an Orthodox priest from Oraştie, a little town

---

*The swastika had nothing to do with Hitler or Nazism. It was the international sign of the struggle against Jewry.

near Alba-Iulia in Transylvania, where he received good training in national-ism.* Moța was a romantic in the early nineteenth-century sense of the word — like Byron, Chateaubriand or Walter Scott, of sincere, idealistic character — but his sincerity was out of place in the twentieth century. Perhaps for that very reason he never wavered in his beliefs and did not scruple to kill for them. It was Moța, however, who conceived some of the practical aspects of the Legionary movement.

Codreanu had to share his time between the tasks in the student movement and those of organizing the L.A.N.C. Professor Cuza, very much of the old school of anti-Semitism, refused to establish any guideline and discipline for the movement: "We do not need discipline — this is not a barrack."[37] But Codreanu steadfastly insisted upon it. The two conceptions, one looking to a political party and the other to a disciplined movement, were to separate the two men later.

On March 26, 1923, the Rumanian Parliament removed Jewish disabilities. Codreanu responded in a fashion that he and his partisans were to repeat countless times in the future. He had tried to convince by arguments; when he failed, he moved in with direct action, in this case against the ghetto of Iași. When he arrived with his group at night, "thousands of Jews woke up and gathered like a nest of disgusting worms. When they received us with shots, we returned the fire. Then we fulfilled our duty and beat everything to the ground which blocked our way. We were determined to show the Jews that Iași, the old capital of Moldavia, was still Rumanian."[38] After this escapade Codreanu was arrested, but he was soon released. Meanwhile, the student strike continued without greatly impressing the Brătianu government. As examination time approached in June, the strike began to lose much of its impetus.

After a L.A.N.C. meeting in Câmpulung, thirty peasants were selected to go to Bucharest to present the anti-Semitic demands in person to Brătianu. Codreanu led the delegation. When officials displayed a reluctance to admit them, Codreanu threatened to tear the whole building apart if the prime minister did not receive them immediately. The unusual and forthright method worked; in a few minutes they were inside the office where Ion Brătianu sat surrounded by his cabinet.[39]

But Brătianu could not or would not initiate anti-Semitic legislation. Codreanu saw no other way but to remove by assassination those Rumanian politicians whom he held responsible for enacting Jewish civil rights. Also marked for removal were a number of Jewish rabbis, bankers and journalists whom he considered not only the leaders of Rumanian Jewry but also cronies and supporters of the dirty Liberal political machine. Six students (Codreanu and Moța included) were to carry through this "purification" of Rumanian national life.[40] When they arrived in Bucharest in October 1923 to carry out

*Moța's father explained that in Transylvania (during Hungarian rule), "Everybody was a right-wing extremist, and we could not be anything else if we wanted to keep our nationality." Rogger and Weber, *The European Right*, p. 521.

their plan, they were betrayed by one of their number and arrested by the police.[41] During the interrogation, Codreanu gave a frank but cunning picture of the plot. He did not deny the conspirators' intent, but he stated that they had not determined the date of its execution. According to the Napoleonic Code, this could not then be considered an assassination attempt.[42]

While he was in the Văcărești prison, Codreanu worked out a plan for the youth organization he would form in case of acquittal. This youth group was to be established within the framework of L.A.N.C. and was to be an educational and fighting community. On November 8, the feast of St. Michael Gabriel, Codreanu pondered what name he should give to the new youth organization. In the chapel of the Văcărești prison there was an image of St. Michael which made an unusually deep impression on him — "as if the Holy St. Michael had stood alive before me." Later on, Codreanu dedicated his movement to St. Michael and named it after him.[43]

Before the jury's verdict, Moța managed to shoot the person who had betrayed them, a fact which did not seem to have impressed the jury adversely. On the contrary, the jury acquitted the plotters amid the hurrahs of a great popular demonstration, a good sign of the unpopularity of the Brătianu government.[44] When Codreanu and his companions returned to Iași in triumph, Moța remained in jail, but he also was acquitted at a later date.

As a result of the new élan acquired during the long solitary incarceration in prison, Codreanu set a new goal for his movements. Violence was not the right way but self-improvement through creative work and discipline, and above all, faith in God and in oneself — this was to be the wave of the future. In Iași on May 6, 1924, Codreanu called together the first Brotherhood of the Cross (Frația de Cruce), as his new group of peasants and students was called, all young men who would fight for a nationalistic renewal. They decided on a construction project. They would build a student center all by themselves in Ungheni, about nine miles from Iași on the banks of the Pruth River.[45] After some weeks of inoffensive construction activity, the prefect of the Iași police, Manciu, attacked the group with his men, dragged them to the Iași police station, and ordered the torture of many of them. Only the personal intervention of Professors Cuza and Sumuleanu saved them from the worst.[46]

Codreanu, who was almost traumatized by the humiliation and degradation of this experience, thought of nothing else and plotted vengeance. Meanwhile, he withdrew to his beloved mountain in the Carpathians, the Rareu. There, beneath the magnificent pines and the slow flight of eagles, he watched the sunset and spent a month and a half alone while shepherds fed and sheltered him. He was overwhelmed in his solitude by thoughts about injustice and the way to combat it. But when he descended from the Rareu, he had no answer.[47]

Returning to Iași, he found out that the prefect Manciu had been decorated in his absence. Codreanu and his friends appealed to public opinion, to the minister of interior, and to King Ferdinand, all in vain. The bureaucrat was always right.[48] Codreanu decided on direct action. On

October 24, he shot Manciu and some policemen in the courtroom in Iaşi.[49] He was arrested, but his popularity was so great that officials dared not try him in Iaşi. In the Rumania of the 1920s, murder was not considered a crime if not committed for personal gain, and the murder of a prefect of the corrupt, arbitrary police, the right arm of an unpopular government, was an act of heroism. Codreanu's trial was first to be held in Focşani, but even that liberal stronghold was not safe any more, so they decided to try him at the other end of the country, in Turnu-Severin on the Yugoslav border. It was to no avail. Codreanu explained to the jury that what he and his friends had done was for God and country and that they would continue the struggle. The jury returned from its deliberations with the swastika emblem of the L.A.N.C. on their coats and pronounced the verdict: not guilty![50]

Codreanu's return to Iaşi was a triumph. Everywhere along the road, his train was greeted with flowers, cheering crowds and songs. The priests blessed him.[51] All this feting, however, did not prove that the Rumanians were Fascists or violent anti-Semites. It was rather a yardstick of the unpopularity of the Liberals. The jury's acquittal was an effective way of showing disapproval of a government and a police force that prevented protest at the ballot box. Shortly after his acquittal, Codreanu married Elena Ilinoiu, the daughter of a railway employee. The wedding was the occasion for a popular feast. Some 2,700 oxcarts and cars covered with flowers brought tens of thousands of people — the procession was four miles long![52] Codreanu's wife was a modest, self-effacing woman, and we shall hear no more of her.

After the wedding, Codreanu returned to his organizing activities within the L.A.N.C. While working, it became clear to him that Cuza's concepts and his own were fundamentally different, not only about the makeup of the L.A.N.C., but also on ideological questions. The essence of the conflict was that Cuza was just a good anti-Semitic bourgeois who wanted a political party on a democratic basis. "Everybody can enter into the L.A.N.C. and stay there so long as he can or desires" was his slogan.[53] But Codreanu wanted a tight-knit, selective combat organization with discipline, whose leader would be a "captain on board a ship," with a magic personality born to command and to be obeyed blindly. He considered Cuza a theoretician and not a practical leader, but at that time he respected Cuza too much to realize in which sphere the essential conflict between them lay. Codreanu's efforts to change things within the L.A.N.C. were fruitless.[54] To avoid an open break, Codreanu and Moţa left for France with their wives to study at the University of Grenoble, but not before a typical incident took place. A Jew attacked Cuza on the street in Iaşi. The students with Codreanu and Moţa went from café to café and hit every Jew they met in the face as a retaliation. A student took some shots at Cuza's assailant but missed, and Moţa went to jail for a month for his part in the retaliatory raid.[55]

While studying in Grenoble, Codreanu searched everywhere for the spirit of Bayard, *"chevalier sans peur et sans reproche."* He avoided the movies, the cafés, the Grenoble of the twentieth century "under the Freemasonic star of the Jewish Hydra." Rather he submerged [in the ramparts of the castle and the old town] in another age and forgot about everything else around me. Here I lived in the France of the past, in the nationalist France. This filled me with deep satisfaction. Here I was not in the Jewish-Freemasonic, Internationalist France! Here I was in the France of Bayard! Not in the France of the present — that of Mr. Léon Blum![56]

And Codreanu had another deep satisfaction in Grenoble: in an old church, he discovered with joy about fifty gilded swastikas as ornaments of the interior.[57]

When Brătianu handed over power to Averescu in the spring of 1926, Codreanu hurried home to participate in the electoral campaign, standing as the L.A.N.C. candidate in Focşani in one of the most outrageous elections in the interwar period. All the arbitrary police action, "quarantines," shameful manipulation of the results, terror and deception (getting prospective voters drunk) were a kind of confirmation of Codreanu's antidemocratic feelings. Although Codreanu, as always, generously practiced his counterterror moves, he wrote:

[All the political parties] are nothing but a gang of tyrants. Under the cover of justice, freedom, human rights, they trample on the country, its laws, freedoms and rights. What road remains open to us in the future?[58]

Although Codreanu himself lost, the L.A.N.C. won 124,778 votes, mostly in the heavily Jewish-inhabited towns of the northeast, and elected ten representatives to Parliament, among them Codreanu's father.[59] But after the elections, the L.A.N.C. collapsed, mainly because of the clash of personalities, who accused each other of having sold out to the Jews, an accusation carefully fostered in the official party paper, National Defense (Apărărea Naţionala). Professor Weber has caught the psychological atmosphere here: to an anti-Semite, his opponents are "if not Jews, then are sold to the Jews. Since he alone is fighting the good fight against the Jews, anyone who disagrees is 'objectively' the tool of the Jewish conspiracy."[60] Consequently, Codreanu's father was also considered a hireling of the Jews.

The miserable failure of the L.A.N.C. had done more than anything else to convince Codreanu of the necessity of founding a different type of movement for the realization of the ideals so close to his heart. He called together his old comrades of the Văcăreşti prison on the evening of June 24, 1927, and issued his Order of the Day Number One, in which he proclaimed the founding of the Legion of the Archangel Michael under his leadership. "He whose faith knows no boundary should enter our ranks. But he who wavers and doubts should stay out."[61] There was a permanent guard appointed to guard the copy of the icon of St. Michael in the Văcăreşti prison that was kept in the student home in Iaşi.

9

The only Fascist movement to be founded under the protective symbol of an icon had a profoundly religious ideology. This ideology blended with nationalism to such an extent that it is impossible to draw the line between them.

The Legion of the Archangel Michael, as Legionaries so often insisted, was not a party but a movement, and more than that it was an order, a militant religious order.[62] Codreanu often stated that "the Church is far above us."[63] Every Legionary meeting, small or large, started with a religious service. Prayer and an appeal to the forefathers was considered by Codreanu as a decisive weapon in the Legionaries' struggle.[64] "It is God who carries us along in his victorious bandwagon,"[65] went the Legionary slogan.

The Legionaries were always aware of their great differences with the Nazis and Fascists on that account. One of their leading intellectuals, Mihai Polihroniade, explained: "Fascism worships the state, Nazism the race and the nation. Our movement strives not merely to fulfill the destiny of the Rumanian people — we want to fulfill it along the road of salvation."[66] Another Legionary intellectual, Garcineanu, called the Legion "the only political movement with a religious structure."[67] Even "the ultimate goal of the nation [must be] Resurrection in Christ."[68] The Legionaries perceived the whole history of mankind, and particularly that of Rumania, as an uninterrupted Passion, a mystical Easter story, in which every step, every motivation, consequently every goal, was a struggle between light and darkness. The road of the Legion must be a road of suffering, sacrifice, crucifixion and resurrection. Moța declared: "As God resurrected Christ in order to help the good to victory, so will the Legion triumph, too — even if only by miracle."[69]

These basic ideas explain to a great extent the extraordinary and powerful death cult which prevailed within the Legion. Some experts call it morbid. But for a Legionary, death was a joyous mystical fulfillment, a reward. One of the leaders of the Legion addressed the student body in the following vein: "I preach to you about death in order to develop in you the taste for Eternity."*

"The most beautiful aspect of Legionary life is death," wrote an Iron Guardist paper. "The Legionary death has nothing in common with ordinary death. Through his death the Legionary becomes one with Eternity; through his death the Legionary becomes the earthly incarnation of history. He becomes a legend. The Legionary must not hesitate before death. Legionary death is dear to his heart; a goal is achieved through it; it becomes a symbol. The death of the Legionary is a symbol, a cult."[70]

The words of a popular Legionary song are:

The Legionary dies singing,
The Legionary sings when he dies,
This is how the Legion triumphs,
The Legionary death is dear to me.[71]

*Ion Popescu Puturi, Gheorghe Zaharia, N. Goldberger, N.N. Constantinescu and N. Copoiu, *La Roumanie pendant la deuxième guerre mondiale* Bibliotheca Historica Romaniae No. 2. (Bucharest, 1964), p. 131. Legionaries often speak in their memoirs about a fallen comrade who fulfilled his Legionary duty so well that his passing away was a "mystical wedding with death." *Dacia,* Anul XII, Număr Festiv (Rio de Janeiro, 1957).

What was the program of the Legion? Legionary leaders rejected with indignation even the mention of the word, which had been made hateful by the dirty politics of the interwar years. "The Legionary movement has faith — not a program," one of the leaders declared shortly when asked a question about a program.[72] Codreanu explained, "This country goes to pieces not because of the lack of programs but because of the lack of men [to carry them out]. In our opinion the task is not to formulate programs, but to create men, a new kind of man!"[73] This famous Codreanu maxim was not entirely unrealistic. Decay was deeply rooted in a popular psychology distorted by centuries of misrule. Codreanu was realistic enough in his evaluation of Rumanians to know that only a fundamental change, a complete, almost evangelical break with the past and present would be able to save his people. So, the goal of the Legion was the creation of a New Man (*Omul Nou* as referred to in Legionary terminology). "The Legion is a revolutionary organization because it goes to the crux of the problems. It not only changes the forms and the appearances, but it changes the essential in men."[74]

In the period when the Legion had no political responsibility, the lack of a program was a definite advantage. By appealing to the intangible, the essential and the irrational, it could reach people more easily on both the lowest and highest levels.

A movement based on the gospel of Christianity as ideology gave a comfortable flexibility to the Legionaries. They sincerely stood for social justice and wished to help the Rumanian lower classes. In that sense, they never left any doubt — their ends were to serve all Rumanians but *only* Rumanians. But their aid to the suffering masses was not to be brought about because social dislocations were an anomaly or because they were ultimately inefficient, but because they were *unjust*. Codreanu proclaimed that the Legionaries "will give the workers more than a program, more than whiter bread or a better bed. They will give them the right to feel themselves the masters of Rumania with the rest of Rumanians."[75] During the brief period of Legionary rule, Legionaries visited Communists in jail and came to the conclusion that it was only their belief in God which separated the Legionaries from Marxism. They then asked the imprisoned Communists to help them organize the workers.[76]

The most degrading accusation in the ranks of the Legion was *ciocoieşte* (puppet of the landowning ruling class). There were fanatical outbreaks against the bourgeoisie during the Legionary rule:

The Legion cannot tolerate the existence of the bourgeoisie, not even in the sense of a linguistic expression, because there is no need to continue the old bourgeois form of life. . . . There can be no thought of a Legion of bourgeoisie; the very thought of bourgeois Legionaries is inconceivable. Between the two realities there is an immense chasm.[77]

Although this attitude is corroborated by the facts — because the Legion never proclaimed any ideology besides integral Christianity or any program besides the spiritual transformation of Rumanians into "new men" (beyond that there were only impulsive actions) — it could also proclaim itself "an antirevolutionary and conservative movement" based on Eminescu's notion of conserving tradition and through it the nation.[78] Understandably, these avowedly conservative aspects of the movement have been emphasized more since World War II than before it, every Fascist movement being desirous to seem as conservative as possible in order to appeal to those by whom it has at least some chance of being tolerated. But the Legion was gaining wide support among the dejected millions, who supported it not because of its conservatism, but because of its impulsive actions on behalf of the poor and the sincerity of its desire to be of help.

But was there any chance to help Rumania in the twentieth century with ideas like those of Moța? "From its very beginning, the industrial age destroyed our spiritual culture but it did not [offer] anything better in its place. It rather established a false culture, which corrupts us and leads us into [a spiritual] perdition." Or: "I and my comrades are like the ghosts of an agonizing world — we carry within us the spectres of fear in the world of today."[79] How far the Legion was willing to go because of its fear that the corruption of Rumania might infect the unspoiled peasant is shown in an article titled "Illiterate Country": "Under the existing conditions our ideal has to be an illiterate country."[80] It should not be surprising that despite its eventual hatred of King Carol and despite Carol's extermination campaign against the Legion, the movement remained staunchly attached to the institution of monarchy.[81] Moța also considered corporative institutions "entirely colorless from the folk point of view." If corporative institutions were established before the creation of the "new man," it would only solidify the existing corruption of Rumanian society. They should come after the birth of the "new man," if at all.[82]

What methods should the Legionaries employ in their struggle? Codreanu answers, "Not bread at any cost — honor at any cost!"[83] In his circulars, Codreanu warns that although Iuliu Maniu was the enemy of the Legion, "according to Legionary dogma, we should not behave dishonestly even with our enemies." But after that Codreanu established the most important operative point of this Legionary code of honor: "As he [Maniu] behaves toward us, we will behave toward him."[84] Moța elaborated this even further: "The state organizes society for the struggle between good and evil. But such a state must adapt itself as much as possible to the existing conditions of life."[85] The Legion, although claiming to stand on the basis of Christianity, did not intend to be an easy target for the police methods and the corrupt bureaucracy of interwar Rumania. They were realistic enough not to turn the other cheek — and they fought back with the violence of men absolutely convinced of the righteousness of their cause. In retaliation, they employed the same methods by which they had been attacked, knowing that they were doing evil. And in expiation of the evil they knowingly committed, they applied a truly original thought process.

Constantin Papanace, a close advisor of Codreanu, explained that, because of the power of darkness (the enemy of the Legion) the Legion as a *political* movement could not do otherwise than retaliate in kind. But in order that it should not fall to the moral level of its adversaries, the Legionary must never forget that he did evil — he must suffer for it in his heart and expiate. "This expiation by suffering constitutes the sacrifice which can reestablish the balance of absolute Legionary purity." Papanace illustrated this with a parable: Several Legionary companies detach themselves to serve as rear-guards in a narrow pass where they engage an enemy deployed in caves and caverns along the way, fighting in them with weapons suitable to such dark recesses.

But their weapons are not the weapons of light. They have lost their candor and their purity. They have had to fight with the arms of darkness. Thanks to them the mass of Legionaries crossed the pass unharmed. They have not known the struggle in the gloom. . . . The others [who have known it] will have to expiate. . . . Their suffering will uplift both them and the Movement.[86]

Suffering and sacrifice was an integral part of the Legionary educational program. According to Codreanu, the Legionary had to climb a mountain of suffering, pass through a forest full of wild beasts, and cross the swamp of despair. Those who did not pass these three trials could not be considered good Legionaries.[87]

It should not be surprising that the Legion believed in elitism. Only the elite were able to follow the "lifeline" of the Rumanian nation; the majority did not count, even when it encompassed 99 percent of Rumanians. "Not in the millions of slaves who bowed their heads under the yoke of foreigners did our people live, but in a Horia, Avram Iancu, in a Tudor and an Iancu Jianu and in the Haiduci . . . it is through them that our people spoke and not through the cowardly or 'reasonable' millions. . . . " And it is of no importance whether this elite wins or loses as long as it follows the "lifeline" of the Rumanian people.* The Legion was to be a "new Rumanian aristocracy," not of material goods or of birth, "but of spiritual qualities; an aristocracy of virtue."[88]

Codreanu did not favor democracy. He said that many nations in the Europe of the thirties "had taken off the clothes of democracy and others 'were in the process' of taking the democratic clothes off in order to put new clothes on. . . . One does not throw away good clothes," he concluded. He regarded democracy with its party system as destructive to Rumanian national unity, as a system which "turns millions of Jews into Rumanian citizens," and as a system unable to carry out any worthy program (what one party builds up, another party will destroy if it comes to power). According to Codreanu, democracy makes it impossible for a politician to fulfill his duty toward his people — electoral obligations and promises distract him from concern with the national interest. Neither can democracy create real authority; it is in the service of the financiers and capitalists. Codreanu continued with examples from the Rumanian village, saying that the

*Codreanu, *Eiserne Garde*, pp. 61-2. Haduci were romantic bandits in the style of Robin Hood, who took from the rich and gave to the poor, and fought the foreign oppressors. They gave great inspiration to the Legion.

overwhelming majority of peasants, who were enfranchised, did not obey even the most elementary sanitary regulations; consequently, they understood party politics even less. If a "true" and a "mendacious" idea confronted each other in an election, and one received 10,000 votes and the other 10,050, "is it thinkable that fifty votes . . . should decide between truth and lie? " Democracy, according to Codreanu, does not allow the election of a real national elite and leadership. Only immoral, unscrupulous people are elected, people who can bribe or be bribed, charlatans or demagogues. A real leader must possess (a) spiritual purity, (b) creativity, (c) courage, (d) Spartan way of life, (e) voluntary poverty, (f) faith in God, (g) love. Democracy is much too individualistic for Codreanu and it therefore recognizes only one of the three dimensions necessary to his concept of a nation. It ignores the two others, i.e., the historic nation and the historic mission of a nation. The Rumanian people were more than so many individuals functioning in the context of present daily life. Rumanian life was seen as consisting of Rumanians living in the present and also of the souls and bones of the dead and the legacy of future generations. In a word, according to Codreanu, democracy is set against the nation as such, because its goal is to satisfy present needs, and the ultimate goal for a nation "is the spiritual Resurrection! The Resurrection of nations in the name of Jesus Christ!"[89] How tragic that Codreanu was right in many aspects of his criticism of the workings of democracy in Rumania, but that it never occurred to him that it was the Rumanian implementation of democracy which was bad, not the idea itself.

If Codreanu did not believe in democracy, he refused to associate the Legion with totalitarian dictatorship. His system was rather an authoritarian one in which the "national religious piety" of the masses would find expression! "The leader will be the embodiment of this invisible spiritual condition [of the nation]."[90] And just to make sure that this voluntary consensus of Orthodox nationalism* would work, Codreanu was inflexibly devoted to discipline and unconditional obedience within the movement. "If discipline means renunciation and sacrifice — then it does not humiliate anybody. Any sacrifice uplifts rather than humiliates . . . . Discipline does not humiliate but renders [the Legionary] victorious!"[91] Transgressions were punished within the movement by a voluntary acceptance of punishment by the members. Codreanu felt that the greatest transgression of all was insubordination, the breaking of discipline.[92]

The mystical nationalism of the Legion, serving as a means and as an end, was inseparable from Orthodox Christianity. It was because of its deep, sincere, sometimes fanatic religious beliefs and goals that the Legion was so uncompromising in its actions later. For crusaders the area of compromise is out of bounds — they must have complete power or none at all. The Legion's mission was a holy crusade; its enemies were not only the enemies of Rumania but also the enemies of God.

*The concept of Codreanu is strikingly similar to the concept of the Slavophiles, especially that of Khomyakov.

These enemies were: (1) dirty politics and politicians and the political parties, (2) Communists, and (3) the equivalent and sum total of the two, the absolute evil: Jews.[93] The Jews were the black in the Legionary spectrum, consequently the religious obsession, the fixed idea. They were the corrupting influence behind the dirty politics, the bearers of capitalist and Communist plague; they were the exploiters of Rumanians, the destroyers of Rumanian culture.[94] And whatever the shabby Legionary rank and file did later with Jewish property, the leadership fought the Jews more in order to expurgate the foremost evil from Rumanian soil than to acquire wealth or position.

Everybody who crossed the path of the Legion was labeled a Jew, including even Lord Rothemere and as many as 1,400 of the 1,800 employees of the hated United Nations thirty years later. To make a Jew out of Lenin would have been too much even for the Legion, so they had to satisfy themselves by deciding that he was merely half Jewish.[95]

10

With the basic Legionary ideas and goals in mind, let us now look at the Legion's organization. The basic unit of the Legion was the nest (*Cuib*).

The leader of a movement must take account of reality and the existing facts with painstaking accuracy. The only tangible reality for me was one single fact: the individual. A poor peasant, suffering bitter privation in his village, an unfortunate sick worker, and a searching intellectual astray — these were my people.[96]

So wrote Codreanu in the 1920s. He wanted to give an opportunity to every individual to gather a circle of men around him and become the leader of that circle. Leaders were to be called not by appointment, but through that inner voice of the intangible that was so important in the Legionary world, coupled with their probity and capacity to lead the groups — the nests. The nest consisted of from three to thirteen individuals; Codreanu refused to use the word "member" since it reminded him of a political party. If there were more than thirteen individuals, the nest automatically split into two nests.[97] Every nest was to have besides its "nest leader" (*şef de cuib*), a secretary to handle the necessary correspondence, a messenger to keep in contact with other nests and the movement's hierarchy, and a treasurer. The six rules of Legionary life within the nest were: (1) the rule of discipline, to follow the nest leader through thick and thin; (2) the rule of work, not only to work but also to love work, not for the sake of gain, but for the satisfaction of having done one's duty; (3) the rule of silence, to be frugal with words; the speech of a Legionary must be action, he must let others act like chatterboxes; (4) the rule of self-education; the Legionary must become through it a heroic man; (5) the rule of mutual aid; Legionaries must not ever abandon each other, and finally, (6) the rule of honor; a Legionary must always act honorably — even honorable defeat was preferable to dastardly victory.[98]

The six rules of the nest must have sounded shocking and strange in Greater Rumania. After all, they were not exactly the principles which characterized the style, philosophy and world outlook of the period. They were probably as disconcerting for the majority of Rumanians as the Quakers' honesty was in the England of Walpole or the morals of ancient Christians emerging from the catacombs was in Rome. No wonder people began to listen!

The meetings of the nest were to be a church where everybody forgot about the petty, sordid problems of everyday life and thought only of the Fatherland. Everyone was to be there punctually and with a good heart.[99] Different topics were proposed for discussion for intellectuals' nests and for peasants' or workers' nests. Some of the topics that would rise in intellectuals' nests: agrarian policy, financial reform, relation between labor and capital, minority questions, the role of the peasant and worker in the Legionary state, etc.[100]

The nest was to be always active, in the village, in town and at the universities. The nest leader had a great deal of initiative, and his orders or the decisions taken at the nest meetings were carried out by every member of the nest unconditionally. Iron discipline, constant action, initiative and obedience characterized the hierarchic order of the Legion from the top to the bottom.[101] An inactive nest was considered a "dead nest."[102] Some nests, depending on their number and the local conditions, might be united in "Legionary families." There was a semi-corporative tendency in the formation of individual nests. Members were not united strictly on professional lines, but the Brothers of the Cross (up to age twenty) were transferred into the Legion in the form of nests. Age and sex were division lines. Girls and women had separate nests, and the Legionary Corps of the ages from twenty-one to twenty-eight were supposed to be the most active members of the Legion. Only the most advanced nests were to conduct political activities.[103]

The Legionary movement was to grow from the grassroots, yet be directed in an authoritarian way from above. But this authoritarianism was not supposed to rest merely on orders from above. Not only were nest leaders to be elevated through the intangible force of their own capabilities and the appreciation of the other nest members, but higher functionaries within the Legion were selected also on the basis of charisma, merit and the same undefined quality within. Codreanu told them, "Go! Conquer [the hearts of] the people! Organize them!" And according to their performance, he confirmed rather than appointed them to the positions they had achieved for themselves.[104] Nevertheless, before the confirmation in a higher position they had to go through an indoctrination stage called School of Cadres.

The hierarchy was established on the following lines: (1) nest leader; (2) leader of the Legionary garrison, encompassing the Legionary families in a town or village; (3) leader of the Plăsa;* (4) leader of different Legionary groups such as detachment, camp, construction project, corps; (5) leader of the Judeţ;** and (6) leader of a Rumanian province.[105] Codreanu, in

*Administrative subdivision corresponding to county or district.

**Corresponding to the French département, after which it was modeled.

principle at least, was very careful about recruiting. Utmost selectivity was to be the rule.[106] The principle was that, out of twenty who wanted to become Legionaries, nineteen should be refused. No Cuzist or Liberal party member or anyone who played a role in party politics was to be admitted. Codreanu was strangely silent about the admissability of the members of the Peasant party of Maniu, whom he respected. His slogan was: "As many friends as possible, as few Legionaries as possible."[107] Even so, the prospective Legionary had a three-year waiting period, and during this time he was a candidate, he was called "member." After that, he became a Legionary, then a head Legionary, assistant commander, Legionary commander, or commander *Buna Veştire*. There was an honorary position for worthy supporters over fifty — they were made Legionary senators. The function a Legionary fulfilled did not necessarily correspond to his grade in the Legion. It was the function which was to give prestige to the grade and not vice versa.[108] It was hard to bring about a unified movement with such a framework. Codreanu saw this, but he was convinced that through mutual love and discipline this difficulty would be overcome.[109]

Initiation into the ranks of the Legion was as dramatic as possible. It took place at night to the accompaniment of songs, torches and oaths, preferably in the middle of a forest or the ruin of a castle. "The chosen one, told that he was entering a world apart, was promised that by following the teaching and practice of this new world, he would become a man of special essence." Thereafter, "there grew in him, out of the excesses of so-called religious practices, a mystic exaltation and the wish to perform some resounding deed."[110] The Legion's uniform, with neat cross belts, included a green shirt, symbolizing the advent of the "spring of the Rumanian nation." The Roman salute accompanied the greetings: *"Sanatate!"* and/or *"Traiăsca Legiuna şi Captanul!"* (Heil! Long live the Legion and its Captain!). On Sundays, both in summer and in winter, hikes and marches through the countryside were to be performed by the nests "in manly step."[111] Codreanu intended the Legion to become much more than a party or a movement — it was to be a way of life.

CHAPTER X

The Legion Against Carolist Rumania

I can show you at this ball ten men who should be condemned as assassins. They have forgotten it, and the world, too.

Stendhal

Show us not the aim without the way. For ends and means on earth are so entangled, that changing one, you change the other, too; Each different path brings other ends in view.

Ferdinand Lassalle

1

In November 1928 an incorruptible man, a convinced democrat and a true patriot, stepped to the helm of the Rumanian state. His leadership was to prove that those commendable qualities are no panacea for the large ills that sometimes plague small and underdeveloped states. They certainly did not answer the needs of troubled Rumania in the years that followed.

Iuliu Maniu came to power with the ardent support and prayers of the great majority of his countrymen. Democracy, the form of government in brotherly France, had been discredited neither at Versailles nor by futile experiments at home in 1918-19, as it was in Hungary. On the contrary, the hope for a peasant democracy inspired the people greatly.

In December, truly free elections were held which caused a marked shift in the existing political balance of Rumania. The results were nothing short of a landslide, a volcanic outburst against the existing Liberal system. The National Peasants, allied with the German party and the Social Democrats, gained 77.76 percent of the votes cast with 77.37 percent of eligible voters participating in the election, an all-time high for Rumania. This gave them 348 seats in the chamber, leaving the opposition with 39 seats. The Cuzists received only 32,273 votes, which meant that they obtained no representation.[1] Maniu announced, "Our first aim will be to give to the principles of the Constitution their real meaning and impart a character of strict legality to the working of the administration."[2]

He tried to be as good as his word. Martial law and censorship were lifted, the xenophobic restrictions on the influx of foreign capital so dear to Vîntila Brătianu's heart were in most instances done away with, and a long overdue process of decentralization started both in the economy and in the administration. A more liberal tariff policy was introduced, designed to promote grain exports and certain imports, which in turn would have helped agriculture. Finally, with the help of large foreign loans, the leu was stabilized at the rate of 167.18 to the dollar. The National Peasant party seemed to act more liberally both in the economy and in internal politics than their predecessors who called themselves Liberals.

But not everything went well. The press, mostly in Liberal hands, started an irresponsible slander campaign against the National Peasant government, using vituperative language and spreading false rumors.* No change was made in Bessarabia's administration, and thus that region remained in something of a permanent ferment. Striking coal miners in the Jiu Valley were fired upon by the army, despite the fact that Maniu tried to be impartial regarding labor and management. A Fascist plot to overthrow the government, hatched by some ambitious army officers, was easily taken care of, but when there was an attempt in 1929 on the life of Vaida-Voevod, an innocent person was arrested in connection with it. The fact that he was crippled by beating and torture while in prison was a good measure of the spirit of the police and administration bequeathed to Maniu by the Liberals, but it reflected poorly on the people in power. Some local elections showed a dwindling enthusiasm for the government as early as March 1930.

The great depression of course dealt a staggering blow to the unfolding of Rumanian democracy — as indeed it did to democratic hopes everywhere in the No-Man's-Land of Europe. The collapse of world grain prices was a severe trial for the Rumanian economy, dependent as it was on grain exports for the well-being of the majority of the population. The newly stabilized currency did not get a chance; it could not have any beneficial influence on the economy with the collapse of international credit.

But all these somber trials and tribulations for Rumanian democracy could have been weathered, perhaps, if not for an event of cardinal importance — the return of Prince Carol from exile on June 8, 1930.

If Maniu and Mihalache were the symbols of integrity, constitutionalism, democracy and the hope of the Rumanian people for a better future, Rumania's only other public symbol, King Carol II, was in the coming decade (1930-40) to do his best to create just the opposite impression. Perhaps it is not an exaggeration to say that Carol was the most corrupt crowned head of twentieth-century Europe. No other king abused the sincere devotion of his people so unscrupulously as he. The other cardinal sin of the country, violence, was the answer of the Legion to Carol's corruption, and the unhappy country found itself caught between the two.

*Perhaps there is no other country in the world where anonymous "well-informed circles" spread sensational rumors in such volume and colorful unreliability as in Rumania before the Communist secret police stopped it in 1948. These rumors appeared in print only during brief spells of relaxed censorship, practicing freedom of speech and press in the most repulsive form. But even spread orally, they tended to make responsible government difficult, if not impossible. It was General Antonescu who set the correct ratio in this flow of irresponsible political gossip, saying that "out of 1,000 rumors, 999 are false." *Pe marginea prăpăstiei*, I, 190-93.

Carol was born in 1893, the first member of the dynasty to be born on Rumanian soil. He received excellent training, mainly because of the insistence of his strict grandfather, Carol I. Tall, slender, cultivated, with an unprejudiced, intellectual mind, a natural charm, and a tremendous capacity for work, he might have made an excellent ruler for his country but for the other aspects of his character. Early in his life, when he was sent to Potsdam, he showed his greed for money in a shocking fashion when he sold at an auction for the officers of his regiment the beautiful Rumanian folklore articles which his mother, Queen Marie, had sent him as gifts for his comrades. During World War I, he donned a Russian uniform and deserted his bleeding country in order to marry a dancer, Zizi Lambrino. After that feat of indiscretion, he was secluded in the Bistriţa monastery in the Carpathians for a while. When the war ended, Queen Marie arranged a match for him with Princess Helen of Greece, the sister of King George II. Carol married her, and Prince Michael was born in 1921. But Carol could not or would not remain faithful. After numerous scandalous liaisons, he met another Helen. The tale of love between this Hohenzollern, the grandson of Queen Victoria and of Alexander II of Russia, and a daughter of the ghetto of Iaşi would read like Cinderella — if only it had not caused so much bloodshed and suffering for Rumania. Carol renounced his throne for Helen (Magda) Wolff, alias Lupescu, divorced Queen Helen and went into exile. His exile was arranged mainly by the Brătianus with the help of the all-powerful favorite of Queen Marie, the *eminence grise* of Rumanian politics, Prince Stirbey. When King Ferdinand died in 1927, the Brătianu clan hoped to establish a Regency for Prince (now King) Michael, a minor. But Maniu and the National Peasants, and above all the Rumanian people, strongly royalist with an almost mystical attachment for their King, fervently desired Carol's return. Maniu stipulated only one condition: Madame Lupescu must stay abroad. Carol promised this, thinking probably that Bucharest was worth if not a mass at least a promise, which in any case was never to be honored. Madame Lupescu practically stepped out of the luggage of the King after the bloodless coup of his return. His son, King Michael, age nine, became Crown Prince and the Great Voevod of Alba-Iulia.

After Carol's flagrant breach of faith, Maniu resigned. As the grand old man explained in private, he would not allow "a royal concubine to defile the Rumanian throne." Maniu's retirement fitted exquisitely into Carol's plans. For the new King had great plans of his own for the salvation of Rumania, as he sincerely believed, and democracy and representative government had no place in them. As he saw it,

> The reason for the political and spiritual crisis of Rumania is to be found in the spell of Western ideas and reforms, [which] were the product of a different tradition, [and of different] economic, historical, national, geographical, and moral conditions.

Carol went on to explain that with the parliamentary tradition, Rumania adopted all the heritage of the bourgeois revolution of 1789 without having a bourgeoisie of her own.

Our political life must pay for this original sin of lies. And this original sin encompasses all spheres of [our] public life, culture, civilization, national economy, administration — all resemble a distorted framework, not fitting into the essential, to the content of those truths which come from the distant past, from the depth of our very existence.[3]

There was plenty of truth in King Carol's words. The question is whether Carol's wrecking of the parliamentary system, and his government by camarillas swayed by his greed for money, his lascivious, suspicious nature, his vanity, his disloyalty — all qualities which blossomed luxuriantly in the Byzantine atmosphere of palace intrigues in Bucharest — offered a better alternative.

Madame Lupescu, or as Carol and her flatterers called her, Duduja, was as cold, as calculating, and as selfish as Carol. She was the most influential royal mistress of the 1930s and the most hated person in Rumania. Although it is hard to imagine a more astronomical difference between the backgrounds of two humans than theirs, she and Carol possessed in their distance a harmony, a deep sympathy for each other. This may be the reason for the strange fact that after their meeting in 1925 they stayed together through thick and thin — and only the death of Carol in 1952 separated them. Apart from Madame Lupescu's indirect, negative, yet effective meddling in politics, the presence of a Jewish mistress at the side of their King, a mistress who drove away their Queen Helen, had a profound effect on the deeply mystical, religious and anti-Semitic Rumanians. The "Jewish female serpent" became the symbol of absolute evil, a viper that would choke off their country.

When Carol, looking like a blond Siegfried, descended from the sky in Transylvania in 1930, the people worshipped him. Millions of Rumanians were so happy to have their dream prince back that they knelt in the dust before him. But Carol was always in a hurry — there was a bridge party at the Alea Vulpache* or a deal to be concluded with Colonel Gavrila Marinescu** or with Max Auşnit.*** In vain did his people proffer their love before the gate of his palace; the King was interested only in such treasures as he could touch. And the cold winds blowing from Moldavia scattered the disprized love of the Rumanian nation.

Maniu's resignation in October 1930 was followed by the appointment of another National Peasant leader, Gheorghe Mironescu, as premier. Carol was meanwhile building up his own positon to deal more effectively in the affairs of the state and ultimately to establish the brand of fascism which he had come to admire since Mussolini's march on Rome. Meanwhile, the deepening

---

*Alea Vulpache No. 2, the home of Madame Lupescu in Bucharest.

**The legendary police prefect of Bucharest, appointed by Carol. Every prostitute, every gambling den, every shoddy dealer paid him a tribute — and after that Carol got his cut. When Mihalache, as minister of interior, tried to remove him from his post, he flatly refused to quit, and it was Mihalache who had to resign, not Marinescu.

***Jewish industrialist, member of the second "industrializing" camarilla, who later fell into disgrace.

depression in Eastern Europe was causing a Fascist upsurge everywhere. Between 1929 and 1932 national income dropped by 45 percent in Rumania. Export revenues fell from 29 billion lei in 1929 to 14 billion in 1933, even though the weight of exports increased from 7 million metric tons to 8 million, reflecting the tremendous drop in prices of agricultural products. Imports fell from 1,102,000 metric tons in 1929 to 450,000 tons in 1932. State revenues declined from 36 billion leis in 1929 to 18 billion in 1933.[4] Despite the fact that petroleum exports preserved an active balance of trade for Rumania throughout the depression, the cumulative consequences of the economic crisis were disastrous, especially for the peasantry. By 1932 the debt per hectare of arable land reached the figure of 6,585 lei.[5] A moratorium on agricultural debt became a pressing issue. But the subsequent reduction of peasant indebtedness was not to be enacted by the National Peasants. In fact, the peasant government did surprisingly little for the peasant masses. They seem to have believed that political democracy and economic liberalism would automatically resolve the difficulties, and their half-hearted support for the cooperative movement and the little financial aid they undertook was not enough. The combination of liberal economics and political democracy were ideas fitting rather the needs of a well-developed middle class than those of Rumanian peasants in the early 1930s.

In April 1931 Mironescu resigned, and the King called upon Professor Iorga to form a new cabinet. Iorga called new elections, which were managed by a sinister figure, Constantin Argetoianu, an unabashed expert at adulterating the electoral process by more than one means. Iorga's party concluded an electoral pact, the National Union, with the Liberals and this, thanks to Argetoianu's activities, got the necessary 47.49 percent of the votes for the premium of the seats. The vote for Maniu's party was duly contained by Argetoianu at 14.99 percent, after which Maniu retired from politics. The Cuzists polled 113,863 votes,[6] mostly in such heavily Jewish-inhabited towns of the northeast as Botoşani, Dorohoi, Iaşi, Succeava and Baia.[7] But the government did little to improve the deteriorating economic situation, which because of its international implications was largely beyond their control. For months the government could not even pay the salaries of the bureaucrats. Because of the failure to obtain a French loan, the government planned to reduce administrative salaries. Carol opposed this measure, so in June 1932 Iorga resigned, and Vaida-Voevod, a rightist peasant leader who was on better terms with the King than Maniu or Mihalache, was called to head a peasant cabinet. New elections were held in July 1932, with considerably less manipulation of the voting process than was customary, and the National Peasants, in alliance with the German party, obtained 45 percent of the vote. The Cuzists increased their strength to 159,071 votes. Codreanu's group gained 70,674 votes.[8] Most of Codreanu's and Cuza's gains came from disaffected Bessarabia. But there was hope for stability neither in the economy nor in politics. Vaida, who became more and more antidemocratic and violently chauvinistic, clashed with Titulescu over the latter's conciliatory attitude towards the U.S.S.R., and there was again a Maniu cabinet for a short while in January 1933. But Carol and Maniu could not get along, and Maniu had to go. Vaida became prime minister again.

Although the peasantry bore the brunt of the depression, the industrial workers also suffered greatly. In January 1933, strikes erupted in the oilfields in Ploeşti and spread to Bucharest. Violent clashes occurred around the Griviţa workshops of the C.F.R. (Rumanian State Railways). The unnecessary violence of the government's measures at the time can be credited to Vaida. He also began to work toward his brand of *numerus clausus,* which he called *numerus valachicus,* directed against Hungarians and to a lesser extent against Jews, these two hated minorities being one and the same in his native Transylvania. But he was too lenient with the growing Legionary Movement for Carol's taste. And the influence of the King was on the increase. By the fall of 1933, Carol had effected a reconciliation with the Liberals, who were in a better position to treat with the King since the death of Vîntila Brătianu in 1930. In November 1933 Carol appointed the Liberal leader Ion G. Duca prime minister, with an understanding that he would manipulate election and crack down on the burgeoning Legionary Movement.

2

We left Codreanu and his embryonic Legion at the end of the Liberal period. On November 8, 1927, the day of St. Michael, the first Legionaries took the solemn oath of initiation into the ranks of the Legion. Codreanu sent some of them to all the Rumanian historic battlefields, where they dug up earth that was supposedly mingled with the blood of heroes fallen there over the centuries. This "earth of our forefathers" *(pămăntul strămoşesc)* was solemnly mixed, and each of the new Legionaries got a small bagful of it to wear around his neck[9] The walls of the room in which the image of St. Michael was guarded were inscribed with Codreanu's slogans, reflecting the ideals of the Legion, all of them taken from the Scriptures: "I will be the Lord of him who will triumph!" "Fight bravely for your faith!" "Guard yourself from the sins of the flesh because they destroy the soul!" "Be watchful!" "Let the hero never die in yourself!" "Brothers in good and bad times!" "He who knows how to die will never become a slave!" Finally, "I believe in the Resurrection of my people and look forward to the destruction of those who betrayed them!"[10] With these ideas and with the four guidelines (1) faith in God; (2) faith in the holy mission of the Legion; (3) mutual love; and (4) song, the Legion set out to bring about a religious national revival and purification in Rumania.[11]

The first months in the life of the Legion were inauspicious. There was very slow progress in the formation of nests, and the financial problems were enormous. The finances were improved through the cooperation of Moţa's father, the Orthodox priest in Oraştie, who put his nationalist paper at the Legion's disposal. By October 1927, as a result of the "struggle" for readers (Codreanu called his every move a struggle, campaign, march, etc.), subscriptions stood at 2,586, so that a modest financial backing was attained.

And not less important was the fact that the Legion had a mouthpiece to propagate the new ideology. The name of the paper was to be *Land of Our Forefathers (Pământul Strămoşesc)*.[12] The Legion even acquired a car. But financial difficulties continued all through 1928. The hope of the Rumanian people in those days was placed in Maniu and a peasant democracy, not in religious mysticism and in violent fantasts. When in January 1929 Codreanu called all the nest leaders to Iaşi for a conference, about forty of them appeared. If the Legion made any headway, it was among the young, and this trend was to continue to the end.[13] "[Codreanu] does not care for the majority of the old, the ones who live for their belly, for pleasures and . . . democracy . . . But he cares for the young generation," said one of the best men the Legion produced, Banea.[14] But all regimes, the corrupt and reactionary, and unfortunately the democratic ones also, more often than not let youth slip through their fingers. The modern totalitarian regimes with broad popular backing, whether of the right or the left, have never committed that mistake. They realized the revolutionary potential in the "lost generations" after the war. Banea spoke of disaffected youth in Rumanian context:

Our generation did not know any happiness or fun in its adolescence, and did not enjoy peace or relaxation in its parental home. On the contrary, it went through all the Calvary of war, privation and pain. It was the music of the [rattle] of arms which delighted its ears . . . In one word: Our generation are the children of war . . . Men of the twentieth century. Our generation does not wish to continue the way we live today.[15]

This youth gathered increasingly around the young men who led the Legion.

Meanwhile, the Legion's embryonic nests, almost unnoticed in Rumania at that time, marched through the countryside, around Focşani and Galaţi. Codreanu traveled all over Rumania, visiting even the proud mountaineers, the Moţi, abandoned to their grinding poverty by successive administrations. What he saw made him cry out: "Can there be a greater tragedy? For ten centuries they resisted outside [Hungarian] pressure in order to perish from hunger and misery in their fatherland, for [the advent of which] they waited for a thousand years!"[16] And the people of Iancu could answer only with the ancient song:

"Gold lies in our mountain's core
But we beg from door to door. . ."*

In December 1929 the Legion was more than two years old, and its quasi-religious activities had not borne the fruit Codreanu expected. In order to solve the Jewish question, " . . . only a political road was open. A road which demanded getting in touch with the broad masses."[17] As always, Codreanu was capable of appraising reality. So the Legion decided to go to the people. Codreanu went through the Pruth Valley, and starting in Bereşti he initiated tactics which were to be followed by the Legion in its political

---

* Old Moţ song. The richest gold deposits of Europe are located in this part of Transylvania.

struggle for years to come. The local authorities, as usual, forbade any meeting which was not a governmental one. Codreanu flatly refused compliance with their instructions. The gendarmerie did its best to keep away people from the neighboring villages who wanted to come to hear Codreanu. Codreanu rode into Berești on horseback, this not only for the sake of romantic appeal but because of the impassable mud. He addressed the crowd in the churchyard. His appearance, his speech made the occasion strikingly different from the political meetings of the past ten years. As he later wrote in his manual, "The Legionary does not make electoral promises." [18] He said in an almost Old Church-Slavonic style, which was to characterize his style to the end:

> Let us all unite, men and women, and let us forge a new fate for our nation and for ourselves. The hour of the redemption and of the Resurrection of our people is drawing nigh! He who believes, he who will fight and suffer, will be blessed by his people. New times are knocking at our doors! A world with a soul which dried up long ago is dying, and a new world is being born — the world of those who are strong and have faith. There will be a place for everybody in this new world, not according to his education or his intelligence or his cleverness, but above all, according to his character and his faith![19]

Afterward, Codreanu continued on to the next village. There a crowd waited for him with candles in their hands. He repeated his speech in village after village. After a while young people up to thirty or thirty-five years of age joined him on horseback until their numbers swelled to more than fifty. They entered the villages with songs. As he wrote, "I felt that I penetrated to undefined depths of their souls, where the politicians with their borrowed programs were unable to descend. There in these depths I stuck the roots of the Legionary Movement."[20] The riders put turkey feathers on their fur caps as a distinctive sign, in the style of the Haiduci, and peasants lined the roads from other villages, asking, "When will you come to our village, young sir? " Everywhere the Christians greeted them with enthusiasm, pouring buckets of water in their way for luck and plenty's sake in the old Moldavian custom.[21] The village lads understood little of what they wanted or who they were, but they sang their songs, and the charisma of Codreanu on horseback with a cross in his hand struck the deepest chords in the mystical, primitive souls of the peasants. They were tired of the fraudulent promises of politicians which were almost invariably accompanied by a great deal of violence.

After the success in January 1930, Codreanu ventured a ride into the perennially dissatisfied "Jewish-Communist" region of Bessarabia. They sewed white crosses on their green shirts and wore the Haiduci turkey feathers and fur hats as they rode through the towns and villages around Cagul, defying the local bureaucracy.

> We looked like Crusaders, and we wanted to be Crusaders who in the name of the Cross entered the struggle against godless Jewish might in order to liberate Rumania.[22]

The tormented and many times shamefully castigated peasantry of this region listened to their speeches with bared heads.[23] Their success was even greater there than in the Pruth Valley.

It was before a second ride through Bessarabia in the early spring of 1930 that Codreanu founded a combat organization to enroll what he called "militant youth organizations to combat Jewish communism." In reality their intended role was to stand up against the interference of the unfriendly, often arbitrary, local authorities. This new subdivision within the Legion was to be the Iron Guard. As Codreanu explained, "When I say Communist, I mean Jew."[24] In order to assure a cooperative reception from the authorities, Codreanu saw the Peasantist minister of interior, Vaida-Voevod. Vaida belonged to the ultranationalist, right wing of Maniu's party, was a seasoned anti-Semite himself, and showed, despite his advice of moderation, great sympathy for Codreanu's goals. Still, Codreanu realized that "the eyes of 1890 see differently from those of 1930."[25] Maybe Vaida's sympathy, like the sympathy of many other elder Rumanian politicians, can be ascribed to the fact that he saw his own youthful dreams revived by the hotheaded, idealistic, nationalistic Iron Guardists, dreams for which he was himself too old, too corrupt, too cautious and too comfortable to fight.

In July 1930, after causing grave disturbances in Maramureş (where according to Codreanu the Jews set a town afire in order to blame it on the Iron Guard*), the Iron Guard began its great march through Bessarabia with the permission of Vaida-Voevod. This second march seems to have taken place in the manner described before, and without significant incident.

But the sympathetic Vaida-Voevod was replaced at the end of 1930 with a very different man, Mihalache. This peasant democrat had not gone through the school of Lueger and Schönerer in Vienna. He had no Fascist sympathies and only one dream — a free, democratic Rumania. When a Legionary who had participated in the Maramureş bestialities, incensed at the comments of some Jewish (and non-Jewish) editors about Legion activities, decided on "direct action" and broke into the office of a Bucharest journalist and fired at him point-blank (he missed), Mihalache dissolved both the Legion and the Iron Guard. Codreanu could not understand: "What was illegal about trying to step on the head of the poisonous Jewish rattlesnake?"** There were searches and arrests. Codreanu himself was arrested, this time because of his alleged involvement in an attempt by Macedonian Rumanian students on the life of the minister of agriculture. Before his customary acquittal, while he was in jail, he won the group for the Legion. This Aroman group became important in the Legion later.***

Meanwhile, the depression cast deeper and deeper shadows over Rumania, and time for democracy was running out. Here, more than in Hungary, the

*Codreanu, Eisérne Garde, p. 351. Eyewitness accounts flatly contradict that of Codreanu.

**Ibid., pp. 360-61. Codreanu almost regretfully observed that because of minor mechanical trouble in the revolver the assailant could not fire his second shot at the journalist.

***Aromans are the Vlachs of Macedonia. They were resettled mainly in Dobrogea. Rogger and Weber, The European Right, p. 544.

road to the Communist left was blocked by nationalism and the party line forced by Stalin on the Rumanian Communists. Also, there was the efficient and cruel *Siguranţa*. If the Labor and Peasant Group, a Communist front organization, gained 73,716 votes and five mandates in the elections of 1931,[26] few of these votes were Rumanian ones. They came mostly from industrial workers in Transylvania and Banat who were Hungarians. The Rumanian Social Democratic party was small and insignificant and had a bourgeois-intellectual character and appeal. Democracy a priori outruled any anti-Semitic measure — not even his long conflict with Madame Lupescu could make an anti-Semite out of Maniu. Even the nondemocratic politicians were closely bound by ties of corruption to Jewish banks and finance, both domestic and foreign. They could offer little of the anti-Semitism desired by middle-class youth and by the masses in the areas of a more unfortunate economic and social stratification of the Jewish community. The bourgeois L.A.N.C., with Cuza's sterile anti-Semitism, was not the answer to the burning social problems either, nor were the burgeoning minor Fascist parties, such as the shortlived Swastika of Fire *(Svastica de Foc)* or the Fascist movement founded in 1933 by Colonel Emanuel Tătărescu, the brother of the Liberal prime minister. The Fascist movement, founded by the attorney V. Emilian, was also distinctly middle class in its composition and world outlook. It operated mainly in Bucharest, imitating N.S.D.A.P. forms and programs, and later joined the L.A.N.C.

The Rumanian masses, especially the young people and the peasants where the National Peasant party was not well organized, found solace and promise in the charisma and the mystical nationalism offered by the Legion. As democracy broke down and depression widened, the Iron Guard rapidly increased its appeal and strength, and the most dissatisfied and militant elements of the Rumanian people joined its ranks. In the elections under Iorga, it participated under the name the Group of Corneliu Zelea Codreanu and gained 30,783 votes and no mandate. But in July 1931, in a by-election in Neamţ, Codreanu was elected.[27] He then entered Parliament, the "cave of the lion," as he called it.

He attacked the lions in the den, demanding the death penalty for misusers of state funds, an investigation of the private finances of leading politicians, and an end to any connection between banks, business firms and politicians. He proceeded to expose some "loans" to leading Rumanian politicians by the greatest private bank of Rumania, the Marmaroş-Blanc. Titulescu led with 19 million lei, Grigore Filipescu with 1,365,000 lei, etc. The "loans" were never denied by these gentlemen, but one deputy assured Codreanu in a rather unconvincing manner that the sums would be paid back.[28]

Obviously, the Iron Guard was beginning to become something more than a moralizing group of mystics or a minor nuisance. In 1932, with its ranks constantly growing, the oligarchy in Bucharest was not able to ignore it any more; something more drastic than the capricious hostility of local authorities was required. This being Rumania, there was a powerful repressive apparatus virtually unrestricted by any law at any government's disposal. The laws, because of the mania for legislation so characteristic of Rumania, stayed on the books. When the Legion tried to run in a by-election in Tutova in the spring of 1932, it was met with all the repression possible. Reinforced gendarme platoons attempted to keep campaigning Legionaries away from the villages, but they did not reckon with two new tactics which the Legionaries introduced into Rumanian politics. First, through their training and marches the Legionaries had the disciplined endurance necessary to play hide-and-run and hit-and-run with the repressive apparatus. Secondly, and perhaps even more significantly, the Legion answered violence with unbridled counterviolence. When captured Legionaries were mistreated, their comrades in a regular streetfight captured the main gendarme outpost and liberated the prisoners.[29] The Legion won the by-election of Tutova, with Codreanu père joining his son in Parliament, and was again dissolved in consequence of its counterviolence this time by the Iorga-Argetoianu government.

In the new elections of July 1932, amid plenty of violence, the Legion more than doubled its votes to 70,674 and won five mandates.[30] The Legion now was campaigning in 36 electoral districts. Most of its votes came from the dissatisfied Bessarabian and Moṭ regions. In Parliament once again, Codreanu flatly refused to become an agent for his constituents in the sense the other M.P.'s were — that is, to procure for them sinecures, etc.[31] Under the sympathetic support of the Vaida government, the Legion was breathing easier and was growing steadily. Codreanu saw the premier again personally, and Vaida suggested "some positive constructive work."[32] Codreanu responded with a construction project in the village of Visani, where the Legion was to build a dam to prevent the flood that every year destroyed crops of poor peasant squatters. Two hundred Legionaries were mobilized for this project, only to be attacked by several companies of gendarmes and trampled to the ground. It was significant that this action was organized by Armand Calinescu, who would meet Codreanu again. Codreanu protested in a letter to Vaida, "We are at the end of our endurance!"[33]

But not only was the Legion at the end of its endurance, the ruling class was, too — with much more powerful means at their disposal. They did not intend to allow any evangelical challenge to the status quo. Unfortunately, the methods they increasingly employed against the Legion only stiffened the latter in its feeling of holy mission. When in the fall of 1933 Carol called the Liberals to power again, the stage was set for the political violence that was to continue throughout the decade.

3

From the fall of 1933 until the first months of 1941, the history of Rumania was thoroughly interwoven with that of the Iron Guard. At the time of the return of the Liberals, the Legion had grown strong enough to be a challenge instead of a nuisance to the ruling corrupt oligarchy. The clash between the corruption of the oligarchy and the camarilla on one hand and the passionate nationalist violence of the Legion on the other dominated the

Rumanian scene until the Legion, which unleashed the fateful struggle, was destroyed.

During the last weeks of the National Peasant government, I. Duca, the head of the Liberals, visited Paris, where he branded the Legionaries an "anarchistic, subversive movement in the pay of Hitler."[34] French political and financial circles were only too glad to hear such language. After Hitler's advent to power, the West feared that the whole of highly unstable No-Man's-Land would tumble into Nazism. Duca and Titulescu gladly gave the necessary guarantee that this would not happen. And after his appointment to head the government upon his return, Duca set to work. The whole police machine was let loose on the Legion, and during the coming elections they were to be kept from the polls. The first two Legionary fatalities occurred during the pre-election campaign. But even the increased terror could not guarantee the desired results; the Legion was by then too popular for that. So ten days before the date set for the election, during the night of the ninth of December, the Legion was dissolved, and in a mammoth roundup 18,000 Legionaries were arrested, chained, and thrown into jail — though not without resistance on their part, a resistance in which eight Legionaries died.[35] General Gheorge Cantacuzino Granicerul warned Duca that with these measures he was signing his death warrant.[36] In the elections, the Liberals, assisted by all the well-known electoral tricks, brutality and falsification, got 50.99 percent of the votes, which assured them 300 seats in the chamber, the Legion having been barred from participation in the election.[37]

But Duca was not destined to enjoy his victory for long. Nine days after the elections, on December 29, three Legionaries shot him dead on the platform of the railroad station in Sinaia. After their deed, they gave themselves up in a state of trance, to expiate. They were the first Legionary legend, the Nicadori, a word formed from the initials of their first and last names.[38] There can be no question that Codreanu had known about their plan; he certainly endorsed it later. In the following weeks he had to go into hiding before the fury of the oligarchy. The whereabouts of Codreanu during this time are still a mystery. One of his close friends, Sterie Ciumetti, was arrested and tortured by police attempting to find Codreanu. Ciumetti kept his silence. His mutilated body was found under a bridge in Bucharest.[39] The most plausible story about Codreanu's whereabouts is that he asked the Jewish industrialist Ausnit to hide him, threatening to shoot him if he refused, a believable threat after the death of Duca. So Ausnit hid him at the place of a cousin of Madame Lupescu.* When he emerged later into a considerably calmer atmosphere to which a semblance of legality had been restored, he was tried by a sympathetic military tribunal (the country being under martial law) and acquitted.[40] The Nicadori drew life sentences in prison.

*Waldeck, *Athene Palace*, p. 32. Apart from this source, other well-informed people have confirmed this version concerning the whereabouts of Codreanu.

After that it was impossible for the Legion to maintain its old form; the new law about "the protection of the order of the state" outruled that. Codreanu was pragmatic enough to form a political party to "make a bid to take power by constitutional means." He even made old General Cantacuzino Granicerul party president. The name of the party was All for the Fatherland (*Totul Pentru Ţara* — *T.P.Ţ.*). The nests, nest families, and all other Legionary organizations were left intact within it. Madame Lupescu was furious and in Bucharest foreign diplomats joked, "The Rumanian Pompadour lost her battle at Rossbach!"

With the new Liberal administration under the premiership of Gheorge Tǎtǎrescu, the most enigmatic and versatile character in Rumanian political life, cooperating with Carol, the Iron Guard, the Nazis, and finally with the Communists, a new period started: a move toward corporatism and fascism. The Liberals seem to have drawn some conclusions from their failure in the late twenties. These conclusions were coupled with the experiences of the depression, not over by far in 1934, to produce the decision that new Liberal policy was to be completely anti-liberal. It meant forcible industrialization emphasizing heavy and armament industries, to be financed not through private banks as in the 1920s, but through the National Bank, an old Liberal stronghold. Most of the new industries were in private hands. The protagonists were Auşnit, the versatile Greek Nicolae Malaxa, Mihai Constantinescu, Dumitriu Mociorniţă and the King, supported by the excellent business talents of Mme. Lupescu, and many less important figures, all members of one camarilla or the other. The new industries were to be protected against foreign competition by high tariffs. The capital was mostly domestic. All these measures put a heavy new burden on the shoulders of the peasantry. Mihail Manoilescu, the president of the National Bank, was the leader of the newly founded (1933) National Corporatist League[41] and the ideologist of this program. As the title of his new party shows, he also drew pertinent conclusions from the Liberal failure of the 1920s. Such burdens could never be accepted voluntarily by the majority of the people, especially in the fashion the industrialization was to be carried through. So the necessary coercion and pressure was proposed in the framework of a one-party system and a corporative Fascist state.[42] But the ultimate consequence of Liberal policy (after 1933 called neo-Liberal) was not realized until 1938, and then only because of the dangerous growth of Iron Guard competition. It was a fascism much more sympathetic to the peasant masses than that of the industrialists of the camarilla. Until then, the repressive apparatus of the regime, thinly veiled with parliamentary trappings, was enough to keep the peasant masses down. Living standards were the lowest in the Balkans, 243 international units in 1934* as compared with 284 in Bulgaria, 455 in Czechoslovakia and 1,069 in England.[43] The agrarian scissors was set at an angle of 59.4 percent as late as 1940, and the living standard was 33-64 percent lower than in 1916.[44] On one hand, the government

*The amount of goods and services that could be purchased in the U.S. for $1 between 1925-34.

promulgated ever-improved moratoriums on peasant debts; on the other hand, it applied its repressive apparatus for the collection of taxes and arrears with a ruthlessness the Rumanian lands had not seen since the time of Phanariote-Turkish rule. Indeed, many of the poor had their last belongings taken away to be sold at public auction. A typical announcement from the official paper, the *Monitorul Oficial,* about a coming auction: "On the eleventh of September there will be a public auction of two shirts, three cracked cups, a damaged glass, a thimble, two cudgels with the name[s] of Costache and Gradu on them, a reel of threads, the saucer-bottom of the damaged glass and a purse with [the content of] 2 lei."[45]

If the people looked for answers, the mystical religious nationalism of the Iron Guard was more easily digestible for the peasants than were Marxist doctrines. So was its social justice based on Christianity, and articulate and inarticulate youth was attracted to the Legion by the image of Codreanu and the many other young men who led it. Not only were the leaders of the Legion young,* but the most popular Legionary leaders came almost without exception from the provincial, just urbanized intelligentsia. The Legion by this time enjoyed a commanding position among Rumanian students,[46] and it received the vociferous support of a stratum whose very existence was a typical Rumanian anomaly. The prodigious increase in enrollment which characterized higher education in Greater Rumania was not an unmixed blessing. Many peasant sons who were admitted as university students were not ready for higher education. This is the main reason for the unprecedented fact that during the period 1921-32, only 8 percent of the students registered ever graduated. These semieducated malcontents (who were, understandably, frustrated on more than one account) joined the Legion in droves during the depression. The Legion succeeded in attracting also an extraordinary number of the lower Orthodox clergy.

Most of the support of the Iron Guard came from perennially depressed, Godforsaken, abysmally poor regions such as the villages of southern Bessarabia and Moldavia, and from the regions of the dense Carpathian forests like Neamț and Câmpulung, areas Codreanu and his friends visited during their long romantic marches, or like their Transylvania stronghold, Turda, the land of the Moți. But not only young officers, students and the peasantry, people from classes where the social anomaly was the greatest, came to the Legion. It also attracted some of the best names of the aristocracy, like Ghyca, Cantacuzino, Sturdza and many others.

Codreanu's most effective propaganda in these years was to be work, action and the example. Hundreds of voluntary labor camps of the Legion, then called the T.P.Ț. party, dotted the map of Rumania, repairing village bridges, roads and churches, building dams, digging wells and working "for the collective and national solidarity."[47] In these camps, the boyar son worked side by side with the son of the laborer and the peasant, creating a powerful feeling of national unity and renovation. If the new intellectuals who

*In 1934, Codreanu was 35, Moța, 32, Vasile Marin, 30, Mihai Stelescu, 27, and Horia Sima, 26 years old.

graduated (or failed to graduate) in increasing numbers from the universities and joined the ranks of the Legion were strongly anti-Semitic because of the Jewish middle classes blocking their way, the lower classes came to the Legion because they hoped to fulfill their desires for a social justice on a national rather than a Russian Bolshevik platform.

And no other nationalist or Fascist party could match the dynamism, the mystique or the popularity of the Iron Guard. In 1934, Vaida-Voevod finally broke with Maniu and, formally abandoning democracy, founded the Rumanian Front *(Frontul Romanesc)* with a frankly authoritarian program. In support of his Romanism, he demanded a chauvinistic restrictive policy against the nationalities, Hungarians and Jews in business, professions and education.[48] But this movement did not attract even a fraction of those who joined the Legion. Neither did the L.A.N.C., with its unbridled attacks on the Legion, its anti-Semitism and its middle-class ideas and membership.

In the years 1934-35, both King Carol and Prime Minister Tătărescu entertained highly dubious relations with the Legion. After all, the Legion was a force which could hardly be ignored, and the general Fascist upsurge indicated that it might easily become the wave of the future. Partly out of sympathy with its goals, partly out of expediency, both the king and Tătărescu were tolerant of its activities and did not exclude a future collaboration. Moreover, with Carol's hold on the country tightening, this lenience was important for the Legion. The king, always wishing to attract youth, founded his own Fascist youth organization in 1934, the Guards of the Fatherland *(Straja Țarii)*, which was heavily subsidized from above and made obligatory for every youth. But it was to remain an empty form without content. It could not steal the thunder of the Legion, for the image of Codreanu was much more appealing to the young. The national leader of the Guards of the Fatherland, Constantin Sidorovici, was later involved in a colossal graft scandal and committed suicide. And as the years went by, parallel with the increase of Carol's influence and interference in politics, the neo-Liberal policies of press censorship, telephone wire tappings and the brutality of the omnipresent secret police, the dreaded *Siguranța,* were steadily on the increase. This was the time of the first camarilla associated with the deceitful personality of Puju Dimitrescu.

In 1935 the L.A.N.C., feeling its own weakness and limited appeal, fused with Octavian Goga's National Agrarian party. Goga was a poet of no mean talent and for a long time had been an outstanding personality of Averescu's People's party, from which he seceded in 1932, to found his own party. He was a Transylvanian, and both in his past and his authoritarian, chauvinist, Fascist tendencies he closely resembled Vaida-Voevod. During his years as a student, he met Lueger and they became close friends.[49] Like so many who thought as he did, Goga showed anti-capitalist and Socialist tendencies as a student at Budapest University.[50] Also, he had the populist touch in those years, being in close contact with Constantin Stere.[51] These foundations bore ample fruits after the war when Goga turned to fascism and a violent anti-Semitism of a conservative Fascist mold, like that of the Szeged Fascists and Imrédists in Hungary. The program of the new party, the National Christian party with its emblem the swastika, proposed a semi-Fascist chamber, with a corporate upper house and a reduced number of representatives. It was devised to appeal to the middle classes, those who were interested in a speedy change of guard. But this being Rumania, they did not confine themselves to a merely anti-Semitic program; the Hungarians, who held a dominant position in Transylvanian towns, were also to be "restricted." The towns were to be Romanized, and the Ukranians, along with the Jews, Bulgarians, and Hungarians, were the "hostile" nationalities, while Armenians and Germans were the friendly ones.[52] And rightly so. Goga and Cuza had a highly successful visit with Hitler as early as 1935, and thereafter the Nazis supported the new Goga-Cuzist formation more than the Iron Guard. The Nazis, where Rumania and Hungary were concerned, were more interested in a subservient, stable, anti-Semitic government than in a group of nationalist mystics and social revolutionaries who promised only conflict of interest and internal upheavals. Docility was a desirable condition in countries they wished to use for their own purposes.*

The Cuzists got 133,205 votes in the elections of 1933, while Goga's National Agrarians polled 121,748, which meant 18 representatives for the new union in Parliament.[53] Most of the patently anti-Semitic vote for the Cuzists came, as before, from the heavily Jewish-inhabited towns of the northeast: Cernauţi, Bâlţi, Succeava, Iaşi.** The Goga-Cuzists adopted the outward Fascist trappings of the Iron Guard, i.e., belts and uniforms, colored shirts (blue instead of green), and parading the symbol of international anti-Semitism, the swastika, a Cuzist insignia of long standing. The party militia, the "lance bearers" (*Lancieri*), were responsible before 1940 for more anti-Semitic brutality and hooliganism than the Iron Guard, especially in the years 1935-37. During the same period, however, almost all anti-Semitic excesses were automatically attributed to the Legion, just as in Hungary they were almost always blamed on the Arrow Cross.

Understandably, relations between the Iron Guard and the Goga-Cuzists were very bad from the outset. No anti-Semite likes it if his monopoly is challenged within his borders. Cuza did not consider that the Iron Guard

---

*In November 1936 Hitler received the neo-liberal leader, Gheorge Brătianu, to whom he explained that if a "stable" Rumanian government were established, he would block any Hungarian revisionist claim. It was Rosenberg's department in the *Wilhelmstrasse* which hoped to carry out in Rumania the Fascist takeover (the *Volksbewegung*) with the help of Goga and Cuza. As in Hungary, they tried desperately at that point to bring together "the head and the body" — that is, a unity between the L.A.N.C. and the Legion, in which they were no more successful than they were in Hungary in bringing together Imrédy with the Arrow Cross, and for the same reasons. Hillgruber, *Hitler, König, Carol und Antonescu.* pp. 10-12.

**Enciclopedia Romaniei*, I, 242-43. It is clear that the Cuzist strongholds were in very different areas from those of the Legion.

"deserved to call itself anti-Semitic," and spoke about the "Judaization of Moța."[54] Codreanu forbade the admission of any Cuzist into the ranks of the Legion.

In the years of the neo-Liberal administration there was more platonic sympathy than fruitful contact between the German Nazis and the Legion, despite the successes of fascism in Europe. In July 1936, after the occupation of the Rhineland, Titulescu, the champion of collective security and Western orientation, was dismissed. Fascism seemed decidedly the spirit of the age, or as Codreanu in his military manner liked to call it, the "Command of the Age."*

The Iron Guard kept growing. As the majority of bourgeois anti-Semites opted for Goga and Cuza, the youth and the peasantry increasingly joined the ranks of the Legion. The year 1936 was an eminently successful one for the Legion, enjoying as it was an uneasy, hopeful toleration by the authorities — uneasy because of the extent of its growth, hopeful because Carol and the oligarchy still hoped to control and use it.

As the Legion increased in importance, it had to take a certain number of stands on practical issues of the day despite its acute revulsion to dealing with the problems of the sordid twentieth-century industrial age. These stands and attitudes were taken on an *ad hoc* basis when the Legion had to face them, and the result was a curious mixture of their ideology and more realistic considerations. Although it concentrated its activities in the villages, the Legion formed the Corps of Legionary Workers in 1936 and in addition to the dozens of labor camps, Codreanu ordered the Legion to enter a very new field for Rumanians, commerce. He wanted to prove that not only Jews could be successful in this area.[55] In less than a year, the Battalion of Legionary Commerce founded a chain of Legionary restaurants, groceries and repair shops covering Bucharest and the provincial towns. The income from these establishments financed vacations for underprivileged children and provided funds for the movement.[56] Besides the commercial establishments, there was a Legionary welfare organization, and steps were taken to organize Legionary cooperatives. At the opening of the Legionary sanatorium in Predeal, different payment rates were established. Everybody was to pay according to his conscience; the poor were not to pay at all. Said Codreanu at the opening ceremony, "A principle of justice says nobody can be his own judge. I answer: This principle humiliates humanity, because it has a weak or greedy man in sight. That's it. But I do not speak of man as he is but as he should or has to be."[57]

The Legion took a closer look at the nationality problem in these years, but its position remained inflexible. Nationalities were simply divided into Christian and Jewish. Regarding the Jews, there is no need to repeat, but even "Christian minorities can enjoy rights only in proportion to their loyalty to Rumania."[58] As for the U.S.S.R., there was no solution or rapprochement possible.[59] As for Hungarian pretensions, they were dismissed contemptuously — "Hungarian revisionist propaganda will not change the boundaries"

*Porunca Vremii, also the name of a Cuzist anti-Semitic newspaper.

290

and lest there be any doubt about the Legion's integral nationalism, Mihail Polihroniade added that Mussolini's words in favor of Hungary would not change the boundaries either.[60] Moța confidently confronted the pretensions of Greater Hungary with the fact of Greater Rumania.[61] When Hitler started to organize his Saxon-Germans in Transylvania during the *Sachsentag* in 1933, Moța remarked somberly that "there is a possibility of animosity between Germany and Rumania. The Germans must remain loyal to Rumania. Rumania will feed [only] loyal nationalities, but enemies will not be tolerated."[62] As another legionary ideologist stated, "The Rumanian is the ruling nation — minorities can have rights only in proportion to their loyalty to the Rumanian state." But he added realistically, "One can no longer denationalize any people in Europe by force."[63] Consequently, despite its acute hatred for democracy, until 1936 the Legion stood ready "to enforce respect of the [peace] treaties with all means. The revisionist states comprised one bloc and the victors another. Therefore, those powers which uphold Versailles must cooperate."[64] But this attitude changed radically during the year, and when in November 1936, after the poor showing of the Western powers in the Rhineland, Ethiopia, Spain and elsewhere, Codreanu addressed the King, we hear a different tune, more fitting to the Legion: "Two worlds confront each other . . . on one side the states of the nationalist revolution — on the other side bolshevism and its hangers-on." Then Codreanu made his point: "There is no Little Entente and Balkan Entente [any more]. He who still believes in it has not understood anything."[65] Codreanu had no reason to reverse this course in his lifetime.

On the pivotal question of financing the burgeoning Legionary movement, Codreanu showed originality. He established the Friends of the Legion *(Prietenii Legionarilor)*, consisting of both domestic and foreign sympathizers who because they were government employees or had business interests or for other reasons could not join the Legion openly. Their contributions were accepted and registered with gratitude.[66] Who were these friends? It would seem that despite the constant noisy accusations against the Legion for "being in German pay," the main contributions came from industrialists like Malaxa, from some rich aristocratic sympathizers, and also from Jewish industrialists and financiers such as Auşnit, Kaufman and Şapiro, as a kind of reinsurance.* What connections the Legion might have had in these years of truce with the *Siguranța* no one can tell. *In the vast underworld of these relations as they existed in Carolist Rumania, one heard many accusations but saw little or no evidence.*

With its growing importance, the Legion found it necessary to form (at its student conference of Tărgu Mureş in April 1936) a new and sinister detachment, the Death Commandos *(Echipa Morții)*, "to avenge the nation" and to "defend the *Capitanul*," which usually meant murdering their enemies.

---

*Despite presentations by Carol to the German ambassador about Nazi help to the Iron Guard, Professor Hillgruber could not establish any concrete data about Nazi financial support to the Legion. Hillgruber, *op. cit.*, p. 13.

Members of this detachment took a special oath over their sacred bags of native land.[67] Their greeting to one another was "Long live death! Long live the Legionary triumph!" They meant business. When Nicolae Stelescu, an old comrade of Codreanu, attempted in 1936 to split the Legion, by forming the Rumanian Crusade, for which he received a generous amount of money and a newspaper from sponsors (allegedly Madame Lupescu was in on it), all ten of the members of his nest participated in his punishment. Every one of them took a shot at the victim as he lay on his hospital bed recovering from an appendectomy. After that, "they chopped his body with an axe, danced around the pieces of flesh, prayed, kissed each other and cried with joy."[68] They surrendered to expiate their deed, and were sentenced to lifelong prison terms. They became another Legionary legend, the Decemviri. Many of their countrymen approved of this savagery: as the national poet laureate Eminescu had explained a long time before, "A political crime committed by a private person ceases to be a crime when it is based on higher views and dictated by the clean notion, even if mistaken, of saving the state." Wide is the range of action for people who are susceptible to such a rationalization. Only Maniu sent condolences to Stelescu's widow.[69]

Attacks on Jews and Hungarians increased, and at the end of the year, Moţa, Marin and five other Legionaries left for Spain to join Franco, leaving a moving testament to their foreboding of and readiness for death, which they offered as a sacrifice for Rumania in the worldwide struggle between good and evil. Shortly after that, in January 1937, Moţa and Marin fell at Majadahonda before Madrid. The nominal head of the T.P.Ţ. party, General Cantacuzino, solemnly handed a sword to General Moscardó, the defender of the Alcázar.

The funeral of Moţa, who was deputy captain of the Legion, and of Marin, leader of the Bucharest Legionary organization, showed the Legion's strength to both friend and foe. Their bodies were brought from Spain to Berlin and then were taken in a solemn procession to Bucharest. On the way to the capital, the train was met by tens of thousands and wherever it stopped the Orthodox clergy turned out to bless it. Mothers raised their children high to look at the fallen heroes. In Bucharest, hundreds of thousands of people, priests side by side with workers, students with army officers, peasants with intellectuals, marched behind the coffins to the little church of Ilie Gorgani, where they were laid to rest.[70] It was the Legionary guard that kept exemplary order in the huge crowds, as they marched along the Calea Victoriei, the main parade street of Bucharest. Their shouts, cheers, and Legionary songs reached the ears of the King and, among other considerations, aroused his savage jealousy. Surprisingly, Carol, despite his unabashed deceit, wanted to be loved by his people, he wanted to appeal to the young, to be a tribune. He wanted to be in the eyes of the Rumanians what his living antipode Codreanu was. In preparation for the coming elections, he used the issue of some Legionary lawlessness* to dismiss the pro-Legionary minister

*The Legion had its own "court" where it terrorized some Liberal student leaders. Rogger and Weber, *op. cit.,* p. 549n.

of interior, Ion Inculeţ. But the growth of the Legion could not be stopped in the framework of the existing parliamentary structure. There were 4,200 Legionary nests in 1935; by January 1937 there were 12,000, and by the end of the year there were 34,000! [71] Codreanu was telling the truth when he proclaimed that the Legion would "never resort to a conspiracy or a *coup d' état.*" There was no need for that. With its feverish activity in connection with the elections in November 1937, almost a dozen newspapers at its disposal, and the sympathetic help of many periodicals — the most important being the *Cuvântul* of Professor Nae Ionescu, whose philosophy was akin to the mystical orthodox Rumanian nationalism professed by the Legion — it could look to the future with confidence. On November 8, 1936, the day of St. Michael, the new Iron Guard headquarters, the Green House, was opened in Bucharest.

To prevent the government from using its terror apparatus in the elections, the T.P.Ţ. party concluded an electoral alliance both with Maniu's party and with right-wing Liberal splinter groups. This did not signal Maniu's conversion to fascism, as the Communists later tried to present it. There was as yet no political agreement or joint electoral list established; the agreement helped Codreanu, harmed Maniu, and confused the peasant electorate.* It also was the testimony of the loss of confidence in democratic ranks. As for the Iron Guard, Codreanu instructed its members that they must not vote for Cuzists under any circumstances in the areas where there were no T.P.Ţ. lists. "The Cuzists are only a different face of the government."[72] There were violent clashes between the Legion and the *Lancieri* of the Cuzists — despite Codreanu's repeated call for a maximum of self-control.[73] But during the election — as before and after it — it was the Legion which proved itself to be the rising political force in Rumania, with its slogans "For every man, half a hectare of land!" or "The hectare and with it the soul!"**Shortly before the elections Codreanu declared:

I am against the great Western democracies. I am against the Little Entente, and the Balkan Entente. I have no use for the League of Nations. In forty-eight hours after the Legionary victory, Rumania will have a close alliance with Rome and Berlin.[74]

Despite sporadic government abuses during the election, the Legion won 16.5 percent of the votes; it got sixty-six deputies into the chamber and became the third largest party in the land.

What was even more important, this relatively decent election brought a crushing defeat to the Liberals. They did not win the 40 percent of votes necessary for the premiership. The Cuzists won 9 percent of the vote, most of

*The clandestine Communist party nevertheless instructed its members to vote for the National Peasants. Roberts, *Rumania: Political Problems of an Agrarian State*, p. 191.

**"*Omul şi pogonul!*" "*Hectărul şi sufletul!*" The pogon being about half a hectare, this promise sounds quite demagogic; although some maintain that the slogans above were to signify the attachment of the peasant to the land rather than a new, impossible distribution of it.

their constituents being the anti-Semitic city dwellers, and people from towns with large Jewish populations.[75] The dissatisfied masses went with the Legion, not with the sterile middle class anti-Semitism of the Goga-Cuzists.

The King was now in a difficult position. He had to dismiss the Liberals, but he did not wish to call upon Maniu's National Peasants to form a government (they received 21 percent of the vote), both because of the extremely bad relations between Maniu and Carol (with Madame Lupescu lurking in the background) and because Carol had little taste for democracy. To appoint an Iron Guard regime was inconceivable. Carol solved the problem by appointing a Goga-Cuzist government (leaving many government posts in the hands of trusted Carolists, Calinescu as minister of interior being the most important among them) under the premiership of the poet Goga. Not only was Goga absolutely loyal to Carol and his camarilla and in her own words a "firm friend" of Madame Lupescu,[76] but he was also considered nationalist and Fascist enough to appease the widespread clamor for fascism. Goga was convinced that his premiership would reassure Germany.[77] If his presence in the government reassured Hitler, the presence of his good friend General Antonescu in the government as minister of defense reassured the English and the French.

General Ion Antonescu, after Codreanu and Maniu the third incorruptible of the interwar period in Rumania, came from a humble family of Pitești in Wallachia. Small, red-haired, strong willed, determined, with a volatile temper and a long vindictive memory which earned him the nickname "Red Dog," he was a true Rumanian patriot in the sense that he looked at Rumania's interests. He was an implacable enemy of communism and considered the U.S.S.R. the hereditary enemy. He was not very enthusiastic about Germany even before the Nazi advent to power. He believed the battles of Tannenberg and Verdun had saved the old world in the great war.[78] And the two heroes of those battles, Marshal Pétain and Field Marshal von Hindenburg, are good keys to Antonescu's ideas of authoritarian conservatism. That he had more vigor than they can be explained by his being some thirty years their junior. Antonescu, as he explained to Hitler later, did not believe in revolutions, only in reorganization. He disdained ideologies. For him "the indispensable thing was an instrument which would guarantee order, tranquility and security."[79] During the long years of his stay in London as Rumanian military attaché, he made strong speeches against the "new barbarisms rising on the banks of the Spree and the Moscow Rivers"; he wished England a new victory in the coming struggle against these evil forces,[80] and he was a good friend of General Maurice Gamelin. But Western performance in the late 1930s shook his faith in English willingness to achieve such a victory. Finally, like Maniu and in large degree Codreanu in Carol's eyes, his undoing was his scrupulous honesty and his flat refusal to pay homage to Madame Lupescu and to permit her meddling in the business of the armed forces.[81] In addition, Antonescu made too much of a nuisance of himself as a kind of Cassandra pointing out the miserable deficiencies, the colossal graft and the unpreparedness of the Rumanian army. Nevertheless, he was as much feared as he was respected in the leading circles of Bucharest in general and the armed forces in particular. Everybody, including the King, knew that he was the kind of person whom one must not cross unless one destroyed him.

Goga and Cuza, after their appointment to the government, unleashed an unprecedented anti-Semitic terror.* Jews were deprived of their citizenship by the hundreds of thousands, their businesses were closed, and they were dismissed from the professions. Good proof of the profitable character of the anti-Semitic boom is that the *Lancieri,* the Jew-baiting ruffians, increased their number from one thousand to tens of thousands within a very short time. The most unrestrained anti-Semites filled the administrative posts of towns like Cernauţi, Iaşi, and others with the heaviest Jewish population. In the realm of the arts, the "Rumanian classic," *Bloodsucker of the Village,* a century-old play depicting Jewish activities in the villages, was hastily dusted off for the cultural enlightenment of the Rumanian public. As Goga explained in an interview granted to a publicity agent of King Carol, "I keep the poet and the politician in two separate rooms." He continued that the door betwen these two rooms was closed. In politics he was a realist, and if the Jews were in truth the salt of mankind, he found the Rumanian dish too salty. He did not intend to deal with the Jews in a poetic manner.[82]

As this shaky government continued its anti-Semitic outrages, the Jews went into an impressive passive resistance, paralyzing business. Their leader, Willy Fildermann, immediately made moves in London and Paris, and in the League of Nations, asking intervention. The French, British, and American ministers protested. When the United States minister, Franklin Mott Gunther, handed a protest to Goga from Jewish organizations in America, Goga remarked: "These [the American Jews] are merely impudent!"[83] The U.S.S.R. broke diplomatic relations. But if Goga was not worried about the West, the King and many other politicians of the non-Nazi line were increasingly so.

With economic disruption on the increase, new elections were ordered to take place in March. A full-fledged war ranged between Cuzists and the Iron Guard in which two Legionaries were murdered, fifty-two gravely wounded, and 450 arrested.** Abruptly, on the eighth of February, the contending parties concluded an armistice. Both the T.P.Ţ. and the Cuzists were to run in the election, but Codreanu withdrew from the campaign.[84] He could afford to; the mood of the country was such that he could be almost certain of an Iron Guardist victory. Carol made a last effort to form a government of national concentration which would suit the popular will and yet be in its majority the tool of the camarilla. He proposed to Codreanu through General Antonescu (a friend of Codreanu) a coalition government of Goga, Vaida and

*This violent campaign was carried out by Professor Cuza much against the wishes of Goga. Hillgruber, *op. cit.,* p. 16.

**Codreanu, *Circulări, scrisori, sfături, gânduri,* p. 82. Goga found it necessary to ask the Germans "not to support the Iron Guard, in order to avoid supporting one rightist party against another." Hillgruber, *op. cit.,* p. 15.

Codreanu. When Codreanu refused, fearing that the people would think that he had become the tool of the King, the die was cast.[85] The versatile, resourceful King had to destroy the Iron Guard by any means at his disposal. On February 12, 1938, Goga was simply dismissed. He departed most disgracefully, ending his farewell address on the radio with the sentence which has become celebrated: "Israel, you have won! " Shortly after that Goga died.

4

The same day, Carol, in his pleasant voice, told his tense, anguished people on the radio that "in hard times only heroic methods can strengthen Rumania, the salvation of which is our supreme law, which I will obey without hesitation!"[86] In order to save his country, the King suspended the democratic constitution, dissolved all political parties, and promulgated a new, frankly Fascist, corporatist constitution, with greatly increased royal prerogatives. These changes were duly endorsed in a referendum in which the open voting yielded some 99 percent of the votes for Carol. The evolution of Liberal economic and political thought and activity had arrived at its logical conclusion: a corporatist Fascist state under the leadership of an industrializing and industrialist clique, with the King established as the virtual dictator of Rumania.

The new government Carol formed was a kind of cabinet of "all talents" — nationalist talents who were loyal to the King. The Patriarch Miron Christea was prime minister,* but the real power in the government was in the hands of the minister of interior, Armand Calinescu, who had defected from the Maniu camp to that of the King and the camarilla. He came from peasant stock in Argeş, the very heart of Wallachia. Anti-Axis, forceful, corrupt, utterly unscrupulous, with a black patch over his right eye (lost through an infection in childhood), he was precisely the desperado Carol needed to stabilize his new system.

The forced industrialization reached an intensity during the royal dictatorship it had not known before, the industrialization process being carried out by the second camarilla, usually associated with the new member of its inner core, Colonel Ernest Urdareanu, the palace marshal. He was as corrupt as anybody in Bucharest — and that is to say much because during the last two-and-a-half years of Carolist rule, that is to say, during the period of Carol's personal dictatorship, corruption reached unheard of proportions. Yet, Urdareanu, perhaps after Madame Lupescu the most hated person in the country, was absolutely loyal to Carol, and he consistently defended the interests of the King and Madame Lupescu, as he saw their interests, with vigor. But here lay the deficiency of his loyalty: he succeeded by doing, in establishing himself as a roadblock between King and nation, to the extent

*The Patriarch was a Transylvanian. It was the irony of fate that the worst persecutions of the ultra-Orthodox Legion took place while the head of the Orthodox Church was the head of the government.

that even Crown Prince Michael called him "Murdareanu"* in private.

Besides the Carol–Lupescu–Urdareanu trio, the camarilla consisted of Calinescu; Professor Iorga, who as an old-style conservative nationalist now participated in the government of national concentration; Marinescu, the prefect of Bucharest; and Moruzov, a shoddy adventurer and former Russian refugee, who became the head of Carol's dreaded personal secret police.** It also included various industrialists (Auşnit, Malaxa), and financiers like Aristide Blank, who were in disgrace from time to time when their business interests or activities clashed with those of the royal industrialist, Carol.

Peasant misery increased, and the unhealthy process of breaking up the peasant holdings into middle-sized holdings and creating an increasing agrarian proletariat continued apace. But the new industrial complexes, the Reşiţa, Malaxa, Titan-Nǎdrǎg-Cǎlǎn, Metaloglobus and I.A.R. (a Rumanian aircraft industry paid for by every Rumanian with an excise tax on postage stamps), guaranteed fabulous profits for the camarilla and those few others near enough to the pork barrel.[87] The unquestioned business talents of Madame Lupescu played more than their share in these schemings; her influence on Carol was tremendous. Codreanu was right when he contemptuously remarked, "Madame orders and the King wishes." But this does not mean that Madame was ever isolated; with a few honorable exceptions Bucharest high society fawned on her, knowing that the road to career and money led through her salon.***

The new Fascist constitution, promulgated by decree, contained one particularly significant paragraph: every minister was selected by the King, was solely responsible to him, and what is more important, had to be of Rumanian nationality for at least three generations. This was obviously aimed at the Zelinski family. Codreanu's answer to all that, taking into account that he had the most powerful mass organization in Rumania under his control, was a surprisingly docile one. He dissolved the T.P.Ţ. party in a protest which

*Murdar in Rumanian meaning the equivalent of merde in French.

**Not the Siguranţa, but a special contingent that looked out for Carol's personal interests, security and business.

***Some letters Madame Lupescu left after her flight, deliberately no doubt, to embarrass her idolators and flatterers, the intrinsic value of whose words were known to nobody better than to this ruthless, cold, clever Jewess, give a good insight into the prevailing Byzantinism of the Carolist era. The greatest ladies and gentlemen of Rumania addressed her as "Darling Duduja." One internationally known Rumanian princess wrote that "the moment today when you allowed me to kiss your hand was the happiest in my life." A high dignitary of the regime addressed her as "Your Majesty," continuing that he had but one wish and that was to see her crowned as the "rightful queen of Rumania." Another high dignitary addressed Lupescu casually as "Ma souveraine." (Waldeck, op. cit., p. 208.) The Legionaries later held these letters as a sort of Damocles sword over the heads of Bucharest high society, which then was making frantic efforts to accommodate itself with the Legion. And, of course, speaking of Madame only as "dirty Jewess."

he transmitted to all members of the government.[88] The reason for Codreanu's seemingly meek compliance was that just a week or two before the *Anschluss* he saw the tide turning in his favor all the way to southeastern Europe. "Does the King intend to govern alone? We don't mind," he said. "We are young, we can wait."[89]

But Carol could not feel comfortable while his brand of fascism had a rival, championed by a much more appealing, popular and charismatic leader than he. With industry and finance behind him, and with the army and police loyal, he moved during the spring against the Iron Guard. Even before the coup of February 12, a plan was forged by the camarilla to assassinate Codreanu. But the foreign minister, Istrate Micescu, selected the wrong instrument for it: the Cuzist prefect of Neamţ, V. Emilian (who tried to found a Nazi movement on an N.S.D.A.P. model himself before he joined the Goga-Cuzists) notified Codreanu immediatley after Micescu's offer. The eruption of scandal was averted by two days through Carol's coup on February 12.[90] With absolute control over the state and with the loopholes of an imperfect constitutional system eliminated, Carol could proceed in other ways. Professor Iorga, in his resurrected *Neamul Romanesc,* started a series of violent attacks on the Iron Guard. When Codreanu replied, he was arrested and sentenced to six months' imprisonment on a libel charge. But this was not considered enough for the security of the regime.

Why did Codreanu not go into exile? A Legionary leader recalls that when prospects of temporary emigration to Italy were discussed as an alternative to incarceration on the Insula Şerpilor, a lonely, barren island at the mouth of the Danube, Codreanu refused to go — he preferred the island.[91] He said to one of the last Legionaries he saw before his imprisonment that "the Legion must retreat now and wait for better days, which will come soon," because "the Carolist dictatorship can not last."[92] Codreanu's analysis was correct; but he was not to see those better days. Soon he was retried on the charge of heading a widespread espionage and terrorist organization in the service of a "foreign power." If part of the accusation, the organized terror, seems to be true, the prosecution certainly did not present any watertight proof of Codreanu's personal responsibility in it. There was no evidence of any foreign-power connection. The connections with Nazi Germany seem to have gone through Goga-Cuzists and even the pro-Fascist, neo-Liberal wing of Gheorghe Brătianu rather than through the Legion.* This time the military tribunal was chosen from the right people. Despite General Antonescu's courageous intervention as a witness on Codreanu's behalf, the sentence was a foregone conclusion.** Codreanu's pro-Axis declarations during the previous

---

*The Legionaries, as they wrote in a letter to Charles Maurras, refused Nazi invitations. Rogger and Weber, *op. cit.,* p. 553.

**General Antonescu's intervention on behalf of Codreanu was the final straw in Carol's eyes. He was retired and kept virtually under house arrest. It was at this time that the Nazis succeeded in establishing their first contacts with Antonescu through the widow of the deceased poet-prime minister, Mme. Veturia Goga. Hillgruber, *op. cit.,* p. 270.

elections and his 1936 letter to the King served as "irrefutable evidence," on the basis of which he was condemned to a ten-year prison term. Immediately after Codreanu's arrest, on April 16, Calinescu struck. About 30,000 Legionary homes were searched and thousands of Legionaries arrested, the police making a good haul. Gheorge Clime, the leader of the Legion appointed by Codreanu after his arrest, and almost the whole Legionary elite were imprisoned in the concentration camps and prisons of Jilava, Miercurea-Ciucului, Râmnicul-Sărăt and Vaslui. The violent persecution of the Iron Guard was intensified during the summer and fall. From then on, the emblem of the Legion, the crossed bars of a prison, was well deserved.

Many of the Legionary rank and file took refuge in the forests of the Transylvanian Alps and the Carpathians, but the ingenious system of nests continued to exist. In many cases, however, the advantage of continued existence was balanced by the obvious disadvantage of isolation once the central command was knocked out by Calinescu. Many Legionary refugees were integrated into the still existing nests in areas where they were hiding.[93]

Despite its confident statements, the government was well aware that the Legion retained the capacity to stir up further trouble. The indefatigable Istrate Micescu contacted the decapitated Legion on behalf of Carol in September 1938, proposing that they accept the King as captain instead of Codreanu. The Iron Guard flatly refused.[94]

Many Legionaries took refuge in Nazi Germany and in Poland. The very route of contact between the nests at home and the exiles in Berlin led through the Poland of the colonels.[95] With its leadership imprisoned, the discipline of the Legion relaxed, both concerning its connections and reliance on Germany, and its activity in Rumania. It is difficult to see how any discipline could have been enforced in the existing fragmented, persecuted, isolated nest system. It was during these months that a rather secondary personality, who because of his relative unimportance was able to evade arrest, became the leader of the Legion.

Horia Sima came from Făgăraş in the Transylvanian Alps; he was the student of Professor Nae Ionescu and the regional Legionary chief of the Banat, and he was thirty years old in 1938. With the elite behind prison walls, he became the commander of the Legion. Sima never had the integrity or the vision of Codreanu. His inflammatory leaflets unleashed a terror campaign, mainly against the Jews, but attacks were made during the months of September and October against gendarme posts, too. Codreanu was most unhappy about these senseless outrages; he felt and rightly so that these bestialities endangered his life. He alternately sent out warnings to Sima and relapsed into a religious fatalism, looking forward to the inevitable that would be the ultimate proof of his devotion, the sacrifice that would be rewarded with the resurrection of Rumania through a Legionary victory.

Codreanu was right in his fears and hopes. The international situation changed steadily in his favor. Munich shifted the whole international balance in the Danube Valley, and there was little question about a future German predominance there. Consequently, right after Munich, Bucharest initiated a cautious course of rapprochement with Germany. But Carol and the camarilla were understandably suspicious about the rise of a great revisionist power, although the friendly German overtures toward Rumania and Yugoslavia put his country in a very different category from that in which Czechoslovakia found itself.[96] The Germans were not interested at that point in establishing a Guardist regime in Rumania.* Their policy, to which they would adhere for the duration of the war, was expressed later by Dr. Hermann Neubacher, their wartime economic dictator in Rumania and the Balkans: "We have but one aim, and that is to maintain quiet in the raw material sphere. We do not wish to Germanize Rumania or to make her Fascist. Any strong government which has the authority to maintain quiet in the raw material sphere will do."[97]

But Carol temporized too long, trying to hold a balance in his relations between the West and Germany, his sympathies being clearly on the Franco-English side. In the end, he exasperated the Germans and did not establish the desired quiet.** An oligarchic government of Carolists with a sprinkling of Goga-Cuzists who effectively controlled the administration and the police and served German interests, supplying the German war machine with the necessary raw materials, would have satisfied Hitler — at least until he had won the war.*** After that, he had his designs on this area, designs of which Gömbös, Imrédy, Szálasi, Codreanu, Sima, Antonescu and the other collaborators never dreamed. So in November 1938, after Carol's trip to London and Paris, he stopped over in Berchtesgaden on his way back to "keep the balance." We have no absolutely reliable account about what happened between him and Hitler. According to one version, Hitler exasperated Carol by contemptuously dismissing his brand of fascism, saying there existed only one dictator for Rumania and that was Codreanu.[98] As the other (and more plausible) version would have it, Hitler stated his intention of basing his policy upon the Carolist dictatorship and reassured him about Hungarian revisionist claims, and went so far in accommodating Carol that when he complained to Hitler about the rather aggressive behavior of the

*Sir Reginald Hoare, the British ambassador in Bucharest, stated that the "Iron Guard was not directed by Germany, and remained a pre-Nazi formation." Rogger and Weber, *op. cit.*, p. 554.

**Carol had an excellent chance to become a proconsul for Hitler in Rumania. And no wonder. Rumania had the *sine qua non* of a modern war: oil. In 1937, Göring frankly stated: "Without Rumania we can not start a campaign." (Lebedev, *op. cit.*, p. 33. Also *Pravda* May 14, 1938.) If Carol had not played both sides in 1939, it is highly improbable that Hitler would have given Bessarabia to the U.S.S.R. in the Nazi-Soviet Pact.

***In April, 1938, Hitler assured the Rumanian ambassador that "he has only economic interests in the Balkan states, and reaffirmed the promise he made concerning Hungarian revisionist claims to Gheorghe Brătianu." (Hillgruber, *op. cit.* p. 18.) German-Rumanian unofficial contacts of consequence went through Mme. Veturia Goga, and Professor Mihai ("Ica") Antonescu (no kin to the general) and Gh. Brătianu in the days of the Carolist dictatorship.

German leader in Rumania, Arthur Konradi,* Hitler agreed in principle to his recall, but ordered both the German Ambassador Wilhelm Fabrizius and Konradi to Berlin before he would take a final decision in the matter.[99] It is possible that the meeting with Hitler left Carol with the impression that he had a free hand to deal with the Iron Guard. It is reasonable to assume that the consequences in either case could be deadly for Codreanu, because despite his repeated warnings to Sima to stop provocations, the Guard went on a vicious rampage, coordinating it, as if as a challenge, with Carol's visit with Hitler.** This time the targets were not only synagogues and Jewish shops; they murdered Professor F. Ştefanescu-Goânga, the anti-Guardist rector of Cluj University, a relative of Calinescu and also Colonel Cristescu, a high official in Cernauţi.***

Carol's response to this challenge was swift and merciless. On November 30, the office of the military attorney attached to the Second Army Corps reported that the night before, Codreanu, the Nicadori and the Decemviri, fourteen men in all, had been "shot while trying to escape."[100] In reality, they were loaded into a truck, tied with ropes, and when the truck stopped on a deserted road they were strangled to death and then shot, brought back to the military prison in Jilava near Bucharest, and buried in a common grave there. Another three Legionaries were murdered on December 3.[101]

5

Hitler was furious about the murder of Codreanu, the more because he thought the world might conclude that Carol carried out the murders in agreement with him. He ordered that all orders and medals which Carol had generously distributed to German officials, especially to Göring, be returned to the Rumanian Embassy. He gave the Nazi press a free hand to abuse Carol,**** and finally the German ambassador was instructed to protest

---

*Konradi, about sixty, paralyzed and directing his activities from bed, was the dreaded head of the Nazi party in Rumania. He had his own spy network, and kept in line even Fabrizius. He represented the party in the ubiquitous conflict with the German state, carrying on a relentless struggle against the evangelical church of the Transylvanian Saxons. He was the most formidable *Volksdeutsch* leader besides Konrad Henlein in the *Südostraum.* Carol saw in him the middle man between the N.S.D.A.P. and the Iron Guard. Hillgruber, *op. cit.*, pp. 275, 109-10.

**Pe marginea prăpăstiei, II, 130; also, the German ambassador Fabrizius observed, perhaps correctly, that "Guardist violence broke out always when other Rumanian politicians who were not Guardists tried to reach an understanding with Germany." Hillgruber, *op. cit.*, p. 276.

***While talking to Hitler, Carol was called to the telephone several times and was told about these Guardist outrages. He never seems to have mentioned them to Hitler. Hillgruber, *op. cit.*, pp. 28-29.

****This permission was taken up by the committed Nazi Germans (especially the party and the SS, from which most of the sympathy for the Legion

301

officially in Bucharest.[102] But ultimately sober realism put an end to this outburst of the nationalist international. In a month or so German-Rumanian relations became normal.[103] During the next eighteen months the Germans did their best to woo Carol.*

On December 20, 1938, amid new and savage Legion persecutions inexorably conducted by Calinescu, Carol proclaimed the foundation of his own Fascist party, with all the trappings and uniforms that went with it. He called it the Front of National Rebirth (*Frontul Renaşterii Naţională*) without, however, promulgating anti-Semitic legislation. Everyone conformed to these new arrangements of the oligarchy with the predictable exception of Maniu and Mihalache, who refused to wear the Fascist uniforms prescribed for deputies and were therefore refused admittance to the Senate.

But behind all the Fascist trappings, the essence of the regime remained the same. At the beginning of 1939, after the death of the Patriarch, the real power in the government, Calinescu, assumed the premiership at last. In February he gave a confident interview to *Paris-Soir*: "The Iron Guard is an old story . . . the Iron Guard no longer exists."[104] Lloyds of London was of another opinion and refused a life insurance policy for Calinescu, an appraisal which was to prove cruelly accurate.[105]

The Legion was not dead. Its new leader (Horia Sima had fled to Germany) was the attorney Ion Victor Voziu,[106] who was soon to escape to the nationalists of Ruthenia before the terror of Calinescu. The nests, though isolated from each other, kept on plotting. The lack of contact often led to confusion so that the same action was planned by two or three nests at the same time, and the members unnecessarily exposed to merciless repression. As for the terror, it more than held its own with that of the Gestapo or the N.K.V.D. Captured Legionaries were tortured, murdered, and their mutilated bodies quietly and efficiently cremated.

Yet the flame of resistance flickered on. In January 1939 some Bucharest nests planned a grandiose attack with flamethrowers on the government buildings, their preparations being in an advanced state when they were apprehended.[107] In June some nests wanted to toss a dozen hand grenades

---

came in the future on an individual basis rather than a matter of policy) with a relish. Editorialized *Angriff*, the paper of the Waffen SS: "The Tale of a King and his Jewish Mistress" (Esther) arriving at a most unbiblical conclusion: "The Jews infected and poisoned his Kingdom and Persia went to pieces! " *Angriff*, December 8, 1938; also, *Time*, December 19, 1938, p. 15.

*Which does not mean that Hitler ever forgave Carol for murdering Codreanu. Years after, in July, 1940, during the Transylvanian crisis, Hitler burst out to the Hungarian delegation (to Teleki and Csáky) "The blood of Codreanu should be avenged on Rumania as a whole." (*Allianz*, p. 274.) And some months later in a conversation with Sztójay he again "most vehemently condemned the murder of Codreanu." (*Ibid*, p. 284). And during the war he still maintained that Codreanu was the "man predestined" to lead Rumania. Ernst Nolte: *Three Faces of Fascism* (New York, Chicago, San Francisco, 1966), p. 455.

into Carol's box during a horse race.[108] Madame Lupescu, a top priority on the list of the Death Commandos, was in constant danger. Isolated outrages against Jews continued on an uninterrupted and increasing scale. One Guardist terror squad murdered Ion Borseanu, the leader of the Transylvanian Agrarian Democrats. Many high government officials received picture postcards from Swinemünde, Germany, showing a group of well-known Guardists with the words, "Don't forget, we are still alive."[109] And in German exile, the Guardists regrouped themselves and waited for a future they believed to be theirs.*

Europe meanwhile moved rapidly toward the renewal of the conflict of 1914-18 after the "armistice of twenty years," as Marshal Foch accurately predicted in 1919. In March 1939 Hitler entered Prague, and Hungary annexed Ruthenia. Carol was worried about the revisionary success of Hungary, which had the largest, most irreconcilable minority in his realm. He ordered a mobilization, which should have demonstrated to him the abysmally poor preparedness of his army, and all over the country proclaimed a slogan which was soon to come home to roost: "[We shall] not [give back] a furrow [of land]! " In the meantime, while accepting an English guarantee of Rumania's independence and territorial integrity, he concluded an all-important economic agreement, the so called Wohlthat Treaty, with Germany. Although the short-term advantages of the treaty, which exchanged Rumanian agrarian products and raw materials for German finished goods, were obvious, it hampered the development of Rumanian industry, and assured a dominant position for Germany in the Rumanian economy; consequently, it restricted the political independence of Rumania greatly.[110] But with an English guarantee and an overwhelming economic commitment to Germany, Carol hoped to have pleased everybody and have secured himself for the time being. Meanwhile, Calinescu tried to imitate in his speeches the style and evangelistic language of the Guardists and to capture their thunder with his social demagoguery.

The German-Soviet agreement was an ominous foreboding of things to come for the whole eastern half of No-Man's-Land. It was not misunderstood in Bucharest — not even in Guardist circles.** After the Russians moved against Poland, Rumania quickly renounced her treaty with Poland, which had purportedly been concluded exactly for such an occasion. At the same time, Polish refugees were welcomed in Rumania and given all assistance to proceed to France and England.

Some days later, in the afternoon of September 21, 1939, the Iron Guard carried through the great feat which in a certain sense was to be its undoing. Six of them ambushed Calinescu's car on an open street in downtown Bucharest, shot him to death and, driving to the headquarters of *Radio Romania,* broke into the studio and announced in trembling, triumphant

---

*Their most famous detachment was the *Rasleţii* (exiles) under the command of Văsilie Iasinschi.

**Even those Guardists in German exile were critical of the pact. Papanace, *Orientări politice in primul exil,* p. 3.

tones: "The Iron Guard killed Calinescu! The murder of the captain has been avenged!" After that, true to Legionary tradition, they gave themselves up to the police in expiation. The fury of Carol and the camarilla knew no bounds. Calinescu was the strongman and the King's most trusted adviser, executioner, friend and administrator; he proved to be irreplaceable. The oligarchy was in a position to show its resentment. The very day of the murder of Calinescu, his assassins and their accomplices were shot on the spot of the murder and left there to rot for days.

But that was not to be all. In every county, a certain number of Legionaries had to be executed or hung from telegraph poles or lamp posts, their bodies displayed in such a state for days for the edification of the people. Some sympathetic prefects handed a few criminals to the execution squads instead of Legionaries, but such cases were rare. It is impossible to tell exactly how many Legionaries perished. Various figures are given. It is reasonable to assume about 250 to 300. But it was not the quantitative side of the extermination campaign which hurt the Legion most. When the regime's terror squads burst into the concentration camps of Râmnicul-Sărăt, Vaslui, Miercurea-Ciucului and the hospital in Braşov, they shot Clime, the T.P.Ţ. leader; Polihroniade, the Legion's foreign policy expert, who had earned the dubious fame of being the Rumanian Göbbels; Prince Cantacuzino (junior); the brilliant attorney Tell; the comrades in arms of Moţa in Spain, Totu and Dobre; perhaps the most admirable man in the Legion after Codreanu, the Transylvanian Ion Banea; the professor of engineering, Ionică; the poets V. Cardu and C. Goga; the student leaders Furdui, Cotigâ, Antoniu and V. Radulescu and the youth leader, Istrati, to name only the most outstanding. This bloodletting was considered by some Legionaries a terrible thing, "but it got the Legion out of a critical situation and restored its faith."[111] Others might agree with the rather sour appraisal the writer heard in comtemporary Rumania: After these massacres the Legion was "like a potato ... the best part of it was under the earth." The Iron Guard still found itself decapitated, leaderless, when a year after the massacres it had to face the responsibilities of power and try to live up to the high ideals it had set out to accomplish.

The German press, despite the fact that the whole plot against Calinescu was planned by Iron Guard exiles in Germany, began such a nauseating campaign against the Legion that Guardist exiles protested to Göbbels.* At home the new Patriarch, Nicodem, condemned the Guard and approved the bloody government reprisals.

*C. Papanace, *Orientări politice in primul exil*, p. 1. Not only did the Germans fail to intervene on behalf of the Legionaries but they never even protested against the massacres. (Hillgruber, *op. cit.*, p. 66.) One may get some idea of the conditions prevailing in Rumania from the fact that the Rumanian state radio read letters demanding the extermination of all the relations and lineage of those who murdered Calinescu, with the comment that the government "will consider the fulfillment of the demands expressed in the letters." *Népszava*, September 25, 1939.

It was hard for Carol to find a worthy successor to "little Hercules," as Calinescu was called. General Gheorghe Argeşanu had succeeded him briefly in order to organize the bloodbath. He died at the hands of the Legion a year later because of this, the fourth premier in a row to be murdered by them in seven years. He was succeeded at the end of September by Constantin Argetoianu, who was succeeded in November by the Liberal leader Tătărescu. Tătărescu headed the government for the rest of the Phoney War, until the collapse of France.

Rumania declared its neutrality in September 1939, and the majority of her press promptly began publishing pro-Allied (i.e., pro-French) editorials predicting the speedy defeat of the ill-fed, ill-trained German hordes. France, mighty France, would take care of them. Meanwhile, Bucharest was the living center of the Balkans. The *douce décadence* was indeed sweet during the winter of 1939-40. There was a lot of money to be made by those who had access to it, for those who had "influential connections." Party followed party, orgy followed orgy. Carol decided to enlarge his palace, and block after block was condemned on the Calea Victoriei; the brother of Madame Lupescu, Constantin (Shloim), made millions on the project. The survivors of the Guard found it expedient to sit out the storm in their nests or in exile. A law was passed promising the death penalty for everyone leading a political organization from abroad.

Despite growing German economic domination, Carol's neutrality leaned toward Paris and London. By the spring of 1940, however, he was growing progressively uneasy. The murderers of Calinescu were permitted reburial according to the rites of the Orthodox Church. Tătărescu and a talented defector from Maniu's party to the camarilla, Mihai Ghelmegheanu, worked incessantly on a reconciliation between the Iron Guard and Carol — but the Iron Guard had moral scruples.[112] The release of the Legionary smaller fry from jails began. In March, Carol announced that the Iron Guard had pledged allegiance to his F.R.N.

Then came the German attack on the West. Although much of articulate Rumania watched the Nazi advance with unfeigned disgust, and although the fall of Paris had a shattering effect, Carol could not afford to waste time on lamentations. He renounced the Anglo-French guarantee and transformed his F.R.N. into a totalitarian party, the Party of the Nation (*Partidul Naţiunei*). He invited the Iron Guard and other Fascist groups to join, announcing that the officials who in recent years had been guilty of killing Iron Guardists would be punished. (That announcement caused considerable hilarity in Rumania). Horia Sima returned to legal political activity and with two other Guardists joined the new government headed by the pro-German Ion Giugurtu, who replaced Tătărescu at the beginning of July. The Fascist ideologist, economist and friend of the Guard, Manoilescu, was foreign minister. Anti-Semitic legislation was introduced in great haste, and the new minister of propaganda, C. Giurgescu, could congratulate his King; "What the Führer has accomplished for Germany, our King has accomplished for us."[113] Sima was less optimistic, although he called upon the Guardists to support Carol's new party, he had some somber forebodings: "The whole world is going topsy-turvy . . . It is possible that our country will meet with misfortune."[114] In August, because of a split within the Legion (the Maximalists insisting on Carol's abdication), Sima resigned from the government, leaving two Guardists behind.[115]

The misfortune predicted by Sima was not long in coming. On June 25, a few days after Carol's move, the intrinsic value of which did not escape the eyes of the Germans, the Russians demanded to be ceded Bessarabia and northern Bucovina. The ultimatum was terse and unequivocal. Carol was in no position to resist. In the ensuing havoc wrought by a disorderly Rumanian retreat, many things happened that ought not to have happened. The Jewish and Ukrainian population, in their elation at the departure of the Rumanian administration from this most misruled part of the country, treated the retreating Rumanians in a manner which was to cost them dearly a year later. Apart from this, they were soon to become acquainted with the N.K.V.D. and other blessings of Soviet power.

Two hot, tense months followed in which Hungary and Bulgaria pressed their claims. If the loss of Bessarabia was not taken very seriously by articulate Rumanians (most of them had never visited it), Transylvania was a battle cry. Not surprisingly, the Soviets encouraged the Hungarians to break up Rumania. For them, the weaker Rumania became, the better chance they had to dominate what was left of it. Germany was in a difficult position. Hungary was a friend, and adamant in her demands for revision — yet at the same time, Germany wanted to keep the best relations with Rumania. Hitler's greatest worry was that a Hungaro-Rumanian war might ensue that could damage the oil fields and bring the Soviets into the picture.[116] So he proposed to Teleki and Giugurtu that they work out the problems by negotiating with each other. When these negotiations did not lead to anything and Carol asked Germany and Italy to arbitrate, the Second Vienna Award was the result.

The Vienna Award of 1940 could be more aptly called an imposed treaty, especially from the Rumanian point of view. The Rumanian delegation was so unaware of what was in store for them that when Ribbentrop and Ciano showed them the map partitioning Transylvania, Manoilescu fainted; they had gone to Vienna to make what they thought would be minor concessions.[117] The award did not solve anything, except that it gave Germany temporary relief in the matter of raw materials. Ribbentrop explained its intrinsic value: "The basic idea of our actual policy toward Hungary and Rumania is to keep two irons in a red hot state and to shape them according to German interests — according to the development of events."[118] In this sense, the Second Vienna Award was a great success in the coming years.

The effect the partitioning of Transylvania had in Rumania, especially in Bucharest, was indescribable. Bitterness filled the hearts of the people. Within two months Rumania had lost large territories where the majority of inhabitants were Rumanians.* In Bucharest on August 30, it was not an unusual sight to see people weeping in public. The mood was a revolutionary one. The system that abandoned one-third of the nation's territory without firing a shot and surrendered millions of Rumanians to foreign yoke (for yoke it was to be and of the most onerous kind) — that system had to go. Great crowds gathered around the statue of Michael the Brave shouting for one man: Maniu. "Let us fight! Give us Maniu! "

It was by no means clear at that point whether or not the events in Bucharest and in the country would follow the course of March 27, 1941, in Belgrade. The eternal dilemma of small nations, "Hácha or Mannerheim? " was not resolved until the next day, when Carol, seeing everything crumble around him,** called on General Antonescu rather than on the democratic hero of Transylvania. Antonescu had been exposed to all kinds of indignities from the camarilla since his disgrace in 1938. He had tried to appeal to Carol's common sense during the Bessarabian crisis and was rewarded with solitary confinement in the Bistriţa monastery for his patriotism.*** But after the Vienna dictate, he was speedily released. Carol did not choose to fight, and the military withdrawal from Transylvania was not an easy task. There was little likelihood that Carol's orders would be obeyed, and he wanted to use Antonescu's authority to carry out this feat.

But some hours after the pro-Maniu demonstrations (the grand old man did not answer the call of the street; he was not the type who could become a revolutionary leader), other songs were sung and other crowds filled the streets. The crowds wore green shirts and they marched on the Elisabeta Boulevard toward the royal palace. They sang about the *Capitanul,* about death and resurrection. Their sad refrains were the expression of the sorrow and frustration of a whole generation. "Give us the King! Give us Lupescu! Don't let them get away with their money!" The Legionary revolution had begun.

In the meantime, Legionary detachments distributed in the barracks Horia Sima's leaflets containing invectives against the King and Madame Lupescu. Attempts were made to seize the public buildings in Bucharest, and the telephone exchange and other government installations in Braşov and Constanţa were in Legion hands by September 3. This supplied General Antonescu with excellent arguments when he asked Carol for dictatorial

*In the territory awarded to Hungary, it was the Jews who held the balance for Hungary — that before 1944.

**The great daily *Universul* came out with a sweeping editorial about "ten years of tyranny under which the young nationalist generation was murdered in a cowardly fashion and billions embezzled under the pretext of rearmament." Taking into account the fact that the censorship allowed this article to be printed made it an open call to revolt. Harald Laeuen; *Marschall Antonescu* (Essen, 1943), p. 40.

***It would seem that only a speedy joint intervention by Fabrizius and Dr. Neubacher before Carol on Antonescu's behalf saved him from the fate of Codreanu. Hillgruber, *op. cit.*, pp. 76-77.

powers. The King hesitated, then yielded; Antonescu went further. He demanded Carol's abdication. A disgusting wrangle followed, mostly about financial questions. How much of his gold, how many of his jewels, his Rubens and El Greco pictures could the King take with him? How much pension would he receive? Crown Prince Michael wanted to leave with Carol.* There could be no question of that; the dynasty had to be preserved. Antonescu firmly refused.[119] Carol decided to leave Rumania.

Carol, Madame Lupescu, and the heart of the camarilla, Urdareanu, contrary to all expectations and probably inspired by their incredible greed, risked the long trip from Bucharest to the Yugoslav border by train. After all, they had been carefully packing their belongings for weeks in anticipation of this exodus[120] — and there was more room for goods on a train than on a plane. So the treasure train started its long, tortuous journey through the Guardist-infested countryside. What followed in the next hours was like a Wild West story. The Guardists made repeated attempts to catch up with the train, and finally, in Timişoara, several miles short of the Yugoslav border, they succeeded. If only the train crew had obeyed the red signal! But for these honest Rumanians (the stationmaster and the garrison of Timişoara) Carol, whether worthy or unworthy, was still their King. They led the train through the marshalling yard under a hail of Legionary bullets, and while Carol, Madame and Urdareanu hid in the bathtub, they allowed it to proceed safely to Yugoslavia.** What worthy people! If only they had had a worthy King! On their arrival to safety, Carol offered the train crew that had saved his life and millions of dollars a tip of two dollars each. Some of them refused it.[121] Perhaps Carol was thinking along the line of Hohenzollern tradition, that "*Sie haben nur ihre verdammte Pflicht getan!*" One thing is certain: His Majesty did not go in for gratitude.

---

*Whatever Carol was like as a King or husband or man, even his enemies admitted that he was a loving and excellent father.

**Waldeck, *op. cit.*, p. 181. According to other accounts, Carol was waiting for the Guardist onslaught with a drawn revolver in his hands protecting Madame Lupescu. (Laeuen, *op. cit.*, p. 50.) All accounts agree that during the trip all three of them indulged in a long recrimination, blaming each other in turn for everything that had happened.

CHAPTER XI

From the Sixth of September to the Sixth of March*

*Cry out loud everywhere that all the evil,
misery and ruin originate in the soul!*

Codreanu

1

When Antonescu was executed in 1946 as a war criminal, he died a much more dignified death than Bárdossy. Although he had acted under a stronger compulsion than Bárdossy in what he did, Antonescu did not call anybody names, nor did he invoke the divinity. He simply said to his mother: "One day history will examine our case. She will be more impartial than our present judges."[1]

On September 6, 1940, the same day Carol made his disgraceful exit with his retinue, the Hungarian Army began a march into Transylvania amid the great rejoicing of the Hungarian and Jewish population and the proud, tormented silence of the Rumanians.** The first thing the Hungarians did was to undo the Rumanian agrarian reform and install a full-fledged neobaroque system.

As the Rumanian Army fell back to southern Transylvania, the whole of Rumania held its breath. What would Antonescu do next? Would he, as some expected hopefully, "pull a De Gaulle"? Not even Maniu wished for that. Yet, on whom could he base his government? On Maniu? That was impossible — the Germans would never accept it. On the Goga-Cuzists? It is true that Goga had been very close to Antonescu, and it was his widow, Mme. Veturia Goga, who both then and after the fall of the Legionary state was the *grande dame* of the regime. Madame Goga and a versatile professor of the Bucharest University faculty of law, Mihai "Ica" Antonescu, *persona grata* in Berlin, did their best to acquaint the Nazi hierarchy with Antonescu, to

*The 6th of September, 1940 to the 6th of March of 1945. The first date marked the advent of Antonescu and the Legion to power, the second, that of the Communists.

**The writer, as a child of ten, was waving at them a Hungarian flag, hidden by the family for 22 years, and he can only add, with the words of Daudet: "Il'y a des moments ou l'histoire rit, et ce rire tantôt discret, tantôt à gorge déployé n'est souvent compris que bien des années après." History plays strangely with her participants. In this case, the departure of Rumanians and the arrival of Hungarians meant death for most of the cheering Jews.

recommend him to Hitler, and to dissipate doubts arising from his pro-French and pro-English past. Although the Goga-Cuzists played a decisive role in Antonescu's regime later, at that point it was impossible for Antonescu to lean on them alone and to snub the Legion. Nor could he turn to the army for support at that time, although no other officer could match his prestige before the armed forces. An army can afford to be beaten and still remain a decisive force; there are plenty of examples of that — for example, in Weimar Germany. But an army that retreats without firing a shot at the three archenemies of the country cannot at the same time have realistic pretensions to power. So the Legion, or what was left of it, remained the logical choice for an ally. It was avowedly pro-Axis and its mystical Christian Socialist revolution, fortified by its martyrdom, made it very popular in these desolate days of September 1940.[2] That for internal politics.

As for foreign policy, the only guarantee Antonescu could see against possible Russian and Hungarian designs on Rumania was cooperation with Hitler; the Axis rainbow had reached its zenith over the No-Man's-Land of Europe. After about a week of negotiations, during which the Germans seem not to have been very enthusiastic about a Legionary takeover, a solution was found. The ministry of interior, a key ministry in any revolution, went to General Constantin Petrovicescu,* calming the bourgeoisie considerably. With a Legionary majority of other cabinet posts, Antonescu became prime minister and *Conducator* (leader) with Horia Sima as vice premier. Southern Dobrogea was ceded to Bulgaria without much ado by the agreement of Craiova, and after that, Germany and Italy guaranteed the boundaries of Rumania. On September 15, Antonescu proclaimed a National Legionary State, in which the Legionary movement was to be the only recognized political party "to be responsible for the moral and material uplifting of the people."[2] After King Michael's radio address to the nation, Antonescu cried, "God help the country, Your Majesty, and me! "[3]

2

In the first week of his rule, Antonescu succeeded in lifting the spirits of his humiliated people. His appeals, written in the monosyllabic language of the peasant and soldier, free of all the nauseating ornaments of the "form without content" language of the last twenty years, penetrated to the very hearts of its hearers. Antonescu understood the Rumanian people's character as well as the Legionaries did. He ordered that the Sunday following Carol's exit be a day of atonement. At 11 a.m., all Rumanians wherever they were had to kneel down, expiate their country's sins, and pray to the martyrs who had died for Rumania. All this religious revival, which characterized the first months of Antonescu's reign, was crowned on September 15, 1940. On that day Queen Helena, Carol's mistreated ex-wife who lived in Rumanian hearts

*This proved to be a portentous choice. The military prosecutor of Codreanu during his trial of 1934, the General was fully devoted to the Legion, but this was not yet known.

as the person who carried a cross (an antipode to Madame Lupescu who was the personification of "Jewish" evil) returned to Bucharest amid great pomp and rejoicing to assume her place at the side of King Michael. All the bells of Bucharest tolled solemnly as the peasants, green-shirted Guardists and the army saluted the *Regina Mama.*

Thus amidst religious revival and a welling public desire to cast off the filth of the past, the Legion began its revolution. Codreanu had not wanted the Legion to take power before it was strong, tight-knit and ready to govern. He gave ample warnings on this point during his life.[4] Yet when the Legion actually did assume the much-coveted power in September 1940, it can be said that it had never in its history been less ready to exercise it. With all the best of its leaders, according to the irreverent joke, under the earth like potatoes, it was Horia Sima who became its commandant.

This third-rate Guardist leader was an "enthusiast" of the worst kind.* He exercised rule as a kind of vicar on earth for Codreanu, because the Guardist movement seemed to be dominated to a remarkable extent from beyond the grave. Sima's faction within the movement was challenged by the one led by Codreanu *père* and his sons Decebal and Horia. Codreanu's father hated Sima and embarrassed him at every possible opportunity from the very beginning of the Guardist regime. And when old Ion Codreanu stood up at meetings and proclaimed, "My son said . . .," it carried a great amount of weight.** There was a third Iron Guardist faction under a certain Cojocaru with its strength in Transylvania, a group vaguely pro-Communist and definitely anti-German. Allegedly, it was this group that established contact with the leftist, later pro-Communist, Ploughmen's Front and its leader Petru Groza. Antonescu had quite a clear picture of their connections.***

Only several hundred of the Legion's old members were alive. In the influx of hundreds of thousands of new members****there were all too many opportunists, Legionaries of a new kind to whom even the older Legionaries referred contemptuously as "Septembrists."[5] They tried to ingratiate

---

*Nazi opinion characterized him as "an enthusiast, a fanatic, for whom dry reality was inconceivable." Laeuen, *Marschall Antonescu,* p. 82.

**When Papanace returned from German exile, he went straight to Codreanu *père,* who called Sima "a Satan, in whom the soul of Stelescu lives" and "an agent of Moruzov." He asked Papanace in despair, "What to do about him? " *Orientări Pentru Legionari,* V, No. 50, November 1961, p. 8.

***Barbul, *Mémorial Antonescu,* pp. 67, 77. Barbul does not indicate the time, nature, or intensity of these contacts. He merely indicates that in November, 1940 (and before that), these contacts existed, certainly with the aim of embarrassing the Groza government, which was in power in Rumania when Barbul wrote his book.

****It is impossible to tell how many new members entered the Legion in these months. Sima says about 500,000. *Cazul Iorga-Madgearu,* p. 75.) If Sima's figure is correct, it certainly indicates a quantity rather than quality. Even so, the figure seems inordinately high.

themselves with Sima by calling Codreanu *père* a traitor[6] — an inauspicious omen for the future of the National-Legionary State. Although the Legion later tried to stop the influx of dubious elements, its new policy recruited members almost exclusively among the common people and all but ignored the suspect middle class.[7] Especially unwelcome were the Cuzists, although Antonescu championed them.[8] Sima dismissed charges that the Legion would be incapable of governing with the statement, "We have proven that we are strong." As for the program of the Legionary government, he stated: "Our program is not worked out yet, but the will is there to convert principles into deeds."[9] In other words, as usual, everything was to follow syllogistically from the archangelic gospel on an *ad hoc* basis.

Whatever noble millenium the Legion had in mind, its tangible efforts were directed toward power and vengeance and the enrichment of too many of its members. Every Legionary request was filled, regardless of whether it was justified.[10] Although there was no sign of the sweeping anti-Semitic legislation everybody expected, "Romanization"* commissions were established which were to carry out the grabbing of Jewish property in typical Rumanian fashion: without any system, in a haphazard, arbitrary fashion, consistent only in an incredible amount of corruption. In foreign policy, the Guardist foreign minister, Prince Mihai Sturdza** proclaimed a Rumanian alliance with the Axis. "Every other political connection near or far falls automatically to the ground from now on."[11] The police apparatus was in most cases put under the control of Legionaries, but that was not all. A special and ever-expanding Legionary police was organized which later became a main point of friction between the Legion and the forces of order.*** These forces, in leather jackets and Haiduc fur caps, many on motorcycles, terrorized, robbed and wrought such mayhem on the population (especially the Jewish segment) that in the next months the whole country was engulfed by anarchy and violence.

Higher on the Legion's list of priorities than enrichment and wholesale robbery was the long-awaited revenge. It was difficult to imagine that once in power the most cruelly persecuted and decimated nationalist movement in Europe would refuse true vengeance — but that was exactly what Antonescu with his conservative military concept of order and his utter inability to recognize a revolutionary situation demanded of the exasperated Legion. The Iron Guard complied, at least in the beginning, but Antonescu's approach proved very costly for the long run. On September 23, Antonescu established

---

*It is significant that the expropriation of Jewish property was never called Aryanization in nonracist Rumania.

**The great number of aristocrats in the Iron Guard became evident. Prince Sturdza, the foreign minister, Alexandre Ghyca, the head of the police in Bucharest, the Cantacuzino family, Constantin Grecianu, the Guardist ambassador to Germany, etc.

***According to Sima, Antonescu asked him to form the *Gărzii Motorizati Legionari* (Motorized Legionary Guard) because he did not trust the Carolist police. *Cazul Iorga-Madgearu,* p. 29.

a special court of investigation to look into the atrocities committed against the Legion during the Carolist era, courts which were to pronounce sentence on the guilty after "due process of law." Sima pushed for a special tribunal of the sort recommended by Codreanu in his Manual, but Antonescu remained adamant. No Legionary was seated on the special court of investigation.[12]

The court started its slow, cumbersome investigation, ordering several dozens of arrests. Carol's flight had come so suddenly that all the culprits guilty of the anti-Guardist terror were still in Rumania, not having had time to flee. Marinescu, the crooked prefect of Bucharest, Moruzov, the head of Carol's personal secret service, General Bengliu, responsible for Codreanu's death, General Argeşanu, who as prime minister carried out the Guardist killings after the murder of Calinescu, and sixty-seven other gendarmerie and police officials were put under Iron Guardist police at the military prison of Jilava. Under a concrete slab in the courtyard of Jilava, the bodies of Codreanu, the Nicadori and the Decemviri lay corroding from the acid which had been poured over them. And still the Legionaries waited on the "due process of law."

In the first weeks, the cooperation between Antonescu and the Legion was rather smooth.* If the General did not believe in revolutionary dynamism or anarchy, he did give the Legionaries a substitute for bread and circuses. Everywhere in Bucharest and in the countryside, gigantic billboards went up showing Codreanu's head against a green background proclaiming: *Corneliu Zelea Codreanu — Prezent!* Huge rallies were held everywhere at which Antonescu appeared with Sima, both wearing green shirts. The greatest of these Legionary rallies was held on October 6 on the square now named Sixth of September Square, below the hill on which Parliament and the Palace of the Patriarch were located. In the colorful cavalcade of uniforms, peasant costumes and green shirts, there was just one discordant element — a large aggregation of relatives of murdered Legionaries, dressed in black, their loved ones still unavenged. This huge black group ominously foretold the things which were to come.

Antonescu sincerely tried to stamp out the evils of the past by legal means. He introduced a stern investigation against officials and businessmen who could not account for their speedy enrichment, and before almost every second or third villa around the fashionable Şosea (Chaussée) area of Bucharest there stood an armed guard, proclaiming that the owner was under house arrest pending further investigation of his misuse of public funds. Only that evil spirit of Carol's reign, heartily detested by Antonescu, the industrialist Malaxa, was beyond reach for the time being. This versatile man had already ingratiated himself with Sima and the Legion by donating huge subsidies, but now he offered them a sports stadium and, infinitely more important, he armed and equipped the Legionary Workers Corps under the leadership of Dmitriu Grozea, whose past was a red rather than a green

*As late as the middle of November, the Legionary press referred to Antonescu as "the glorious son of Legionary Rumania." *Buna Veştire,* November 19, 1940.

one.[13] Before taking power, the Legionaries had rallied the peasantry. But after they were in possession of large cities, they became aware of the dynamic revolutionary qualities of the workers, and Sima, with the help of Grozea, now welcomed the workers into the ranks of the Legion.[14] Their number soon reached 13,000,[15] and their role became important.

Meanwhile, the Legion's excesses multiplied. In fact from October on, it became increasingly clear that the Legion had reached an uncontrollable state. Deprived of vengeance, it consoled itself with wholesale robberies and individual arbitrary outbursts, and Sima had to condone it if he wanted to preserve a semblance of authority. British subjects were arrested and brutally mistreated.[16] Foreign diplomats, among them those from the United States, France, Turkey, Argentina, Brazil and the U.S.S.R., protested on behalf of their citizens exposed to Legionary arbitrariness.[17] The Greek Embassy was attacked by the Aroman Legionaries, who had a special grudge against their former country, and particularly after war broke out between Greece and Italy, many Greeks were kidnapped, robbed and physically mistreated. Antonescu was very unhappy, because he feared retaliatory English air attacks.[18] Cuzists were molested, their homes invaded, and their swastikas broken by Legionary police.[19] And through it all, the main targets of the outrages were, of course, Jewish lives and property. Every evening in Bucharest and the provinces, the Motorized Legionary Guards set out to rob and kill Jews, and to attack and plunder their homes.* Knowing it was hopeless to seek defense against them, in most cases the Jew kept quiet; if he reported to the police, he was next day dragged to the Guardist police station and tortured to silence or worse.** Amid this chaos and lawlessness, the positive aspects of Legionary activity shrank to negligible proportions. But the Legionary welfare did try its best to help the needy, and Sima limited the maximum salary of officials to 20,000 lei.*** Spartan, archangelic socialism was clearly on the march, and as we shall see, more so with every passing week. By then, however, the bourgeoisie and the Cuzists were more frightened than admiring of any and all activities of the Legion.

*Item: The Guardist mayor of the Bucharest suburb Șerban Voda alone committed 87 murders and took 70 truckloads of booty from Jewish homes. *Time*, February 10, 1941, p. 29.

**The very incomplete list of Guardist outrages (even the Antonescu account stated that Jews never dared to report, and even non-Jews seldom), not including the worst excesses committed during the Guardist uprising on the days of January 21-23, 1941, or the Jilava massacres in November, 1940, enumerate 450 mistreatments, 323 kidnappings, 9 murders, 88 private homes violated, 1,162 cases of property acquisitions by "forcible sale," 1,081 cases of confiscation, 65 wanton devastations and 260 cases of forcible occupation of property. *Pe marginea prăpăstiei*, II, 131-33.

***Universul*, October 7, 1940. The value of the lei in dollars was rather elusive in those days. Official course was $1 = 210 lei; on the black market, 500 lei.

At the end of October, the much-vaunted German military mission arrived, and German troops began to enter Rumania in strength "to train the Rumanian army." But they stopped virtuously before the Focşani gap. They kept respectfully away from the borders of Russia — at least before the Hitler-Molotov meeting the following month. With the arrival of German troops, the Rumanians felt safer concerning both the Russians and the Hungarians, and the Legion rejoiced in the mistaken belief that the German army reinforced its position. Sima and the Legion made incessant attacks against Hungary, denouncing alleged (and real) Hungarian atrocities in Transylvania and proclaiming that "the Vienna arbitration belongs to the past."[20]

3

It was the month of November that proved decisive in the unfolding of the tensions in the National-Legionary State. General Antonescu watched with increasing dismay the hectic atmosphere created by the Legionary enthusiasts and opportunistic criminals. "Long live death! " the Legionaries proclaimed ever more often. But a man like Antonescu, a conservative military man with a strong sense of order and discipline, had to consider the preservation and the assurance of life rather than death the prime responsibility of a government. And by November something more disquieting than attacks on Jews began to develop. Although the Legion had no professed program of social change, this being both its strength and its weakness, as its archangelic doctrine confronted practical realities the conclusions it drew were sweeping and radical. With every week that passed, it leaned more and more to the complete refusal of capitalism, the middle classes, and a radical overhaul of economics and society. "The Enemy: Capitalist Individualism," editorialized the Legion's daily, expressing the opinion that capitalist individualism was the only, indeed, the main enemy of the Legion.[21]

The increasing anarchy, the flight of Jewish capital, the insecurity about what the Legion would do next progressively disorganized the economy. The dislocations led to a meteoric rise in prices — food prices rose 300–400 percent during the few months of Legionary rule. When Antonescu expressed anxiety at the situation, Sima's response was revealing: "A Legionary regime cannot coexist with a liberal economic structure. Here is the difficulty — two concepts, two worlds clash." Economic and political ideas must coincide, the state must control on the model of Germany and Italy. Antonescu's rejoinder was a categorical one. He explained to Sima that in Germany and Italy, Nazism and fascism not only did not destroy bourgeois economy but supported it. He (Antonescu) could not destroy Liberal or even Jewish economies, because they were the essence of Rumania.[22] Sima kept up a relentless pressure, professing that "the Legion believes in a directed economy, and not in 'experts' who receive directives from the banks and the old party men."[23] He then attacked that fortress of the Cuzist bourgeoisie, the daily *Porunca Vremii*, as a "blackmail paper" (which, of course, was true), and demanded its immediate suppression.[24] It was more and more obvious that the conflict between Antonescu and the Guardists was too serious to be resolved. But it was also clear that the balance between them was not in Rumanian hands. Whom would the Germans support?

As far as the Germans in Rumania are concerned, there were several hierarchies established on the well-known lines of the Nazi party and the Nazi state. Konradi and the Gestapo represented the party. The German Embassy, with the fatherly, old-school diplomat Fabrizius, the German envoy, represented the state. Later the German Army came into the picture with the Wehrmacht and SS and the usual division lines among them. But Rumania, being the most important country in the *Südostraum's* raw material zone, had another embassy in the Strada Wilson (in the building once occupied by the Austrian Embassy) just opposite the Ministry of Propaganda, and this was decidedly "new order." Headed by Dr. Hermann Neubacher, the German minister plenipotentiary for economic questions in the Balkans, and staffed by economists from Section "W" *(Wirtschaft —* economy) of the Wilhelmstrasse, it was more important than all the other German hierarchies combined. Dr. Neubacher was an Austrian, and he liked to pretend to be an old revolutionary (he had spent some months in Schusschnigg's concentration camps for Nazi activities). The Nazis preferred to employ Austrians in dealing with the *Südostraum,* provided their loyalty to Nazism was beyond doubt. The Austrians had dealt with the complex problems of No-Man's-Land for centuries, and had a tact and understanding in dealing with these nationalities that the Prussians notably lacked. Dr. Neubacher was the virtual economic dictator of Rumania, the most important single Nazi. Hitler, as usual, arbitrated between factions rather than giving his unconditional support to one hierarchy or the other.

The Iron Guard had the sympathies of the SS and of Himmler, but the individual sympathies of even the most extreme Nazis were never so strong as to prejudice German national interest. The Guardists for their part were also nationalists and by no means blindly subservient to the Germans. Especially in the economic field, a field where German imperialism expressed itself in the most blatant form in Rumania, did the Guardists have strong reservations about German influence. Sima remarked in dismay that "Germany . . . was about to take the place of Jews in the economic exploitation of Rumania."[25] The remark proved apt in a literal sense. German businessmen swarmed into Bucharest and purchased the enterprises of the hard-pressed Jews for a farthing. Or rather, they thought they had purchased them. Because at that point the whole Legionary resistance, not daring an outright refusal, went into passive action. The ministries first sent back the papers for "correction and confirmation"; then they conveniently discovered that a new decree had been issued. Finally, the Legionary police arrested the Jew in question and forced him to "Romanize" the enterprise he had sold to the German; that is, he must "sell" to a Rumanian, preferably to a Legionary. Commented Dr. Neubacher in dismay: "The Rumanians are so very, very oriental."[26]

The Germans, essentially conservative in their economic-political ideas for the *Südostraum*, were alarmed by the disrupting effect on the economy of archangelic radical socialism and meddling, in addition to their frustration and annoyance over not even getting their share of the loot. The Legion's lawless plunder dismayed them even more. After one extreme night of outrage by the leather-clad motorized Legionary police, Neubacher asked Sima, "Did your captain die so that the worst criminals should get the richest spoils? "[27] When some decent Legionaries asked Sima to put an end to the pilfering and robbery, he shrugged his shoulders and said, "I can't. They would not go for it."[28] Deprived of the satisfaction of vengeance, the Septembrists wanted at least to secure for themselves the advantages of quick enrichment.*

Antonescu's conviction that something had to be done about the Legion was maturing. He had violent clashes with Prince Sturdza, the Guardist foreign minister, about the latter's efforts to fill every post in the foreign service at home and abroad with Guardists.[29] There was an armed clash between Guardist factions around the Green House in Bucharest and also in the countryside. On November 8, Codreanu *père* made a violent outburst against Sima in Iaşi, and he and his son Decebal were fired upon by would-be assassins three days later.[30] Antonescu said several times that he could not continue to live in this anarchy, but he could do nothing without first securing German support. "You must talk to the *Führer*," advised Fabrizius every time Antonescu saw him.** And in the middle of November Antonescu set out for Rome and Berlin. His first meeting with Hitler was to be combined with the adherence of Rumania to the Tripartite Pact. Antonescu arrived at the right moment. Molotov had left Berlin several days before, and the complete divergence of the German and Soviet positions resulted in Hitler's decision to invade Russia. From then on Hitler had an interest not only in the Rumanian economy; his new need for a healthy, strong Rumanian army as an auxiliary for his designs gave him one more reason to reestablish order and put an end to Legionary anarchy. Although Antonescu seemed skeptical about being able to sway the *Führer* to his side in the conflict with the Legion (he said goodbye to his friends with the words, "I will return either ... in the guise of Hácha or in the uniform of Mannerheim."***) he was an

---

*This was a far cry from the morality of Codreanu, who was most unhappy and punished severely some young Guardists who once pointed a gun at a Jewish innkeeper instead of paying their bill. Codreanu, *Eiserne Garde*, p. 328.

**Barbul, *Mémorial Antonesco*, p. 35. The Guard reacted to Antonescu's criticism of Legionary anarchy in characteristic fashion: They decided that they "shall not force him to live in anarchy," and formed a Death Commando group in order to assassinate him. *Ibid.*, p. 66.

***People close to Antonescu were pessimistic before his trip to Berlin, telling him that he was like a man who wishes the support of the Pope in a quarrel with the Catholic Church. Barbul, *op. cit.*, p. 76. As an aftermath, one may ask today: Was it merely accidental that in April, 1968, the Rumanian government delegation, during a state visit to

eminent success with the *Führer*.[31] Not that he was subservient or abject — on the contrary. Antonescu started out with a sharp attack on the Vienna arbitration, whereupon the *Führer* comforted him that "the last chapter in the history of Transylvania is not yet written," even promising "in the framework of a general settlement" to regain Bessarabia for Rumania.* Hitler did not promise Antonescu his full support against the Legion, nor did he reveal his intention of invading the U.S.S.R., but a personal contact was made on the basis of which their mutual trust could be built later, a trust which would last to the end.

In Bucharest, Antonescu was received by noisy Guardist crowds, which were convinced that he had brought back Transylvania, or at least Cluj, in his pocket. Mass demonstrations and meetings were held to this effect before the German and Italian Embassies, causing much embarrassment to their occupants. When Antonescu faced his friend Mihai Antonescu, "Ica" confronted the General with a military intelligence report that a group of Death Commandos had been assigned to assassinate him because of his criticism of Guardist anarchy.[32]

More sinister events followed. On the tenth, Bucharest was badly damaged by a violent earthquake. Many a Legionary considered this a punishment for their failure to avenge their martyrs.** In November, as before, funeral followed on funeral as the Legionaries exhumed and solemnly reburied their dead. These events took place under the aegis of the Legion's death cult, accompanied by such an all-absorbing macabre pomp that the Legionary regime was called both by Rumanians and foreigners the "regime of funeral processions." But the greatest funeral of all, the reburial of Captain Codreanu, the Decemviri and Nicadori, was to take place on November 30, the second anniversary of their murder.

Could the Captain and his companions be laid to eternal rest without being avenged? According to Sima, Codreanu had not left any directive for the

Helsinki, deposited wreaths on the grave of Field Marshal Mannerheim? This Rumanian act provoked the hitherto angriest attack by *Pravda* against the Rumanians. *Pravda* reminded them that Mannerheim, like Antonescu, fought on the side of Hitler. *San Francisco Chronicle*, May 1, 1968. Apparently Maurer and Manescu saw other parallels when they decided to commit the "outrage."

*Barbul, *op. cit.*, pp. 51, 63. Also Hillgruber, *Hitler, König Carol und Antonescu*, pp. 113-15. Although there is some reason to believe that by this time Hitler was disillusioned with the Iron Guard. On November 20, 1940, when Teleki and Hitler met in Vienna he told the Hungarian prime minister: "I fared badly with the National Socialist leaders of south-eastern Europe — I regret that I gave them a chance ... and I shall [abandon] this experiment ..." Lackó, *Nyilasok, nemzetiszocialisták*, p. 245.

**The earthquake unveiled another bit of corruption — the skyscraper Carlton, like many other new buildings, collapsed, showing in its debris what kind of cheap, unfit material they were built from because of the prevailing graft.

rumored "three days of vengeance" the Legion was clamoring for. But, he continued, who knew which of the many tormented and shamefully murdered Legionaries wished such a vengeance in his agony during the horrors of 1938? As the relations between Antonescu and the Legion deteriorated, by the beginning of November Antonescu seems to have experienced a change of heart toward the prisoners in Jilava: he did not want death sentences to be pronounced. Sima warned that such an outcome would make it impossible to restrain the Legion, but apparently the mood of the Special Court of Investigation also changed during the second half of November. Marinescu and General Bengliu were to be transferred to a sanatorium, and a murderous officer of the gendarmerie was to be allowed to go free. Sima warned Mihai Antonescu, but to no avail.[33]

When the exhumation of Codreanu and his thirteen companions took place, the atmosphere (with their murderers only a few feet away) was tense. The inmates felt the danger and sent urgent messages to Antonescu to substitute the military guard for the Legionary guard at Jilava. When the team of Legionaries working on the exhumation found out about this, they were mad with rage. "Antonescu sold us out! They will never be punished! " was the furious cry. They entered the cells and massacred the inmates, and after that they lined up before Codreanu's open grave and saluted, crying "*Capitanul*, we have avenged you! "[34] These gruesome events of the night of November 26 shocked the country, especially the Rumanian middle classes. And well they might be shocked, because more was to follow.*

The General, urged by Mihai Antonescu, was furious when he found out about the massacre, the more so because the next day the famous prefect, Colonel Zavoianu,** ominously ordered the arrest of many other leaders of the old regime. Tătărescu, Ghelmegheanu, Argetoianu, and General C. Iliaşievichi and Giugurtu were dragged to the Prefecture and only the speedy personal intervention of A. Rioseanu, a pro-Antonescu official of the Ministry of Interior, and Sima himself spared them.***

After that, during a violent clash in the Council of Ministers, Antonescu demanded the leadership of the Legion for himself; there could not be two authorities, he and the Legionaries. He brought up Franco's role in Spain as an example. But such a change seemed inconceivable to Sima — the leader of the Legion could not come from the "outside." That masterful Macchiavellian, Mihai Antonescu, stepped forward to try to convince Sima that the

---

*According to the Antonescu regime, it was not those who disinterred Codreanu who commited the murders but Grozea and his Legionary Workers Corps — although this *mise en scène* seems rather artificial. *Pe marginea prăpăstiei*, II, 137.

**Although Zavoianu was executed by Antonescu after the Legionary rising, Sima claims that it was not he but the *Chestor* (Questor) Stânga who ordered the arrests as an *agent provocateur. Cazul Iorga-Madgearu*, pp. 46-47.

***Ibid. According to German sources, it was Fabrizius and Dr. Neubacher whose personal intervention saved at least two of them, Tătărescu and Guigartu. Hillgruber, *op. cit.,* p. 307.

change would be only a formal one, but Sima insisted that nobody in the Legion could obey Antonescu.* As the General kept pressing his demand, as Sima balked and a break seemed inevitable, Dr. Neubacher entered the picture, trying to mediate. He explained that "things should not be taken too tragically," that "revenge is the order of the day when radical changes of the regime take place and Antonescu should understand the situation."** Antonescu withdrew his demand.[35] Nevertheless, from that time on Antonescu treated Sima as a "chief of bandits."[36] He would have liked to crush the Legion then, but it was impossible because of his uncertainty concerning the German attitude, and the imminent and well advertised ceremony of Codreanu's reburial, to be held two days later on November 30. Meanwhile Antonescu and Sima, in a joint public statement, disavowed the murders.[37]

But the Legion's thirst for vengeance was still unslaked, especially after their prisoners were released from the Prefecture. On November 28, Sima made categorical promises to Antonescu that the outrages would stop and appealed to the Legion in that vein. However, when he returned from the country the next day, where he had gone to stop some Legionary violence at the last minute, he found in Madame Lupescu's former villa a death squad (eight men under the leadership of engineer Traian Boeru) who informed him that they had just murdered Professors Iorga and Virgil Madgearu. Iorga, eighty years old, was revered as "the teacher of the nation"; Madgearu was an innocent economist. As Sima recalls, the killers seemed to be in a state of transfiguration. A kind of other-world calm was reflected on their faces. Boeru spoke in mystical terms in the name of all of them about avenging the *Capitanul.* He spoke of the treachery of Professor Iorga and that of Professor Madgearu and of Codreanu's alleged order that he be avenged.*** He also spoke of the "twenty years of suffering" the Legion had to endure. Sima was moved and discarded the idea that any provocation was involved. He condoned the "revenge for three days," after which the Legion was to return to normalcy. Sima reported that the death squad had first looked for Tătărescu and Argetoianu, but they were in "protective custody."****So the "new men" had to expend their emotions on Iorga and Madgearu. That same night a macabre "vengeance feast" was celebrated in the Green House.[39]

*Antonescu seems to have had long-standing designs to take over Legion leadership, a design coinciding with Hitler's, as we shall see later. He even invented a new salute, "Long live the Legion and the General!" (instead of "the Captain").

**Dr. Neubacher spoke out of experience. As the mayor of Vienna after the *Anschluss,* he permitted and condoned the worst outrages against Jews as a "necessity of revolutionary dynamism." Waldeck, *Athene Palace,* p. 77.

***Professor Iorga's past and anti-Legionary attitude and role in Codreanu's first condemnation should be clear to the reader. The well-known economist and partisan of Maniu, Professor Virgil Madgearu was hated by the Legion because he was of Hungarian descent and an alleged culprit in anti-Legionary intrigues. *Cazul Iorga-Madgearu,* pp. 17, 20.

****Ibid., pp. 59-64. Inside the German-controlled premises.

Next morning, Bucharest and all Rumania awoke in horror to the new outrage. The discovery of the mutilated bodies of Professor Iorga and Madgearu, in the forests near Ploeşti and Bucharest respectively, struck terror into the bourgeoisie.

With all this, the careful arrangements for the funeral of Codreanu and the Nicadori and Decemviri had been made. A solemn procession, miles long, marched from the little church Ilie Gorgani all the way to the Green House on the outskirts of Bucharest, where the martyrs of the Legion were to be laid to rest. Envoys of all Axis countries (with the exception of Hungary) participated in the funeral procession. Hitler was represented by Baldur von Schirach and Ernst Wilhelm Bohle. The perpetrators of the Jilava murders and those of Iorga and Madgearu marched along with the rest. There was no attempt made to apprehend them.* This was to be the last great display by the National-Legionary State. A grim-visaged Antonescu marched in the icy wind and light snow, wearing a green shirt for the last time. He walked between Sima and the Axis dignitaries behind the coffins of the *Capitanul* and the others, which were covered with Rumanian flags. German planes dropped wreaths on the grave in the courtyard of the Green House. Next morning Bucharest returned to the normalcy of Legionary rule.

If the bourgeoisie were terrified during the last week of November, the popular masses were not. Sima actually had to declare an enlistment halt to the influx of new members who tried to enter the Legion in the first part of December.[40] If up to that time all crimes and indecencies of corrupt politicians had gone unpunished, as Sima explains, "Jilava destroyed the myth of this immunity, which had been enjoyed up till then by all the rascals of the Rumanian land," a fact that seemed to impress the masses favorably.[41] Believing that it had the support of the masses behind it, and unconvinced that there would be an adverse German reaction, the Legion became even bolder and more radical.** Meetings, festivities and funerals continued

---

*Sima explained to Antonescu that only if there were a thorough purge of the old politicians would he consider the punishment of Legionaries who committed atrocities — which, of course, Antonescu was less than willing to do. *Ibid.*, pp. 73-75.

**Some days after the murders, Himmler, speaking more for the SS than for Hitler, wrote to Sima that "such a measure was a just one, because it could never be carried out [through] ordinary justice, which is bound by paragraphs and depends always on the formalities of paragraphs." Himmler continued that both in his capacity as the *Reichsführer* of the SS and of the German police, he stood squarely behind the Legionary movement. *Biblioteca Historica Romaniae, No. 2*, p. 40. Nor was this the only encouragement the Legion received from Germany in those days. After the funeral of Codreanu, Baldur von Schirach and Bohle had a long conversation with Sima during which they suggested that the Legion "should follow a more active course." They invited Sima in the name of Hess to Germany in order to discuss with some top Nazis what this "more active course" should be. Legionary representatives were invited to all official N.S.D.A.P. festivities, and Antonescu became "painfully aware"

throughout December. The wholesale robbery and extortion of Jewish property, countless criminal attacks on Jews in Bucharest, and arbitrariness in the countryside, where every Legionary was a kind of divine right ruler responsible only to God, seemed on the increase.* In Constanţa, a new structure, the Column of Infamy, was erected, to which people, mostly Jews, were tied for days, castrated amid the howls of mobs, and ultimately frozen to death. Jewish stores were broken open all over the country; Jews were drowned in icebound rivers in Brăila, Bacău and other places as a kind of "Christmas celebration," despite the protests of Antonescu.[42] Meanwhile, the "new men" created by the Legion indulged in self-congratulation, confident that their role in Rumanian history was a kind of *fait accompli*, their cause a crusade above the criticism and reproach of mortals. Wrote a Sibiu paper in December, "The Horia of our days is greater than the mountains. He looks like an angel [and carries] the sword of an archangel. Horia is the idea, Horia is the feeling, he is our will, our [right] arm. We believe in Horia fanatically and will continue to do so until we die."[43] A grandiose monument was planned for the Legionary dead in Predeal, and the Legionaries started a movement to canonize Codreanu, only to be advised by the Orthodox hierarchy to come back a few centuries later, by which time the question could be ruled upon. There were suggestions that a new nationalist capital be founded, to be named Codreni.[44] But more ominous than the Legion's anarchy or its anti-Jewish activities or its self-confident tone and uncompromising language, were its encroachments in the army,** and among the students and faculty in the schools.*** And although the

---

that the Boeru group, which was an illegal movement, and other Legionary terror squads, obtained the arms with which they carried out the murder of Iorga and Madgearu from the Germans. (Hillgruber, *op. cit.*, pp. 116-17.) Ignorant of the personal ties which developed between Antonescu and Hitler, having no idea about Operation Barbarossa, and being also "enthusiasts," the Legion had no difficulty in interpreting these German manifestations as a sign of the most ardent and unqualified Nazi support.

*After the massacres and on Antonescu's demand, Sima dissolved the Legionary police. *Cazul Iorga-Madgearu*, p. 60. Like too many Rumanian laws, this one remained a dead letter. Some weeks later, announcements appeared in the Legionary press about new training courses for the most vicious police, the *Gărzii Motorizati*, promising future expansion. *Buna Veştire*, December 12, 1940.

**A sample: "The officer must no longer belong to a separate caste. He must preoccupy himself with all social, political, economic and cultural problems that affect the nation's soul. The army must belong to the people. The officer must no longer be a chief appointed by orders and regulations, he must be elected, or considered as elected by the soldiers under his command." Rogger and Weber, *The European Right*, p. 562.

***One-thousand-one-hundred-and-nine professors were absent from their classes during four months of Legionary rule because of their activities on behalf of the Legion, an immense amount of arms and ammunition was

higher echelons of the church hierarchy were always opposed to the Legion, the lower clergy was more than cooperative.* Just as disquieting were the already mentioned contacts established between the Legion and some Communist leaders in prison. And the completely uncontrollable Legionary horde planned a gigantic St. Bartholomew's Night for the coming New Year, during which all former politicians would be exterminated so that the New Year could begin, as they said, "purified of the leprosy of the past." Sima personally hurried to Bucharest to avert this slaughter and to issue a *dementi* for the benefit of the terrified public.[45] By then it was clear to the forces of law and order that something had to be done and done fast.

On New Year's Day, Antonescu made his last appeal to the Legion. "The country needs quiet, work, and brotherhood. Remember that the fall of others came from greedy pursuit of worldly goods and interest. . . . Do not inflict upon others the sufferings you have suffered."[46]

It did no good — one could not reason with the Legion. They were supremely confident about their strength within Rumania, and in regard to the Germans, after the few encouragements they had received they could not conceive that the nationalist international would not work. They believed only what they wished to believe, that is, that the Germans were with them and not with Antonescu and the "rotten past." They acted and reacted accordingly. When as a sign of important things to come the conservative diplomat Fabrizius was replaced by Freiherr Manfred von Killinger in a move to upgrade the German Embassy in Bucharest, the Legion remained unperturbed.** Legionary police raided the home of Fabrizius' mistress in a show of contempt for Antonescu's friend, who was particularly hated by the Legion because they believed he could have prevented the massacres of the Carolist era if he had wished to do so.

During January, the Legion was radicalizing the revolution with every day that passed. "There can be no place in Legionary terminology for the bourgeoisie," wrote the Legion's daily, "not only in the linguistic sense, but

---

recovered from sixteen secondary schools (even from theological seminaries!) after the fall of the National-Legionary State. (*Pe marginea prăpăstiei*, I, 142; II, 183.) As December came, the Legionary press editorialized about "The Students — the Revolutionary Guard of the Nation." *Buna Veştire*, December 14, 1940.

*Two-hundred-and-eighteen priests were prosecuted for participating in the armed Legionary insurrection in January, 1941, attacking gendarme posts, disarming soldiers, fighting on the barricades. In the higher hierarchy of the Legion alone there were 54 Orthodox priest office holders. *Pe marginea prăpăstiei*, II, 102-5.

**This ruffian, the former German consul at San Francisco, and a *Freischärer* in the early 1920's, was a guarantee for Hitler that no nonsense would be permitted which might be detrimental to German interest. Von Killinger showed the Slovaks what the New Order was like. His book *Fröhliches aus dem Leben eines Putschisten* gives a good insight into his character.

because of a more imperative and rational cause: the ethical concept of the Legion. In its essence, the bourgeoisie is nothing. It is the expression . . . of a way of life hostile to the Legionary existence: individualism. The Legion will resolve radically the problem of the bourgeoisie. By its very name, the 'Legion of Archangel Michael' is at loggerheads with bourgeois individualism."[47] Even more revolutionary was the tone of the new daily *Legionary Worker (Muncitorul Legionar)* started for the growing workers corps. It proclaimed that for "the first time [in Rumanian history] the worker has triumphed over his exploiter," and it will be "the workers' children . . . who will become the leaders of the Rumanian nation."[48] And as the forces of law and order, Antonescu, Church dignitaries, the army, and the Germans (although the Legion did not know that) drew together, Sima prepared his blow. On January 14, he appealed to the Legion, promising "an imminent disclosure of material about masonic machinations against the interests of Rumania plotted with the help of British intelligence."[49] On the same day, Grozea, the leader of the Legionary workers, demanded the dismissal of Rioseanu and accused him (and through him, of course, General Antonescu) of being a "hireling of the Jews." Two days later, Patrascu, secretary general of the Legion, convoked the nest leaders of Bucharest, flatly told them that "the breach between Antonescu and the Legion is irremediable," and predicted a Legionary victory in a coming armed showdown. "He is alone and there are many Legionaries. . . . The senior officers will be with him . . . but the young officers will be with us."[50] What Patrascu forgot to tell his comrades was on whose side the *Führer* would be.

Sima seems to have considered that all he had to do to convince Hitler and win his support was to write him a letter in January in which he pointed out that collaboration between the Legion and Antonescu was impossible because of the reactionary spirit of the latter, and because Antonescu, being an old Anglophile, counted secretly on Germany's ultimate defeat. As proof, Sima cited the famous address delivered by Antonescu while he was military attaché in London. Hitler was furious for two reasons — first, on account of the patent disloyalty of Sima, and secondly because Sima had shown such little respect for the German intelligence in fancying that he could tell the *Führer* anything about Antonescu's past that he did not already know.[51]

When at Fabrizius' prodding Antonescu visited Hitler on January 7, the *Führer* told him about Operation Barbarossa and the role the Rumanian army was to play in it.* In light of both the coming operations in the Balkans and the attack against Russia, the disorder and chaos caused in the rear of German armies by the Legion in Rumania was intolerable. When Antonescu asked Hitler what to do about the fanatics, Hitler answered curtly, "One must get

*Barbul, *op. cit.*, p. 94. According to German sources, it was Antonescu who asked for the meeting with Hitler. Neither Sima nor Antonescu wished to pay him a visit in the company of the other, and it was Sima who remained in Bucharest. Hillgruber sets the date of the meeting between Hitler and Antonescu on the fourteenth instead of the seventh of January, the date indicated by Barbul. Hillgruber, *op. cit.*, pp. 117-19.

rid of them." He then treated Antonescu to a lecture about the salutary power of a machinegun. Antonescu was pleased. He told Hitler that he was once warned that to visit him was like "trying to win the support of the Pope in a quarrel with the Church." "The fate of heretics is harder than that of schismatics," said the *Führer* with a smile.*

Having settled the issue in such unequivocal terms, Antonescu moved on his return to deprive the Legion of its economic and power bases. The infamous Romanization Commissions, responsible not only for unabashed pillage and corruption but also for wreaking havoc with the country's economy were abolished. This destroyed the Legion's revenue apparatus and ended the plunder that had served the greed of the "new men." Next day, the minister of the interior, General Petrovicescu, who had revealed his unconditional support of the Legion, was removed from his post, and the Legionary chief of police Ghyca, the prefect Mironovici, and the Legionary chief of the Siguranţa, Maimuca, were suspended from their duties. Similar measures followed in the countryside. Sima saw the coming of the counterrevolution forestalling his own *coup d'état*, and he was not prepared to allow such a thing to happen.

On January 18, 1941, a German major was assassinated in Bucharest, apparently by a Greek who was a British agent. This murder provided an excuse for gigantic Legionary rallies all over the country protesting against the inability of Rioseanu to protect the lives of German officers. These demonstrations were only rehearsals for a general armed insurrection. That evening all nest leaders were instructed to maintain hour-by-hour contact with the leadership. Grozea was trying his best to mobilize the workers. The students were organized by the Legionary student leader, Viorel Trifa.** Mass demonstrations followed in Bucharest under the slogans: "We want a Legionary government! " "Long live Prime Minister Horia Sima! " "Death to freemasons and Jews! "[52] The suspended Legionary police functionaries barricaded themselves in the gendarmerie headquarters and the Prefecture (next door to Antonescu's office) and refused to give up their posts. Legionary workers occupied the telephone exchange, the radio station and other important points in Bucharest, and fighting erupted when army units tried to dislodge them.[53]

The next three days, January 21, 22 and 23, were a closing chapter that was fitting to the National-Legionary State. The Legion could not offer more than it had. And what it had — a fanatic "enthusiasm" at its best and a sordid criminality at its worst — was always essentially mystical, unrealistic, and irresponsible.

The rebellion was almost exclusively a Bucharest affair; the countryside remained relatively quiet, despite incitement and deceptive reports broadcast

*Barbul, *op. cit.*, pp. 73-76. According to Hillgruber, Hitler was more reserved. Nevertheless, Hitler said to Antonescu in the presence of Fabrizius: "You are no Franco! You are [a real] Mussolini! " Hillgruber, *op. cit.*, pp. 118-19, 305.

**Trifa is a bishop of the Rumanian Orthodox Church in the United States.

over the Legion-held *Radio Romania.** The Legion appealed to German soldiers in Rumania during the rising in order to prod them into supporting the Legion.[54]

The capital, however, was engulfed by rapine and murder. With the exception of the barracks, the main (northern) railroad terminal, some ministries and Antonescu's headquarters, Bucharest was in Legionary hands, and at long last the Legionaries could carry through the pogrom and pillage that Antonescu had denied them! Swarms of Legionaries descended on the Jewish district around the Strada Lipscani, broke open and looted shops, set synagogues afire, and forced their way into homes, where they raped women before their husbands and afterward tortured the men to death before their dishonored wives, daughters and parents. Some victims were dragged to the police stations in order to be tortured to death there; others were taken to the forests around Bucharest and shot. But all of these fared better than those (among them a girl of five) who were taken to the municipal slaughter yard in Baneăsa where the "new men" invented something original indeed. As Fascist mobs outside mockingly chanted Jewish prayers, the Jews were slaughtered in a Jewish ritual reserved for beasts. While still alive, they were put through all the phases of dissection of cattle, and finally their decapitated torsos were hung on the hooks marked "Kosher meat."[55]

In other parts of the city, sporadic fighting continued while the radio exhorted listeners to form Legionary Alcázars and to hold fast, every broadcast ending with the slogan "Long live death! " Bareheaded Legionary columns singing Orthodox Church hymns marched with mystical fearlessness straight into what seemed to be a hail of bullets. Whenever one of them fell, the bells of Bucharest churches rang out. The great bell of the Church of the Patriarchate, pulled by twenty-nine men, tolled steadily. Wherever a Legionary fell, a candle was lit. Some Legionaries went mad — one of them, a young lad in a frenzy of joy, emptied his gun at passers-by at the intersection of Calea Griviţei and Calea Victoriei in the very heart of Bucharest, while tears ran down his cheeks. A soldier captured by the Legion was soaked in kerosene and set afire.**

Sima disappeared when the first shots were fired. Antonescu was confident — he could have crushed the uprising with loyal troops, but he wanted to wait "until the disorder disrupts the railroad network. Then the Germans will ask me to restore order."[56] The German commander in Rumania, General Erik Hansen, and Ambassador Fabrizius begged him several times to move the full strength of the army against the Legion. Antonescu waited for encouragement from higher quarters. The *Führer* personally called on the evening of the twenty-third. "I don't need fanatics, I need a healthy Rumanian army,"

---

*In one instance the Legionaries let Bucharest know that 40,000 Rumanian soldiers had joined them and were marching on Bucharest from Braşov — this news was false. *Pe marginea prăpăstiei,* II, 20-21.

**The Associated Press correspondent St. John observed at close range the agony of this miserable human torch and the bestial joy of his tormentors. *Foreign Correspondent,* p. 180.

he said, and he offered German troops to restore order if necessary. "The Rumanian army is healthy and will restore order," answered the *Conducator.* "Heil, Antonescu!" came Hitler's reply.* After that the Rumanian army and tanks went into action and crushed the Legion within hours. Only the Green House offered some prolonged resistance; there the Workers Corps and the Legionary detachments, the diehards of *Vestiitori* and *Rasleţii* tried to hold out for a while — but of course to no avail.

With the uprising under control, in order to forestall any complications and disagreeable surprises detrimental to German interests, Dr. Neubacher called on Sima** and announced that "Antonescu represents a guarantee for the war aims of Germany. . . ." "There was no arguing after that" remembers Neubacher. "I dictated an appeal . . . a cease fire order, and Horia Sima signed it."[57] Sima's appeal to the Legionaries to return to civil life and end the struggle "which the Legionaries do not want" and which "only serves the ends of the enemies of Rumania and of the Axis"[58] provided the epitaph under which the Legion was buried forever, becoming paradoxically the first Fascist movement to fall in a Europe where Germany reigned supreme.***The same day the German forces saluted Antonescu in a parade before his office.

The toll of Legionary fury will never be exactly known. The official report lists 21 military dead and 53 wounded, and 374 dead and 380 wounded among civilians.****Mass arrests followed. Of the 3,999 arrested, 1,333 persons were released within two weeks; the rest awaited trial.*****The versatile Malaxa, for one, had not bet on the right horse; Antonescu was happy to send him to jail for arming and financing the Legion. While an almost incredible amount of loot was recovered from Legionaries, those who were not

*Barbul, *op. cit.,* pp. 103-5. In the first stage of the uprising, according to German sources, Antonescu was not so self-confident. He feared that the expected reinforcements from Craiova would not arrive in Bucharest on time, and he asked the help of German tanks. Hillgruber, *op. cit.,* p. 120.

**The whereabouts of Sima were known only to von Bolschwing, the head of the Gestapo in Bucharest, who shortly after the Legion's failure was thrown into a concentration camp for the support he gave to the Legionaries during and after the rebellion. Hillgruber, *op. cit.,* pp. 120, 309.

***According to the Legionaries, on the night of January 22-23, Neubacher communicated to Sima an ultimatum from Hitler that if resistance to Antonescu's forces did not cease, the German army would intervene on his behalf. *Sentinela,* Munich, November, 1963, pp. 2-3.

*****Porunca Vremii,* February 13, 1941. The same official report lists 118 Jews killed, yet the Jewish community organization of Bucharest on January 27, 1941, identified 630 Jewish dead and 400 missing. Hilberg, *The Destruction of the European Jews,* p. 489.

*****Porunca Vremii,* February 21, 1941. Neubacher tried to save the Legionaries from the worst, feeling himself morally responsible for them. He said so to Antonescu, and his intervention on their behalf spoiled their relations forever. Hillgruber, *op. cit.,* p. 121.

apprehended by loyal army units (mostly the leadership, like Sima, Iasinschi, etc.) were dressed in SS uniforms and smuggled out of the country on German military trains.* In Germany they were put into relaxed concentration camps, mainly in Berkenbrück, but also in Buchenwald and Dachau. In Rumania, those Legionaries who had not compromised themselves during the rising hastened to proclaim their loyalty to Antonescu. Codreanu *père*, never a great friend of Sima, disavowed the rising in forceful terms. Antonescu established military courts for almost every delinquency, with a trial within twenty-four hours and execution after another ten hours. The new German ambassador, von Killinger, arrived at his new post on January 24, 1941, the day after the crushing of the Legion, with Hitler's categorical instructions: "To support General Antonescu with all the means at his disposal."[59] From then on Archangelic Socialism belonged to the past.

5

January 27, 1941, was a bleak winter day in Bucharest. Snow flakes fell gently, almost compassionately, as if to hide the dastardly deeds of men. Life crept back to the deserted, shattered streets, people began to clear away the debris, the fires of the synagogues were burning low, and special teams went about their work of disinfecting the municipal slaughter pens in Baneăsa.

On that day Antonescu established a full-fledged personal dictatorship based on the Rumanian army. Most of the new cabinet ministers were army generals. The rest of the posts were filled by Antonescu's friends, the most prominent being Mihai "Ica" Antonescu. The Rumanian army had never played as prominent a role in politics as the other Balkan armies did, but now it came into its own as a bulwark of conservative stability. The character of the new regime being a conservative military dictatorship, political parties were outlawed and on February 15, 1941, the National-Legionary State was officially abolished.

The new government and its administration paid due lip service to Fascist ideas, and for the next three and a half years or so its members were classic examples of what one could call Rumanian fellow travelers of Fascism. The Legionaries were cruelly persecuted, their Archangelic Socialist ideas thoroughly discredited. The Goga-Cuzists became the backbone of the new regime, though not as a political party; in Antonescu's system there was no room for political life or for ideologies. But thanks to their ideas and their

*Von Papen's son, a German officer of Rumania during that time, seems to have been very active in the expatriation of Legionaries, *Dacia*, XII, Numar Festiv (Rio de Janeiro, January 1957), p. 18. It would seem that because Hitler's position in the conflict was known to few even among the initiated Germans, in the ensuing confusion, many high-ranking Germans sided with the Legion. Antonescu demanded the recall of several high-ranking German functionaries, among them the German consuls in Ploeşti and Constanţa, and above all, the recall of Konradi. His request was granted. Hillgruber, *op. cit.*, p. 310.

previous contacts with the Germans, they were in the appropriate position to collaborate, and Mihai Antonescu managed to fill many posts with them. Goga-Cuzist Fascist fellow travelers represented the best the Antonescu course and German interests could hope for under the circumstances. They were ready to be apolitical; they were conservatives,* much more unreserved friends of Germany than the Iron Guard was. Moreover, although they were nationalists they did not seek to establish a nationalist millenium, an Archangelic panacea with "new men." Thus every bureaucrat or exponent of the old regime who could adapt himself to the new government, which most were embarrassingly eager to do, was welcome to jump on the bandwagon and grow rich.** Hitler for his part was not entirely happy about the purely military dictatorship based on a single person rather than a one-party mass movement, but under the circumstances this was the best he could hope for, and he knew it.***

The economic policy of the new regime, both because of Antonescu's personal preferences[60] and because of the demands of the German war machine, favored agriculture over industry. The Germans did much for the mechanization of Rumanian agriculture and for raising its productivity.[61] All these changes were ratified by a so-called plebiscite, which gave Antonescu a too-impressive 99 percent of the votes. However, although that mandate is almost certainly exaggerated, it might be said that the misrule by the Legion, and its total inability to live up to the high expectations it had excited in the people for more than a decade, gave Antonescu and his conservatives a chance. The overwhelming majority of Rumanians truly acquiesced in the changes, and not only because they had no other choice.

The Legionary movement disappeared from the Rumanian scene almost

*The editorials of the Goga-Cuzist *Porunca Vremii* were written by Ilie Radulescu, the most abject idolator of Hitler. Sample: When Hitler in July, 1940, made his famous peace bid to England, Radulescu considered this "the greatest manifestation of human spirit since Christ." Also an unmitigated anti-Semite, for whom to find parallels one must go to Milotay and Rajniss, he discussed the popular participation in the Legionary rising under the meaningful title: "Vermin of the City," calling the common people *mahalaua*, a Turkish word meaning scum of skid row. *Porunca Vremii*, February 3, 1941.

**Sima complained bitterly, realizing too late that "when the Legionaries were removed from power, the Germans lived in excellent friendship with the old world that was their enemy before. They substituted us in the alliance with the Axis with those representatives of the old world which Berlin considered more flexible, easier to maneuver, and more subservient to the demands of German imperialism." *Cazul Iorga-Madgearu*, p. 65.

***Even while encouraging Antonescu to destroy the "fanatics of the Iron Guard," he added that "a state without a movement based on ideology is a soulless state." Barbul, *op. cit.*, p. 76. And after long years, he remembered with nostalgia: "Antonescu ought to have made the Legion the basis of his power — after shooting Horia Sima." *Hitler's Secret Conversations*, p. 227.

overnight. Grozea and sixteen of his companions were tried and executed for their alleged participation in the Jilava murders. In May the Bucharest Military Tribunal passed sentence on 225 Guardists. Thirty, including a lieutenant and fifteen members of the police, drew life sentences; 23 got from five to twenty years, and 138 were sentenced to lesser terms; 33 were acquitted.[62] When the Rumanian national holiday came on the tenth of May, in the Faculty of Law of Bucharest University, the Legionary-minded students rioted, cheered Horia Sima, and sang Legionary songs. The disorders were quashed with an iron hand by the authorities, who coupled their action with an ultimatum that unless the culprits' names were divulged the university would be closed.[63] It was the last Legionary demonstration. The jails were overflowing with them, and the movement was dead for all practical purposes.

6

Nevertheless, Sima once more contacted Antonescu in a letter written from Germany at the end of March, offering reconciliation and assuring Antonescu (probably with Himmler in mind) that such a reconciliation would be welcomed in German and Italian circles. Antonescu had no reason whatsoever to look for any reconciliation with the Legion, so he refused Sima's peace feeler in the sharpest terms.[64] Contacts were never resumed between him and the Guard. And although no ally of Germany (with the exception of Mussolini) enjoyed such prestige before Hitler as Antonescu, the Iron Guard exiles were kept dangling over his head like a sword of Damocles. Hitler used it with skill and ruthlessness, as he used the Transylvania issue in relation to both Hungary and Rumania, when Antonescu balked at toeing the line in the new order.*

Antonescu joined Hitler in the attack on the U.S.S.R. on June 22, 1941. Because he was a hater of Slavs and of communism, because Russia was Rumania's hereditary enemy and just a few months before had grabbed Rumanian territories, Antonescu undoubtedly had as good reasons to oppose the Soviet Union as any national leader who espoused the "crusade against

---

*Early in 1943, when the Germans owed many billions of lei to Rumania for petroleum and grain deliveries, but hesitated to deliver industrial goods in their turn, Antonescu halted further raw material deliveries. At that point, Himmler let Sima "escape" to Italy and let Rumanian intelligence "find out" about his whereabouts. After Antonescu protested violently, the Gestapo quickly "recovered" Sima and put him back in a concentration camp, and Antonescu was offered three box cars of gold bars to redress the balance, unfavorable to Rumania. (Barbul, *op. cit.,* pp. 172-75.) According to German sources, Sima escaped to Italy because the Germans (at Antonescu's request) began to hold the Legionaries, who had enjoyed considerable freedom until then, in concentration camps. When Antonescu found out about Sima's escape, he ordered the imprisonment of at least 1,000 Legionaries, who were released after the Gestapo "recovered" Sima. Hillgruber, *op. cit.,* pp. 227, 331.

bolshevism." Rumania participated in the war against Russia with more than a dozen divisions, with Antonescu himself in command of both the Rumanians and the strong German formations on the southern wing of the front. In one month after the attack was launched, Rumania recovered Bessarabia. Maniu and Constantin Brătianu demanded that the Rumanian troops stop on the Dniester line, but Antonescu sent them deep into the Ukraine, where they besieged and annexed Odessa and all the territories between Bug and Dniester as a Rumanian "Transnistrian" province. After the fall of Odessa, Antonescu promoted himself to the rank of marshal. Rumanian troops continued their advance all the way to Stalingrad, only to meet their doom there a year later.

At the outbreak of the war with the U.S.S.R., Antonescu asked the Germans to put the rather leniently treated Guardists in Germany into detention camps. In Rumania, imprisoned Legionaries could volunteer to serve on the front in special detachments under permanent surveillance, though they could not be promoted or decorated.[65]

Meanwhile the Rumanian press and propaganda was quite reasonable in its attitude toward the Western Allies* with whom Rumania was at war by the end of 1941. But toward Russia, the press started a revolting campaign about the "civilizing mission of the Latin race among the barbarians of the Scythian steppes, etc.," presenting Rumania's poorly equipped, poorly fed, cruel army as Roman Legions bringing *Ius Romanum* and *Pax Romana* to the lands they profaned.**

But far worse things occurred inside Rumania. Crusades in the past had often started with the massacre of Jews, and the next "crusade" was to be no exception in Rumania, where as elsewhere in Nazi-controlled Europe, the real anti-Jewish horrors started with the attack on Russia. They were soon to dwarf all the Guardist outrages of the past. They can be laid straight at the doorstep of Antonescu and his Goga-Cuzist Fascist fellow travelers. Only he could have stopped them. When he deemed it necessary to do so, he did.

The anti-Jewish excesses of the year 1941 in Rumania bore the distinct characteristics of a pogrom rather than the cold, systematic efficiency of the

*Antonescu's instructions to the Rumanian press were as follows: "I am the ally of the Reich against Russia. I am neutral between Great Britain and Germany. I am for the Americans against the Japanese. Did you understand?" They did. There was no parallel to the vulgar tone of the Hungarian press toward the West in Antonescu's Rumania. When Rumania under heavy German pressure had to declare war on the United States, the first secretary of the foreign ministry, Gheorghe Davidescu, explained to the American chargé d'affaires, Benton, that "Rumania does not make this step by her own choice," and the two embraced when they parted. Barbul, *op. cit.*, pp. 140-41.

**One could see as a part of the *Mission Civilisatrice* the streetcars in Galaţi, which the Rumanians stole from Odessa. Although no other country had as much justification to be anti-Russian as the Rumanians or the Poles, the Rumanian outrages in Russia compare favorably with those of the Germans. The Hungarians and Italians lagged far behind them.

Final Solution as it was administered by Germans and Hungarians: although they were horrible, in the ultimate analysis they were more spectacular than efficient. Despite the horrors, the majority of Rumanian Jews survived. The disorganized haphazardness of the action, its arbitrariness, and the colossal corruption that attended it, all proved mitigating factors.*

After the repeal of the Goga decrees, it was the decree of the Giugurtu government which began to restrict Jewish rights. Under the Guardist regime, except for the decrees that authorized expropriation of Jewish-owned lands, there was little anti-Semitic legislation. Jewish veterans of World War I were exempted from expropriation, and the definition of the Jew was more a religious than a racial one. Racism never excited the Rumanians much; even the expropriation of Jewish property was called rather "Romanization" than "Aryanization." And even considering the billions of lei of forced contributions Antonescu levied on the Jewish community, and the forced labor service, from which most of the Jews could buy their way out officially by paying a head tax, the legislated anti-Semitism was insignificant compared with nonlegislated actions.

But the persecution of the Jews during the Antonescu regime was by no means indiscriminate. Geographically, the dividing line that separated a relatively decent Rumanian attitude from unmitigated horrors runs along the line that separates the Bessarabia and Bucovina areas which were ceded by Rumania to the U.S.S.R. in June 1940. If the treatment of Jews in the Regat and southern Transylvania was reasonable, the Jewish masses of the formerly Soviet areas went through a nightmare.

This differentiation is significant. The abjectly poor proletarian Jewish masses there, mistreated by Rumanian anti-Semitic misrule and corruption for twenty-two years, did not lose much when Soviet troops came in 1940. Many of the populace had greeted the Soviets as liberators and set upon their former tormentors with the help of the N.K.V.D. When the Rumanians returned, they were not prepared to exercise "self-criticism" and to examine the intrinsic causes of Jewish disloyalty very closely. They saw both a good pretext and an opportunity to rid Bessarabia of a hateful, disloyal minority, whatever the cost. Shortly after the recapture of Bessarabia the Jews were driven across the Dniester by the tens of thousands, put into camps in the Golta Prefecture and in Vapniarca, Dumanovca, Acmecetca, and Vertujen in Transnistria. In the camps they were starved, tortured and shot to death. Bread could be bought only for gold, and potato peelings were a veritable delicacy. But exemptions from deportation could be bought, obtained on the basis of "economic necessity," or even awarded through conversion — 40,000 religious Bessarabian Jews chose to convert in order to live. The general arbitrariness and corruption and the lack of organization led to horrors unprecedented, often provoking even German disapproval,[66] but the lack of

---

*Rumania was the only country where the mayor of the capital city and his deputy in addition to the colonization minister, General Zwiedeneck (an ethnic German), had to be dismissed for "dark" transactions with Jewish property. Hilberg, *op. cit.*, p. 480n.

a systematic approach saved the lives of tens of thousands. When the Rumanian troops captured Odessa, they celebrated the occasion with a formidable massacre of the Jews there, killing about 15,000. By the spring of 1942, the fury of the extermination process had calmed down. Because of the confusion, it will never be known how many of the deported perished. Their number could be about 100,000. The treatment of those who survived improved, and the Jews of the Regat were allowed to supply them with food and clothing. Most of these 50,000 to 80,000 Jews were still alive when the war ended; Antonescu even allowed them to reenter Rumania when the front again reached the Transnistrian region.* Much of the improvement in the fate of these Transnistrian deportees, and finally, the dissolution of the camps, was accomplished through American pressure and bribes. For example, Alexandre Crețianu, the Rumanian ambassador in Ankara, was promised, and later received, a U.S. visa for himself and family as a price for his cooperation in the alleviation of the fate of those unfortunates.[67]

Antonescu himself knew about the deportations and doubtlessly also about the horrors of Transnistria.** But even in the Regat, things happened which ought not to have happened. Several days after the attack on the U.S.S.R., the news was spread in Iași (then some ten miles from the front) that Jews and army deserters had opened fire somewhere on Rumanian soldiers. A brutal pogrom followed in which 4,000 to 7,000 Jews perished.*** Haphazard arbitrariness characterized the evacuation of Jews from the areas near the front. They were carried on "death trains" around the country, without food or water, until most of them perished.****The Jews of Dorohoi

*It is an irony of fate that the overwhelming majority of them chose to do so in 1944. Disillusioned with Communism, they came to Rumania, which was not Communist yet, and from where they could freely emigrate to the West and Israel. In 1949, the Russians forcibly repatriated these unfortunates to the U.S.S.R., considering them "deserting Soviet citizens." *Ibid.*, pp. 500-7.

**Called "forced emigration" by Rumanian bureaucrats, Antonescu approved it. "I am ever ready to risk not to be understood by certain traditionalists . . . I am for the forced emigration. It is indifferent to me if in history they will consider us barbarians." *Biblioteca Historica Romaniae*, No. 2, p. 49. Only Maniu protested resolutely against these horrors.

***Ibid., p. 50. Curzio Malaparte was an eyewitness to the horrors of Iași, and according to him, the SS carried out these massacres with Rumanian civilian "volunteers," armed with crowbars and knives, who pursued the hordes of Jews to the Piața Uniri (the center of town), murdered them in droves on the pavement "until their feet slipped in blood." Other SS men and Rumanians threw hand grenades into the cellars of Jewish homes, where the people tried to hide. The horrified Jews leaped to death from the windows of their houses; "screaming, disheveled women drop on the pavement, their faces hit the asphalt with a dull thud!" The SS men and the Rumanian "volunteers" accompanied this scene with laughter . . . *Nicht Wahr?* (New York, 1966), p. 8.

****Sartori, the Italian consul, hurried to the aid of the tormented Jews with

in southern Bucovina, an area not occupied by Russians in 1940, were also deported to Transnistria for one reason or another. The Gypsies fared worse; 26,000 of them were put into concentration camps, about 8,000 of them were massacred there, and 3,000 starved to death.[68] All these horrors occurred in the Regat during the "enthusiasm" of the first days of war; later, things seemed to return to "normalcy." Antonescu never censored or punished the perpetrators of these nightmares.* He was certainly no Kállay and did not put on trial the infamous Modest Isopescu, Corneliu Calotescu, or other Rumanian military who were guilty of these horrors as Kállay put on trial the Hungarian officers responsible for the crimes of Novi Sad.**

To the Germans, Rumanian methods left much to be desired. They wanted efficiency and thoroughness instead of ebullience or haste.***By 1942, the Final Solution was on its way and Auschwitz, Maidanek and Treblinka were

---

all his authority as a representative of Fascist Italy. He reached the "death train" at the station Podolea, and the silence inside it alarmed him. He ordered the station master to open one of the boxcars. The horrified consul was buried under the Jewish corpses which fell out of the overcrowded boxcar. Later he and the rabbi of Podolea counted 2,000 corpses, women, children and babies included. *Ibid.*, pp. 9-11.

*In one case, he sent an officer responsible for a hideous massacre of Ukrainian and Jewish women and children to front line duty as punishment. Barbul, *op. cit.*, p. 123.

**Willy Filderman, the courageous leader of Rumanian Jews, wrote him a letter in October, 1941, describing what was going on in Transnistria. Antonescu answered that those Jews deserved such treatment for being pro-Soviet, and called on Filderman to support and to approve the measures taken. Later, when Filderman still felt like protesting, this time about a forced contribution levied on the Jewish community, he himself was deported to Transnistria. Laeuen, *op. cit.*, pp. 103-6.

***The German attitude was summarized some weeks later during a conversation between Hans Frank, the notorious governor of the Polish *Generalgouvernement,* Ludwig Fischer, the military governor of Warsaw, and Otto Wächter, the military governor of Cracow, a conversation at which Malaparte was present. When somebody mentioned that during the Iaşi massacres 7,000 Jews were killed, everybody nodded approvingly that the figure was "considerable"; *but they objected to the manner in which it was carried out,* expressing their opinion that the "Rumanians are not civilized people." "We Germans," as they expounded to Malaparte, "are guided by reason, method and organization — not by bestial instincts," *Nicht Wahr?,* p. 13. Referring many times to German disapproval of the anti-Jewish brutalities of the Hungarian gendarmerie or of the Rumanian military in Transnistria, this conversation should be remembered. Only in the sense of the conversation overheard by Malaparte can there be a question of Nazis disapproving anti-Jewish massacres. Considering the Jews harmful insects, potato beetles, bacilli or rabbits, they wished to exterminate them. But to derive a sadistic pleasure from this "necessary sanitation" was not considered by them as a "civilized attitude." Nor did they consider it efficient.

334

functioning full blast. During the summer of 1942, Radu Lecca, the newly created general commissar for Jewish affairs, was invited to Berlin in order to negotiate with the Germans about the "evacuation" of Rumanian Jews to Poland (Auschwitz), an action to which both Antonescus seem to have agreed in principle. It is not clear what happened between Lecca and the Germans in Berlin; the fact remains that after his return from Berlin there was never any further talk about Jewish deportations in Rumania, a situation which chagrined Eichmann tremendously.* But Antonescu was more valuable, loyal, and had more authority before Hitler than did Horthy or Kállay during the same period, and never did the *Führer* or any other German dare to tell him what to do about his Jews. The Rumanian Jews were fated to survive; the "Romanization" process slowed down to a crawl by 1942, and often behind the appointed Rumanian manager it was the Jewish owner who conducted the business.** Many Rumanian Jews grew rich during the war, and they were able in 1944 to help the Hungarian Jews who escaped to Rumania before the much more consistent and much more merciless Hungarian variant of the Final Solution. All of these escapees, despite Hungarian Fascist reports to the contrary, were received well in Rumania.

The defeat at Stalingrad — a defeat even more instructive for Bucharest than for Berlin — initiated the machinations of Mihai Antonescu to achieve a Western-oriented separate peace and to escape the clutches of the hereditary enemy, on much the same lines as Kállay's efforts.***Antonescu knew about these efforts as he also knew about the similar efforts by Maniu and Brătianu. Being a Rumanian patriot, he never interfered with any of them. But the Red Army's advance cast a deepening shadow over Rumania. Stalin might have had doubts about what he was going to do in Budapest, Prague or Vienna, but he seems never to have had the slightest doubt what fate he had in store for

*Hilberg, *op. cit.*, pp. 500-5. Professor Hilberg expresses the probability that it was the discourteous reception accorded by Martin Luther and Karl Rademacher to Lecca in Berlin which changed Antonescu's mind about the impending deportation. The writer, without pretending to be an expert on the Rumanian mind in general and that of Antonescu in particular, considers the de-Judaization of Rumania too important a goal of nationalists to have been influenced by such trivialities — especially before Stalingrad. It is more reasonable to assume that Antonescu found out what fate awaited the Jews, once deported. And these Jews, not considered traitors as were those in Bessarabia, he did not wish to see die.

**In 1940, 28,225 "Romanizations" were carried out in 1941, 16,971, and in 1942, merely 6,506. *Ibid.* p. 499.

***It is interesting that in the framework of his efforts, Kállay, in June, 1943, sent the Transylvanian grandee Miklós Bánffy to Bucharest in order to contact Maniu (Bethlen was behind the mission of Bánffy). They both agreed that the Axis had lost the war and that the national interests of their respective countries demanded a break with the Axis; nevertheless, no cooperation could be decided upon because of Transylvania. *Allianz*, pp. 92-93.

Rumania.* Because Antonescu knew this, he wanted ironclad guarantees from the West before he ceased to fight, guarantees the West was neither willing nor able to give.

Never was the *douce décadence* so sweet in Bucharest as during the year 1943 and the first half of 1944.** There seemed to be a market for every possible kind of merchandise, and there were some who made fantastic fortunes overnight while the majority of Rumanians bled and suffered. Their suffering was considered perhaps regrettable but not very important. It seemed as if the whole system could feel its deserved end and would try to make the best of its time as long as it could still do so, dancing over a volcano covered with a leaf of paper. When Bucharest became dangerous because of the American air attacks, "society" moved to the beautiful mountain resorts in the Transylvanian Alps and continued their high life in Sinaia, Călimăneşti, Predeal, Azuga and Buşteni.

In April, the Red Army penetrated deeply into Rumania, taking Cernauţi, Bălţi, and Hotin, and reaching the outskirts of Iaşi. And there they stopped for four months, with Molotov proclaiming that the U.S.S.R. had no designs on Rumanian independence or self-determination and would not impose its social system on her either. Whether Rumanians believed Molotov's promises or not, that was the moment when Communists, Socialists, Liberals and National Peasants got together with young King Michael to save the country. There were no parties, only Rumanians, in this grave moment. Old Prince Stirbey was sent to Cairo to negotiate, and the diplomat Creţianu, who was initiated as to the plans, became the head of the key Rumanian Embassy in Ankara. The heart and soul of the negotiations was the old democrat Maniu. Once again Antonescu knew about all this and again he did not interfere. He tried to find his way to the Russians rather than to the West, not by preference, but because he knew that the key to the future lay in Moscow rather than in Cairo or Algiers. Maniu and the young King, supported by his devotedly patriotic camarilla,*** realized that too. When on August 20 the Russians opened their attack on the Rumanian front and Antonescu still fancied that Rumanian troops could withdraw into Transylvania and go on fighting, the King lost patience. He saw that nothing could be gained that way

*In the famous "percentage agreement" with Churchill, Rumania rated a solid 90 percent as compared with 50 percent in Hungary and Yugoslavia.

**Allied bombings started with the daring U.S.A.F. air raid on the Ploeşti oilfields in August, 1943, but they became systematic only after the all-out heavy daylight raid on Bucharest on April 4, 1944. From them on, heavy air attacks wrought havoc on Ploeşti, Bucharest, Galaţi, Turnu-Severin, Braşov, and other towns. Captive U.S. airmen were never mistreated and no stories of "explosive toys" scattered allegedly by U.S. planes were invented in Rumania.

***Consisting of his marshal of the court, Baron Ionel Mocioni-Stircea, his personal secretary, the young, faithful Ioniţiu, and his contact to the foreign ministry, Grigore Niculescu-Buzeşti, all of them supervised and helped in a motherly fashion by Queen Helen.

except the utter destruction of Rumania. On the other hand, taking into account the outrageous Hungarian behavior after March 1944, now was the time to reannex northern Transylvania.* The fateful step was executed in a master stroke by the young ruler himself — there was no Horthy-like nonsense about playing fair with Hitler or von Killinger to the detriment of the country's interests. Antonescu was invited to the palace in the afternoon of August 23, while victorious Russian troops were marching through the streets of Iaşi. When he showed reluctance to accept the realities of the situation and to abandon his personal designs for Rumania's salvation, King Michael ordered his arrest, handing him over for safekeeping to the Communist leader, Emil Bodnaraş, and his detachment. The same evening, the King read over the radio the news of Rumania's capitulation and the coming liberation of Transylvania.** He also announced the appointment of General Constantin Sanatescu*** as head of the new coalition government of National Peasants, Liberals, Socialists and Communists.

The Rumanian army obeyed loyally the order of its King.**** The Germans were taken by complete surprise — twenty-one of their divisions perished. Von Killinger committed suicide in the German Embassy; he had no illusions about his fate in Soviet hands, or even in case of a possible return to the Reich. Since July 20, ambassadors who failed in their missions had become expendable. The Germans savagely bombed Bucharest in their mad fury, aiming at the royal palace, which they succeeded in destroying.***** But their

---

*The Russians, in whose hands rested the fate of Rumania, clearly favored Hungary over Rumania both on emotional and rational grounds. They detested the Rumanians and considered the country's decrease in size to be in the interests of the U.S.S.R. It was the immense service Rumania rendered to Russia by her successful *renversement dés alliances* and Hungary's unequivocal Fascist stand which made the Russians — albeit, reluctantly — turn northern Transylvania back to Rumania. And even so, they hesitated, using it as a blackmail device against Maniu to help to install the Communists. Only after the coup of March 6 did the Russians turn northern Transylvania over to the Petru Groza government.

**The whole process of preparing Rumania's exit from Hitler's camp is told in a reliable fashion by Reuben H. Markham in *Rumania Under the Soviet Yoke* (Boston, 1949), and by one of the protagonists, Alexandre Cretzianu himself in his *The Lost Opportunity* (London, 1957).

***It was he, as the commander of the Bucharest garrison, who in January, 1941, crushed the rising of the Iron Guard.

****Although on the front some Rumanian officers were disagreeably surprised by the move of King Michael and offered their resignations, when the commanding German general made overtures towards them, they declared their determination to remain true to their oath to King Michael. Hillgruber, *op. cit.*, p. 346.

*****It is Lieutenant-General Altred Gerstenberg who was responsible for this outrage. He left Bucharest in order to carry out an armored attack on the capital in addition to the bombings; *he did this by breaking his word of honor previously given the Rumanians to the effect that he would not*

would-be punishment resulted only in a Rumanian declaration of war on Germany, and in two or three weeks the last German soldier was cleared out of Rumania. In another month, Transylvania was taken back from the German-Hungarian army.

There was little reason to rejoice, however. The arriving Russians behaved in Rumania no better than they did elsewhere, and the Rumanian Communists wrecked the coalition government of General Sanatescu. In January, after getting their instructions from Moscow, they provoked incidents and clashes, forcing General Sanatescu's successor, General Nicolae Radescu, to retire. Following the blunt personal intervention of Andrei Vyshinski, a completely Communist-controlled government under Petru Groza was installed in Rumania on March 6, 1945.* Thus, the vision of liberty passed only flickeringly over Rumania, like the phantom of a dream.

7

The Legion got a chance to write a brief, disgraceful epilogue to its history. On August 24, 1944, they were dusted off by the Nazis, brought to Vienna in haste from the concentration camps, and a Legionary government was formed under Sima.** This government, which never controlled so much as a square inch of Rumanian territory, made frantic appeals to Rumanians to revolt against their King, roundly abusing the courageous ruler in the most vulgar terms.*** The Sima government organized a regiment of Legionaries, which some sources claim arrived in time to fight the Russians in the area of

---

engage in such activities. Ibid., p. 220. General Gerstenberg was a member of the chivalrous Richthofen Squadron during the First World War.

*It is not without significance that the minister of culture and education in the Groza government, the Orthodox priest Burducea, had a Legionary background and had to be removed from the cabinet at a later date because of it.

**The formation of this Rumanian National Government was not an easy task. The Nazis wished to form a broadly based "national" government with the participation of other Rumanians, notably General Ion Gheroghe, Antonescu's ambassador in Berlin, who flatly refused to have anything to do with the Legion. Therefore, although the German radio proclaimed the formation of the Rumanian National Government on August 24, the government was established only on December 10, 1944. The Legionaries assured the Nazis that they could easily organize from their supporters in Rumania a guerilla movement sixty- to eighty-thousand strong. This boast was quickly unmasked by the Germans as not corresponding to the facts. Hillgruber, *op. cit.*, p. 228.

***In 1949, Sima wrote an abject apology to King Michael, speaking of "the former Legionary Movement," and while recognizing the illegality of his Vienna government in 1944, asked to be allowed to participate in the Rumanian National Committee in exile. *Memoriu adresat M.S. regului Mihai I* (Madrid, 1949).

Stettin in the last weeks of the war.* The Guardists also led an "enthusiastic" activity among the Rumanian P.O.W.'s captured by the Germans (by that time the Rumanian army was fighting with the Russians), urging them to return to their units and stir up revolt against the Rumanian government.** When the Red Army approached Vienna, the Sima government was evacuated to Alt-Aussee, and after the collapse of the Third Reich, they went into illegality. It was not difficult for them to submerge for a while. Removed by Antonescu from the Rumanian scene as early as 1941, they were prevented in spite of themselves from becoming war criminals and from sharing the fate of war criminals.

8

Greater Rumania began her existence at the end of World War I with shining prospects. Victorious, with her nationalistic goals satisfied, with rich resources and her most nagging problem, the agrarian question, seemingly resolved, she had chosen a democratic structure for herself — and why not? She had no reason to be dissatisfied with the war allegedly fought to make the world safe for democracy, nor even with the ultimate outcome, which tried to make the world safe for France instead. Rumania had her place in that framework, too; every great moment in her history had been connected with France in one way or another.

The peculiarity of democratic institutions seems to be that they flourish best in their native Western soil. The prerequisites for democracy are not only a strong middle class, which carries out industrialization by its own efforts and not with the help of the state, or the only possible substitute — a conscientious, independent, prosperous peasantry. In addition, a high literacy rate and a high living standard are also desirable. But all these factors by no means guarantee a working democracy, as the example of Weimar so painfully demonstrates. A long continuity of growing self-government and a gradual growth of democratic institutions, moderation in politics, respect for the law, and the assumption of civic responsibilities are at least as necessary, and they cannot be transplanted from Danish, English or French soil to Dobrogea or Moldavia.

*Dacia, XII, Numar Festiv, (Rio de Janeiro, January 1957), p. 22. Sima insisted that these troops should not be sent to fight there, where they would confront Rumanian troops, fighting then on the Soviet side. Hillgruber, op. cit., p. 228.

**The writer met several of these unfortunate Rumanian soldiers during his stay in Siberian labor camps (1949-1956). They said that when they returned to the Russian Army after their release across the lines at Banska-Bystrica in Slovakia, the Russians would not believe in their innocence and their unwillingness to foment revolution, and sentenced them to twenty-five years of forced labor as spies.

Rumania had none of these. Underdeveloped industrially, with an abysmally poor, backward peasantry, with a middle class alien in blood, religion and spirit, with half of the population illiterate and with no experience or tradition of her own in self-government, with venality replacing civic responsibility in those who ruled, the Western institutions grafted to Rumania's medieval foundations bore strange fruits — the structure was deprived from its very outset. The system became more and more untenable as the years advanced. Calinescu, Ghelmegheanu, Vaida-Voevod, Manoilescu, all these apostles of authoritarianism or fascism began their careers in the National Peasant party, that is, in democratic ranks. Certainly, it was something more than just opportunism that made them desert the cause of democracy. And the people in Rumania, which is to say the peasantry, became more and more disillusioned, not with democracy as such — they never understood what it meant in the first place — but with the system. Because the frequent changes of government did not help, they understood that a change of government alone would not bring alleviation. Something radically new was desired, something very different from the other parties. Thus, democracy failed. Communism with the handicaps Stalin imposed on the Rumanian party was unthinkable, and not on nationalistic grounds alone. Communism had so little to offer the peasant in the 1930s. Rumania was much closer to the collectivization process and the famine across the Dniester than other countries. It is doubtful that even a Rumanian Lenin could have bridged this widespread antipathy — the genius of Madame Anna Pauker certainly did not. Many of the disillusioned, searching people seemed to find the answer in Codreanu's mystical, nationalistic social justice.

The Legion tried to carry populist doctrines to their ultimate conclusion — not by trying to bridge the chasm between Bucharest and the shepherd in Făgăraş, but by refuting Bucharest and everything it stood for. This refusal of a without doubt distasteful, sad reality was to be not only a reaction to it, but an answer and a solution, too. Yet, this movement was not a spontaneous peasant protest. Its leadership and its staunchest militants came from those who had been uprooted from the old agrarian society but who had not yet found an equilibrium in the new society. If the borderline cases of nationality are often the zealots of nationalism, the class borderlines produce no less violent people as a consequence of their lack of security. Regarding this, one should consider the relative youth of the Legionaries, most of them in the cadres being students. They were the unemployed intellectual or semi-intellectual proletariat, produced by Rumanian universities quite out of proportion to the needs of the country, and also young army officers — in a word, the most disoriented elements in society.

In the West there is, thanks to the slow evolutionary process, the possibility for two intelligentsias to live together. Even there, this coexistence is an increasingly uneasy one. But in Rumania, as in the forty or fifty newly independent nations of our age, the new intelligentsia emerged from the patriarchal atmosphere for the very purpose of opposing itself to the old intelligentsia, which was also the ruling elite. This process in Rumania was

340

similar to that in the colonial countries, where it was always the Westernized natives who led the revolt against the colonial power.

On the political level, the ensuing struggle had to lead to extremism, because for these people the victory had to be complete, and could only be achieved through the utter destruction of the enemy. This is the explanation for the ruthless brutality of the corrupt oligarchy and for the violence of the Legion. Half-measures for the Legion would not do. Codreanu was a deeply religious, mystic nationalist more than he was a nationalist politician. Since for him the Rumanian people were the community of those alive, dead, and yet unborn, he did not consider the state more than a garment, and a very bad one for Rumania. To strengthen the body of the people by first creating a new soul was for him more important than programs. Although ever realistic as to the short-run objective, he did not pay attention to long-range practical goals. Perhaps he saw the crux of the problem — that the existing moral standards of the society made it unlikely that anything good could be accomplished for the majority of Rumanians of the 1920s or 1930s, that only a thorough transformation of the whole value system and world outlook could change their orientation and their lot.

But the best is often the enemy of the good, and this was surely the case of the Legion. Its refusal to consider political realities led to its undoing. These young people thought they were capable of accomplishing everything just because they had faith in the righteousness of their cause. After all, God was on their side, and their opponents were the enemies of God.

The "new man" — for the leadership of the Legion considered itself already the "new man" — would solve all the problems when he confronted them. When he confronted poverty or exploitation or injustice, he would fight it — and that is what the Legion set out to do. Middle-class individualism was inconceivable to their medieval romanticism. Their hatred for the Jew had nothing to do with racism; it was a nationalist reaction against an irritating alien particle in the Rumanian body. But of course economic and nationalistic considerations did not explain everything. The Jews were the antithesis of the Legion's dream world; they seemed to destroy the absolute which was the very essence of the Legion. Marx, a Jew, conceived a society outside of the natural boundaries of nation and country; Freud, a Jew, exculpated sin and guilt by the concept of an innocent unconscious, and thereby dealt a blow to the Church; Einstein, a Jew, pulverized the concept of time and tradition. No wonder the Jew in the eyes of men like Moţa and Codreanu was the absolute evil and must be treated accordingly.

Not everybody who became disillusioned with the performance of democracy in Rumania chose the hard road of the Legion. There were those in the developing Rumanian middle class who were more interested in "changing the guard" of the Jewish middle class, and who chose to follow Cuza and Goga. Fascism in Rumania had also a bourgeois and a popular branch, with the splinter Fascist movements joining up sooner or later. If they were student groups, like the *Fascia Naţionǎlǎ Romana*, they joined Codreanu; if they were of a predominant bourgeois character, like Vaida's or

341

Emilian's movements, they joined Goga and Cuza. The Goga-Cuzists had no real conflicts with the ruling oligarchy. On the contrary, they were "the other face of it" and were more than ready to reconcile themselves with Carol or Antonescu; and in turn they helped to accommodate them to the spirit of the age.

Carol's F.N.R. does not deserve to be called Fascist. It was a convenient and seemingly up-to-date structure for the oligarchy, carrying the singularly unliberal policies of the Rumanian Liberals to a logical conclusion. It was a personal dictatorship of the Trujillo type rather than a Fascist one. There was no popular support behind the clique of industrialists, court favorites, and police bullies. Even Moruzov's secret police looked out for Carol's personal interests more than anything else. It was the army and police which kept the Carolist structure from collapse and did a good job of it. When it did collapse, the blow came from outside, not from the inside.

If we question the constructiveness of a democratic solution, the extremely grave and complex problems of Rumania demanded not only honesty and patriotism and willingness to sacrifice, but also cool heads, realism, and a great deal of economic knowledge and planning: more than just faith in the intangible, and the creation of a "new man" as an answer to all problems. For whether Moţa, Codreanu or the others liked it or not, Rumania had entered irreversibly into the twentieth century. Whoever wished to help the Rumanian people could not do it without considering the realities attendant upon this rather unpleasant fact. Politics, as Bismarck said, is the art of the possible. But it is exactly politics in which Codreanu did not wish to engage. For the short run, this refusal gained him many admirers; later it led him and almost all the few devoutly "new men" the Legion created to a terrible fate.

When the Legion finally had the chance to prove itself, there were practically no "new men" available, just riffraff. And they were not adequate to the task to lead Rumania in the middle of the twentieth century in the very focal point of a world war. As the Germans so often said during the hectic months of Legionary rule, "These men have too many Horst Wessels but not a single Schacht, Todt or Wohlthat." But it is difficult to see how the Legion could ever have acceded to power under any circumstances other than the black despair of September 1940. Even then, it could assume power only in an uneasy coalition with Antonescu; that is, with the army.

When they came to power they had the fickle and transitory support of the masses, but this support was not well enough established yet to challenge the bourgeoisie, the Germans, the Jews, and all the other minorities, and finally all the forces of law and order simultaneously.

Lenin fomented chaos in order to give his tight-knit professional revolutionary group the only chance it had to take power; by contrast, the Legion was unable to control its own membership, which brought chaos to the country after it took power. Considering the activities of Legionaries during their brief rule, one is at a loss to see any of the "new men" the Legion was supposed to create. But one can see abundant manifestations of all the very old Rumanian qualities against which Codreanu strove with such passion and vigor: corruption, lack of discipline, greed.

As the weeks passed, there was a distinct radicalization in the social and economic activities of the Legion. Its reforming zeal was sincere, and its Archangelic Socialism as applied *ad hoc* to existing problems was as radical as anything in Rumania before the Communists' advent to power. The pronounced Legion preoccupation with the workers once it was in power is also significant. The Bucharest rising in January 1941 was led by Sima, Grozea and Trifa, respectively the commanders of the Legion, the workers and the student organizations, all of these forces being the most unmistakably revolutionary forces, not only in Rumania, but in any revolutionary movement anywhere. It was this combination of social strata against which the ruling class carried out its counterrevolution with the help of Antonescu and the army at the end of January. And the Legionary revolutionaries who substituted chaos for organization and discipline were in no position to offer a successful resistance to the counterrevolution. But it would be mistaken to assume that only the greed and lack of discipline of the Legionary rank and file were responsible for the failure. Third-rate leadership was an even more vital shortcoming. Especially inadequate to the demands of the day was Sima, whose lack of political and revolutionary experience certainly did not warrant his enormous ambitions and pretensions, and whose weak catering to the Legion activists led to such bloodshed. General Antonescu contributed to it, too, by his inability to conceive the revolutionary dynamism of a movement which had emerged from the nightmare of the torture chambers of the Carolist police and had for a party emblem a prison bar. And the Germans were also responsible. They did not proclaim their stand until it was too late. They kept everybody guessing, until the events of the end of January 1941 forced their hand to defend their interests.

Yet despite its failure as a movement and an idea, the Legion belonged to the series of revolutionary movements which today determine the face of our earth. It is interesting to guess what reforms the Legionaries would have carried out if Antonescu had not stopped them. There is little reason to doubt that their revolution would have been the most radical and sweeping in Rumanian history up to 1941.

The Germans were interested in neither Rumanian fascism nor the welfare of the Rumanian people through Archangelic social reforms. They never believed in the nationalist international any more than Stalin believed in the Communist International — that is, they believed only to the extent they could use the nationalist (or Communist) forces outside Germany (or Russia) in the German (or Soviet) national interest. And German national interest could be assured in the most satisfactory fashion through Antonescu and the many Goga-Cuzists who filled the administrative posts under him for the duration of the war.

Nothing could be more erroneous than to consider the Antonescu regime Fascist after February 1941. It was an old-fashioned military dictatorship, the personal dictatorship of Antonescu. This dictatorship lacked anything that could be compared to the ideologies which were the very moving force of the political system of Italy and especially of Germany. And for the ruling class this dictatorship, which was endorsed by the Germans, seemed to be infinitely better than experiments in Archangelic Socialism. It was an updated *status quo ante,* and it seemed to be best for the national interest. In the first eight months after Antonescu's advent to power, Bessarabia and northern Bucovina had been recovered, and while still hoping to regain Transylvania, the *Conducator* helped himself to Transnistria and Odessa.

Antonescu differentiated between Jew and Jew. The Jew was not considered *ipso facto* a traitor or a subhuman. Indeed, the treatment of Jews west of the Pruth was surprisingly decent as compared with other Nazi-controlled areas in Europe. As a result there is less hatred between Rumanians and the Rumanian Jews than there is between Jews and Hungarians.

Despite the fact that he was Hitler's choice, Antonescu was never a puppet. He defended Rumanian national interests against the *Führer* more than any other Nazi satellite leader. When he refused to capitulate in 1944 despite the fact that he knew the war was lost, it was not because he wanted to prolong his rule or the rule of the oligarchy or his own life; he wanted a guarantee for his country as far as Soviet designs were concerned. And it was here that he grossly misunderstood both his own potential and the implications of Rumania's international situation. Being committed to his policy and being an imperious, self-righteous man, he could be removed from his post only in the fashion in which King Michael removed him on August 23, 1944.

The young ruler and his companions need not be ashamed for what they did on that day, despite the sad aftermath. They did all that they could under the circumstances for their country, and no leader or patriot can do more. It is difficult to see how Rumania could have avoided becoming the scene of German rearguard action, and what is more important, how she could have reannexed northern Transylvania if not for the action of King Michael. And communism and Soviet domination would have been the end anyhow.

But, as the events of the last years show, March, 6, 1945, was not yet the end. Rumanians possess an indestructibility that is sometimes beyond the comprehension of the Westerner. Long experience of survival has taught them that each fall results in unforeseen opportunities, and they somehow always manage to rise to their feet again. Those fatalistic, flexible, realistic people on the borderline between the West and the Orient have profited from the great lesson their history has taught them: they have cultivated a superb sense of the temporary and transitory quality of everything.

CHAPTER XII

Conclusions and Parallels

Revolution is an idea that found bayonets.

Napoleon

Few historical phenomena have been so utterly discredited as fascism. This fact certainly does not facilitate the adoption of an attitude of scientific objectivity toward it even a quarter of a century after its downfall. Of those scholarly works that have been published on the subject, most have concentrated on the Fascist movements of international importance — Italian fascism and German National Socialism. Little or nothing has been written about Fascist movements in No-Man's-Land, especially in Hungary and Rumania, regardless of the fact that only in that region did fascism assume the proportions of a mass movement.

Until the pioneering work of Professor Eugen Weber, one could differentiate among five categories of opinions concerning fascism in Hungary and Rumania:

1. The opinion of A. Crețianu, first secretary in the Ministry of Foreign Affairs of Rumania and one of the chief architects of Rumania's successful *renversement dés alliances* in 1944, exemplifies the viewpoint of the former ruling class. He maintained that the Iron Guard "was made up largely of pseudo-intellectual riffraff, unable or unwilling to make a decent living, and who sought refuge in a mystic nationalism, the only reality of which was a ferocious anti-Semitism."[1] Such evaluation can be found in almost every statement of the representatives of the Carolist regime and are corroborated by the descriptions of the Goga-Cuzist-Antonescuites (see Barbul's work).

If one adds to the profile depicted above some derisive references to Szálasi's "lunacy," coupled with some contemptuous epithets as to the "trashy rabble" character of the Arrow Cross rank and file, Crețianu's picture of the Iron Guard would fit the descriptions of Kállay and Horthy on the one hand and that of the Szeged Fascist Imrédists of the Arrow Cross on the other.

2. The second evaluation is that drawn by Jews. Based on the most horrifying of human experiences, it is understandable that it emphasizes anti-Jewish terror and little else.*

*A good example of such an analysis is *Blood Bath in Rumania*, published by *The Record*, 4, No. 6-7, New York, July-August, 1942, to which a great number of parallels exist, published by Hungarian Jews in and outside of Hungary, giving exaggerated credit to the Arrow Cross for anti-Jewish horrors, credit which really belongs to the Imrédists.

3. The Communists have changed their position on fascism several times; but they have maintained inflexibly that any Fascist approach to social justice was nothing but demagoguery, anarchy or retrogression. No true proletarian could find anything attractive about it.*

4. The "enthusiast" apologists, Hungarian and Rumanian Fascist émigrées since 1945 more often than not, emphasize the "conservative" aspects of revolutionary Fascist movements, e.g., religion, nationalism, and above all, anti-communism, for obvious reasons.

5. As for scholarly thought, the words of Prof. Hugh Seton-Watson are as good an example as any. He saw a dividing line between different Fascist currents within Hungary and Rumania, "the first type being practiced by reactionary governments who aped Mussolini and Hitler, partly to ingratiate themselves with those gentlemen, and partly because they felt that Fascism 'is

*The fluctuation of the party line during the last forty years concerning fascism, especially its East Central European manifestations, are revealing. The Comintern defined fascism in 1928 as "using the discontent of the petite bourgeoisie, the intelligentsia ... recruiting the most backward strata of the workers." After taking power, however, fascism "casts aside its anti-Capitalist rattle and discloses itself as the terrorist dictatorship of big Capital." Quoted by R. Palme Dutt, *Fascism and Social Revolution,* (London, 1934), pp. 88-9. By the mid-thirties, however, Fascist movements — among them those in Hungary and Rumania — acquired unmistakable mass support. Georgiy Dimitrov had these movements in mind when he addressed the VII Congress of the Comintern in 1935, pointing out that "because of their appeal to the most urgent needs of the masses it was possible for the Fascists to line up part of the population at their side in every country." *Izbrannie Proisvedenia* (Gospolizdat, 1957) I, 377. What a "great part" of the population the Fascists succeeded in lining up at their side was understandably not pointed out by Dimitrov. With the entry of the Red Army into Hungary and Rumania and communization well under way, there could be no question anymore about Fascist "appeal to the most urgent needs of the masses," or true proletarians ever answering such an incongruent appeal. Any past connection between the Arrow Cross and Iron Guard on one hand and proletarian masses on the other had to be refuted. The Iron Guard became, in the words of Lucreţiu Patraşcanu, "a conjunction of déclassés and Lumpenproletariat." (*Lumpenproletariat* being the traditional Communist repository, where everything that does not fit into the Marxist scheme can be stored.) Patraşcanu, *Probleme de baze ale Romaniei* (Bucureşti, 1946), pp. 259-60. The Arrow Cross was described almost verbatim in the same way by Hungarian Communist historians of the Stalinist Era. With the stabilization of the system (the crushing of the Hungarian Revolt in 1956 being the turning point), Communist historians are undertaking more detailed studies of the popular Fascist movements. By the mid-sixties, they freely recognize the participation of genuinely popular broad masses in them. (Concerning the Iron Guard, see Lebedev, *Rumy'nia v godi vtoroy mirovoy voyny,* p. 43.) As far as the Arrow Cross goes, the work of Professor Lackó gives ample testimony to this changed Communist interpretation.

the up-to-date thing.' " They therefore fit out their old reactionary regimes with new trappings. They had no intention of transforming them into totalitarian states. The second type of Fascist movement, with broad popular support and pretensions to social justice, was dismissed by Professor Seton-Watson as "demagogic."*

There were some isolated voices in the first score of years after the war, like that of Prof. Henry Roberts, who, when reflecting about the Iron Guard as early as the late forties, saw in it something more than just demagoguery and hooliganism. According to Roberts, "It was a very important aspect of Rumanian political and social life," and he protested against the then current opinion which tended to dismiss it merely as a German Fifth Column or a superficial phenomenon.[2]

Speaking of the Arrow Cross, Professor Macartney explains that its members were

> honestly seeking true social and political reform and genuine remedies for real grievances, and that they were attracted to Nazism because, besides its anti-Semitism, it also, as preached in Southeastern Europe, advocated such reforms. To ignore these facts, which were systematically concealed by those hostile in their own interests, both to the bad and the good sides of Right Radical movements, is not only to do them injustice but to leave their appeal incomprehensible and to distort the whole political picture of the period.[3]

Even yet, the Fascist phenomena in Hungary and Rumania are not concisely defined. Those scholars who have pioneered the assault on existing walls of established opinion concerning fascism, like Professors E. Nolte and Eugen Weber, freely recognize that their works are by no means conclusive and that the subject demands "further investigation,"[4] especially as regards Hungarian and Rumanian fascism.**

*Hugh Seton-Watson, *The East European Revolution* (New York, 1951), p. 43. Under the impact of Professor Weber's recent studies, Professor Seton-Watson made some important amendments to his sweeping criticism of the popular Fascist movements as voiced above. See the *Journal of Contemporary History*, No. 1, 1966, p. 184n.

**Nolte, *Three Faces of Fascism*, p. 462. How badly this investigation is needed is evident from the question asked by Professor Nolte: Commenting on the fact that as war is the basic component of fascism, he continues that Hungarism could never have been implemented without war: "How could a philosophy of war become of paramount importance in a country like Hungary which could never have started a war on its own?" Professor Nolte also asks a second question: "How could a certain kind of subtle culture critique have become a vital political factor in Rumania at the edge of Europe?" It is interesting that for some scholars, Europe still ends almost with the Landstrasse. Marburg and der Lahn seems to be far away from the huts of Moldavian peasants and the *douce décadence* of Bucharest so far away that the icy abyss which existed between them is invisible even to such brilliant scholars as Nolte. However, Nolte points out the essence of the problem in his next phrase: "It is not Fascism itself, but the clear development of certain essential

347

Apart from the widespread antipathy which was and is felt toward the Fascist phenomenon, the difficulty in understanding and explaining it lies in the astounding variety of Fascist or quasi-Fascist movements that existed in Europe before and during World War II, ranging from the frankly anti-Christian Nazis to the fanatically religious Iron Guard. If one considers the common denominator (perhaps the only common denominator) of all Fascist movements, namely intolerant ultranationalism, the astounding variety of these movements should follow syllogistically. But it should be pointed out that the phenomena based on the philosophies of Christianity, democracy, liberalism or Marxism are in reality not so universal as they would seem. There are many approaches to the Christian ideal; considerable differences exist between parliamentary democracies; and there is an ever-growing divergency between states which claim to be Marxist. Most of these differences are based on national characteristics.

The key to the understanding of fascism in Hungary and Rumania lies in their national history, both recent and remote. Nations, as Lenin grudgingly conceded, are "stubborn facts," and Metternich's refusal to recognize this failed to prevent people from thinking along the lines of nationalism.

In the No-Man's-Land of Europe, an excessive dose of nationalism does not make a movement extremist; it is a basic ingredient of all politics; it is thought to be the very condition of survival. Even the Communists had to learn this the hard way. Perhaps it was not an accident that the monolithic Communist bloc suffered its first split on nationalistic lines in Eastern Europe in 1948. But nationalism in itself does not mean dictatorship, much less a Fascist one. It can be compatible with humanity, even with a democratic process. The example of modern France (despite some considerable convulsions and updatings of her institutions) or of Britain clearly shows this. But during the interwar period, ultranationalism was fatefully related to another problem in Hungary and Rumania, a problem which was perceived by Borkenau as early as the late 1930s.

Commenting on Lenin's failure to establish a "democratic dictatorship" of the peasantry and the workers, Borkenau saw the cause in the absence of a strong and self-confident bourgeoisie. This lack, he said, existed not only in Russia, but also in Spain, China, and Latin America — in short, wherever industrial progress was mainly due not to efforts at home but to pressures from the industrialized West. Then, in the same vein, Borkenau continues,

> In all those countries the impact of Western capitalism shattered the *Ancien Régime* without creating modern classes which would take the lead in reconstruction, and they are therefore compelled to choose either interminable and futile convulsions, or the establishment of some sort of dictatorship to execute the task in which the bourgeoisie fails, namely to modernize the country. Whether the dictator calls himself Lenin or Atatürk or Chiang-Kai-Shek*   matters less than may appear; it is not

characteristics, which is dependent on the size of a country and the significance of its spiritual traditions."

*Borkenau referred to the early, revolutionary stage of the Kuomintang.

decisive whether he starts from a dogma of proletarian revolution, of national or religious revival. The fact of modernizing dictatorship is decisive.[5]

Professor Weber defined twentieth-century fascism as "a by-product of disintegrating liberal democracy."[6] Perhaps in the industrialized West, fascism could be considered as such, but during the interwar years democracy did not have a chance in Hungary and Rumania; consequently there can be little talk of its disintegration, or of fascism as the by-product of this process.

The similarities between Hungary and Rumania are often deceiving. First, and above all, the line separating Rome and Byzantium runs between the two nations, this division being the clearest in Transylvania where the two cultures come to blows. Hungary may be a backward part of the West, but it still belongs to it. The short Turkish rule over part of Hungary did not change this. The Rumanian historical experience, the fusion of Byzantine, Turkish, and Phanariote heritages created something very different, especially in the Regat.

It is true that both Hungary and Rumania are small nations and both exist in the same hectic atmosphere of No-Man's-Land, but while Rumania historically accepted her status and shrewdly acted according to it, Hungary, because of her independent, proud, Westernized aristocracy, never submitted to her fate in passive oriental fashion. Indeed, until the advent of the industrial age, this aristocracy could more than hold its own for itself and for Hungary.

Both countries were underdeveloped economically — Rumania more than Hungary — but as a result of her historical experiences, the problems created by underdevelopment in Hungary resembled the problems of Poland, Spain or Portugal. In Rumania the same ills created problems much like the ones that developed in newly emerging nations in Africa and Asia, where Western institutions proved very alien to the new soil in which they were expected to flourish. It is not from such soil that working democratic institutions grow — no more in Rumania than in Pakistan or Ghana.*

Rumania woefully lacked either a strong, self-conscious middle class of Rumanian origin or the only possible substitute: a strong, land-owning

*This can be illustrated by the words of an Indonesian student leader, who made the following statement to an American correspondent in January, 1967, after Indonesia had gone through its great convulsion in which, according to conservative estimates, 200,000 Communists were massacred in cold blood. Commenting on the interim government's intention to hold democratic elections, the student activist spoke in a language which could have been repeated verbatim in interwar Rumania: "The future for us has become so dark. Where shall we go? We saw how the old academicians lived. They were parasites of the state, working in overpopulated departments. The trouble is that Sukarno's revolutionary indoctrination was not thorough, and, of course, we read books. We inherited the university system from the West and along with it we learned fundamental logic. But what shall we do with it? How shall we apply it? Sukarno's passing will not solve our problems, it will only be the

prosperous peasantry. Hungary's only middle class in the Western sense was Jewish, and despite their assimilation, the Jews were not to prove a substitute for a native middle class. It is doubtful that even the most loyal assimilated alien middle class can serve as a substitute for a native middle class, if the process of modernization is to be democratic. What is more, in 1919 democracy in Hungary could be based on little more than the five percent of the population who were Jews, and a working democracy by its very definition needs a broader native basis than that. It is almost certain that Hungary's other middle class, the "middle class of Hungarian gentlemen," was able effectively to silence the Western-minded middle class after the upheavals of 1918-19 as it did largely because the latter was so easily identified by its Jewish origin. If there had been a middle class of Hungarian peasant origin, the Hungarian Nation and its Swabian recruits could not with impunity have identified every Western idea of reform with Judaism, whether it was, as Gömbös called it, the "Gold International" (that is, "Jewish" capitalism) or the "Moscow International" (that is, "Jewish" bolshevism).

Nor was the lack of a strong native bourgeoisie or of a prosperous peasant middle class the only obstacle on the road to democratic evolution. The situation was further aggravated by the presence in Hungary of an all-powerful, historic ruling class, and in Rumania by an adroit oligarchy; consequently, the people were quite inexperienced in the art of self-government.

After World War I, Rumania belonged to the satisfied nations, but the Russian menace, combined with Hungarian and Bulgarian revisionist claims, gave her a feeling of insecurity, and she sought security for the maintenance of the status quo in the West — which meant France. Hungary, on the other hand, underwent a great, although perhaps to a certain extent justifiable, mutilation at Versailles, and she looked for redress to Italy and later to the much more powerful Germany of Hitler. But if France and the West were of little help to Rumania, German help for Hungary definitely had the characteristics of a Trojan horse: the role of Hungary in a Nazi-controlled southeastern Europe was a distinctly subordinate one. Rumania, on the other hand, belonged to the Russian sphere (in Stalin's and Churchill's evaluation to the extent of 90 percent), and Rumanians could find little solace during those years if they looked to the East. Hitler was ready to treat Rumania, and did treat her, with consideration. One cannot overestimate the significance of the accommodating German attitude on one hand and the Russian menace on the other when considering Rumanian politics in general and Rumanian fascism in particular.

During this time, the fact that the Communist left in Rumania was invariably identified with the number one national enemy was by no means the fault of the Rumanian element in the party ranks — Communists like

beginning.. It is all very romantic to talk in terms of democracy, but one-man, one-vote would be fatal in a nation that is 70 percent Javanese. A democratic election in an underdeveloped country is always cata-strophic." *Saturday Review,* February 4, 1967, p. 81.

Lucreţiu Patraşcanu, Gheorghe Gheorghiu-Dej or Nicolae Ceauşescu. By one means or another, Stalin imposed his line on the Rumanian Communists. Consequently, in the party membership the hostile minority groups were overrepresented — to say the least — and a working class deserving the name was lacking. Nor was either Ilie Moscovici or Madame Pauker a Lenin, nor even a Trotsky or a Zinoviev. In addition to these factors, one must remember the ruthless and efficient secret police. For a number of reasons, then, the Communist left did not have a chance in Rumania.*

As for the Rumanian Social Democratic party, it was a docile, bourgeois-intellectual group with a program proclaiming the necessity of building capitalism in Rumania first. Only after that would it consider the building of socialism. Thus it had what Lenin calls a "trade union consciousness" at its best; in the meantime, it helped to build capitalism. No wonder it did not attract the masses, that is, the peasantry. In addition, the camp of democratic socialism was split: there was a Unitary Socialist party and a Rumanian Socialist party in addition to the "regular" Social Democrats.[7]

In Hungary, the workers' movement was strong before World War I, but the Communists and radical Social Democrats, under predominantly Jewish leadership, were so thoroughly discredited during 1918-19 that between that date and the Communist takeover of 1947 Hungarian nationalism did not have to oppose itself to Russia or a communism based on Russia as did Rumanian nationalism. The extent of the early leftist failure insured that the Hungarian ruling classes considered even a democratic, let alone leftist, answer to the country's problems contrary to the Christian national spirit, which was to guide and sustain the neobaroque edifice. A brutal, watchful secret police and an even more brutal gendarmerie were not absent in Hungary either. After exiling, imprisoning or destroying the more radical leaders of the Social Democrats, Bethlen made his peace with the remaining rump of the party. The result was disheartening. The Social Democratic party became the party of the organized, relatively prosperous "aristocracy" of the working classes, an almost middle-class element within the vast disinherited masses. Not only were the miserable agrarian proletarians, the "three million beggars" of Hungary, beyond its reach; so were the unskilled workers and the numerous lower echelons of state employees. So the Hungarian masses had little solace or chance to air their grievances when they looked to the left.

Liberal democracy was not discredited in Rumania in 1919. On the contrary, it was an example to be looked to, almost a fashion. But the establishment of working institutions must be based on more than fashion or imitation. They must originate and develop out of a fusion of ideology and the experience of a people's past. Since Rumania did not have a Hungarian Nation which would be equally irreconcilable to democracy and communism, she gave the benefit of doubt to Western institutions. Under Brătianu's Liberal reign, a mixture of Western trappings and Phanariote methods were

*There are various estimates of the membership of the illegal Communist party in Rumania during the interwar period, none giving a higher figure than 1,000 members, many of them non-Rumanians.

tried, but these two traditions being too contradictory, the Brătianu system broke down. There was a genuine attempt at Western democratization during the brief National Peasant period. It was crushed by the great depression, but it is highly improbable whether even under the most favorable circumstances the National Peasants could have solved the problems of Rumania, the personality of Carol and the intransigent integrity of Maniu supplying not the least of reasons. After their fall, the liberals, calling themselves "neo-Liberals," progressed to the logical conclusion of their economic and political ideas as expressed by Professor Manoilescu: they began to do away with the cumbersome democratic institutions. The Fascist trappings of the Carolist dictatorship, as Hugh Seton-Watson saw it, were the ultimate consequence of this trend, the Antonescu dictatorship being the latest and last updating of the old structure.

For Hungary, a defeated nation, the Trianon Treaty imposed by the great democracies did not make a democratic transformation easier. The too-recent memories of the Károlyi republic, which ended, according to Borkenau's formula, after futile convulsions on the extreme left, did not help establish democracy either. But all these drawbacks would not have been decisive roadblocks on the way to another experiment with democracy if it had not been for that cardinal, centuries-old factor in Hungarian politics: the political nation – the Hungarian Nation.

Sometimes in semideveloped countries, the bureaucracy forms a class by itself, being a state within a state. In Hungary, not only was the bureaucracy a state within the state, but there was a nation within the nation. And the bureaucracy and this nation were identical. When an adroit ruling class has monopolized political power from time immemorial to the extent that, while representing only four to five percent of the population, it dares to call itself the "nation" and gets away with it into the mid-twentieth century; when this class inflexibly identifies its own interests as being those of Hungary, then this class has to develop a political philosophy which recognizes first and foremost its own class interests. So it was in Hungary. Democracy, by its very definition, would have challenged the rule of the tiny minority over the majority; consequently, it had to place in the Hungarian Nation's philosophy in 1919 or after. Democracy, therefore, had to be identified with its only representatives in Hungary, the arch enemy of the majority of the Hungarian Nation, the Jewish middle classes. These, in their turn, had to be identified with their kinsmen in Moscow and the City of London – and with the antinational Kun regime, to add length to the tail of the monster. Under such circumstances, the establishment of any kind of democracy (except for whatever such existed in the workings of the political nation itself) was, of course, out of the question. Hungary did not even experiment with democracy after the Hungarian Nation was restored to its monopoly of political power in 1919. It swung to the right long before the rest of the No-Man's-Land of Europe, or for that matter any part of Europe.

Although a unified political nation faced the democratic and Communist challenge, after the *status quo ante* was restored it became clear that conflicts of interest existed within its ranks and that it could not remain "unitary and indivisible" (*egységes és oszthatatlan*, a favorite boast of the political nation). It was Vienna against Szeged; that is, the Bethlen system consisting of the magnates, the land-owners and their allies, the great Jewish capitalists, who possessed real wealth and power, against the "middle class of Hungarian gentlemen," the destitute gentry, the refugee civil servants and the Officers Corps. The Szeged group had an all-quiet-on-the-western-front psychology best represented by Gömbös and Eckhardt,* in which reason gave way to a mixture of short-term class interests and irrational ultranationalism. While refusing democracy, the Szeged men considered themselves worthy of supplementing the Bethlenites and simultaneously moving into the positions held by the Jewish middle classes. But they were effectively contained under the strong, versatile hand of Bethlen; it remained for depression and that by-product of the depression, German Nazism, to give them their chance.

As a consequence, by the 1930s the political spectrum of Hungary and Rumania was strange, indeed almost unique. Democracy and communism had disappeared almost entirely from politics as forces of consequence. The staggering problems that remained had to be coped with outside the framework of these ideas. What followed afterward does not fit into the classical definition of the political right or left.

The Bucharest ruling class, perhaps because of its relatively fluid, flexible character, seemed to find consensus in a solution that amounted to a Fascist (to be sure, conservative Fascist) updating of the system. Called "neo-Liberalism" by its adherents, this new system forced economic liberalism on an unwilling people in the only way possible: by denying political freedom. In Hungary, on the other hand, where the lines of controversy within the ruling class were much more rigid than those in Bucharest, there was a rift between the Szeged Fascists and the Bethlenites long before the depression.

The question in Rumania was not so much *how* the country was to be run; the King, Calinescu, Vaida-Voevod, Goga, Cuza, Tătărescu,** all of them, were ready to reconcile themselves with the ideas of Manoilescu; the question was rather *who* was to run the country. The conflict in Hungary was not only of personalities but also of ideology and of social structure. The lower echelons of the political nation demanded a Fascist change of guard, a full political and economic takeover, and discarded the neobaroque system in favor of a Fascist, perhaps even a totalitarian, dictatorship. This was irreconcilable with the interests of the Bethlenites and their Jewish capitalist

*Hungary fought longer and suffered much more under the psychosis of World War I than Rumania, despite the fact that the latter was occupied by the enemy. Hungarian liability was much greater — she was defeated, occupied, torn by revolution and mutilated.

**Not in vain did Codreanu refer to the Goga-Cuzists as "the other face of the government" (the Tătărescu government of neo-Liberals). After the failure of the Legionary revolution, the Goga-Cuzists became the actual government, not its alter ego.

allies.* With a rift so clear, there could be no permanent cooperation between the two factions of the Hungarian Nation. After the unifying emergency of 1918-19, the Szeged men and those of Vienna parted. The other great emergency, the depression, brought an uneasy coalition, but Gömbös increasingly made it clear that he wanted absolute control; only his death prevented an earlier showdown between the factions.

In Hungary, the Szeged Fascists represented the 400,000 members of the middle class of Hungarian gentlemen. In Rumania, the line between the upper and middle strata of the oligarchy in power between 1933 and 1944 cannot be drawn so clearly. It is true that during the Carolist corporate state, the uppermost stratum of the oligarchy seemed to benefit more than before or after. But if one excludes the short Legionary interlude, it is hard to find any representation of interests of the people as a whole during these eleven years.

There was a predominantly middle-class Fascist answer to Rumania's problems, too, whether in the form of Vaida's Rumanian Front or in the ideas of the Goga-Cuzists, in the neo-Liberal framework of Manoilescu, Tătărescu, or the Manoilescu-conceived Carolist dictatorship.

A middle-class movement in Rumania always meant a strong dose of anti-Semitism, and the roots of Rumanian conservative fascism reach back to the L.A.N.C. with its sterile, exclusively anti-Semitic program that still held to the framework of parliamentary process.** When Goga, who like many others was not especially impressed with the performance of democracy in Rumania, fused his agrarian party with the L.A.N.C. in 1935, the resulting organization became the backbone of a Rumanian middle-class fascism based mainly on anti-Semitism. After the end of the First World War, the middleclass of Hungarian gentlemen had as much, if not more, conflict with the Jewish middle classes as the Rumanian middle class did — the assimilation and loyalty of the Hungarian Jews notwithstanding. Consequently, anti-Semitism was to be the very motive force of the Szeged Idea right from its birth in 1919. If the other programs of Hungarian and Rumanian middle-class fascism were quite vague, the anti-Semitic program in both was violent and clear, dominating and frequently replacing in reality all promised social reform. This was anti-Semitism at its most uncompromising: the ferocious, undying hatred of those who feel deprived of their profits by their neighbors.

But despite the existing similarities between the social stratification of Jews in Hungary and Rumania, with which the prevailing anti-Semitism in

*Despite the fact that Jewish money was instrumental in bringing Gömbös to power, by 1935 the good instincts of Ferenc Chorin, Leo Goldberger, and Jenö Vida foretold the things which were in the making, and they quickly returned to the Bethlenite fold, where they were welcomed with more pragmatism than enthusiasm.

**The first anti-Semitic nationalist party, as we remember, called itself National Democrats under the leadership of Professor Cuza, Iorga, and Codreanu père. The character of the Jewish question in Rumania being a national and social one, many Rumanians did not find anti-Semitism incompatible with a parliamentary system.

these two countries is usually explained, there are some marked differences between the two Jewish communities which should be pointed out. The similarities seem rather superficial and the differences become basic if one considers, for example, that there were more Jewish war dead in Hungary during World War I than there were Jewish servicemen serving in the Rumanian army during the same period. There are in all things degrees in degeneration; consequently, there are degrees in anti-Semitic degeneracy. Moreover, there is a difference between a loyal, useful, zealously patriotic Jewish community like that of Hungary, and the unassimilating, often hostile Jewish minority of Rumania. Whereas the Jewish question seemed to be a national problem in Rumania and the apparent threat posed by the Jews was by no means restricted to the middle classes, in Hungary until 1945 the Jews were considered a real problem almost exclusively by the Hungarian Nation, which after the First World War saw in the Jewish middle class an obstacle and challenge to itself. The Hungarian people had no economic conflicts of interest with the Jews and were little infected by this disease until 1944.*

*The reader may be surprised at seeing one of the most violently anti-Semitic people of the world being absolved of anti-Semitism, so this point needs some clarification. Although the answer goes beyond the scope of our subject, which ends in 1945. When the surviving Jews returned from Auschwitz to Hungary in 1945, they entered a hostile environment which "could not forgive them what it did to them." Only a year before when the Jews left for Auschwitz, nobody, not even Horthy, had believed they would ever return. Many Hungarians of all classes had helped themselves to Jewish property. In 1945, they seemed somewhat less than enthusiastic to return it to their rightful owners. A revolting, disgusting haggling started, causing much bitterness on both sides. Jews looked for protection in this situation to the Soviet Union and to its agents in Hungary, the Communists. At that point, they challenged not only the class interests of the Hungarian Nation but the national interests of the Hungarian people; hence, the rising tide of popular anti-Semitism. The Communists' skill at using dissatisfied minorities for consolidating their power does not restrict itself to the use of Jews alone. Although no 60-70 percent of Transylvanian Hungarians had been exterminated with the eager cooperation of their countrymen a year previously, the Hungarian minority of Transylvania, when threatened by Rumanian reprisals for the period of 1940-44, accepted the blandishments of the Soviet-sponsored Groza puppet regime, and contrary to their kinsmen in Hungary, became the obedient servants of the Communists, brutalizing the Rumanian majority in the most hideous fashion under the protection of the Russians. Nor was this a spontaneous move on behalf of the Hungarians in Transylvania. This "pragmatic" move was decided by none other than the cousin of the former prime minister, Count Béla Teleki! It is he who decided that "the only way open to salvation for the Hungarians in Transylvania is: To initiate, in agreement with the Communists [of Rumania] an opening to the Left." *Allianz,* p. 397; also, Macartney, *October Fifteenth,* p. 484. On the other hand, the Rumanian Communists, being Rumanians with a long historical experience behind them, knew the intrinsic value of such support and did not put up with it

In Rumania, there was a tradition of anti-Semitism based on nationalism, which in its turn had been based since time immemorial on Orthodox Christianity, and which could be employed against an unassimilating Jewish community with relative ease. The Szeged Fascists were not so lucky. There, the Jews were Hungarians. Many had converted to Christianity and intermarried with Christian Hungarians. An anti-Semitism based on Christianity or nationalism would not do; a highly successful process of assimilation had to be undone. Consequently, Hungary was the only country outside of the German ethnic bloc which introduced racial anti-Semitism for much the same reason as the Viennese or the Germans did. This was the achievement of Gömbös and Eckhardt. Rumanian bourgeois Fascists took a violent stand against other nationalities in addition to the Jews, especially those that blocked the advancement of the middle classes and refused to become Rumanians as well, like the Hungarians in Transylvanian towns. With more than 70 percent Rumanians within their boundaries, they thought they could press for a "Romanization" (as it was called) of the trades and professions. The Szeged Fascists, on the other hand, did not have a nationality problem. Acceptance into the ranks of the Hungarian Nation took assimilation for granted, whether it was assimilation from the lower classes (Antal) or an assimilation of nationality (Gömbös). Because it did not have a nationality problem in its ranks, the political nation had little sympathy or understanding for it. If anyone claimed that one existed, whether his name was Szálasi, Professor Jászi, or for that matter Professor Jakob Bleyer,* it was a treasonable utterance for the police or the gendarmerie to handle in an administrative manner. So the old policy of assimilating the elite of nationalities (excluding Jews) was continued by the Szeged Fascists.

The Bethlenites were rigidly committed to an old tradition expressed in the neobaroque restoration. This system was less flexible than that of the Rumanian oligarchy. For Carol it was not the form but the essence of power that mattered. He exchanged in quick sequence the democratic Maniu system with neo-Liberal pseudofascism — later his own kind of corporatism — and if the choice had been his, he would have remained in Bucharest during the Legionary state and even after. After liquidating the pretensions of Archangelic Socialism, the oligarchy arrived at a pragmatic arrangement with Antonescu. In neobaroque Hungary, one could not change the form without also changing the content of the system. Consequently, the showdown between the *csáklyások* and the changers of the guard was inevitable.

Manoilescu was the ideologist of the Rumanian middle-class Fascists, but the coherence of the ruling class prevented other bourgeois Fascists from developing any radical social reforming zeal. Here, neither social reform nor

---

any longer than was strictly necessary. Hence, the news of the "persecution" of Hungarians in Transylvania.

*He was the moderate leader of the nonassimilating Swabian peasants in Hungary, who until the advent of Hitler were required to assimilate if emancipated and educated.

totalitarianism was contemplated beyond updating the trappings and the institutions of the system with the help of corporatism. Not so in Budapest. The immobility and archaic character of the neobaroque edifice made it easy for Gömbös to present his partisans as the Reform Generation and his tenure in office as the Reform Era.* Although anti-Semitism dominated their social program both in theory and practice, they nevertheless brought a little social mobility into a rigid caste system. This gave some hope to newly educated peasant and lower middle-class sons. The Szeged Idea spoke vaguely of land reform, but it had precise words concerning Jewish banks and industry. Above all, it gave at least some lip service to the notion that everyone was a part of the nation as a whole. It is in this that the Szeged men were at their demagogic best.

Gömbös was the only truly charismatic leader the Szeged Fascists ever had. Rumanian middle-class fascism had ruthless operators like Calinescu and lyrical pseudo-Fascists like Goga, but none of them could be compared with the personality of Gömbös. With his dynamism (another quality which was absent in Rumanian bourgeois Fascist leaders) and with the help of Hitler, he could have turned Hungary into a corporate, totalitarian state. And in strong contrast to his opposite numbers in Bucharest, Gömbös really wished to do just that. In no sense did he intend merely to "update" the neobaroque edifice; he was dedicated to its demolition. Under his leadership, the Government party's transformation into a one-party Fascist system could have served this purpose much better and much more sincerely than the various one-party systems created by Carol. Such a party could have rallied much popular support in Hungary if for no other reason than that it would have put an end to long immobility. But Gömbös missed his moment during the years of the depression. The Bethlenites tied his hands in the beginning; his "revisions" confused everybody; there was also too much individualism and democracy within the political nation; and meanwhile the Arrow Cross rose. The *csáklyások* were shaken but not broken. Gömbös died, and his "orphans," in the ensuing disarray, found themselves in very different circumstances with a very different new leader.

Imrédy was an economist imbued with a dry and ruthless logic, more conservative than Gömbös and entirely lacking his charisma and sincere Hungarian patriotism. He replaced the dynamism of Gömbös with unrelenting ambition. Under the rapidly changing circumstances of the late 1930s and World War II, he drew his conclusions from the march of events. He was not a Fascist by conviction despite his professed National Socialism. He reduced Gömbös' frankly totalitarian plans to mere Fascist trappings. But believing in the necessity of "updating" the neobaroque system by a change of the guard, he considered the possibility of carrying out some long overdue Szeged Fascist reforms. In order to accomplish his program, he had to crush the

*Using the traditional name of the period between 1830-48 and the name of that Hungarian generation, which, it is true, consisted also of the lower echelons of the political nation, who were protagonists of the Reform Era.

Bethlenites, the Jews and the Arrow Cross. The Szeged Fascists could not do this by themselves alone: there were only 400,000 of them, and by no means all of them were militants. Imrédy needed help from the outside. As far as possible Western support goes, he knew very well that the West would never support his goals. Hungary's Western connections were maintained almost exclusively through the Jewish middle classes and the Bethlenites. Soviet help was excluded automatically, so he had to rely on the only chance he had: Nazi ascendancy and victory. Imrédy and his partisans often proclaimed that Hungary stood or fell with a German victory and made much of the "common Hungarian-German destiny." From the Szeged point of view, the logic of this stance is unassailable. In the light of such logic, one may understand the unconditional subservience of the March Men and their ghastly record.

There was no such all-or-nothing attitude in the flexible Rumanian bourgeois Fascist camp. Apart from the very different Rumanian tradition in conducting foreign affairs, there was one marked leadership difference between it and the Szeged Fascists: Goga, Cuza, Vaida, Manoilescu, and the two Antonescus, Gheorge Brătianu, Calinescu and the other Rumanian middle-class Fascist sympathizers were without exception Rumanians. It cannot be said with much certainty of Szeged Fascist leadership and the Hungarian officer corps that they were Hungarians. It would be hard to establish with accuracy how far and how deeply they were influenced in their decisions in 1944 by their non-Hungarian, or to be exact, by their German descent. It would seem that their Hungarian patriotism was by no means as sincere as they claimed it was. The absence of a predominantly Hungarian middle class avenged itself in 1944 as much as if not more than it did during the years 1918 and 1919.

Both middle-class Fascist movements were Hitler's choice for collaboration. The Nazis followed only their interests in this area and these seemed to be safeguarded in the best possible way by the accommodating attitude of Imrédy or the iron hand of Antonescu. Not being hampered by any commitment to a "holy mission" in this area, the Germans did not wish to experiment during the war, and their traumatic experience with the Legion only strengthened them in this determination. But there is little in common between the unconditional, disreputable subservience of the Hungarian March Men and Rumanian relations with Germany. The Antonescu regime was at no point the equivalent of the government Hungary was governed by after March 19, 1944. Much of this can be credited to the personality and robust patriotism of General Antonescu, but even without him it is not easy to imagine that the Goga-Cuzists would have debased themselves to the level of a Baky or an Imrédy. It is quite possible that without Antonescu there would have been more subservience to Hitler. Even so, the saying current in Bucharest in 1967 (after another seemingly collaborating regime had declared its independence at the right moment from the national enemy) may explain the likely Rumanian attitude: "We Rumanians are ready to sell even our country if necessary, but we do not make delivery." It should be pointed out that in 1944 the democratic and Communist camps in conjunction with the King and the two Antonescus worked feverishly to extricate Rumania from the approaching holocaust and disaster. There is no evidence of any disreputable traffic developing between Killinger's office and any Rumanian politician, bourgeois Fascist or other. There were no traitors to be found among the Goga-Cuzists (old Professor Cuza was still alive and kept informed of the preparations, which he approved fully). Veesenmayer had no such difficulties. A constant stream of informers, most of them Szeged Fascists, reported Kállay's every move and later Horthy's to him and to the R.S.H.A. Even on the Jewish question, the Rumanian middle-class Fascists, their anti-Semitism mitigated more by opportunism and corruption than by humanistic considerations, proved themselves in the ultimate analysis more moderate toward their unassimilated Jews than their opposite numbers in Hungary were toward their assimilated ones.

As far as any possible cooperation between the two middle-class Fascist camps was concerned, there could not be any. The one in Rumania was an updated oligarchy; that in Hungary was the Hungarian Nation supposedly rejuvenated through the spirit of the age. These changes were not sufficient to diminish even an iota the existing Hungaro-Rumanian hatreds on either side, so the controversy was relentlessly pursued by each side without a shred of sympathy for the other.*

In the matter of Fascist fellow traveling during Hitler's ascendancy in the *Südostraum*, the whole Rumanian oligarchy was ready to go along, but never all the way. Although democratic institutions had failed when superimposed on Rumanian realities, thus giving birth to a great disenchantment, the quasi-Fascist Rumanian oratory of the era does not have a sincere ring. There was a quest for an answer, and the trappings or approaches of fascism seemed the best solution as of 1938, and for that matter until 1942. But this was not considered the final answer to Rumania's problems even by those who were at the helm. It was one more station on the long Rumanian road — it was not the millennium.

In Hungary, because of the conflict between the Bethlenites and the Imrédists, there were many politicians, bureaucrats and officers in important positions who sympathized more with Imrédy than with Horthy or Kállay, but while the conservatives were still powerful, they did not avow their sympathies very loudly until March 1944. This vast opportunistic camp can be safely defined as Fascist fellow travelers, the best examples being Antal, Marton, Mecsér, Endre, the Officers Corps and (on a different level, no doubt) the distinguished historian, Hóman.

While we have considered the efforts of the Rumanian oligarchy to accommodate to the "command of the times" and those of the lower echelons of the political nation in Hungary to acquire the Bethlenite positions of power and Jewish wealth with the help of the spirit of the age, we have not

*The only tangible exception being the strange participation of Professor Cuza in 1925 in the work of the Budapest Anti-Semitic World Congress organized by Gömbös and Eckhardt.

mentioned the reaction of the majority of Hungarians and Rumanians to the tribulations of the depression. Hungarian and Rumanian middle-class fascism hardly resulted in a "modernizing dictatorship" or a "development dictatorship," as Professor Nolte calls the phenomenon.* According to Borkenau's formula, after the attempt to establish a working democracy in these two countries predictably failed, and with the road to communism solidly blocked by a number of insurmountable barriers, Rumania and Hungary swung to the right and the ruling classes in both countries tried to enforce the kind of rightist solution which served their interests. These interests were by no means identical with those of the common people. Rumanian peasants could not identify themselves with the interests of the camarilla or of the corrupt, city-dwelling, "Romanizing" middle classes any more than the Hungarian workers and peasantry could identify with the interests of the Aryanizing *nouveau riches,* the Szeged Fascist bureaucrats or the Officers Corps.

It was precisely the failure of the bourgeois Fascists to establish a modernizing dictatorship in Rumania that gave the Iron Guard its chance.** In Hungary, it seems certain that Gömbös could have established some kind of dictatorship, whether a bourgeois Fascist or a totalitarian one, which would have carried out a very limited modernization, but for one reason or another, he failed to do so. So the popular desire for modernization produced a desperate, stillborn effort in the form of the Arrow Cross.

It was impossible after the ordeal of the depression to leave the majority of the people out of politics and to settle the affairs of Hungary and Rumania as if they concerned exclusively the Hungarian Nation and the oligarchy. When such an attempt was made, the people protested vigorously and began a peculiarly violent class struggle*** in the form of the Arrow Cross and

*Professor Roberts pointed this out when, in assessing the achievements of the Carolist corporative state, he maintained that while industrialization was definitely desirable, the manner in which it was carried out by Carol, Malaxa and the others was not." ... it would appear ... that the Rumanian people were not paying temporarily for the establishment of industries which would benefit them subsequently, but were instead being drained of their resources for the profit of a small group of industrialists, politicians, and court favorites, in no way responsible to them." *Rumania: Political Problems of an Agrarian State,* pp. 344-45. Looking at the Szeged Fascist record before and during 1944, it is difficult to give them even as much credit as Professor Roberts gave to Carol. Imrédy sold the lion's share of Hungarian industry lock, stock, and barrel to the SS and Göring.

**In Turkey, Kemal Ataturk succeeded in establishing a dictatorship which served the people as a whole rather than merely a clique; consequently, no significant opposition could be mobilized against his harsh, unprecedented reforms.

***After the considerable Arrow Cross success in the elections of 1939, the Bethlenites freely conceded that "the masses of leftist radicalism are now on the extreme right." *Népszava,* June 3, 1939. Also Lackó, *Nyilasok, nemzetiszocialisták,* p. 176.

Legionary movements.* This social protest was carried out in the very name of these two factors which Marxism denied, two factors all-important for common Hungarians and Rumanians alike: nationalism and religion. To call such phenomena "rightist" or "leftist" would seem meaningless, and to identify these currents with the classical definition of the left or the right would be to take them out of context. Such identification might serve certain contemporary political interests (as it did in its time), but it would be small contribution to understanding. The other current definition category, that of "revolutionary conservatism," fits these movements only with important qualifications.

Neither of these popular movements was spontaneous; their leaders and instigators came from those segments of society which were uprooted from the old agrarian, patriarchal way of life but had not yet secured a place in the new society — or where the anomalies of Rumanian and Hungarian social structure were most striking. They were unemployed intellectuals, dismissed civil servants, young army officers, students, lower middle-class shopkeepers and artisans, all borderline cases in society. Their insecurity could and did generate as violent a fanaticism as one might observe among the inhabitants of a border area between hostile nations or cultures.

The ideologies of both movements are inseparable from the personalities of the leaders, Codreanu and Szálasi, who conceived them. It is proper and fitting that it should be so; in such movements, only the ideas and orders of the leader matter. There is a similarity between the background of Szálasi and that of Codreanu. They came from non-Rumanian and non-Hungarian stock respectively. In addition, each had a mother who was of different national background from the father. Both mothers were very religious, and their influence on their young sons was great. Both leaders came from the lower middle classes, so that they were borderline cases socially as well as ethnically. Both were relatively young as leaders (they were almost the same age), and each had a pronouncedly military background. Both were mystics and what a philosopher of the Enlightenment would call "enthusiasts," but their enthusiasm had different roots. Codreanu's enthusiasm was of the religious kind. He considered himself the emissary of the Archangel Michael, the tool of God to stamp out evil in Rumania. Szálasi was more self-contained. It was from the "secret force within himself" that he derived his monotonous, stubborn logic and strength.

While Codreanu, thanks to his Rumanian upbringing and environment, could combine his "holy mission" and his irrational ends with a hard-headed appreciation of the underworld of Rumanian politics for the short run, Szálasi was, considering his means, his ends, his tactics and his strategy, constantly in the clouds — and his inflexibility cost his movement dearly.

*Professor Nolte maintains that "apart from the awkward problem of Perónism," all Fascists movements were movements of the middle classes. *Op. cit.,* p. 401. To this writer the phenomena of the Arrow Cross and in particular of the Legion would seem not less "awkward" than that of Perónism.

Indeed, no other Fascist leader in the world could rival Szálasi for lack of realism.

In its concepts of organization, the Legion seemed more elitist and more imaginative than the Arrow Cross. Its elitism was based on recognition for merit and a mystical calling to lead. While there is no doubt about the sincerity of Szálasi's belief in his calling, the rest of the Arrow Cross hierarchy was selected according to worldly and very much less elitist criteria, to say the least.

While Szálasi had an inflexible program in Hungarism, the Legion refused with indignation to formulate any program. Every step the Legion took was to follow from Orthodox Christianity on an *ad hoc* basis, and because these steps were rooted in Orthodoxy, they were to be the only correct ones toward the solution of a given problem. The Legionary state was to be a distinctly Orthodox Rumanian one. The ultimate goal of the state was salvation, which meant the salvation of the individual by way of the salvation of the collective.

Both movements were, by their very *raison d'être*, strongly nationalistic. But when Szálasi and Codreanu spoke about the nation, they meant the whole nation, especially its lower classes. They couched their attack against the ruling classes in ultranationalistic terms. Until this became obvious to the Rumanian oligarchy and the Hungarian Nation they could get away with such social criticism; however, when the "tendency" of their nationalism, as Gömbös called it, became clear, the reprisals taken against them were matched in Hungary only by the measures taken against Communists and in Rumania they far exceeded the persecution of Communists.

Hungarism's nationalism had some vague Turanian and Aryan nostalgia. But though the Legionairics often proclaimed the brotherhood of Latin nations, they did not appeal to the glories of Rome. Their nationalism tried to go back to the nation equated with the peasantry, and in Rumania a nationalism based on the peasant had to be identical with Orthodoxy. While Hungarism was, in general, respectful of Christianity,* and while the teachings of the Iron Guard supposedly were based on Orthodox Christianity (a debatable contention), the fact remains that Rumania was the only Orthodox country where a Fascist movement received mass support. Although the hierarchy of the Rumanian Orthodox Church was traditionally a part of the ruling class, the extent of the lesser clergy's participation in Legionary activities was very great indeed.

While Hungarism was frankly racist and there was talk among its proponents about an "Aryan-Turanian membership, country, policy," etc., this racism was not of the same stripe as that which supported the German superman complex. It was directed only against Jews — against nobody else. The Legion, on the other hand, because of its identification with Orthodoxy,

---

*Although Szálasi indulged in the perversion of the Bible, and some Hungarist ideologues, like Vágó, were quite hostile to "Jewish" Christianity. It is therefore that the churches kept the Arrow Cross at arm's length. Only a few priests were members, some later defrocked.

had to reject racism and did. Rumanians are as ethnically mixed as the Hungarians, but they have always drawn different conclusions from this fact. The Rumanian Iron Guard took its violent anti-Jewish stand on the basis of the existing national and social problems presented by the Jewish question. It is difficult to imagine Codreanu ordering mandatory anthropological examinations of prospective Legionaries (complete with skull measurements) of the sort which Szálasi ordered for Arrow Cross members in 1942-43, and even in 1945!

But Codreanu, while not a racist, was nevertheless a much more violent anti-Semite than Szálasi. Codreanu considered the Jew the irreconcilable enemy of his own special utopia. Szálasi was not a pathological Jew-hater. The Jews simply did not fit into Hungarism; knowing his ideas on one hand and the Jews on the other, this was quite understandable. Consequently, he wished to get rid of them. This (at least in theory) had nothing to do with humiliation, despoliation or extermination. But anti-Semitism, despite Codreanu's hatred or Szálasi's racism, was by no means as important a factor in attracting support in the Arrow Cross or the Iron Guard as it was in the middle-class Fascist movements. The majority of Hungarians and Rumanians who were attracted to the Arrow Cross and the Iron Guard were attracted by the sincere concern Szálasi and Codreanu felt for their plight much more than they were by anything else, anti-Semitism and even nationalism included.

The social program of Hungarism was vague, almost as vague as those of the bourgeois Fascist parties. But in contrast to Codreanu, Szálasi spoke positively and unequivocally of socialism and a *socialnationale* (as a modified socialist international). Codreanu never employed the word "socialism." Yet the Legion's dedication to and affinity for Orthodoxy created an Archangelic Socialism that made it more radical than any other Rumanian party save the Communists. During the interwar period, it was their forceful criticism of obvious and long-standing abuses and their determination to take steps on an *ad hoc* basis, not their respective social programs, which clearly distinguished the Iron Guard and the Arrow Cross on the one hand from the middle-class Fascists on the other, with their lip service to social reform. And it was the manifest sincerity of their dedication to social reform rather than the social criticisms themselves which attracted the simple Hungarian and Rumanian folk to these radical Fascist movements.*   The ruling classes as

*There is no need to elaborate the sincere devotion of Szálasi or Codreanu to social justice here again. Let's only record a typical, almost quasi-Marxist outburst by Sima. When he recalls that the strongly pro-German neo-Liberal chief, Dinu Brătianu, in 1938 approved the murder of Codreanu on the basis that "from the point of state interest it was justifiable," Sima asks in fury: "Which state? The one which was conducted from the salon of Mme. Lupescu? Or the exploiting state of the neo-Liberal government?" (*Cazul Iorga-Madgearu*, p. 25.) And how painful it must have been for the few Social-Democratic deputies, when after the crushing defeat in the elections in 1939 (with the poor in the camp of the Arrow Cross) they entered Parliament only to be greeted by

363

well as the masses understood this. The persecution of the Legion and of the Arrow Cross was always proportional to its popularity and mass support.

While the attitude of the Legion had a strong Populist content with its love for the "unspoiled peasant," and a deep hostility not only toward capitalism and industrialization (an attitude which had clear origins in Stere and Eminescu), Hungarism had practically no precedent or roots in Hungarian political history.* For good or bad, Szálasi's trend of thinking was an original one. It was by no means anti-industrial, nor did it emphasize agriculture rather than industry. It wished rather to establish a balance between the two.

Szálasi wanted to reorganize Hungary within her historical boundaries in the framework of a voluntary, multinational federation of the Great Carpathian-Danubian Fatherland. This makes him almost the only Hungarian leader outside the democratic or Communist camp who recognized the existence of a nationality problem inside the boundaries of the Lands of the Holy Crown of St. Stephen.** He was willing to recognize the separate existence of other national groups by granting rights and autonomy to them without forcing them to become Hungarians first.

Szálasi, like the rest of his countrymen, had not the slightest doubt about the voluntary acceptance of his K.D.N.H. by the nationalities. This would bring about the *Pax Hungarica* without which the peace of Europe, the solution of world problems and the triumph of National Socialism would be unimaginable and also impossible.*** This was the ultimate goal of Hungarism. Codreanu's attitude was a more exclusive one as far as membership and the treatment of nationalities were concerned. Here again, as in the case of Rumanian bourgeois fascism, the fact that 70 percent of Rumania's population consisted of Rumanians was a decisive factor. In Hungary, not

---

the solid block of Arrow Cross deputies, seated on the extreme left, with such derisive outcries as: "What do you want here anyway?" "Is there still any business left for Socialists? " "Ridiculous, obsolete (position)!" *O.N.K.*, June 21, 1939.

*Recent Communist historical study of the Arrow Cross tries to identify it with populism (agrarianism) — being, according to Marxists, the most reactionary trend in socialist thought. (Lackó, *op. cit.*, pp. 36-39.) It is possible to maintain that such an interpretation contradicts the facts. There was a Hungarian Populist movement at the beginning of the twentieth century. But the teachings of the leading Hungarian Agrarian Socialists, Achim and Mezöfi, have nothing in common with Hungarism. If the quasi-Populist agrarian proletarian supporters of Böszörmény rallied behind Szálasi, this was not because of Hungarism but out of necessity.

**There remains also the *Völkisch* solution, carefully fostered by the R.S.H.A. type of nationalists in the bourgeois Fascist camp like Baky and Imrédy. Such a solution would have destroyed not only historic Hungary but even Trianon Hungary.

***This should answer Professor E. Nolte's understandable question: How did the Arrow Cross imagine it could implement its program without a major war? Nolte, *op. cit.*, p. 462.

even the wishful thinking of Szálasi could envision an exclusively Hungarian solution. The best he could hope for (the Hungarians constituted only 45 percent of the total inhabitants of the K.D.N.H.) was Hungarian supremacy in a framework of voluntary federation.

Szálasi wished to create a new Hungary, but in Rumania the Legion wished first to create a "new man." It was this "new man" who was to create a new Rumania. Therefore, Moţa refused corporatism which, as he saw it during the neo-Liberal era, would only perpetuate the existing corruption of society. Corporatism should come only after the creation of the "new man," if at all. On the other hand, Szálasi accepted corporatism without hesitation or reservation (as a good Fascist should) as the framework of Hungarist society.

During the Arrow Cross meetings, the humble members were with their own kind, not amid gentle folk, as in the other Fascist movements. Also their desperation at not finding any better, more constructive outlet for their desire for social justice had much to do with their rallying to Szálasi's banner. The archangelic gospel as preached by Codreanu was highly effective in acquiring the support of the peasantry. Its simple, almost Church Slavonic language was refreshingly different from the usual artificial language of the politicians. It was the peasant's own language; it penetrated to his heart and soul. It gave him a quasi-religious experience and above all, it gave him hope.* This cannot be said of Szálasi's bewildering prose, directed as it was to the working class rather than to the peasantry.**

And even if the Arrow Cross and the Legion failed to fulfill the expectations and hopes of simple Hungarians and Rumanians, we must agree with Professor E. Weber concerning these two movements, that "the identification between Fascism and reaction is widely off the mark."[8]

While the rank and file of the Legionaries and of the Arrow Cross were peasants and workers respectively,*** the leaders of both movements came

*Although the workers' revolutionary potential was perhaps recognized before 1940, the large industrial centers were firmly controlled by the Carolist corporate state, and the Legion could not take advantage of it until the advent of the National-Legionary State. The proletarian character of these movements is further emphasized by the steady fluctuation of Iron Guardists and Arrow Cross men to and from the Communist party of their respective countries after 1945 and even before. There is as yet no evidence of such a traffic between the Communist party and the Szeged Fascists or the Carolist Goga-Cuza-Antonescu supporters.

**The Hungarian peasantry, despite its miserable life, is one of the least revolutionary of all peasant groups in Europe. Even during the revolution in 1956, although much more affected by collectivization than the workers, and admittedly sympathetic to the goals of the revolution, they gave it little active support. Almost all the fighting was done by workers and students.

***In connection with the massive popular participation in these movements, two accusations so often raised against them should be answered: (1) Legionary violence, and (2) the large criminal element present in the

almost exclusively from the lower middle classes. There were few, indeed very few, intellectuals in either the leadership or the rank and file of the Arrow Cross;* the students in Hungary were in the majority Szeged Fascists. But a very considerable proportion, if not the majority, of Rumanian students during the interwar years sympathized with the Legion, and its leadership included many intellectuals of good standing. Both the Arrow Cross and the Legion had a youthful leadership (the Legion even more than the Arrow Cross), a characteristic trend in all radical Fascist movements in contemporary Europe. This youthful leadership explains in part the recklessness of the Legion; its rank and file, especially the militants, also consisted of very

---

ranks of both the Arrow Cross and the Legion.

As far as Legionary violence goes, it was more often than not greatly provoked by the initial violence and corruption of the Rumanian ruling classes. It is they who credit the Legion with initiative, but in most cases one can speak (if one disregards the anti-Jewish horrors) of retaliation only. It would seem that the Rumanian oligarchy had a monopoly on violence before the Legion challenged it, and monopoly is always considered the best policy by those who have it. The other root of Legionary violence lay in Orthodoxy. Diminished personal responsibility coupled with the rectification of the collective ego could and did easily unleash a violence which in the 1930s raged in Rumania like an elemental storm, a storm in which the Iron Guard itself found its bloody doom.

Concerning the rate of crime in the membership of these popular movements, one should not be surprised if the Hungarian Nation or the Bucharest oligarchy emphasizes that aspect. After all, they always referred to the simple folk in the ranks of the Arrow Cross and the Legion in the most contemptuous terms. While the moral standards of the Hungarian Nation during the interwar period left a lot to be desired and those of the Bucharest oligarchy warrant a loud moralizing even less, the most surprising criticism of Arrow Cross morality comes from an unexpected quarter. Professor Lackó indulges in the publication of elaborate charts proving that a very considerable proportion of Arrow Cross rank and file had a criminal record. (Lackó, *op. cit.*, p. 134.) Apart from the fact that during the communization process in Hungary Arrow Cross toughs were welcomed in the Communist shock troops which ruthlessly crushed the democratic parties, Professor Lackó should remember the ratio established by Lenin concerning revolution: For every honest revolutionary there are a hundred dishonest ones.

*Ferenc Fiala, the ex-Communist, Arrow Cross journalist, recalled a rather depressing incident. When Szálasi visited his apartment, he noticed on his bookshelf the works of Dezső Szabó, Endre Ady and Atilla József — without doubt the three greatest representatives of Hungarian literature in the twentieth century. Dezső Szabó represents the Populist, Endre Ady the Westernizing and Attila József the Socialist current. Szálasi remarked: "These works must disappear from Hungarian literature." Szálasi also met several writers — the meeting was a very unsuccessful one. Lackó, *op. cit.*, p. 261n.

young people.* The prevalence of youth in the rank and file of the Arrow Cross was much less pronounced.

The relations between the popular Fascist movements and Germany were almost uniformly unfavorable; the Nazis considered them a last trump in their game. The National-Legionary State did not come into being because of any German demand. The Nazis were never so naive as to believe in a Nationalist International; consequently, Germany never demanded the establishment in Hungary and Rumania of regimes copied from Nazism, and as we have seen, the popular Fascist movements in both countries were not copies of the N.S.D.A.P.

Hitler was by no means unaware of the conflicts that might arise from the intransigency of other integral nationalist movements, even from their economic development on nationalistic lines.** What he wished in this area — as elsewhere — was collaboration and subservience. This he found in those middle-class Fascist movements which depended on him for their very existence.

Not compelled to fight on as many fronts as the Szeged Fascists and feeling the support of the masses behind them, Szálasi and Codreanu (and even Sima) did not depend on Hitler alone to maintain their eventual rule. Hence Szálasi's inflexibility and the Legion's more passive, subtle, "Rumanian" resistance as compared with the flexibility of Goga-Manoilescu and of the Antonescu regime toward Hitler.

Perhaps the flexibility of the bourgeois Fascists can also be explained by their political maturity. Imrédy and his partisans were certainly not "enthusiasts," and the oligarchy in Bucharest was even less prone to "enthusiasm" than Imrédy. Inflexible nationalism in Hungary and Rumania was more characteristic of the lower classes than of the educated classes. Yet despite their blood-and-thunder oratory both before and after the war against "German imperialism" (a phrase unheard in bourgeois Fascist terminology), both Szálasi and Sima did give way to the blandishments of power offered by the Nazis. Szálasi accepted the unenviable role offered to him in October 1944, with half of Hungary under Soviet control, and Sima was ready to play an even more ridiculous role in Vienna during the same period.

Connections and sympathies between the two popular Fascist movements were more numerous than the contacts and sympathies between the Fascist movements of the Budapest and Bucharest ruling classes. There were at least some manifestations of sympathy between the Arrow Cross and the

*While investigating the nominal role of an admittedly not absolutely representative Legionary group of militants exiled after their failure of January, 1941, Professor E. Weber found that in 1940 the average age of 226 Legionaries was 27.4. *Journal of Contemporary History,* 1966, No. 1. p. 108.

**He remarked at the height of German-Italian relations that if Mussolini's reforestation program were carried out, it might be necessary in a hundred years to wage war on Italy. Nolte, *op. cit.,* p. 410.

Legion,* based rather on a common fate at the hands of their ruling classes than on a compatibility of ideas. Such feelings of vague solidarity were expressed at times by Codreanu himself.** And there was also the mysterious agreement in the spring of 1945 between the Arrow Cross Foreign Minister, Kemény, and his Iron Guardist colleague, Prince Sturdza. The agreement could not be taken very seriously: the very substance of Legionary doctrine and Hungarism was an inflexible insistence on the boundaries of Greater Rumania and the Lands of St. Stephen respectively. Since the desired limits overlapped, any meaningful cooperation was automatically excluded.

Did either the Arrow Cross or the Iron Guard represent an attempt to establish a modernizing dictatorship?

The Archangelic Socialism of the Legion and its categorical repudiation of the twentieth century suggest that it could not and would not establish such a dictatorship. While this was not so much the case with the Arrow Cross, Szálasi lacked the basic qualities required to lead a successful modernization process, such as a realistic appreciation of the situation and the ability to compromise. Since they attained power under the most unfavorable circumstances and held it only for a short time, it is difficult to imagine what might have been accomplished under less hostile conditions and a more protracted rule, but neither their programs nor their records once in power suggest great success. A process of modernization requires something more than sincerity and good intentions coupled with anarchy. Far from being positive, self-motivated forces to carry out a process of modernization in which the bourgeoisie had failed, the popular Fascist movements seem to have been products of the extent of ruling-class failure to establish a truly modernizing dictatorship.

When compared with the two great Western Fascist movements, Italian fascism and German National Socialism, the Legion seems to resemble the

*After the murder of Codreanu, Hubay, acting as regent for Szálasi during his imprisonment, wrote a sympathetic editorial titled "Codreanu Will Shoot Back," predicting the eventual victory of the Legion in Rumania. (*Magyarság*, December 5, 1938.) Hubay warned that if a similar attempt were made against the Arrow Cross, it would be met with force. An Arrow Cross paper published the translation of Codreanu's diary, and several other Arrow Cross papers adopted a moderate tone toward the Iron Guard. When attacked by other chauvinistic papers for this, they answered that "they must familiarize the Hungarian people with the enemy." Budaváry László, *Zold Bolsevizmus* (Budapest, 1941), pp. 54-58, 73-76. The former Communist, and in 1940 one of the chief Arrow Cross publicists, Fiala, wrote euphoric editorials in July, 1940, hoping for an Iron Guardist takeover and "the transformation of Rumania into a totalitarian state." *Pesti Újság*, July 6, 1940.

**In 1937, Codreanu made his contribution to the idea of the Nationalist International, saying that "There exists a feeling of solidarity between people who serve their nations in the different parts of the world exactly like the solidarity of those who work respectively for the destruction of their nations. Charlé, *op. cit.*, p. 99.

former. Both Mussolini and Codreanu preferred action to theory and programs, and relied largely on an emotional and sentimental appeal.* Both movements could be pragmatic in their approach to the problems of the day. But one all-important reservation should be made at that point: Orthodoxy, at least in theory, was the very motivation of the Legion's actions, even (if we remember the "expiation" procedure) of its pragmatism. Such pragmatism has its root in both Italy's and Rumania's long historical experiences in which inflexibility was not very helpful in the struggle for survival. The absence of racism, despite violent Legionary nonracial anti-Semitism, also suggests a Latin trend in Italian and Rumanian fascism rather than a Nordic one.

For Szálasi, theory mattered as much as it did for Hitler. He was as inflexible in his Hungarism as the Nazis were in their race doctrine. It would seem that not only did theory count for Szálasi as much as action, but in most cases it replaced action. Szálasi bridged the immense gulf that existed between his theory and Hungarian reality by ignoring it. In addition to his patent racism, more reminiscent of Nazism than Italian fascism, Szálasi, like the Nazis, incurred great sacrifices for the Hungarist idea.

Completely lacking in the ideas of the Arrow Cross and the Iron Guard was the Nietzschean spirit, the proclamation of Eternal War, the quest for *Kultur* of Nazism and Italian fascism. In the case of the Legion, Orthodox Christianity automatically ruled out such ideas. But even Szálasi, who professed to be a racist, never exploited the race doctrine beyond rejection of the Jews in a rather passive fashion. *Pax Hungarica* was Szálasi's goal and salvation was the Legion's. Not "race planning," which envisioned the extermination of millions of Slavs and the virtual enslavement of tens of millions, but brotherhood within the Great Carpathian- Danubian Fatherland was the solution Szálasi had in mind for the nationality problem. Even the rather exclusive, intolerant Legion was ready to "feed loyal nationalities."

It is, however, unfair to compare Fascist movements that did not succeed in establishing power for more than a few months with movements which wielded great power for twelve and twenty-one years respectively. Both Italian fascism and Nazism underwent great alteration as compared with their original concepts, alteration that occurred when theory had to be translated into practice — and few things in politics can become so disillusioning as that. There is little doubt that if the Legion and the Arrow Cross had been confronted for a long time with the harsh realities of the governing process, these movements, which thrived on the availability of an uncommitted

---

*"No ideology restrained fascism," wrote Mussolini. "It was born out of a lack of action, and it was *action*. In the first two years [of its existence] it was not [even] a party, but it was an antiparty, a movement." Mussolini further explains that during the following years, fascism developed a framework of action and principles, which were nationalist-syndicalistic, antipacifist, and glorified the nation and combat. These principles were also elitist, authoritarian, anti-individualist. They represented force and action, rejected liberalism, democracy and socialism, and propagated "unity within the nation." *Enciclopedia Italiana*, Vol. XIV, p. 848.

public, would have had to rest on rigidity and regimentation. And there is likewise little doubt that, confronted with such a contradiction, such movements would fail, because as Professor E. Weber has observed, they would either have lost to opponents or given up their ideals.[9] Szálasi's performance during the winter of 1944-45 and Sima's role during the same period (but also the story of the National-Legionary State) should be an instructive indication of the gulf existing between Arrow Cross and Legionary promises and the possibility of their fulfillment. Szálasi's and Codreanu's responsibility for this should be emphasized: their honesty and belief in the ideas they preached does not exculpate them. They alone with their irrational dreams brought into motion the broad popular masses, with dire consequences for Hungary and Rumania. That they were not corrupt personally makes them an exception to the rule. There can be hardly a question of any posthumous rehabilitation to be granted to Szálasi and Codreanu on the basis of their sincerity and incorruptibility when these qualities are balanced off against their roles and responsibilities.

Fascism, as in any other country where it prevailed, did not come to Hungary and Rumania fifty or a hundred years earlier, when with all the curses of life in No-Man's-Land, they were even worse off than they were between 1919 and 1945. Professor Henry Roberts points out:

Fascism . . . is not the creation of a nation or a social group which is at the bottom of the heap, but rather appears among those nations, social groups or individuals which have advanced to the extent of being aware of their position and at the same time being resentful and frustrated.*

Finding themselves at an intermediary stage of development, Hungary being at a higher level than Rumania, and with corresponding social structures, these two countries nevertheless tried to come to terms with the twentieth century. The economic aspect of this problem had to be resolved in terms of the geopolitical, ethnic and historical framework of the region and the countries' respective positions within it, without any democratic or Communist solution available to them.

The psychological problems consequent in the transition from a traditional to a semi-industrial society are by no means simple ones, even under circumstances more favorable than those prevalent in and around Hungary and Rumania during the interwar period. The inherent woes of these countries only increased the psychological problems.

*Roberts, op. cit., pp. 223-24. The closest parallel to the problems of Hungary and Rumania is contemporary Latin America, where the woes inherent in a feudal society combined with a pseudo-democratic system superimposed on a colonial past are combined to corroborate the words of Professor Roberts. Perón's fascism did not rise in abysmally poor, backward Eucador, Bolivia or Perú, for example, but in relatively developed Argentina. The Brazilian Fascist movement, the Integralistas, did not have its stronghold in the parched, overpopulated, backward lands of the northeast, but in the much more but not sufficiently developed areas of São Pãolo, Santa Catarina or Rio proper. This movement is led by borderline cases in social and national background and leans on borderline groups for support.

Today, peoples emerging from traditional societies, standing on the threshold between tomorrow and yesterday, are apt to feel strange in the present. They try to save or recapture values that are submerging and receding in the ugly world of modern industrial civilization. All these conflicts create fear, fear of the present and of the future. This "mood," a primary ingredient of fascism, is not so much the product of underdevelopment per se as it is a product of a certain *stage* during the modernization process. There is a transition zone between the world that is passing away and the world that is emerging. During this transition stage, the process of change is reflected in economic and social structures as in a mirror. Depending on local circumstances and conditions, and on how painful the transition becomes, there is a class of people which is the very focal point of the process of transition and is by its very nature the most unstable element of the whole social structure.

This class, the lower middle class, may step forward to mobilize the hysteria, the insecurity, the fear, which arises from the incapability of the average person to comprehend the infinitely complex nature of the modernization process. After they mobilize this incomprehension, they turn it into an irrational bravado.

Trotsky referred to the lower middle class as "human dust." And as the role of these people in twentieth-century society would seem more often than not a very negative one, Trotsky did not discern any need to qualify his harsh statement. Their negative record is by no means entirely of their own making. They are pawns in a very sensitive stratum of human social development, caught by the force of development itself, which is an irresistible force.

Development, by its own dialectic, is a never-ending process; therefore, no one is entirely spared its accompanying fears. Not only the underdeveloped or developing societies, but, as we painfully become aware, even the most industrialized societies must endure the trauma of social change as they enter the *second industrial revolution*: the process of automatization, computerization, and large-scale urbanization of society. This second industrial revolution promises to be no less fundamental and disruptive than the one which followed the invention of the steam engine. It creates the same psychological problems as the first did: the average person is incapable of understanding what is really happening to him and around him during the process of transition. Other aggravating factors, such as a frightening nuclear balance, doubts about national existence and purpose, and racial tensions, compound these fears. Unscrupulous men and pressure groups who are both willing and able to appeal to and exploit these fears, this mood, are not lacking in either developed or underdeveloped societies. Frequently these politicians come from and appeal to the lower middle classes. They encourage them to end their "silence" and insipidness and give vent to their hysteria in active protest, or possibly in a sham patriotism. These politicians do this in disregard of historical experience, which by the late 1960s has produced ample evidence of the dangers inherent in mobilizing an unstable, insecure, uprooted and inwardly antagonistic social group.

This is what happened in Hungary and Rumania and elsewhere, too, during the first half of this century. The German Nazis must have felt the negative character of the mood created by fear of the twentieth century when they proclaimed their celebrated slogan: "Fear is not a world outlook." Unfortunately, fear became the basic undercurrent of the world outlook of almost every Fascist movement. In Hungary and Rumania, vague, diverging anxieties found a convenient rallying point in the common denominator and the most inflamed wound of all: nationalism. The mood itself, like the stage of development which caused it, would have been, like the mood of Poujadism in France, a transitory one.* It is true that the impossibility of making Hungary accept Trianon and guaranteeing Greater Rumania in a satisfactory manner against Russian, Hungarian and Bulgarian claims perpetuated the mood caused primarily by economic factors. The genius of Szálasi and Sima was not adequate to the task of stabilizing this mood, which Professor E. Nolte has called a "metapolitical phenomenon."[10] More able and more ruthless leaders might have been able to consolidate and express it much more effectively, as indeed such leaders might exploit favorable circumstances at any time. If and when that happens, national relations become very complicated, because conventional relations are all but impossible with governments who depend at home on the exploitation and maintenance of an exceptional circumstance and the perpetuation of a mood which otherwise should be overcome, the sooner the better.**

Because Hungary and Rumania had no Hitler or Mussolini to mold this mood into one huge impulse, it was reflected differently in the different

*That the Iron Guard and the Arrow Cross, despite their appeal and despite the large masses they were able to mobilize, did not have solid foundations in Hungarian and Rumanian society but were rather the expression of a despair and a mood is illustrated by their meteoric rise in the years 1936-37 and 1938-39 respectively and their anticlimax-like collapse. That of the Legion occurred quickly under the blows of Carolist police — certainly a different kind of behavior could have been expected from them after their brave talk a year before. The Arrow Cross collapsed through apathy during the early years of the war. The great hopes and expectations fizzled out as fast as they arose. The National-Legionary State and the rule of Szálasi during the winter of 1944-45 increased party membership, but the presence of opportunists entering the ranks for the purpose of looting is not a reliable yardstick in establishing the extent of popular support. How different, for example, is the stubborn protest of the French and Italian proletariat expressed in an almost unchanging 25 percent of Communist votes for the last twenty years.

**Describing a huge Nuremberg rally in September, 1937, staged in the name of this mood, complete with enormous military and civilian parades, the difference being almost unnoticeable between the two, a spectacle which could have signified only one thing for those who wished to understand, Professor E. Nolte asks: "But was everyone aware of the sacrifice necessary to make this blessing a lasting one? Hitler knew it; two months after his Reich party congress, he summoned the chiefs of staff to the Hossbach conference." *Op. cit.*, p. 387.

social strata. The middle classes and the upper classes looked back to the past, a past in which it was their birthright to rule the dejected masses. This they were not prepared to surrender to the change which was in the making. While trying desperately not to slip down, they hoped to stabilize their position with the kind of system Manoilescu and the everchanging Szeged Idea envisioned. They were no "enthusiasts." They did not reject the twentieth century as long as they could accommodate themselves to it. The Carolist regime and the Szeged Fascists, especially in 1944, went a long way on this road of accommodation with (as they saw it) the modern age. But a truly modernizing dictatorship, if successful, must ensure accommodation to the changing times not only by a ruling class but by the nation as a whole. Historical experience shows that it is unreasonable to expect that a certain class of society will commit political and economic suicide for the benefit of another group of fellow citizens.

Taking into account the staggering problems of No-Man's-Land, perhaps one could object to the harsh criticism in these pages against the middle-class Fascist movements in Rumania* and even those in Hungary. If failure is accepted as a fact, the only fair way to determine how much positive content there was in the concept or policy which failed would be to take a close look at the causes and extent of the failure. The actions of the Szeged Fascists differed from the efforts of the Bethlenites and the Goga-Cuzists in degree rather than in kind, but the Imrédists were certainly consistent in their efforts — so consistent that they were ready to destroy Hungary rather than to lose it, something neither Horthy nor Antonescu nor the Goga-Cuzists were prepared to do.

Codreanu looked back to the past, too, but his nostalgias were not the nostalgias of those who have lost their privileges. It was as if he were trying to give substance to his dream of the past. But while an individual can afford such an attitude without compromising himself, for a mass movement in the twentieth century, such an approach to problems means more than defeat and ridicule. It also brings moral disaster because such a Quixotic struggle with the modern world sets off a chain reaction of moral degradation in which all the positive qualities of the movement are outdistanced by the negative ones.

While Codreanu tried to help his people by rejecting the twentieth century and tried to prevent the corruption of the industrial age from ravaging the soul of the unspoiled peasant, Szálasi refused even to consider the existence of the twentieth century. He built his dream world and spent most of his days in it. It must be considered a proof of the extent of the desperation of all too many Hungarians that *faute de mieux* they followed him into the clouds.

According to Nolte's definition, "Fascism is anti-Marxism which seeks to destroy the enemy by the evolvement of a radically opposed and yet related ideology, and by the use of almost identical and yet, typically modified

---

*Rumania's position in general, and that of General Antonescu in particular, warrants a great deal of consideration to his regime, a consideration which should be categorically denied to the Imrédists.

methods; always, however, within the unifying framework of national self assertion and autonomy."* This definition, related to that of Professor Gustav Adolf Rein's "conservative revolution," does not adequately cover the phenomena of fascism in Hungary and Rumania because they were, in most cases, not so much fighting Marxists (the Marxists had been rendered powerless before) as they were fighting each other, the radical Fascist movements conducting a violent class struggle with their own ruling classes which professed to be not only anti-Marxist but also Fascist. Would it be possible to consider Hungarian and Rumanian popular fascism as *inconsistent Fascist movements, imbued with a desperate, infantile romanticism?* It was the inconsistency of their own ideas, their failure to foresee the consequences of their theories, and either the lack of a plan of action or the unworkability of the existing plan even for the short run, which were the main reasons for their meteoric rise (the dream world they created served well in a situation where every rational approach failed.) The same factors were responsible for their quick downfall. If Hitler and Mussolini achieved at least a temporary success, this was the result of their temporary acceptance of the requirements of an industrial age reality. It was the Bethlenites and the middle-class Fascist movements who rallied industry, the military and the Germans, not the Arrow Cross or the Legion.

Professor Nolte attributes to fascism an epochal character, having in mind the interwar epoch in which the impact of various influences and factors — World War I, defeat, unsatisfactory victories, disconcerting changes, irritating stages of development, and the general discredit the war brought to reason — created a metapolitical phenomenon all over Europe. Since then, according to him, one can speak of fascism, but the Fascist era is over.[11] Such a forecast seems justified in regard to Europe. But modernization, like other historical phenomena, did not and does not arrive everywhere at the same time and in the same form. The mood of that intermediary stage of development when underdeveloped societies abandon their traditional standards and values and try to make the inevitable transition to an industrial age is occurring only now in many of the nations of the world. An excessive dose of nationalism is not absent anywhere in the second half of the twentieth century, especially in countries presently engaged in their own process of modernization. For those countries that must now come to grips with the problems that plagued Hungary and Rumania during the interwar period, it would be worthwhile to study the history of the Hungarian and Rumanian Green Shirts and the history of middle class Fascist movements. Like every individual, so every nation carries within itself a noticeable amount of irrationality. Under the heavy burden of modernization, the lamps of the Enlightenment may easily flicker or go out altogether. Whether those new

*Nolte, *op. cit.,* p. 20. The definition of National Socialism was, according to Professor Nolte, "the death throes of the sovereign, martial, inwardly antagonistic group ... a practical and violent resistance to transcendence." Such definition fits Hungarian and Rumanian Fascism even less than did Professor Nolte's first definition of fascism. p. 421.

movements which may arise from such circumstances will be called Fascist is doubtful and quite unimportant; fascism never claimed to be a universal idea. But the mood which creates it comes from the very depth of the human psyche. In this sense fascism is a universal phenomenon. And here lies the danger of this mood, because it believes it can give an answer to problems, but its very irrationality prevents it from doing so.

There is little likelihood that the problems of the twentieth century will be settled in the fashion in which the Congress of Vienna settled the problems of Europe a century-and-a-half ago. The masses have entered, or are on their way to entering, the arena of decision making on an ever-increasing scale. Consequently, such moods may arise as easily elsewhere as they arose in the 1930s in Central and Eastern Europe. But now the implications of such a mood in view of mankind's advancement in technology are much more dangerous than they were thirty years ago. In the second half of the twentieth century, the celebrated saying of the hero of the Vienna Congress, *"tout ça qu'est excessif est insignifiant,"* can be accepted only with great reservations. The excesses caused by such a mood can become significant — and not necessarily in the positive sense as Tallyrand defined significance. Today this "metapolitical phenomenon," if not checked, could cause incomparably more damage than was caused by that largest holocaust in recorded human history — and that disaster was unleashed on unsuspecting mankind by such a mood, the mood known in our time as fascism.

Notes

Notes to Chapter I

1. Oszkár Jászi, *Dissolution of the Habsburg Empire* (Chicago, 1929), p. 299.
2. Macartney, *October Fifteenth*, I, 7.
3. It is surprising that Hungarians achieved so much in this field — having so many non-Hungarian or Magyarized people among the leadership of their fight for freedom in 1848-49. Even Prof. H. Friedjung, by no means a friend of Hungary, wrote in surprise: "One should also count among the best political qualities of the Hungarians that they know how to attract the best sons of other nationalities and that they treat them with all the warmth of their temperament as brothers." *Österreich von 1848-1860* (Stuttgart-Berlin, 1908), I, 227.
4. Jászi, *op. cit.*, p.334.
5. *Ibid.*, p. 328.
6. B. Hóman and Gy. Szekfü, *Magyar-Történet*, V, 579.
7. Imre Lukinich, László (Ladislaus) Gáldi, and Ladislaus Makkai, *Geschichte der Rumänen*, (Budapest, 1942), p. 360.
8. *Ibid.*, p.393.
9. L. S. Stavrianos, *The Balkans since 1453* (New York, 1961), p. 354.
10. *Ibid.*, pp. 490-91.
11. Conştantin Daicoviciu, Ştefan Pascu, Victor Chereşteşiu, Ştefan Imreh, Alexandru Neamţu, Tiberiu Morariu Cornelia Bodea, Bujor Surdu, Camil Mureşan, Conştantin Nuţu, Acaţiu Egyed and Vasilie Curticăpeanu, *Din istoria Transilvaniei* (3rd ed.; Bucureşti, 1963), I, 262-72.
12. Stavrianos, *op. cit.*, pp. 361-62.
13. Winston Churchill, *The World Crisis, 1915* (New York, 1929), pp.1-2.
14. Erich Maria Remarque, *All Quiet on the Western Front*, trans. A. W. Wheen (Boston, 1929), p. 290. Permission to quote kindly granted by Mr. Remarque.
15. Franz Borkenau, *The Communist International* (London, 1938), p. 111.
16. Macartney, *op. cit.*, I., 22.
17. Borkenau, *op. cit.*, p. 113.
18. Dezsö Sulyok, *A magyar tragedia* (Newark: Privately published, 1954), p. 242.
19. Ödön Málnási, *A Magyar nemzet igaz története*, (Munich, 1959), p. 149. The statistics of Dr. Málnási were used with the greatest reluctance in the absence of other data.
20. Borkenau, *op. cit.*, p. 115.
21. Sulyok, *op. cit.*, p. 251.

22. Lukinich,Gáldi and Makkai, *op. cit.,* p. 399.
23. David Mitrany, *The Effect of the War in South Eastern Europe* (New Haven, 1936), p. 101.
24. *Din istoria Transilvaniei, op. cit.,* II, 452.
25. Henry Roberts, *Rumania: Political Problems of an Agrarian State,* (New Haven, 1951), p. 30.
26. Roberts, *op. cit.,* p. 366.
27. *Ibid.,* p. 367.
28. *Enciclopedia Romaniei,*(Bucureşti, 1938-43), I, 149.
29. *Ibid.*
30. *Ibid.*
31. Roberts, *op. cit.,* p. 361.
32. *Ibid.,* p. 54
33. *Great Britain and the Near East, August 4, 1938,* II, p. 118.
34. *Economic Development in South Eastern Europe,* Study Group under David Mitrany (Oxford, 1945), pp. 14-15.
35. *Enciclopedia Romaniei, op. cit.,* IV, 957-64.
36. R. G. Waldeck, *Athene Palace* (New York, 1942) p. 242.
37. *Economic Development in South Eastern Europe, op. cit.,* pp. 14-15.
38. Octavian Goga, *Mustul care fierbe,* (Bucureşti, 1925), pp. 44-45,

Notes to Chapter II

1. Macartney, *October Fifteenth,* I, 18.
2. Karl Barth, *Dogmatics in Outline* (London-Toronto, 1949), p. 70.
3. Max Weber, *The Protestant Ethic and the Spirit of Capitalism,* (New York, 1958), p. 271.
4. Oscar Jászi, *Revolution and Counter-Revolution in Hungary* (London, 1924), pp. 188-9.
5. Jenő Lévai, *Fekete könyv a magyar zsidóság szenvedéseiröl* (Budapest, 1946), p.48.
6. *Ibid.*
7. *Ibid.*
8. Macartney, *op. cit.,* I, 20,

Notes to Chapter III

1. Macartney, *October Fifteenth,* I, 28n.
2. *Ibid.,* pp. 75-77.
3. *O.N.K.,* January 10, 1924, p. 107.
4. Súlyok, *A magyar tragédia,* pp. 272-75.

5. *Ibid.*, p. 274.
6. *Ibid.*, p. 266.
7. F. Stephen Kertész, *Diplomacy in a Whirlpool* (West Bend, Ind., 1953), p. 21.
8. *Ibid.*, p. 19.
9. *Porunca Vremii*, April 19. 1941.
10. Súlyok, *op. cit.*, p. 223.
11. Gyula Illyés, *A puszták népe* (Budapest, 1937), pp. 125-26.
12. *Ibid.*, p. 92.
13. *Ibid.*
14. *Ibid.*, pp. 142-43.
15. Súlyok, *op. cit.*, pp. 322-23.
16. Horthy, *Ein Leben für Ungarn*, p. 153.
17. Tormay, *An Outlaw's Diary, passim.*
18. Horthy, *op. cit.*, p. 127.
19. Tormay, *op. cit.*, I, 86-87.
20. *Ibid.*, pp. 102-3.
21. *Ibid.*, II, 58-60.
22. *Ibid.*
23. *Ibid.*
24. *Ibid.*
25. (Princeton, 1964), p. 66.
26. *O.N.K.*, November 16, 1943, p. 336.
27. *Ibid.*, March 22, 1928, pp. 236-37.
28. Jászi, *Revolution and Counter-Revolution in Hungary*, p. 225.
29. Raul Hilberg, *The Destruction of the European Jews* (Chicago, 1961), p. 11
30. Lévai, *Fekete Könyv a magyar zsidóság szenvedéseiről*, pp. 48-49.
31. Macartney, *op. cit.*, I, 77.
32. Lévai, *op. cit.*, p. 8.
33. *Ibid.*
34. Súlyok, *op. cit.*, p. 281.
35. Málnási, *A Magyar nemzet igaz története*, p. 164.
36. *Három nemzedék és ami utána következik* (Budapest, 1935), p. 451.
37. *A fajvédöpárt programmja*, pamphlet (Budapest, 1927).
38. Szokoly, *És Gömbös Gyula, a kapitány*, pp. 319-21.
39. Macartney, *op. cit.*, I, 72-73.
40. Szokoly, *op. cit.*, pp. 234-35.
41. This was Tisza's remedy for the agrarian question twenty years before.
42. *O.N.K.*, May 5, 1931, p. 361; December 7, 1923, p. 367.
43. *Ibid.*
44. *Ibid.*, April 17, 1928, p. 22.
45. *Ibid.*, March 22. 1927, p. 85.

46. Macartney, *op. cit.*, I, 77.
47. *O.N.K.*, April 17, 1928, p. 22.
48. Szokoly, *op. cit.*, pp. 253-54.
49. Wilbert Ellis Moore, *Economic Demography of Eastern and Southern Europe*, (Geneva, 1945), p. 26.
50. Jászi, *Revolution and Counter-Revolution in Hungary*, p. 203.
51. Miklós Horthy, *titkos iratai*, (Budapest, 1963), p. 33.
52. Macartney, *op. cit.*, I, 85.
53. See Chapter IV.

Notes to Chapter IV

1. Macartney, *October Fifteenth*, I, 89.
2. Horthy, *titkos iratai*, pp. 82, 95.
3. *O.N.K.*, July 30, 1931, pp. 181-82.
4. *Ibid.*, December 16, 1931, p. 490.
5. Macartney, *op. cit.*, I, 90.
6. *O.N.K.*, November 11, 1931, p. 133-35.
7. *Ibid.*, April 6, 1932, pp. 185-87.
8. Macartney, *op. cit.*, I, 92.
9. *Ibid.*, p. 99.
10. *O.N.K.*, December 16, 1931, p. 485.
11. *Ibid.*, October 11, 1932, p. 51.
12. *A Gömbös kormány nemzeti munkaterve*, (Budapest, 1932.) A pamphlet available also in English, *The National Programme of the Gömbös Government.*
13. *O.N.K.*, October 22, 1936, p.35.
14. *Ibid.*, June 13, 1933, pp. 264-65.
15. Macartney, *op. cit.*, I, 106.
16. *Ibid.*, p. 118.
17. *Ibid.*, p. 119.
18. *O.N.K.*, May 19, 1933, pp. 64-65.
19. *Ibid.*, March 7, 1934, pp. 277-79.
20. *Ibid.*, May 3, 1933, pp. 32-33.
21. Macartney, *op. cit.*, I, 181-82.
22. *O.N.K.*, May 27, 1935, p. 56.
23. *Ibid.*
24. *Ibid.*
25. *Ibid.*, May 17, 1933, p. 551.
26. *Ibid.*, February 19, 1936, p. 463.
27. Macartney, *op. cit.*, I, 125.
28. *Ibid.*, p. 128n.

29. *Ibid.*, p. 148.
30. *Ibid.*, p. 132.
31. *Ibid.*, p. 134.
32. Horthy, *Ein Leben für Ungarn*, p. 174.
33. *O.N.K*, May 23, 1934, pp. 134, 148, 150.
34. *Ibid.*, December 12, 1934, p. 401.
35. Macartney, *op. cit.*, I, 138-40.
36. *Allianz*, pp. 109, 112-13, 115-16.
37. Súlyok, *A magyar tragédia*, p. 444.
38. *O.N.K.*, May 7, 1934, p. 221.
39. Macartney, *op. cit.*, I, 148.
40. *Ibid.*, I, p. 152.
41. *O.N.K.*, October 11, 1932, pp. 51, 114.
42. *Ibid.*, p. 116.
43. *Ibid.*, May 11, 1938, p. 471.
44. H. Rogger and E. Weber (eds.), *The European Right, A Historical Profile*, (Berkeley, 1965), p. 10.
45. *Ibid.*, p. 384.
46. *Ibid.*, p. 385.
47. András Török, *Szálasi álarc nélkül*, (Budapest, 1941), p. 11.
48. Lackó, *Nvilasok, nemzetiszocialisták*, pp. 18-19.
49. Macartney, *op. cit.*, I, 159.
50. Rogger and Weber, *op. cit.*, p. 386.
51. Macartney, *op. cit.*, I, 159.
52. *O.N.K.*, July 10, 1932, p. 31.
53. Macartney, *op. cit.*, I, 158.
54. *Ibid.*, p. 158n.
55. Török, *op. cit.*, p. 13.
56. *Ibid.*, p. 11.
57. Ferenc Barbácsi-Simon, *Az enyingi nyilasház*, (Enying, 193?), pp. 50-65.
58. *Ibid.*, p. 3.
59. *O.N.K.*, April 25, 1934, p. 395.
60. *Ibid.*
61. *Ibid.*, June 12, 1933, pp. 195-99.
62. *Ibid.*, May 17, 1933, p. 551.
63. *Ibid.*, June 13, 1933, pp. 264-65.
64. *Ibid.*, p. 263.
65. *Ibid.*, May 7, 1934, p. 221.
66. *Ibid.*
67. Machiavelli, *Discorsi*, I, Chapter 58.
68. *O.N.K.*, April 26, 1938, pp. 38-40.
69. Török, *op. cit.*, p. 16.

70. Ferenc Szálasi, *Út és Cél* (Budapest, 1936).
71. Macartney, *op. cit.*, I, 160-65; Weber, *op. cit.*, 157-64; Rogger and Weber, *op. cit.*, pp. 388-96; Lackó, *op. cit.*, pp. 46-59, and Szálasi, *Út és Cél.*
72. Török, *op. cit.*, pp. 17-18.
73. Macartney, *op. cit.*, I, 166.
74. *Ibid.*
75. *Cél és követelések* (Budapest, 1935).
76. Lackó, *op. cit.*, pp. 65-66.
77. Macartney, *op. cit.*, I, 168n.
78. Súlyok, *op. cit.*, p. 441.

Notes to Chapter V

1. Horthy, *Ein Leben für Ungarn*, p. 174. Also, Macartney, *October Fifteenth*, I, 173.
2. Macartney, *op. cit.*, I, 177.
3. *Ibid.*, p. 174.
4. *O.N.K.*, October 22, 1936, p. 35.
5. Macartney, *op. cit.*, I, 177.
6. *Ibid.*, pp. 181-82.
7. Lackó, *Nyilasok, nemzetiszocialisták*, pp. 124-25.
8. *Ibid.*
9. *Ibid.*
10. *Ibid.*, p. 133.
11. *Ibid.*, p. 120.
12. Török, *Szálasi álarc nélkül*, p. 10.
13. *Ibid.*, p. 4.
14. *Ibid.*, p. 37.
15. *Ibid.*, p. 64.
16. *Ibid.*, p. 43.
17. Macartney, *op. cit.*, I, 175. Also, Lackó, *op. cit.*, p. 66.
18. Török, *op. cit.*, p. 16.
19. Macartney, *op. cit.*, I, 189. Also Lackó, *op. cit.*, pp. 101-2.
20. Macartney, *op. cit.*, I, 202-5
21. *Ibid.*
22. *Ibid.*
23. *Ibid.*
24. *Ibid.*
25. *Ibid.*, pp. 213-14.
26. *Ibid.*
27. *Ibid.*

28. *Ibid.*
29. *Ibid.*, pp. 187-88.
30. Nicholas Kállay, *Hungarian Premier* (New York, 1954), p. 185.
31. Macartney, *op. cit.*, I, 195n.
32. *Ibid.*, pp. 217-19; also, Lackó, *op. cit.*, p. 105-7.
33. *Ibid.*, both sources.
34. *Ibid.*
35. Súlyok, *A magyar tragédia,* pp. 355-56.
36. Horthy, *titkos iratai,* p. 170.
37. Macartney, *op. cit.*, I, 219-20. Also, Lackó, *op. cit.*, pp. 105-9.
38. Macartney, *op. cit.*, I, 106, 308.
39. *Ibid.*, p. 227.
40. Málnási, *op. cit.*, p. 289.
41. *Ibid.*, p. 292.
42. Macartney, *op. cit.*, I, 170-71.
43. *Ibid.*, pp. 171, 228-29.
44. *Ibid.*
45. *Ibid.*
46. Török, *op. cit.*, pp. 88-89.
47. *Népszava,* June 21, 1939, p. 6.
48. Lackó, *op. cit.*, pp. 125-36.
49. *Ibid.*
50. *Ibid.*, p. 143.
51. *Ibid.*, p. 151.
52. Török, *op. cit.*, p. 64.
53. *Ibid.* p. 40.
54. Horthy, *Ein Leben für Ungarn,* p. 200.
55. Kertész, *Diplomacy in a Whirlpool,* p. 35.
56. Horthy, *titkos iratai,* pp. 185-87; also *Allianz, op. cit.*, p. 193.
57. Macartney, *op. cit.*, I, 274-75.
58. *Ibid.*, I, 306.
59. *Ibid.*, p. 307.
60. *Ibid.*, p. 308.
61. *Ibid.*, p. 310.
62. *Ibid.*
63. *Ibid.*, pp. 309-14. Also, in detail, *Allianz,* pp. 202-5.
64. Súlyok, *op. cit.*, p. 364.
65. Macartney, *op. cit.*, I, 318.
66. Súlyok, *op. cit.*, p. 366.
67. Hilberg, *Destruction of the European Jews,* p. 514.
68. Lévai, *Fekete könyv a magyar zsidóság szenvedéseiről,* p. 74.
69. *O.N.K.*, February 28, 1939, p. 39.
70. *Ibid.*

71. Lévai, *op. cit.*, p. 39.
72. Macartney, *op. cit.* I, 325n.
73. *O.N.K.*, January 18, 1939, p. 305.
74. Horthy, *titkos iratai*, p. 205.
75. Súlyok, *op. cit.*, p. 490.
76. Macartney, *op. cit.*, I, 327-28.
77. *Ibid.*, pp. 328n.
78. Súlyok, *op. cit.*, p. 368.
79. *O.N.K.*, February 22, 1939, pp. 496-500.
80. Macartney, *op. cit.*, I, 351.
81. *Népszava*, June 23, 1939.
82. Macartney, *op. cit.*, I, 350.
83. Lackó, *op. cit.*, p. 171.
84. *Pesti Napló*, June 8, 1939.
85. *New York Times*, August 2, 1939, p. 11.
86. *Ibid.*, August 21, 1939, p. 5.
87. *Ibid.*, October 17, 1939, p. 1.
88. *Allianz*, pp. 247-50.
89. Macartney, *op. cit.*, I, 367.
90. R. C. Waldeck, *Athene Palace* (New York, 1942), p. 76.
91. Macartney, *op. cit.*, I, 374.
92. *Ibid.*, p. 353.
93. Kállay, *op. cit.*, p. 418.
94. Horthy, *titkos iratai*, p. 362.
95. *Ibid.*, p. 464.
96. *O.N.K.*, November 30, 1939, p. 500.
97. Lackó, *op. cit.*, p. 210.
98. *Ibid.*, p. 211.
99. *Ibid.*, p. 207.
100. *O.N.K.*, April 24, 1940, p. 339.
101. Macartney, *op. cit.*, I, 397.
102. *Ibid.*, p. 401. Also, *Népszava*, June 1, 1940.
103. *O.N.K.*, June 7, 1940, p. 470.
104. *Ibid.*, June 17, 1940, p. 287.
105. Macartney, *op. cit.*, I, 402.
106. Horthy, *titkos iratai*, p. 256.
107. *O.N.K.* November, 11, 1940, p. 208.
108. Macartney, *op. cit.*, I, 428.
109. *Ibid.*
110. *Ibid.*, p. 434.
111. *Ibid.*, pp. 434-35.
112. *O.N.K.*, November 26, 1940, p. 859.
113. *Ibid.*

114. *Ibid.*, July 2, 1941, p. 443.
115. *Ibid.*, November 25, 1941, p. 554.
116. Macartney, *op. cit.*, I, 437.
117. *Ibid.*
118. Lackó, *op. cit.*, pp. 236-41.
119. Horthy, *titkos iratai*, p. 260.
120. *Ibid.*, p. 272.
121. Macartney, *op. cit.*, I, 431-38.
122. *Ibid.*, p. 346.
123. *Pester Lloyd*, March 26, 1941; also, Macartney, *op. cit.*, I, 473.
124. *Time*, April 7, 1941, p. 35.
125. Macartney, *op. cit.*, I, 475.
126. *Ibid.*, pp. 481-82.
127. *Allianz*, p. 301-6.
128. In 1926 Horthy made a conciliatory speech there to Yugoslavia.
129. Horthy, *titkos iratai*, p. 292.

Notes to Chapter VI

1. Kállay, *Hungarian Premier*, p. 9.
2. Súlyok, *A magyar tragédia*, p. 376.
3. Macartney, *October Fifteenth*, II, 12-13, 39.
4. Hilberg, *The Destruction of the European Jews*, p. 512.
5. Macartney, *op. cit.*, II, 19-23.
6. Súlyok, *op. cit.*, p. 381.
7. Macartney, *op. cit.*, II, 23.
8. *Ibid.* pp. 26-31.
9. *O.N.K.*, June 27, 1941, pp. 305-28.
10. Macartney, *op. cit.*, II, 31.
11. *Ibid.*, p. 33.
12. *Ibid.*, p. 36.
13. Elek Karsai, *A budai vártól a gyepüig* (Budapest, 1965), p. 31.
14. Macartney, *op. cit.*, II, 41.
15. *Ibid.*, I, 456.
16. *Ibid.*, II, 43-44.
17. *Magyarság*, September 14, 1941.
18. *Ibid.*, September 26, 1941.
19. *Ibid.*
20. Macartney, *op. cit.*, II, 45.
21. *Ibid.*, p. 42.
22. Lackó, *Nyilasok, nemzetiszocialisták*, pp. 265, 269-70, 285.

23. Horthy, *titkos iratai*, pp. 300, 439.
24. Macartney, *op. cit.*, II, 64.
25. *Ibid.*, pp. 64-68.
26. Kállay, *op. cit.*, p. 110.
27. Horthy, *Ein Leben für Ungarn*, p. 241.
28. Macartney, *op. cit.*, II, 73-74.
29. *Ibid.*
30. *O.N.K.*, December 2, 1942, p. 490.
31. Macartney, *op. cit.*, II, 291n.
32. Lackó, *op. cit.*, p. 277.
33. Horthy, *titkos iratai*, op. cit., p. 321.
34. Kállay, *op. cit.*, p. 8.
35. Horthy, *titkos iratai*, p. 309.
36. *O.N.K.*, March 19, 1942, p. 103.
37. *Ibid.*, November 25, 1942, p. 263.
38. Kállay, *op. cit.*, p. 24.
39. Karsai, *op. cit.*, p. 168-83.
40. Lévai, *Fekete Könyv a magyar zsidóság szenvedéselről*, pp. 276-78.
41. *Ibid.*
42. *Ibid.*
43. Macartney, *op. cit.*, II, 100-1.
44. *Ibid.*
45. *Ibid.*, p. 155.
46. Hilberg, *op. cit.*, p. 473.
47. *Ibid.*, p. 485.
48. Karsai, *op. cit.*, p. 204.
49. Hilberg, *op. cit.*, pp. 522-23.
50. Macartney, *op. cit.*, I, 165.
51. Horthy, *titkos iratai*, pp. 261-62.
52. Kállay, *op. cit.*, p. 122.
53. *O.N.K.*, November 19, 1941, p. 434.
54. Hilberg, *op. cit.*, p. 524.
55. Macartney, *op. cit.*, II, 148n.
56. *Ibid.*
57. Kállay, *op. cit.*, pp. 100-90.
58. Macartney, *op. cit.*, II, p. 149.
59. Kállai, *A magyar függetlenségi mozgalom* (1936-1945), p. 190.
60. Horthy, *titkos iratai*, pp. 338, 343.
61. *Ibid.*
62. *Ibid.*, p. 386.
63. Macartney, *op. cit.*, II, 195.
64. Súlyok, *op. cit.*, p. 505.

65. Karsai, *op. cit.*, p. 352.
66. Macartney, *op. cit.*, II, 202.
67. *Ibid.*, p. 209; also, Kállay, *op. cit.*, pp. 229-36.
68. *Ibid.*, both sources.
69. *Ibid.*
70. Horthy, *titkos iratai*, p. 408.
71. Macartney, *op. cit.*, II, 220.
72. *O.N.K.*, July 2, 1941, p. 443.

Notes To Chapter VII

1. Macartney, *October Fifteenth*, II, 225-29.
2. Kállay, *Hungarian Premier*, p. 422.
3. *Ibid.*, p. 418.
4. Macartney, *op. cit.*, II, 245.
5. *Ibid.*, p. 246.
6. *Ibid.*, pp. 103-4.
7. Lackó, *Nyilasok, nemzetiszocialisták*, p. 273.
8. *Ibid*, pp. 251-52.
9. Horthy, *titkos iratai*, p. 368.
10. Kállay, *op. cit.*, p. 223.
11. Macartney, *op. cit.*, II, 199-200.
12. *Ibid.*
13. Árpád Henney, *Hungarist Pro Memoriam, 1953* (London, 1953), p. 11.
14. Macartney, *op. cit.*, II, 258n.
15. József Darvas, *Város as ingoványon*, (Budapest, 1945), p. 91.
16. Súlyok, *A magyar tragédia*, p. 507.
17. *Hitler's Secret Conversations, (1941-1944)* (New York, 1962) p. 60.
18. *Ibid.*, p. 91.
19. *Ibid.*, P. 580.
20. *Ibid.*, p. 326.
21. *Ibid.*, p. 620.
22. *Ibid.*, p. 580.
23. *Ibid.*, p. 423.
24. Macartney, *op. cit.*, II, 290-96.
25. *Ibid.*
26. *Ibid.*, pp. 295-99.
27. *Ibid.*
28. *Összetartás*, April 22, 1944.
29. *Time*, May 2, 1961.
30. Hilberg, *The Destruction of the European Jews*, p. 527.

31. *Ibid.*, pp. 528-31.
32. Lévai, *Fekete könyv a magyar zsidóság szenvedéseiröl*, p. 106.
33. *Ibid.*, pp. 115-16.
34. *Ibid.*, p. 101.
35. Macartney, *op. cit.*, II, 276.
36. Hilberg, *op. cit.*, p. 530.
37. Karsai, *A budai vártól a gyepüig*, p. 471-72.
38. Lévai, *op. cit.*, p. 132.
39. Macartney, *op. cit.*, II, 279-82.
40. Lévai, *op. cit.*, pp. 140, 172.
41. *Ibid.*, p. 175.
42. *Ibid.*
43. Aladár Vozáry, *Így történt!* (Budapest, 1945), pp. 22-75; also, Lévai, *op. cit.*, p. 112.
44. Lévai, *op. cit.*, p. 132.
45. *Ibid.*, p. 138.
46. *Ibid.*, p. 140.
47. *Ibid.*, p. 145.
48. Vozáry, *op. cit.*, pp. 50-75; also Lévai, *op. cit.*, p. 142.
49. Lévai, *op. cit.*, p. 176.
50. Macartney, *op.cit.*, I, 106, 308.
51. *Ibid.*, II, p. 286.
52. Hilberg, *op. cit.*, p. 539.
53. Lévai, *op. cit.*, p. 73.
54. *Ibid.*, p. 170.
55. Hilberg, *op. cit.*, p. 539.
56. Súlyok, *op. cit.*, pp. 460-63.
57. Hilberg, *op. cit.*, p. 540.
58. Súlyok, *op. cit.*, pp. 462-63.
59. Hilberg, *op. cit.*, p. 538.
60. Lévai, *op. cit.*, p. 150.
61. *Ibid.*, pp. 167-68, 179.
62. *Ibid.*, p. 66.
63. *Ibid.*, p. 176.
64. *Ibid.*, p. 50.
65. *Ibid.*, p. 51.
66. *Ibid.*, p. 66.
67. Kállay, *op. cit.*, pp. 444-45.
68. Macartney, *op. cit.*, II, p. 283n.
69. *Ibid.*
70. *Ibid.*
71. Lévai, *op. cit.*, pp. 165-68.

72. *Ibid.*
73. Macartney, *op. cit.*, II, 303.
74. *Ibid.*
75. *Ibid.*
76. *Ibid.*, p. 490.
77. Hilberg, *op. cit.*, p. 547.
78. Macartney, *op. cit.*, II, 303-7.
79. Horthy, *titkos iratai*, pp. 440-44.
80. *Ibid.*
81. Ira Hirschmann, *Caution to the Wind*, (New York, 1962), p. 177.
82. Hilberg, *op. cit.*, pp. 542-45.
83. *Ibid.*, pp. 548-49.
84. Horthy, *titkos iratai*, pp. 457-65.
85. Macartney, *op. cit.*, II, 307, 310.
86. *Ibid.*, pp. 310-13.
87. *Ibid.*, pp. 323-24.
88. *Ibid.*, pp. 330-31.
89. *Ibid.*, p. 343.
90. *Ibid.*
91. *Ibid.*, p. 326.
92. *Ibid.*, pp. 356-60.
93. *Ibid.*
94. *O.N.K.*, September 21, 1944, p. 259.
95. *Ibid.*, p. 263.
96. Macartney, *op. cit.*, pp. 360-62.
97. *Ibid.*
98. *Ibid.*, p. 367.
99. *Ibid.*, pp. 368-69.
100. *Ibid.*, pp. 369-71.
101. *Egyedül Vagyunk*, October 7, 1944, p. 1.
102. Macartney, *op. cit.*, II, 380.
103. *Ibid.*, pp. 385-86.
104. *Ibid.*
105. *Ibid.*, p. 403.
106. Horthy, *titkos iratai*, p. 324,
107. Macartney, *op. cit.*, II, 421-22.
108. *Ibid.*, pp. 411-12.
109. *Ibid.*, pp. 414-15.
110. *Ibid.*, p. 427.
111. Horthy, *Ein Leben für Ungarn*, p. 289.
112. *Ibid.*

113. *Ibid.*, p. 293.
114. Macartney, *op. cit.*, II, 438.

Notes to Chapter VIII

1. Macartney, *October Fifteenth*, II, 448.
2. Karsai, *A budai vártól a gyepüig*, pp. 618-19, 648-50, 652.
3. Lévai, *Fekete könyv a magyar zsidóság szenvedéseiröl*, pp. 215-17.
4. *Ibid.*, pp. 225-26.
5. *Ibid.*
6. *Ibid.*
7. Macartncy, *op. cit.*, II, 450-51.
8. Hilberg, *The Destruction of the European Jews*, pp. 552-54.
9. *Ibid.*, p. 553.
10. Kállay, *Hungarian Premier*, pp. 473-74.
11. Súlyok, *A magyar tragédia*, p. 539.
12. Lévai, *op. cit.*, pp. 76-77.
13. Karsai, *op. cit.*, p. 618.
14. József Horváth, János Nemes, István Pintér and László Szabó, *Az utolsó felvonás*, (Budapest, 1958), p. 499.
15. Macartney, *op. cit.*, II, 455-57, 462.
16. *Ibid.*, 461-62.
17. Karsai, *op. cit.*, p. 623.
18. *Ibid.*, p. 624.
19. Macartney, *op. cit.*, II, 451n.
20. Karsai, *op. cit.*, p. 641.
21. Rogger and Weber, *The European Right*, p. 403.
22. Horváth, *et. al., op. cit.*, p. 516.
23. Macartney, *op. cit.*, II, 468.
24. Karsai, *op. cit.*, p. 589.
25. Kertész, *Diplomacy in a Whirlpool*, p. 86.
26. Even Arrow Cross Foreign Minister Baron Kemény was not spared. His property was plundered and he and his family went through wholesale indignities, as did other similar cases in Austria. Karsai, *op. cit.*, p. 678-80.
27. Macartney, *op. cit.*, II, 468.
28. *Ibid.*
29. *Összetartás*, March 14, 1945.
30. Macartney, *op. cit.*, II, 468.
31. Karsai, *op. cit.*, p. 648.
32. Hilberg, *op. cit.*, p. 542.
33. *Ibid.*, p. 400.
34. Lévai, *op. cit.*, p. 316.

35. Macartney, *op. cit.*, II, 490.
36. Lévai, *op. cit.*, p. 129.
37. Horthy, *titkos iratai*, p. 468; also *Allianz*, p. 385.
38. Horthy, *titkos iratai*, p. 389.
39. Horváth, *et. al.*, *op. cit.*, p. 137.

Notes to Chapter IX

1. Rogger and Weber, *The European Right*, p. 515.
2. Roberts, *Rumania: Political Problems of an Agrarian State*, pp. 143-47.
3. *Crez de generaţie* (2nd ed., Bucureşti, 1937), p. 39.
4. Codreanu, *Eiserne Garde*, p. 11.
5. *Ibid.*, pp. 12-13.
6. *Ibid.*, p. 9.
7. *Ibid.*, p. 14.
8. *Ibid.*, p. 25
9. *Ibid.*
10. *Ibid.*, p. 18
11. *Ibid.*, p. 20-25.
12. *Ibid.*
13. *Ibid.*, pp. 33-34.
14. *Ibid.*, p. 35.
15. *Ibid.*, pp. 40-52.
16. *Ibid.*, p. 53.
17. *Ibid.*
18. *Ibid.*, p. 39.
19. *Ibid.*, pp. 54-59.
20. *Ibid.*
21. *Ibid.*, p. 60.
22. N. I. Lebedev, *Rumy'nia v godi' vtoroy mirovoy voyni* (Moscow, 1961), pp. 12-13.
23. Roberts, *op. cit.*, pp. 114-15.
24. *Politics and Political Parties in Rumania* (London, 1936), p. 9.
25. Lebedev, *op. cit.*, p. 33.
26. *Politics and Political Parties in Rumania*, pp. 311-14.
27. Codreanu, *op. cit.*, p. 63.
28. *Ibid.*, pp. 123-26.
29. *Ibid.*, pp. 70-83.
30. *Ibid.*, pp. 227-29.
31. *Ibid.*, p. 65.
32. *Ibid.*, p. 111.
33. *Ibid.*, p. 89.

34. *Ibid.*, p. 91.
35. Titus P. Vifor, *Doctrina Fascismului Roman și Anteproectul de Program* (București, 1924).
36. Roberts, *op. cit.*, p. 226n.
37. Codreanu, *op. cit.*, p. 94.
38. *Ibid.*, p. 99.
39. *Ibid.*, p. 127.
40. *Ibid.*, p. 129.
41. *Ibid.*, p. 133.
42. *Ibid.*, p. 137.
43. *Ibid.*, p. 144.
44. *Ibid.*, p. 158.
45. *Ibid.*, pp. 163-67.
46. *Ibid.*, pp. 169-74.
47. *Ibid.*, pp. 175-78.
48. *Ibid.*, pp. 179-84.
49. *Ibid.*, pp. 184-85.
50. *Ibid.*, p. 206.
51. *Ibid.*, pp. 207-8.
52. *Ibid.*, pp. 211-12.
53. *Ibid.*, p. 216.
54. *Ibid.*, pp. 214-24.
55. *Ibid.*
56. *Ibid.*, p. 229.
57. *Ibid.*
58. *Ibid.*, pp. 230-37.
59. *Politics and Political Parties in Rumania*, p. 55.
60. Rogger and Weber, *op. cit.*, pp. 526-27.
61. Codreanu, *op. cit.*, pp. 259-60.
62. *Ibid.*, p. 275.
63. Corneliu Codreanu, *Circulări, scrisori, sfături gânduri*, p. 35. (In mimeographed form.)
64. Corneliu Codreanu, *Cartica șefului de cuib, 1944 (Manual for the Nest Leader)*, Article No. 54. The writer is obliged to Professor E. Weber for this mimeographed copy of the original manual, therefore, quotations will be made by article, not by page number, and this source will be referred to as the *Manual*.
65. Codreanu, *Eiserne Garde*, p. 271.
66. Charlé, *op. cit.*, p. 67.
67. *Ibid.*
68. *Ibid.*, p. 79.
69. *Ibid.*, p. 73.
70. *Pe marginea prăpăstiei, 21-23 Ianuarie 1941* (București, 1942), II, 53-54.

71. *Ibid.*

72. Traian Herşeni, *Mişcarea legionără şi ţărănimea* (Bucureşti, 1940), p. 3.

73. Codreanu, *Eiserne garde*, p. 273.

74. Ernest Bernea, *Stil Legionar, Collection "Omul Nou"* (Exile Edition), p. 16.

75. *Dacia*, Annul XIII Număr Festiv (Rio de Janeiro, December, 1958).

76. *Pe Marginea Prăpăstiei*, op. cit. I, pp. 113-14.

77. *Buna Veştire*, January 10, 1941, p. 1.

78. Vasilie Iasinschi, *În faţa cu adevărul*, (Madrid, 1961).

79. Ion Moţa, *Crani de lemn* (3rd ed., Bucureşti, 1937), pp. 9-10, 247.

80. *Buna Veştire*, February 28, 1937.

81. Codreanu, *Eiserne Garde*, p. 398.

82. Charlé, *op. cit.*, p. 93.

83. *Ibid.*, p. 72.

84. Codreanu, *Circulări, scrisori, sfături, gănduri*, p. 20.

85. Moţa, *Crani de lemn*, p. 99.

86. Rogger and Weber, *op. cit.*, pp. 533-34.

87. Codreanu, *Manual*, Articles 56, 57, 58.

88. Codreanu, *Manual*, Article "Legionar."

89. Codreanu, *Eiserne Garde*, pp. 373-99.

90. *Ibid.*, p. 301.

91. *Ibid.*, p. 293.

92. Codreanu, *Manual*, Article 41.

93. *Ibid.*, Articles 64, 65, 66.

94. Banea, *Rănduri către generaţia noastra* (Omul Nou, November 1951), pp. 14, 15.

95. Rogger and Weber, *op. cit.*, p. 521; also Horia Sima, *Le procès Eichman et la conscience mondiale* (Madrid, 1962).

96. Codreanu, *Eiserne Garde*, pp. 302-3.

97. *Ibid.*

98. Codreanu, *Manual*, Articles 1, 2, 3.

99. *Ibid.*, Articles 6, 7, 8, 9.

100. *Ibid.*, Article 12.

101. *Ibid.*, Articles 13, 14, 15, 16.

102, Charlé, *op. cit.*, p. 60.

103. Codreanu, *Manual*, Articles 20-25.

104. Codreanu, *Eiserne Garde*, p. 304.

105. Codreanu, *Manual*, Article 39.

106. *Ibid.*, Article 36.

107. Charlé, *op. cit.*, p. 62.

108. Codreanu, *Manual*, Article 39.

109. Codreanu, *Eiserne Garde*, p. 307.

110. Rogger and Weber, *op. cit.*, p. 522.

111. Codreanu, *Manual*, Articles 16/bis, 37.

Notes to Chapter X

1. *Politics and Political Parties in Rumania*, pp. 56-57.
2. *Times* (London), November 12, 1928.
3. *Enciclopedia Romaniei*, I, 937.
4. Roberts, *Rumania: Political Problems of an Agrarian State*, p. 176.
5. *Ibid.*, p. 179.
6. *Politics and Political Parties in Rumania*, p. 57.
7. *Enciclopedia Romaniei*, I, 242-43.
8. *Politics and Political Parties in Rumania*, p. 58.
9. Codreanu, *Eiserne Garde*, pp. 307-9.
10. *Ibid.*, p. 271.
11. *Ibid.*, p. 268.
12. *Ibid.*, p. 294.
13. *Ibid.*, p. 315.
14. Banea, *Rânduri către generaţia noastra*, (Omul Nou, November 1951), pp. 16-17.
15. *Ibid.*, pp. 1-2.
16. Codreanu, *Eiserne Garde*, p. 321.
17. *Ibid.*, p. 329.
18. Codreanu, *Manual*, Article 42.
19. Codreanu, *Eiserne Garde*, pp. 332-34.
20. *Ibid.*
21. *Ibid.*
22. *Ibid.*, pp. 338-48.
23. *Ibid.*, p. 349.
24. *Ibid.*, p. 349-50.
25. *Ibid.*
26. *Politics and Potitical Parties in Rumania*, p. 57.
27. Codreanu, *Eiserne Garde*, p. 373.
28. *Ibid.*, pp. 373-76.
29. *Ibid.*, pp. 399-402.
30. *Politics and Political Parties in Rumania*, p. 58.
31. Codreanu, *Eiserne Garde*, p. 408.
32. *Ibid.*, p. 431.
33. *Ibid.*, pp. 415-28.
34. *Ibid.*, p. 428.
35. *Ibid.*, p. 434.
36. Rogger and Weber, *The European Right*, p. 547.
37. *Politics and Political Parties in Rumania*, p. 59.
38. Codreanu, *Eiserne Garde*, pp. 434-35
39. *Ibid.*
40. Codreanu, *Eiserne Garde*, p. 435.

41. *Politics and Political Parties in Rumania,* p. 208.
42. Mihail Manoilescu, *Die Einzige Partei als politische Institution der neuen Régime.* (Berlin, 1941). This work expounds the ideological foundations of the process.
43. Roberts, *op cit.,* p. 80.
44. Lebedev, *Rumy'nia v godi' vtoroy mirovoy voyny.* p. 16.
45. *Ibid.* Two lei were about 1.5 cents U.S.
46. *Journal of Contemporary History,* No. 1, 1966, p. 106.
47. Codreanu, *Eiserne Garde,* p. 436.
48. *Politics and Political Parties in Rumania,* p. 179.
49. Ciprian Doicescu, *Viaţalui Goga* (Bucureşti, 1942), pp. 130-31.
50. *Ibid.,* p. 76.
51. *Ibid.,* pp. 375-78.
52. *Politics and Political Parties in Rumania,* p. 171.
53. *Ibid.,* p. 59.
54. Moţa, *Correspondenţia cu "Serviciul Mundial,"* p. 18.
55. Codreanu, *Eiserne Garde,* p. 437.
56. *Ibid.,* p. 438.
57. Charlé, *Die Eiserne Garde,* p. 88.
58. Banea, *op cit.,* pp. 14-15.
59. Mihail Polihroniade, *Tineretul şi politica externa,* (Bucureşti, 1940), p. 3.
60. *Ibid.,* p. 13.
61. Moţa, *op. cit.,* p. 30.
62. *Ibid.,* p. 138.
63. Ion Covrig-Nonea, "Mişcarea legionără şi minoritatea," *Randuiala,* II, No. 1, 1936, 9-10, 375-76, 379.
64. Mihail Polihroniade, "Politica externa Romaniei," *Randuiala,* II, 1936, p. 1.
65. Codreanu, *Eiserne Garde,* p. 440.
66. Codreanu, *Manual,* Article: *Asociaţia prieţenii legionarilor.*
67. *Pe marginea prăpăstiei,* I, 53-54.
68. Rogger and Weber, *op cit.,* p. 548.
69. *New York Times,* July 16, 1936.
70. Codreanu, *Eiserne Garde,* p. 443.
71. *Ibid.,* p. 436.
72. Codreanu, *Circulări, scrisori, sfături, gânduri,* p. 5.
73. *Ibid.* pp. 78-80.
74. Codreanu, *Eiserne Garde,* pp. 440-41.
75. C. Enescu, "Semnificăţia alegerilor din decemvrie 1937 în evoluţia politică a neamului romanesc," *Sociologia Romaneasca,* II, No. 11-12, November-December, 1937, p. 523.
76. *Time,* January 17, 1938, p. 27.
77. Gheorghe Barbul, *Mémorial Antonesco (Le IIIe homme d l' axe)* (Paris, 1950), p. 23.

78. *Ibid.*, p. 25.
79. *Ibid.*, p. 75.
80. *Ibid.*, p. 82.
81. *Ibid.*, pp. 20-21.
82. Bolitho, *Rumania under King Carol*, pp. 43-49.
83. *Time*, January 24, 1938, p. 16.
84. Rogger and Weber *op. cit.*, p. 551.
85. *Pe marginea prăpăstiei*, I, 33-34.
86. Codreanu, *Eiserne Garde*, p. 447.
87. Roberts, *op. cit.*, pp. 206-14, 344-45.
88. Codreanu, *Eiserne Garde*, pp. 448-451.
89. *Cazul Iorga-Madgearu*, Declarations made by Horia Sima to the periodical *Carpaţi* (Madrid, 1962), p. 13.
90. Codreanu, *Eiserne Garde*, p. 445.
91. Constantin Papanace, *Despre Capitan Nicadori şi Decemviri*, Biblioteca Verde, No. 10 (Rome, 1963), p. 13.
92. *Cazul Iorga-Madgearu*, p. 12.
93. *Dacia*, Anul XII, Număr Festiv (Rio de Janeiro, 1957).
94. C. Papanace, *Orientari politice in primul exil.* Biblioteca Verde (Rome, 1953), p. 12.
95. The National Radical party and Polish Patriotic Youth had great sympathies toward the Legion, overlooking rather carelessly the implications of a Legionary takeover to Poland's security.
96. Hillgruber, *Hitler, König, Carol und Antonescu*, pp. 23-27.
97. Waldeck, *op. cit.*, p. 76.
98. *Ibid.*, p. 28.
99. Hillgruber, *op. cit.*, pp. 26-29.
100. Codreanu, *Eiserne Garde* (Appendix), p. 455.
101. *Ibid.*, p. 459.
102. Hillgruber, *op. cit.*, pp. 29-31.
103. *Ibid.*
104. Rogger and Weber, *op. cit.*, p. 556.
105. *Time*, October 2, 1939, p. 22.
106. *New York Times*, December 5, 1938.
107. Rogger and Weber, *op. cit.*, pp. 556-57.
108. Their leader was none other than Dr. Ion Păslaru, a Ph.D. in theology.
109. *New York Times*, September 24, 1939.
110. Roberts, *op. cit.*, p. 214; also, in detail, Hillgruber, *op. cit.*, pp. 42-48.
111. Rogger and Weber, *op. cit.*, p. 558.
112. *Cazul Iorga-Madgearu*, p. 22.
113. *Time*, July 1, 1940, p. 25.
114. *Ibid.*
115. Rogger and Weber, *op. cit.*, p. 557.

116. Macartney, *October fifteenth*, I, p. 419n.
117. *Ibid.*, p. 415n.
118. *Biblioteca Historica Romaniae*, No. 2, *op. cit.*, p. 15. Also: *Les archives secrètes de la Wilhelmstrasse* (Paris, 1954) Vol. V, Book I, p. 376. Also: Hillgruber, *op. cit.*, p. 28.
119. Harold Laeuen, *Marschall Antonescu* (Essen, 1943), pp. 42-48.
120. *Ibid.*, pp. 42-50.
121. *Time*, November 25, 1940, p. 25.

Notes to Chapter XI

1. Barbul, *Mémorial Antonesco*, p. 11.
2. Laeuen, *Marschall Antonescu*, p. 51.
3. Barbul, *op. cit.*, p. 34.
4. Rogger and Weber, *The European Right*, p. 561.
5. *Orientări Pentru Legionari*, p. 10.
6. *Ibid.*
7. *Pe marginea prăpăstiei*, I, 10.
8. *Ibid.*, p. 181.
9. *New York Times*, September 10, 1940.
10. *Pe marginea prăpăstiei*, I, 10.
11. *New York Times*, September 29, 1940.
12. *Cazul Iorga-Madgearu*, pp. 31-35.
13. *Pe marginea prăpăstiei*, I, 12.
14. *Ibid.*
15. Rogger and Weber, *op. cit.*, p. 561.
16. *New York Times*, Sept. 29, 1940.
17. *Pe marginea prăpăstiei*, II, 141.
18. *Ibid.*, pp. 190-93.
19. Rogger and Weber, *op. cit.*, p. 562.
20. *Buna Veştire*, October 11, 1940; also, November 17, 1940.
21. *Ibid.*, October 22, 1940.
22. *Pe marginea prăpăstiei*, I, 145-46.
23. *Ibid.*, p. 154.
24. *Ibid.*
25. *Cazul Iorga-Madgearu*, p. 28.
26. Waldeck, *Athene Palace*, p. 218.
27. *Ibid.*, p. 279.

28. *Ibid.*
29. Laeuen, *op. cit.*, p. 84.
30. *Orientări Pentru Legionari*, p. 4.
31. Barbul, *op. cit.*, p. 69.
32. *Ibid.*, p. 66.
33. *Cazul Iorga-Madgearu*, p. 64.
34. *Ibid.*, pp. 36-44.
35. *Ibid.*, pp. 48-59.
36. Barbul, *op. cit.*, p. 37.
37. *Buna Veştire*, November 29, 1940.
39. *Pe marginea prăpăstiei*, II, p. 143.
40. *Cazul Iorga-Madgearu*, p. 69.
41. *Ibid.*, p. 81.
42. *Pe marginea prăpăstiei*, II, 223-27.
43. *Glasul Strămoşesc*, December 15, 1940; also, *Pe marginea prăpăstiei*, I, 255.
44. *Pe marginea prăpăstiei*, II, pp. 223-27.
45. *Ibid.*, pp. 139-40.
46. Rogger and Weber, *op. cit.*, p. 564.
47. *Buna Veştire*, January 10, 1941,
48. *Muncitorul Legionar*, No. 5, January 15, 1941. Also, *Pe marginea prăpăstiei*, I, 56.
49. *Curentul*, January 14, 1941.
50. *Pe marginea prăpăstiei*, II, pp. 16-17.
51. Barbul, *op. cit.*, pp. 80-81.
52. *Pe marginea prăpăstiei*, II, 18-20.
53. *Ibid.*
54. *Ibid.*, p. 334.
55. Robert St. John, *Foreign Correspondent*, (London, 1960), pp. 176, 180.
56. Barbul, *op. cit.*, p. 103-5.
57. Herman Neubacher, *Sonderauftrag Südost* (Göttingen, 1956), p. 56.
58. Laeuen, *op. cit.*, p. 92.
59. Hillgruber, *op. cit.*, p. 121.
60. Laeuen, *op. cit.*, p. 112.
61. Roberts, *Rumania: Political Problems of an Agrarian State*, p. 236.
62. *New York Times*, May 13, 1941.
63. *Ibid.*
64. *Pe marginea prăpăstiei*, II, 285-94.
65. *Dacia, XII*, Număr Festiv (Rio de Janeiro, January 1957), p. 21.
66. Hilberg, *The Destruction of the European Jews*, pp. 492-500.
67. Hirschmann, *Caution to the Wind*, pp. 152-60.
68. *Biblioteca Historica Romaniae*, No. 2, pp. 50-51.

Notes to Chapter XII

1. Cretzianu, *The Lost Opportunity*, p. 20.
2. Roberts, *Rumania: Political Problems of an Agrarian State*, p. 232.
3. Macartney, *October Fifteenth*, I, 157.
4. Weber, *Varieties of Fascism*, p. 145.
5. Borkenau, *The Communist International*, p. 42.
6. Weber, *op. cit.*, p. 139.
7. *Politics and Political Parties in Rumania*, p. 241.
8. Weber, *op. cit.*, p. 141.
9. *Journal of Contemporary History*, No. 1, 1966, p. 126.
10. Nolte, *Three Faces of Fascism*, p. 427.
11. *Ibid.*, pp. 1-9.

Bibliography

"The nature and the major characteristics of [Fascist] movements," wrote Professor Eugen Weber, ". . . encompass a vast area of contemporary experience. Conceived in Europe, like Nationalism and Marxism, Fascism and National Socialism have become articles for export. The circumstances in which they grew, the sentiments that inspired them, the characteristics we have noted, all may be found with variations in most political life of the world today. Neither sympathy nor dislike are by themselves a satisfactory reaction to attitudes and ideas with which we must learn to cope. Fascist movements demand further investigation if we are to understand the many problems which confront us here and now." (*Varieties of Fascism*, p. 142.)

The sources mentioned below do not represent a comprehensive bibliography of Hungarian and Rumanian fascism — not even of the present work, for which only the chief sources of information are included. A number of other relevant works exist, of course. And the complete picture of Hungarian and Rumanian fascism will be drawn only when Hungarian and Rumanian archives and libraries are opened and the materials placed at the disposal of historians, a process now well under way. Only in the possession of the whole evidence will it be possible to write a full history of these remarkably peculiar responses to the challenges of the modern age, works which in the hopeful words of Professor Ernst Nolte, will be "something other than angry accusations or whitewashing apologies."

General Studies and Works Useful for an Introduction to Fascist Phenomena in Hungary and Rumania

Arendt, Hannah. *The Origins of Totalitarianism.* New York and Toronto, 1951.

Borkenau, Franz. *The Communist International.* London, 1938.

Ciano, Galeazzo. *Ciano's Diary, 1937-1938.* London, 1952.

_____. *The Ciano Diaries, 1939-1943.* New York and Toronto, 1946; London, 1947.

Dumitriu, Petru. *The Prodigals.* New York, 1962.

Enciclopedia Romaniei. 4 vols. Bucharest, n.d.

Goga, Octavian. *Mustul care fierbe.* Bucharest, 1925.

Guderian, Heinz. *Erinnerungen eines Soldaten.* Heidelberg, 1951.

Hitler's Secret Conversations, 1941-1944. New York, 1962.

Hóman, Bálint and Szekfü, Gyula. *Magyar történet.* Budapest, n.d.

Illyés, Gyula. *A puszták népe.* Budapest, 1936.

Iorga, Nicolae. *Geschichte des Rumänischen Volkes.* 2 vols. Gotha, 1905.

_____. *Histoire des Roumains et de la romanité orientale.* 4 vols. Bucharest, 1937.

Jászi, Oszkár. *Dissolution of the Habsburg Empire.* Chicago, 1929.

_____. *Revolution and Counter-Revolution in Hungary.* London, 1924.

Kohn, Hans. *The Idea of Nationalism: A Study of Its Origins and Background.* New York, 1944.

Kovács, Imre. *A néma forradalom.* Budapest, 1938.

Macartney, C.A. *Hungary: A Short History.* Edinburgh, 1962.

Madgearu, Virgil. *Evoluţia economiei româneşti dupa războiul mondial.* Bucharest, 1940.

Mitrany, David. *The Effect of the War in Southeastern Europe.* New Haven, 1936.

_____. *The Land and the Peasant in Rumania: the War and Agrarian Reform (1917-1921).* London and New Haven, 1930.

Moore, Wilbert E. *Economic Demography of Eastern and Southern Europe.* Geneva, 1945.

Nazi Conspiracy and Aggression. 11 vols. Washington, 1946.

Nolte, Ernst, (ed.). *Theorien über den Faschismus,* (Wissenschaftliche Bibliothek, Vol. 21.) Berlin and Cologne, 1967.

_____. *Three Faces of Fascism.* New York; Chicago; San Francisco, 1966.

Politics and Political Parties in Rumania. London, 1936.

Remarque, Erich Maria. *All Quiet on the Western Front.* Boston, 1929.

Roberts, Henry. *Rumania: Political Problems of an Agrarian State.* New Haven, 1951.

Schmidt, Paul. *Statist auf diplomatischer Bühne, 1922-1945.* Bonn, 1951.

Seton-Watson, Hugh. *Eastern Europe Between the Wars, 1918-1941.* 2d ed., Cambridge, Eng., 1946.

_____. *The East European Revolution.* New York, 1951.

Szekfü, Gyula. *Három nemzedék és ami utána következik.* Budapest, 1934.

Voinea, Şerban. *Marxism oligarhic, contributie la problema desvoltarii capitaliste a Romaniei.* Bucharest, 1926.

Zeletin, Ştefan. *Burghezia româna, origina şi rolul ei istoric.* Bucharest, 1925.
_____. *Neoliberalismul.* Bucharest, 1927.

A Short Bibliography
of
Fascism in Hungary

Ábrahám, Ferenc, and Kussinszky, Endre (eds.). *Ítél a történelem: (a)* Bárdossy per, Budapest, 1945; *(b)* Imrédy per, Budapest, 1945; *(c)* Szálasi per, Budapest, 1946.

Allianz: Hitler, Horthy, Mussolini: Dokumente zur ungarischen Austenpolitik (1933-1944). Budapest, 1966.

Barbácsi, Simon Ferenc. *Az enyingi "nyilasház": Festetics nyilaskeresztes vezér vallomásai.* Budapest, n.d.

Budaváry, László. *Zöld Bolsevizmus.* Budapest, 1941.

The Confidential Papers of Admiral Horthy. Budapest, 1965.

Darvas, József. *Város az ingoványon.* Budapest, 1945.

A Fajvédöpárt programja. Pamphlet. Budapest, 1927.

A Gömbös kormány nemzeti munkaterve. Pamphlet. Budapest, 1932.

Henney, Arpád. *Hungarist Pro Memoriam.* London, 1953.

Hídfő. Series published by Hungarian Fascist exiles in Munich.

Horthy Miklós titkos iratai. Documents. Budapest, 1963.

Horthy, (Admiral) Nicholas. *Memoirs.* New York, 1957.

Horthy, Nikolaus. *Ein Leben für Ungarn.* Bonn, 1953.

Horváth, József, Nemes, János, Pintér, István, and Szabó, László. *Az utolsó felvonás.* Budapest, 1958.

Hubay, Kálmán. *Két forradalom.* Budapest, 1941.

Juhász, Gyula. *A Teleki kormány külpolitikája, 1939-1941.* Budapest, 1964.

Kállai, Gyula. *A magyar függetlenségi mozgalom, 1936-1945.* Budapest, 1965.

Kállay, Nicholas. *Hungarian Premier: A Personal Account of a Nation's Struggle During the Second World War.* New York, 1954.

Karsai, Elek. *A budai Sándor palotában történt (1919-1941).* Budapest, 1965.

_____. *A budai vártól a gyepüig (1941-1945).* Budapest, 1967.

Kékessy, Rudolf. *Vádak és a valóság.* Budapest, 1941.

Kertész, Stephen. *Diplomacy in a Whirlpool: Hungary between Nazi Germany and Soviet Russia.* Notre Dame, 1953.

Kisbarnaki, Farkas Ferenc. *A Tatárhágó visszanéz.* Buenos Aires, 1955.

Lackó, Miklós. *Nyilasok, nemzetiszocialisták, 1935-1944.* Budapest, 1966.

Macartney, C.A. *October Fifteenth: A History of Modern Hungary 1929-1945.* Edinburgh, 1961.

Málnási, Ödön. *A magyar nemzet igaz története.* Munich, 1959.

Montgomery, John F. *Hungary, the Unwilling Satellite.* New York, 1947.

Nagy, Ferenc. *The Struggle Behind the Iron Curtain.* New York, 1948.

The National Programme of the Hungarian Government. Pamphlet. Budapest, 1932.

(1) *Országgyülési Napló; Képviselöház (1919-1945);* (2) *Felsöházi Napló (1924-1945).* Parliamentary Diaries of the Lower House (1), and of the Upper House (2).

Pushkash, A. I. *Vengriya v godi vtoroy mirovoy voyni.* Moscow, 1966.

Ránki, György. *1944 március 19.* Budapest, 1968.

Rogger, Hans and Weber, Eugen, (eds.). *The European Right (A Historical Profile).* Berkeley, 1965.

Roósz, József. *Földreform vagy parasztpolitika.* Budapest, 1960.

Rozsnyói, Ágnes. *A Szálasi puccs.* Budapest, 1963.

Saly, Dezsö. *Szigorúan bizalmas.* Budapest, 1945.

Súlyok, Dezsö. *A magyar tragédia.* Newark, 1954.

Szakács, Kálmán. *Kaszáskeresztesek.* Budapest, 1963.

Szálasi, Ferenc. *Ut és cél.* Budapest, 1936.

_____. *A Magyar állam felépítésének terve.* Budapest, 1933.

Szirmai, Rezsö. *Fasiszta lelkek.* Budapest, 1946.

Szokoly, Endre. *És Gömbös Gyula a kapitány.* Budapest, 1960.

A tízhónapos tragédia. Documentary. Budapest, 1945.

Tormay, Cécile. *An Outlaw's Diary.* New York, 1923.

Török, András. *Szálasi álarc nélkül.* Budapest, 1940.

Ullein-Reviczky, Antal. *Guerre Allemande, paix Russe.* Neuchatel, 1947.

Vozáry, Aladár. *Igy történt! (1944 március 19 – 1945 január 18).* Budapest, 1945.

Vágó, Dr. Pál. *Munkanélküliség, hitel, országépítés.* Budapest, 1939.

_____. *Nyilt levél C.A. Macartney professzor úrhoz.* Beccar, 1960.

Út és Cél. Series published by Arrow Cross exiles in Buenos Aires.

Weber, Eugen. *Varieties of Fascism (Doctrines of Revolution in the Twentieth Century).* Princeton, N.J., Toronto, New York, London, 1964.

A Short Bibliography
of
Fascism in Rumania

Adevărul în procesul lui Corneliu Z. Codreanu. Bucharest, 1938.

Amazar, D.C. *Lupta mantuitorului.* Bucharest, 1937.

Asesinatele de Jilava. Documentary. Bucharest, 1942.

Banea, Ion. *Capitănul,* Bucharest, 1936.

Barbul, Gheorghe. *Mémorial Antonesco, le IIIe homme de l'axe.* Paris, 1950.

Bernea, Ernest. *Cartea capitanilor.* Bucharest, 1938.

Biblioteca Verde (Caiete Verzi). Series edited and published by Constantin Papanace in Rome. Mimeo.

Câtre români. Bucharest, 1941.

Charlé, Klaus. *Die Eiserne Garde.* Berlin, 1939.

Codreanu, Corneliu Zelea. *Cârtica şefului de cuib.* Bucharest, 1933.

_____. *Eiserne Garde.* Berlin, 1939.

_____. *Îndreptarul frăţiilor de cruce.* Bucharest, 1935.

_____. *Pentru legionari.* Bucharest, 1936.

Comnène, N., P.. *I responsabili.* Verona, 1949.

_____. *Preludi del grande dramma.* Rome, 1947.

Covrig-Nonea, Ion. *Mişcarea legionară şi minoritaţile.* Bucharest, 1937.

Cretzianu, Alexandre. *The Lost Opportunity.* New York, 1957.

Dacia. Series published by Iron Guardist exiles in Rio de Janeiro, Brazil.

Doicescu, Ciprian. *Viaţalui Goga.* Bucharest, 1942.

Eastermann, A., L. *King Carol, Hitler and Lupescu.* London, 1942.

Escolar, Tomás. *Vida y doctrína de C.Z. Codreanu.* Barcelona, 1941.

Finotti, Alfonso, P. *La Guardia di Ferro.* Florence, 1938.

Gafencu, Grigore. *Last Days of Europe. A Diplomatic Journey in 1939.* New Haven, 1948.

_____. *Prelude to the Russian Campaign.* London, 1945.

Gărcineanu, G.P. *Din lumea legionară.* Bucharest, 1937.

Georgescu, Titu. *Nicolae Iorga împotriva hitlerismului.* Bucharest, 1966.

Gheorghe, Ion. *Rumäniens Weg zum Satelitenstaat.* Heidelberg, 1952.

Hersheni, Traian. *Mişcarea Legionară şi muncitorimea.* Bucharest, 1937.

_____. *Miscarea Legionară şi ţaranimea.* Bucharest, 1940.

Hillgruber, Andreas. *Hitler, König Carol und Marschall Antonescu; Die Deutsch-Rumänische Beziehungen, 1938-1944.* Wiesbaden, 1954.

Laeuen, Harald. *Marschall Antonescu.* Essen, 1943.

Lebedev, N.I. *Padenie diktaturi Antonescu.* Moscow, 1966.

_____. *Rumy'nia v godi vtoroy mirovoy voyni: Vneshnepoliticheskaya i vnutripoliticheskaya istoriya Ruminii v 1938-1945 gg.* Moscow, 1961.

Manoilescu, Mihai. *Die einzige Partei als politische Institution der neuen Régime.* Berlin, 1941.

Marin, Vasile. *Crez de generaţie.* Bucharest, 1937.

Markham, Reuben H. *Rumania Under the Soviet Yoke.* Boston, 1949.

Moţa, Ion. *Cranii de lemn.* Bucharest, 1937.

Neubacher, Hermann. *Sonderauftrag Südost.* Göttingen, 1956.

Noul regim. Bucharest, 1939.

Omul Nou. Series published by Horia Sima's friends in Germany.

Palaghiţă, Ştefan. *Garda de fier.* (Spre reinvierea Romaniei) Buenos Aires, 1951.

Patrăşcanu, Lucreţiu. *Problemele de bază ale României.* Bucharest, 1946.

_____. *Sous trois dictatures.* Paris, 1946.

_____. *Sub trei dictaturi.* Bucharest, 1946.

Pe marginea prăpastiei. 2 vols. Documentary. Bucharest, 1942.

Polihroniade, Mihail. *Tineretul şi politica externa.* Bucharest, 1940.

Popescu-Puţuri, Ion, Zaharia, Gheorghe, Goldberger, N., Constantinescu, N. N., and Copoiu, N. *La Roumanie pendant la deuxiéme guerre mondiale.* Bibliotheca historica Romaniae No. 2. Bucharest, 1964.

Rogger, Hans and Weber, Eugen. *The European Right: A Historical Profile.* Berkeley, 1965.

Saleo, Eminardo. *Mussolini e Codreanu.* Palermo, 1942.

Seicaru, Pamfil. *Un junimist Antisemit: A.C. Cuza.* Madrid, 1961.

Sima, Horia. *Cazul Iorga-Madgearu.* Madrid, 1961.

_____. *Destinée du nationalisme.* Paris, 1951.

Tharaud, Jean. *L'envoye de l'archange.* Paris, 1939.

Waldeck, R.G. *Athene Palace.* New York, 1942.

Weber, Eugen. *Varieties of Fascism.* (Doctrines of Revolution in the Twentieth Century). Princeton, N.J., Toronto, New York, London, 1964.

405

A Short Bibliography
of the
Jewish Question in Hungary
and
Rumania

Blood Bath in Rumania. Published by *The Record* (New York), vol. 4, no. 6-7 (July-August, 1942).

Braham, Randolph. *The Destruction of Hungarian Jewry.* New York, 1964.

Dubnow, S.M. *Die neueste Geschichte des jüdischen Volkes.* 3 vols. Berlin, 1920.

Ébredö Magyarok Egyesülete. *Anti-Semitism in Hungary.* Budapest, 1920.

Hilberg, Raul. *The Destruction of the European Jews.* Chicago, 1961.

Karsai, Elek, (ed.). *Fegyvertelenül álltak az aknamezökön.* Budapest, 1962.

Lévai, Jenö (Eugene). *Black Book on the Martyrdom of Hungarian Jewry.* Zurich, 1948.

_____. *Eichmann in Ungarn.* Budapest, 1961.

_____. *Fehér könyv. Külföldi akciók zsidók megmentésére.* Budapest, n.d.

_____. *Fekete könyv a magyar zsidóság szenvedéseiröl.* Budapest, n.d.

_____. *Szürke könyv a magyar zsidóság megmentéséröl.* Budapest, n.d.

The Contemporary Hungarian
and Rumanian Press, Fascist or
Otherwise

A very important source of information in investigating Hungarian and Rumanian fascism is the contemporary press. The main sources are, of course, the stacks in Hungarian and Rumanian libraries. But these materials, even if accessible, demand the command of the Hungarian and Rumanian languages. Fortunately, there were daily and weekly papers printed in more easily accessible languages, in Hungary in German and in Rumania in French.

L'Independence Roumaine (weekly). Bucharest.

Le Moment (weekly). Bucharest.

Moniteur Oficiel (daily). Bucharest.

Pester Lloyd (daily). Budapest.

There are two books in Hungarian about the Fascist press in Hungary which contain valuable information and quotations:

Major, Róbert. *25 év ellenforradalmi sajtó.* Budapest, 1945.

Kún, Andor. *Berlinböl jelentik.* Budapest, 1945.

Outside of the United States, the Österreichische Nationalbibliothek in Vienna, the Bibliothéque Nationale in Paris, and the Biblioteca Universitaria

Alessandrina in Rome have a considerable Hungarian and Rumanian newspaper collection, and a large number of titles by Fascist or Iron Guardist sympathizers.

Newspapers and periodicals in Hungarian and Rumanian that are available in the Library of Congress are listed in *Newspapers of East Central and South Eastern Europe in the Library of Congress* (Washington, 1965) containing 787 titles. The *New York Public Library* also has a considerable number of Hungarian and to a lesser extent Rumanian newspapers.

And the rather tiresome sampling of *The New York Times*, with much less result, is always possible and useful.

Index

Absolutism, in Hungary (1849-67), 8
Acţiunea Romaneasca (Rumanian Action), 261
Á.D.O.B., see Committee of Unemployed University Degree Bearers
Adrianople Treaty (1829), 13
Advance Guards (Élharcosok), 95, 110
Ady, Endre, 336 n.
Aggteleki, Gen. B., arrest of, 227-28
Agriculture: in Hungary, 10n.; during depression (1930s), 83, 84; first Fascist-type party and, 70-71; in Rumania, 16; See also Land reforms
Albrecht of Habsburg (Archduke), 72, 175, 180, 189; Final Solution and, 184
Alecsăndri, Văsilie, 14
Alexander (King of Yugoslavia), 257; murder of, 102, 168
Alexander II (Tsar of Russia), 26, 276
All for the Fatherland (Totul Pentru Ţara), 286; See also Legion of the Archangel Michael
Alliance Israelite, 69, 259
Alliance of the Veterans of the Eastern Front, see K.A.B.Sz.
All Quiet on the Western Front (Remarque), 20
Anatal, István, 93, 95, 97, 136n., 356; arrest of, 235
Anti-bolshevism, in Hungary, 77
Anti-Comintern Pact, 152
Anti-Jewish Law (Hungary): first, 136; second, 147-49; third, 171-72
Anti-Semitism: in Austria, 65-66; in Hungary, 58, 64-69, 70, 74-77, 86, 93, 100, 126, 151, 258n., 259; in Rumania, 44-45, 47, 65, 248-50, 252-54, 258n., 289, 295, 354; World Anti-Semitic Congress (1925), 72, 359n.

Antonescu, Ion, 29, 172, 183, 211, 275n., 298; execution of, 309; as minister of defense, 294-95; as premier, 307-37, 342-44, 352, 356, 358; arrest of, 337; declares war on U.S.S.R., 330-31, 339
Antonescu, Mihai "Ica," 309, 319, 329; Premier Antonescu and, 318, 328, 335
Apărărea Naţionala (National Defense) (newspaper), 265
Apor (Bishop of Györ), 209, 210
Argeşanu, Gen. Gheorge, 305, 313
Argetoianu, Constantin, 278, 305
Arnauts (Moslem troops), 4, 12
Arrow Cross Militia (Fegyveres Pártszolgálat) 230, 233, 237, 238
Arrow Cross party, 55, 110, 145, 152-61, 191n., 374, 360-70, 372n.; Black Front of, 141; co-operative of (Marok), 155n.; dissolution under Teleki of, 151; in government, 230-40; groups in, 127-28; miners strikes of, 154, 166-67; plot of, 163; reorganization of, 152; rise of, 125, 357; R.S.H.A. infiltration of, 142, 175; Swabians and, 165; Szálasi and, 93, 120-22, 134-38, 140-43, 166, 180, 188, 194-96, 201-2, 219-29, 345, 361-70; See also Party of National Will
Arsenic women, 108
Ashkenazic Jews, see under Jews
Association of Awakening Hungarians, see É.M.E.
Association of Hungarian Life (Magyar Élet Szövetsége), 131
Association of Hungarian National Defense, see M.O.V.E.
Atäturk, see Kernal Atäturk
Atlantic Charter, 75
Auşnit, Max, 277, 285
Austria: anti-Semitism in, 65-66;

409

Hungary's relations with, 22, 79; Nazi Germany and, 103, 132, 133, 135; Socialists in Parliament of, 11n.; in World War I, 20-21

Austro - Hungarian - German Treaty (1883), 16

Averescu, Gen. A.: government of, 256, 265; land reforms and, 29, 253, 254; in peasant revolt (1907), 17; political party of, 288; in World War I, 26

Az Est (Jewish press), 104n.

Bacsó, Béla, assassination of, 55

Bagulescu (Fascist group leader), 261

Bajcsy-Zsilinszky, Endre, 100; during German occupation, 193; execution of, 235, 236; as leader of Smallholders party, 186; protest of Novi Sad massacre by, 179-80

Bakay, Gen. Szilárd, kidnapping of, 225

Baky, László, 124, 134-35, 140, 152, 164, 187n.; in Arrow Cross party, 142, 176, 191n.; during World War II, 155; German occupation and, 193, 216, 221; Jews and, 185-86, 204, 205; plot of, 214; R.S.H.A. and, 180, 196; under Szálasi, 231-32

Bălcescu, Nicolae, 14

Balkan War (1913), 17

Balogh, István, 40n.; political party of, 112, 131

Banea, Ion: on Jews, 259n.; on Rumanian youth, 280; shooting of, 304

Bánffy, Miklós, 335n.

Banking system, in Hungary, 10n.

Bárczy, István, 214

Bárdossy, László, 187, 201; as premier, 171-75, 177, 181, 182; death of, 309

Bărnuţiu, Semeon, 18, 28

Baross, G., 97, 125

Bartha, Károlyi, 183

Barthou, Louis, 257; murder of, 102, 168

Basch, Franz, 165

Battalion of Legionary Commerce, 290

Battle of Britain, 167

Battle of Mohács, 80

Bebel, August, on anti-Semitism, 64

Belgian Charter (1831), 16

Bem, Gen. József, 40n.

Beneš, Eduard, 104, 257; on Trianon Treaty, 56

Bengliu, Gen., 313, 319

Benicky, Ödön, 55n.

Benton (chargé d'affaires), 331n.

Beregffy, Károly (minister of defense), 236

Berthelot, Gen. Henry, Rumanian Army under, 26

Bessarabia, 252, 275; Codreanu in, 281-82; Jews in, 258n.-59n., 332; Rumanians and, reannexation of, 15, 331; in World War I, 26, 27; in World War II, 306; Russians in, 13, 16, 257, 306

Bethlen, Count István, 71, 77, 78, 89, 92, 98, 105, 124, 136, 149, 150, 152, 167, 181, 335n., 353; during German occupations, 197, 235; Horthy and, 216-17, 220; on Gömbös, 90; Jews and, 184-85; as leader of Vienna counterrevolutionists, 50, 53; on 1939 election, 154; as premier, 58-59, 64, 68, 70, 73, 74, 81, 87, 110, 351; attitude toward Succession States, 79-80; during depression (1930s), 83-85; resignation of, 85; restoration of prewar Hungary by, 69

Bibescu, Prince, 14

Bienenstock, Capt., shooting of, 233

Birthrate: among Hungarian peasants, 60; in Rumania, 31

Bismarck, Otto von, 1, 16, 45, 342; on alliances, 82, 171, 227; on history of Europeans, 123

"Black Death," Jews and, 38

Black Front, 141

Black Hand, 71

Black Hundreds, 258n.

Black Shirts of Hungary (Eagles), 74

Blank, Aristide, 297

Bleyer, Jakob, 356

Bloodsucker of the Village (play), 295

Blum, Léon, 55

representative of Catholicism, 185; R.S.H.A. and, 193; Szeged movement and, 92, 111, 135, 142, 155, 191; during World War II, 155; in army, 163, 182

Imrédy, Madame, 150

Inculer, Ion, 293

Incze, Antal, 186

Independent Smallholders, Agricultural, and Bourgeois party, *see* Smallholders party

Indonesia, 349n.-50n.

Industrial revolution, 370-71

Industry: in Hungary, 10n.; in Rumania, 17, 31; *See also specific industries*

Institute of Racial Biology, 196

Institute of Research on the Jewish Question (*Zsidókutató Intézet*), 198

Integralistas (Brazilian Fascist movement), 370n.

Ionescu, Nae, 293, 299

Ionescu, Take, 257

Ionică, Prof., 304

Ionițiu (secretary of King Michael), 336n.

Iorga, Nicolae, 12, 45, 47; murder of, 320, 322; in National Democratic party, 248, 252; as premier, 278, 283; in second camarilla, 297, 298

Iron Guard, 176, 223, 286, 345, 347, 372n.; Codreanu and, 155, 246-47, 250, 259, 282-84, 293, 295-96; exiles in Germany of, 303, 304, 330; F.R.N. and, 305; Goga-Cuzists and, 289-90, 295; Jews and, 259; Stere and, 249; support of, 287; *See also* Legion of the Archangel Michael

Isabelle (Archduchess), 72

Israel, Eichmann and, 128n.

Istrati (Legionary), shooting of, 304

Italy: Hungary's relations with, 80-82, 102; Gömbös and, 101; in war with Ethiopia, 103, 104n.; in World War I, 20, 21n., 25; in World War II, 168, 187-88

Jacquerie (1514), 2; (1907), 17; in Transylvania, 17-18

Janissaries, 61

Japan, in World War II, 177

Jaross, Andor, 149, 179, 191, 225; on Arrow Cross party, 232; Jews and, 148, 185, 204, 207, 209, 213

Jászi, Oszkár, 10, 43; as minister of nationalities, 22, 27-28

Jews: Ashkenazic, massacres of, 38-39; in Austria, 65-66; in Bessarabia, 258n.-59n., 332; in Bucovina, 258n., 332, 334; in Bulgaria, 183; in Czechoslovakia, 67, 148; in France, 241; in Hungary, 9, 39-44, 105-6, 111, 245n., 350, 354-56; anti-Jewish laws, 136, 147-49, 171, 172; anti-Semitism and, 58, 64-69, 70, 74, 75, 76-77, 86, 93, 100, 126, 151, 258n., 259; Arrow Cross terrorist attacks on, 141, 142, 230-31, 232-34, 238; Final Solution and, 183-86, 202-17, 240-43, 335; financing of Gömbös by, 88-89, 90, 97, 112, 354; Italian fascism and, 104n.; press and, 158n.-59n.; radicals among, 42-43; Red Terror and, 25, 65; statistics on, 41n.; Szálasi's views on, 116, 119, 223, 363; during World War II, 171, 175, 178, 181, 182-83, 187, 222; nationalism of, 37-38; in Poland, 39; in Rumania, 30, 44-48, 67, 68, 258n.-59n, 354-56; anti-Semitism and, 44-45, 47, 65, 248-50, 252, 253-54, 258n., 289, 295, 354; Codreanu and, 253, 254, 259-62, 264, 269, 282, 341, 363; Final Solution and, 334-35; Legionary attacks on, 314, 322, 325, 327n.; legislation against, 305, 332; "Romanization" and, 312, 332, 335; statistics on, 44n., 46n., 47n.; during World War II, 211, 220, 331-35, 344; Sephardic, 38n.; in Succession States, 67; Cécile Tormay on, 43n., 63; in Transylvania, 163n., 211, 258n.,-59n., 309; in Yugoslavia, 67

Jodl, Gen. Alfred, 188

Joseph (Archduke), 22, 25, 224

Joseph II (Holy Roman Emperor), 4, 17; Jews and, 40

Imrédy, 146; in Rumania, 29-31, 253, 254
Landstrasse (Vienna), 1
Lansing, Robert, 21n.
Lassalle, Ferdinand, 274
Latin America, 370n.
Laval, Pierre, 102
Lavoro Italia (newspaper), 74-75
Law III (1921), applied to Village Explorers, 139
Lawyers, in Rumania, 35
Lázár, A., 91
League of National Christian Defense, see L.A.N.C.
League of Nations, Hungary in, 74, 83, 84, 96, 103, 152
Lecca, Radu, 335
Legion of the Archangel Michael: Battalion of Legionary Commerce in, 290; Carol II and, 268, 275, 288, 290, 292, 305; Codreanu and, 254, 265, 267-73, 279-93, 294, 298, 311, 340-42, 360-70; Corps of Legionary Workers in, 290, 313, 319n.; ideology of, 265-71; death cult in, 266, 318; Iron Guard of, see Iron Guard; under Nazis, 338-39; organization of, 271-73; persecution of, 299-305; revolution of, 307-30, 342-43, 353n.; in World War II, 331
Legionary Worker (Muncitorul Legionar) (newspaper), 324
Legionary Workers Corps, 290, 313, 319n.
Lenin, V.I., 23, 24, 231, 342, 348, 351, 366n.; on nationalism, 52; Third International and, 249
Leon, Gheorghe, 34
"Lidérc" (secret weapon), 236n.-37n.
Liga Apărării Naționăle Creștine, see L.A.N.C.
Lincoln-Trebitsch (Jewish adventurer), Gömbös and, 88n.
Lloyds of London, 302
London Daily Mail (newspaper), 79n.
London Daily Telegraph (newspaper), 143
Louis Napoleon, Rumania and, 14, 15

Ludendorff, Erich, 79
Lueger, Karl, 17, 19, 28, 66
Lungulescu (Fascist group leader), 261
Lupescu, Madame (Helen [Magda] Wolff), 276, 277, 283, 285, 286, 292, 294, 296, 297, 303, 305, 307, 308, 311
Lupescu, Constantin (Shloim), 305
Luther, Martin, 335n.
Lutz, Gizella, 114
Lutz (Swiss ambassador), 234

MacArthur, Douglas, 159n.
Macartney, C.A., 42, 48, 87n., 125, 156, 174, 199, 289; on Arrow Cross, 347; on Hitler, 104; on Hungarian National Socialist party, 164; on Imrédy, 137, 208; on Jews, 37, 183
Machiavelli, Niccolò, on the masses, 113
Mackensen, August von, 26, 123, 125n.; on Bucharest, 31-32
Madách, Imre, 92
Madgearu, Virgil, 31
Magyar Élet Mozgalom, see M.É.M.
Magyar Élet Szövetsége, see Association of Hungarian Life
Magyar Futár, 157n.
Magyar Megújulás Pártja, see Party of Hungarian Renewal
Magyar Nemzeti Függetlenségi Front, see Hungarian National Independence Front
Magyar Nemzeti Függetlenségi Párt, see Party of Racial Defense
Magyar Örszem, see Hungarian Sentinel
Magyar Megújulás Pártja Nemzetizocialista Pártszövetség, see Party Alliance of the Party of Hungarian Renewal and National Socialists
Magyar Országos Véderő Egyesület, see M.O.V.E.
Magyarság (newspaper), 140, 157, 164, 176
Madgearu, Virgil, murder of, 320, 322n.
Maimuca (Legionary), 325
Malaparte, 334n.

419

Malaxa (industrialist), 291, 313, 327
Malinovski, Marshal Rodom, 226
Málnási, Ödön, 127-28, 139, 194; on Red Terror, 25; trial of, 138
Malraux, André, 198
Mănăstire Dealului (school), Codreanu at, 252
Manciu (prefect of police), 263-64
Maniu, Iuliu, 19, 28-29, 283, 292, 302, 307, 309, 331, 333n., 335n., 336, 337n., 352, 356; Legion of Archangel Michael and, 268, 273; political party of, 256, 280, 282, 288, 294, 305, 320n.; as premier, 274-75, 276, 277, 278
Mannerheim, Field Marshal, 318n.
Manoilescu, M., 286, 352, 353, 356; as foreign minister, 305, 306; on Trianon Treaty, 56
Marghiloman, Alexandre, 27
Maria-Teresia (Queen of Hungary and Bohemia), 27
Marie (Queen of Rumania), 25-26, 276
Marin, Vasile, 251; funeral of, 292
Marinescu, Gavrila, 277, 313, 319; as police prefect, 277n., 297
Marmaroş-Blanc (bank), 283
Marok (Arrow Cross cooperative), 155n.
Maróthy, Károly, 152
Marseille murders, 82, 96, 102, 257
Márton, Béla, 92, 94, 99n., 100, 124, 125, 146, 154n., 202
Marty, J., 226
Marx, Karl, 6, 63, 341
Masaryk, T.B., 21n., 56, 67, 80
Matolesy, Mátyás, 100
Maurras, Charles, 240
Mecsér, András, 101, 124, 155, 188; as ambassador to Germany, 236
Mefhosz (student organization), 97
M.É.M. (*Magyar Élet Mozgalom;* Movement of Hungarian Life), 149, 151
Mendelssohn, Moses, 63
Meskó, Zoltán, political party of, 109-10, 111, 112, 152
Metternich, Prince Klemens von, 1, 12, 13, 348
Micescu, Istrate (foreign minister),

298, 299
Michael (King of Rumania), 199, 217, 226, 256n., 276, 297, 308, 310, 311, 336-37, 338, 344
Michelet, Jules, 14
Miczkiewicz, Adam, 14
Mihalache, Ion, 248, 275, 278, 302; on land reforms, 29; as minister of interior, 277n., 282
Milotay, István, 112, 157, 160, 161, 167, 197; Jews and, 185
Milotay, Madame, 157
Mindszenty, József Cardinal, 93n.; arrest of, 235
Miners' strikes: in Hungary, Arrow Cross and, 154, 166-67; in Rumania, 275
Mirabeau, Count Honoré de, 63
Mironescu Gheorghe, as premier, 277, 278
Mironovici (prefect), 325
Mocioni-Stircea, Baron Ionel, 336n.
Moldavia, 25n.; bolshevism in, 252; Jews in, 44n.; Moldavian Republic, 27; Russians in, 13
Molnár, Ferenc, 203
Molotov, Vyacheslav, 317; in World War II, 173-74, 336
Monitorul Oficial (newspaper), 287
Móricz, Zsigmond, 139
Moruzovi (adventurer), 297, 311n., 342
Moscardó, Don José, 133, 229n., 292
Moscardó, Luís, 229n.
Moscovici, Ilie, 351
Mosonyi, K., 179
Moţa, Ion, 251, 259n., 263, 264, 266, 291, 341, 365; funeral of, 292; on industrial age, 268; Iron Guard and, 261-62; Legion of Archangel Michael and, 279, 280
M.O.V.E. (*Magyar Országos Véderö Egysület;* Association of Hungarian National Defense), 50, 71, 87, 97, 125; plot of, 130
Movement of Hungarian Life, *see* M.É.M.
Muncitorul Legionar, see Legionary Worker
Mussolini, Benito, 120, 132, 161, 253, 254, 291, 367n., 369; fall of,

420

187; Hungary's relations with, 81, 82, 103, 106, 168; Gömbös and, 71, 74, 95*n*., 101, 102; Jewish middle class and, 104*n*.; Szálasi and, 137; Rome-Berlin Axis proclaimed by, 131

Nagy, Ferenc, 100
Nagy, Vilmos (minister of defense), 183
Nagyatádi-Szabó, István, 60, 69, 105; as leader of peasants, 55, 58
Napoleon Bonaparte, 39, 121, 230, 345
Nation, Die (newspaper), 210
National Agrarian party, 288, 289
National Christian party, 289
National Council (Hungary), 22
National Corporatist League, 286
National Defense (newspaper), 265
National Democratic party, 248, 354*n*.
National Labor Center (*Nemzeti Munkaközpont*), 99
National Legionary State, 310-28, 367, 370, 372*n*.
National Peasants, 254, 273, 293*n*., 294, 340; government of, 275-78, 285, 352; in 1928 election, 274
National Socialist (newspaper), 109
National Socialist Agricultural Laborers and Workers party, 110
National Socialist party (Hungary), 111; during World War II, 155
Nationalism, 348; in France, 6; in Hungary, 2, 6, 61, 362; Szeged movement and, 76; Jewish, 37-38; in Rumania, 2, 47, 247-51, 362
Nationalist International, 52, 140, 368*n*.; Germans and, 191, 367; Gömbös and, 71, 74, 102
Nationality laws (1868), 8
Nazis: Gömbös and, 71, 90*n*., 103; journalism of, 159*n*.; in Rumania, 316; Goga-Cuza and, 289; Legion of the Archangel Michael and, 290, 291*n*.; Swabians and, 139; *See also* Germany; Hitler, Adolf; National Socialist party (Hungary)
Neamul Romanesc, see Rumanian Nation

Németh, László, 139
Nemzeti Egység Pártja, see Party of National Unity
Nemzeti Munkaközpont, see National Labor Center
Nemzeti Összefogás Pártja, see Party of National Coalescence
Nemzeti Számonkérő Szék, see Chair of National Retribution
N.E.P., *see* Party of National Unity
Neubacher, H., 156, 300, 307*n*., 316, 317, 319*n*., 320, 327
Neue Zürcher Zeitung (newspaper), 210
Neurath, K. von, 132*n*.
New Hungarian Worker (Új Magyar Munkás) (newspaper), 129, 130
Newspapers: Hungarian Fascist, 108, 158*n*.,-59*n*., 167*n*. See also specific newspapers
Ney, K., 217, 221, 231
Nicadori (Legionary terrorists): funerals of, 318, 321; murders of, 301, 313; shooting of Duca by, 285
Nicholas, Prince (regent), 256
Nicholas I (Tsar of Russia), 13, 14, 19
Nicholas II (Tsar of Russia), on Rumania, 31
Nicodem (patriarch), 304
Niculescu-Buzeşti, Grigore, 336*n*.
"1938 Club," Imrédy and, 146
N.K.V.D., 306, 332
Nolte, E., 347, 360, 372, 373-74
Novi Sad (Ujvidek): massacre at, 171, 178-80, 197; trial of, 189
Nuremberg Laws, 147, 204

Oberbäck, Baron von, 141
Officer Detachments (*Tiszti különítmény*), 71, 78, 92, 122, 134; murder of policemen by, 57*n*.; White Terror of, 53, 54-55, 87, 95, 141*n*.
Official Gazette, see Budapesti Közlöny
Oil industry, in Rumania, 17
Omelka, Ferenc, 127, 180*n*.
Operation Barbarossa, 172, 324
Operation Margarethe, 190, 192
Order of Heroes (*Vitézi Rend*), 87*n*.